Encyclopedia of Modern
Christian Politics

ENCYCLOPEDIA OF MODERN CHRISTIAN POLITICS

Volume 1, A–K

Edited by
Roy P. Domenico and Mark Y. Hanley

GREENWOOD PRESS
Westport, Connecticut • *London*

Library of Congress Cataloging-in-Publication Data

Encyclopedia of modern Christian politics / edited by Roy P. Domenico and Mark Y. Hanley.

    p. cm.

  Includes bibliographical references and index.

  ISBN 0–313–33889–2 (v. 1 : alk. paper) — ISBN 0–313–33890–6 (v. 2 : alk. paper) — ISBN 0–313–32362–3 (set) 1. Christianity and politics—History—Encyclopedias.

I. Domenico, Roy Palmer. II. Hanley, Mark Y.

BR115.P7E58   2006

320.008´27—dc22   2006015695

British Library Cataloguing in Publication Data is available.

Library of Congress Catalog Card Number: 2006015695

ISBN: 0–313–32362–3 (set)
    0–313–33889–2 (vol. 1)
    0–313–33890–6 (vol. 2)

First published in 2006

Greenwood Press, 88 Post Road West, Westport, CT 06881
An imprint of Greenwood Publishing Group, Inc.
www.greenwood.com

Printed in the United States of America

The paper used in this book complies with the Permanent Paper Standard issued by the National Information Standards Organization (Z39.48–1984).

10 9 8 7 6 5 4 3 2 1

Contents

List of Entries

Preface

We developed this work for the purpose of illustrating the breadth and significance of Christian activism in, and influence on, modern politics rather than as an attempt to include everyone and everything from every corner. Our rationale for defining "modern" as the period after 1789 is detailed in the introduction below. We asked our authors to write in a jargon-free style accessible to the general educated reader. Most importantly, we reminded them of their essential task: to produce entries that *focus primarily on how Christianity substantively shaped their subject's outlook, actions, and political influence.* For broader considerations or concentration on different themes, the reader must turn to additional resources, beginning with the suggested readings at the end of most entries. Note, however, that for many contemporary activists and groups that information is often widespread and fragmentary rather than the stuff of numerous neatly bound volumes.

Another challenge we tackled was the question of whom or what was authentically Christian. Was Francisco Franco more or was he less sincerely Christian than, say, Dorothy Day? There cannot be an answer to such questions, let alone one that satisfies everyone. Therefore, we approached the question liberally. Franco frequently insisted that his was a holy crusade, and he enjoyed enough Catholic, *as Catholic,* endorsement and support that to include an entry on him in this work was warranted. Few would doubt Day's sincerity, although her cause for canonization is problematic. On the other hand, while Adolf Hitler was technically a Christian, there is no evidence that he ever sincerely incorporated Christian principles into his political vision or applied them as answers to Germany's problems. Nevertheless, some figures sympathetic to Hitler, such as Carl Schmitt or Houston Stewart Chamberlain, are entries in this work. We have also included some figures whose own Christian devotion was vague or complex, such as Giuseppe Mazzini and Charles Maurras, yet whose political visions clearly betrayed, in very different ways, significantly Christian aims. In sum, this liberal approach gives full scope to the surprising diversity of Christian activism.

By employing a global strategy and devoting attention to Catholic, Protestant, and Orthodox communities, we had to rule out a goal of comprehensiveness. To make this work as useful as possible, we have also included the following: an introductory essay and a substantial bibliography of general works on Christianity and politics; a full index that includes both proper names and relevant topics;

entries with boldface cross-references; and, finally, a comprehensive contributor section that includes the credentials and entry list for each author. While the 557 entries give substantial place to American and European topics, we also devote considerable attention to Christian activism beyond those shores to include Canada, Australia, Asia, Africa, and Latin America. Our emphasis is on prominent individuals whose Christian faith significantly shaped their public lives, but also included is a substantial sampling of the many political parties and reform groups that openly identified with Christianity. Many less well-known figures whose contributions are nonetheless significant have also earned a place. Taken as a whole, these entries provide a compelling story of Christian activism that was *central* rather than peripheral to the development of modern political cultures. In other words, Christian activism did not just *reflect* cultural change; it was integral to it.

We wish to thank the 159 authors who collaborated with us on this project. Without their expertise, cooperation, and friendly assistance, there would have been no encyclopedia. Beyond their contributions, generous help came from many quarters. At the University of Scranton, Elliot Gougeon and Stephanie Longo kindly helped translate certain entries. Jane Wesloski of the Scranton History Department, furthermore, provided crucial help at key moments, for which we extend our sincere thanks. Scranton's Weinberg Memorial Library delivered help when it was needed most, and, there, we are particularly indebted to Sheila Ferraro and Magdalene Restuccia. Wilson Miscamble of the University of Notre Dame gave valuable advice early in the project. Thanks also to student assistants J. Mark Leslie and Matthew A. Magruder at Truman State University and Trish Ross at Scranton, who provided help with correspondence, proofreading, and fact-checking. Truman State University provided a needed semester of sabbatical leave to complete this project. Finally, we must thank our wives, Janet and Robin, and our children for cheerfully enduring our peculiar and chaotic work schedules and burdens throughout this project.

Introduction

Since the twin towers of the World Trade Center fell on September 11, 2001, at the hands of a terrorist network claiming divine guidance toward religio-political aims, the West has scrambled with an unprecedented sense of urgency to better understand a fundamentalist Islam that, with few exceptions, cannot conceive of a political order not guided by Islamic law.

The experience of a political culture thoroughly intertwined with religious purpose is certainly not unfamiliar to Western observers. Queen Elizabeth II remains the titular head of church and state in the United Kingdom, where Anglicanism maintains something of its old sanctioned status. Despite the diminution of papal power over the last centuries, Pope Benedict XVI can still claim absolute authority as the nonhereditary, elective monarch of Vatican City. Control of the Papal States had given Roman pontiffs real vestiges of political power until 1870, and the church continues to wield a contributing influence on political parties and activist groups throughout the world. Within the secular political cultures of modern Europe, state sponsorship of national churches remains common. Germany, for example, provides constitutional guarantees of religious freedom but still grants Catholic and Evangelical Lutheran churches privileged access to public places and state administrative structures. The United States, a nation particularly jealous of its historic guarantees of separation of church and state, is nevertheless embroiled in perennial debates as to whether constitutional rights mandate merely an institutional divide or a radical separation of religion from policy making and public space.

For the millions who reside in nations historically linked to Christendom, then, a resurgent interest in understanding how religion shapes political culture ought to begin not in Baghdad or Tehran but in their own backyards. This volume encourages that aim and focuses on the *modern* era of Christianity's relationship to national political cultures. We chose the late 1780s as a starting point for three reasons. First, the French Revolution—begun in 1789, and in its most radical phase controlled by leaders contemptuous of all religious institutions—served clear warning, mainly to the Catholic Church, that future political upheavals in Europe would only diminish the power of organized religion. As reaction replaced revolution, and Europe entered the long peace between the Congress of Vienna (1815) and the outbreak of World War I in 1914, the old aristocratic regimes slowly disintegrated. Christian influence came to depend increasingly upon accommodative posturing based on moral suasion and assimilative tactics rather than cultural complacency and state guarantees.

Secondly, in the same year that French malcontents stormed the Bastille prison, the nation destined to become the most powerful arbiter of global politics in the twentieth century put into effect a Constitution that provided no formal nods to religion. As amended by the Bill of Rights, it guaranteed a national government that "shall make no law respecting an establishment of religion, or prohibiting the free exercise thereof." With the United States, thoroughly Protestant at the time, the nation's leaders reached easy consensus that the European model of state churches would never sink roots in American soil. Consequently, two of the world's great political revolutions seemed to point the way toward final victory for the secular political state ruled by Enlightenment reason and a rational public morality uninformed by Christian faith.

Finally, these transatlantic political upheavals occurred on the eve of the Industrial Revolution and the rise of free-market capitalism. Such economic transformations brought rapid urbanization with accompanying labor and social unrest, paving the way for modern party politics, union movements, and powerful ideological assaults on the standing order. Christians responded aggressively to these material changes and popular demands for power. More importantly, and as these volumes fully reveal, their stunning diversity of aims and methods yielded sharp internecine clashes and gave prominent place to Christian activism at almost every political turn.

Since the time of Constantine and Theodosius, Europe was commonly considered the land of the Christians, or Christendom. Other religions existed, of course, and held important places within that Christendom. Pagans occupied significant stretches of land, notably across northern and northeastern Europe, into the second millennium. Jews and Muslims, moreover, played key roles, particularly in Iberia, Sicily, and the Balkans. Sooner or later, nonetheless, Christian churches weaved their influence through all states. Disputes frequently disrupted relations between throne and altar, such as the eleventh-century Investiture Controversy, and, on fewer occasions, Christian rulers might submit to infidels as they did in Constantinople, Sicily, Muscovy, or the Crusader states. That a principality would freely abandon its Christian foundations, however, was unthinkable. Medieval bureaucracies rested predominantly, often exclusively, in the hands of Christian clerics. Lordly and royal symbols often recalled Christian images, as many still do. Ceremonies, coronations, and accessions to the nobility held Christian components. Despite secularizing ideas in science and moral philosophy, the rise of the nation-state, and Christian fragmentation—first between Rome and the Greek East and then between Rome and the Protestant north—the alliance between the church and the state remained in one form or another as a universal European truth until the shock of the French Revolution.

The French Revolution opened new political vistas and methods that seemed alien to Christians. Activism in mass politics was a new idea, and far removed from any experience. Christian response was initially clumsy, either marked by tentative and short-lived clubs and societies or by heavy-handed reactionary oppression characterized by Alexander I's Holy Alliance. The Age of Reaction from 1815 until 1848 was essentially a hope among Christian traditionalists that some form of the old order would return through a reliance on the tattered ties between church and state. Prince Metternich in Austria, Russia's Czar Alexander, and the restored Bourbon monarchy in France employed their troops to squash liberal and nationalist uprisings across Europe. The church in Rome rejected the legacy of the French Revolution and the new liberalism in a string of *zelanti* popes who identified with reactionism. The greatest of these pontiffs was Pius IX, whose "Syllabus of Errors" (1864) may be considered the definitive antimodern manifesto of the nineteenth century.

It was not until the 1840s that the work of Felicité Lamennais and others showed Christians that they could adapt to liberalism and the new politics and organize to achieve Christian-inspired goals. Despite the condemnation by Pius's predecessor, Gregory XVI, the spirit of Lamennais remained alive. The Malines Convention of 1867 served as a Catholic version of the workers' International at about the same time that that rallying event was held in London. By the end of the century, Christian political parties had begun to emerge across the European continent. Some of the first were the German Center Party, peasant parties, and various Christian Social or Christian Socialist Parties in central Europe. More often than not, these organizations were confessional, tightly linked to the churches and the hierarchy, and committed to the protection of their embattled religion. They identified with religion and maintained an interclass vision that gave them a potential leg up over socialist parties anchored to the working class or liberal parties associated with the middle classes. Observers, however, frequently doubted their commitment to democracy and suspected them of reactionary and ultramontane goals. But it was a first step. Lamennaise and others represented a new Christian openness to liberalism, while nationalism was another nineteenth-century idea that owes a debt to Christian thinkers and activists.

Although earlier, reactionary Christian thinkers rejected nationalism as antithetical to Christian universalism, others embraced it. In the struggle for Italian unification, for example, Giuseppe Mazzini bestowed both a religious and a democratic patina on his portrait of what his nation would become. Beyond Europe, the United States, and some additional, mainly Anglophone nations such as Australia, New Zealand, and Canada, the history becomes more difficult. In most Muslim areas Christian presence was an imperial imposition and of negligible importance among the indigenous peoples. In other places, such as sub-Saharan Africa and East Asia, Christian politics resembled some of its European manifestations and worked toward national liberation. Independence movements in South Africa and India, and Chinese nationalism, all contained important Christian elements.

Anti-Semitism, furthermore, emerged as a factor in some Christian politics of the late nineteenth and early twentieth centuries. As a young man in Vienna, for example, Adolf Hitler's hatred was cultivated in part by his exposure to Karl Lueger's Christian Social Party. Historians have noted, furthermore, the anti-Semitism of Charles Maurras' Action Française. While the organization touted its Christian aims, some scholars have been more interested in identifying its protofascist character.

The First World War augured important changes for Christian politics. In the Soviet Union, of course, it ended them. Not only did the Communist regime crush Christian political movements and kill many of their leaders and adherents, but the remnants of the churches that were allowed to survive were forced to become mere sycophants to the dictatorship of the proletariat. In the West, the communist menace affected, some might say blinded, Christian political activity. In his 1937 encyclical, *Divini redemptoris,* Pope Pius XI left no doubts of the Catholic Church's total condemnation of the Moscow regime. It also reiterated Rome's belief, still very much alive, that liberalism had only itself to blame for the birth of the red monster.

Such opinions led certain Christians to view emergent right-wing figures of the 1920s and 1930s—Benito Mussolini, Antonio Salazar, and Francisco Franco, among others, and, to some extent, even Hitler—as saviors from or at least safeguards against the radical Left. The Center Party bears no small responsibility in paving the way for the National Socialist dictatorship, although it ended in shame as one of the Führer's early victims. Philippe Pétain's puppet Vichy government was another that enjoyed significant Christian support. Pope Pius XII, moreover, has received criticism for his alleged silence on Nazi racism, although the story contains some twists. His predecessor, Pius XI, for example, chastised the Mussolini regime in his *Non abbiamo bisogno* (1931) and Hitler's in *Mit brennender Sorge* (1937). Indeed, many Christians suffered at the hands of the fascists and their collaborators. Lay Christian political leaders such as Austria's Chancellor Kurt Schuschnigg joined clergy in Nazi concentration camps. The ranks of the Resistance during the Second World War contained many names of those who fought as Christians. Remnants of the Center Party or Luigi Sturzo's Italian Popular Party, disbanded by Mussolini with the connivance of Pius XI, consequently formed nuclei of struggle and by the 1940s comprised much of the core of the Christian Democratic (CD) parties that materialized after the fall of Fascism.

The United States prior to the Revolutionary era had been a patchwork of colonies, each developing its own rules of accommodation between religion and politics. The ever-increasing cultural diversity of settlers, wide geographic separation, and a prevailing preoccupation with economic development assured that England's meager attempts to enforce Anglican loyalties would invariably meet with failure. The prevailing cultural winds during the seventeenth and eighteenth centuries blew decidedly in favor of denominational proliferation within the Christian fold and the elimination of religious restrictions on voting and political participation. The growing consensus in America was that religious privileges and qualifications had no formal place in the political process.

Not that individual colonies and determined religious groups within them failed to test alternatives. Early in their history, Massachusetts Bay's Puritan leaders made political participation contingent upon church membership. In 1685, England anointed Edmund Andros as colonial governor charged with uniting New York, New Jersey, and New England under a single administration. Among the many ways that Andros managed to irritate colonists was with the mandate that Anglican services be materially supported throughout the region. Puritans, as any student of American history quickly learns, did not cross the Atlantic in order to establish religious freedom and certainly not to play host to an Anglican establishment they regarded as synonymous with religious and political corruption. They expected their corner of America to serve like-minded settlers who wanted to worship God in the one best way—the Puritan way. In the middle colonies, William Penn's heavily promoted "Holy Experiment" in Pennsylvania, brimming with substantial guarantees of religious freedom featured in the Charter of Liberties (1701), still betrayed the proprietary expectations that the colonial order would give favored place to Quaker interests and beliefs.

Such efforts, however, are notable for their failure, not success. Massachusetts backed away from tying voting privileges to church membership in 1647; Andros was arrested, and his Dominion of New England dissolved in the wake of England's Glorious Revolution; the seventeenth-century resistance to Puritan political proscriptions by Anne Hutchinson and Roger Williams (who founded Rhode Island in protest) signaled the long-term vulnerability of the Puritan order; and on the eve of the American Revolution, Pennsylvania's increasingly diverse population had made Pennsylvania a fiercely democratic state bearing little resemblance to a holy commonwealth. Consequently, the constitutional separation of church and state emerges as something less than a surprising outcome of early American political development. In 1802, President Thomas Jefferson explained just how prominent the barrier was when he told Connecticut's Danbury Baptist Association that the framers had built nothing less than a "wall of separation" between church and state. His words caused little political stir at the time, but in 1879 the Supreme Court took formal notice of the phrase, and in the 1947 case *Everson v. Board of Education,* Justice Hugo Black, writing for the court majority, described a wall that "must be high and impregnable. We could not approve the slightest breach."

Rather than ending debate, however, Black's seemingly unambiguous declaration only fueled an ongoing controversy that has spanned two centuries. In other words, while Americans have historically endorsed the institutional separation of church and state, in practice the Christian community has broadly resisted the idea that religion should neither inform their public engagements nor be acknowledged in public space. On that point, the faithful have regarded Jefferson's wall as permeable, even porous, and their efforts have given shape to the practice of modern Christian politics in America. Yet as Christian activism in its European context found wide expression through formal party organization and state churches, the American system has proved hostile to such arrangements. First Amendment obstacles and the obvious political liabilities of a narrow religious identity in a two-party system encouraged Christian strategies based on moral suasion and independent activism designed to influence the political process rather than directly control it.

The importance of this political maneuvering can scarcely be exaggerated. Nevertheless, as America embraced the separation of church and state, so too historians have often presented Christian activism as an occasionally interesting sideshow or a topic best suited for believers or specialists—tangential, in other words, rather than integral to the broader story of American political development. Fortunately, that has begun to change in light of the work of such scholars as Mark Noll, Nathan Hatch, Richard Carwardine, and Jonathan Sassi. Similarly,

George Marsden, Stephen Carter, and Christopher Lasch have eloquently explained the distortions inherent in cultural studies that marginalize the role of religious belief. This volume gives global reach to that effort, and while most entries shed light on people and political organizations outside the United States, American entries comprise the largest single national group. Taken together, they provide a useful window onto the rich diversity of Christian political commitments.

Early in the nation's history, Christian denominations, jealous of their respective positions in a free society, were content to mark sharp differences between civic and Christian duties to protect against state meddling in church affairs and denominational solicitations of government favors. A few New England states provided modest support for Congregational churches into the 1830s, but such remnants of colonial days eventually bowed to the national model of separation. Nevertheless, Christian denominations still retained a strong interest in public morality, optimistically citing a practical harmony between reason and revelation in the shaping of a virtuous citizenry. After all, both sacred and secular theorists at the time of the nation's founding seemed united in calling for public virtue as the linchpin of republican stability. Christians, however, considered personal faith and transcendent biblical truths as the preferred partner in this cooperative venture.

This understanding of morality, coupled with a continuing conviction that nation-states remained providential players in God's divine plans, set the stage for Christian activism. Indeed, Protestant leaders had heady expectations for the new republican order. With constitutional guarantees providing security from Catholic political intrigues, mainstream leaders predicted complete victory for the fundamental truths of orthodox Protestant Christianity in the new marketplace of ideas. Beyond that lay a global concert of faith that would ultimately initiate Christ's millennial reign of peace and prosperity. That plan did not work out. By the 1830s, various Christian groups were formally protesting government delivery of Sunday mail, organizing antislavery societies, and fueling the early temperance movement, but they labored within a Christian community that proved as vulnerable to the fractious tendencies of democratic choice as was the larger culture. From the ranks of imported European traditions, new groups such as Alexander Campbell's Disciples of Christ and Joseph Smith's Church of Jesus Christ of Latter-day Saints (Mormons) were springing wholecloth from the unpredictable fabric of American freedom. In short, Christian political activism did not mean Christian consensus.

The course of the antislavery movement is also instructive. By the 1830s, Northern Christian luminaries such as Frederick Douglass, Gerrit Smith, and Arthur and Lewis Tappan were breaking public silence on the slavery issue to denounce an American political system that tolerated human bondage. South of the Mason-Dixon line, James Henley Thornwell, Thornton Stringfellow, and like-minded angry Southerner evangelicals upbraided their Northern counterparts for polluting the Gospel with politics. The Mormons clashed with Protestant and Catholic orthodoxy for multiple reasons, but they shared common ground with antislavery activists, and that moral stand helped spur their expulsion from Missouri in the 1840s. When Sarah and Angelina Grimké rejected cultural proscriptions against women speaking in public and began stumping for abolition, Catharine Beecher, noted author and daughter of Presbyterian leader Lyman Beecher, denounced their methods as inconsistent with Christian teaching. Southern believers were outraged when Catharine's sister, Harriet Beecher Stowe, deployed her evangelical sympathies in *Uncle Tom's Cabin* (1854). Her moral tirade against slavery became the most politically inflammatory publication of the age. When John Brown stood trial in 1859 for attempting to seize a U.S. military arsenal and foment slave rebellion, his openly Christian motivations enraged Southerners. On the day of his execution, however, church bells across the North tolled to honor his moral courage. Abraham Lincoln deliberately veiled the particulars of his own religious faith, perplexing more than a few ministers, but his personal letters and political speeches reveal a man steeped in biblical knowledge and ably applying Christian teaching to illuminate political and military objectives during the Civil War. Sociologist Robert Bellah calls Lincoln the most able practitioner of an American "civil religion," separate from but decidedly influenced by the nation's Christian tradition.

Such examples of both chaos and community continued beyond the war and into the twentieth century, with Christian leaders encamped across the political terrain. In *Christianity and the Social Crisis* (1908), Walter Rauschenbusch called upon turn-of-the-century Christians to embrace the Social Gospel and keep churches culturally relevant in a modern industrial age. His more conservative rivals invested equal enthusiasm in attacking public education's drift toward evolutionary thought and secular pedagogy. As the war against evolution in education devolved upon the trial of John T. Scopes in Dayton, Tennessee (1925), Frances Willard's Woman's Christian Temperance Union was enjoying the results of the Eighteenth Amendment that began the nation's short-lived experiment with Prohibition. On yet another Christian front, Catholics, convinced that their political protests against Protestant influence in public schools could never yield full satisfaction, set about constructing the most elaborate system of private parochial education in the nation.

Perhaps no example better reveals the politically diverse application of Christianity to political causes in the twentieth century than the Ku Klux Klan revival of the 1920s and the civil rights movement at mid century. The Klan emerged after the Civil War as the self-proclaimed defender of white Anglo-Saxon Protestant culture in the South. After being suppressed in the early 1870s under Ulysses S. Grant's presidential watch and remaining moribund for decades, the secret enclave emerged again in the 1920s, its ranks filled with Protestant ministers, mostly from the Midwest and South. Leaders targeted Jews and recently arrived Italian Catholic immigrants as especially dangerous threats to Protestant civilization. But Klan resurgence proved ephemeral, and by the 1950s, black Protestant leaders powerfully redirected Christian political energy toward the injustices of the South's segregated society. With the Reverend Martin Luther King at the helm of the Southern Christian Leadership Conference, black Christian activists pursued their goals through King's strategy of nonviolent direct action. In *Why We Can't Wait* (1963), King justified his methods with a number of historical precedents, but he also made clear that

Christian faith was the predominant source of his moral foundation and commitment to nonviolence.

Significantly, disparity between the Klan and the American civil rights movement was repeated or mirrored in European and Latin American politics that divided Christians over ideologies and conflicts. After the Second World War, for instance, some Italian Christians sympathetic to Communism, followers of Adriano Ossicini and Felice Rodano, faced the wrath not only of Catholic political figures like Luigi Gedda and Mario Scelba, but of no less than the figure of Pope Pius XII. Catholic Mexicans and Orthodox Russians fought the radical secularism of their governments after 1917, while Brazilian and French clergy sometimes alienated the hierarchy when they stood shoulder to shoulder with workers after the Second World War.

When the U.S. Supreme Court handed down its decision in *Roe v. Wade* (1973), the legalization of abortion jolted conservative evangelicals from their recent political slumber and introduced the most politically significant era of Christian activism since the antislavery and civil rights movements. The ruling facilitated an unlikely alliance between evangelicals and conservative Catholics who shared their antiabortion position. The Religious Right became a potent political force, usually aligned with Republican politicians, especially Ronald Reagan. Yet as Pat Robertson, Jerry Falwell, and Ralph Reed became national celebrities in the cause, the tradition of political action marked by internal dissent continued. Catholic traditionalist Richard John Neuhaus, for example, maintained a sympathetic but decidedly independent voice disseminated largely through his publication *First Things*. Likewise, liberal voices such as Jim Wallis, Martin Marty, and Robert Bellah called upon Christians to refocus their activism on the abuses of American power and the structural injustices inherent in capitalist society. Through all the tumult, "America's evangelist," Billy Graham, somehow managed to stay mostly above the fray, maintaining his historic role as the most visible Christian link to the arbiters of American power.

At the opening of the twenty-first century, Christian activism in the United States shows no signs of departing the public square. The election of George W. Bush placed in the White House a president more committed than any previous chief executive to building connections between faith communities and government social action. Bush refined his vision of "compassionate conservatism" while serving as Republican governor of Texas, and as president he called for Congress to formally endorse "faith-based initiatives." The plan would offer government funds to religious (not necessarily Christian) groups providing public material assistance consistent with government objectives. Congress was still withholding endorsement in 2005, and Christians, as usual, were not united in supporting the plan. By 2006, liberal Protestant and Catholic leaders, strongly opposed to the war in Iraq and Bush's foreign policy, had little interest in supporting the administration. Evangelicals offered a friendlier hand but looked beyond faith-based initiatives to their most pressing expectation—the presidential appointment of Supreme Court justices who would overturn the *Roe v. Wade* decision.

On the other side of the Atlantic, secular consumer society accelerated by spectacular economic growth—the economic miracles of Germany and Italy, or

France's "thirty glorious years"—presented new cultural challenges. While Christian Democratic parties or thinkers tended to be economically progressive in support of planned markets, welfare states, or workers' participation in decision making, many Christians remained culturally conservative. In Italy their politics played themselves out over such issues as censorship, divorce, and abortion battles, all of which they ultimately lost. Women's liberation created anxiety among Europe's Christians as it did on other continents, in part because the question divided them. Women in the workplace, per se, were not roundly condemned. Italian Catholic Action, for example, even reacted favorably at the end of the 1950s toward female police units. Women, after all, usually supplied the majority of Christian Democratic votes, and leaders from CD women's organizations advocated expanded roles in much the same way that lay feminists did. On the other hand, most closed ranks over preserving the honored role of motherhood and the sanctity of the unborn. These controversies should not cloud the fact that Christian Democrats enjoyed extraordinary successes in both Latin America and through much of postwar Europe. In such diverse states as Chile, Bolivia, Germany—before and after unification—post-Communist Poland, the Low Countries, Italy, and even notoriously secularized France, Christian Democracy was a force to be reckoned with and often dominated the political scene.

In sum, the larger history of modern political development cannot be understood apart from the history of modern Christian politics. And as the entries in these volumes reveal, that story can be at once enlightening, inspiring, contradictory, or even troubling.

A

ABERNATHY, RALPH (1926–1990).
A Baptist pastor and civil rights leader, Abernathy oversaw the successful movement to desegregate the American South. The bureaucratic foil to **Martin Luther King**'s charismatic authority, Abernathy played a critical role in the formation and maintenance of the **Southern Christian Leadership Conference** (SCLC).

Abernathy was born in Linden, Alabama, in 1926. Although embedded in the segregated South, the Abernathy family had some financial independence due to a prosperous farm. While he was young, his father instilled in him a respect for the virtues of U.S. citizenship, a citizenship that Abernathy would always interpret as implicitly linked to a profound moral vision. This loyalty encouraged Abernathy's overseas service during World War II. Upon his return, he began his lifelong professional commitment to the ministry and in 1948 was ordained as a Baptist minister. With financial assistance from the G.I. Bill, he completed a bachelor of science in mathematics from Alabama State University (1948) and a master of arts in sociology from Atlanta University (1951). Following the completion of his master's degree, Abernathy took a pastorate at the First Baptist Church in Montgomery, Alabama. It was there that his path merged with King's, and the modern civil rights movement began.

A conservative in politics and theology, Abernathy was not a likely activist. But his commitment to Christianity motivated an unending frustration with the crass impieties of discrimination. He was known to say, "Christians should be ready for a change because Jesus was the greatest changer in history." After meeting in Montgomery, King and Abernathy forged a productive working relationship, and in 1955 they organized a boycott of that city's bus system. For thirteen months, the 17,000 African Americans inhabiting that city walked or carpooled to work. White Montgomery resisted the protest, bombing the homes and churches of those blacks in charge, including Abernathy. The nonviolent strategy prevailed, however. Desegregation of the buses in 1956 encouraged more-forceful protests and more efficient organization.

King and Abernathy hoped to repeat their Montgomery success throughout the South. In order to do so, they gathered a group of Southern black ministers from eleven states to form the Southern Christian Leadership Conference (SCLC) in 1957. The central purpose of the organization was to arrange nonviolent resistance to segregation. their motto was "Not one hair of one head of one person should be harmed." With King as president and Abernathy as secretary-treasurer, the SCLC organized

marches, sit-ins, boycotts, and voter registration drives in the fight against systematic
discrimination. Abernathy labored as the
bureaucratic mainstay, eventually moving
the SCLC headquarters to Atlanta in 1961.
Though primarily responsible for the pragmatics of protest, Abernathy did his share
of demonstrating. During his stints as secretary-treasurer and vice president, he was
arrested nineteen times.

The Civil Rights Act of 1964 signaled the
legal success of the SCLC's efforts, and its
passage altered the direction of the movement. Abernathy and King turned to the
social aspects of discrimination, including
income and housing disparity. Just as their
war against black poverty was taking shape,
King was assassinated in 1968. Abernathy
was forced to step further into the spot-
light, taking over King's position as the
president of the SCLC. But the devastation
of King's death and the grinding persistence of the Vietnam War undermined the
progress of the civil rights movement.

Abernathy went on to lead the Poor
People's Campaign in Washington, D.C.
(1968), the Atlanta sanitation workers'
strike (1968), and the Charleston hospital
workers' strike (1969), but none of these
efforts matched his earlier successes.

By 1970, Abernathy had shifted the
SCLC's direction, focusing more on legal
advocacy and fundraising. He headed that
organization until his resignation in 1977,
at which point he made an unsuccessful
bid for a Georgia congressional seat. The
last ten years of his life were spent at his
ministry in Atlanta.

In later years, younger black leaders criticized Abernathy for his conservative politics (he endorsed **Ronald Reagan**'s
presidential bid). However, such commentaries fail to recognize the essential conservatism of the SCLC and its primarily Baptist
leadership. For Abernathy, civil rights were
a moral necessity more than a political revolution. His careful management of the
Southern Christian Leadership Conference

Rev. Ralph Abernathy, leader of the Poor People's Campaign, addresses a
group of protesting squatters, citizens of "Resurrection City," 1968. © Costa
Manos / Magnum Photos

guided the early success of the American civil rights movement.

Bibliography. Abernathy, Ralph. *And The Walls Came Tumbling Down.* New York: HarperCollins, 1989. Garrow, David J. *Bearing the Cross: Martin Luther King, Jr., and the Southern Christian Leadership Conference.* New York: Quill, 1999.

Kathryn Lofton

ABOLITIONISTS (UNITED STATES). The American abolitionists' pursuit of emancipation is a story of the fusing of religious and political energies. Most of the militant men and women who made up the small but swelling minority of immediate abolitionists in the antebellum years drew their inspiration from a vital Protestant evangelicalism. Many, though by no means all, believed that the United States' political system, infused with the republican values of the Declaration of Independence and the federal Constitution, provided the means of laying siege to the most potent slave economy in the Atlantic world.

Earlier, during the Revolutionary era, proponents of natural rights philosophy had joined with those radicalized by the mid-eighteenth century "awakenings"—Quakers and other evangelicals—to bring about gradual abolition by political means. Emancipation was in progress in most of the Northern states by 1784, and in all by 1804. Yet even as reformers celebrated these successes, plantation slavery was tightening its grip. As the cotton culture expanded, many questioned the effectiveness of schemes of gradual reform, most notably the American Colonization Society's program of settling free blacks abroad.

From the later 1820s a new generation of heart-warmed Christians made Southern slavery a target for the outworking of their faith. The movement that took institutional shape in the American Anti-Slavery Society (AASS) in 1833 was conditioned by a strain of millennialist revivalism associated with

Charles Grandison Finney's "burned-over district" of upstate New York and parts of the New England diaspora, as well as the rest of New England itself. Liberal Protestants and antinomians were represented within the movement, but orthodox evangelicals constituted its main body. Believing in the perfectibility of American society, they regarded slavery as much more than a social evil to be stoically endured while it withered away; it was a sin jeopardizing the souls of all—non-slaveholders included—and they demanded immediate efforts for its extirpation.

From the start, many in the AASS proved sympathetic to "Calvinist" views of citizenship and looked beyond moral suasion. Most respected the constitutional right of slave states to control their domestic institutions but believed that Congress could tackle slavery wherever the federal government exercised sole authority. They circulated petitions house-to-house. They questioned candidates for public office and won antislavery pledges. White male abolitionists voted, while black and many female reformers drew the lessons of their own disfranchisement and began their own campaigns for voting rights.

At the same time, a minority of abolitionists followed **William Lloyd Garrison** and Henry C. Wright down the road of Christian anarchism, nonresistance, and perfectionism and refused to vote or fulfill other conventional civic obligations. Garrison's anti-governmentalism—part of a broader complex of antiauthoritarian, anticlerical, antinomian, and iconoclastic ideas—invited an avalanche of criticism from conservative reformers for his "transcendental nonsense" and contributed to fissures in the AASS that would split the movement from top to bottom in 1840.

At first, abolitionists aimed to act as a lever on the two major parties and thereby secure an influence beyond their numbers. But with Whig and Democratic leaders appearing unable to escape the thralldom of the slave power, Myron Holley and others proposed an antislavery third party. They met resistance not just from Garrisonians but also from more conservative abolitionists like **Lewis Tappan.** But with Joshua Leavitt's and **Gerrit Smith**'s influence thrown into the scales, the balance tilted toward independent action for Bible politics. At Albany in April 1840, a convention of political abolitionists nominated James Birney as presidential candidate of what would become the Liberty Party.

In program, modus operandi, and composition, the new party was an expression of revivalist Protestantism. To avoid the judgments of the Almighty, Liberty men argued, the federal government should disconnect itself from the sin of slavery by sponsoring abolition in the District of Columbia and in the Florida Territory, ending the interstate slave trade, repudiating the congressional gag laws that silenced discussion of abolitionist petitions, and resisting Southern expansionists' demands for the annexation of Texas. A few even argued that the federal government, as the constitutional guarantor of republicanism, had the power and duty to prosecute abolition within the boundaries of the slave states. The party's activists formed a religious brotherhood, with "come-outers," notably Wesleyan Methodists and Free Presbyterians, strongly represented alongside vigorous minorities from Congregationalist, New School Presbyterian, Freewill Baptist, and other mainstream churches.

Liberty men made little impact during the Log Cabin Campaign of 1840, and the party's vote in the presidential contest of 1844 totaled a meager 65,608. As a one-idea movement, it failed to serve those whose political concerns extended beyond abolition. It had to address anxieties over a "wasted" vote. Likewise it had to face up to its uneven impact on the two main parties, weakening Whiggery, the force more sympathetic to humanitarian reform,

more than it did the Democrats. In 1844 Birney's candidacy had attracted enough Whig ballots to hand the pivotal state of New York, and thus the presidency, to the avowed annexationist and slaveholder James Knox Polk.

Abolitionists saw enhanced opportunity for political action in the wake of the Mexican war (1846–1848). Liberty men coalesced with dissident so-called Conscience Whigs and Democratic Barnburner enemies of the Polk administration into a Free Soil Party committed to choking slavery and keeping it out of the lands ceded by Mexico. The Free Soilers' stress in the 1848 election on the interests of Northern white labor, and their ambivalence toward racial equality, spurred a few around Gerrit Smith, William Goodell, and the black radical Henry Highland Garnet to form a dissident fourth party, the Liberty League. But a majority of political abolitionists treated the new movement as a crusade founded on "the idea of right and justice and the truth of God." Even the fugitive-turned-abolitionist **Frederick Douglass** endorsed it, despite the racism of its Barnburner nominee, Martin Van Buren. Although the party lacked the moral purity of the Garrisonians, it seemed a more realistic route to freedom than the self-segregation of those who wanted "no Union with slaveholders." During the campaign the third party drove Northern Whig and Democrat leaders as never before onto explicitly antislavery ground, to the alarm of the parties' Southern wings. Its intervention denied victory to the Democrats in the presidential contest and secured the election of a dozen of its congressional candidates.

The Compromise of 1850 (by which conservative Unionists resolved the political crisis over the Mexican cession) took the electoral wind out of radical antislavery politics and yet provided the issue, the new Fugitive Slave Law, on which a fractured and interracial abolition movement could begin to draw together again. During the 1850s, this draconian measure spurred alleged runaways and their abolitionist allies to new heights of resistance. The nasty Civil War in Kansas—blamed by abolitionists on "slaveocrats" deemed to have plotted a slave future for the territory—served only to convince nonresistant Garrisonians of the need to embrace violence. **John Brown**'s raid on Harpers Ferry in 1859, widely supported by black and white activists, was the logical result of abolitionists' growing appetite for confrontation with an apparently insatiable slave power.

Abolitionists did not abandon the political arena in the 1850s, but as sectional issues came to take over the politics of the mainstream parties and left little room for a third antislavery force, so their political influence shrank (in the North, that is. It was a different matter in the South, where an exaggerated idea of abolitionist power nourished an ever-more potent Southern radicalism.) The racial conservatism of the new Republican coalition and its prioritizing of the needs of Northern white labor led some immediatists to endorse Gerrit Smith's independent abolition party in 1860, but most abolitionists saw enough Protestant righteousness and vision in the party of **Lincoln** to deliver to it their energies and their votes. Once war broke out in April 1861, the final traces of abolitionist nonresistance and disunionism dissolved. Immediatists readily engaged in a struggle they were determined to turn into a war for emancipation; they became the Union's radical conscience. Through the pulpit, and the platform, petitions, and editorial columns of the New York *Independent* and other mass-circulation religious and secular newspapers, abolitionists maintained an insistent moral drumbeat for freedom, racial equality, the use of black troops, and civil and political rights for freedmen.

When emancipation came, in the shape of Lincoln's proclamation of January 1, 1863, it opened the door to final freedom but did not affect the revolution in racial attitudes that the abolitionists had sought. Nor was it the immediatists' political pressure and moral suasion that had affected it. Battlefield realities and the actions of the Confederates' slaves themselves played a much larger role than the abolitionists in creating the emancipationist tide that shaped the Union's future. The same limits to the abolitionists' influence were evident in the postwar world, when their racial egalitarianism impelled many of them into the politics of Reconstruction. There they confronted mainstream Republicans committed to the fight against Andrew Johnson's conservative policies but reluctant to move ahead of opinion in race-conscious Northern constituencies. As in the antebellum years, abolitionists' religious inspiration and moral ambition outran their political influence.

Bibliography. Carwardine, Richard J. *Evangelicals and Politics in Antebellum America.* New Haven, CT: Yale University Press, 1993. McPherson, James M. *The Struggle for Equality: Abolitionists and the Negro in the Civil War and Reconstruction.* Princeton, NJ: Princeton University Press, 1964. Stewart, James Brewer. *Holy Warriors: The Abolitionists and American Slavery.* New York: Hill & Wang, 1976.

Richard J. Carwardine

ACCIÓN CATÓLICA MEXICANA. *See* Mexican Catholic Action

ACTION FRANÇAISE. From its founding in 1899 to its dissolution at the end of World War II, Action Française was the most significant French royalist movement of its time and a key component of an emerging radical (or new) right in France in the years before the First World War. Behind the leadership of **Charles Maurras,** and with a predominantly Catholic membership, Action Française promoted a politics of violent anti-republicanism, monarchism, nationalism, and anti-Semitism—some of which would come to the fore during the period of German occupation and rule from Vichy.

Founded at the height of the Dreyfus Affair to combat the republican supporters of Alfred Dreyfus, a Jewish officer who had been falsely accused of delivering military secrets to the Germans, Action Française took its name from the newspaper of the same name edited by Maurras. Along with Paul Déroulède and Maurice Barrès, Maurras was a chief exponent of what has come to be called integral nationalism. It was Maurras (and his newspaper) who did most to formulate a coherent doctrine of integral nationalism, the components of which included militant nationalism, racism and anti-Semitism, anti-republicanism, and authoritarianism. According to Maurras's brand of nationalism, France was a superior motherland, worthy of the unqualified devotion of all "genuine" Frenchmen and women (excluding "alien" elements such as Jews, Protestants, Freemasons, and naturalized French people). But, according to Maurras, France was no longer a great power; it had become "a masterpiece of littleness." For Maurras, this decline from great-power status was the fault of republicanism, as France's true interests were not (and could never be) represented by the men of the republic. His recipe for the recovery of France's greatness was the overthrow of the republic and a return to monarchy.

Maurras's support for the army at the time of the Dreyfus Affair reflected as much his belief in the role of the army as guarantor of domestic order as it did his opposition to Dreyfus the Jew. For Maurras admired order, hierarchy, and authority. Although he was a nonbeliever, he (like Marshal **Philippe Pétain** in the early 1940s) looked to Roman Catholicism to provide a moral foundation for national salvation. His monarchism reflected a belief in a hierarchical social order rather than any allegiance to the Bourbon dynasty.

Following the Law of Separation of 1905, and for purely political reasons, Action Française took up the defense of the Catholic Church. Only then did it become a true mass movement, able to mobilize thousands in the streets. It received open support from leading French bishops and, on the eve of war in 1914, 90 percent of its members were Catholics.

The half-dozen years following the end of World War I saw the apogee of Action Française's influence among lay Catholics and religious alike, to the extent that it was sometimes identified with the French Catholic Church (and vice versa). Little wonder then that Pope **Pius XI**'s condemnation of the movement—for subordinating religion to politics and nationalism—in December 1926 dealt an enormous blow to Action Française. Catholics were instructed to abandon the movement and its newspaper. Three months later, the sacraments were denied to members of the movement. Even though many Catholic laymen ignored the Vatican's directive, the French clergy generally submitted. By the end of 1927, *Action française* had lost half of its readers. Yet Rome's condemnation of *Action Française* did not come out of the blue. As early as 1914, **Pius X** had warned the movement against idolatry of the nation. The condemnation of 1926 marked another decisive episode in the long gallican-ultramontane struggle.

By the mid-1920s Action Française—with its commitment to the church and the monarchy—appeared faintly old fashioned, especially compared to Benito Mussolini and his Fascists in Italy, whose admirers and imitators in France included dissident members of Action Française who yearned for a fascism *à la française*. For although it had recognizably fascist traits, and notwithstanding its leading role in the anti-parliamentary riots of February 1934, Action Française was not fascist. Maurras was more a man of ideas than a man of action. Indeed, much of the movement's appeal to intellectuals (Catholic and otherwise) in the interwar years testified to the quality of the newspaper's literary pages rather than the appeal of its political doctrine.

Dissolved (although not dismantled) by Leon Blum's Popular Front government in 1936 and disowned by the Bourbon pretender in 1937, Action Française was removed from the Index by **Pius XII** in 1939. Increasingly drawn to a kind of anti-Bolshevik pacifism following the Munich conference of September 1938, most of its members welcomed what Maurras referred to as the "divine surprise" of defeat in 1940 and supported the Vichy regime.

Bibliography. Nolte, Ernst. *Three Faces of Fascism: Action Française, Italian Fascism, National Socialism.* London: Weidenfeld & Nicholson, 1965. Prévotat, Jacques. *L'Action Française.* Paris: Presses universitaires de France, 2004. Prévotat, Jacques. *Les Catholiques et l'Action Française: Histoire d'une condamnation 1899–1939.* Paris: Fayard, 2001. Weber, Eugen. *Action Française: Royalism and Reaction in Twentieth-century France.* Stanford, CA: Stanford University Press, 1962.

Ramesh J. Rajballie

ACTON, JOHN EMERICH EDWARD DALBERG (1834–1902). Lord Acton (later first Baron Acton) was an important British historian and lay Roman Catholic who played a role in both religious and secular politics. He was one of the leading historians of the nineteenth century, though he never published a major book during his lifetime. He became known for his scholarly articles and reviews, however, many of which concerned the history and politics of the Catholic Church, ranging across the history of modern Europe from the Reformation onwards. Dedicated to the history of liberty, he is remembered for his epigram: "power tends to corrupt and absolute power corrupts absolutely."

In some respects, Acton was a European as much as a British figure. He was born in Naples, the son of an English baronet. Raised as a Catholic in England, Acton's life was transformed at the age of sixteen

when he studied in Munich under the tutelage of Professor Johan Ignaz von Döllinger, who became his mentor. At the time, Döllinger was an ultramontane priest and defender of the pope, though he and Acton later became rebels. From Döllinger, Acton acquired his fascination with history. Döllinger taught him the new methods of German historical scholarship characterized by intense research in archives.

Settling in England, Acton was elected to parliament in 1859 for an Irish constituency, but his political career ended uneventfully in 1867. He barely spoke in debates and failed to have any impact. At the same time, he became coproprietor and editor of the *Rambler* (later *Home and Foreign Review*), which he established as the leading liberal Catholic periodical of the 1860s in Britain. Acton provided lengthy articles on historical and religious issues, demonstrating that Catholics were capable of serious intellectual inquiry. He showed off the latest techniques of scientific history, which he imported from Germany. Acton aimed to link Catholicism with the forces of progress. The Catholic hierarchy was alarmed by such independence of thought, and Acton stopped the journal in 1864.

Liberalism (meaning here a dislike for absolutism as well as support for the Liberal party) informed Acton's writings. He became a close friend of the Liberal leader **William Gladstone,** who raised him to the peerage in 1869. Acton was skeptical of contemporary nationalist movements in Europe. He disliked states based around a dominant racial group and favored those that included a variety of races, which, he believed, promoted liberty.

Acton was also opposed to ultramontanism in the Catholic Church. He was active at Rome in opposing the proclamation of papal infallibility at the first Vatican Council in 1869–1870. His efforts to prevent the decree failed, although (unlike Döllinger, who publicly opposed the doctrine) he was not excommunicated. Acton thereafter devoted less time to religious affairs. He claimed to belong to the soul rather than the body of the church.

His reputation as a scholar increased. In 1886, he helped establish the *English Historical Review,* which became the most important historical journal in Britain. Through his connection with Gladstone, he was appointed lord-in-waiting to Queen Victoria in 1892. Then, in 1895, he was made Regius Professor of History at Cambridge University. He helped launch the *Cambridge Modern History* (an influential series of historical surveys), though he did not live to contribute to it. In later life, he was known to be writing a history of liberty, which he never completed. When he died in 1902, he was admired as an important Catholic intellectual, but most of all as a scholar who reshaped the study of history through scrupulous archival research.

Bibliography. Chadwick, Owen. *Acton and History.* Cambridge: Cambridge University Press, 1998. Hill, Roland. *Lord Acton.* New Haven, CT: Yale University Press, 2000.

Rohan McWilliam

ADDAMS, JANE (1860–1935). A tireless advocate for immigrants, orphans, and the working classes, Addams emerged in the late nineteenth century as a leader in the American settlement movement. Best known for the creation of Hull House, the first social settlement in America with male and female residents, Addams spent her life attempting to reconcile economic disparity through cultural reform. Although she was continually at odds with her own faith and religious authority, Addams remains a major moral figure in the pantheon of Protestant activism. Many interpret her political and organizational labors as enactments of the **Social Gospel** theology popularized during her era.

Addams began her life in a world of middle-class morality and material comfort.

She was born in Cedarville, Illinois in 1860, where her father was a prominent citizen and prosperous banker who helped found his state's Republican Party. Among the first generation of American college women, Jane Addams attended the Rockford Female Seminary (later Rockford College) at her father's insistence. Though John Addams was a Hicksite Quaker, he saw in seminary education the opportunity for women to find a meaningful vocation in a world of limited professional options.

Jane Addams struggled throughout her life with religion, acknowledging alternatively its necessity as a moral compass and danger as a pacifying delusion. Her education at Rockford instilled in Addams a commitment to the passion and pragmatic labor of missionary work. She attempted to manifest that devotion through a medical education, briefly attending the Women's Medical College of Philadelphia in 1881, but she was forced to return home following an incapacitating spinal condition. She would eventually recover from this particular ailment, although from 1881 until 1888 she suffered from a nervous disorder (known as neurasthenia) that accompanied a prolonged depression. The death of her father in 1881 left her aimless in the world of middle-class Victorian womanhood, and she sought resolution through meaningful labor.

In 1889, she found resolution with the formation of Hull House. Addams originally conceived of Hull House as an educational site for other women like herself, where the educated wealthy could encounter the impoverished. Throughout her forty-six years of management, Addams reiterated that the mission of Hull House was to assist both the resident workers *and* those served. Founded on Chicago's west side, Hull House mirrored other settlement houses in its construction of programs to encourage economic mobility among the poor. What made Hull House unique was its pairing of these activities with arts education. Addams sought to improve not only physical conditions for the immigrants flooding Hull House but also their overall quality of life. She believed that the poor needed trained integration into society rather than remaining unendingly in geographic and material exile. Thus, she provided job training, public baths, day care, and citizenship classes alongside coursework in literature and art. This forged an impressive educational combination, one that gained Addams a national profile as a compassionate laborer among the urban poor.

Aside from its social service work, Hull House also became an important launching pad for related movements to reform the conditions of the American factory worker. Historians point to Addams as the creator of urban sociology, as she collected data on sweatshops and housing, sewage systems, and educational disparity in her effort to construct clear arguments for necessary legislative change. As a result of this research, she and her co-workers were able to encourage the creation of factory and tenement codes in Illinois, as well as the formation of several women's labor unions.

Addams's reputation fostered her role as a major progressive fundraiser and organizer. In the age of urban reform, she was a headlining advocate who could garner votes, monetary support, and middle-class empathy for her causes. She did not always take popular positions, siding with the workers during the Pullman Strike and opposing U.S. acquisition of the Philippine Islands. Moreover, she endorsed a diverse array of national candidates, including Theodore Roosevelt, Eugene Debs, and Herbert Hoover. She served in multiple local and international capacities, from garbage inspector for Chicago's Nineteenth Ward to leadership positions in the National Peace Congress and Women's International League for Peace and Freedom. Her labors were rewarded with the 1931 Nobel Peace Prize.

In an age suffused with theologies of social responsibility, Jane Addams sought to realize Protestant moral ideals. Eschewing corporate models of social service, Addams attempted to create thoughtful citizens. Her moral vision and pragmatic sensibility remain paradigmatic expressions of American social activism.

Bibliography. Elshtain, Jean Bethke. *Jane Addams and the Dream of American Democracy.* New York: Basic Books, 2002. Lasch, Christopher, ed. *The Social Thought of Jane Addams.* Indianapolis, IN: Bobbs-Merrill, 1965.

Kathryn Lofton

ADENAUER, KONRAD (1876–1967). Longtime chairman of the **Christian Democratic Union** (1950–1966), Adenauer embodied the struggle to integrate the Federal Republic of Germany with the West and ultimately achieve German reunification following World War II. He realized a

Jane Addams. Courtesy of the Library of Congress

lifetime of political involvement as *Oberbürgermeister* (lord mayor) of Cologne (1917–1933), president of the Prussian Council of State (1921–1933), chairman of the **Christian Democratic Union** in the British zone of occupation (1946), member of the Landtag (state parliament) of North Rhine-Westphalia (1946–1950), president of the Parlamentarischer Rat (Parliamentary Council) (1948–1949), federal chancellor (1949–1963), foreign secretary (1951–1955), and member of the Bundestag (federal parliament) (1949–1967).

Adenauer was the son of a civil servant and grew up in Cologne as one of four children in a modest household. Following his *Abitur* (school-leaving exam) in 1894, he studied law and economics in Freiburg, Munich, and Bonn. After his finals, he worked as a lawyer and judge in his hometown. Through his marriage in 1904 to Emma Weyer, he came into contact with members of the upper-middle class in leading Rhineland social and political circles. His background and upbringing as a Catholic led him to membership in the **Center Party** (Zentrum), the party of German political Catholicism. In 1906 he was elected to the Cologne City Council and became lord mayor in 1917. His wife, who had borne him three children, died in 1916. In 1919 he married Auguste Zinsser, with whom he had four children.

In the first German (Weimar) republic, Adenauer was one of the nation's strongest political personalities. For sixteen years he determined Cologne's fortunes and made the city into a metropolis in the west of Germany by refounding the university, reviving the Cologne trade fairs, and encouraging industry, such as the Ford Motor Company, to locate to the area.

After the end of World War I he advocated the detachment of the Rhineland from Prussia but not from Germany, which brought him the unjustified accusation from nationalist circles of being a separatist. He sought, furthermore, to link heavy industry in the west of Germany with that of adjacent countries, thereby easing fears among those countries toward the German Reich. From 1921 to 1933 he belonged to the Prussian council of state, the central organ representing the towns and provinces in Prussia, of which he was elected president each year. He was repeatedly considered for the position of chancellor. As president of the Munich Catholic Conference (Katholikentag) of 1922, he recommended that Catholics and Protestants work together long before the founding of an interdenominational party was considered.

Adenauer opposed National Socialism and as a result was dismissed from his position as lord mayor of Cologne on March 12, 1933 and banished from his hometown. During the years of Hitler's dictatorship and the war, Adenauer remained in banishment and under threat and surveillance. He survived with his family in his house in Rhöndorf, near Bonn. Following the attempt to assassinate Hitler in 1944, Adenauer was imprisoned for several months by the Gestapo.

After the fall of Nazism in 1945, the American military authorities permitted Adenauer, a politician with an unblemished record, to resume his old appointment as lord mayor of Cologne. He energetically approached his task of rebuilding the ruined city. However, British military authorities dismissed Adenauer and forbade him any form of political activity following his criticism of their occupation policies. When he was again allowed to return to politics, Adenauer concentrated on building up the CDU, formed in 1945. He very soon held all offices of leadership within the CDU in North Rhine-Westphalia and the British zone of occupation. After the creation of the Federal Republic of Germany in 1949, he was elected chairman of the CDU (1950) and was regularly reelected with a vast majority up until he resigned in 1966. With his election in 1948

The German Federal Chancellor Adenauer on the way to the Office of the Federal Chancellor, 1957. © National Library of Vienna

as president of the Parliamentary Council, the task of which was to work out the *Grundgesetz* (Basic Law) for the newly created state, Adenauer undertook a key role with more than just regional importance. After the first parliamentary elections, he was elected federal chancellor in 1949.

In Adenauer's fourteen years as chancellor—years marked by the East-West differences and the cold war—the foundation was laid for the successful development of West Germany's second, or federal, republic. In 1949 the highest authority over the young democracy lay with the Allied High Commissioners of the occupying forces, the United States, Great Britain, and France. Adenauer succeeded within a few years in reestablishing German political and moral credit in the Federal Republic— a republic mostly in ruins, flooded with refugees and exiles, and democratically still in the process of development. He sought to anchor all of free Germany within the circle of Western democracies. He did not seek the reunification of the divided country for its own sake. For him, the preservation of freedom had priority over unity; the military defense contribution was aimed at securing this freedom. The respect he won with this policy opened up successively greater areas for maneuver for the fledgling republic until finally in 1955 the Federal Republic became a fully sovereign state.

Adenauer's Christian convictions nurtured his antipathy toward communism and kept him constantly concerned about Soviet expansionism. Adenauer always pleaded for the integration of the Federal Republic in the community of Western democracies, which he saw as an idealistic unity. To this end he pursued both the development of federal armed forces as defense against the Red Army of the Soviet Union and the integration of Western defense organizations. He also worked for European integration, which received its formal foundation in the European Economic Community (EEC) in 1957 by the Treaty of Rome. He encouraged reconciliation with France, which culminated in the signing of the Franco-German treaty in 1963. Adenauer's policies consolidated and stabilized the young democracy first by providing for the assimilation of the millions of exiles and refugees. Secondly, they developed the social market economy—together with his economics minister **Ludwig Erhard**—which combined the promotion of free enterprise with social security and with compensatory measures. Within a short time, the defeated and devastated country had produced the most efficient European economy, the German "economic miracle."

The respect Adenauer earned as a modernizer with the epoch-making direction of his domestic and foreign policies during his chancellorship from 1949 to 1963, was reflected in major election victories. In the 1953 federal election, Adenauer's CDU—together with its Bavarian sister party, the **Christian Social Union (CSU)**—won the majority of seats in parliament, and in 1957 they won the majority of votes cast (50.1%). Under his chairmanship, which he relinquished in 1966, the CDU/CSU became the strongest political force in Germany. The party stood for Christian values was oriented toward the West. Its domestic and foreign political aims for the Federal Republic were a modern landmark for the future.

Adenauer has often been criticized for giving the safeguarding of freedom and the integration of the Federal Republic into the western community of states priority over the reunification of Germany. In actual fact he never lost sight of German unity. Western integration was supposed to make reunification possible without the loss of freedom and peace in Europe. He could only imagine the restoration of German unity linked with the end of East-West antagonism and with a unified European continent. His aim

was "that Europe will become a large, common house for all Europeans, a house of freedom." A year before his death, he described the fact that global politics did not allow him to achieve this goal as "very distressing." He died at the age of ninety-one in his house in Rhöndorf.

Bibliography. Adenauer, Konrad. *Briefe 1945–1959.* 7 vols. Berlin: Siedler, 1983–2000. Adenauer, Konrad. *Erinnerungen.* 4 vols. Stuttgart, Germany: DVA, 1965–1968. Adenauer, Konrad. *Teegespräche 1950–1963.* 4 vols. Berlin: Siedler, 1984–1992. *Adenauer und die Hohen Kommissare.* 2 vols. Berlin: Siedler, 1989/1990. Buchstab, Günter, ed. *Die Protokolle des CDU-Bundesvorstands 1950–1965.* 4 vols. Düsseldorf, Germany: Droste, 1984–1998. Köhler, Henning. *Adenauer: Eine politische Biographie.* Berlin: Propyläen, 1994. Schwarz, Hans-Peter. *Adenauer. Der Aufstieg 1876–1952. Der Staatsmann 1952–1967.* 2 vols. Stuttgart, Germany: DVA, 1986–1991. "Zum 125 Geburtstag von Konrad Adenauer." *Die politische Meinung* 45 (December 2000): 373.

Günter Buchstab

ALBERTARIO, DAVIDE (1846–1902). An Italian Catholic priest and journalist, Albertario was a fiery foe of liberalism and a leader of the so-called intransigents, who rejected any reconciliation with the Italian state after the loss of the temporal power of the papacy in 1870.

Born in Filighera, in the province of Pavia, Albertario graduated with a degree in theology from the Gregorian University in 1868 and was ordained in 1869. In July of that year, he joined the editorial board of the *Osservatore Cattolico,* a Milan-based daily that aimed at curbing liberal feelings within the Lombard clergy. He became coeditor of the newspaper along with Enrico Massara in 1873.

Albertario took issue especially with Milan's archbishop, Luigi Nazari di Calabiana, a senator and staunch stalwart of the House of Savoy who opposed the doctrine of papal infallibility proclaimed in 1870. Albertario was harshly criticized for a vicious obituary of Italy's King Victor Emmanuel II, in which he stressed that the sovereign had indeed fulfilled his promise to remain in Rome but only as a corpse.

Albertario was an outspoken and vitriolic polemist, but the backing of Pope **Pius IX** enabled the *Osservatore Cattolico* to continue publication. As papal support for Albertario declined under **Leo XIII,** Albertario's subsequent campaigns against the Rosminians as well as against moderate bishops Geremia Bonomelli and Giovanni Battista Scalabrini resulted in a number of lawsuits on moral, religious, and libel charges.

Unlike other intransigents who advocated a return to the pre-Risorgimento past, Albertario argued that Catholics had to compete with the socialists and the liberals in order to make inroads within the youth and the working class. Thus, he urged a less restrictive interpretation of the *Non expedit* (the papal formula that prohibited Catholics from voting and standing as candidates at parliamentary elections) and was instrumental in securing the election of seventeen Catholics to Milan's City Council in 1895. Albertario also embraced reforms such as workers' ownership of the means of productions, which brought him close to the Socialists. That stand helped to place Albertario among the subversives in the eyes of the authorities. In the wake of the Milan rioting of 1898, the *Osservatore Cattolico* had to cease publication for a few months, and Albertario was sentenced to three years in prison.

Upon his release, Albertario took a backseat in politics but supported the Christian Democrats of **Romolo Murri.** He remained a controversial figure even after his death and became an example for anti-Fascist Catholicism in the mid-1930s.

Bibliography. Pecora, Giuseppe. *Don Davide Albertario campione del giornalismo cattolico.* Turin, Italy: SEI, 1934.

Stefano Luconi

ALEXANDER I (1777–1825). Czar Alexander I ruled the Russian Empire at a time of religious ferment and diplomatic instability. Drawn toward mysticism, he turned to Christianity to help shape his country and Europe.

Alexander came to the throne as a result of a court rebellion against his unpopular father, Paul I (r.1796–1801). Though he had almost certainly assented to the overthrow, he was shocked when he learned that his father had been murdered during the course of the event. Many historians believe the sense of guilt and repentance this caused in the new ruler created a heightened interest in religion for the remainder of his life.

Though a member of Russia's official Orthodox Church, he became deeply influenced by Protestantism. Like many educated Russians of the time, he was drawn to Western religious and intellectual currents such as German pietism, which emphasized sentimentality and a reliance upon the Bible alone. This and the shock of Napoleon Bonaparte's invasion of Russia in 1812 produced in Alexander a deeply sensitive and even erratic religious character that expressed itself in government.

In domestic policies Alexander was guided by one of his most trusted advisors, Alexander Golitsyn. The czar appointed Golitsyn to the important position of chief procurator of the Holy Synod, an administrative body of the Orthodox Church introduced by Peter the Great (r. 1682–1725) and modeled upon the Protestant system of church-state relations found in Prussia. Later, Alexander placed Golitsyn at the head of a newly created Ministry of Spiritual Affairs and Enlightenment. Golitsyn used his influence to promote the formation in 1813 of the Russian Bible Society, which, inspired by the British Foreign Bible Society, sought to disseminate Bibles to the common people. As part of its program it sponsored the translation of scripture from the traditional Church

Slavonic language, which common Russians had once used, to modern Russian. Though this goal was not realized until later in the century, Golitsyn did succeed in eliminating some of the policies that protected the Orthodox Church from competition with Western forms of Christianity.

The spirit of religious universalism that characterized domestic policies also shaped foreign policy under Alexander. In the wake of Napoleon's invasion, Russia had mobilized to expel the French and to chase them back to Paris. Peace was finally established at the Congress of Vienna in 1815. Alexander had solemnly vowed never to make peace while French forces occupied Russian soil, and the experience of fighting a secular France added to his sense of religious idealism. As Russia's representative at the Congress of Vienna, therefore, he introduced a treaty known as the Holy Alliance that reflected his desire to create a universal Christian civilization in post-revolutionary Europe. The main partners of this treaty were Roman Catholic Austria and Protestant Prussia. It called upon European rulers to honor the traditional role of Christianity in Europe and to act in concert to defend religion in the face of secularization. Though it lacked concrete obligations and soon fell into obscurity, the Holy Alliance would shape diplomacy in Europe during the first half of the nineteenth century.

Bibliography. Florovsky, Georges. *Ways of Russian Theology*. Trans. Robert L. Nichols. Vol. 1. Belmont, MA: Nordland, 1979. Martin, Alexander M. *Romantics, Reformers, Reactionaries: Russian Conservative Thought and Politics in the Reign of Alexander I.* DeKalb: Northern Illinois University Press, 1997.

John Strickland

ALEXANDER III (1845–1894). Czar Alexander III ruled the Russian Empire (1881–1894) during a time of political uncertainty. Motivated both by personal devotion and political calculation, he used Christianity as a force for restoring order.

Alexander came to the throne in an environment of political crisis following the assassination of his father, Alexander II (1855–1881). This shocking event discredited the series of measures introduced by his father and known as the Great Reforms. Aided by conservative advisors at court, Alexander III brought a halt to the reform movement and sought ways to strengthen Russia's traditional political order. For this he turned in particular to the Orthodox Church, which in times past had provided a basis for Russian civilization.

Though the church administration had not remained unaffected by the spirit of reform prior to the assassination of Alexander II, many of its members were sympathetic to the new czar's conservative course. The nineteenth century had seen the rise of numerous sectarian bodies hostile to Orthodox Christianity. One such body was the Dukhobors (spirit wrestlers), who would soon affiliate themselves with the popular yet apostate novelist Leo Tolstoy (d.1910). The church was also challenged by a growing indifference to religion among many of the population, particularly the nobility and the urban workers. Thus the call to return to an earlier pattern of rule in which the czar served as the defender of the church was appealing.

Some of Alexander's policies were of great benefit to the church. His support for missionary activities, for instance, helped it establish the largest network of training and evangelism in its history. The size and finances of the Orthodox Missionary Society were greatly expanded, and in distant Tokyo the Russian Orthodox missionary Bishop Nicholas (d.1912), later canonized as a saint, began work that would result in the conversion of tens of thousands of Japanese. In Palestine, ruled for centuries by the Muslim Turks,

Alexander also supported the establishment of a missionary organization called the Orthodox Palestine Society, which was dedicated to building hospitals, churches, and monasteries in the region, and to disseminating literature on pilgrimages to the Holy Land within Russia. Finally, in 1888 Alexander actively supported the church's organization of a large national commemoration of the baptism of Kiev (traditionally attributed to Prince Vladimir's directive in 988).

Alexander's support for the church could sometimes, however, be heavy handed. His reliance upon the reactionary layman **Konstantin Petrovich Pobedonostsev,** who held the governmental office of chief procurator of the Holy Synod (the body of bishops governing church administration), contributed to a pernicious bureaucratization of church life. His advocacy of Russification, a policy by which Orthodoxy was used as an instrument to create loyal subjects, alienated many Roman Catholics and Protestants living in Russia's western borderlands.

Thus, at the time of his early death, Russia continued to face uncertainty, a condition that would be resolved tragically during the reign of his son Nicholas II (r.1894–1917).

Bibliography. Rogger, Hans. *Russia in the Age of Modernization and Reform, 1881–1917.* London: Longman, 1987.

John Strickland

ALIOTO, JOSEPH LAWRENCE (1916–1998).

Attorney, Catholic lay activist, and mayor, Joseph Alioto was born in San Francisco, California, the only son of Giuseppe and Domenica Lazio Alioto. He graduated from Sacred Heart High School in 1933 and received his bachelor's degree magna cum laude from St. Mary's College in Moraga in 1937. Alioto's lay activism began in 1936, when he addressed the Ignatian Council of the Young Men's Institute and called for a "Catholic Internationale" to meet the challenges posed by the international Communist movement. He attended law school at the Catholic University of America in Washington, D.C., serving as an administrative assistant to Monsignor **Francis J. Haas,** dean of the university's School of Social Science. He received his LLB degree in 1940.

In both his private law practice and as an appointed and elected public official, Alioto—a Democratic Party activist—consistently and explicitly drew upon Roman Catholic social justice principles. After earning his law degree, he served as a special assistant in the Antitrust Division of the Justice Department and as a member of the wartime Board of Economic Warfare. Back in San Francisco after the war ended, he began a law practice that specialized in private antitrust suits, a practice that proved successful for decades and brought him national renown.

In 1948 Alioto accepted the first of several appointments to city government positions, serving on the board of education from 1948 to 1954, and then as chairman of the city's Redevelopment Agency from 1955 to 1959. At a time when San Francisco mayors and most members of the board of supervisors (city council) practiced fiscal conservatism, Alioto championed social justice for the disadvantaged and aligned himself with reformers willing to spend public money to improve social conditions. As member and president of the School Board, he supported patriotism in the curriculum and teacher pay raises, while criticizing teachers who praised socialism and communism in the classroom.

During his term as redevelopment chair, and later as mayor from January 1968 through December 1974, Alioto advocated policies rooted in principles derived from Catholic social theory. He successfully campaigned for the return of control of the Port of San Francisco from the state of

California to the city of San Francisco. He supported local control over decisions about how the increased volume of inter-city automobile traffic should be accommodated and defied federal and state highway agency proposals for cross-town freeways. He advocated urban renewal while opposing the destruction of entire neighborhoods and serviceable old housing and called for equity for those displaced by redevelopment. He insisted that down-town commercial redevelopment had to be accomplished with human needs, as well as aesthetic and environmental considerations, in mind. In responding to sometimes violent actions for black, brown, and red power during student strikes in 1968 and 1969 and to the notorious racially motivated "Zebra" serial killings that stretched over 179 days beginning in 1973, Alioto insisted on both aggressive mainte-nance of social order and renewed efforts to achieve racial justice for all San Franciscans. He left public life to resume his law practice in 1975. Alioto continued to be an active patron of the arts of his native city until his death in 1998.

Bibliography. Issel, William. "Liberalism and Urban Policy in San Francisco from the 1930s to the 1960s." *Western Historical Quarterly* 22 (November 1991): 431–50. Wirt, Frederick M. *Power in the City: Decision Making in San Francisco.* Berkeley and Los Angeles: Univer-sity of California Press, 1974.

William Issel

ALLEN, RICHARD (1760–1831). African American preacher, community leader, and founder of the African Methodist Epis-copal Church, Allen was born the slave of Benjamin Chew, a prominent Phil-adelphia attorney. He was later sold to a Delaware farmer, who eventually allowed Allen to buy his freedom. In 1777, while he was still a slave, Allen joined the Meth-odist Society. He was licensed to preach in 1782 and two years later attended the first Methodist General Conference held in

America. He began preaching at St. George's Methodist Church in Philadel-phia in 1786, and consequentially the number of black parishioners increased dramatically. Allen organized prayer and exhortation meetings for people of African descent but met with strong opposition from white church leaders. The situation at St. George's reached a crisis in 1787, when black parishioners, led by Allen and Absa-lom Jones, walked out during a worship service after being denied freedom of seat-ing. White church leaders had accosted Jones during a congregational prayer and forcefully urged him to move to a different area of the church. This incident increased support for an independent church, and an African American church was estab-lished; however, the majority of its found-ers opposed affiliation with the Methodists. Allen respected the Methodists for bringing the Gospel to enslaved African Americans and believed that Methodist doctrine was well suited to people of African descent. In 1793, he was asked to be the new church's minister but declined on account of his commitment to Methodism. Determined to build a church for people of African descent, Allen personally broke the ground for Bethel Church, which was officially opened by Methodist Bishop Francis Asbury in July 1794. Asbury ordained Allen in 1799. Although Allen felt indebted to the Method-ists, ongoing interference by the denomina-tion led him to call a conference of black churches in 1816. The churches decided to unite, and the African Methodist Episcopal (AME) Church was founded. Allen was elected bishop of the new denomination and served the AME in that capacity until his death.

Allen's writings, particularly his autobi-ography and articles on contemporary issues, broadened the extent of his reli-gious and political influence. His addresses and articles, some of which were pub-lished in *Freedom's Journal,* opposed both slavery and efforts to establish colonies in Africa for people of African descent. Rejecting plans for African repatriation and colonization, he maintained that freed slaves had a responsibility to those who remained in bondage and that African Americans were an integral part of the newly formed United States. Methodist doctrine forms the basis for Allen's anti-slavery writings, but he was also influenced by the political and social thought of the Revolutionary War era. He urged slaves to be charitable to their masters, even if their masters were cruel, and to refrain from bearing any ill will toward them. He insisted that God would reward those slaves who were faithful to the Gospel with eternal life. At the same time, he warned slaveholders that God, the protector of the oppressed, would avenge the mistreatment of people of African descent. Allen argued that slavery was not only hateful to God but also destructive of human potential. Citing the contrary effects of liberty and bondage, he insisted on the importance of liberty and equal opportunity, especially in regard to education. Allen's emphasis on liberty illustrates his use of political philosophy as well as religious doctrine in his arguments on behalf of African Americans.

Bibliography. George, Carol V. R. *Segregated Sabbaths: Richard Allen and the Emergence of Independent Black Churches, 1760–1840.* New York: Oxford University Press, 1973. Wesley, Charles H. *Richard Allen: Apostle of Freedom.* Washington, DC: Associated Publishers, 1935.

Susan J. Hubert

AMERICAN TEMPERANCE SOCIETIES (UNITED STATES). In the nineteenth century, concern in America over consumption of alcohol rose to the level of a widespread reform movement, probably the largest and most significant reform movement of the century. First appearing during the early years following the American Revolution, the reform manifested itself in a variety of organizations in

the antebellum decades, to be taken up once again after the Civil War by the better-known **Woman's Christian Temperance Union.** From the beginning, the temperance movement was infused with a sense of urgency by Christians and their churches. Biblical injunctions against drunkenness combined with a post-Revolution civic morality called republicanism to fuel the effort to reduce alcoholic consumption.

Drinking was widespread in colonial America. Alcoholic beverages were considered nourishing stimulants, though drunkenness was condemned, and alcohol was regulated through licensing. Drinking was challenged soon after the Revolution, and attitudes began to change. One early voice was that of prominent physician and Declaration of Independence signer Benjamin Rush, whose pamphlet in 1784 cited distilled liquor as harmful to the human body. Evidence of rising alcoholic consumption caused alarm and inspired the appearance of organized efforts to curb imbibing. In 1812, Connecticut clergyman **Lyman Beecher** made a report to the Presbyterian General Association on "the ways and means of arresting the tide of intemperance." Beecher was appalled at the prevalence of drinking at clergy ordinations. His report urged that clergy and church members abstain from the use or sale of distilled liquor (Beecher, *Autobiography,* 247–48). The next year the Massachusetts Society for the Suppression of Intemperance, one of the earliest temperance organizations, was established to curb intemperance and immorality. Fifty-six of its 115 original members were clergy.

In 1825 Beecher preached a series of six sermons on intemperance. "Intemperance is the sin of our land," he declared, "and if anything shall defeat the hopes of the world, which hang upon our experiment in civil liberty, it is that river of fire which is rolling through the land" (Beecher, *Six Sermons,* 7). He proposed efforts to turn public sentiment against the traffic and sale of distilled liquor, after which prohibition legislation would be acceptable. Beecher had reason to be concerned. Alcoholic consumption was rising dramatically as new western regions beyond the mountains found their grain easier to transport if distilled into whiskey. As whiskey replaced the more expensive rum, consumption of absolute alcohol may have risen to as much as 7.1 gallons per capita among the population fifteen and older during the first three decades of the nineteenth century. Beecher and other religious spokesmen believed that, to succeed, America's experiment in civil liberty required responsible individualism, participatory democracy, and Christian morality. Alcoholic intemperance threatened to undermine all three personal attributes. The next year another temperance society was formed in Boston, the American Temperance Society (ATS), claiming national scope and a divine mission to preach the gospel of abstinence. In explaining their action, the organizers passed as their first resolution "that it is expedient that more systematic and more vigorous efforts be made by the Christian public to restrain and prevent the intemperate use of intoxicating liquors" (ATS, *Permanent Temperance Documents,* 11).

Although churches were disestablished during the Revolutionary era, and the states abandoned support of religion at public expense, the conviction remained that society needed a unifying religious perspective and a broadly accepted morality. The overwhelmingly Protestant consensus in America allowed the different denominations to affirm, if not join hands together in, reform efforts. Attacking alcoholic intemperance was a cause upon which they agreed. Drunkenness was biblically condemned, and all denominations disciplined drunken members. Not surprisingly, temperance leaders were usually clergy or prominent laymen, and of the

sixteen founders of the ATS in 1826, seven were clergy.

In its initial form the temperance message preached voluntary abstinence from distilled liquors, known as "ardent spirits." As the reform evolved, it developed different strategies, including total abstinence from all intoxicants, affirmed by a teetotal pledge, and beginning in the late 1830s, efforts at prohibitive legislation. The support of Christians was essential to these temperance efforts. They joined individually, but institutional support was evident as well in denominational responses. Church denominations, while supportive of temperance overall, differed in their emphases and participation in the phases of the temperance movement. Attitudes among three of the largest antebellum denominations, Baptists, Methodists, and Presbyterians, are illustrative.

Methodist prohibitions against drinking dated from Charles and John Wesley's work among the unchurched lower classes of England in the 1730s. Moreover, Wesleyan theology of sanctification emphasized individual spiritual progression toward perfection. Abstinence was generally a term of church membership, and individuals joined temperance societies, although there was hesitation among some Methodists to join secular societies, implying, as it might, a criticism of the church.

Baptists were more diverse in their responses, a reflection of the Baptist tradition of congregational autonomy. In general they supported the movement, but while some churches demanded abstinence as a term of membership, others did not.

Presbyterians, overall a more upscale population, allowed greater latitude for private judgment and the drinking of wine during the 1830s. The denomination split into Old School and New School factions in 1837–1838. New School Presbyterians favored the modifications of Calvinism articulated by Samuel Hopkins and the

New Haven Theology of Nathaniel W. Taylor, including sympathy for revival evangelism and cooperation with nondenominational benevolent societies. Old School Presbyterians looked askance at organizations and societies outside the church. Overall, it is impossible to imagine the temperance movement prior to 1840 without the support of Christians, both denominationally and individually.

After 1840, the temperance movement took a new direction with the appearance of the Washingtonians, followed shortly by the Sons of Temperance. These societies were more secular in orientation and often appealed to the unchurched, at least in their early years. The Washingtonian movement began in Baltimore in 1840 by six reformed tipplers. With all the zeal of an evangelical revival, reformed drunkards testified to redemption from demon rum. The new movement initially targeted drunkards, whom the churches ignored. Long on fervor but short on organization, the movement flashed then faded; but its impetus was picked up and given structure in the Sons of Temperance movement, which appeared in the mid-1840s. Shedding a specific emphasis on drunkards, the Sons became a more mainstream movement, a full-fledged, somewhat secret, oath-bound society that spread throughout the country and beyond. Its offer of mutual support for sobriety, benevolent aid to members, and a sense of belonging appealed to thousands. Churches responded ambivalently to both of these organizations and debated whether joining was appropriate for Christians. Their secular orientation, and the secrecy and oaths of the Sons, troubled church members, and the Sons were occasionally perceived by churches as competition. Nonetheless, by the end of the 1840s, many Christians were to be found it their ranks. In its peak year of membership, the Sons claimed 238,000 members.

The final phase of the antebellum temperance effort was the prohibition crusade of the 1850s. As moral persuasion to temperance reached its limits, zealous reformers turned to legislation. The Maine Law of 1851, a full-fledged prohibition law, became the model for state campaigns across the country. While numerous states passed some version of prohibitive legislation, the success was short lived, as laws were overturned or repealed. American politics of the mid-1850s presented confusing crosscurrents of issues, including growing sectionalism, slavery and its extension, nativism, and the splintering of the Whig party. Temperance politics added one more dynamic. Christian influence at this stage of the reform is not easily discerned.

The Civil War marked both a pause and a turning point in the effort against alcohol. Following the war a national Prohibition Party was formed, and, more significantly, the Woman's Christian Temperance Union, providing more voice in the crusade against alcohol to those who were often its innocent victims. The antebellum temperance effort, however, had succeeded in defining and addressing alcoholic intemperance as a serious domestic and social problem, and reducing consumption of absolute alcohol by the 1840s to one to two gallons per capita, a consumption level that continued for the rest of the century. Christians, through the behavioral standards of their organized churches, through their individual participation in societies, and their collective vision of America as a Christian republic, provided the backbone of the antebellum movement.

Bibliography. Abzug, Robert H. *Cosmos Crumbling: American Reform and the Religious Imagination.* New York: Oxford University Press, 1994. American Temperance Society. *Permanent Temperance Documents of the American Temperance Society.* Vol. 1. New York: Arno Press, 1972. Beecher, Lyman. *Autobiography,* ed. Charles Beecher. 2 vols. New York: Harper, 1863. Beecher, Lyman. *Six Sermons on the Nature, Occasions, Signs, Evils and Remedy of Intemperance.* 4th ed. Boston: T. R. Marvin,

1828. Blocker, Jack S. *American Temperance Movements: Cycles of Reform.* Boston: Twayne, 1989. Tyrrell, Ian R. *Sobering Up: Prohibition in Antebellum America, 1800–1860.* Westport, CT: Greenwood Press, 1979.

Douglas W. Carlson

ANDREOTTI, GIULIO (b. 1919). Seven-time **Christian Democrat** prime minister and a member of thirty-four out of his country's forty-eight governments between 1946 and 1992, Giulio Andreotti is the epitome of the pervasive Catholic presence in postwar Italian politics.

As a young man, Andreotti served as president of the *Federazione Universitaria Cattolica Italiana,* a Catholic organization for university students. After the fall of Fascism, Andreotti became a protégé of Christian Democrat Premier **Alcide De Gasperi,** who appointed him undersecretary to the president of the council of ministers (prime minister) in 1946. Support from the Vatican subsequently aided Andreotti's political rise and his consolidation of power. In turn, he championed a few Catholic campaigns such as the crusade against divorce in the mid-1970s. As premier, he made sure that Italy's participation to the 1991 first Gulf War, which Pope **John Paul II** opposed, was mainly symbolic.

While he was always known as a devout Catholic, Andreotti's widespread political following was based less on his voters' religious concerns than on an effective political machine that relied on the distribution of government patronage. Likewise, pragmatism rather than Christian values shaped Andreotti's career. Though a moderate with a large following within the right wing of his party, Andreotti endorsed the Christian Democratic government's opening to the Socialists in 1962. Ten years later, however, that commitment did not prevent him from forming a center-right cabinet that included the conservative Liberal Party for the first time since 1957 and relegated the Socialists to the opposition for the first time since 1962. Yet Andreotti was also the premier of the national solidarity governments that benefited from the abstention of the Communist Party in the mid- and late 1970s while he established connections to *Comunione e Liberazione* (**Communion and Liberation**), an influential conservative Catholic association. Furthermore, between 1989 and 1992, he presided over two additional cabinets resulting from an alliance with Socialist leader Bettino Craxi, who pursued an anticommunist strategy.

Untouched by the "clean hands" investigation into corruption that swept away Italy's political leadership in the early 1990s, Andreotti was indicted on charges of Mafia connections in 1993. Cleared of such accusations twice, in 2002 he was convicted of the 1979 murder of Mino Pecorelli, a muckraking journalist who had allegedly threatened to reveal Andreotti's supposedly shady deals in the 1970s. An appeals court eventually overturned this latter verdict in October 2003 because the case lacked proof. Though appointed a senator for life in 1991, however, Andreotti no longer played a prominent political role since the killing of Salvo Lima, his Mafia-related lieutenant in Sicily, ruined his own bid for the Italian presidency in 1992.

Bibliography. Galli, Giorgio. *Il prezzo della democrazia: La carriera politica di Giulio Andreotti.* Milan: Kaos, 2003.

Stefano Luconi

ANTHONY, SUSAN BROWNELL (1820–1906). An indefatigable political organizer and reformer, Anthony was an early advocate and leader of the nineteenth-century women's rights movement. From the 1850s to the end of her long life, Anthony stood at the forefront of agitation for women's right to vote. She spent fifty years in service to the goal, first as cofounder in 1869 of the National Woman

Suffrage Association (NWSA), and later as an officer of the National American Woman Suffrage Association (NAWSA), formed in 1890.

Although not overtly religious, Anthony's interest in social reform was linked to her Quaker upbringing. Her father, Daniel Anthony (1794–1862), was raised and educated in the Society of Friends. In 1817, he married Baptist Lucy Read (1793–1880) in Adams, Massachusetts. Lucy Read Anthony never converted to Quakerism, but she raised her children in a Quaker household. As a Quaker, Susan was taught that God dwelled within each human being, a belief that had radical implications. Many Quakers, including the Anthonys, were led to join nineteenth-century reform movements. Indeed, Susan Anthony's family attended a women's rights convention before she did, traveling to an early convention near their home in Rochester, New York.

Anthony's approach to social issues was egalitarian and nonsectarian, influenced by Quaker ideology and her family's passion for reform. Her interest in women's rights grew out of her own experiences, however. After her father declared bankruptcy following the Panic of 1837, she began teaching to support herself. She taught for twelve years. On her own in Canajoharie, New York, she joined the Daughters of Temperance and delivered her first public speech on their behalf in 1849. Shortly thereafter, Anthony resigned her position as headmistress of Canajoharie Academy and started a career as a political activist. Yet her experience as a teacher stayed with her throughout her life and led her to champion working women's causes.

In the early 1850s, Anthony confronted the limitations society placed on women speaking in public. Denied a voice in an 1852 Sons of Temperance meeting in Albany, New York, Anthony walked out of the meeting and formed the Woman's State Temperance Society. In 1853,

Anthony spoke out about the disparity in female teacher's wages at the annual convention of the New York State Teachers' Association. She later reported that the men present debated for over thirty minutes before allowing her to address the assembly.

Over the next thirty years, Anthony had ample opportunity to hone her oratorical skills in front of approving and disapproving audiences. She began her activist career as an agent for the American Anti-Slavery Society (see **Abolitionists**) and became skilled at organizing meetings, fundraising, and public speaking. After the war, she continued her work with the American Equal Rights Association (AERA). In the 1870s, she traveled the country as a lyceum lecturer.

Before Congress passed the fifteenth amendment in 1869, women's rights leaders advocated universal suffrage, or extending the vote to women as well as African American males. After it passed, thus

Susan B. Anthony. Courtesy of the Library of Congress

granting the right to vote regardless of "race, color, or previous condition of servitude," woman suffrage became a separate issue. During the late 1860s and early 1870s, women tested the new amendment by voting in state and local elections, arguing that it extended the vote to them as well. In 1872, Anthony tested it by voting in the national election. When she was convicted of the crime of voting "without having a right to vote," because she was a woman, this avenue of protest was effectively shut down.

In the 1880s, Anthony and other suffrage leaders moved to preserve the history of their movement. Anthony, **Elizabeth Cady Stanton,** and Matilda Joslyn Gage collaborated on the first three volumes of *The History of Woman Suffrage.* Anthony also made her papers available to journalist Ida Husted Harper for a biography, published as the *Life and Work of Susan B. Anthony* (1898). In addition, Anthony recognized the necessity of training younger leaders to take the movement into the twentieth century. She nurtured the speaking skills and political talents of a new generation of women's rights activists.

Susan B. Anthony remained active in the organized woman suffrage movement until 1906, speaking at a NAWSA convention just one month before she died in March. During her lifetime she earned the affection of countless women across the United States. She had become "Aunt Susan," a beloved figure in the movement and its personification in the popular imagination.

Bibliography. Barry, Kathleen. *Susan B. Anthony: A Biography of a Singular Feminist.* New York: New York University Press, 1988. Gordon, Ann D., ed. *The Selected Papers of Elizabeth Cady Stanton and Susan B. Anthony.* 3 vols. New Brunswick, NJ: Rutgers University Press, 1997–2003. Pellauer, Mary D. *Toward a Tradition of Feminist Theology: The Religious Social Thought of Elizabeth Cady Stanton, Susan B. Anthony, and Anna Howard Shaw,* ed. Jerald C. Brauer and Martin E. Marty. Brooklyn, NY: Carlson, 1991.

Meg Meneghel MacDonald

ANTI-REVOLUTIONARY PARTY (THE NETHERLANDS). The Anti-Revolutionary Party (ARP) in the Netherlands was a significant political movement among evangelical Reformed Protestants from 1827 to 1980.

The worldview foundations for the party were laid by the parliamentarian **Guillaume Groen van Prinsterer** in his important book *Unbelief and Revolution* (1847). Based on a principled rejection of the secularist worldview of the French Revolution in its liberal and radical forms, Groen argued for a Christian worldview on Augustinian/Calvinist lines as the basis for all of life including politics. Groen believed that if democratic voting procedures were divorced from biblical moral values and the national heritage, the result would be the end of true constitutionalism, with a pragmatic secularism as the final norm. Around this ARP worldview Groen began to gather a national following, especially on the issue of full freedom for Christian schools. His slogan was "The Gospel versus the Revolution" (or the Bible's principles versus secular humanism). Theocracy was rejected in favor of constitutional democracy.

The ARP's organizer was Dr. **Abraham Kuyper.** He popularized Groen's worldview and emancipatory reformism in about ten thousand editorials in *De Standaard* daily newspaper between 1872 and 1918. He also led more than a dozen national parliamentary campaigns during that period. For example, during the 1873 campaign he wrote, "The other parties campaign for parliamentary seats, more or less. We campaign for our principles!" Between 1872 and 1879, Kuyper organized the ARP around the program of principles, a central committee under his chairmanship, and scores of local voters' clubs. It was Europe's first nationally organized Christian Democratic party. The ARP's most basic principle was that state authority derives from divine institution, not popular consent. Kuyper deepened the ARP worldview with the concepts of sphere sovereignty; common grace; the ordinances of God for family, church, and state; and the Kingship of Christ over all of life. Kuyper adopted a principled pluralism and saw the complete equality of Christian schools with all others funded by a voucher system as a key ingredient of that pluralism. Parity was achieved in the constitutional reforms of 1917. At elections between 1937 and 1972, the ARP received over 200,000 votes on average and was a major governing party with 16 percent of the national vote.

After World War II, the ARP persisted in carrying on with its worldview in spite of secularist pressures to introduce only pragmatic parties. During 1945–1952 the party stayed out of the government in protest against the surrender of Indonesia. At the same time, the party endorsed European federalism, NATO, and a provisional welfare state. By 1968 the party leaders decided to merge with two sister parties (one Catholic) with moderate policies to bring greater stability to governing coalitions. The public debate between the Catholic "open party" concept of all people of good will and the AR "closed party" of self-confessed Christians grabbed headlines during 1973–1976. The open party won, with no official place for the ARP worldview.

The formal end of the ARP came in 1980, when it merged with the **Christian Democratic Appeal** party. While the party could be credited for supporting social emancipation, educational pluralism, a benevolent colonial policy, and a responsible governing record, it also tolerated triumphalism, imperialism before 1949, and some poor judgments in crisis situations.

Bibliography. Langley, M. R. "Emancipation and Apologetics." Ann Arbor, MI: UMI Dissertation Services, 1995. Langley, M. R. *The Practice of Political Spirituality.* Jordan Station, ON: Paideia Press, 1984.

McKendree R. Langley

ANTONELLI, GIACOMO (1806–1876). This last of the "lay cardinals" played a key role in the pontificate of **Pius IX,** seconding the reformism of the early years as well as the reaction following the restoration of 1849. Secretary of state for almost three decades (1848–1876), and effective head of the papal state until its collapse in 1870, he orchestrated the counter-Risorgimento, which opposed Italian unification.

Pope **Gregory XVI** appointed him apostolic delegate to Orvieto (1835), Viterbo (1836), and Macerata (1839). In 1841, Antonelli became Gregory's undersecretary of state for the Interior, receiving sacred orders up to the deaconate. He later served as Gregory's minister of finance (1845), retaining the post under Pius IX. In 1847, Antonelli was named cardinal deacon. Supportive of Pio Nono's reformism, he presided over his consultative chamber. In 1848, Antonelli helped to draft the Constitution of the Papal States, and Pius IX made him secretary of state and effective head of his constitutional ministry.

Constrained to resign when his cabinet called for war against Austria, the cardinal arranged the pope's flight from Rome to the Kingdom of Naples (or Two Sicilies) at the end of 1848. He invoked the intervention of the Powers (France, Austria, Spain, and Naples) that defeated **Giuseppe Mazzini**'s Roman Republic and restored papal power in 1849. At the pope's behest, Antonelli resisted French Emperor Louis Napoleon's pressure to liberalize his state, drafting a decree (September 1849) that assured political power would remain in the hands of the pope and his appointees. Assuming many of the burdens of state (1850–1870), Antonelli allowed Pius IX to concentrate on church affairs. Unable to prevent Piedmont's unification of the peninsula in 1859–1861, the cardinal persuaded Napoleon to retain French troops in Rome, preserving it for the papacy until the Franco-Prussian War (1870) and the French withdrawal.

Antonelli provided the diplomatic justification for the pope's intransigent position on the Roman Question, over papal sovereignty and territory after 1870, and his refusal to recognize the Kingdom of Italy. After 1872, he proved helpful in resisting the Kulturkampf in Bismarck's Germany and in protesting the laical policies of the French Republic. He offered the pope his economic experience as well as his diplomatic expertise, revising the collection of Peter's Pence and converting it into the primary source of papal income. Despite his long and loyal service, Antonelli has been maligned as the Villain of the Risorgimento. Many who hesitated to criticize the pope for Rome's polices blamed his minister instead. Liberals disliked the cardinal for making papal absolutism viable after 1850, nationalists for his attempt to block Italian unification, and conservative Catholics for his failure to do so.

Bibliography. Coppa, Frank J. *Cardinal Giacomo Antonelli and Papal Politics in European Affairs.* Albany: State University of New York Press, 1989.

Frank J. Coppa

ANTONY, BERNARD (b. 1944). This former member of the European Parliament (1984–2004) and of the French National Assembly (1986–1988) also uses the pen name Romain Marie and is the leader of the Catholic Traditionalist wing of the extreme-right Front National party in France.

He was strongly influenced in his student years by the French Thomist philosopher Louis Jugnet, who during World War II was a staunch supporter of **Philippe Pétain,** and by the integralist movement Cité Catholique, founded in 1946 by Jean Ousset. He also supported the Algérie Française movement before becoming in 1972 a follower of Bishop **Marcel Lefebvre** in his fight against the reforms voted by the Vatican II Council. He parted ways with Lefebvre and his St. Pius X Fraternity in 1988 after Pope **John Paul II** declared Lefebvre to be a schismatic because he had consecrated bishops without the pope's consent. Antony founded the Chrétienté-Solidarité lay movement in 1980 and cofounded the integralist far-right daily newspaper *Présent* two years later.

His ideology is that of the pre–Vatican II church, blended with a fascination for the authoritarian and corporatist doctrine of the Vichy regime during World War II, the Christian mystique of Spanish Falange, and the Romanian **Iron Guard.** Antony is also known in France as a staunch supporter of Samir Geagea's Lebanese Forces. Within the Front National, he is an outspoken opponent of the "modernist" wing and refuses any change on the party's stand on such issues as the family, abortion, and divorce (the FN is pro-life and frowns on divorce, homosexuality, and gender equality). He is also an exponent of the conspiracy theory, with a special concern for Freemasonry and the "Jewish lobby." He remains vocally anticommunist and sees communist "subversion" at work behind everything that challenges his beliefs. He is chairman of the Alliance Générale contre le Racisme et pour le Respect de l'Identité Française et Chrétienne (AGRIF), which brings to court those he sees as undermining the values of Christianity and promoting "anti-French racism," and of the Centre Henri et André Charlier. He publishes the monthly *Reconquête.*

Bibliography. Daoudal, Yves. *Romain Marie sans concession.* Paris: Éditions Dominique Martin-Morin, 1985.

Jean-Yves Camus

APESS, WILLIAM (1798–1839). Apess, a Methodist minister who wrote one of the first American Indian autobiographies, helped lead the Mashpee revolt. His writings and actions stood at the intersection of religious, ethnic, and political redemption. Apess was born to a Pequot mother and a "mixed" father, both laborers. When he was three, his parents divorced, moved away, and left him with his maternal grandparents. Soon, his drunken grandmother badly beat him; Apess would later blame whites for addicting American Indians to alcohol. Rescued by an uncle, he was indentured to various Anglo-Americans (like so many other "colored" children) until he ran away in 1813 to enlist in the army. After several campaigns, he left in 1815. Apess was baptized after his return to Connecticut in 1818. During the following six years, he traveled and labored, married and had children, and served as a leader in Methodist classes. In 1825, he obtained a license from the Methodists and began to preach in the region among congregations of poor people of color.

In April 1829, Apess was ordained by "radical" Protestant Methodists and months later published *A Son of the Forest,* perhaps the first American Indian autobiography. The book reflected concerns of ethnicity and class, recounting his redemption as a member of a mistreated minority, and protesting against the moral problems of early industrial New England. He was licensed to preach in 1831 and published *The Increase of the Kingdom of Christ,* which revived the idea that American Indians were descendants of Jews. His next book, *The Experiences of Five Christian Indians* (1833), combined conversion narratives with strident condemnation of white racism. Subsequent books celebrated the Mashpee revolt and feted Metacom (a Wampanoag chief known to the English as King Philip), while condemning the Puritan colonists. All used evangelical rhetoric to call for religious and political liberation.

Apess's most significant action was leading the Mashpee revolt. The Christian Wampanoag community on Cape Cod was established in 1665, and by 1800 it had become the largest tribe in the region. Beginning in 1746, Massachusetts appointed guardians for American Indians, who had extensive powers over community resources. The Mashpees resisted, regaining their autonomy in 1763 but losing it in 1788 due to the influence of their minister Gideon Hawley. Most Mashpees then abandoned the orthodox church and embraced Baptist ministers who were part Indian. In May 1833, Apess attended the American Indian meetinghouse and was shocked to find only whites and an unsympathetic Phineas Fish, who had replaced Hawley in 1811. He later preached to the American Indians on their oppression, inspiring meetings and a petition to the governor to dismiss Fish and end the guardianship. When there was no reply, the Mashpees agreed to bar whites from the reserve, dismiss their guardians, and take control of the church, raising alarms of an Indian uprising. A state investigator was met by nearly a hundred Mashpees, many carrying muskets, but he cooled tempers by promising a legislative hearing. In January 1834, Apess and two others went to Boston to press their case. The Mashpees heard their case discussed and gave speeches to the legislature and at various public venues. In March, the legislature abolished the guardianship and made Mashpee a district with the power to elect town officials.

As a result, Apess became a celebrated speaker, and was invited back to Boston to eulogize King Philip. Unfortunately, within two years he was sued for debt and fled Mashpee for New York. There he died on April 10, 1839, apparently of apoplexy.

Bibliography. O'Connell, Barry, ed. *On Our Own Ground: The Complete Writings of William Apess, a Pequot.* Amherst: University of Massachusetts Press, 1992. O'Connell, Barry, ed. *A Son of the Forest and Other Writings by William Apess, a Pequot.* Amherst: University of Massachusetts Press, 1997.

Daniel R. Mandell

AQUINO, CORAZON (b. 1933). Aquino was born the daughter of a wealthy family. Her father was Don Jose Cojuangco of Tarlac, and her mother Dona Demetria Sumulong (daughter of distinguished Don Juan Sumulong of Antipolo). She received a convent education in the Philippines and went to the United States, where she obtained a bachelor of arts degree in French and mathematics from the Catholic College of St. Vincent, run by Sisters of Charity in New York. After graduation, she returned to her homeland, where she met and married Benigno S. (Ninoy) Aquino, Jr., on October 11, 1954. She led the quiet life of a deeply Catholic housewife and mother of five children. Ninoy Aquino became a national hero in the Philippines for sacrificing his life to fight against the martial law regime of Ferdinand Marcos (1972–1986).

On August 21, 1983, the former senator Benigno Aquino returned from a three-year exile in the United States to run for president against Ferdinand Marcos. On his arrival at Manila International Airport (now known as Aquino International Airport), Ninoy Aquino was arrested and assassinated on the spot by one of Marcos's soldiers, who was sent to "guard" him. The brutal assassination of Ninoy galvanized the nation into a massive Peoples' Power movement, led by Corazon, that received broad support from the nation's Catholic Church and ousted the dictator from power through a bloodless revolution. Corazon Aquino was democratically elected as the new president of the republic on February 25, 1986, which was the last day of the people's revolution. The election was contested by many, and a monitoring agency, the National Movement for Free Elections, which was staffed by Catholic clergy, reported fraud but could not stop it. President Aquino pledged herself, nevertheless, to fighting corruption and easing Philippine poverty, although by 1991, after repeated attempts to overthrow her government, she left power short of her goals. She is best remembered for her restoration of democracy after the Marcos regime.

Bibliography. Reid, Robert H., and Eileen Guerrero. *Corazon Aquino and the Brushfire Revolution.* Baton Rouge: Louisiana State University Press, 1995.

Kathleen Nadeau

ARCHER, JOHN KENDRICK (1865–1949). Archer was the most prominent Baptist labor activist in twentieth-century New Zealand. Born in England, he claimed John Ruskin and the Italian **Giuseppe Mazzini** as important influences. He was also associated with the Baptist activist John Clifford.

Archer was thus formed in an environment in which churches claimed a direct role in political affairs. In 1908, after holding three pastorates, he emigrated to New Zealand, attracted by its reputation for social experiment. Here he found a very different situation. While a number of Baptist leaders were interested in labor issues, there was no organized forum. Archer soon turned his attention to party politics. He was a founding member of the New Zealand Labour Party, serving as president from 1928 to 1929.

In the decade following the First World War, Archer stood unsuccessfully for election to Parliament four times. Through this period he continued as a minister in Baptist churches and held important denominational posts. His most significant political offices came late in life. In 1925, while minister of the Sydenham Baptist Church, he was elected mayor of Christchurch, in the South Island. He held both posts for six years and led the city's early response to the Great Depression.

In 1935 the first Labor government was elected. Two years later Archer was appointed to the upper house of the New Zealand parliament, the Legislative Council, where he served until just before his death. Here he maintained a strong advocacy for labor legislation and social change. Archer was a renowned polemicist, happy to admit he relished a fight. He was open to modernist theology and insisted that the New Testament was a radical document and the only creed necessary for Christians.

Bibliography. Sutherland, M.P. "Pulpit or Podium? J.K. Archer and the Dilemma of Christian Politics in New Zealand." *New Zealand Journal of Baptist Research* 1 (October 1996): 26–46.

Martin Sutherland

ARCHER, PAULINE NEE. *See* Vanier, Georges–Phileas

ARFEL, JEAN LOUIS [JEAN MADIRAN] (b. 1920). The French journalist and writer Jean Arfel, who uses the pen name Jean Madiran, is one of the most influential thinkers of the Catholic integralist movement. Born into a middle-class family that was conservative but did not belong to the **Action Française,** he became a follower of the thought of **Charles Maurras** during high school. He then studied philosophy at Bordeaux University, where he discovered the writings of St. Thomas Aquinas. Those influences, together with his education in the Scout movement, shaped his ideology for the rest of his life.

During World War II, Arfel became one of the most promising young intellectuals of **Philippe Pétain**'s Vichy regime. He was one of the leaders of the Étudiants d'Action Française and from 1943 on wrote in the daily newspaper *L'Action Française* and in the *Revue universelle,* another organ of the royalist movement. He also wrote some very harsh articles about the Jews in France in *L'État nouveau,* but he always opposed National Socialism (which he thought was a pagan ideology) and after 1945 never denied the truth of the Holocaust.

A milestone event in his life was the 1944 general meeting of the Étudiants d'Action Française, when Maurras publicly named him as one of the young people he saw fit to continue his work. The same year, Madiran was awarded the *Francisque,* the highest civil decoration of the Vichy regime, of which he was the youngest recipient. Undoubtedly, if the outcome of the war had been different, Madiran would have become an important figure. The Allied victory meant a broken career, and after 1945, he became a teacher of philosophy in an upper-class private school, École des Roches. He also worked for an anticommunist think tank founded by the former collaborationist Georges Albertini, who at the height of the cold war became influential in conservative right circles. Arfel also contributed to several of the many semi-clandestine publications that blossomed after 1946 on the French Far Right. In 1956, he founded the monthly review *Itinéraires,* which became the main organ of the French traditionalists who opposed the Second Vatican Council. At this time, Madiran was the main thinker of the Cité Catholique movement. His most important books against modernism and liturgical reform were *Ils ne savent pas ce qu'ils disent* and *Ils ne savent pas ce qu'ils font* (1955). After the Vatican Council, he wrote the two-volume *L'Hérésie du XXe siecle* (1968 and 1974), which contained what was to become the slogan of Bishop **Marcel Lefebvre**'s followers: "Give us back the Holy Scriptures, the Catechism and the Mass".

In 1980, Madiran cofounded the newspaper *Présent,* which was the first nationalist, Catholic, and far-right daily publication in France since the Action française was banned in 1944. Madiran supported Le Pen's Front National, of which he was once a candidate in a local election. His thought shaped what is known as the nationalist-Catholic wing of the party. After the integralist schism in 1988 between Marcel Cardinal Lefebvre and Pope **John Paul II,** he chose to remain within the Roman Catholic Church and disavowed Bishop Lefebvre's conduct and support for Saint Peter's Fraternity. He is still the chief editor of *Présent.* His political ideal is a Catholic, nationalist, and corporatist authoritarian regime, grounded in Maurras's thinking and the social doctrine of the Catholic Church.

Bibliography. Masson, Danièle. *Jean Madiran.* Maule, France: Éditions Difralivre, 1989.

Jean-Yves Camus

ASOCIACIÓN CATÓLICA NACIONAL DE PROPAGANDISTAS (ACNP). *See* National Association of Propagandists

AUBERT-PICARD, JEANNE (1909–2003). Drawing on her experience in French Catholic associations, Aubert-Picard became committed to women's rights and democratic planning. After World War II, she implemented her ideals as a member of government organizations and consumer leagues. Her transition from Catholic leader to social activist thus had national ramifications.

In 1927, while working as a secretary in a Parisian factory, Aubert-Picard met Georges Quiclet, an assistant bookkeeper who was a member of the **Young Christian Workers** (JOC), a Catholic youth group that strove to Christianize and improve the lives of young laborers. Quiclet and his priest, Georges Guérin, convinced Aubert-Picard to initiate a female branch of the movement, the JOCF, for which she served as general secretary from 1928 to 1939.

Aubert-Picard espoused many traditional concepts, such as the ideal of the housewife, but she also defended the right of women to control their sphere, leading her, rather ironically, to devise opportunities for women outside the home. Aubert-Picard organized the JOCF into sections run by *jocistes* themselves, promoting democratization and encouraging women to become leaders. She also forced women to think independently by asking them to investigate and propose solutions for such social problems as housing, hygiene, and factory safety.

During World War II, Aubert-Picard directed home economics programs for **Philippe Pétain**'s Vichy Regime. She left that position in 1942 but continued working with women and families as a member of the Popular Movement of Families (MPF), an organization established by former members of the JOCF to defend working-class rights, including the right to decent housing and a say in how those homes were designed.

Membership in the MPF propelled Aubert-Picard into other organizations, including the National Union of Family Associations and the Economic and Social Council (CES), two consultative assemblies that brought her to the attention of Pierre Sudreau, **Charles de Gaulle**'s first minister of construction. In 1958 Sudreau asked Aubert-Picard to investigate female opinion on housing. To do that, she organized a referendum on home design, initiating the nation's first step toward democratic planning.

Aubert-Picard left the Construction Ministry in 1962, but she remained a member of the CES until 1974, working on issues as diverse as pollution control and garment labeling. From 1965 to 1974, Aubert-Picard also served as president of the Federal Union of Consumers and as editor of the association's journal, *Que choisir.*

Bibliography. Dermenjian, Geneviève. "La première jociste de France." *Notre histoire* 121 (1995): 40–44.

W. Brian Newsome

AVERILL, ALFRED WALTER (1865–1957).
Averill served as Anglican reverend archbishop, bishop of Auckland (1914–1940),
and primate and archbishop of New
Zealand (1925–1940). Born in Stafford-
shire, England, he studied theology successively at St John's College (Oxford), Ely
Theological College, and Oxford University, where he received an honorary doctorate of divinity in 1912. Named vicar of
the Church of St. Michael and All Angels in
Christchurch, New Zealand in 1894, he
vigorously encouraged Christian engagement with the community and supported
such organizations as the Red Cross, Royal
Empire Society, New Zealand Society for
the Protection of Women and Children,
District Nursing Association, and Auckland
Rotary Club.

As a New Zealand cleric, Averill pursued
the middle ground between traditionalism
and modernism. He also advocated complete autonomy from the Church of
England and pursued adjustments to the
constitution of the New Zealand church in
defense of that aim. On the political scene,
he formulated strong declarations against
the inhumanity of World Wars I and II.
Most of his sermons, well publicized in the
newspapers at the end of the thirties,
focused on international affairs. He
insisted on the vital importance of a
collective security policy and called for
global unity in opposing brutal dictatorial
regimes.

His involvement in politics was perilous
and sometimes popularly condemned.
Upon the signing of the Munich Pact in
1938, Archbishop Averill supported a
thanksgiving meeting, initiated by the
mayor of Auckland, celebrating this alleged
"immense chance" for the peace. Within
New Zealand society, he emerged in ecclesiastic circles during the interwar years as
the protector of underprivileged people.
He denounced the inequalities of the social
system and the deprivations experienced
by New Zealand's indigenous population,
the Maori. Convinced that they needed
self-directed religious institutions, Averill
worked throughout his career to strengthen
communication between the Anglican
Church and the indigenous population.
Averill retired from public life in 1940.

Bibliography. Averill, A. W. *Fifty Years in
New Zealand.* Christchurch, NZ: Whitcombe &
Tombs, 1945. Limbrick, W. E. "Averill, Alfred
Walter." *Dictionary of New Zealand Biogra-
phy.* Vol. 3. Wellington, NZ: Allen & Unwin,
1996.

Jérôme Dorvidal

AZIONE CATTOLICA ITALIANA. *See* Italian Catholic Action.

B

BACHEM, KARL (1858–1945). One of the key figures in Wilhelmine and Weimar German Catholic politics, Bachem came from one of the best-known Catholic families in Prussia. His father owned a publishing company, which included the daily *Kölnische Volkszeitung,* among the most important Catholic newspapers in Germany.

From an early age, Bachem became aware of the discrimination against Prussian Catholics. After completing a law degree in 1880, he embarked on a career as lawyer, which he abandoned soon after being elected to the German parliament and the Prussian state legislature in 1889. Bachem focused most of his early political efforts on maintaining and protecting the role of the church in education. During the 1890s, in addition to often serving as a liaison between the Vatican and the German Catholic leadership, Bachem played a vital role in the preparation and passing of the new German Civil Code. He stressed the importance of Catholics' support for this set of laws, since it would demonstrate their willingness to integrate into the Second Empire.

The issue of Catholic assimilation remained one of his highest priorities throughout his political and publishing careers. Although poor health forced him to leave parliament in 1905, Bachem continued to publish a great number of books,

articles, and pamphlets, preserving his status as one of Germany's leading Catholic politicians. In the last decade before the First World War, he attempted to convince his fellow Catholics to open up Catholic trade unions to Protestants. Bachem viewed this as a necessary step in order to prevent workers from supporting the increasingly popular Social Democrats. He was one of the strongest proponents of broadening the appeal of the **Center Party** (Zentrum) to attract Protestants as well. In this, he was ahead of his time, as was his vision of a Christian party that drew support from both confessions, which did not materialize until the founding of the **Christian Democratic Union** in 1945.

During the First World War, Bachem became a controversial figure as he led the aggressive annexationist faction within his party. Especially toward the end of the war, he was involved in fierce debates with more moderate Catholics over German war aims. Because only a minority supported his ideas, he was forced to adapt to the official party line that advocated suing for a peace without territorial acquisitions. Most of Bachem's important writing took place in the interwar period. The monumental nine-volume history of the Center Party constitutes his most significant publication. It remains one of the best sources for the history of political Catholicism.

With the ascent of National Socialism, which Bachem rejected, his opportunities for publishing vanished. Thus, he spent the last decade of his life out of the lime-light. Bachem died in December 1945, only a few weeks after the formation of the interconfessional Christian Democratic Union, which constituted a political party closely resembling the ideals that he had been striving for during most of his life.
Bibliography. Bredohl, Thomas M. *Class and Religious Identity: The Rheinish Center Party in Wilhelmine Germany.* Milwaukee, WI: Marquette University Press, 2000. Kiefer, Rolf. *Karl Bachem, 1858–1945: Politiker und Histo-riker des Zentrums.* Mainz, Germany: Matthias-Grünewald-Verlag, 1989.

Pontus Hiort

BALBO, CESARE (1789–1853). A leading figure of Italy's nation building, and an exponent of the Italian form of European liberal Catholicism, Balbo was born into a Piedmontese noble family. During the French regime in Italy he could not refuse to collaborate with the Napoleonic admin-istration, which liquidated the old states on the peninsula, including the temporal dominion of the church. For that, Balbo, together with many others, was excommu-nicated.

With the end of Napoleon's empire, Balbo entered a military and diplomatic career but fell again in disgrace and was sent into exile because of his constitu-tional ideas and friendship with leaders of the Piedmontese revolt of 1821. Forced to suppress a vocation for a *vita active,* he dedicated himself to the study of Italian history, literature, and language, even after returning home in 1824. He considered a scientifically conceived historiography necessary for the much hoped-for intellec-tual rebirth of the nation. In numerous treatises (such as *History of Italy under the Barbarians, Summary of Italian History,* and *Reflections on Italy's History,* as well as a series of open *Letters* on the

progress of literature and civilization in general), he discussed the reasons for Italy's decline in the early modern age and its chances for rising again. In this perspec-tive, it is not astonishing that he admired Machiavelli, whose antipapal polemic he refused, but whose patriotic ideas he tried to integrate into a Christian vision of prog-ress that, in Italy's case, meant national unification coupled eventually with consti-tutional guarantees.

For Balbo, modernity did not have to be in contrast with Christian faith and Catholicism; on the contrary, rightly under-stood, modern liberty and its constitu-tional protection had to be considered the political and social outcome of real prog-ress stimulated by Christian revelation. Similar positions were called neo-Guelf, since they also favored an active participa-tion of the pope's authority in the planned Italian Federation.

Balbo's writings helped create a public opinion open to reforms and inclined to moderate patriotism without the revolu-tionary excesses of **Giuseppe Mazzini**'s movement. He gave further impulses to overcome the paralyzed atmosphere of the Restoration era with the famous treatise *On Italy's Hopes* (1844). Together with Camillo Cavour, he created the leading political review, the title of which became the synonym of the entire unification pro-cess: Risorgimento (1848). Balbo clearly identified the Habsburg Empire as a main obstacle to Italian unification, and he felt that a shift of Austrian interests to the Balkans might offer a solution to the Italian question. Influenced by the English model, he found in representative monarchy the best form of the state.

Balbo returned to Piedmontese politics shortly before 1848 and was for a short time chief minister of the first constitu-tional government. He was entrusted with the war against Austria, though he favored a more cautious policy that aimed at a Federal Union of Italian States including the reestablished State of the Church. Piedmont's King Victor Emmanuel II sent him on a mission to Pope **Pius IX** in connection with the renewal of the concordat, which failed. In later years Balbo fought against anticlerical politics of the national liberal movement.

Bibliography.   Balbo, Cesare. *Storia d'Italia e altri scritti editi e inediti.* Ed. Maria Fubini Leuzzi. Turin, Italy: Einaudi, 1984. De Rosa, Gabriele, and Francesco Traniello, eds. *Cesare Balbo alle origini del cattolicesimo liberale.* Rome-Bari, Italy: Laterza, 1996.

Christiane Liermann/
Francesco Traniello

BALMES, JAIME LUCIANO (1810–1848). Two names dominate Spanish Catholic apologetics in the first half of the nineteenth century—Jaime Balmes and Donoso Cortes. Although they often appear together, they were of very different temperaments. The fiery and ardent Donoso contrasted with the calm and moderate Balmes, the "Doctor Humanus" ("If I can be a philosopher," he wrote, "but not a man, I renounce philosophy"). Born in Vich, Catalonia, his short life was one of great intensity. He studied in the seminary of his native city (1817–1826) and continued at the University of Cervera (1826–1835) and later in its seminary library, where he concentrated on the Thomas Aquinas's *Summa Theologica.*

As a journalist, he founded and edited *La civilizacion* (1841–1843) and later *La sociedad* (1843–1844). In 1844, he moved to Madrid, where, with Jose M. Quadrado, he collaborated on *El pensamiento de la nacion* (1844–1846) and founded a newspaper, *El conciliador,* to bring together the Carlists with the Constitutionals. In Madrid, Balmes previously published his *Sobre el celibato del clero católico,* and the following year (1840), in Vich, his *Observaciones sociales, politicas y economicas sobre los bienes del clero.* That year he also published in Barcelona his *Consideraciones politicas*

sobre la situacion de Espana. A collection of political writings was published in 1847 under the title *Esritos politicos.* Both in the social and political fields, Balmes had many genial insights. In his four-volume *Filosofia fondamental* (1846), he tried to overcome the errors of his time: sensualism, materialism, rationalism, and idealism. He was concerned with the foundation of certainty as a first philosophical step, and he might be considered the founder of scholastic criteriology. However, he paid too much attention to Descartes, which influenced his psychological and subjective approach. He also wrote a four-volume textbook, *Curso de filosofia elemental* (1847).

Balmes wrote a "code of good sense" in his *Criterio* (1845), a practical guide for the practical life based on realism and objectivity. "A good logic must be of the whole man," he insisted. Balmes's greatest work, *El Protestantismo comparado con el Catolicismo en sus relaciones con la civilizacion europea* (1842–1844), was a work of the philosophy of history and apologetics. This critique of Guizot's *Histoire generale de la civilisacion en Europa* contains Balmes's definition of civilization as the confluence of material, intellectual, and moral progress and examines Catholicism's role in this achievement. Of apologetic character were his *Cartas a un exceptico en materia de religion* (1846) and his last work, a defense of Pope **Pius IX**'s liberal measures at the beginning of his reign, which gave his critics the opportunity to embitter the last days of his life.

Balmes advocated the subordination of politics to the moral order as well as to reality and was consequently known as a master of conciliation without compromising fundamental principles. He inclined toward dialogue and rejected positions of "all or nothing." An outstanding example of Balmes's efforts for conciliation was his unsuccessful project of a marriage between Spain's Bourbon queen and the son of the Hapsburg pretender, Juan Carlos.

Bibliography. Casanovas, Ignacio. *Biografía de Balmes: Obras Completas de Balmes.* Madrid: Biblioteca de Autores Cristianos, 1948.

Edward J. Capestany

BARELLI, ARMIDA (1882–1952). A central figure in the organization of Italian Catholic women in the twentieth century, Barelli became active among the Catholic laity in Milan in 1910 when she joined a group under the leadership of the Franciscan **Agostino Gemelli.**

In the following years, Barelli played a key part in at least three major projects to restore the church's declining popularity in Italian society: in the tragic year of 1917 the consecration of the Italian Army to the Sacred Heart of Jesus, the creation in 1918 of the Catholic Young Women Section (*Gioventu' Femminile,* GF) for women ages eighteen to twenty-five (later thirty-five) as a separate branch of the **Italian Catholic Action**'s women's movement, and the founding of the Catholic University, inaugurated in 1921 by Cardinal Ratti, later Pope **Pius XI.**

GF was born out of a project of spiritual retreats in Milan for young women filling jobs in growing numbers as office clerks, shop attendants, and service employees of all kinds. The birth nationwide of a Catholic association for young women was regarded with great favor by Pope **Benedict XV**—who insisted that Barelli should be president—and by his successor Pius XI, as it addressed the church's concerns about the incipient women's emancipation as a threat to family, the stronghold of traditional values. Recruitment of young women from all walks of life, the extension to girls ages six to twelve (1923), the capillary circulation of the GF bulletin, the use of slogans, and spectacular parades (visibly outdoing the ones staged by Fascist youth organizations) give witness to Barelli's foresight and intuition about mass mobilization. These organizational successes also made GF a main target when, in June 1931, Benito Mussolini's regime banned for four months all youth organizations unconnected to the Fascist Party.

As a board member of the Catholic University, Barelli employed her remarkable managerial skills to amass financial support for the institution. In 1920, she convinced Pius XI to institute University Day (*Giornata Universitaria*), when GF women in all parishes would collect funds for the benefit of the institution.

Pope **Pius XII** appointed Barelli vice president of Catholic Action in 1946. Despite her failing health, she spared no effort in leading Catholic Action and GF in complying with the role the church assigned to women in winning back the masses in a postwar period marked by the rise of mass party politics. In 1962, ten years after her death, a process for her beatification was initiated.

Bibliography. Sticco, Maria. *Armida Barelli: Una donna fra due secoli.* Milan: Editrice Vita e Pensiero, 1967.

Margherita Repetto-Alaia

BARTH, KARL (1886–1968). The most important Protestant theologian of the twentieth century, Barth was deeply concerned and intimately involved in many of the social and political events that shook the European continent during the last century.

Born in Basel, Switzerland, to moderate Pietist parents, Barth studied in Bern, Berlin, Tübingen, and Marburg. He was ordained in 1908 and after further academic work and a brief pastorate in Geneva (1909–1911), he became pastor to the Reformed congregation of Safenwil in the Aargau from 1911 to 1921. Barth's experience in the industrial village of Safenwil was crucial to his theological and political development.

In the working conditions of the local factories, Barth was directly confronted with the unjust practices and conditions characteristic of rural laissez-faire capitalism.

Under the influence of the Swiss Religious Socialists **Leonhard Ragaz** (1868–1945) and Hermann Kutter (1863–1931), Barth became a pastoral and political advocate for the workers, giving lectures on labor issues and human rights, leading readings of books on economics and socialist politics, and holding informal talks on practical issues like domestic finances, work schedules, and women in the workplace. Theologically, Barth's essay "Jesus Christ and the Social Movement" (1911) is characteristic of his thought during this early period.

His theological and practical endeavors were much appreciated by the local workers, who in 1913 asked him to consider joining the Safenwil Worker's Association as their president. Though he declined their offer, he continued to give guidance to the workers through his pastoral office, helping them to establish at least three different unions in Safenwil. He would eventually join the Socialist Party in 1915. The response of those who sided with the factory owners was equally passionate, as illustrated by a highly critical and public attack on Barth by the son of a local factory owner in a regional newspaper in 1912.

As for many of his contemporaries, the outbreak of the First World War was a shock for Barth, causing him to question his theological (Protestant Liberalism) and political (Religious Socialism) orientations. Barth was disheartened and disgusted by the collapse of many of the leading theological and political representatives of Protestant Liberalism and Socialism in the face of the German war policy of Kaiser Wilhelm II. Under the influence of **Christoph Blumhardt** (1842–1919), with whom Barth had a decisive meeting in 1915, Barth would retrieve and critically reconstruct his socialist commitment. Though he would no longer see socialism as *the* sign of the coming kingdom of God, he would argue that socialism was a parable of the kingdom, thus allowing it a provisional, penultimate importance. His controversial Tambach lecture of

1919, "The Christian's Place in Society," as well as the second edition (1922) of his *Römerbrief* reflected his new orientation, his break with the Religious Socialists, and the development of a new theological orientation that would come to be known as dialectical theology.

With the invitation to join the faculty of the University of Göttingen as honorary professor of reformed theology in 1921, Barth's political engagement became less overt, though no less important—until 1934. In his struggle against Nazism, Barth's engagement with political issues reached its zenith. Though Barth had publicly attacked fascism and anti-Semitism as early as 1925, his greatest contribution to the struggle against National Socialism came in the form of the *Theological Declaration of Barmen* (1934), perhaps the single most important politico-theological document of the twentieth century. Written in response to the German Christian movement within the German Evangelical Church, and unanimously adopted by the Confessing Church Movement, *Barmen,* the principle author of which was Barth, argued for the theological *and* political independence of the church and of the individual Christian vis-à-vis the state. According to *Barmen,* any political allegiance demanded by the state was penultimate at best and could never be regarded as another revelation of God. But neither could the church nor the individual Christian allow the state to simply go its own way, as though it had no responsibility before God. *Barmen* attacked Nazi ideology, and by implication all political ideologies, as a form of idolatry that the church must resist. Unfortunately, *Barmen* gave no clear repudiation of the Nazi policies against the Jews, a fact that Barth later lamented.

Dismissed from his post at the University of Bonn in 1935 for failure to give the oath of loyalty to the führer required by all state employees, Barth was immediately offered a position at the University of Basel, where he would remain until his retirement in

1962. In Switzerland Barth remained an active supporter of resistance against the Nazis both in Germany and without. His numerous lectures, open letters, publications, and radio addresses during this period attest to the seriousness with which he saw the situation. His protest and advocacy of armed resistance became so loud that in 1941–1942, under pressure from the German foreign ministry, he was censured by the Swiss government, though his publications and radio addresses would continue to be heard and read in Great Britain during the war.

After the war, Barth was a vocal advocate for responsible friendship with Germany. He stayed out of the debates over the cold war, calling both Communism and anticommunism dangerous ideologies. He continued to write and speak on issues like poverty and nuclear disarmament, though his stance over the cold war would remain largely misunderstood in the West. Barth died in 1968.

Bibliography. Barth, Karl. *Against the Stream: Shorter Post-war Writings, 1946–1952.* London: SCM Press, 1954. Barth, Karl. *Community, State and Church: Three Essays.* Gloucester, UK: Peter Smith, 1968. Hunsinger, George. *Karl Barth and Radical Politics.* Philadelphia: Westminster Press, 1976. Jehle, Frank. *Ever Against the Stream: The Politics of Karl Barth, 1906- 1968.* Trans. Richard and Martha Burnett. Grand Rapids, MI: William B. Eerdmans, 2002.

Christian T. Collins Winn

BASIC ECCLESIAL COMMUNITY (PHILIPPINES). The Philippine Basic Ecclesial Community (BEC) is a grassroots activist movement that offers an alternative approach to society and ecology. It identifies with the nationalist struggle against colonial and neocolonial dominance by Spain (1565–1898), the United States (1898–1946), and the Filipino elite.

The contemporary movement arose in reaction against Marcos' martial law dictatorship (1972–1986). Church leaders referred to Vatican II (1962–1965) social teachings to fight for the rights of the oppressed inside the nation. They worked to organize and increase the class consciousness of the poor and to improve their circumstances. Latin American liberation theologies influenced these social action workers who paved the way for the BEC movement. The Maryknolls institutionalized this movement in Davao province on the southern island of Mindanao in 1967. From there the movement spread out to the rest of the nation.

The BEC was formalized at the Mindanao-Sulu Pastoral Conference in Davao City, Mindanao, in 1971 after the Conference of Latin American Bishops in Medellin, Colombia, in 1968. The Catholic Bishops Conference, the National Secretariat for Social Action, and the United Church of Christ (a coalition of Protestant churches) endorsed the movement in 1977. The annual Mindanao-Sulu Pastoral meeting provided a forum for bishops to discuss their ideas with other clergy and lay participants involved in the BECs. They debated about issues such as the question of the degree of lay participation the BEC and the organizational structure of the church. Initially, the BEC model was introduced as a way to encourage the laity to become more actively involved in the liturgy. Later, some bishops stressed the importance of lay leadership and organization training programs directed at issues of social justice and liberation of the poor. This led to a controversy that portended to divide the movement. On one side, some bishops perceived the BECs to be an encroachment on the institutional power of the church. On the other side were those who stressed the ecclesiality of the BECs. The term "ecclesial" refers to the people of God as the body of the church. This disagreement between the conservatives (those advocating the hierarchical church) and the progressives (those promoting the popular church) resulted in a deadlock that closed the meetings in 1983, when the bishops met apart from the lay board.

Many progressive clergy involved in the earlier Mindanao-Sulu Pastoral meetings were transferred to conservative parishes in the Visayas and Luzon, while conservative bishops were transferred to replace them, and in theory, their programs, a reshuffling that continues into the new millennium. In this context many of the Christians critical of the martial law regime and involved in the BEC movement and its task forces for social justice were forced underground during that period, meaning they were under military surveillance and had reason to fear for their lives.

After Ferdinand Marcos was ousted from power by the well-known People's Power Revolution in 1986, the BEC continued to thrive, and in 1991 at the Second Plenary Council held in Cebu in the Central Philippines, the BEC model was officially decreed by the church hierarchy as "the new way of being a church." The new model was added to diocesan management networks throughout the nation, but some conservative archdiocesan centers began to stress the liturgical over the liberational aspect. Today there are both kinds of BECs in the Philippines.

Bibliography. Kinne, Warren. *A People's Church? Mindanao Sulu Church Debacle.* Frankfurt am Main, Germany: Peter Lang, 1990. Nadeau, Kathleen. *Liberation Theology in the Philippines: Faith in a Revolution.* Westport, CT: Praeger, 2002.

Kathleen Nadeau

BASQUE NATIONALIST PARTY (PARTIDO NACIONALISTA VASCO). The birth of Basque nationalism traditionally dates to an 1895 speech made by Sabino Arana (1865–1903) at Larrazábal on July 3, the feast of St. Ignatius of Loyola. The year before his discourse, Arana formed a recreational society, the Euskaldun Bastokija, which historians consider the forerunner to the Partido Nacionalista Vasco (PNV). From its creation,

the party has maintained a decisively confessional character with strong roots and inspiration in the fundamentalist Catholicism of Carlism and with God and Ancient Law as its motto.

At its beginning, the PNV existed only at Bilbao and its province (Vizcaya). In 1899, a moderate group joined the PNV and the ship owner Ramón de la Sota became the party's leader. After 1899, the PNV would be characterized by two opposing elements: one that calls for the unification of the "seven historic territories" in a *Euskadi* (or *Euskal Herria*) independent from Spain and France, and the newer, more moderate element that calls for political autonomy without formal separation from Spain. The Catholic hierarchy at first kept its distance from the PNV, although the party found an ample following in the lower members of the clergy. While it was born from traditionalist premodern beliefs, the PNV also took an important modernizing role in politics.

Until the 1930s, it remained a moderate party linked to the Spanish right regarding social programs and ideology. During the Second Republic (1931–1936), however, the centralism and nationalism of the Spanish right pushed the PNV toward the Left. At the outbreak of the Spanish civil war, the PNV defended the republic against **Francisco Franco**'s military rebels, switching from its moderate Catholic stance to a pronounced antifascist position. In return, on October 1, 1936, the Spanish Cortes approved the first Basque statute of autonomy, and shortly thereafter the first Basque government was installed under J. A. Aguirre. Upon learning of this, the Vatican did not quite understand what was happening and then criticized the arrangement. However, in spite of Franco's wishes, Rome did not formally condemn the new government. Basque nationalist troops (*gudaris*) were overwhelmed by Franco's forces in the summer of 1937. Before this, the symbolic city of the Basques, Gernika (Guernica), was bombed by Nazi and Fascist air units. The destruction contributed to the myth of the heroic fight of the Basques against Fascism.

Following Franco's victory, the PNV went into an active exile, especially after the 1960s, when it undertook clandestine actions against the government. A large number of young people from the youth organizations of the PNV founded Euskadi ta Askatasuna (ETA) in 1959. The territorial reorganization of the Spanish state after Franco's death in 1975 and the return of democracy in 1978 contributed to the Basque Country's becoming one of the seventeen autonomous regions in Spain. Since 1980, the Basques have had their own Statute of Autonomy. Either alone or in coalition, the PNV has always headed the Basque government, especially with the militant *lendabari,* who is the president of the autonomous government.

Bibliography. De Pablo, S., L. Mees, and J. A. Rodriguez Ranz. *El péndulo patriótico: Historia del Partito Nacionalista Vasco.* 2 vols. Barcelona: Critica, 1999–2001.

Alfonso Botti

BATISTA, CÍCERO ROMÃO (1844–1934). Batista (Padre Cícero) is considered a personal patron saint and godfather throughout Brazil's northeast (an area embracing the states of Bahia, Sergipe, Alagoas, Pernambuco, Paraíba, Rio Grande do Norte, and Ceará) and is regarded by some today as a forerunner of liberation theology's preferential option for the poor.

Padre Cícero owes much of his fame to a disputed miracle that occurred in 1889. Ordained in 1870, he was at that time a generally well-regarded but little-known parish priest in Juazeiro do Norte, a small settlement located in the interior of the state of Ceará. On March 1, 1889, a *beata* (a member of a lay, penitent sisterhood) named Maria de Araújo took communion from him, and, according to onlookers,

the host was transformed into blood. This occurred several more times throughout Holy Week.

Dom Joaquim Vieira, the bishop of Fortaleza (Ceará's capital) sent a commission to investigate the events in Juazeiro. The commission corroborated the miracles, but Dom Joaquim rejected that verdict. Padre Cícero's supporters have ascribed the bishop's actions to jealousy and the fear that Padre Cícero's fame would undermine his own authority. Detractors also suggest that the miracles were an elaborate hoax perpetrated either by the priest himself or by some of his followers. Scholarly accounts tend to focus on the Romanization or ultramontane movement then gripping Brazil's Catholic Church. They also cite the elite's disdain for the masses, who were generally seen as ignorant, prone to mysticism and superstition, and easily misled.

After a second commission declared the miracles to be false, the bishop suspended Padre Cícero's holy orders. In 1894, the Holy Office in Rome also condemned the miracle. Though never formally defrocked, Padre Cícero lost his right to preach and administer the sacraments. In part this resulted from his continued assertion of the miracle's verity, including the declaration that the blood was that of the Christ. In addition, he refused to leave Juazeiro permanently, a condition that the bishop had stipulated if Padre Cícero were to have any chance of reclaiming his full priestly rights. In the eyes of his followers, he became a martyr who suffered because of his devotion to the humble people of the interior. Juazeiro became known as a holy city and pilgrims came in ever-larger numbers to seek Padre Cícero's blessing and counsel.

As Juazeiro grew in importance, Padre Cícero also became a regional political actor. In one celebrated incident commonly known as the Juazeiro Sedition (1913–1914), forces loyal to Padre Cícero helped depose the sitting state executive.

This also secured Juazeiro's political autonomy as a county seat. Padre Cícero himself held several elected offices, including mayor of Juazeiro. During the last decades of his life, he received numerous state and national officials and office seekers who hoped to receive his political blessing.

Religious pilgrimages, now on an enormous scale, continue in the present day, marking both significant religious dates as well as important moments in Padre Cícero's life. The pilgrimages have contributed greatly to the growth and prosperity of Juazeiro, which boasts a statue of Padre Cícero that is the second-largest religious image in Brazil, second only to the famous statue of Christ the Redeemer on Corcovado Mountain in Rio de Janeiro.

Bibliography. Comblin, José. *Padre Cícero de Juazeiro.* São Paulo, Brazil: Edições Paulinas, 1991. Della Cava, Ralph. *Miracle at Joaseiro.* New York: Columbia University Press, 1970.

Gerald Michael Greenfield

BAUDRILLART, HENRI MARIE ALFRED (1859–1942). Baudrillart was a French scholar, teacher, cleric, and Catholic propagandist. Born into a religious family in Paris and ordained in 1893, he was elected to the Academie Française in 1918, appointed bishop in 1921, and elevated to cardinal in 1935. He was rector of the Paris Institut Catholique between 1907 and 1942 and skillfully guided it through the difficult period following the separation of church and state in 1905 and the so-called modernist crisis that challenged the church's authoritative claims.

The Institut Catholique became a premier institution of higher learning under his leadership in the interwar years. Renowned for his deep patriotism during the First World War, Baudrillart founded the Comité catholique de propagande française à l'étranger and was invited to write leading articles promoting the cause of France for forty-five American newspapers reaching a readership of over fifteen million people. Baudrillart became an ardent anticommunist in the 1920s, believing, as did most Catholics, that Bolshevism's atheism and internationalism posed a threat to French values and French identity.

While conservative, during the turbulent period that culminated in the Popular Front he nonetheless advised students at the Institut Catholique that neither socialism nor the French embodiment of the traditional Far Right, the **Action Française** (condemned by the papacy in 1926), was an option for Catholic voters. Baudrillart believed Hitler's ascendancy ominous and vigorously denounced Nazi error, notably its neopaganism. He spoke out against German aggression as war approached and maintained this patriotic line for the duration of the hostilities.

Baudrillart, however, is now largely remembered for having gone beyond traditional Catholic support for **Philippe Pétain** and his Vichy regime during the occupation and advocating collaboration with the Germans. Baudrillart's strident anticommunism clouded his judgment in the last years of his life. He encouraged young Catholic men to join the Légion des Volontaires Français (LVF), a group dedicated to joining the German "crusade" against Bolshevism. While it never became a mass movement, the LVF nevertheless provided the Germans and French collaborators with valuable propaganda, diverting attention away from their anti-Semitism.

Baudrillart's stance was not representative of the collective voice of the church in France at this time. Many of his coreligionists, including members of the hierarchy, regretted and were embarrassed by Baudrillart's excesses, while others discounted his actions as those of an imprudent elderly man who had lost his bearings.

Bibliography. Christophe, Paul, ed. *Les carnets du cardinal Alfred Baudrillart.* 9 vols. Paris: Le Cerf, 1994.

Vesna Drapac

BAUER, GARY L. (b. 1946). Bauer is a Christian Right leader and political activist who campaigned for the Republican nomination for president of the United States in 2000. Born in Covington and raised in Newport, Kentucky, he is the son of an ex-marine who held a variety of jobs during Bauer's youth. Following his father's wishes, Bauer worked hard in school in Newport, graduating in 1964. After graduating from Georgetown College in Georgetown, Kentucky, he moved to Washington, D.C., to take a job with the Republican National Committee during the Watergate scandal. In 1973, Bauer received a law degree from Georgetown University Law School.

Disenchanted with party politics after Watergate, he found a position with the Direct Mail Marketing Association, a lobbying firm. Bauer reentered Republican Party politics in 1980 when he became a senior analyst for the **Ronald Reagan**-George Bush presidential campaign. In October 1982, Bauer was appointed deputy undersecretary of education for planning, budget, and evaluation. He was promoted to undersecretary of education in 1985. In that position, he opposed value-free curriculums in public schools. He blamed such curriculums for the moral breakdown of American society. Bauer became President Reagan's chief adviser on domestic policy in 1987.

When Ronald Reagan left the White House in 1989, Bauer became president of the Family Research Council, a conservative political advocacy group created by Dr. **James Dobson** of Focus on the Family. Bauer also served as senior vice president of Focus on the Family. He grew the Family Research Council into an influential organization in Washington. When he arrived, the organization had a budget of $200,000, three thousand members, and three employees. By 1998, the Family Research Council's budget had increased to $14 million with 450,000 members and

ninety-three paid employees. In 1992, the council legally split from Focus on the Family and Bauer stepped down as vice president of the latter group. This move allowed the Family Research Council to become more involved in political advising and lobbying.

Spurred by the Republican Party's defeat in the 1996 presidential election, he founded a political action committee, the Campaign for Working Families (CWF). This PAC funded candidates who were pro-life, pro-family, and pro-free enterprise. In 1997, the PAC raised $2.6 million, leading Bauer to claim that it was the second-largest PAC in the United States.

Bauer's success with the Family Research Council and the CWF, and his disgust with the Republican Party's inability to enact its pro-family and pro-life agenda, led him to launch a bid for the 2000 Republican presidential nomination. In April 1999, he officially announced his candidacy from his hometown of Newport, Kentucky. He took a leave of absence from the Family Research Council and CWF. Shortly after coming in last in the New Hampshire Republican primary in February 2000, Bauer ended his campaign and endorsed Arizona senator John McCain. He continued in politics after his failed bid for the White House by establishing American Values, a pro-family, pro-life organization, and joining with Rabbi Daniel Lapin to launch the American Alliance of Jews and Christians.

The ultimate goal of Bauer's campaign for president was "a society that's stable, where marriage means something, where the virtue deficit is being dealt with, where kids are being taught reliable standards of right and wrong." During the campaign, he regularly related the story of his first political activity in Newport, usually telling the story as a form of moral lesson. A regular worshipper at the local Baptist church because of his grandmother's prodding, he learned of an effort to clean up his hometown. In 1957, *Esquire* magazine had labeled Newport "Sin City" because of the town's gambling, official corruption, and generally "wide-open" atmosphere. As a sophomore in high school, Bauer joined the effort to end corruption in city government and reduce the influence of organized crime. The reform effort was largely successful, electing a "Switch to Honesty" ticket to city hall by 1961. Bauer gave up the chance for a lucrative career as a high-powered Washington lawyer or lobbyist in order to help turn America around in the same way that he helped clean up Newport.

Bibliography. Cottle, Michelle. "The Making of a Crusader." *New Republic,* 15 March 1999, 16–18. Oldfield, Duane M. *The Right and the Righteous: The Christian Right Confronts the Republican Party.* Lanham, MD: Rowman & Littlefield, 1996.

John David Rausch, Jr.

BEECHER, CATHARINE ESTHER (1800–1878). The eldest of thirteen children born to Presbyterian luminary **Lyman Beecher,** Catharine stands among the most forceful and influential nineteenth-century women who attempted to define the female role in the new American Republic. That she steadfastly opposed women's entry onto the political stage makes her a particularly important window onto the diversity of female advocacy in antebellum America.

Catharine's early education at home was augmented by her study at Sarah Pierce's Female Academy in Litchfield, Connecticut, where her father ministered. Following her mother's death in 1816, she assumed a full measure of domestic responsibility in becoming a surrogate parent for Lyman's seven younger children until the patriarch remarried a year later. A spiritual struggle to come to terms with her father's Calvinist faith accompanied these steps into adulthood. When her fiancé drowned in 1822, still uncertain of his own salvation, Catharine shouldered that burden partly by rejecting Calvinism's harsher determinist

elements. This standing quarrel with her father's faith, coupled with her decision to remain single, turned Catharine in a fiercely independent direction.

In establishing the Hartford Female Seminary in 1823, Beecher broke the finishing-school mold and developed a diverse curriculum that respected women's capacity for intellectual stimulation and academic rigor. She joined her father in Cincinnati in 1832 and devoted herself to promoting education in the west and especially to the recruitment of female teachers. For single women, she believed, the school was an appropriate extension of female domestic responsibilities.

With the publication of *Suggestions Respecting Improvements in Education* (1829) and *The Elements of Mental and Moral Philosophy* (1831), she embarked on a publishing career that vigorously promoted women's domestic roles. Her flagship volume, *A Treatise on Domestic Economy* (1841), linked republican stability directly to the moral influence of women in the home.

Beecher's lifelong opposition to women's suffrage can easily obscure her contributions to the nation's political discourse. By 1870, she could still deliver shrill denunciations against the increasing stridency of suffragist leaders such as **Elizabeth Stanton** and **Susan B. Anthony.** Most American women, she chided, would view the ballot "not as a privilege conferred, but as an act of oppression, forcing them to assume responsibilities belonging to man, for which they are not and cannot be qualified" (Boydston, Kelly, and Margolis, 253). Yet if Beecher's intransigence put her behind the times, her advocacy of the Christian family carried political overtones that still resonate in modern political debate.

In her moral and political philosophy, Beecher measured cultural power on her own terms. Politicians, she believed, expected to achieve social stability by using the legislative system to compel morality and punish wrongdoers. Beecher though women delivered the more potent blows against public corruption simply by sustaining a Christian home. This application of domestic power could infuse the political system with virtuous leaders bearing a keen sense of responsibility for women's needs. Presiding over this haven from worldly immorality, women delivered pre-emptive strikes against destructive behaviors that government had to address through more costly and less effective means. In sum, political responsibility would draw women away from the natural, god-given source of their power, forcing them onto the public stage and draining the domestic sphere of its restorative power. Women and men were intellectual equals, she regularly insisted, but such equality did not erase male responsibility to lead in the family and the political arena. Women such as **Angelina Grimké** who defied such proscriptions in order to publicly denounce slavery drew special fire from Beecher. If women find laws to be unjust and unequal, she chided, they should use their "influence with the lawmakers, and *in an acceptable manner,* and these laws would speedily be changed" (Boydston et al., 141).

Beecher's moral formula gave little attention to the personal aspirations of single women or women attracted to the challenges of the marketplace and professional world. The dismal working conditions that marked mid-nineteenth-century American industry only fueled her conviction that women who ventured into the workplace faced myriad exploitations. Although the marriage bond affirmed male prerogatives, it also obligated men to use their "power of physical strength" and "power of the purse" to insulate women from such abuses (Boydston et al., 141).

Beecher's utopian plan to realize the "*Bible rights* of woman" drew from moral and spiritual values broadly shared in mid-nineteenth-century America. The reformers who met at Seneca Falls, New York, in 1848 to found the modern women's rights movement had little patience with such spiritual boundaries and saw better than Beecher that women would not accept political impotence indefinitely. Nevertheless, Beecher's core principles—support of universal public education as a mainspring of cultural stability, assaults on exploitative labor practices, and a vigorous defense of the family as the foundation of moral character—continue to inform modern political debate and legislative initiatives.

Bibliography. Beecher, Catharine. *True Remedy for the Wrongs of Woman.* Boston, 1851. Boydston, Jeanne, Mary Kelly, and Anne Margolis. *The Limits of Sisterhood: The Beecher Sisters on Women's Rights and Women's Sphere.* Chapel Hill: University of North Carolina Press, 1988. Sklar, Kathryn Kish. *Catharine Beecher: A Study in American Domesticity.* New Haven, CT: Yale University Press, 1973.

Mark Y. Hanley

BEECHER, HENRY WARD (1813–1887). It was as a compelling lecturer, preacher, and popular essayist—not as a profound theologian or original thinker—that Beecher enjoyed public recognition in mid-nineteenth-century America. The ninth child of the preacher-reformer **Lyman Beecher,** Henry Ward was as much at home on the political platform and lyceum circuit as in the pulpit, ministering to the aspirations of self-improving middle-class citizens. Some found him gushing, facile, and vulgar; others delighted in the power, wit, and emotional range of his appeals; none could doubt his capacity to charm and electrify an audience.

Beecher modified the Calvinism into which he was born by stressing not God's power but his love and mercy. But he remained faithful to the claims on orthodox Calvinists to embrace active Christian citizenship as a means of advancing God's kingdom. His concern for the democratic and political needs of the Mississippi Valley led him after graduating from Amherst to follow his father westward. During his Indiana pastorates in Lawrenceburg (1837–1839) and Indianapolis (1839–1847) he won praise for his energetic civic engagement. His main focus was church growth and community improvement through moral suasion. But as a leading minister in the state capital he also established easy relations with political figures, including Samuel Bigger, Whig governor and fellow Presbyterian, and helped secure state-supported provision of institutions for deaf-mutes and the blind.

Beecher's period of most influential political activity proved to be the first half of his four decades as Congregationalist pastor of Plymouth Church, Brooklyn (1847–1887), the years of the Union's crisis over slavery. By the standards of the day, he was no conservative. He regarded slavery as a real social ill; he came to question the practicality and underlying motivation of schemes for colonizing ex-slaves in foreign lands, and he sought to improve the lot of free blacks. He deprecated the violence meted out by antiabolitionists. But at the same time he condemned as counterproductive the invective of **William Lloyd Garrison** and other radical abolitionists. He thought slavery would gradually perish through economic forces and feared moving too far ahead of mainstream Protestant opinion. Until the outbreak of the Mexican War in 1846, Beecher avoided taking any stand that might be deemed controversial. But distrust of Southern expansionism drove him onto more advanced ground, as did the terms of the 1850 compromise. He began to pursue a Free-Soil agenda in the columns of the new Congregationalist weekly, the New York *Independent*. He addressed the American Anti-Slavery Society (see **Abolitionists),** called for passive disobedience to the new Fugitive Slave Law, and conducted mock auctions to raise funds to free slaves.

The repeal of the Missouri Compromise in 1854, and the voting fraud and violence surrounding the setting up of a proslavery legislature in Kansas, further radicalized Beecher, now convinced that a slave power was plotting to control the nation. As well as promoting the emigration of antislavery settlers to the new territory, he pledged money to buy Sharps rifles (so-called Beecher's Bibles) for their self-defense against "border ruffians." Equally, he saw the need for a new antislavery political force and, despite his previous scruples, threw himself publicly into party-based activity. In 1856 his church (the Church of the Holy Rifles) gave him time off to campaign for the presidential candidate of the new Republican Party, John C. Frémont.

That party, devoted to the ideal of social mobility, provided Beecher with a natural ideological home. He championed the interests of self-disciplined and aspiring workingmen, while deprecating the moral blight that slavery inflicted on education, industry, thrift, and family life in the South. Beecher was only one of thousands of evangelicals who brought a sharp moral, millennialist edge to the Republicans; he also contributed a reputation and a reach that few could match. Though perceived by many as a radical abolitionist, he actually represented the moderate mainstream of Republicanism in seeking the slow strangulation of slavery. His sanction of defensive violence in Kansas did not extend to support for slave rebellions or **John Brown**'s raid at Harpers Ferry. He rejoiced in **Abraham Lincoln**'s victory in 1860.

During the lower South's secession in 1860–1861 Beecher stood firm against compromise. He welcomed war as a means of vindicating democracy and republican government. His sermons strengthened patriotism by linking God's purposes and national mission. He did not at first urge a struggle for emancipation but, after taking up the editorship of the *Independent* in September 1861, increasingly criticized Lincoln's reluctance to broaden the war's aims. His sometimes fierce assaults on the administration during 1862 gave way to approval once the Emancipation Proclamation was issued. His justly acclaimed speaking tour in Britain during the fall of 1863 did not so much change attitudes as gave further impetus to already-improving Anglo-American relations. Following Lincoln's nomination for a second term, Beecher energetically campaigned for his reelection. When the Union flag was raised at Fort Sumter on April 14, 1865, Beecher gave the main address.

Reconstruction revealed Beecher's ambivalence and social moderation, and the conflict in his mind between equal rights and laissez-faire principles. He advocated education, limited suffrage, and modest economic help for freedmen but feared that too much federal "nursing" of Southern blacks would undermine self-help and antagonize Southern whites. He supported Andrew Johnson's aim of promptly readmitting the seceded states and ending the federal military government in the South. His criticisms of the Radical Republicans in his misguided "Cleveland Letter"—addressed to a pro-Johnson convention during the elections of 1866—exposed him to heated attack and public rejection.

This experience, and a nation-gripping scandal over his alleged adultery with Elizabeth Tilton, colored but did not end his public standing. He continued to support women's suffrage, temperance, and free trade. He maintained his connections with Republican leaders during the 1870s and, despite his concerns over corruption, supported James Garfield for the presidency in 1880. But in 1884, believing that the Republicans could not be trusted over civil service reform or "the rights of labor as against combined capital," (Clark, 253) he helped the Democrat Grover Cleveland secure the presidency. When he died, the state legislature recessed, national leaders paid their respects, and tens of thousands

came to view his body—a measure of his persisting public esteem.

Bibliography. Beecher, William C., and Samuel Scoville. *A Biography of Rev. Henry Ward Beecher.* New York: C. L. Webster, 1888. Clark, Clifford E. *Henry Ward Beecher: Spokesman for a Middle-Class America.* Urbana: University of Illinois Press, 1979. McLoughlin, William G. *The Meaning of Henry Ward Beecher: An Essay on the Shifting Values of Mid-Victorian America, 1840–1870.* New York: Alfred A. Knopf, 1970.

Richard J. Carwardine

BEECHER, LYMAN (1775–1863). During the first four decades of the nineteenth century, Beecher was a leading evangelical revivalist of the Second Great Awakening in America and the premier reform clergyman of his generation. An energetic and pugnacious advocate for his principles, he engaged in a host of campaigns—including anti-dueling, moral reform, temperance, and Sabbatarianism—as both spokesman and organizer.

Beecher sought to apply Christian morality in defense of free republican government. As he observed, "From the beginning my mind has taken in the Church of God, my country, and the world as given to Christ. It is this that has widened the scope of my activities beyond the common sphere of pastoral labor" (*Autobiography,* 46). Moreover, Beecher led New England Congregationalism from its establishment roots to voluntary activism and worked to unite evangelicals from various denominations against Unitarians, other liberals, and Roman Catholics. However, more radical elements in the reform camp and conservatives in the church eventually scorned him. His remarkable children—including the preacher **Henry Ward Beecher,** the writer **Harriet Beecher Stowe,** and the educator **Catharine Beecher,** to name just three—constituted one of his greatest legacies.

Beecher's mother died soon after his birth in New Haven, Connecticut, and his maternal aunt and uncle raised him in North Guilford. He entered Yale in 1793, where President **Timothy Dwight** became his mentor. As an undergraduate, Beecher experienced conversion and graduated in 1797. In the year following, he studied theology with Dwight, adopting his teacher's style of evangelical Calvinism that would later be more fully articulated in the New Haven theology of his friend, Nathaniel William Taylor.

Beecher became pastor of the Presbyterian church in East Hampton, Long Island, in 1799 and ignited a revival the following year. He first came to prominence with the publication in 1806 of *The Remedy for Duelling,* which laid out several key themes and tactics of his subsequent activism. Dueling Beecher labeled murder and a land-defiling sin. He concentrated his denunciation on its threats to republican government, namely that it was contrary to the rule of law, destructive to the political leadership, and inimical to free speech and the press. He identified the recently emerged first party competition between Federalists and Jeffersonian Republicans as a twofold cause, since political contention generated the insults that led to challenges and because partisans would overlook their candidates' involvement. Instead, Beecher exhorted his listeners not to vote for duelists. "If only the members of christian churches, become decided in their opposition to duelling [*sic*], it will produce a sensation through the state. The votes of professing christians, of different denominations, are too numerous and important to be thrown away" (*Lyman Beecher,* 35). He limned further solutions that would become standards of his later organizing, calling for ministers to speak out, the distribution of publications, and the organization of voluntary societies.

Pleading an inadequate salary, Beecher left East Hampton in 1810 for a pastorate in Litchfield, Connecticut. He returned to his home state as its Congregational establishment, or standing order, was nearing its end. (Disestablishment would occur finally in 1818.) He helped found the Connecticut Society for the Suppression of Vice and the Promotion of Good Morals in 1812. In the same year he preached *A Reformation of Morals Practicable and Indispensable* and called for repentance. Since elected officials would not pursue the unpopular course of tackling vice, Beecher called for "local voluntary associations of the wise and the good to aid the civil magistrate in the execution of the laws . . . [and to act as] a sort of disciplined moral militia" (*Lyman Beecher,* 18). Accepting the results of disestablishment, Beecher warned Christians to stay above mere party politics and only pursue issues of great moral import. He played a leadership role in the organization of local, state, and national missionary organizations, including the American Bible Society.

In 1826 Beecher became pastor of Boston's Hanover Street Church. In the center of Unitarianism, he engaged in revivals and helped launch the periodical *Spirit of the Pilgrims* as a voice of orthodoxy. He assisted in organizing the American Temperance Society in 1826 and published two years later *Six Sermons on the Nature, Occasions, Signs, Evils, and Remedy of Intemperance;* indeed, it was Beecher's temperance preaching that launched the reform career of **William Lloyd Garrison.** Beecher also played a prominent role in the organization of the General Union for the Promotion of the Christian Sabbath in 1828.

From Boston Beecher moved to Cincinnati in 1832, based on the belief that the future of the United States would be determined in the west. He assumed the presidency of Lane Theological Seminary that year and published *A Plea for the West,* in which he argued that only education and enlightened piety could save the Republic from the threats of benighted Catholic immigrants and their conspiratorial leaders; he called for stricter naturalization requirements. At Lane, however, Beecher became caught in the middle of a dispute between abolitionist students and conservative trustees, who in 1834 voted to shut down antislavery discussion on campus for fear of inciting the city's residents to mob violence. The result was that most of the student body departed for Oberlin. In 1835 Beecher also suffered a trial for heresy on account of his New Haven doctrines that foreshadowed the 1837 schism of the Presbyterians into Old School and New School factions, although the case was dropped on appeal. A firm Whig during the Jacksonian era, Beecher supported William Henry Harrison in the election of 1840. Four years later, Democrats reissued Beecher's old anti-dueling sermon in order to embarrass Henry Clay, who had fought duels earlier in his life. Beecher remained as president of Lane until his retirement in 1850.

Bibliography. Abzug, Robert H. "Lyman Beecher and the Cosmic Theater." In *Cosmos Crumbling: American Reform and the Religious Imagination*. New York: Oxford University Press, 1994. Beecher, Lyman. *Autobiography.* Ed. Barbara M. Cross. 2 vols. Cambridge, MA: Belknap Press of Harvard University Press, 1961. Beecher, Lyman. *Lyman Beecher and the Reform of Society: Four Sermons, 1804–1828.* New York: Arno Press, 1972. Harding, Vincent. *A Certain Magnificence: Lyman Beecher and the Transformation of American Protestantism, 1775–1863.* Brooklyn, NY: Carlson, 1991. Howe, Daniel Walker. *The Political Culture of the American Whigs.* Chicago: University of Chicago Press, 1979.

Jonathan D. Sassi

BEKKERS, WILHELMUS (1908–1966). A Roman Catholic Bishop and ecumenical leader, Bekkers was born in Sint Oedenrode, in the Dutch province of Brabant. After serving as a parish priest in the towns of Hertogenbosch and Tilburg, Bekkers was appointed coadjutor to Bishop Mutsaerts of Den Bosch in 1956 and succeeded him in 1960.

As bishop, Bekkers focused on issues concerning marriage and the family. In his weekly television show, Bekkers often emphasized the supremacy of conscience and remarked that while all methods of birth control have "unsatisfactory elements," they often fell under the rule of conscience. Bekkers's willingness to engage in dialogue about issues concerning marriage, sexuality, and the family earned him the respect of organizations such as the Society for Sexual Reform that had long understood Catholic attitudes toward sexuality as hopelessly retrograde.

Bekkers was perhaps most beloved in Holland for his ecumenical openness. His efforts to encourage in ecumenical dialogue and his specific work to engage Reformed churches before the convocation of the Second Vatican Council marked an important moment of rapprochement between Dutch Catholicism and Protestant denominations. Bekkers also exerted a crucial influence in annotating conciliar schemas that encouraged discussions among European bishops before the Second Vatican Council was convened. Bekkers's motto as bishop was *Caritas pro armis* (Love as a weapon).

Bibliography. Van Hess, Nico. "Everyone's Bishop." In *Those Dutch Catholics,* ed. Michel van der Plas and Henk Suèr. New York: Macmillan, 1968.

Mathew N. Schmalz

BELLAH, ROBERT NEELLY (b. 1927). Perhaps no American scholar elicits greater respect and commands more influence in the liberal Christian community than does Robert Bellah. While the retired University of California, Berkeley, sociologist and public philosopher has published widely in a career spanning half a century, his reputation rests chiefly on a pair of extraordinarily influential works—the 1967 essay "Civil Religion in America," and the collaborative effort *Habits of the Heart,* published in 1985. At the core of Bellah's worldview is a conviction that the prevailing ethos that currently drives American political and economic development is rooted in flawed assumptions about the nation's past and an unwarranted faith in individualism as a basis for moral order.

Bellah carries lasting scars from his early academic career. As a young undergraduate at Harvard, he drifted widely from his traditional Protestant upbringing to become a member of the American Communist Party in 1947. His party activity focused mainly on his leadership of Harvard's John Reed Club until internal party discord in 1949 compelled him to abandon his communist affiliation. Bellah completed his doctoral work at Harvard in sociology and Far Eastern languages in 1955 under the direction of Talcott Parsons but not before his graduate career was marred by the Red Scare investigations of that era.

Pressed by McGeorge Bundy, dean of Harvard's Faculty of Arts and Sciences, to cooperate with the House Un-American Activities Committee and provide information about communist efforts beyond his own experience, Bellah refused and ultimately turned down a faculty appointment that required compliance with government investigations. After Harvard backed away from this contract proviso in 1957, Bellah accepted a faculty appointment.

In 1967, he left his full professorship for a faculty appoint at Berkeley, where he remained until retiring in 1997. That same year, Bellah published his essay on civil religion in the scholarly journal *Daedalus.* Borrowing the term itself from the writings of Jean-Jacques Rousseau, he described a ritualized public process of synthesizing religious and patriotic rhetoric to identify ultimate meaning in national purpose and destiny. In America, he argued, this "public religious dimension" constituted "a set of beliefs, symbols, and rituals" that existed quite apart from particular theological traditions. Bellah traced the progress of this civil religion from the nation's founding and cited **Abraham Lincoln** as its most worthy practitioner. It was Bellah's forceful cautions, however, that resonated most readily for an audience steeped in the cultural turmoil spawned by the Vietnam War. While civil religion properly reined might sustain the nation's highest principles, it could also identify Americans as a "chosen people" and ironically promote their enslavement to a host of unholy causes—economic injustice, racism, and a predatory geo-political agenda fueled by the "arrogance of power."

Bellah's lifelong study of the sociology of religion eventually included a revitalized interest in his Christian roots and a deep commitment to seeing organized Christianity become a bulwark of moral and cultural alternatives to the prevailing values of market capitalism and global power politics. For Bellah, the emergence in the 1980s of the Christian Right under the aegis of leaders such as **Pat Robertson** and **Jerry Falwell** and organizations like the **Christian Coalition** and **Moral Majority,** constituted an egregious prostitution of authentic Christian values to American capitalism and nationalist aims. As contributor to and presiding editor for *Habits of the Heart,* as well as its sequel, *The Good Society* (1991), Bellah and his intellectual companions called unequivocally for a revolution in American cultural values. Reflecting Bellah's Marxist past and Christian sympathies, the chapters point to a deep-seated structural disease in America with market capitalism and an accompanying ethos of radical individualism as the chief infectious agents.

By allowing the means of production to define ultimate human values, Americans had become servants of a false god, and true democracy was lost. Bellah offers salvation in a collective admission that such idolatry cannot lead to genuine community. Moreover, Bellah complains that modern capitalist culture justifies its selfish ethos through erroneous ancestral claims to the nation's founding philosophy. The most potent philosophical center of the nation's first citizens, he argues, was a Christian tradition focused on community and a classical republican ideal that elevated public service above self.

Consequently, Bellah's plan for cultural survival encompasses both revolution and restoration to restore true participatory democracy. This new political morality could then create "democratic institutions, within which we citizens can better discern what we really want and what we ought to want to sustain a good life on this planet" (Bellah, *Good Society,* 9).

In December 2000, President Bill Clinton awarded Bellah the United States National Humanities Medal, citing his commitment to "reminding Americans and of the dangers of individualism unchecked by social responsibility."

Bibliography. Bellah, Robert N. "Civil Religion in America." *Daedalus* 96 (Winter 1967): 1–21. Bellah, Robert N. *The Good Society.* New York: Alfred A. Knopf, 1991. Bellah, Robert N., et al. *Habits of the Heart.* Berkeley and Los Angeles: University of California Press, 1985.

Mark Y. Hanley

BELLOC, HILAIRE PIERRE (1870–1953). Belloc was a major British author, poet, controversialist, and onetime member of Parliament. His politics were rooted in the Catholic faith, and he made his reputation above all as a polemicist for libertarian economics and as a major popularizer of conspiratorial anti-Semitism.

Born in St Cloud, France, Belloc was naturalized as a British subject in 1903 and educated at the Oratory School under **John Henry Newman,** and at Balliol, Oxford. From early on, he was engaged in various social reform and antiwar movements, in which he gained sufficient recognition to be elected a Liberal member of Parliament in 1906. After four years' service in the House of Commons, Belloc lost faith with parliamentary democracy, and he essayed into the vigorous libertarian, anti-Semitic, and Christian polemic for which he is best remembered.

Together with his friend and fellow Catholic **G. K. Chesterton,** Belloc made up the so-called Chesterbelloc group, which advocated a Distributist system of economics and governance. This system was predicated on the Christian assumption that capitalism and Socialism alike were rooted in unacceptably materialist values and that they encouraged loss of independence and appreciation for the Christian virtues. Instead, the Distributists hoped to effect a return to a neo-medievalist system of locally autonomous communities composed of peasant proprietors, craftsmen, and shopkeepers. Belloc preferred such a system to modern collectivist liberalism, which he assailed with great force in his major theoretical book, *The Servile State* (1912).

A convinced anti-Semite, Belloc did much to popularize modern conspiratorial anti-Semitism in the English-speaking world. His anti-Semitism was shaped by Christian, racialist, and economic prejudices, and he believed in the existence of a worldwide Jewish conspiracy, supposedly masterminded by international finance and burrowed into the structures of governance of every Western nation. Consequently, in 1911–1914 Belloc passionately publicized the so-called Marconi Affair, a complicated bribery scandal, which according to him proved that leading Liberal politicians were being paid by Jewish financiers.

Above all a Catholic neo-medievalist, Belloc yearned for a return to preindustrial, supposedly more Christian paradigms and social structures, and together with Chesterton, he exerted great influence on a range of similarly minded British thinkers of many religious and political persuasions. His forceful anti-Semitism and frequently narrowly doctrinaire theories, however, severely limited his impact on public policy.

Bibliography. Corrin, Jay P. *G. K. Chesterton and Hilaire Belloc: The Battle against Modernity.* Athens: Ohio University Press, 1981. McCarthy, John P. *Hilaire Belloc: Edwardian Radical.* Indianapolis, IN: Liberty Press, 1978.

Markku Ruotsila

BENEDICT XV [GIACOMO DELLA CHIESA] (1854–1922). Born of a noble Genoese family, Della Chiesa graduated from a secular university with a law degree (*dottorato di legge*). His ecclesiastical education was at the Capranica College, the Gregorian University in Rome, and at the prestigious Academy of Noble Ecclesiastics, the training ground of Vatican diplomats and curial bureaucrats.

He soon caught the eye of **Rampolla Cardinal del Tindaro** and served in the Madrid nunciature from 1883 to 1887 and then as *minutante* to that great secretary of state. He became substitute secretary of state (*Sostituto*) in 1901, and thus one of the most powerful men in the Vatican. But the death of **Leo XIII** and the election of **Pius X** in 1903 spelled the beginning of the end of Della Chiesa's influence in the Vatican, as he found himself increasingly at odds with the policies of Papa Sarto and his very young secretary of state, **Raphael Cardinal Merry del Val,** particularly on the questions of handling relations with France and modernism.

It is alleged that when he was elected pope he found a denunciation of himself for "modernism" among Pius X's papers. There was something of a personality clash between the *Sostituto* and his new boss. Eventually, in 1907, Merry Del Val managed to get him out of the way by sending him to be archbishop of Bologna. Serving in one of the largest dioceses in Italy was a crucial formative experience. It enabled him to rule a diocese in the heart of Italy's "red belt," with all the problems that entailed, including the "de-Christianization" of large areas under the control of the Socialists and their trade unions and peasant leagues.

Benedict XV. Courtesy of the Perry-Casteñeda Library

It seems likely that it was at this time that he became a "closet" Christian Democrat with remarkably progressive ideas on social questions, in contrast to those of Pius X, who came close to banning Catholic trade unions toward the end of his reign.

Made a cardinal, rather late, in May 1914, Della Chiesa was elected pope only four months later after a three-day conclave, despite the opposition of Merry Del Val and the more intransigent cardinals. In fact, he was eminently *papabile* and was the front-runner from the beginning.

From the outset of his pontificate, Benedict declared the papacy to be neutral and impartial in the First World War and engaged in considerable humanitarian relief for civilians and military alike on both sides of the conflict. He also vigorously protested against the Turkish massacres of Armenians. Benedict and his secretary of state, **Pietro Cardinal Gasparri,** also engaged in unceasing diplomatic efforts to bring the war to an end, culminating in his

Peace Note of August 1917. The note prefigured much of Woodrow Wilson's later "Fourteen Points" but was rejected by both sides. He was frequently denounced as the *pape boche* in France and less often as *der französiche Papst* in Germany. He was not much liked in Italy either, especially after the Italian defeat at Caporetto, which was blamed on defeatism generated by the Peace Note.

Partly because of the brevity of his reign, but also because of the lack of success of his peace diplomacy during the First World War, and the opposition it aroused in both camps, Benedict is little known. Nevertheless, Benedict's pontificate ranks as an important one in the history of the modern papacy. Although he failed to bring peace to Europe, he brought peace to the church after the terrible antimodernist persecutions of his predecessor. He promulgated the Code of Canon Law in 1917 and began the policy of concordats with states based on that code. He revitalized papal diplomacy and consequently the international influence of the papacy. He also renewed the Roman Catholic Church's missionary outreach and its relations with the Eastern churches in communion with Rome.

In Italy, he was instrumental in finally abolishing the *Non expedit,* the Vatican's ban on Italian Catholics voting or standing as candidates in parliamentary elections, thus opening the way for the massive electoral affirmation of the *Partito Popolare Italiano* (PPI, **Italian Popular Party**) in November 1919. He also permitted Catholics to form their own trade union, the Confederazione Italiana del Lavoro, in 1918 but warned against Catholic cooperation with Marxist parties and against the threat of Communism.

It is a tribute to the soundness and importance of his policies that they were all continued by his successor, even to the extent that **Pius XI** retained Benedict's secretary of state, Pietro Cardinal Gasparri.

Bibliography. Pollard, John F. *The Unknown Pope: Benedict XV (1854–1922) and the Pursuit of Peace.* London: Chapman, 1999. Rumi, Giorgio, ed. *Benedetto XV e la pace, 1914–1918.* Brescia, Italy: La Morcelliana, 1990.

John F. Pollard

BENNETT, WILLIAM JOHN (b. 1943). A former academician and U.S. Cabinet secretary, Bennett became "America's self-appointed moral guardian" in the 1990s (Starr, 62). Born in Brooklyn, New York, and raised in a broken Catholic home, Bennett enjoyed baseball and rock and roll until he found a deeper meaning for his life through classical literature.

Graduating from Williams College in 1965, Bennett went on to the University of Texas to obtain his PhD in philosophy in 1970. After a succession of academic assignments, he earned a degree from the Harvard Law School in 1971 and moved to Boston University, where he was assistant professor of philosophy (1971–1976). He was a capable professor, although his own experience in teaching convinced him that genuine education must develop his students' character and not just impart facts.

Bennett came into public prominence as an advocate of humanities education. While executive director and president (1976–1981) of the National Humanities Center, he vigorously promoted the humanities as essential to the development of the well-rounded student. During this period, Bennett coauthored his first book, *Counting by Race* (1979), which argued that affirmative action programs were ultimately destructive to American democracy. The book also brought Bennett, a former Democrat who had once dabbled in radicalism, to the attention of conservative Republicans.

In 1981, Bennett was appointed to the chair of the National Endowment for the Humanities (NEH) by President **Ronald Reagan**. Almost immediately, he provoked a political firestorm at the NEH by adopting a narrow interpretation of humanities, which ended the funding of many controversial projects. Bennett's major accomplishment at the NEH was the production of a study entitled "To Reclaim a Legacy: A Report on the Humanities in Higher Education" (1984). The report was critical of the contemporary status of the humanities in American colleges and universities and urged schools to return to a stress on the humanities, particularly with an emphasis on Western civilization.

President Reagan appointed Bennett education secretary in 1985 despite the vocal opposition of various liberal organizations that criticized his stance on civil rights and his ultraconservative biases at the NEH. Bennett spent much of his term as secretary of education (1985–1989) antagonizing the educational establishment by supporting a greater role in public education for parents, teachers, and local governments. He also backed education vouchers and tax credits for parents of school-age children, as well as merit pay for outstanding teachers. In consonance with his most primary beliefs, Bennett strongly favored curriculum reform in schools that emphasized "the three C's": content, character, and parental choice.

In 1989, President George H. W. Bush appointed Bennett director of the Office of National Drug Control Policy. Although he occupied the position for only twenty months, Bennett was able to use his role as "drug czar" to emphasize his core themes of individual responsibility and local enforcement of policy. By the 1992 presidential election, Bennett was finally out of government. As codirector of the Empower America think tank and a fellow at the conservative Heritage Foundation, Bennett uniquely positioned himself to comment on the American sociopolitical climate of the 1990s.

The commentary came in a flurry of books, published within a ten-year period. Notable among these works were *The De-Valuing of America* (1992), *The Book of Virtues* (1993; editor), *Body Count* (1996; coauthored), *The Death of Outrage* (1998), *The Educated Child* (1999; coauthored), *The Broken Hearth* (2001), and *Why We Fight* (2002). All these works reiterated support for traditional values. Unlike many conservative critics, however, Bennett moved beyond mere jeremiad in his writings to offer constructive societal reforms. To that end, *The Book of Virtues,* which has sold millions of copies, was especially significant. Organized under ten virtues (self-discipline, compassion, responsibility, friendship, work, courage, perseverance, honesty, loyalty, and faith) the collection of 320 moralistic stories for children led to several other books and a PBS cartoon series.

His formidable intellect and strong convictions established Bennett as a doyen of neoconservatism by the turn of the century. On the other hand, his forcefulness and brusque manner also made him a lightning rod for the liberal establishment, which equated his prescriptions with reactionary and nostalgic conservatism. Still, his pronouncements carried sufficient political weight that Bennett was asked to run for national office in 1996 as Bob Dole's vice presidential running mate.

A serious blow to Bennett's reputation came in 2003 when it was revealed that he had lost $8 million through gambling in the 1990s. Although Bennett insisted that no harm was done by his gambling and that he would give it up, the news triggered much consternation among his Protestant evangelical constituency.

Bibliography. Alter, Jonathan, and Joshua Green. "Bennett: Virtue Is as Virtue Does?" *Newsweek,* 12 May 2003, 6. "Bennett, William (John) 1943– ." *Contemporary Authors.* New Revision Series 111. Detroit: Thomson Gale, 2003. Goodgame, Dan. "The Chairman of Virtue Inc." *Time,* 16 September 1996, 46–49. Starr, Alexandra. "Bully Pulpit. Lucrative, Too." *Business Week,* 5 March 2001, 62–66.

Robert H. Krapohl

BERGAMÍN Y GUTIÉRREZ, JOSÉ (1895–1983).

A Spanish poet, essayist, and playwright, Bergamín was born in Madrid and died in San Sebastián. Considered a member of the 1927 Generation, Bergamín was able to unite Republican progressive leftist political militancy with his personal Catholic religious beliefs, which were influenced by the writings of **Jacques Maritain** and Unamuno. In 1933 he founded *Cruz y Raya,* one of the most important Catholic cultural journals of the era, and served as its editor until 1936. He joined the small number of Catholic intellectuals who sided with the republic during the civil war against **Francisco Franco**'s insurrectionary forces. At the end of the war, Bergamín was exiled and went to Mexico, where he founded Seneca publishers, and then to Argentina and Uruguay. Bergamín returned to Spain in 1959 but was once again forced into exile in 1963 because he signed a petition supporting a miners' strike in the Asturias region of Spain. He then lived in Paris until 1970, when he permanently returned to Spain, settling in the Basque Country, where he gradually became a follower of Herri Batasuna's radical nationalism. Besides his numerous collections of poetry, his most important religious works include *Detrás de la cruz: Terrorismo y persecución religiosa en España* (1941), in which he distinguished religion from clericalism, citing Unamuno, Etienne Gilson, Alessandro Manzoni, and the papal condemnation of the traditionalist French organization **Action Française.** He explains the title of this work on page 41, where he remembers a statement from a Catalan priest, "The anarchists in Spain are burning the churches; the Catholics have burned the church." In response to this, Bergamín asks, "Does one die in front of the cross or does one kill from behind it?" Another of Bergamín's major religious works was *El clavo ardendo* (1972), a collection of reflections on Vatican II.

Bibliography. Canamiñana Ruiz, M. *José Bergamín, ensayista.* Madrid: Editorial de la Universidad Complutense, 1999. Memdiboure, J.-M. *José Bergamín: L'Écriture à l'épreuve de Dieu.* Toulouse, France: Presses Universitaires du Mirail, 2001.

Alfonso Botti

BERNADIN, JOSEPH (1928–1996).

Born to Joseph and Maria (Simion) Bernadin, immigrants to the United State from northern Italy, Joseph and his only sibling, Elaine, attended both public and parochial schools. His father, a stonecutter, died in 1934, leaving his wife to raise the two children. After a brief stint at the University of South Carolina, the young Joseph decided to enter the seminary. Upon finishing his theological studies at the Catholic University of America in Washington, D.C., he was ordained a priest for the diocese of Charleston, South Carolina, in 1952.

As a young priest, Bernadin was quickly recognized for his talent and served in several church leadership positions, including chancellor and vicar-general, and attended the fourth session of the Second Vatican Council (1962–1965) in Rome as a *peritus* (theological advisor) for his bishop. In 1966 he was ordained an auxiliary bishop for the Archdiocese of Atlanta and served under Archbishop Paul J. Hallinan, a leading American at the recent council, who also had a profound impact on his new assistant bishop. In 1968, Bernadin was elected general secretary of the National Conference of Catholic Bishops (NCCB), and in 1972 he was named archbishop of Cincinnati. Two years later he was elected president of the NCCB.

As chair of the bishops' committee that authored the pastoral letter "The Challenge of Peace" during the last, tense years of the cold war, Bernadin acted as a much-needed mediator for a committee that contained members with very different views on nuclear arms. When in 1983 a final draft was approved by the entire conference, it occasioned wide debate on war and peace, both inside and outside Catholic circles, and propelled Bernadin onto the national stage.

In July 1982, Bernadin was transferred again to become archbishop of Chicago. With the use of a gentle touch that emphasized listening and collaboration, Bernadin quickly set out to heal deep wounds left by his autocratic predecessor, John Cardinal Cody. However, this is not to say that he eschewed all controversy. When he initiated a badly needed reorganization of diocesan institutions, Bernadin stood firm despite strong protests from Catholics and some of his own priests whose parishes or schools were due to close.

On February, 2, 1983, Pope **John Paul II** elevated Bernadin to the college of cardinals. Also that year, as chair of the NCCB's Pro-Life Activities Committee, Cardinal Bernadin spoke of the need to support a consistent ethic of life, or "seamless garment," a statement that angered conservatives in the church who felt that this watered down the gravity of abortion by placing it in a wider ethical conversation that included capital punishment, euthanasia, poverty, and other social justice issues.

In June 1995, Cardinal Bernadin learned that he had pancreatic cancer. Despite this news, he maintained a full schedule. Even as his prognosis worsened the following year, he helped launch the Catholic Common Ground Project, an effort to support dialogue among increasingly polarized camps in the American Catholic Church. On September 9, 1996, President Bill Clinton awarded Bernadin the Medal of Freedom.

Bibliography. Kennedy, Eugene. *My Brother Joseph: The Spirit of a Cardinal and the Story of a Friendship.* New York: St. Martin's Press, 1997.

Anthony D. Andreassi

BERNANOS, GEORGES (1888–1948). Bernanos was a French novelist and pamphleteer whose devout Catholicism and rightist politics inspired his literary vision during the first half of the twentieth century. He is best known for his novel *Diary of a Country Priest* (*Le journal d'un curé de campagne,* 1936; film version directed by Robert Bresson, 1950). Bernanos maintained in that work as well as in his other writings a moralistic focus less preoccupied with the particulars of right and wrong actions than with a more profound vision of earthly life as a struggle between forces of good and evil. As he saw it, evil found its best opportunities for success within the complacent hearts of modern bourgeois Pharisees, or *bien-pensants,* as characterized in his 1935 pamphlet *La grande peur des bien-pensants.*

Born the son of a prosperous upholsterer in Paris in 1888, Bernanos' ancestral roots lay in the northern soil revisited in his novels. Raised in an antirepublican and anti-Dreyfusard household, he spent much of his youth engaging in street brawls as a member of the Camelots du Roi, the militant wing of the monarchist and anti-Semitic **Action Française.** He also studied rhetoric, law, and letters. He fought in the 1914–1918 war, receiving both wounds and decorations. After the armistice he found employment as a national insurance inspector to support himself and his family as he began work on his first novel. The success of *Sous le soleil de Satan* (1926) gave Bernanos enough financial security to devote himself fully to writing. He also gradually distanced himself from **Charles Maurras,** whose **Action Française** movement suffered papal condemnation at the end of 1926.

Without ever renouncing his monarchist and anti-Semitic sentiments, Bernanos increasingly came into conflict with the rising tide of fascism and the moral paralysis of his middle-class French compatriots. Having witnessed Italian Fascist and Spanish Falangist atrocities on Majorca in 1936, he emerged as one of the few French Catholic critics of **Francisco Franco** during the Spanish civil war, as evidenced in *Les grands cimetières sous la lune* (1938). Bernanos, who had broken irrevocably with Maurras, moved his family to Brazil in 1938, both out of moral disgust and in search of a less expensive home. During World War II he hurled invective at both the "disgusting monstrosity" of Nazi racism and the "curse" of **Philippe Pétain**'s collaborationist Vichy regime, characterizing the bourgeois Catholic supporters of the latter as "the Marshal's pious parishioners."

In 1945, Bernanos returned to France and for the fourth time rejected the Legion of Honor. Quickly becoming disenchanted with **Charles de Gaulle**'s postwar leadership, he departed for Tunisia. He later succumbed to cancer in a hospital outside Paris. His last major novel, *Monsieur Ouine* (1946; originally published in Brazil, 1943), continued to probe his main concerns: the dying parish, a faithless bourgeoisie, and evil's terrifying yet doomed offensive against the power of God's grace.

Bibliography. Gaucher, Guy. *Georges Bernanos et l'invincible espérance.* Paris: Cerf, 1994. Speaight, Robert. *Georges Bernanos: A Study of the Man and the Writer.* New York: Liveright, 1974.

Richard Francis Crane

BERRIGAN, DANIEL (b. 1921) AND PHILIP (1923–2002). The Berrigan brothers were the most prominent radical American priests of the Vietnam War era and beyond. The brothers Berrigan adapted the traditions of nonviolent civil disobedience to modes of direct action so prevalent in the 1960s and 1970s. They forced Catholics and others to confront the radical implications of Gospel-based personal witness in the era of atomic weaponry and racial inequality.

Daniel and Philip Berrigan were born in Minnesota and grew up in Liverpool, New York (near Syracuse) the fifth and sixth of six sons born to Freda Fromhart, a German American, and Thomas Berrigan, a mercurial Irish American steam-boiler operator and farmer. He was a subscriber to the radical *Catholic Worker* newspaper and founded the Catholic Interracial Council's Syracuse chapter, movements that prefigured his sons' dominant concerns. Thomas Berrigan's occasionally violent outbursts later prompted Dan Berrigan to remark, "It's enough to make you nonviolent, or very violent I guess" (Polner and O'Grady, 57). Dan Berrigan entered the Society of Jesus in 1939, while Philip Berrigan entered the Josephite Order in 1950 after service in the U.S. Army during World War II and graduation from the College of the Holy Cross. Both brothers underwent the conventional priestly training of the period, but Philip Berrigan's experience with segregation in New Orleans in the 1950s helped transform his worldview, along with that of his brother. Dan Berrigan was a poet and an intensely intellectual admirer of the Trappist monk Thomas Merton and **Dorothy Day** of the Catholic Worker movement, who in very different ways called Christians to apply their spiritual convictions to social injustices.

By 1965 the Berrigans were central figures in the burgeoning "Catholic Left." At the end of that year Daniel Berrigan was exiled by the Jesuits—under pressure from New York's **Francis Cardinal Spellman**—after he seemed to condone the self-immolation of a young protestor against the Vietnam War, a former student of his. Philip Berrigan decided to express his revulsion for the Vietnam War with a gesture unprecedented for an American priest: he participated with three other antiwar activists in a raid on the U.S. Customs House in Baltimore, where they poured a concoction of blood from ducks and humans on draft records of the Selective Service. Daniel Berrigan returned from exile to become a charismatic antiwar leader as chaplain at Cornell University. On May 18, 1968, the Berrigan brothers and seven others (including Elizabeth McAlister, a nun who married Philip Berrigan the following year in an unofficial ceremony) invaded the Selective Service office in Catonsville, Maryland, where they poured homemade napalm on draft records. In October of that year they each received prison sentences of three years (concurrent in Philip's case with a six-year sentence for his part in the 1967 raid). Rather than surrender to authorities and begin his sentence in April 1970, Daniel Berrigan went underground and confounded his pursuers for four months before being apprehended by FBI agents posing as bird watchers on Block Island, where he had found refuge.

The Berrigans spent time in and out of prisons in the 1970s and 1980s (especially Philip, who spent nearly a decade incarcerated); there were more actions, trials, and sentences. They were parodied, lionized, and condemned, both inside and outside the Catholic Church. The central theme in the life of both brothers was *witness*. As Daniel liked to say, "Don't just do something, stand there." They stood squarely against the tools of violence and war, with Philip as the rugged organizer and Daniel as existential poet. They produced no formal treatises on Christian pacifism, though Daniel was a prolific writer of poems and memoirs. Through the power of their personal witness they reduced the scale of global issues to a human size. Few agreed with all their actions, but even their critics had to acknowledge the constancy of their witness.

Bibliography. Polner, Murray, and Jim O'Grady. *Disarmed and Dangerous: The Radical Lives and Times of Daniel and Philip Berrigan.* New York: Basic Books, 1997.

James T. Fisher

BETHUNE, MARY JANE MCLEOD (1875–1955).

Imbued with the missionary spirit at an early age, Bethune spent her life trying to better the condition of African Americans. She founded the historically black Bethune-Cookman College, served in the administration of President Franklin D. Roosevelt, and headed the two largest African American women's organizations of her era. Throughout her life, Bethune emphasized self-help, racial pride, and religious faith.

Born near Maysville, South Carolina, as the fifteenth of seventeen children of former slaves, Bethune overcame the handicaps of poverty and a dark, heavily African appearance. She received a scholarship to attend the Scotia Seminary for Negro Girls in Concord, North Carolina. Bethune later adopted the highly regimented Christian-centered learning style of Scotia for her educational philosophy. Following graduation in 1894 from Scotia, Bethune attended evangelist Dwight Moody's Institute for Home and Foreign Missions with the aim of becoming a missionary in Africa. After being rejected for a posting because no black missionaries were needed in Africa, Bethune decided to become an educator.

Educated black women of the late nineteenth century believed strongly in racial uplift, an ideology that offered an opportunity to prove that blacks deserved to take a respected position within American society. Racial uplift emphasized self-help, racial solidarity, temperance, thrift, chastity, and social purity. Bethune worked for racial uplift.

Recruited by a Presbyterian minister to open a school in Palatka, Florida, Bethune left her teaching job at a mission school in Georgia. At Palatka, she started a community school that took her to teach in the jails and in the sawmills. She stayed in Palatka for five years, until another minister persuaded her to move to Daytona. Bethune became the first black woman to found an institute of higher learning when she opened her college in 1904.

Bethune believed that racial uplift would lead to integration and rights of citizenship for African Americans. The argest organization of

Mary McLeod Bethune with a line of girls from the school, 1905. © Florida State Library and Archives

black women at this time, the National Association of Colored Women (NACW), promoted intensive social service at the local level to boost the quality of African American home life and educate the mothers of the race. Bethune served as its head from 1924 to 1928. Deciding that the NACW did not focus enough on political activities, she founded the National Association of Negro Women (NCNW) in 1935 to lobby the government. The NCNW encouraged blacks to participate in civic, political, and educational activities; served as a clearinghouse for information concerning women; and developed projects to promote integration.

A close friend of Eleanor Roosevelt and a convener of the Black Cabinet in the Roosevelt administration, Bethune headed the Division of Negro Affairs of the National Youth Administration from 1935 to 1943. This position enabled her to channel funds to black education. In her last years, Bethune joined the conservative evangelical Protestant group Moral Re-Armament.

Possibly the most influential black woman of the twentieth century, Bethune publicly pronounced her faith throughout her life and dedicated herself to bettering the lives of others.

Bibliography. King, John T., and Marcet H. King. *Mary McLeod Bethune: A Woman of Vision and Determination.* Lake Junaluska, NC: Commission on Archives and History, United Methodist Church, 1977. McCluskey, Audrey Thomas, and Elaine M. Smith, eds. *Mary McLeod Bethune: Building a Better World.* Bloomington: Indiana University Press, 2001.

Caryn E. Neumann

BETTO, FREI (b. 1944). Carlos Alberto "Betto" Libânio Christo was born in Belo Horizonte, Brazil. After his first activist experiences in the Catholic Youth Movement, he joined the Dominican order in 1965. Known as Frei Betto, he became a prolific theologian of liberation, a journalist, philosopher, writer, and the mentor of Luiz Inácio Lula da Silva, who won Brazil's

2002 presidential election. Frei Betto has continued his struggle for social justice in Brazil and Latin America. He is known internationally for his campaigns that link Christianity to projects for political change, and for his journalistic and scholarly writing, especially his book of interviews with Fidel Castro, *Fidel and Religion* (1987).

As a young man, Betto took a more outspoken revolutionary turn when Brazil succumbed to military rule in 1964. He enrolled in the School of Journalism at the University of Rio de Janeiro and gained increasing popularity through media exposure with articles on Catholic Church renewal. In 1965, he joined the Dominican order, where he picked up the study of philosophy while still a novitiate. By 1968 he pursued his studies in theology in Rio Grande do Sul.

A Dominican friar concerned about human rights, Frei Betto was imprisoned by the military dictatorship at twenty-five, accused of helping dissidents escape the country. In 1971, after twenty-two months in prison awaiting trial, he was charged and sentenced to four additional years.

Betto has spread liberation theology for over forty years, actively publishing and organizing advocacy for a specifically Latin American brand of social justice informed by Christian principles. He remains an outspoken theologian who defends Brazil's street children, assists popular movements of the poor and landless, and advocates grassroots education. In 1997, he was chosen Intellectual of the Year by the Brazilian Writers Union and won the national literary Jabuti Award.

Bibliography. Betto, Frei. *Fidel and Religion.* New York: Simon & Schuster, 1987.

Jadwiga E. Pieper Mooney

BIDAULT, GEORGES (1899–1983). A leading Catholic politician of the third and fourth French republics as well as the head of the homeland Resistance during World War II, Bidault was born into a middle-class family at Moulins. He did army service briefly at the end of World War I, took a degree in history from the Sorbonne, and then taught, first at a secondary school and later at a university.

With **Francisque Gay** he founded the leftist Catholic daily, *L'Aube* (The Dawn) in 1932 and was its foreign editor until 1939. Taken prisoner when the Germans invaded France in 1940, he escaped and joined the Gaullist resistance in 1941. Following the execution of Jean Moulin in 1943, he became head of the National Council of Resistance. **Charles de Gaulle** indicates in his war memoirs that Bidault would not have been his first choice but nonetheless terms him "an eminent resistance leader having in the highest degree the taste and the gift for political life, well known before the war for his talent as a journalist and his influence among the Christian Democrats, and ambitious to see this little group become a great party with himself as its head."

Indeed, in 1944 Bidault founded the **Popular Republican Movement** (*Mouvement Républicain Populaire,* MRP) with the blessing of the general. Later that year, he became foreign minister in de Gaulle's provisional government and, in 1945 in San Francisco, signed the United Nations Charter on behalf of France, miraculously winning for his nation one of the five permanent seats on the Security Council and the veto power that went with it. He later served as premier in both the provisional government following de Gaulle's retirement and then during the Fourth Republic (1949–1950), when the MRP was one of the three dominant parties in France, along with the Socialists and Communists. He was foreign minister (1947–1948) and defense minister (1951–1952) and appeared frequently in the various cabinets that sprung up every six months during this era. His hardline policy on Vietnam was greatly responsible for the French debacle there in 1954.

In 1949, Bidault was elected chairman of the MRP. Despite the fact that both he and de Gaulle had attended Jesuit schools at a time when the Jesuits had been banished from France (de Gaulle in Belgium and Bidault in Italy), the two prominent Catholics parted ways over the Algerian revolution (1954–1962), a contentious issue that doomed the Fourth Republic and brought the return of the general from Colombey as its last premier (1958) and as founder and first president (1959–1969) of the Fifth Republic.

The more pragmatic de Gaulle eventually recognized that the Algerians must be given their independence, while Bidault actively supported the colons and French army elements that refused to cede Algeria to the insurgents. Doubtless, Bidault's concern was for the one million Europeans in Algeria as well as for the native Algerians who had become Christians and collaborators with France, the result of 125 years of colonial rule. As events were to prove, Bidault's concerns were well founded.

In 1956 Bidault joined the Union for the Safety and Resurrection of French Algeria. He and Jacques Soustelle later created the Conseil national de le Résistance. Eventually Bidault allied himself with the Organisation Armée Secrète (OAS) and, much like **Philippe Pétain,** pronounced de Gaulle a traitor and was implicated with OAS efforts to assassinate him. Thus, Bidault was forced into exile in 1962. The general's presidential memoir was less complimentary of Bidault than were his war memoirs, referring to "Bidault and his henchmen" as some of "the usual agitators of the so-called 'extreme Right.'" Nonetheless, he granted Bidault amnesty in 1968, and Bidault died in 1983 on French soil.

Bibliography. Bidault, Georges. *Resistance: The Political Autobiography of Georges Bidault.* Trans. Marianne Sinclaire. New York: F. A. Praeger, 1967. Demory, Jean-Claude. *Georges Bidault: 1899–1983, biographie.* Paris: Julliard,

1995. Irving, R.E.M. *Christian Democracy in France.* London: Allen & Unwin, 1973.

William J. Parente

BIDAWID, MAR ROUPHAEL (1922–2003). For twenty-three years, Bidawid headed as patriarch the Chaldean Catholic Church, which constitutes roughly 75 percent (250,000) of the Christian population in Iraq. The Chaldean Catholics are descended from the fifth-century heretical group the Nestorians.

Bidawid was born in 1922 in Mosul (Iraq), where he completed his primary and secondary studies. After he completed a doctorate in theology in Rome, where he lived and studied for ten years, he was ordained priest in 1944. Between 1950 and 1956, Bidawid was priest chaplain for the Christians working for the Iraq Petroleum Company (IPC). In 1957, Bidawid was elected bishop and, in 1962, was transferred to the Chaldean diocese of Beirut, where he served as his community's patriarch for twenty-three years. Bidawid was very involved in fostering ecumenical relations with other Iraqi Christian churches, such as the Assyrian Church of the East. He was one of the founders of the Council of Catholic Patriarchs and Bishops in Lebanon. During the regime of Saddam Hussein, given his personal concern for the Christian community in Iraq, Bidawid was a strong opponent of Western (mostly U.S.) policy toward his country. Following Saddam Hussein's invasion of Kuwait (1991), he openly criticized the UN-imposed sanctions against his country. Like other Christian religious leaders in the Middle East, Bidawid's paramount concern was the survival of his community and its role as a major player in Iraqi society. During his patriarchate, Bidawid established Babylon College, which became an instrumental educational institution for the Chaldean Church.

Bibliography. Cragg, Kenneth. *The Arab Christian: A History in the Middle East.* Louisville, KY: Westminster/John Knox Press,

1991. Sennott, Charles. *The Body and the Blood: The Middle East's Vanishing Christians and the Possibility for Peace.* New York: Public Affairs, 2001.

George Emile Irani

BIGELOW, HERBERT SEELY (1870–1951). Minister and reformer, Bigelow served on Ohio's Fourth Constitutional Convention (1912), in the Ohio state legislature (1913–1914), on the Cincinnati City Council (1936, 1940–1941), and in the U.S. Congress (1937–1939).

He was born in Elkhart, Indiana, to Edwin and Anne Pratt Seely. After an unhappy childhood on his father's farm, he was adopted at the age of fifteen by Alpheus and Emma Bigelow, devout Presbyterians from Cleveland, Ohio, who were impressed by the boy's interest in religion. He attended Oberlin College's preparatory school, followed by Western Reserve College (Cleveland) and Lane Theological Seminary (Cincinnati). Called to minister to the Vine Street Congregational Church in 1895, he spent the rest of his life in Cincinnati crusading for social justice through his preaching and political involvement.

Bigelow embraced the **Social Gospel** during his seminary training, when his work at a settlement house convinced him that it was a clergyman's duty to fight poverty and inequity. A fervent admirer of **William Jennings Bryan,** Bigelow was anti-imperialist and antiwar. He constantly fought against corrupt city and state politics and championed measures that ensured the people's control over their own government, such as municipal ownership of utilities, voters' use of the initiative and referendum, workman's compensation, pensions, and woman suffrage. He was also a lifelong advocate of Henry George's single-tax theory. Bigelow soon earned a reputation as a radical reformer. Despite Vine Street Church's proud abolitionist history, the elders found him too liberal and too political. After many disagreements, Bigelow severed his connection with the Congregational Church and moved his flock, renamed the Peoples' Church, to a new location that could accommodate political discussions as well as church services.

Bigelow's first important political role came when Cleveland mayor Tom Johnson recruited him to campaign for Bryan in 1900. In 1906, as secretary of the Ohio Direct Legislation League, Bigelow helped bring about a constitutional convention in Ohio. Elected president of the convention, he mediated effectively among the delegates' disparate views, and the new constitution passed in 1912, incorporating many of the reforms Bigelow endorsed—but without his favorite plank, the single tax. His success with the convention resulted in his election to the Ohio House of Representatives in 1913.

His outspoken opposition to the United States' entry into World War I enforced Bigelow's radical reputation and probably provoked a notorious 1917 incident in which he was beaten by unidentified thugs. It took many years for Bigelow to overcome the antiwar stigma and regain a political position, although he never stopped preaching municipal reform and the single tax. In 1933 he successfully lobbied for an old-age pension law in Ohio. In the mid-1930s, with the support of Father **Charles Coughlin,** Bigelow was elected first to the Cincinnati City Council and then, for one term, to the U.S. Congress. Bigelow broke off his association with Coughlin in 1937 and was not reelected. Although his official political career effectively ended in 1941, after a second term on the city council, he continued to speak and preach until his death.

Like his hero, Bryan, Bigelow was a masterful orator. This skill served him as minister and politician, although he did not mark a distinction between his pastoral and political duties, believing as he did that

"citizenship, too, is a religion. . . . For by the votes of a free state God answers the prayers of His people" (Bigelow, 93–94).
Bibliography. Beaver, Daniel R. *A Buckyeye Crusader.* Cincinnati, OH: Author, 1957. Bigelow, Herbert S. *The Religion of Revolution.* Cincinnati, OH: Daniel Kiefer, 1916. Herbert S. Bigelow Papers. Historical Society Library, Cincinnati, Ohio.

Janet C. Olson

BLACK HUNDREDS (RUSSIA). The Black Hundreds was a loosely affiliated body of monarchist political activists that came into existence during the final years of the Russian Empire. Reacting against a growing revolutionary movement, they upheld loyalty to the monarch and devotion to Orthodox Christianity as the hope for Russia. Because of their occasionally violent activities, however, they failed to win the complete support of either czar or church.

The term "Black Hundreds" originally applied to Russian townspeople in ancient times who demonstrated loyalty to the ruler and to the Orthodox Church at moments of political disorder. At the beginning of the twentieth century, new social tensions related to peasant land-hunger, worker impoverishment, and reverses in the Russo-Japanese War (1904–1905) exploded in the revolution of 1905. Though unsuccessful in overthrowing Czar Nicholas II (r.1894–1917), this event was accompanied by enormous popular violence and resulted in the creation of a representative assembly called the State Duma. This new body placed restrictions on the customary autocratic authority of the monarch and introduced Russia's first political parties. It also sought to reduce the influence of the Orthodox Church, to which the majority of Russians belonged.

Within the troubled order that arose after the revolution of 1905, a variety of political groups that sought to preserve autocracy and the influence of the Orthodox Church emerged. Officially calling themselves "patriotic unions" (in an effort to minimize their partisan character), they were soon likened to the ancient Black Hundreds, a name they accepted. They included the Union of Russian Men, the Union of the Archangel Michael, and, most influentially, the Union of the Russian People.

The latter group was established in 1905 by a physician named Alexander Dubrovin. His hope was to appeal both to the loyal nobility and the common peasantry to protect Russia from the challenges posed by the Duma. Though he initially managed to win the approval of the czar and some members of the clergy, his movement soon tested their support. In fact, though highly conservative in his political ideology, Dubrovin used the broad membership of the Union of the Russian People to organize public demonstrations that occasionally degenerated into mob violence. The most common targets of these outbursts were university students, Socialists, and Jews. Due to this, Nicholas II never officially endorsed the Black Hundreds, and many of the clergy, such as Metropolitan Antony of Saint Petersburg (d.1912), publicly denounced them. Other hierarchs, such as Metropolitan Antony of Kiev (d.1936), sought to persuade them to abandon their anti-Semitism.

In the end, the Russian Revolution of 1917 swept both Nicholas and the Orthodox clergy from Russia's political order, and along with them the Black Hundreds was destroyed.
Bibliography. Geifman, Anna, ed. *Russia under the Last Tsar: Opposition and Subversion, 1894–1917.* Oxford: Blackwell, 1999.

John Strickland

BLISS, WILLIAM DWIGHT PORTER (1856–1926). Episcopal priest, Christian socialist, and social reformer, Bliss was born in Constantinople into a Congregationalist missionary family. After studying at Robert College (Constantinople), he came to the United States to attend Amherst College

(BA, 1878) and Hartford Theological Seminary (DD, 1882). He served as a minister in Denver and then in South Natick, Massachusetts, where his exposure to the condition of workingmen, as well as his reading of Henry George's *Progress and Poverty,* aroused his interest in socialism. At the same time, he was inspired by the Anglican Christian Socialist thought of the 1840s and by the activism of contemporary Anglicans such as Stewart Headlam.

Bliss came to believe that socialism, combined with spiritual force, could bring about the kingdom of heaven on earth; for the rest of his life, he considered himself a Christian socialist. He left the Congregational Church and in 1886 was ordained an Episcopal priest. To him, the Protestant Episcopal Church was the church of social Christianity: less individualistic and more worldly than other Protestant denominations, it was better able to take responsibility for healing society's ills and advocating social justice in the material world.

Over the next forty years, Bliss held pastorates in Massachusetts, California, New York, and New Jersey but spent most of his time and effort working to educate people about social injustice and to enlist them into one or more of the nearly twenty organizations he participated in or founded. He helped establish the Church Association for the Advancement of Industry and Labor (CAIL) in 1887 and then went on to join Edward Bellamy's Nationalist Club. He started the Society of Christian Socialists and the Church of the Carpenter, organized for Richard T. Ely's Christian Social Union, and formed the American Fabian Society, the Union Reform League, and the Social Reform Union. He also wrote for **Josiah Strong**'s American Institute for Social Science and the magazine *Gospel of the Kingdom* and participated in the Christian Socialist Fellowship. Bliss also started a settlement house; wrote lectures, articles, pamphlets, and Sunday School lessons; edited a series of classic socialist works; conducted surveys for the Federal Labor Bureau; and, during World War I, worked with the YMCA in Europe.

Each organization Bliss formed had an executive board filled with well-known political and social reform names, a publication (usually edited by Bliss), an educational program, and a political agenda. Many welcomed secular and non-Christian members. With remarkable energy, Bliss traversed the country promoting his organizations, which were unvaryingly ephemeral. Still, his comprehensive *Encyclopedia of Social Reform* (1897, revised 1908) remains an invaluable resource, as well as a reflection of his personality and method. While experts from **Jane Addams** to Victor Yarros contributed discussions of organizations, individuals, and theories to the encyclopedia, Bliss wrote many of the entries himself.

Bliss never ran for political office. He saw himself as an educator and organizer, not a politician, but his objectives were ultimately political. Despite his support of the Populist Party in 1892 and the Socialist Party in 1912, he had no confidence in the potential of a third party. His goal was the establishment of a national reform coalition that would consolidate the power of the era's innumerable individual reform groups, generating the force of a political party without the politics. As an evolutionary socialist, Bliss hoped that an enlightened citizenry would vote to revolutionize American society. To him, socialism meant a government run not by political machines or for the benefit of the wealthy, but by and for the people. Christian socialists were citizens who saw it as their Christian duty to enact such equitable policies as fair labor laws, national ownership of industry, and woman suffrage.

Late in his life, Bliss lamented that the Christian social action of the day was still limited to charity in an unjust environment; the kingdom of heaven on earth that he had worked so hard to inspire was still far distant. With his agendas and platforms inclusive to the point of ineffectuality, Bliss has been dismissed by contemporaries and historians alike as a promoter of idealistic schemes that were bound to fail. Bliss's sincerity, faith, and energy, however, are uncontested. The motto on the masthead of his Christian socialist newspaper, the *Dawn* (1889–1896), expressed the principle that Bliss lived by: "He works for God who works for Man."

Bibliography. Frederick, Peter J. *Knights of the Golden Rule: The Intellectual as Social Reformer in the 1890s.* Lexington: University of Kentucky Press, 1976. Markwell, Bernard K. *The Anglican Left: Radical Social Reformers in the Church of England and the Protestant Episcopal Church, 1846–1954.* Brooklyn, NY: Carlson, 1991. Webber, Christopher. "William Dwight Porter Bliss: Priest and Socialist." *Historical Magazine of the Protestant Episcopal Church* 28 (1959): 9–39.

Janet C. Olson

BLUMHARDT, CHRISTOPH FRIEDRICH (1842–1919). A shining example of the possibility of linking a deep spirituality with radical social involvement, Blumhardt was the spiritual forefather of Religious Socialism in Germany and Switzerland. Unlike J. H. Wichern (1808–1881) and the Inner Mission Movement, or the Evangelical Social Congress of Adolf Stöcker (1835–1909), Blumhardt's thought and engagement were far more radical and centered on the conviction that the kingdom of God was breaking into history in the form of Socialism.

Born into the eschatologically oriented Pietism of Württemberg, Christoph was deeply influenced by the ministry and theology of his famous father, Johann Christoph Blumhardt (1805–1880). Christoph studied theology at the University of Tübingen (1862–1866) and was ordained in 1866. By the late 1880s he had begun to undergo a profound change as he reconsidered the more conservative eschatological expectations of his father. This reconsideration led him to the conclusion that the kingdom of God was breaking into the world, though not in ways his father would have recognized. He came to the conviction that the struggle for the kingdom of God was to be found in the struggle over the "Social Question" that was taking place throughout Europe in the latter half of the nineteenth and first part of the twentieth centuries.

Seeking to be faithful to this new theological paradigm, Christoph would create enormous controversy by publicly identifying himself with the Social Democrats (SPD) in 1899. He would eventually run for office in the district of Göppingen for a seat on the Württemberg Landtag, which he held from 1900 to 1906. As a representative of the SPD, Blumhardt engaged in debate over wage increases, trade tariffs, and education. He also gave public lectures to Christian groups in which he explained his understanding of the relationship between Christianity and Socialism. In these presentations, Blumhardt often argued that Socialism was both God's judgment on a culture and economy predicated on the worship of money and at the same time a true though provisional form of the coming kingdom of God, in which all people, especially the poor, would share in the blessings of the earth.

At the same time, Blumhardt began to receive pressure from within the SPD to take sides over the growing debate surrounding the revisionism of Eduard Bernstein (1850–1932). Though Blumhardt initially rejected Bernstein, his theological framework and abhorrence of violence naturally led him in that direction. A definite turn away from politics began to occur in 1903 after the Dresden Party Day conference at which August Bebel (1840–1913) and the revolutionaries argued violently against the revisionists. This event, coupled with a growing conviction that political activity was not the way to usher in the kingdom of heaven, led Blumhardt to withdraw from politics.

Even out of the public eye, Blumhardt continued to exert influence through his publications and ministry at Bad Boll. He interpreted the outbreak of the First World War as God's judgment on Europe, though he was hopeful that God might somehow work through it to bring the kingdom.

Though the latter half of his life was marked more by quiet reflection, he influenced a number of prominent Swiss individuals who sought to bring together a theological vision of the kingdom of God with the political reality of Social Democracy. Among his successors were Hermann Kutter (1863–1931), **Leonhard Ragaz** (1868–1945), Howard Eugster-Zeust (1861–1932), and **Karl Barth** (1886–1968).

Bibliography. Lejune, Robert, ed. *Christoph Blumhardt and His Message.* Rifton, NY: Plough, 1963. Meier, Klaus-Jürgen. *Christoph Blumhardt: Christ, Sozialist, Theologe.* Bern, Germany: Peter Lang, 1979.

Christian T. Collins Winn

BOEGNER, MARC (1881–1970). Boegner was a leader of French Protestantism who worked for ecumenism and the application of Christian principles to public life. He grew up in the house of the prefect of Orleans and planned to become a naval officer but had to give up this intention due to a sight defect. He studied jurisprudence for a year, but a conversion experience in 1899 convinced him to dedicate his life to Christ.

Boegner redirected his studies to theology and took over a parish in the little community of Aouste in the Alps. In 1906, he was forced to look after himself for a while because of a heart disease and used this illness to prepare a dissertation. In 1911 the Missionary Society of Paris called him to work as a teacher and head of the home of missionary students. He published his dissertation, *The Unity of the Church* (1914), in English. The title summarized his lifelong concern.

During the First World War he served wounded soldiers as a paramedic. After the armistice, he took over the parish of Passy in west-end Paris and kept it for thirty-five years. Also, after 1948 he served as president of the Fédération Protestante de France, of the Reformed Church of France, and of the Mission of Paris. Furthermore, he became one of six presidents of the **World Council of Churches** (WCC). Up to his old age he remained chairman of the Missionary Society of Paris as well as head of the Relief Committee of the French Protestant youth organizations (Comité inter-Mouvements auprès des Evacués).

Boegner's dissertation claim that "Christian truth" was "represented in its entirety only by a universal Church" pushed him to strive for Christian unity. Believers should become aware of their union in Christ and tolerate certain dogmatic differences for the benefit of the harmony of the church. Boegner started with his own splintered Reformed Church and the Methodists. In 1938, after five years of troublesome negotiations, he called for a synod in Lyon, which moved to reunite the divided sections and to constitute the Reformed Church of France. As a tribute to his merits, Boegner was elected president of this church, an office he kept until 1950. Until 1960, he also remained head of the Fédération Protestante de France, since it was his intention to bring together Reformed and Lutheran Protestants to form a United Church. He welcomed with great joy the cause of ecumenism adopted by the Roman Catholic Church in its Second Vatican Council in 1965 and took part as an observer in the third session of the Council.

By that point, Boegner had become well known as a leading figure of the ecumenical movement based in Geneva. He had assumed significant roles in the 1937 World

Conferences on Life and Work as well as that on faith and order in Oxford and Edinburgh, and in 1939 he was nominated vice president of the then-forming World Council of Churches and charged with the supervision of the general secretariat. World War II, a time of persecution under the German occupying power and the Vichy regime, delayed the process. Boegner put it back on track, however, when he proposed to the assembly in Amsterdam in 1948 that the founding of the WCC should be announced. Representatives of Protestant, Anglican, and Orthodox churches unanimously accepted this resolution and elected Boegner one of six presidents of the organization. Until his death he strove relentlessly to bring the WCC to life.

As a minister of a middle-class parish in Paris, Boegner struggled also to realize the **Social Gospel.** "The Church's task is getting to the sources of all misery and to remind its believers of their duty to raise their forces to counter—if in any way possible—the destructive effects of certain 'structures' of the modern world," he wrote in 1932. During the Algerian War of Independence he frequently visited the French president and the minister of justice to protest against torture and to request better treatment for Muslim prisoners. Furthermore, he offered to mediate an end to the hostilities.

Bibliography. Boegner, Marc. *L'Église et les questions du temps présent.* Paris: Éditions Je Sers, 1932. Boegner, Marc. *L'Exigence œcuménique.* Paris: A. Michel, 1968. Boegner, Marc. *The Unity of the Church.* Paris: Free Faculty of Protestant Theology, 1914.

Gerhard Besier

BOFF, LEONARDO (b. 1938). The Brazilian Boff is, together the Peruvian **Gustavo Gutierrez**, probably the best-known Latin American liberation theologian, and the first to situate liberation theology within a broader social, political, ecological, indeed holistic context. He was born in Concórdia,

Santa Catarina, Brazil to second-generation Italian immigrant parents. After theological training in Rio de Janeiro, he entered the Order of the Friars Minor (Franciscans) in 1959 and was ordained in 1964 to the priesthood.

After finishing a doctoral degree in Germany in 1971, he returned to Brazil and served for twenty-two years as professor of theology and ecumenics at the Franciscan institute at Petrópolis. During this period he pioneered the development of Brazilian liberation theology and was active in the formation of ecclesial base communities (CEBs). These lay-led groups became a means of organizing the urbanizing poor on the peripheries of Brazil's cities, both in terms of church affiliation and political organization. This remarkable phenomenon generated much sociological and political scientific interest as observers speculated whether liberation theologies would support the leftist Workers Party in free elections in 1991.

Boff's remarkable publishing activity includes serving from 1970 to 1985 as senior editor of the publisher Editora Vozes, and coordinating the publication of the sixty-volume collection *Theologia e Libertação* and the Portuguese edition of the collected works of Carl G. Jung. He also served as editor of the *Revista Eclesiástica Brasileira* (1970–1984), the *Revista de Cultura Vozes* (1984–1992), and of the international journal *Concilium* (1970–1995), and in addition is the author of over sixty-five books. He served as professor of ethics, philosophy of religion, and ecology at the State University of Rio de Janeiro (UERJ) from 1993 until his recent retirement. He has also been a visiting professor at numerous universities including Lisbon, Basel, Salamanca, Heidelberg, and Harvard and holds honorary doctorates from Turin and Lund.

Boff's first work, *Jesus Christ Liberator: A Critical Christology for Our Time* set out his basic understandings of history, the recognition of the value of the spiritual and material dimensions of life, and the value of persons and thus of human rights. Deeply influenced by the example of his order's founder, St. Francis, Boff's theology has offered an alternative to the individualism, materialism, and social and political oppression characteristic of much of the modern world. Thus his focus is on "the underside" of modernity, the poor and oppressed, rather than on the first-world problem of atheism. Boff was most concerned about the "non-personhood" of the vast majority of Latin Americans. Such a focus is not impartial. It represents a commitment expressed in the methodological step of the "option for the poor," whereby their oppression is exposed through social scientific (Marxist class) analysis, evaluated in the light of faith, and then opposed through available political means. Boff's involvement with the CEBs resulted in two controversial works, *Church: Charism and Power* (1981) and *Ecclesiogenesis: The Base Communities Reinvent the Church* (1976). In these works, the emphasis on the role of the laity led him to question church teachings and, by the late 1980s, to accept a participatory form of democracy in place of a state socialism. These positions led to his summoning to Rome by the prefect of the Sacred Congregation for the Doctrine of the Faith, Cardinal Ratzinger, in order to explain sections of his book, *The Church: Charism and Power.* His subsequent disciplining and silencing focused worldwide attention on the political implications of liberation theologies.

In the early 1990s, after his resignation from the active priesthood, he reconceptualized liberation theology by developing a more inclusive ecological liberation paradigm, one that includes as the poor all beings whose relationality is denied. Drawing on the holism philosophy articulated by the South African leader Jan Christian Smuts, Boff argues in *Ecology and Liberation: A New Paradigm* for this new paradigm of relatedness. By situating the poor within this wider ecological paradigm, he reveals the interactions between the ecological, social, political, and spiritual aspects of life.

Bibliography. Boff, Leonardo. *Ecology and Liberation: A New Paradigm.* Maryknoll, NY: Orbis Books, 1995. Boff, Leonardo. *St. Francis. A Model for Human Liberation.* New York: Crossroads, 1982. Cox, Harvey. *The Silencing of Leonardo Boff. The Vatican and the Future of World Christianity.* Oak Park, IL: Meyer-Stone Books, 1988. Maclean, Iain S. *Opting for Democracy? Liberation Theology and the Struggle for Democracy in Brazil.* New York: Peter Lang, 1999.

Iain S. Maclean

BONALD, LOUIS DE (1754–1840). Viscount Bonald's career as publicist and politician gives him dual significance for modern Christian politics. He was both a major theorist of the counterrevolution and an influential player in French Restoration politics in the period from 1814 to 1830.

Born into an old noble family in southern France, Bonald received an excellent education from the Oratorian Fathers at Juilly, served a short period of military service, and by the eve of the Revolution was a respected estate owner and the mayor of Millau. In the early years of the Revolution it appeared that he might retain a position of leadership in local politics. With the collapse of the old royal administration in the summer of 1789, he took a leading role in the organization of a special commission and a militia to maintain law and order locally and proposed "federation" with other municipalities in the region for the same purpose. He was elected mayor of Millau in February 1790 but resigned in July following his election to the new departmental Council of Aveyron. He was then elected president of that council. The

National Assembly's decision to enforce its new Civil Constitution of the Clergy by requiring the clergy to take an oath of loyalty proved to be the turning point in Bonald's relation to the Revolution. He announced he could not enforce the oath and resigned his position. In October 1791 Bonald and two of his sons emigrated, and he joined the counterrevolution at Colbenz.

Following the failure of the counterrevolutionary royalist army in 1792, Bonald settled in Heidelburg, where he devoted himself to the education of his sons and to the composition of his first major work, *Théorie du pouvoir politique et religieux,* which was published in Constance in 1797. Despite the fact that the work was suppressed in France, Bonald returned to Paris, where in 1801 he published *Du divorce,* designed to influence the drafting of the Civil Code under Napoleon, and probably the most accessible of his theoretical works. In 1802 he published *La législation primitive,* a reworking of his *Théorie du pouvoir.* Although he collaborated with **François-René de Chateaubriand** in political journalism and finally accepted a position from Napoleon on the Council of the University, Bonald's most active period as a journalist and politician came during the Restoration period.

Bonald welcomed the Bourbon Restoration, served as a deputy from Aveyron from 1815 to 1822, and was made a peer in 1823. A spokesman and leader of the ultraroyalists, he successfully proposed a law against divorce (1816) as well as legislation severely restricting liberty of the press (1822), and served for a time as president of a censorship committee. He was also active as a journalist, writing for the *Conservateur* and the *Défenseur.* Following the Revolution of 1830, Bonald refused the oath to King Louis-Philippe, gave up his peerage, and retired to his native province.

Like other conservatives, such as **Joseph de Maistre** and Chateaubriand, Bonald wrote in support of monarchical government and Catholicism. He was distinctive, however, in his response to the challenge of Enlightenment rationalism, which he sought to co-opt rather than reject. Building on certain fundamental assumptions about the nature of language (which he believed man received as a gift from God, along with his being) and the temporal and logical priority of society to the individual, Bonald self-consciously developed a "science of society" that depicted all social and political relationships as a series of triads reflecting what he saw as the natural order of the universe. In the political order, for example, the triad always consists of a power, the minister of that power, and the subject. These fundamental ideas were developed in great detail in his lengthy and dryly scholastic writings. In contrast to the ultramontane Maistre, Bonald was a Gallican who was quite ready to subordinate the church to the authority of the state. He was also ready, for the sake of creating obedient and loyal subjects, to put all education under strict state supervision.

Though no longer much read today (as evidenced by the lack of new editions of his works, only one of which has appeared in English), his significance has been generally recognized. His "structuralist" approach to social and political issues clearly influenced the functionalist sociology of Auguste Comte, **Frédéric Le Play,** and Emile Durkheim. Some scholars believe that his "corporatism" and authoritarianism found its most complete fulfillment in France in the Vichy regime's attempt to create state-directed organizations that would leave no area of human life unsupervised.

Bibliography. Bonald, Louis de. *On Divorce.* Ed. and trans. Nicholas Davidson. New Brunswick, NJ: Transaction Publishers, 1992.

Klink, David, *The French Counterrevolutionary Theorist Louis de Bonald (1754–1840)*. New York: Peter Lang, 1996. Reedy, W. Jay, "Maistre's Twin? Louis de Bonald and the Counter-Enlightenment." In *Joseph de Maistre's Life, Thought, and Influence: Selected Studies,* ed. Richard A. Lebrun. Montreal: McGill-Queen's University Press, 2001.

Richard A. Lebrun

BONHOEFFER, DIETRICH (1906–1945). Bonhoeffer was one of the leading Lutheran theologians in the Confessing Church during the Third Reich.

After earning his doctorate and Habilitation in theology, he served briefly at the German Lutheran parish in Barcelona, Spain, and then spent a year at the Union Seminary in New York before accepting the post of university chaplain at Berlin University in 1931. These experiences, particularly his time at Union Seminary, introduced him to the ecumenical movement, in which he participated for the rest of his life. In 1933, Bonhoeffer publicly opposed the National Socialist regime and its anti-Semitism, both of which he considered to be fundamentally incompatible with the gospel message. While some have criticized him for his continued supercessionism, that is, his belief that the Jewish people would eventually be redeemed by conversion to Christianity, Bonhoeffer's position defines him as one of the least compromising members of the Confessing Church. Bonhoeffer remained committed to a statist view of society and was not opposed to the idea of a state church, but he insisted that the legitimacy of state action should be measured by religious values.

From 1933 to 1935, Bonhoeffer served as pastor of the German Lutheran community in London, where he renewed his ecumenical ties and in particular became closely connected with Bishop George Bell of Chichester who supported international recognition of the Confessing Church in Protestant organizations. In 1935, Bonhoeffer became director of the Confessing Church's pastoral seminary and continued his work even after Berlin University withdrew his license to teach in 1936. In 1939, the Gestapo banned Bonhoeffer from teaching or even publicly speaking because of his refusal to accommodate the regime.

Even though Bonhoeffer sailed to America in 1939 to take up a teaching position at Union Seminary, he returned to Germany to remain close to those pastors whom he had trained. Largely in order to protect Bonhoeffer, friends arranged for him to serve in German military intelligence, the *Abwehr,* whose officers actively sought to warn the west about Hitler's intentions and to facilitate the escape of German Jews. Bonhoeffer himself became involved in circles plotting against Hitler. In 1942, he led a group formulating a moral vision statement for a postwar social order. In connection with his *Abwehr* activities, the Gestapo arrested Bonhoeffer in 1943 but did not discover his deeper involvement in the resistance until after the attempt on Hitler in 1944. Bonhoeffer remained incarcerated until an SS flying court-martial ordered his execution at Flossenbürg concentration camp on April 9, 1945. Bonhoeffer's theology can best be understood in his statement that resistance is "something of which only someone completely committed to faith, beyond reason, principle, conscience, freedom and virtue, is capable, committed only to act in faithful obedience to God."

Bibliography. Bethge, Eberhard. *Dietrich Bonhoeffer: A Biography: Theologian, Christian, Man for His Times*. Rev. and ed. Victoria Barnett. Minneapolis: Augsburg Fortress Press, 2000. Bonhoeffer, Dietrich. *Dietrich Bonhoeffer Works*. 16 vols. Minneapolis: Augsburg Fortress Press, 1996-2006. Schlingensiepen, Ferdinand. *Dietrich Bonhoeffer, 1906–1945: Eine Biographie*. Munich: C. H. Beck, 2005.

Martin Menke

BOOTH, WILLIAM (1829–1912) AND CATHERINE MUMFORD (1829–1890). The Booths founded the **Salvation Army** in 1865 in London, England. They were both raised in devout Methodist households. They met through their association with the Reform movement, a loose affiliation of Methodists seeking a more democratic structure and a more zealous membership. From the time of their engagement in 1852, they formed an evangelical partnership dedicated to working for God in all aspects of their lives. They were married on June 16, 1855, in London.

William was ordained by the Methodist New Connexion in 1855 and he worked as a circuit preacher and independent evangelist. Catherine Mumford Booth published the widely read pamphlet "Female Teaching" in 1859. It was occasioned by the tour of Mrs. Phoebe Palmer, the American Holiness advocate. Mrs. Palmer's work was denounced by many clergy, and the pamphlet was a reply. Catherine's argument rested on what she called a common-sense reading of scripture that considered passages in light of other biblical writings and the historical context in which it was written. She proclaimed a woman's right to preach the Gospel. Unlike most of her contemporaries, including Mrs. Palmer, she believed women's preaching was sanctioned in scripture and was an absolute necessity given the dire state of the world. Soon after publishing this pamphlet, she began preaching by invitation, and in 1860 she took over William's pulpit when he fell ill for some months. This highly unusual arrangement was praised by the New Connexion's newspaper, but a local newspaper claimed she wore her husband's clothing while preaching.

In 1861 William Booth resigned from the New Connexion to work as an independent revivalist. The debates between those who favored orderly services that would build a stable congregation and those who believed zealous preachers must seek out the lost had divided Methodists for generations. The Booths were particularly influenced by the work and writing of Americans James Caughey and **Charles Finney.** They favored strong preaching that led listeners to seek conversion in that moment. The techniques the Booths employed during their four years as revivalists would later help them to build the Salvation Army.

In 1865, William was invited to preach in London by the editors of the evangelical newspaper the *Revival.* The success of the campaign convinced him to remain in London. It not only offered the Booths a stable home, but with its vast population, London's East End seemed an ideal place for evangelical work. That small mission grew into the Salvation Army, with William Booth as its general. By 1885, the Army was at work in Great Britain, Europe, North America, and parts of the British Empire.

In 1890, William Booth published *In Darkest England and the Way Out,* a book that proposed a solution to poverty and unemployment by drawing upon the ideas of social imperialism and **Social Gospel.** Booth's scheme was widely supported in Britain, and the social service programs were the most prominent aspect of the Army's work by the early twentieth century. Catherine Booth, known as the Army Mother, never held an official rank but preached frequently at Army meetings and served on many committees. She was the author of many published sermons and books on child rearing, Holiness, and the Army's work. Her unwavering call for women's right to preach opened the way for other women to preach and hold positions of authority in the Army, and many Salvationist women claimed she had inspired their work. She was also the mother of eight children, all of whom served in the Salvation Army, two as general. Catherine died in 1890 and William in 1912. They are buried together at Abney Park Cemetery, in London.

Bibliography. Ervine, St. John. *God's Soldier: General William Booth.* 2 vols. London: Heinemann, 1934. Walker, Pamela J. *Pulling the Devil's Kingdom Down: The Salvation Army in Victorian Britain.* Berkeley and Los Angeles: University of California Press, 2001.

Pamela J. Walker

BOURASSA, HENRI (1868–1952). A self-taught man with great oratory skills and an extensive knowledge of history, politics, and law, Bourassa was a Canadian politician who fiercely opposed the British Empire and the widespread Imperial Federation movement. He also crusaded against the Americanization of Canadian moral and cultural life. A man of deep political convictions and unwavering faith, he also had the power to electrify crowds. Though his nationalism did not really reach an English Canadian audience before the 1930s, French Canadians saw him as their hero from the turn of the century up to the mid-1920s.

What Bourassa called the "nationalist doctrine" was a combination of Catholic conservatism and Liberal principles. But it must be said that in his thought, the Catholic element did not contradict the Liberal one; instead, both were integrated within a consistent system. His religious faith was that of a Catholic ultramontane for whom the papal voice is half human and half divine: the pope expresses the will of God on earth. This explains why, during World War I, Bourassa doubted that the League of Nations could bring about a fair and lasting peace, since he saw no indications that the nascent League would recognize the illuminating teachings of the pope.

For the nationalist leader, the fight against the British Empire did not imply the renunciation of the British Crown because they were two different things. The former was a monstrous outgrowth of English economic power, while the latter embodied the sound political principles Bourassa embraced: liberty, decentralization, and a respect for minorities. For him, these principles appeared in perfect harmony with basic Christian values. In addition, he saw Canada as a British country comprising an Anglo-French nation, a definition suggesting that French and English Canadians were legally equals regarding language and religious educational rights. From Bourassa's Catholic viewpoint, Americans had no ideals except the worship of the wealth and luxury. Their influence over the Canadian nation would only lead to extreme individualism and fragmentation, with the aggravating outcome of destroying French Canadian public good, imbued as it was with Catholic values such as justice, charity, and probity. By continually denouncing the pervasive influence of English imperialism and American materialism on Canadian life, Bourassa tragically played the prophet of doom in Parliament and on the public scene.

Bibliography. Lacombe, Sylvie. *La rencontre de deux peuples élus: Comparaison des ambitions nationale et impériale au Canada entre 1896 et 1920.* Quebec: Presses de l'Université Laval, 2002.

Sylvie Lacombe

BROOKS, PHILLIPS (1835–1893). Brooks was one of the greatest preachers in the history of the American pulpit. Oliver Wendell Holmes proclaimed Brooks "the ideal minister of the American gospel," and Julia Ward Howe, after hearing Brooks preach, exclaimed, "What a pity that everybody cannot hear Phillips Brooks."

He was one of six sons born to William and Mary Brooks in Boston. Both parents could trace their roots back to the Puritans of Massachusetts Bay. Four of the sons became Episcopal clergymen. Phillips Brooks was educated at the Boston Latin School and Harvard, where he proved himself to be a superb scholar, writer, and poet and excelled in the classics. After graduating from Harvard he became a teacher at the Boston Latin School, where, unable to maintain discipline, he was a failure. He then went on to the Virginia Theological Seminary to prepare himself for ministry in the Episcopal Church. Brooks never married.

His first parish was the Church of the Advent (1859–1861) in Philadelphia. He then moved on to Holy Trinity Church (1862–1869) in the same city, the most prestigious Episcopal church in Philadelphia. During those years he wrote the beloved Christmas carol "O Little Town of Bethlehem" and delivered his best-known sermon, "**Abraham Lincoln.**" This sermon was delivered on April 23, 1865, when the body of the slain president lay in state in Philadelphia. Though this eloquent memorial to Lincoln may well represent Brooks at his best, the sermon was not typical of the great preacher, for he seldom addressed political and social issues from the pulpit. Of the approximately 550 sermons of Brooks that remain, only a very few speak to social issues. During the Civil War years he did speak out in support of the Union and vigorously opposed both Southern slavery and Northern discrimination. He was disgusted with his denomination for its failure to take a stand against slavery and secession. However, within a year after the Civil War, Brooks adopted a policy of never taking an offending stand on almost any social issue. Society would change, Brooks thought, when people understand their kinship with God. One writer has observed, "He shrank from discussion of current affairs; his business was with eternity."

During his college and seminary years, Brooks came to have great reservations about the worth of classes on rhetoric and homiletics. He felt that such studies developed artificial and unnatural tendencies in the speaker. It was in his Philadelphia years that Brooks developed his unique style of preaching. He spoke rapidly, at the rate of over 200 words per minute. Some listeners found it difficult to adjust to such rapidity of speech. On most occasions Brooks read his sermons from a manuscript, but in his latter years, because of great demands upon his time, some sermons became more extemporaneous in nature. Hours of preparation preceded delivery, whether extempore or read. For Brooks, preaching was serious business. Unlike his contemporary, **Henry Ward Beecher,** Brooks disdained the use of humor in the pulpit. In a denomination that placed great importance on ritual, Brooks made preaching the focal point of worship. Standing six feet and four inches in height and weighing about 250 pounds, Brooks was an imposing figure in the pulpit.

In 1869 Brooks accepted a call to become rector of Trinity Church in his hometown, Boston, a position he would occupy until 1891. His years at Trinity were his most notable. He published many books, most of them collections of his sermons and addresses. In 1877 he delivered and published his renown *Yale Lectures on Preaching.* He received honorary doctorates from Harvard and Oxford Universities. Early in 1877, the congregation of Trinity Church consecrated a new building on Boston's Copely Square, one of the most beautiful examples of Romanesque architecture in the United States. The building still stands today, housing a large and active congregation, one of many historical showpieces in the city. In 1880 Brooks delivered a sermon before Queen Victoria, becoming the first American to preach a sermon before an English monarch.

In theology Brooks was a "Broad Churchman," meaning he stressed a oneness with other religious expressions rather than their differences. For such a stance he was criticized by the more conservative elements in the Episcopal Church, an opposition that was sometimes loud but never large in numbers. In 1891, Brooks was elected to become the bishop of Massachusetts, a position he would hold for only fifteen months due to his death from diphtheria on January 23, 1893.

Bibliography. Albright, Raymond W. *Focus on Infinity: A Life of Phillips Brooks.* New York: Macmillan, 1961. Allen, Alexander U. G. *Life and Letters of Phillips Brooks.* 3 vols. E. P. Dutton, 1901.

David B. Chesebrough

BROTHERHOOD OF SAINTS CYRIL AND METHODIUS (UKRAINE). This secret Ukrainian society was established in Kiev in 1845. Inspired by pan-Slavic federalism and Christian ideas of justice, liberty, fraternity, and equality, it strove to implement them within a social reform program. It advocated the emancipation of serfs, the democratization of education, and linguistic and cultural equality within a proposed political union of Slavic peoples in one federation.

The Brotherhood's driving force, historian Mykola Kostomarov (1817–1885), drafted the programmatic documents, the "Statutes and the Books of the Genesis of the Ukrainian People." The core dozen members included educators, writers, and lawyers, while a larger group of sympathizers included the prominent writer Panteleimon Kulish and the poet Taras Shevchenko.

Recent studies identify elements of the Brotherhood's Christian ethos. Its patrons were the Byzantine missionaries to the Slavs, Saints Cyril and Methodius, who epitomized Slavic unity as a historical memory and as a model for the future. The seal of the Brotherhood contained the evangelical dictum "You will know the truth and the truth will make you free" (John 8:32). The notion of a brotherhood evoked the Christian fraternal egalitarianism that was central to the society's reformist ideas. Kostomarov's "Statutes" called for a political and spiritual union of Slavs grounded in Christian principles. The fraternal federation would be a just alternative to the master-slave relations that existed within autocracies.

In addition to pan-Slavic and Christian values, the Brotherhood supported Ukrainian national values, but there was no consensus on the question of Ukrainian autonomy. Some members sought independence from Russia, while others held fast to the pan-Slavic vision.

Regardless of its commitment to nonviolence, the Brotherhood's secrecy and opposition to czarist autocracy gave it an aura of subversion, while the pursuit of political, not merely cultural, goals placed it outside the law. Denounced in 1847 to the czarist authorities, its leaders were exiled or detained. The severest punishment—ten years in Siberia—went to Shevchenko. Czar Nicholas I personally commanded that he be prevented from writing and sketching. Czar Alexander II's amnesty in 1856 freed the leaders of the Brotherhood. Many returned to active cultural work, but the Brotherhood's political project was effectively put to rest.

Despite the Brotherhood's short-lived existence (fourteen months), it set a precedent in the history of Ukrainian political thought. For the first time, political ideas had been mobilized to promote autonomy and independence from Russian domination. The Brotherhood's advancement of national values in the political sphere also set an example for later adherents of Ukrainian nationalism.

Bibliography. Zaionchkovskii, P. A. *Kirillo-Mefodiivskoe obshchestvo 1846–1847.* Moscow: Izd-vo Moskovskogo Universiteta, 1959.

Andrii Krawchuk

BROWN, JOHN (1800–1859). Convicted of treason for attempting to seize a United States military arsenal and ignite a slave insurrection, Brown has been variously marked as a religious zealot, a crazed fanatic, and a courageous martyr to the antislavery cause since he went to the gallows in 1859. His raid on Harpers Ferry, Virginia, in October of that year shocked a nation already reeling from political jolts that came in rapid succession following the Mexican-American War (1846–1848) and the breakdown of political compromises that had historically held the nation together.

Brown fronted moral outrage born of Christian faith and an absolute determination to realize social and political justice for enslaved blacks. His worldview was long in the making. Born in Connecticut, Brown was raised in Hudson, Ohio, where meager opportunities for formal education blended with early estrangement from denominational Christianity. When in 1836 Franklin Congregational Church elders rebuked Brown for offering his own pew to black worshippers during a revival meeting in Ohio's Western Reserve, the young abolitionist resolved never to enter a church again. Brown's skepticism regarding institutional solutions to the slavery problem only increased over time. Indeed, several of Brown's twenty children (born to two wives) gradually accepted their father as a leader specially ordained by God to be an instrument of slave liberation.

Certainly Brown's ill-fated financial ventures and perennial struggle to survive economically did not provide clear evidence of a special status with God. Real estate schemes, cattle farming, and tanning all became unfortunate steps on his way to bankruptcy in 1842. By the late 1840s, he was in Springfield, Massachusetts, exploring opportunities in the American wool trade. It was there that Brown's life-long abolitionist ideals began to overwhelm his financial pursuits and he began to focus his complete attention on the slavery question.

When the Kansas-Nebraska Act (1854) opened up the possibility of slavery in the territory, Brown at last had a national stage worthy of his grand design of liberation. With support of such benefactors as **Gerrit Smith,** Samuel Gridley Howe, and Theodore Parker, Brown claimed his role as Christian defender of free-state settlers in Kansas, even as proslavery forces proved equally determined to secure the territory for themselves. Following the sacking of Lawrence in May 1856 by proslavery forces, Brown declared himself an instrument of divine vengeance. At Pottawatomie Creek, he authorized four of his sons to carry out the brutal slaying of five proslavery men. Amid the broader chaos of "Bleeding Kansas," however, Brown managed to elude punishment, eventually finding his way to the East Coast to seek support for more ambitious ventures.

The final plan had always been immediate liberation of all the slaves, and Brown believed God's patience had run out. In the middle of 1859, he and a small band of supporters positioned themselves in Maryland, just a few miles from the United States arsenal at Harpers Ferry. The October 16 assault on the facility by seventeen whites and five blacks yielded no general slave rebellion

John Brown. Courtesy of the Library of Congress

and left Brown and his supporters in the hands of U.S. Marines under future Confederate generals J. E. B. Stuart and Robert E. Lee.

Brown's trial, conviction, and execution provided the basis for generations of controversy. While publicity about the Pottawatomie Massacre dimmed Brown's star for many eastern supporters, his cool, deliberative defense of his actions at trial, grounded in Christian moral principles, earned his redemption for many Northerners (notably **Ralph Waldo Emerson**). For Southerners, such sympathy—bows, as they saw it, to a madman and murderer—was a political abomination. Secessionists could only revel at being handed so glaring an example of Northern perfidy.

Brown's letters and declarations made clear the principles that defined him as a radical of the age. Though clearly in the minority among **abolitionists,** Brown wanted slavery's end to be accompanied by full social and political equality for blacks. Even women's equality figured in his planned future of social justice. While many abolitionists lamented the social condition of blacks, they also doubted their cultural and intellectual potential. Brown, on the other hand, exuded confidence that they had the intelligence, moral sense, and raw desire for individual opportunity that rendered them fully capable of effecting their own freedom and standing equal to whites at every level.

Brown's faith assumed the common condition of humanity before God, a condition that made racist ideologies an affront to divine authority. He spoke boldly of a national political heritage that mandated black freedom, but at the deepest level, Christian principle and biblical example remained the mainspring of his egalitarian ideals and sense of mission. His very personal understanding of New England Calvinism convinced him above all else that he had been predestined by

God to lead in the eradication of American slavery. Brown welcomed the opportunity for martyrdom in the days before his execution, leading Emerson to compare his death to Christ's sacrifice. His refusal to speak with the many clergymen who offered their services was a symbolic expression of contempt for the nation's institutional authority. At bottom, his was never truly a political fight, because his principles of action ultimately lay beyond the realm of politics.

Perhaps no individual in American history has exhibited a more culturally significant application of Christian belief to political action than did Brown. Indeed, his most recent biographer, while acknowledging a multiplicity of factors contributing to the Civil War, nevertheless marks Brown's assault on Harpers Ferry as the essential spark that ignited the great conflict (see Reynolds).

Bibliography. Oates, Stephen B. *To Purge with Blood: A Biography of John Brown.* 2nd ed. Amherst: University of Massachusetts Press, 1984. Peterson, Merrill D. *John Brown: The Legend Revisited.* Charlottesville: University Press of Virginia, 2002. Reynolds, David S. *John Brown, Abolitionist.* New York: Alfred A. Knopf, 2005.

Mark Y. Hanley

BROWNING, ROBERT (1812–1889). Browning was one of the most important British poets of the Victorian period. The public hailed him during his lifetime as prophet to an unbelieving and materialistic age, and after his death his innovative poetic techniques influenced modernist poets such as Ezra Pound and T. S. Eliot. More has been written about Browning as a religious than as a political thinker and about his innovative use of dramatic monologue in his most popular poems, such as "My Last Duchess," "Fra Lippo Lippi," and "Andrea del Sarto," and especially in his epic masterpiece *The Ring and the Book* (1868–1869). While not overtly political,

Browning is often revolutionary minded in his poetry.

Browning's early works dealing directly with political themes reveal a love of freedom and hatred of tyranny, and his association with his wife Elizabeth Barrett's attachment to the Italian nationalist cause during their life together in Venice gave him a reputation as a champion of liberty during his lifetime. After his death, opinions about the political implications of his religious beliefs and poetic style caused some controversy. The Boston Browning Society, which attracted leaders of American thought such as John Dewey and William James, read Browning as a philosophical pragmatist with a commitment to Christian socialism.

Many other critics, especially George Santayana and **G. K. Chesterton,** on the other hand, read Browning as an individualist, a liberal, and a democrat. Browning's rejection of Platonic idealization and his attachment to the mundane and grotesque as subjects of his religious and poetic vision signal a democratic sensibility similar to Walt Whitman's. Browning's use of a series of soliloquies in *The Ring and the Book* shows a liberal commitment to freedom of speech. At the same time, Browning's poetry reveals a persistent skepticism about political and institutional machinery as a solution to human problems. His poetry gives preeminent place to religion, art, and the personal obligations of friendship and human love. Browning was raised in a devout evangelical family and, as is particularly evident in his collection *Christmas-Eve and Easter Day* (1850), he did not consider the world an end in itself but a means to man's supernatural end.

Bibliography. McNally, James. "Browning's Political Thought." *Queen's Quarterly* 77 (1970): 578–90.

Susan E. Hanssen

BROWNSON, ORESTES AUGUSTUS (1803–1876). Brownson's career as a New England editor was marked by a singular passion to align America's political and cultural development with the divine will. While he eventually rested his hopes for such harmony on a foundation of Roman Catholicism and republicanism, the wild philosophical and religious turns that led to this conservative ground left his audience confused and subsequent historians unsure as to Brownson's contemporary impact and long-term significance.

Born in Stockbridge, Vermont, Brownson quickly absorbed the strict Presbyterian morality of the elderly couple who cared for him following his father's death in 1809. His precocious and inquisitive nature was guided by sparse opportunities for formal schooling. A brief teaching career gave way to preaching under the Universalist banner in 1826. Brownson found the broad and lenient Universalist path to salvation more appealing than the gloomy Calvinism of his youth, but it proved insufficient in his relentless and unflinching pursuit of certainty about the human condition. He flirted with skepticism in the 1830s but found greater attraction in the humanistic optimism of the Unitarians, transcendentalists, and early socialist labor leaders, especially Robert Owen and Frances Wright. These contacts fired his hopes for progress through popular politics, and he became an ardent Democrat. He supported Martin Van Buren's presidential bid and expected his essay "The Laboring Classes," a vigorous assault on concentrated wealth, to help seal a Democratic victory over the Whigs in 1840. Van Buren's defeat, however, convinced him that the poor and the weak were as incapable as the wealthiest classes of recognizing true morality and acting virtuously for the common good.

His faith in popular democracy gone, Brownson turned again to religion and found in Roman Catholicism the spiritual and cultural compass that guided the remainder of his life. His conversion in 1844—shocking even to those readers of *Brownson's Quarterly Review* who had grown accustomed to the editor's unpredictable turns—made him the most prominent and controversial Catholic voice in the nation.

Warming to the Roman Catholic Church's institutional coherence and doctrinal stability, Brownson nevertheless kept his independent stripes. As the American Party (Know-Nothings) constructed its nativist, anti-Catholic platform in the 1850s, Brownson earned papal accolades for defending the compatibility of his new faith with American republicanism. Just as easily, however, he chastised Irish Catholics who eschewed acculturation and envisioned the church as an oasis of Celtic culture.

Catholicism consolidated Brownson's guiding belief that the political and spiritual worlds could not be separated, but he gave his views a distinctly American cast. Since sovereignty ultimately lies with God, any political system that assigns absolute authority to the people or the state is inherently flawed. National progress requires deference to the divine will as revealed on this earth by the church. This alliance of church and state requires neither force nor formal ties. Rather, as the Constitution's framers enshrined natural principles of equality and right, Americans should now embrace the church's universal claims as merely the superior, spiritual foundation of their own national aspirations.

This unifying logic cast Brownson in an outsider's role, however, and yielded anything but harmony in primarily Protestant America. Amid rising sectional tensions over slavery, he variously attacked both **abolitionists** and Southern slaveholders for their disruptive disregard of established law. In the 1844 presidential election, Brownson called upon John C. Calhoun, the South's preeminent defender of slavery and states rights, to accept the nomination and restore the "lustre" to presidential leadership. Initially convinced that a divinely sanctioned hierarchy of human relations might give the Southerner "a valid right to the services of his slave," he finally sided with Northern principles against the political chaos threatened by Southern secessionists. When war finally came in 1861, Brownson pronounced slavery as the cause and chided President **Abraham Lincoln** for not immediately recognizing the link between Union and emancipation. When Republican radicals convinced Brownson in 1864 to join an anti-Lincoln movement, he supported John C. Fremont until the Pathfinder withdrew from the race. Now bereft of political home and audience, the editor abandoned his *Quarterly Review*.

Brownson's retirement provided the reflective opportunity to consolidate his thought in *The American Republic* (1865). America's destiny, he concluded, was to complete the civilizing process begun by Greeks and Romans. Americans were now uniquely free to harmonize religion and politics, to obey God's will without submitting to the "barbaric" and oppressive political systems that had historically marred the human struggle. No constitutional violations tarnished this high calling, he argued. The business of church and state could remain forever separate because what matters is the "intrinsic unity of principle" and that "while moving in separate spheres, each obeys one and the same Divine law" (Brownson, 250). Brownson maintained the courage of his convictions long after most of his contemporaries cared to listen.

Bibliography. Brownson, Orestes. *The American Republic.* Ed. Americo Lapati. New Haven, CT: College and University Press, 1972. Carey, Patrick W. *Orestes A. Brownson:*

American Religious Weathervane. Grand Rapids, MI: William B. Eerdmans, 2004. Lapati, Americo D. *Orestes A. Brownson.* New York: Twayne, 1965. Schlesinger, Arthur M. *A Pilgrim's Progress: Orestes A. Brownson.* Boston: Little, Brown, 1966.

Mark Y. Hanley

BRUINS SLOT, J. A. H. J. S. (1906–1972). Bruins Slot was a major leader of the Dutch Calvinist underground resistance movement during World War II, editor of the prominent newspaper *Trouw,* and lawmaker of the **Anti-Revolutionary Party** (ARP) in the postwar period in the Netherlands.

In 1931 Bruins Slot received his doctorate from the Free University of Amsterdam. His thesis described ARP founder **Groen van Prinsterer** as a leader convinced of the essential justness of the 1853 reestablishment of the Roman Catholic hierarchy within the country. Then he served as mayor of Adorp in the northern Groningen province until resigning during the German occupation. In 1943, he worked with ARP leader **Jan Schouten** and became the editor of a new resistance paper for the banned ARP entitled *Trouw* (Faithful). The paper printed unsigned articles that denounced the Nazi worldview as anti-Christian, gave resistance instructions, carried statements by exiled Queen Wilhelmina, denounced anti-Semitic policy, and reported the D-day invasion. The Germans executed 120 hostages when their threats failed to stop the courageous editor from publishing the paper. In 1946, Bruins Slot was also elected to Parliament and served as ARP delegation chair from 1956 to1959.

Bezinning en Uitzicht (Thinking about Our Times," 1949) was his case for European federalism (now called the European Union) to promote the unity of Western Europe and oppose communism. He wanted to see a Reformation influence along with Catholicism and humanism in it. "The law-abiding community of nations is a Christian ideal. Nationalism is heathen We are God's co-workers in building a better world," he observed.

During and after the war, Bruins Slot wanted to regain the Dutch East Indies occupied by the Japanese in 1942 and given independence in 1945. During the Dutch police actions there, he made battle inspection tours with Schouten. But after Queen Juliana granted legal independence to Indonesia, Bruins Slot changed his mind to embrace anticolonialism, and a more critical view of ARP tradition. During 1967 his editorials supported anticolonialism, civil rights for American blacks, and food aid for India. While thankful for what America did in the Marshall Plan and NATO, he was critical of U.S. policy in Vietnam.

Bibliography. Bruins Slot, J. A. H. J. S. *En Ik was Gelukkig.* Baarn, Netherlands: Bosch & Keuning, 1972.

McKendree R. Langley

BRÜNING, HEINRICH (1885–1970). An unusual combination of Catholic piety and reverence for the Prussian state molded Brüning's upbringing in Münster, Westphalia. He lost his businessman father at an early age and grew up admiring an older brother who became a priest. Brüning earned a doctorate in economics in 1915 and then fought as an infantry officer on the western front. At the war's end, he renounced any thought of marriage in order to dedicate himself completely to politics, feeling a vocation to rescue Germany from the consequences of defeat.

In 1920, he became executive secretary of the umbrella organization for Germany's Christian trade unions, which sought to promote cooperation between Catholic and Protestant workers. He also championed Adam Stegerwald's unsuccessful campaign to transform the Catholic **Center Party** (Zentrum) into a broadly ecumenical "German, Christian, democratic, and social" party, to cite a slogan from a famous speech by Stegerwald in November 1920. It was largely written by Brüning and influenced the later founders of the **Christian Democratic Union.**

Brüning was elected to the Reichstag for the Center Party in 1924 and gained respect for the unrivaled diligence with which he studied fiscal policy. He became the Center's parliamentary leader in 1929 and was summoned by President Hindenburg to the chancellorship at a fateful moment in March 1930, when the last majority parliamentary coalition of the Weimar Republic collapsed as the result of a quarrel between Social Democrats and liberals over the financing of unemployment benefits.

Brüning's record in office has long fueled controversy. He felt compelled to govern by presidential emergency decrees and responded to the Great Depression with a policy of fiscal austerity and deflation. Influential figures around Hindenburg hoped to exploit his good name to implement authoritarian constitutional reforms, but Brüning himself denied emphatically that the democratic constitution of the Weimar Republic was responsible for Germany's problems. Instead he always blamed the worldwide economic crisis and the reparations provisions of the Versailles Treaty. Many historians reproach Brüning for deliberately aggravating the economic crisis to strengthen his case that reparations must be abolished, but this accusation is unfounded. Due largely to circumstances beyond his control, Brüning could do little more in domestic policy than seek to distribute the suffering caused by the Great Depression as fairly as possible among all social classes. The unemployment rate soared to over 40 percent by January 1932, a development that promoted explosive growth by the Nazi Party.

Brüning did labor skillfully to persuade the British and Americans that reparations harmed the entire world economy, and he deserves much credit for the Hoover Moratorium of July 1931 and the final abolition of reparations in June 1932. He also thwarted Hitler's attempt to gain power through election to the presidency by rallying a broad coalition behind the reelection of Hindenburg, and then he responded to the spread of street violence by outlawing the organization of Nazi storm troopers. This action provoked a fatal quarrel with the army leadership, however, and Hindenburg's personal advisors persuaded him in May 1932 to replace Brüning with the blatantly reactionary Franz von Papen, whose disastrous policies ruined any foundation for a broad coalition against Hitler.

Chancellor Brüning rarely spoke of God in public, but all his thinking about politics was inspired by the ideals of *Rerum novarum* and the Catholic social movement, which he tried to synthesize with maxims learned from the great statesmen of Prussian history. He believed fervently that all Christians should support the emergence of trade unions to counterbalance the dominant economic power of capital, and that the state was obliged to protect the economically weak. His admirers considered Brüning an exemplary Christian statesman because of his self-denial. He never used his government limousine for personal errands and gave a large portion of his salary to charity. For Brüning, his faith also implied an obligation to resist the spread of the Machiavellian attitude that the end justified the means in political struggle. Police agents once brought him photographs of homosexual acts by the commander of the storm troopers, Ernst Röhm, but Brüning immediately ordered them burned. In retrospect, questions arise as to whether his ascetic streak hindered empathy with ordinary Germans, and whether the goal of discrediting the Nazis did not justify more ruthless methods than Brüning was prepared to employ. Brüning's last political battle was an unsuccessful campaign in the spring and summer of

1933 to persuade the Center Party not to approve Hitler's Enabling Act and the Vatican not to sign a concordat with Hitler. The Nazis were essentially pagan and had a limitless appetite for power, Brüning argued, and they would inevitably persecute the church; Catholic leaders must not confuse the German people about the evil character of their new government. Brüning was compelled to flee Germany in 1934, however, and eventually joined the faculty of Harvard University. His ideas for promoting social partnership between the classes, a more active role for the laity in religious life, and ecumenical cooperation between Catholics and Protestants had little chance to succeed in the highly polarized atmosphere of the Great Depression.

His reverence for the great statesmen of Prussian history also encouraged a dangerous overestimation of the landowning nobility in general and President Hindenburg in particular. Most of the later founders of the Christian Democratic Union turned their backs on the Prussian tradition, but in other respects they returned under more favorable conditions to the successful pursuit of ideas first outlined by Heinrich Brüning.

Bibliography. Hömig, Herbert. *Brüning: Kanzler in der Krise der Republik.* Paderborn, Germany: Schöningh, 2000. Patch, William. *Heinrich Brüning and the Dissolution of the Weimar Republic.* Cambridge: Cambridge University Press, 1998.

William Patch

BRUNNER, EMIL (1889–1966). Brunner was one of the most influential moral and political Protestant thinkers of the twentieth century. Despite a youthful attraction to religiously based socialism, the emergence of totalitarian regimes in the aftermath of World War I convinced the Swiss theologian to reassert the relevance of historic Reformation theology as the moral alternative to both radical democratic individualism and particularly the collectivist state.

Christian faith is not merely theoretical, he argued, but should be an operative global principle.

An ordained minister in the Swiss Reformed Church, Brunner came from modest material circumstances and a strictly pietistic and dissenting theological background. His almost fundamentalist spiritual training did not preclude broader intellectual interests, including such modern theories as Darwinism.

Brunner completed most of his theological studies in Zurich and in 1913 sojourned briefly in England as a teacher. From 1916 to 1924, he ministered to a rural congregation in Eastern Switzerland and began a close relationship with **Karl Barth.** However, their relationship would later become strained by a passionate debate over natural theology. Brunner defended the claim that human reason provided some basic knowledge of God even outside divine revelation, which Barth pointedly refuted in his famous "Nein!" Yet Brunner's position would have implications for his political theology, which was based partly on natural law. Brunner's warmly received publications led to a thirty-year appointment as full professor of systematic and practical theology at the University of Zurich (1924–1953).

Of great political significance is Brunner's book *The Divine Imperative* (1932). Here he devoted attention not only to the importance of marriage and the family in sustaining Christian social principles but also to the just organization of labor, the state, law, science, art, and the church. In *Justice and the Social Order* (1943), Brunner reintroduced Aristotle and advocated natural law, contending that there are unwritten eternal rules that every human, as individuals and within the context of the community, must observe. Mere positive law is not a sufficient basis for sustaining a just community.

Together with the Scottish theologian Joseph H. Oldham, Brunner was one of the most influential figures of the ecumenical Life and Work movement. Focusing on the destructive potential of authoritarian regimes, Brunner told a Paris audience in 1934 that "the Christian seeks always democracy," because "the possibility of limiting the coercive powers of the state by Law on the one hand and the active control by the people who are governed on the other hand, is a direct consequence of how Christianity conceives the State. . . . The notion of a totalitarian state contradicts the Christian thought that there are different realms of life, each of which carries its own rules and limit each other."

One the eve of World War II, Brunner's friendship with Princeton Theological Seminary president John Alexander Mackay led to an offer of a professorship, but health problems and the unsettled political climate forced him to return to Switzerland. Subsequently appointed president of Zurich University, he preached and published widely in an effort to promote spiritual resistance to Nazism in Switzerland. He helped Jewish refugees, especially university professors who had been expelled from Germany, and advocated the death penalty for traitors who assisted German forces.

Following the war, Brunner's influence was largely eclipsed by the theological influence of such luminaries as Karl Barth, **Paul Tillich,** and Rudolf Bultmann. In 1948, he was denied an opportunity to assert his anticommunist views before the new **World Council of Churches.** As counselor on evangelism for the World's Alliance of YMCAs, however, Brunner received warm receptions from Asian audiences and eventually served for two years as professor of Christian ethics and philosophy at the newly founded International Christian University in Tokyo.

His last political fight came during the cold war when he warned against appeasement of the Soviet Union by the West.

"Through the renouncement of atomic weapons," Brunner cautioned in 1958, "the danger of an atomic war is not removed, rather on the contrary, it is brought closer. Because for those who are brutal and violent [the Soviet Union] there is no greater temptation than the defenselessness of the other party."

Above all, Brunner insisted that the state must fully acknowledge the individual's singular importance and dignity in the divine plan and premise the development of community on that reality.

Bibliography. Brunner, Emil. *Ein offenes Wort.* Ed. Rudolf Wehrli. 2 vols. Zurich: Theologischer Verlag Zürich, 1981. Brunner, Hans Heinrich. *Mein Vater und sein Ältester: Emil Brunner in seiner und meiner Zeit.* Zurich: Theologischer Verlag Zürich, 1986. Jehle, Frank. *Emil Brunner: Leben und Werk.* Zurich: Theologischer Verlag Zürich, 2006.

Frank Jehle

BRYAN, WILLIAM JENNINGS (1860–1925). Bryan was one of the most influential political and religious leaders of the late nineteenth and early twentieth centuries. He served in the U.S. House of Representatives (1891–1895) and as secretary of state (1913–1915) and ran for the presidency on the Democratic Party ticket in 1896, 1900, and 1908. Despite losing all these elections, Bryan remained a dominant ideological force in American life from his surprising emergence into national prominence at the Democratic Convention in 1896 until his unexpected death in 1925.

During his early political career, Bryan emphasized the need for economic and political reform along a Progressive model. After his last presidential defeat in 1908, he turned his attention to moral and cultural issues, such as the prohibition of alcohol, women's suffrage, and banning the teaching of evolution. Despite his early interest in lower tariffs, an increased money supply, and reducing corporate influence, all of Bryan's political and economic ideas were profoundly shaped by the Protestant evangelical values of his youth.

Bryan was born and raised on a small farm just outside Salem, Illinois, the seat of Marion County. His father, Silas, was a circuit judge and a deacon of the Baptist Church. His mother, Mariah Jennings, was a Methodist. Rural southern Illinois in the late 1800s was thoroughly Protestant in culture. Bryan's beliefs in free will and perfectionism—the idea that each individual's achievement of moral excellence would cause most social evils to disappear from the world—reflected this. When he was fourteen, Bryan experienced a religious conversion at a revival and became a lifelong member of the Presbyterian Church. He was never much interested in theology but always emphasized a personal commitment to Christ. Throughout his life, he was a model of evangelical behavior, avoiding alcohol, gambling, swearing, dancing, and theaters. Bryan was a graduate of Illinois College and received his law degree from Union Law School in Chicago. In 1884, he married Mary Elizabeth Baird, who was helpful to his political career, shared his spiritual interests, and was his constant companion on the Chautauqua lecture tour, where Bryan often chose to speak on religious subjects.

In 1887, Bryan moved to Lincoln, Nebraska, intending to establish a more profitable law practice, but was soon drawn to politics. His entrance into the political world was eased by his opposition to "moral reform"—the mostly Republican, Protestant, and evangelical attempt to use the coercive powers of state and local governments to improve the behavior of Americans. Early in his career, Bryan subscribed to the "personal liberty" ideology of the Democratic Party. He based his opposition to government intrusion into the moral lives of Americans on the demands of electoral politics. Most Nebraska Democrats were Irish, Czech, and Polish Catholics or German Lutherans, who were strongly opposed to so-called moral reform because they regarded it as an attack on the immigrant cultures of the Gilded Age. Bryan was elected to Congress in 1890 and 1892 mostly because of his support for low tariffs and the use of silver to inflate the currency. But his opposition to prohibition was also important to his success.

Bryan's 1896 campaign for the presidency also emphasized economic issues, especially the demand for the monetization of silver. His stand against prohibition did not help him, because his opponent, Republican William McKinley, was also opposed to prohibition. McKinley's rejection of moral reform helped him gain the votes of middle-class German Lutherans in the crucial swing states of the Midwest, thus throwing the close election to the Republican candidate. Bryan's presidential rematch with McKinley in 1900 also mostly ignored moral and cultural issues.

William Jennings Bryan. Courtesy of the Perry-Casteñeda Library

His final attempt at the presidency in 1908, against Republican William Howard Taft, was completely Progressive in conception, but Bryan justified his proposals for political and economic reforms with a call for "applied Christianity," a willingness to help one's fellow man. Bryan was bitterly disappointed by this third defeat. Some Catholics who normally supported the Democrats' defense of immigrant cultures voted for Taft because of his effective governorship of the Catholic Philippines. Bryan felt betrayed because he had fought anti-Catholic bigotry and had numerous Catholic friends. He vowed never to run for the presidency again.

Beginning in 1910, Bryan tackled the great moral and cultural issues of the early twentieth century. He had become convinced that his religious influence was greater than his political clout, and that the former was best exercised as a lobbyist for the moral and social improvement of the United States. In Nebraska, he fought for a "county option" law, legislation that would give counties the choice whether to regulate or ban alcohol. At the federal level, he worked tirelessly for a constitutional amendment outlawing alcohol nationwide. When prohibition was finally achieved in 1919, both supporters and opponents credited Bryan as the single individual wielding the greatest influence on the issue. During these years, Bryan also became an advocate for women's suffrage. He based his support for women's voting rights on the need for equality among human beings in a "Christian brotherhood." Bryan's appointment as secretary of state in 1913 by Democratic president Woodrow Wilson redirected his work on moral improvement to the international arena. Bryan's Christian principles also appeared in his management of American foreign policy. He worked for international peace by negotiating thirty conciliation treaties with other nations. He believed that working for good over evil and substituting the use of reason for force would lead eventually to the elimination of war. Bryan resigned as secretary of state in 1915 because he believed that Wilson's strong protest against the German sinking of the *Lusitania* violated American neutrality in the early years of World War I.

In the 1920s, Bryan became involved in a national movement to ban the teaching of evolution in schools. He had long believed that the Darwinian concept of the survival of the fittest was un-Christian because it justified hurting the weak in favor of the strong. It was a "law of hate," while Christianity was the "law of love" by which human progress was achieved. He also believed that Darwinism had produced the cruelties of the recent war and the ongoing struggle between labor and capital in the modern industrial world. Bryan participated in the so-called Scopes monkey trial in 1925, the famous prosecution of a Dayton, Tennessee, high school teacher for violating the state's law against teaching evolution. This trial has come to symbolize the great culture wars of the 1920s, such as the conflicts between rural and urban life, religion and science, and traditional Christianity and modernism. Physically exhausted by the trial, Bryan died in his sleep a few days after its conclusion.

Whether Bryan was supporting economic, political, or moral reform, evangelical Protestantism inspired his work. His belief in political equality and economic opportunity for all Americans was founded in the idea of a Christian brotherhood of mankind. His devotion to democracy and the common man came from his faith that God had created people to be fully capable of self-governance. To believe otherwise would be to cast aspersions upon the Almighty. Bryan believed that moral and physical courage are derived principally from religious faith in "a righteous cause." Moral law came from God, not from the self-interested concerns of human beings.

Bryan differed from other evangelicals of his era mainly in his high degree of tolerance for other religions, especially Catholicism and Judaism. His belief in the intimate connection between the religious and political worlds continues to inspire many people today.

Bibliography. Cherny, Robert W. *A Righteous Cause: The Life of William Jennings Bryan.* Norman: University of Oklahoma Press, 1994. Coletta, Paolo E. *William Jennings Bryan.* 3 vols. Lincoln: University of Nebraska Press, 1964–1969. Smith, Willard H. *The Social and Religious Thought of William Jennings Bryan.* Lawrence, KS: Coronado Press, 1975.

Michael S. Fitzgerald

BUCHANAN, PATRICK JOSEPH, JR. (b. 1938). American conservative journalist, television commenter, and politician, Buchanan may be best remembered for his speech at the 1992 Republican Convention when he declared, "There is a religious war going on . . . for the soul of America." The speech was controversial for calling upon religious conservatives to "take back the culture, and take back our country" from a secular liberal elite. From his writings and press appearances, Buchanan's political positions have been described as traditionally conservative or paleoconservative, although a more accurate account would be a social and cultural conservative combined with a populist economic outlook and a realpolitik, almost isolationist, view of American foreign policy. He also is known for his controversial views on restricting immigration, defending some Nazi war leaders, labeling Dr. **Martin Luther King** "a criminal," and criticizing U.S. support of the state of Israel, which has caused some to accuse him of anti-Semitism.

Buchanan was born on November 2, 1938, in Washington, D.C., where he was educated in the Roman Catholic school system, graduating from Georgetown University in 1961 with degrees in English and philosophy. In 1962 he earned a master's degree

at Columbia University in journalism and that same year became an editorial writer for the *St. Louis Globe Democrat* newspaper. He was an early supporter of Richard Nixon and became an advisor to the Nixon campaign in 1966, landing him the positions of advisor and speechwriter in the Nixon White House until 1974. Buchanan returned to the White House in 1985, serving as communication director under President **Ronald Reagan** until 1987. When he is not serving or running for the presidency, Buchanan writes as a syndicated political columnist and makes appearances as a commentator on national television news shows such as *The McLaughlin Group, Crossfire, Buchanan and Press, Scarborough Country,* and *MSNBC News.*

Buchanan campaigned for the Republican presidential nomination in 1992 and 1996, and as the Reform Party presidential candidate in 2000. Having lost the 1992 primary campaign to President George H. W. Bush, Buchanan criticized the liberal views of Bill Clinton in his famous "culture war" speech at the Republican Convention. In 1996, he again lost the Republican nomination to Senator Bob Dole. Believing the Republican Party had abandoned traditional conservative principles in favor of neoconservative ones—a philosophy that favors an expansive federal government and a preemptive military foreign policy—Buchanan left the Republican Party in 2000 and campaigned for the presidency on the Reform Party ticket, winning 0.4 percent of the popular vote.

Buchanan's political and religious views are best presented in his own books, such as *Right from Beginning* (1988), *The Great Betrayal* (1988), *A Republic, Not An Empire* (1999), *The Death of the West* (2000), and *Where the Right Went Wrong* (2004). In these works, as well as in his numerous press appearances, Buchanan has advocated a conservative social agenda. Staunchly antiabortion, Buchanan favors a strictly pro-life Supreme Court as well as school prayer, tax breaks for two-parent families, and bans on gay marriage. These social and cultural views are often religiously based and seek to impose a conservative Christianity upon a liberal political culture. But if Buchanan's social positions are rooted in a conservative Christianity, so are his populist views on economic relations, which have prompted him to call for higher tariffs on imports and a repeal of NAFTA to protect domestic industries and the working families that sustain them. Finally, Buchanan's isolationist foreign policy also can be understood as part of the American Christian tradition as seeing the United States as "a city on a hill," aloof from world affairs so as to remain untainted by its political and moral corruption.

Bibliography. Buchanan, Patrick J. *Right from Beginning.* Washington DC: Regnery, 1990. Grant, George. *Buchanan: Caught in the Crossfire.* Nashville, TN: Thomas Nelson, 1996. Scotchie, Joseph. *Street Corner Conservative: Patrick J. Buchanan and His Times.* Alexander, NC: Alexander Books, 2002.

Lee Trepanier

BUCHEZ, PHILIPPE JOSEPH BENJAMIN (1796–1865). A physician by training, Buchez's Christian and Catholic foundations, as well as his Saint-Simonism, helped lay the basis for his engagement in revolutionary politics. During the Restoration period that followed the defeat of Napoleon's empire (1814/15–1830), Buchez cofounded several anti-Bourbon secret societies and only by chance avoided a death penalty for conspiracy in 1822. He participated in the revolutions of 1830 and 1848, whereby he justified his revolutionary activities and his fight for a democratic-socialist (not in the Marxist sense) society by his Christian belief. In his *Parliamentary History of the French Revolution,* he argued that the revolutionary process, including Robespierre's Terror

(1793–1794), was the fulfillment of the Christian Revelation.

In 1827 Buchez for the first time founded a journal (*Journal des progrès des sciences et institutions médicales,* 1827–1830), to be followed by several others in later years. The most important of these publications was *L'Atelier* (1840–1850), which was one of the earliest journals to give workers a voice. Buchez's social doctrine was condensed in the *Revue nationale* (1847–1848). With the Revolution of 1848 Buchez engaged in a parliamentary career, which brought him to the presidency of the French Constitutional Assembly within weeks. When on May 15, 1848, popular masses entered the Assembly building, President Buchez seemed to be shocked by the events and failed to act. Therefore he was not reelected and *L'Atelier* and *Revue nationale* declined within months. He was soon arrested after the coup d'etat by Louis-Napoleon in December 1851. His public career over, Buchez returned to scientific writings.

Bibliography. Cuvillier, Armand. *Buchez et les origines du socialisme chrétien.* Paris: Presses Universitaires de France, 1948. Cuvillier, Armand. *Un journal d'ouvriers: "L'Atelier."* Paris: Éditions Ouvriers, 1954. Geissberger, Werner. *Philippe-Joseph-Benjamin Buchez.* Winterthur, Switzerland: Keller, 1956. Guccione, Eugenio. *Philippe Buchez e la rivoluzione francese.* Palermo, Italy: Palma, 1993. Isambert, François André. *De la Charbonnerie au Saint-Simonisme: Étude sur la jeunesse de Buchez.* Paris: Éditions de Minuit, 1966.

Oliver Benjamin Hemmerle

BUCKLEY, WILLIAM F. (b. 1925). The conservative path that brought **Ronald Reagan** to power was paved by Catholic conservative William F. Buckley, editor of the *National Review* and political commentator for more than forty years. In the conservative wilderness years of the 1950s, Buckley became the voice for an avowedly respectable form of conservatism, one that eschewed the populist excesses of McCarthyism for a more cerebral anti-statism. Rejecting the welfare state in favor of competitive individualism, traditional morality, and classical laissez-faire economics, Buckley crafted the elements of the conservative ethos that coalesced in the 1960s.

Born in 1925 to a devout Catholic family headed by a father who had accrued his wealth in the oil industry, William F. Buckley grew up in an atmosphere of intense religious devotion and material privilege. The young Buckley absorbed his political values from his father, Will Buckley Sr., who inculcated his children in the virtues of anticommunism, Catholic orthodoxy, intolerance for government regulation, restricted democracy, and unrestricted free enterprise. As the United States edged toward war in 1940, he also converted his ten children into vigorous defenders of isolationism.

After serving in the army, Buckley attended Yale University and excelled as a debater, newspaper editor, and general man-about-campus. It was here that his conservative views blossomed in dialectical opposition to what he considered the anti-Christian, liberal bias of the college's faculty. After graduating, Buckley channeled his views into the polemical *God and Man at Yale* (1951), a book that pitted individualism and Christianity against atheism and collectivism. The book quickly made Buckley into a pariah for liberals and a lightning rod for conservatives. It became the basis of his claim to conservative intellectual leadership in the 1950s. It also exposed his predilection for free-market capitalism, the alleged merits of which he explained in his 1959 *Up from Liberalism*. State intervention, high taxes, and the growing power of trade unions threaten individual rights more than corporate expansion, Buckley argued, since the state is more likely to undermine a person's liberties than is a company. Operating on the assumption that a rising tide lifts all boats, he posited that the disadvantaged benefit from the prosperity generated by unfettered capitalism. *Up from Liberalism* featured a feisty defense of economic individualism, but it was rooted in a religious worldview that stressed unlimited economic freedom as the foundation for obedience to God and the moral authority of tradition.

Economic disputes were subsumed by the struggle over communism. Buckley had been conditioned toward anticommunism by his father and by a Catholic tradition that viewed communism as an atheistic, materialistic adversary that threatened Western civilization itself. In 1954 he and Brent Bozell, future coeditor of the *National Review,* published *McCarthy and His Enemies,* a defense of the vitriolic senator that the benefits of anticommunist "McCarthyism" outweighed the liabilities of McCarthy himself. But Buckley and Bozell assembled a book that did more than excuse McCarthy's histrionics; it entertained the possibility of "coercive sanctions" being used against not only the Communist Party but communist ideas as well. Supportive of government loyalty tests based on ideological conformity, Bozell and Buckley offered what historian John Judis has described as a "balanced authoritarianism" (Judis, 107) directed at fundamentally altering rather than protecting the status quo.

It was in the *National Review,* however, that he found the most powerful vehicle for his oppositional views. The magazine appealed to conservative elites and offered a forum for younger conservatives roused by McCarthyism. Unveiled in 1955, it soon became a leading voice of anticommunism, often of the most stringent brand. The *Review* castigated the Eisenhower administration for its support of New Deal programs and for its unwillingness to follow through on its policy of communist "roll-back." Although the journal was not sectarian, it was religious in the sense that it provided an outlet for Catholic conservatives and others who opposed American abandonment of Christian Eastern Europe to the jackboot of Stalinist domination.

Buckley and the *National Review* continued to play the role of gadfly to the liberal "establishment" and intellectual color guard for the emerging conservative movement in the 1960s and 1970s. They opposed John F. Kennedy, despite his Catholicism, and supported Barry Goldwater, largely because of his nuclear militancy. They championed Ronald Reagan's gubernatorial candidacy in 1966 and considered the war in Vietnam a struggle to preserve the virtuous Catholic South against the infidel communist North. Buckley had little sympathy for the civil rights movement and at one point endorsed black disfranchisement. In 1966, he became the host of the nationally broadcasted *Firing Line,* a talk show featuring debates, interviews, and Buckley's incisive wit, a combination that kept the program on the air until 1999.

Buckley enthusiastically supported Reagan's ascent to power and enjoyed close relations with him once in power, but by the late 1980s, he was becoming more of an icon than the iconoclast who had penned *God and Man at Yale.* His significance lay in his ability to fuse conservatives from across the ideological spectrum into a mainstream coalition. Christian traditionalists, free-market ideologues, and libertarians anguished over government intervention in the economy, and vigilant anticommunists found common ground in Buckley's *National Review* and through organizations such as Young Americans for Freedom, a group that he helped found in 1960.

Bibliography. Allitt, Patrick. "The Bitter Victory: Catholic Conservative Intellectuals in America, 1988–1993." *South Atlantic Quarterly*

93 (Summer 1994): 631–58. Allitt, Patrick. *Catholic Intellectuals and Conservative Politics in America, 1950–1985.* Ithaca, NY: Cornell University Press, 1993. Judis, John. *William F. Buckley: Patron Saint of the Conservatives.* New York: Simon & Schuster, 1988. Schulman, Bruce J. *The Seventies: The Great Shift in American Culture, Society, and Politics.* Cambridge, MA: Da Capo Press, 2002.

Michael Dennis

BULGAKOV, SERGEY NIKOLAEVICH (1871–1944). Bulgakov was a philosopher, economist, Russian Orthodox theologian, and a well-known public figure whose ideas evolved from "legal Marxism," through Christian socialism and Idealism, to Christian Orthodox theology. Bulgakov was born in Livny, in Russia's Orel *guberniya* and studied at the Orel seminary and at Elets gymnasium. Influenced by Marxism, he broke with the church and became a law student at Moscow University, where he graduated as a specialist in political economics and statistics (1894). Bulgakov's marriage to Elena Ivanovna Tokmakova in 1898 produced four children. After study in Berlin (1898–1899) and a dissertation on *Capitalism and Agriculture* (Moscow, 1900), he secured a position at Kiev University (1901–1906) and contributed to liberal and Marxist journals. During this period Bulgakov's disillusionment with Marxist philosophy was reflected in his book *The Problems of Idealism* (1902) and a collection of articles, *From Marxism to Idealism* (1903). Together with N. A. Berdyaev, he became coeditor of the political and philosophical journal *Voprosy zhizni* (The Questions of Life), then *Novyj put'* (New Way). In 1905, together with V. Sventsistkij, V. F. Ern, A. S. Glinka (Volzhskij), K. M. Aggeev, and others, Bulgakov collaborated in the establishment of a Christian Socialist party—the Union of Christian Politics—and was elected a deputy of the Second Duma as an independent Christian Socialist (1906). He became a professor at Moscow University (1906–1917), defended his doctoral dissertation on the *Philosophy of Economics* (1912), continued his evolution to Orthodoxy, and described his conversion in *The Undying Light* (1917). Bulgakov was ordained a priest in 1918, but the Bolshevik government prevented his return to teaching and expelled him from the Soviet Union in 1922. He moved to Prague, where he taught church law and theology at the Russian People's Institute (1923–1924). He was later a professor of theology and dean of the Russian Orthodox Theological Institute of Paris (1925–1944). During the last twenty years of his life, Bulgakov developed sophiology, a philosophical-theological system built around the concept of *sophia* (Greek for "wisdom"). He outlined these ideas in his *Wisdom of God* (1937).

Bibliography. Naumov, K. *Bibliographie des oeuvres de p.Serge Boulgakov.* Paris, Institut d'études slaves, 1984. Zander, L.A. *Bog i mir: Mirosozertsanie o.Sergiya Bulgakova.* Paris: YMCA, 1948.

Irina Novichenko

BURTON, ORMOND EDWARD (1893–1974). Burton was a Methodist minister, historian, and decorated World War I veteran. Raised near Auckland, New Zealand, he received a religious education at the Remuera School.

Writer of the official history of the New Zealand Division in World War I, he was horrified by the soldiers' experiences in the trenches. In the final years of the war, he was attracted to the philosophy of the Brotherhood of Men of Goodwill. Later, he condemned the New Zealand Church's quiet resignation toward the New Zealander infantry's sacrifice "for British interests" and estimated that the greatest debacle on the western front had been

that both sides vigorously aligned their cause with Christianity.

The Treaty of Versailles, regarded by Burton as a moral and political failure, facilitated his conversion to pacifism. Close to the Young Men's Bible Class movement, and teacher at the Methodist Wesley College in 1930, he was soon nominated minister of the Webb Street Church in Wellington. At the same time, he initiated a widely popular public forum each Sunday afternoon near the Bassin Reserve that frequently included pacifist and religious themes. Involved in the foundation of the New Zealand Christian Pacifist Society in 1936, Burton was arrested during an oration at Pigeon Park in 1940. Convicted along with other clergymen for "obstructing the police," he spent over two years in prison as a result of their dissenting declarations (over eight hundred conscientious objectors were sent to detention camps). Despite his popularity, his cultural marginalization prompted his eviction from the Methodist Church in 1942. He remained outside the fold for fourteen years and did not find a new position until 1955.

Burton's writings that reveal both the intensity of his pacifist convictions and his devotion to the Christian faith include *Shall We Fight?* (1923), *The Silent Division* (1935), *In Prison* (1945), *A Testament of Peace* (1965), *The Ways of God to Man* (1966), and *To Whom Shall We Go?* (1968).

Bibliography. Burton, O.E. *Against Conscription.* Auckland, New Zealand: Pelorus Press, 1949. Locke, Elsie. *Peace People: A History of Peace Activities in New Zealand.* Christchurch, New Zealand: Hazard Press, 1992.

Jérôme Dorvidal

BUSH, GEORGE WALKER (b. 1946). American presidents have routinely recognized the ornamental and inspirational potential of religious rhetoric. Bush, far more than any previous American chief executive, has sought to make religious ideas and language politically respectable and practically significant in shaping government policy. Whether he is restoring religion's rightful place in the public square or threatening historic constitutional barriers between church and state, this has become a thematic flashpoint in assessments of the Bush presidency.

Bush came relatively late to the deep spiritual awareness that now guides both his public and private life. In his youth, he discovered Christianity through the staid rituals and reserved spirituality of the Bush family's New England Presbyterian roots. The process of his rediscovery of Christianity, however, took place not in the land of the Puritans but in Midland, Texas, where George Herbert Walker Bush moved his young son and family in 1948. Together with wife, Barbara, the senior Bush found financial security and eventually wealth from the light, sweet crude that fueled Texas's booming economy. And while the oil business eventually took the family to Houston, the younger Bush would always claim Midland, its capitalism softened by small-town values and Bible Belt Christianity, as his cultural home.

By the 1980s, however, Bush's life had come up decidedly short as a measure of Christian virtue. In line with family tradition, he was educated in New England, first at Phillips Academy in Andover and then Yale University, where he graduated as a history major in 1968. Following a stint in the Texas Air National Guard during the Vietnam War years, Bush entered Harvard Business School, where he finished a master's of business administration degree in 1975. His mediocre academic performance at all levels contrasted sharply with the high marks friends gave him for knowing how to have a good

time. "When I was young and irresponsible," Bush freely admits, "I was young and irresponsible" (Mansfield, 161). By the time he married Laura Welch in 1977, his list of embarrassments included a 1976 arrest for drunk driving, which reflected a serious drinking problem.

The spiritual transformation that shaped Bush's political career came in the mid-1980s when a private conversation with **Billy Graham** left him seeking a deeper, more personal religious experience. Upon returning to Midland, he followed his wife's lead and joined the United Methodist Church. By 1986, alcohol and good times had given way to serious Bible study and spiritual renewal along conservative evangelical lines. A new sense of moral purpose and direction, however, made his profitable departure from Harken Energy and five years as managing general partner of the Texas Rangers in the early 1990s seem less than satisfying. Then in 1994, his successful bid for the Texas governorship finally convinced Bush that his spiritual calling was linked to public service.

As governor, Bush developed a framework for social policy centered on what he called "compassionate conservatism." While conservative critics argued that this call to action implied an inherent moral void in conservatism, Bush denied the charge and concentrated his energy on the operative principle of his philosophy: the faith-based initiative. While Bush's plan did not deny government's role in providing social services, he turned to private faith-based organizations as a vast and underappreciated resource that deserved access to government funds. Under his watch in Texas, private and religious charities could request state funding for welfare services and compete for social service contracts. One state prison became a private enterprise directed by noted Watergate figure turned evangelical leader Charles Colson. So-called Second Chance groups under faith-based leadership gave support to unwed mothers. For Bush, such efforts empowered the faithful without violating constitutional boundaries between church and state.

As a presidential candidate in 2000, Bush seemed to transform his Texas experience into a "faith-based candidacy." He invigorated conservative evangelical supporters when he declared in a Des Moines, Iowa, debate that Jesus Christ was the historical figure he most admired. Far more than **Jimmy Carter** or even **Ronald Reagan,** Bush was regarded as someone who would act broadly upon his spiritual convictions rather simply privatizing them. On the other hand, opponents winced at the possibility that a new religious order might threaten hard-won victories, especially the defense of abortion rights.

In his 2001 inaugural address, Bush laid out policy-making guideposts clearly inspired by his own spiritual experience. Infusing the language of the Declaration of Independence with an intimate spirituality far from Thomas Jefferson's deistic leanings, Bush declared that Americans "are guided by a power larger than ourselves who creates us equal in His image." Noting that "public interest depends on private character," and that God's "purpose is achieved in our duty," Bush promised that policy would trump platitudes: "Church and charity, synagogue and mosque lend our communities their humanity, and they will have an honored place in our plans and in our laws."

As president, Bush has been unable to extract from a divided Congress a solid legislative affirmation of his inaugural commitments, but his creative use of executive power has yielded proximate victories. On his first day in office, Bush halted U.S. support for all international agencies that offered abortion services. He declared a National Day of Prayer and Thanksgiving and placed in Cabinet and high-level White House posts a myriad of openly religious people. Cabinet meetings in the Bush White House opened regularly with prayer, and Bible studies became commonplace among White House staff.

Almost immediately, Bush asked Congress to provide the legislative legs to give stride to faith-based charities seeking government funding. By 2003, both the House and Senate had passed their own plans for funding faith-based charities, but cooperation proved elusive. Disagreement focused particularly on whether faith-based organizations that accepted federal funds could still discriminate in hiring on the basis of religious affiliation.

His congressional hopes dimmed, Bush used executive authority instead to open administrative channels to federal aid for religious groups. The plan mandated no religious restrictions on beneficiaries and ruled out coercive proselytizing in the distribution of aid. Religious discrimination, however, could be a factor in the hiring of employees and appointment of board members. Bush also attached Centers for Faith-Based and Community Initiatives to several federal agencies and told the Federal Emergency Management Agency to accept aid applications from religious nonprofit organizations. For Bush, public humanitarianism born of faith communities celebrates precisely the Constitution's framers' original intent: the state can promote neither institutional religion nor faith, but the charitable private character that faith produces is a public resource worthy of public support.

Although the terrorist attacks of September 11, 2001, on New York's World Trade Center kept foreign policy at the forefront of Bush's executive agenda, religion again played formidably in his ordering of events. Most controversial was his willingness to present the war on terror in biblical proportions as a battle between good and evil. Yet he made clear to an audience in the Islamic Center of Washington that he called for a "crusade" against religious extremists, not Islam itself. "Islam is peace," he insisted, "a faith that brings comfort to a billion people around the world."

Central to Bush's worldview is a concept of democratic freedom that blends sacred and secular meaning to create a powerful sense of mission. It is, as he said in his first inaugural address, not a limited "creed of our country" but an "inborn hope of humanity." Once a "rock in a raging sea," the nation's ideals are now a "seed upon the wind, taking root in many nations" (second inaugural address). Bush makes no claims to a messianic role and freely acknowledges the nation's flaws. Rather, he believes he has been "called" to sustain the nation's role as the leading light of a global democratic movement. From the toppling of the Taliban government in Afghanistan to the invasion of Iraq, the war on terror has only hardened that conviction.

Not surprisingly, the political Left and liberal Protestant critics such as **Robert Bellah, Jim Wallis,** and Jimmy Carter find no divinely anointed mission in Bush's policies. Instead, they see a clear assault on constitutional guarantees of separation between church and state and an unholy alliance between Christianity and an abusive American foreign policy. Particular troubling for these critics is the Bush doctrine of national security based on preemptive war and the open pursuit of regime change in countries deemed hostile to U.S. interests. Similar concerns focus on administration policies that open federal coffers to charitable groups who discriminate on the basis of religion in hiring decisions.

At bottom, Bush's secular opponents view religion as primarily private, individual, and reflective in character, not as raw material for formulating public policy. Bush's plans, they argue, open federal doors to openly sectarian organizations whose intensely religious outlooks will necessarily violate constitutional sanctions. For many Christian groups, however, the humanitarian and communitarian impulse of faith represents a wellspring of social responsibility that the state can no longer afford to ignore. The Christian Left, on the other hand, embraces Christian community and outreach as an ideal radically separate from American economic and political aims.

Whatever the outcome of this debate, Bush made his presidency a standing call for revising religion's relationship to the state, and changes in the Supreme Court in 2005 promised to add another dimension to public scrutiny of Bush's blending of faith and politics. The retirement of Supreme Court justice Sandra Day O'Connor, the death of Chief Justice William Rehnquist, and the appointment of John G. Roberts, Jr., to replace him gave Bush's evangelical and Catholic supporters hope that a more conservative court would overturn *Roe v. Wade,* the 1973 decision that more than any other single factor had politicized conservative Christian groups in the 1980s.

Bibliography. Aikman, David. *A Man of Faith: The Spiritual Journey of George W. Bush.* Nashville, TN: W Publishing Group, 2004. Black, Amy E., Douglas L. Koopman, and David K. Ryden. *Of Little Faith: The Politics of George W. Bush's Faith-Based Initiatives.* Washington, DC: Georgetown University Press, 2004. Bush, George. "First Inaugural Address." January 20, 2001; Bush, George. "Second Inaugural Address." January, 20, 2005. Kengor, Paul. *God and George W. Bush.* New York: HarperCollins, 2004. Mansfield, Stephen. *The Faith of George W. Bush.* New York: Penguin, 2003. Singer, Peter. *The President of Good and Evil.* New York: Penguin, 2004.

Mark Y. Hanley

BUSHNELL, HORACE (1802–1876). Bushnell was one of the most influential and controversial pastor-theologians in nineteenth-century America. From his pulpit at the Congregational North Church in Hartford, Connecticut, he preached and published his way into the center of long-standing theological controversies that divided nineteenth-century New England churches. Although claiming the mantel of orthodoxy against such challenges as Unitarianism, transcendentalism, and Darwinism, Bushnell was also a thorny presence among his establishment compatriots, who, he believed, spent too much time parsing Calvinism's doctrines rather than preaching a personal faith of lifelong spiritual growth, supernatural experience, and vigorous social and political engagement.

Born in 1802 in Litchfield, Connecticut, the precocious and intellectually curious Bushnell graduated from Yale in 1827. A year as editor of the *New York Journal of Commerce* led to a brief flirtation with a law career before Bushnell returned to Yale for theological training. Ordained in 1833, he accepted the pastorate at North Church and remained there until health problems forced his resignation in 1859. Pulpit and pen gave Bushnell ample outlet to drill a consistent theme: conserving the faith's historic doctrines required liberation from outmoded defenses. In *God in Christ, Discourses on Christian Nurture,* and *Nature and the Supernatural,* Bushnell described an experiential faith that rejected both the revivalist's emphasis on flash-point conversion, and the moralist's dependence on reason and human striving. He called for an organic, deeply personal understanding of spiritual and cultural growth that would replace the atomistic tendencies of democratic individualism with true Christian community.

Despite his early sympathies for Jacksonian democracy, he sharply rebuked the cultural and political arrogance that he found among both Whigs and Democrats. "Under any and all forms of government you will have unholy work," he chided in an 1840 sermon. "For man is unholy, your democracy is unholy, full of mischiefs, treacheries, cruelties, and lies." Only Protestant Christianity, he argued, provided an adequate basis for principled political engagement. His 1845 trip to Europe only hardened this position. In his sermon "Barbarism the First Danger," published amid the turmoil of the Mexican-American War, Bushnell celebrated the civilizing tendencies of American republicanism and equality and counseled Protestant vigilance against Roman Catholic influence upon poor and ignorant populations in the western United States.

Amid the rising sectional crisis of the 1850s, Bushnell gave quarter to neither slaveholders nor abolitionists, pronouncing both groups guilty of excessive individualism and political demagoguery. Slavery would disappear peacefully only as steady spiritual progress enlightened humanity and made the institution culturally untenable. As strident Southerners defended their interests through secession in 1860, however, Bushnell's political sympathies settled squarely with the North and the new Republican Party.

Still, he viewed the war as symptomatic of a political failure even deeper than slavery. The war must end the institution, he insisted, but it must also expose the weaknesses in a democratic system devoted to courting the whims of a fickle and selfish electorate. Salvation lay in a deeper public faith in God's sovereignty, historic constitutional principles, and the unchanging moral truths from which they derived. Bushnell joined **Abraham Lincoln** in defining the American union as an organic entity that transcended constitutional arrangements.

A cultural conservatism deeply respectful of immutable moral laws and organic principles of human development, however, also limited Bushnell's vision of racial justice. He expressed uncertainty about the freed people's social and political potential and identified the black community's best hope in embracing the superiority of Anglo-Saxon culture. Only in his later years was Bushnell willing to speculate that God's sovereignty might allow for the "uplifting and spiritual new birth of the African race" (Mullin, 226).

Bibliography. Cheney, Mary Bushnell. *The Life and Letters of Horace Bushnell.* New York, 1880. Cross, Barbara. *Horace Bushnell: Minister to a Changing America.* Chicago: University of Chicago Press, 1958. Mullin, Robert Bruce. *The Puritan as Yankee: A Life of Horace Bushnell.* Grand Rapids, MI: William B. Eerdmans, 2002.

Mark Y. Hanley

BUTTERFIELD, HERBERT (1900–1979). Butterfield was an English Methodist historiographer and diplomatic, religious, and cultural historian. He is best known for his analysis and critique of the Whig, or progressive, conception of history, in which past events are understood and judged in terms of their effects in the present. Although this has been expressed in a more theoretically compelling form by philosophers like R. G. Collingwood and Michael Oakeshott, Butterfield's critical evaluation of the Whig interpretation of history was far more influential on practicing historians because of his status as a working academic historian.

Butterfield was born in Yorkshire, England, in 1900, the son of working-class Methodists. He attended Peterhouse College at Cambridge University and was subsequently a fellow and eventually the master of Peterhouse. He was also a professor of modern history and ultimately became Regius Professor of History at Cambridge. Before going up to Cambridge, Butterfield qualified as a Methodist lay preacher and acted in this capacity in his native Yorkshire and in Cambridge throughout his life. He was knighted in 1968.

Although it initially received mixed reviews, Butterfield's *The Whig Interpretation of History* (1931) was his most significant contribution to the field of historiography and his most influential work. In it, Butterfield criticized the tendency of historians to understand past events solely in terms of their contribution to present circumstances. Instead of transporting the concerns of the present into the past, Butterfield insisted that historians should study the past for its own sake. As part of the general argument and in a specific critique of **Lord Acton,** he also claimed that historians should refrain from making moral judgments about the actions of historical individuals. Butterfield's conclusions were based, in part, upon his particular conception of historical explanation, which is necessarily connected with an imaginative sympathy for historical actors that precludes value judgments. Implicit in his account of sympathy is an understanding of Christian charity and the recognition that sinfulness is a condition common to all human beings.

Butterfield became a well-known public figure as the result of a series of public lectures and radio addresses on the connection between history and Christianity. These were ultimately published as *Christianity and History* in 1949. In it, Butterfield articulates a conception of history that, while distinct from religion, presupposes certain Christian ideas. First, the primary unit of analysis for the historian is the human individual. It is neither societies nor institutions but individual human beings with unique personalities and souls that are truly real. These individual human beings are corrupted by sin yet have free will. Thus, according to Butterfield, historical events ought to be understood as the result of the complex interactions of flawed personalities, not as a dualistic narrative of good versus evil. However, in a concession that complicated his conception of history greatly,

Butterfield acknowledged that the results of these complex interactions can be conceived in a larger way as the result of Providence, which gives ultimate meaning to history.

Butterfield also made significant contributions to the field of international relations theory as one of the founders, along with Martin Wight, Hedley Bull, and Adam Watson, of the so-called English School of international relations. Butterfield's work on international relations stressed the importance of traditional diplomacy and the balance of power. Butterfield emphasized the relation of these traditions to limitations on war and on the vilification of other states. He was also highly critical of the ideological claims of both blocs during the cold war, citing the inherent sinfulness of human nature as a warning against self-righteousness in foreign affairs.

Critics have suggested that Butterfield's later historical work contradicted some of his own earlier methodological strictures, especially his critique of the intrusion of moral judgments in historical writing. For example, in *The Englishman and His History,* which can best be understood as Butterfield's contribution to the English war effort, he explicitly praises the Whig tradition of liberty. Although he distinguishes between Whig politicians, whom he praises, and Whig historians, whom he disparages, Butterfield's account of the particular character of English liberty as resulting from the Whigs' willingness to compromise and their non-ideological style of politics certainly appears to manifest a moral judgment about the value of humility and modesty in politics and life. Indeed, it is this moral judgment, which is taken from his understanding of Christianity, that informs Butterfield's notion of sympathetic imagination and his late work on international relations.

Bibliography. Cowling, Maurice. "Herbert Butterfield, 1900–1979." *Proceedings of the British Academy* 65 (1979): 595–609. McIntire, C.T. *Herbert Butterfield: Historian as Dissenter.* New Haven, CT: Yale University Press, 2004. Sewell, Keith C. "The 'Herbert Butterfield Problem' and Its Resolution." *Journal of the History of Ideas* 64 (4): 599–618.

Kenneth B. McIntyre

C

CAMERON, JOHN (1827–1910). Roman Catholic priest, bishop, and educator, Cameron was born in South River, Antigonish County, Nova Scotia, Canada. He attended St. Andrews Grammar School and was then educated at the Urban College, Rome, where he qualified for the PhD and the doctor of divinity. He studied in the Holy City for ten years and was ordained priest there on July 26, 1853.

Upon returning to his native diocese the following year, he became rector and professor at St. Francis Xavier's College, and later rector for the adjacent St. Ninian's Parish. In 1863, he was assigned as rector for Notre Dame de l'Assomption Cathedral, Arichat, and also acted as vicar-general to Bishop **Colin Francis MacKinnon.** He was then made coadjutor to MacKinnon in 1870 and succeeded him seven years later. Due to his unwavering devotion to Rome, Cameron was asked to settled ecclesiastical disputes in Canada in 1871, 1880, and 1885. In 1886, he relocated the seat of the diocese from Arichat to Antigonish, a decision that significantly antagonized the Acadians. Once he gained full control of the diocese, its unhealthy state became immediately obvious to him. Through effective administration, and with the financial and moral support of the clergy and the people, he reinvigorated and fortified the diocese to a firmer position.

Cameron had interfered in politics since the 1870s, but he was especially calculating in the 1896 federal election. His deliberate meddling on behalf of his close friend Sir John Sparrow David Thompson triggered a hostile response from the clergy and others. Thompson, a convert to Catholicism, established his political career as attorney general of Nova Scotia and ended it as prime minister of the country. Cameron ordered a pastoral letter be read in all diocesan parishes immediately prior to the 1896 election. It contained the directive that the electorate should vote Tory in order that remedial legislation concerning the Manitoba School Question could be successfully introduced by Thompson's party. Cameron demoted clergy and disciplined others who contravened his decree. His actions were to have a detrimental effect upon his career. This situation was not resolved until 1900 and then only upon the intervention of the apostolic delegate. As a result of Cameron's last major dalliance with politics, he was chastised by Rome and his reputation was deemed tarnished by the church hierarchy. He sustained, however, the deference and respect of his people until his death in 1910.

Bibliography. Johnston, A. A. *Antigonish Diocese Priests and Bishops, 1786–1925.* Ed. Kathleen M. MacKenzie. Antigonish, NS: Casket, 1994. MacLean, R. A. *Bishop John Cameron: Piety and Politics.* Antigonish, NS: Casket, 1991.

Kathleen M. MacKenzie

CAMPBELL, ALEXANDER (1788–1866). An Irishman by birth, Campbell was the early leader of the Disciples of Christ movement. He had little interest in American politics until he developed a passion to put an end to the institution of slavery. That fervor developed after Campbell witnessed slavery firsthand when he settled in western Virginia. In 1814, Campbell and his wife, Margaret, received a farm and a few slaves from her father, who wished to keep the couple from moving to Ohio. When he had taught the slaves to read and converted them to Christianity, Campbell emancipated them and provided each with a pension. In *Millennial Harbinger,* the religious journal he founded, Smith explained that "They have souls as well as bodies; they have powers of reason; they have consciences, moral feelings, moral instincts, and are susceptible of spiritual enjoyments, of immortality and eternal life. They have the rights of husbands and of wives, of parents and of children; and any code which takes these away from them is not of God, but of man. Moral training, religious and moral instruction, they must have among their inalienable rights and privileges" (*Harbinger,* May 1845).

After traveling across the South on his many preaching tours, Campbell denounced slavery as "that blighting and blasting curse under which so fair and so large a portion of our beloved country groans" (*Harbinger,* February 1832). Even so, his opposition to slavery was a stark contrast to the extreme views advocated by many abolitionists, because Campbell based all social reform on the synthesis of Christian unity, biblical primitivism, and postmillennialism.

Though Campbell was sympathetic to a Lockean view of natural rights, he insisted that, for the Christian, all conclusions reached from any political theory must be subordinate to the teachings of scripture. Thus, he believed that Christians were free to vote, hold political office, and associate with political parties of their choosing, as long as their votes and associations were governed by biblical precepts.

Campbell's revival movement sought to unite all Christians by replacing complicated, man-made creeds with the simple apostolic gospel of the first century, and by restoring the pattern of worship and church government found in the New Testament. If these principles were followed by enough Christians, he believed, the resulting spiritual revival would eventually produce a thousand years of worldwide peace, social justice, and religious harmony. "Crimes and punishments will cease," Campbell said, and "governments will recognize human rights, and will rest on benevolent principles" (*Harbinger,* January 1841).

To Campbell, the greatest obstacle both to Christian unity and to the onset of the millennium was slavery, for it threatened to divide churches along sectional lines. Hoping to prevent such division, he made his only venture into politics as a delegate to the 1828 Virginia Constitutional Convention. There he intended to present a plan to use the federal surplus to emancipate slaves and colonize them in Africa. Failing to gain a hearing for his proposal, Campbell turned his attention to publishing the *Millennial Harbinger* in 1830. In this religious journal he pledged to write about "the *injustice* which yet remains in many of the political regulations under the best political governments, when contrasted with the *justice* which Christianity proposes, and which the millennial order of society promises," and to make "disquisitions upon the treatment of African slaves, as preparatory to their emancipation, and exaltation from their present degraded condition" (*Harbinger,* January 1830).

Over the next thirty years, Campbell wrote frequently on the subject of slavery, always from a biblical perspective. Thus, he maintained that slavery was not inherently evil, since the New Testament regulates, rather than rejects, the practice. Moreover, Campbell defended the Fugitive Slave Law, arguing that abolitionists who openly violated the law were in rebellion against God-given authority. At the same time, he argued that Christians needed to lead the way in immediately reforming and gradually eliminating all slavery in America, lest it divide the church and the nation. Following the same logic, Campbell denounced the secession of the Southern states, saying, "Secessionism once instituted is not our union dissolved! Secessionism is only another name for disunion" (*Harbinger,* February 1862).

In other areas of social and political concern, Campbell consistently sought to conform his views to scriptural precedent, even if those views were unpopular in nineteenth-century America. Consequently, he opposed the forced relocation of the Cherokee Indians on the grounds that the United States had made treaties pledging to protect the Cherokees' God-given property rights, and such rights could not revoked by a change in government policy.

At a time when many Americans defended the use of military force, Campbell was a pacifist, arguing that New Testament teaching prohibited Christians from participating in war, and that there was no such thing as a truly just war. In 1848, in the aftermath of the Mexican War, Campbell proposed that a congress of nations and a high court of nations be formed to adjudicate international complaints and to remedy grievances before they escalated into armed conflict.

As the national debate over slavery began to degenerate into violence in the 1850s, Campbell began to despair that his dream of peace and religious harmony would not be fulfilled in his lifetime. By 1858, he had pushed back the predicted beginning of the millennial age nearly into the twenty-first century. The coming of the Civil War, however, made even that prediction seem overly optimistic. In 1864, at the height of the conflict, Campbell lamented, "For forty years we have been not an unfaithful nor an unwatchful sentinel upon the walls of Zion, and we had, with perhaps unwarranted fondness, cherished the hope of closing our service beneath peaceful and hopeful skies" (*Harbinger,* January 1864).

Bibliography. Bailey, David T. *Shadow on the Church: Southwestern Evangelical Religion and the Issue of Slavery, 1783–1860.* Ithaca, NY: Cornell University Press, 1985. Harrell, David E., Jr. *Quest for a Christian America: The Disciples of Christ and American Society to 1866.* Nashville, TN: Disciples of Christ Historical Society, 1966. Lunger, Harold L. *The Political Ethics of Alexander Campbell.* St. Louis, MO: Bethany Press, 1954.

Richard A. Koffarnus

CARDENAL, ERNESTO MARTINEZ (b. 1925). Nicaraguan poet, priest, and philosopher Cardenal eloquently represented the burgeoning connections between Marxist and Christian revolutionary ideology during the violent Central American political conflict of the second half of the twentieth-century. While Cardenal's advocacy of liberation theology drew criticism from some sectors of the Catholic hierarchy, his poetry and participation in the Nicaraguan Revolution established him as a hero for revolutionary-minded Christians throughout Latin America.

After a Jesuit secondary education in Managua, Cardenal studied literature at Mexico City's Universidad Nacional Autónoma de México (UNAM) from 1942 to 1946, and at Columbia University in New York from 1948 to 1949. Following a brief stint in Europe, he returned to Nicaragua, where he published various poetic works and became actively involved in the political opposition to the corrupt dictatorship of the Somoza family. After participating in an abortive assault on the presidential palace in 1954 known as the April Rebellion, Cardenal traveled to the United States and entered the Gethsemane Monastery in Kentucky, where he studied with the Trappist monk and fellow poet Thomas Merton. After an illness forced him to complete his religious studies in Mexico and Colombia, he was ordained in 1965. In consultation with Merton, Cardenal then founded a Christian commune at Solentiname, Nicaragua, encouraging other Christian artists and thinkers to join him.

Opposition to the Somoza regime increased throughout the 1970s, eventually culminating in the 1979 overthrow of Anastasio Somoza Debayle and the triumph of the Sandinista National Liberation Front (FSLN). Having gradually become convinced of the compatibility of Christian faith and violent social revolution, Cardenal joined the FSLN in 1977 after the destruction of the Solentiname commune in a government reprisal. He then traveled throughout Latin America, Europe, and the Middle East, gathering support for the Nicaraguan opposition. With the toppling of the Somoza regime in July of 1979, the new Sandinista-led government appointed Cardenal head of the newly established Ministry of Culture, in which capacity he served until 1988. During Cardenal's remaining tenure as Nicaragua's minister of culture, he established programs to promote literacy and the arts but also continued to encourage social and political action among Christians in Nicaragua and throughout the world. His embrace of the more Marxist elements of liberation theology invited a reprimand from Pope **John Paul II** during a papal visit to Central America in 1983. He has since garnered numerous accolades, both for his sociopolitical activism and his writings.

Bibliography. Uriarte, Iván. *La poesía de Ernesto Cardenal en el proceso social centroamericano.* Managua, Nicaragua: Centro Nicaragüense de Escritores, 2000.

Barry Robinson

CARTER, JAMES EARL "JIMMY," JR. (b. 1924). Carter superseded the traditional prejudices of his native Georgia to become the thirty-ninth president of the United States. His foray into national politics presaged a more prominent political role for American evangelicals than in the early twentieth century. Ironically, the so-called Religious Right, which propelled Carter into the White House in 1976, deserted him four years later in favor of **Ronald Reagan,** a person whose record as an active churchman paled next to Carter's.

The son of a peanut farmer, he derived his moral and spiritual bearings from his immersion in the ethos of the local Southern Baptist church in Plains, Georgia. Consonant with the individualistic and pietistic strains of Baptist teachings, Carter was born again at age eleven. He was subsequently baptized and welcomed into the local church. As he matured, Carter assumed the role of Sunday school teacher in his church, a task he continued to enjoy even after he became president.

Carter grew up among blacks and, thus, dissented against the racism that infected many of his fellow white Southerners. The biblical teaching that "God is no respecter of persons" was strongly reinforced by Carter's mother, Lillian, who was probably the dominant familial influence on him. Carter's academic bent, ambition, and predilection for personal discipline led him to the U.S. Naval Academy (1942–1946), where he studied nuclear engineering. Although the navy took him away from the South, the roots that bound Carter to Georgia ran deep, as evidenced by his marriage to Rosalynn Smith, his childhood sweetheart, in 1946. Carter embarked on a naval career but resigned his commission in 1953 to manage the family farm upon the death of his father.

Three traditions synthesized to form Carter's mature religious perspective: Southern evangelicalism, a dissenting tradition that emphasized separation of church and state, and the political realism popularized by **Reinhold Niebuhr.** By the 1960s, Carter's pietism and Niebuhrian perception that politics was an instrument to establish justice in a sinful world had led Carter into a political career. He was elected to two terms in the Georgia State Senate (1962–1966), and the governorship in 1970.

When Carter decided to run for the presidency in 1976, he was essentially a political unknown. Yet, events in the mid-1970s conspired to boost him to the pinnacle of American political power. National unrest, culminating with an unsatisfactory end to the Vietnam War, racial upheaval, and the Watergate scandal, soured many Americans on professional political "insiders." In addition, Carter's promise of "I'll never lie to you," buttressed by his modest lifestyle, seemed refreshing after the disgraced Nixon administration. Carter was also assisted by an evangelical subculture that was coming of age politically. Disgusted by societal trends that they equated with moral depravity, evangelicals organized to redress political indignations like the *Roe v. Wade* decision (1973) of the U.S. Supreme Court. Many of them hoped that an evangelical president like Carter would finally check the social and political liberalization of the age. Carter also appealed shrewdly to the pride of Southerners to elect one of their own to the presidency and thus end the political ostracization of the South that had been in effect since the Civil War.

Although the evangelical aspects of his character helped Carter achieve the presidency, the same traits contributed to his undoing as president. Following Niebuhr, Carter believed that power tends to corrupt sinful human beings. Hence, his insistence on human rights and social justice in foreign

Jimmy Carter, 1977. Courtesy of the Library of Congress

affairs evinced a moderation that some saw as indecisive. Additionally, his historically Baptist view of strict separation between church and state made Carter reluctant to use religious symbolism to promote his political agenda. Critics interpreted his stern moralism as self-righteousness and a stubborn unwillingness to compromise. As Carter had few natural allies in Washington, the outsider status that got him elected was a liability when political coalitions were needed to govern.

Carter's record as president was mixed. Domestic success, particularly in the area of governmental reform, was outweighed by high inflation, unemployment, and federal deficits. The situation was brighter in foreign affairs: full diplomatic recognition was accorded to the People's Republic of China; a new Panama Canal treaty was ratified; and the Camp David peace accord ended the ancient conflict between Israel and Egypt. Unfortunately, the successes were largely undone by the taking of American hostages in Iran by followers of Ayatollah Khomeini in 1979. More than any other event, Carter's preoccupation with the hostages and his inability to recover them shook the faith of the American people in his presidency.

To win reelection in 1980, Carter needed the continued support of Southern evangelicals. However, his inclination to govern as a political moderate ran against the growing conservative impulse in evangelicalism. Groups like the **Moral Majority** succeeded in vilifying Carter for the "selling out" of Taiwan, the "giveaway" of the Panama Canal, and his ineptitude in handling the Iranian hostage crisis. In the 1980 campaign, Carter lost much of the evangelical vote to Reagan, who voiced a religious agenda that harmonized more fully with the values of the religious right. Losing his reelection bid in a landslide, Carter returned to Georgia to assume the life of a private citizen.

After 1981, Carter experienced a public rehabilitation. His establishment of a research center, service as diplomatic envoy, and work for Habitat for Humanity displayed the better characteristics of his evangelical persona. His post-presidential years were not universally triumphant, however. Failing to unify the various theological wings of the Southern Baptist Convention, Carter left the church of his forebears in 2000 to affiliate with the moderate Cooperative Baptist Fellowship. On balance, though, retirement was good for the "best ex-President" of all time (Yancey, 88). Awarded the Nobel Peace Prize for 2002, Carter finally found vindication for himself and the fundamental principles of his evangelical worldview.

Bibliography. Carter, Jimmy. *Keeping Faith.* New York: Bantam, 1982. Holifield, E. Brooks. "Three Strands of Jimmy Carter's Religion." *New Republic,* 6 June 1976, 15–17. Miller, William Lee. *Yankee from Georgia.* New York: Times Books, 1978. Orecklin, Michele. "People (Noble Edition): Jimmy Carter." *Time,* 21 October 2002, 90. Yancey, Philip. "Servant in Chief." *Christianity Today,* 21 May 2002, 88.

Robert H. Krapohl

CARTER, STEPHEN L. (b. 1954). Carter is William Nelson Cromwell Professor of Law at Yale University, where he has taught since 1982. He was born in Washington, D.C., and attended public schools there, as well as in New York City and Ithaca, New York. His undergraduate degree is from Stanford University, and his JD is from Yale. Before accepting a teaching position at Yale, he clerked for Judge Spottswood J. Robinson, III, of the U.S. Circuit Court of Appeals and Justice Thurgood Marshall of the U.S. Supreme Court.

He is the author of eight books (including one best-selling novel) and numerous scholarly articles. He also writes an occasional column for *Christianity Today,* a leading evangelical magazine. His scholarly interests focus on the First Amendment religion clauses, religion in American public life, and the politics of federal judicial appointments.

He has written three books on the general subject of religion and politics: *The Culture of Disbelief: How American Law and Politics Trivializes Religious Devotion* (1993), *The Dissent of the Governed: A Meditation on Law, Religion, and Loyalty* (1998), and *God's Name in Vain: The Wrongs and Rights of Religion in Politics* (2000). The first book garnered a lot of attention, winning praise across the political spectrum from conservative **William F. Buckley** to then-president Bill Clinton.

For Carter, the preeminent role of religion in a pluralistic liberal democracy is to offer an alternative to the dominant secular culture. He repeatedly argues that the quintessential religious stance is oppositional or subversive and that the quintessential religious voice is prophetic—speaking truth to power and calling the authorities to account for their shortcomings. He does not deny that some religions have (in the past) fallen prey to the Constantinian temptation to avail themselves of the coercive power of the state in order to enforce and put into practice their vision of the true and the good, thereby mistaking and ultimately corrupting that vision. But this is not our threat here and now. Instead, we live in a secular welfare state, "in which regulation is everywhere" and "the state gets in the way of almost everything, in the sense that few areas of life escape the administrative apparatus" (Carter, 1993, 144; Carter, 1997, 1643). Our task is to defend the institutions that generate alternative meanings that interfere with the "hegemonic" tendencies of liberalism.

Carter defends pluralism and diversity because it is the best arrangement under which *fallen, finite,* and *fallible* human beings can live their lives on earth. Our task, he argues, is to discern God's will as best we can and live in accordance with it. We undertake our task of discernment with the humble awareness that we are fallible, something that the powerless are more likely to recognize than are the powerful. But we can catch glimpses of God's will: we can know the difference between right and wrong and thereby prophetically identify instances of injustice.

For Carter, then, it is not sufficient for communities of faith to protect themselves from the state in order to provide the centers of difference and resistance. They must and will also venture out of the garden and into the wilderness to bear witness. And in bearing witness, they will "inevitably" have some sort of impact on their fellows: "When religion presses back against the dominant culture, both are changed as a result of the encounter" (Carter, 2000, 172).

He reminds his readers that "the civil rights movement and the abolition movement were church-led revolutions, and they were accomplished because the garden was largely left alone: raised to ideas radically different from the wisdom of the moment, the leaders of those movements, as well as the rank-and-file, put their faith

into practice and changed the nation" (Carter, 2002, 302–3).

In sum, Carter offers a vision of religious freedom that does not reduce it to a matter of individual or communal privacy. He cherishes the public role of religion and insists that it be permitted and indeed encouraged to criticize and transform the larger culture. As a result, he is difficult to categorize. Unlike many progressives, he is not a secularist or a separationist, and unlike many "religionists," he is not simply a conservative.

Bibliography. Carter, Stephen L. *The Culture of Disbelief: How American Law and Politics Trivialize Religious Devotion.* New York: Basic Books, 1993. Carter, Stephen L. *The Dissent of the Governed: A Meditation on Law, Religion, and Loyalty.* Cambridge, MA.: Harvard University Press, 1998. Carter, Stephen L. "The Free Exercise Thereof." *William and Mary Law Review* 38 (July 1997): 1627–1661. Carter, Stephen L. *God's Name in Vain: The Wrongs and Rights of Religion in Politics.* New York: Basic Books, 2000. Carter, Stephen L. "Reflections on the Separation of Church and State." *Arizona Law Review* 44 (Summer 2002): 293–312.

Joseph M. Knippenberg

CATHOLIC BISHOPS' CONFERENCE OF THE PHILIPPINES COMMISSION ON SOCIAL ACTION, JUSTICE AND PEACE (PHILIPPINES). Changes within the Roman Catholic Church during the papacies of John XXIII and Paul VI and the deliberations of the Second Vatican Council (1962–1965) prompted the Catholic Bishops' Conference of the Philippines (CBCP) in 1966 to establish the Episcopal Commission on Social Action (ECSA) and an administrative arm, the National Secretariat of Social Action (NASSA), known after 1969 as the National Secretariat of Social Action, Justice and Peace. Between 1969 and 1974, the Mindanao-Sulu Secretariat of Social Action (MISSSA), the Visayas Secretariat of Social Action (VISSA), and the Luzon Secretariat of Social Action (LUSSA) were established to coordinate social action programs regionally.

A major goal of ECSA and NASSA was the creation of social action centers (SACs) in every diocese in the country to organize and coordinate social action activities and to stimulate the development of SACs at the parish level. In the years just after ECSA and NASSA were founded, the bishops focused on initiating self-help programs among poor farmers, agricultural workers, and fisherfolk and on teaching the meaning of social justice. Over the past thirty years, however, the social action activities of ECSA and NASSA have expanded dramatically.

By 2003, there were no fewer than eighty SACs throughout the country that initiated, implemented, and directed social action projects in local churches and basic ecclesial communities (BECs). Currently, NASSA is involved in a multiplicity of social action programs and campaigns, including building BECs, improving the conditions of women and children affected by globalization, protecting the environment for sustainable development, educating Filipinos for responsible democratic government, and helping improve agricultural productivity among poor peasants. Additionally, NASSA (which maintains a Web site) engages in relief and rehabilitation work and remains an important advocacy agency of the Catholic hierarchy's social action efforts.

Bibliography. Fabros, Wilfredo. *The Church and Its Social Involvement in the Philippines, 1930–1972.* Quezon City, Manila: Ateneo de Manila Press, 1988. Giordano, Pasquale T. *Awakening to Mission: The Philippine Catholic Church 1965–1981.* Quezon City, Manila: New Day, 1988. National Secretariat for Social Action. 2003. www.nassa.org.ph.

Robert L. Youngblood

CATHOLIC POLITICAL PARTIES (ECUADOR). The Partido Conservador Ecuatoriano (Ecuadorian Conservative Party), formed by the caudillo Gabriel García Moreno in 1869, long represented Catholic political interests in Ecuador. As president of Ecuador (1861–1865, 1869–1875), García Moreno allowed the Jesuit order to be reestablished in Ecuador, negotiated a favorable concordant with the Vatican, and greatly expanded the power of the Catholic Church in all aspects of Ecuador's political, social, and educational institutions.

After García Moreno's death in 1875, the Conservative Party continued his policies. The Liberal Revolution of 1895, led by General Eloy Alfaro, broke the Conservative's hold on the state and reduced the Conservative Party to secondary status. During much of the liberal period (1895–1925), Catholic political power was represented by the influential archbishop of Quito, **Federico González Suárez,** who opposed liberal reforms. In 1919 the Conservative Party reaffirmed its commitment to Roman Catholicism by consecrating itself to the Divine Heart of Jesus. Its agenda was approved by Archbishop Aurelio Espinosa Polít, who along with his brother, José Espinosa Polít, also an archbishop, zealously fought for the integration of Catholic dogma in state policy.

In 1925, Dr. Julio Tobar Donoso attempted to remold the Conservative Party in the image of the **Italian Popular Party;** nevertheless, the bishops continued to exert their influence over the party well into the 1950s. In 1956 the Conservative Party gained influence by backing a rightist coalition knows as Alianza Popular (Popular Alliance), which elected Dr. Camilo Ponce Enríquez president of Ecuador. Ponce had formed his own Catholic party, Movimiento Cristiano Social (MSN, Christian Social Movement), in 1951.

In the 1960s another party, the Partido Demócrata Cristiano (Christian Democratic Party) was formed with official affiliation with the international Christian Democratic movement. The Coalición Institucionalista Demócrata (CID, Institutional Democratic Coalition), founded in 1965, was a party that also professed to represent Catholic political interests in Ecuador. While right of center like the MSN, the CID, however, was formed to promote the political career of a particular candidate.

In the last quarter of the twentieth century, Catholic politics in Ecuador had been fragmented and represented by various parties that usually formed coalitions during presidential elections. For example, in 1984 the Conservative Party joined forces with the Partido Social Cristiano (Christian Social Party) and the Liberal Party to form the Frente Nacional de Reconstrucción (National Reconstruction Front), which elected León Febres Cordero president. However, while conservative candidates such as Febres Cordero appeal to Catholic officials and voters, it is evident that church control of particular political parties in Ecuador has waned in recent years.

Bibliography. Bialek, Robert W. *Catholic Politics: A History Based on Ecuador.* New York: Vantage Press, 1963.

George M. Lauderbaugh

CATHOLIC WORKER MOVEMENT (UNITED STATES). Founded in 1933 in New York City by Peter Maurin and **Dorothy Day,** the Catholic Worker movement continues today as a lay apostolate serving the poor. In his famous essay "What the Catholic Worker Believes," Maurin described the principles of the movement as "gentle personalism," "the personal obligation of looking after the needs of our brother," "the daily practice of Works of Mercy," and "Houses of Hospitality for the immediate relief of those who are in need."

The Catholic Worker criticizes both socialism and capitalism as dehumanizing systems of social and economic organization. It advocates a decentralized and simpler society based on communitarian Christianity and the practice of love in action. The movement does not oppose technology per se but does call for its use in ways that foster human dignity and community. The movement is also committed to Christian pacifism. This commitment caused some friction during World War II, when Day refused to compromise on this central tenet of the movement.

This radical approach to social justice has been a defining hallmark of the movement since its inception. In contrast to liberal Catholic social thinkers like John Ryan, who was the dominant reform advocate in the American church during the early twentieth century, Day and Maurin did not seek moderate social reform through political means. They instead advocated the creation of what Maurin called "a new society within the shell of the old." Epitomizing the evangelical strand of Christian social action, the Catholic Worker believes Christians are called to perform radical acts of sacrifice and charity in imitation of Christ.

The best-known aspects of the movement remain the *Catholic Worker* newspaper and the Houses of Hospitality. The first issue of the paper, which sought to popularize the church's position on social justice, was distributed on May 1, 1933, in New York's Union Square at the price of a penny per copy.

The first House of Hospitality was also opened in 1933 in New York City. The movement now operates over 175 Catholic Worker houses throughout the world, with 155 in thirty-six U.S. states. The houses serve as a source of food and shelter for the poor and a residence for members of the movement. Catholic Workers live in voluntary poverty and dedicate themselves to serving the poor and pursuing social justice in conformity with the program of the movement.

The movement is almost exclusively urban in its focus. Maurin originally called for the creation of farming communes, to be called agronomic universities. One such farm was formed in 1936. This aspect of the movement, however, has never flourished, particularly in comparison to the Houses of Hospitality.

Bibliography. Day, Dorothy. *The Long Loneliness: An Autobiography.* San Francisco: Harper & Row, 1952. Roberts, Nancy L. *Dorothy Day and the Catholic Worker.* Albany: State University of New York Press, 1984.

Zachary R. Calo

CENTER FOR PUBLIC JUSTICE (UNITED STATES). The Center for Public Justice is a public policy organization, now located in Annapolis, Maryland, which undertakes to bring the principles of a Christian worldview to bear on the political realm. It is rooted in the European Christian democratic tradition, particularly as developed in the Netherlands by **Guillaume Groen van Prinsterer** (1801–1876), **Abraham Kuyper** (1837–1920), and Herman Dooyeweerd (1894–1977).

The principle of "sphere sovereignty," or what has more recently come to be called "differentiated responsibility," is the most characteristic feature of this tradition and undergirds a nonliberal approach to the limited state. Sphere sovereignty has three primary implications: (1) ultimate sovereignty belongs to God alone; (2) all earthly sovereignties or authorities (including state, church, family, marriage, and voluntary associations) are subordinate to and derivative from God's sovereignty; and (3) there is no earthly sovereignty from which the others derive. This third point most sharply distinguishes sphere sovereignty from its otherwise similar Roman Catholic counterpart of subsidiarity and undergirds what might be called a nonhierarchical conception of civil society.

The center was founded in 1977 as the Association for Public Justice (APJ), which grew out of two predecessor organizations, the National Association for Christian Political Action and the Christian Action Foundation, both of which had their beginnings at Dordt College in Sioux Center, Iowa. The work of APJ was divided for tax purposes between two legal entities, APJ proper and the APJ Education Fund. While the former was intended to engage in direct efforts to influence the policy process, the latter undertook the sort of policy analysis characteristic of a think tank.

In 1990 the APJ board of trustees undertook a major reorganization, essentially putting the lobbying arm on ice and shifting virtually all its activities to the Education Fund, which was renamed the Center for Public Justice. In 1994 the center sponsored a major conference on welfare policy, the proceedings of which were eventually published as *Welfare in America.* Since then it has been active in supporting the charitable choice provisions of the Welfare Reform Act of 1996, which prohibit the federal government from discriminating against overtly religious social service organizations in its disbursement of public welfare funds. More recently the center has been working on issues related to international justice and governance and at this writing is preparing to undertake a major study of healthcare policy. But probably its most enduring commitment has been securing public support for parental control of education, a position rooted in Kuyper's understanding of sphere sovereignty.

The center cannot be understood apart from the efforts of James W. Skillen, formerly its executive director and now president. Having received a PhD in political science at Duke University under John Hallowell, Skillen taught at Messiah, Gordon, and Dordt colleges before taking up the leadership of APJ in 1981.

The center has an approximate counterpart in Canada, Citizens for Public Justice, which was established in 1963 and is located in Toronto.

Bibliography. Carlson-Thies, Stanley W., and James W. Skillen, eds. *Welfare in America: Christian Perspectives on a Policy in Crisis.* Grand Rapids, MI: William B. Eerdmans, 1996. Center for Public Justice. 2005. www.cpjustice.org. Skillen, James W. *Recharging the American Experiment: Principled Pluralism for Genuine Civic Community.* Grand Rapids, MI: Baker Books and the Center for Public Justice, 1994. Skillen, James W. *The Scattered Voice: Christians at Odds in the Public Square.* Edmonton, Alberta: Canadian Institute for Law, Theology and Public Policy, 1996. Skillen, James W., ed. *The School-Choice Controversy: What Is Constitutional?* Grand Rapids, MI: Baker Books, 1993.

David T. Koyzis

CENTER PARTY [DEUTSCHE ZENTRUMSPARTEI] (GERMANY). From the 1860s until 1933, the German Center Party, the Deutsche Zentrumspartei, claimed to be the political representation of Germany's Catholic laity. From the very beginning, its founding leader, Ludwig Windthorst, insisted on the party's independence from the Catholic hierarchy, which the party maintained until its dissolution.

The party's members and supporters came from backgrounds as heterogeneous as German Catholicism itself. It included Westphalian aristocrats (until 1918 most Bavarians and Rhinelanders) but also Silesians, as well as some Poles in Prussia's eastern provinces. From 1871 until 1918, the Center Party also enjoyed support in Alsace-Lorraine. During the course of its history, the party increasingly lost the support of working-class Catholics to other parties, and the most conservative nationalists switched their allegiance to the DNVP, the German Nationalist Party. Nonetheless, unlike most other nonsocialist parties, the Center was able to retain and even increase its share of the votes in the last elections of the Weimar Republic, largely by attracting those of newly enfranchised women.

Throughout its history, the Center Party actively defended the particular needs of its Catholic members. Thus, during the Kulturkampf, the party was a target of Chancellor Otto von Bismarck's failed efforts to establish a protestant-nationalist-Prussian alliance against socialists and Catholics. Instead of breaking the political will of German Catholics, Bismarck succeeded only in drawing them closer to the Center Party than they would ever again draw to any Catholic political party. When Bismarck's successors realized that their struggle against socialism was doomed by demographics, they included the Center Party when assembling parliamentary majorities. By this means, Center Party leaders could dismantle most anti-Catholic legislation and preserve particularly Catholic interests.

In the early 1900s, the party increasingly asserted itself, for example, by demanding an investigation into the misconduct of German colonial authorities. Nonetheless, the party continuously struggled against anti-Catholic discrimination, particularly in the Prussian army and civil service, which included academic institutions as well.

After the revolution, conditions for the Center Party changed as radically as they did for any other party. The party fought against socialist efforts to end the denominational nature of the public schools. Its conservative members decried the concept of popular sovereignty as blasphemous, and the revolution itself as a sin against a divinely mandated order. Its former Bavarian members founded the more conservative particularist Bavarian People's Party (Bayrische Volkspartei) and some members of the party's right wing moved to the German Nationalist People's Party (Deutschnationale Volksparei).

Without success, Adam Stegerwald of the Christian labor movement urged the Center Party to transform itself into a broadly Christian-based party. Newly enfranchised women became crucial electoral supporters for the party. Despite deep internal divisions that cut several ways between Catholic workers representatives, Westphalian and Silesian magnates, and political progressives and conservatives, the Center Party became one of the Weimar Republic's most important supporters, primarily out of a sense of responsibility, rather than from a sincere commitment to Weimar's parliamentary democracy.

The Center Party participated in almost every cabinet and led nine of the twenty governments between the revolution of 1918 and the Nazi seizure of power. Germany's first labor minister, for instance, was a Catholic priest and member of the Center Party. Thus, Germany was one of the first countries to introduce unemployment benefits. In domestic politics, the party continued its Wilhelmine policies of fierce and repeated obstruction by insisting on maintaining Catholic values in social, educational, and moral legislation. In foreign policy, the party resented the Versailles Treaty and its consequences as much as any other, but its commitment to Catholic values of serving the people's needs above all permitted it to produce parliamentary majorities for the treaty, and for acceptance of the 1921 reparations ultimatum, the Dawes Plan, and the Young Plan. It was a Centrist chancellor, **Josef Wirth,** who concluded the Rapallo agreement to prevent the Allies from playing Russian and German interests against each other. Cologne's Center Party lord mayor and post-1945 chancellor **Konrad Adenauer** forced Foreign Minister Stresemann to consider the needs of the Rhenish population in concluding temporary agreements with the French occupation forces.

In the later twenties, the party increasingly shifted to the right, isolating progressives such as Wirth who were sincerely committed to a republican democracy rather than to the Weimar Republic for lack of a better alternative. Between 1930 and 1932, the party supported **Heinrich Brüning** as technocratic chancellor by presidential fiat without parliamentary legitimacy. Without much mourning, the republic had fallen; Centrists now wondered what would replace it.

The final year before the party's dissolution in July 1933 is, historiographically, its most controversial. As early as August 1932, Center Party leaders sought talks with the Nazis to form a broad anticommunist coalition government, even though party leaders and the German hierarchy both had condemned National Socialism. These talks ended fruitlessly. In the first and only fairly free elections after Hitler's appointment as chancellor, the Center Party was the only non-nationalist party to increase its share of the vote by winning votes as the only remaining realistic noncommunist and non-Nazi alternative.

In late March 1933, the new parliament passed Germany's most controversial legislation ever, the Enabling Act, which gave the regime very broad powers, and on the basis of which it governed until Germany's defeat twelve years later. Center Party votes were crucial to provide the two-thirds majority necessary for this constitution-changing legislation. Many historians have argued that this vote was a quid pro quo for Nazi guarantees for Catholic civil servants and for the long-sought Concordat between Germany and the Holy See, concluded in June 1933. Speaking for such an arrangement is the fact that the Center Party leader Monsignor **Ludwig Kaas,** was a Catholic cleric who decamped to Rome shortly after the crucial vote, as well as the subsequent limited endorsement of the new regime by the German bishops. There is, however, no documentary evidence to support the existence of such an arrangement. Furthermore, the party's fierce independence from the Catholic hierarchy, the existing evidence of protracted agonizing debates among Center Party leaders—which was concluded only by an appeal to party unity—and the evidence that Hitler had promised the Center Party additional legal safeguards against abuse of the Enabling Act, safeguards that never appeared, make it unlikely that the Center

Party sacrificed Germany to the Nazis for narrow particularist interests.

The party officially disbanded in July 1933. Many of its members suffered persecution by the Nazis; some engaged in resistance. After Germany's defeat in 1945, some former members refounded the party, but its time had passed. Its heir, the **Christian Democratic Union**, was an interdenominational party based on broad Christian interests and values.

Bibliography. Cary, Noel D. *The Path to Christian Democracy: German Catholics and the Party System from Windthorst to Adenauer.* Cambridge: Cambridge University Press, 1996. Evans, Ellen Lovell. *The German Center Party, 1870–1933: A Study in Political Catholicism.* Carbondale: Southern Illinois University Press, 1981. Morsey, Rudolf. *Die Deutsche Zentrumspartei, 1917–1923.* Düsseldorf, Germany: Droste, 1966. Morsey, Rudolf. *Der Untergang des politischen Katholizismus: Die Zentrumspartei zwischen christlichem Selbstverständnis und "Nationaler Erhebung" 1932/33.* Stuttgart, Germany: Belser, 1977. Ruppert, Karsten. *Im Dienst am Staat von Weimar: Die Deutsche Zentrumspartei 1923–1930.* Darmstadt, Germany: Droste, 1992.

Martin Menke

CEREJEIRA, MANUEL GONÇALVES (1888–1977). The head of the Portuguese Catholic Church during the lengthy Salazar dictatorship, Cerejeira backed the regime's main policies, including the wars it fought from 1961 to 1974 to try to retain its African colonies. Thanks to his close relationship with Salazar, the church enjoyed state patronage, but it came at the price of alienating many liberal-minded Catholics active in social movements.

Cerejeira grew up in northwest Portugal, the main stronghold of Catholicism. He was ordained a priest in 1911 shortly after the installation of a republican regime (1910–1926) which was strongly anti-clerical. By the time he obtained his doctorate in medieval history in 1918, he was a prominent figure in Catholic politics and had struck up what would be a durable alliance with Antonio de Oliveira Salazar, the country's future ruler.

Cerejeira became a bishop in 1928 when Salazar was already in government. A conservative military coup in 1926 had become the launching pad for a right-wing dictatorship which Salazar civilianized in the early 1930s after he stabilized Portugal's chaotic finances. The dictator drew his most reliable political support from the nation's Catholics, headed by Cerejeira since August 1929, when the Vatican appointed him cardinal patriarch of Lisbon. A period of Catholic revival got underway, crowned by the 1940 Concordat with the Vatican; but Salazar was constrained by the fact a section of the political elite was still anticlerical and was committed to the retention of civil marriage and civil divorce.

Cerejeira strove to prevent Salazar's right-wing dictatorship from moving in a totalitarian direction. It is believed that Pope **Pius XII** had given instructions for him to take charge of the Catholic Church if the forum had been detained by the Nazis. But Cerejeira refused to support any return to democracy after 1945, when Portugal was increasingly seen as an archaic survivor from the fascist era. Progressive clergy were driven out of the church, which prevented it from becoming a church of resistance, as in Franco's Spain. In 1967, Cerejeira arranged the visit to Portugal of Pope **Paul VI** for the fiftieth anniversary of the Miracle of Fatima. He retired in 1971, a year after the death of his secular ally Salazar and three years before the overthrow of the dictatorship. The secularism that he had long opposed once more reasserted itself, and Catholicism lost much of its influence in a rapidly urbanizing society.

Bibliography. Braga da Cruz, Manuel. *As Origens da Democracia Cristã e o Salazarismo.*

Lisbon, Spain: Editorial Presença/Gabinete de Investigaçōes Sociais, 1979.

Tom Gallagher

CHALMERS, THOMAS (1780–1847). Chalmers is most famous for his leading of the Disruption of the Established Church of Scotland in 1843, resulting in the creation of the Free Church. He also played a pivotal role in the shaping of the modern transatlantic debate about poverty and its attendant problems in an industrial age. Chalmers was born in 1780 in the fishing village of Anstruther in Fife. Educated at St. Andrews and then Edinburgh universities, he was influenced by the moral philosophy of the Scottish Enlightenment thinkers and by the economic writings of Thomas Malthus and Adam Smith. He returned to east Fife in 1803 to become the minister of the small rural parish of Kilmany, and there he converted from a somewhat tepid moderate Christianity to an evangelical outlook. Inspired by works such as **William Wilberforce**'s *Practical View of Christianity* and **Hannah More**'s *Practical Piety,* he moved in 1815 to the Tron parish, set in the emerging industrial heartland of the city of Glasgow.

Once in Tron, Chalmers quickly gained recognition as a dynamic preacher. Between the end of 1815 and October 1816, he gave a midweek series of sermons entitled the *Astronomical Discourses* before packed congregations of the Glasgow middle classes. Published in 1817, these quickly became bestsellers, and Chalmers's fame as a dynamic preacher spread. Invited to London to preach, he journeyed there in 1817 and became the evangelical toast of the city. He was introduced to Wilberforce and the **Clapham Sect,** and on his triumphant journey back to Scotland, he visited Hannah More in Bristol and stayed in Liverpool at the home of the Scottish-born John Gladstone, father of the future prime minister **William Ewart Gladstone.**

On his return to Glasgow, Chalmers became increasingly aware of the limitations of his ministry to the poor. He concluded that his efforts to evangelize were being thwarted by declining church attendance and a demoralized populace. Part of that demoralization, he believed, was the growing breakdown of the traditional Scottish system of poor relief, which had relied mainly on church collections gathered in the Established Church of Scotland and the strict limiting of official relief controlled by the kirk sessions to the deserving poor: widows, orphans, the lame, and the insane. However, how could the deserving poor be identified in a large urban parish where anonymity prevailed, where church building could not keep pace with the growing urban populations, and where the ensuing low church attendance meant collections that were inadequate for the official parish inhabitants they were supposed to serve? In addition, the increasing pressure from large-scale unemployment was encouraging the civic authorities to provide official public relief to the able-bodied unemployed, thus turning them into paupers, that is, official recipients of charity. Chalmers argued passionately that the latter action would result in a lazy, dependent, immoral population as automatic public relief could be relied upon, and independence and hard work were not their own rewards. His aim became the development of a method to relieve poverty without creating pauperism.

As Chalmers's ideas developed, he urged the city authorities to give him the chance to test his theories. Indeed, by 1819 a new parish, St. John's, was created, and Chalmers set about demonstrating the viability of his emerging vision of a "godly commonwealth" (Brown, 112). His solution was to re-create a more "natural" system of social interaction—the rural idyll within the darkness of the city—by using his "locality principle" to break the inner city into small, manageable units where a team of elders, deacons, Sunday school teachers (male and female), the minister, and his assistant would combine in a "moral police force" that would ensure that all other possible means of private charity from neighbors and relatives had been exhausted before any official parochial relief was proffered (Chalmers, 14:25–71, 92–93, 119, 133–41, 208–9, 250).

As Chalmers worked on his social experiment, the popularity of his next series of midweek sermons, *The Application of Christianity to the Commercial and Ordinary Affairs of Life,* and the publication of his *Christian and Civic Economy* between 1819 and 1826 illustrate his growing stature as an authority on the new urban conditions. Due to his identification as an expert on poor-relief management, Chalmers was called to testify before the Royal Commission on Poor Laws in England and Wales, and the Royal Commission on Poor Laws in Scotland. Although both commissions in the end produced Poor Relief Acts for England (1834) and Scotland (1845) that would not support Chalmers's ideal of exclusive reliance on voluntary relief, the rigor of the "workhouse test" in rooting out malingerers reflects some of the spirit of his ideas and the mood of the times.

Chalmers left St. John's in 1823 but continued to write and preach about poverty and pauperism. Although he conducted another parochial experiment in the West Port of Edinburgh in the 1840s, his ministerial career after St. John's was mainly academic, not pastoral, as he took up positions in turn as professor of moral philosophy at St. Andrews University, and then as professor of divinity at the University of Edinburgh in 1828. In 1829 he entered the political arena directly as he campaigned alongside the Scottish Whigs for the Catholic Emancipation Act. Chalmers was by no means a Whig by inclination, but he believed nonetheless that Catholic emancipation was vital in order to facilitate the education and thus moral responsibility of the growing Catholic population in Scotland alongside the Protestant majority. In support of the latter and as part of his bid to section the cities into microcosms of the countryside, Chalmers also became an active advocate for the provision of new churches and for state aid in the expansion of education. Between 1834 and 1841, Chalmers headed the Church of Scotland's Church Extension campaign, which ultimately resulted in the creation of over 220 parish churches in Scotland. Ultimately, however, the tensions between the moderate and evangelical parties within the Church of Scotland and the government in London over patronage would be exacerbated in these years. Eventually, a monumental clash with the state resulted concerning the rights of male parishioners to at least veto, if not directly select, their ministers. As Brown and Fry point out, Chalmers and the Scottish evangelical party came to perceive the issue as one of spiritual independence as opposed to secular control, and in 1843, Chalmers led over 450 Church of Scotland ministers and nearly half of the lay membership in their historic abandonment of their parishes and kirks into the Free Church of Scotland (Brown and Fry, viii).

Chalmers was in many ways physically weakened by the ecclesiastical struggle. However, his books and pamphlets continued to be popular in Britain, continental Europe, the United States, and Canada as each area in turn dealt with the phenomenon of modern industrial society. American philanthropists and churchmen such as James Lennox, John Griscom, Joseph Tuckerman, and **Lewis Tappan** read his *Christian and Civic Economy* and were influenced by it in their work in New York and Boston. Chalmers's impact can also be seen in the origins and philosophy of the Charity Organization Society in both Britain and the United States, and his visitation principles in many ways underpinned the development of the casework approach embraced by modern social work. In addition, his inclusion of women in his local visitation cadres added to the respectability emerging on both sides of the Atlantic concerning the direct involvement of middle-class women in philanthropic work in the slums of the industrial age.

The wounds caused by the Disruption would by and large eventually heal. The problems of alleviating want in industrial and industrializing societies have proven more resilient. It is remarkable that despite the fact that Chalmers's vision of voluntary charity would not materialize on either side of the Atlantic, echoes of his rhetoric and practical solutions are still heard in the political debate over poverty today.

Bibliography. Brown, Stewart J. *Thomas Chalmers and the Godly Commonwealth.* Oxford: Oxford University Press, 1982. Brown, Stewart J., and Michael Fry, eds. *Scotland in the Age of Disruption.* Edinburgh: Edinburgh University Press, 1993. Chalmers, Thomas. *The Works of Thomas Chalmers.* 25 vols. Glasgow, 1835–1842. Cheyne, A. C., ed. *The Practical and the Pious: Essays on Thomas Chalmers.* Edinburgh: St. Andrew Press, 1985. Hanna, William. *Memoirs of Dr. Chalmers.* Edinburgh, 1849–1852. Mohl, Raymond A. *Poverty in New York 1783–1825.* New York: Oxford University Press, 1971.

Mary T. Furgol

CHAMBERLAIN, HOUSTON STEWART (1855–1927). The expatriate son of a British admiral, Chamberlain became one of the leading advocates of an extreme nationalist and racist form of Christianity in Germany at the beginning of the twentieth century. An ardent follower of the composer and cultural reformer Richard Wagner, who propagated moral regeneration through art, the superiority of the German race, and a return to "authentic" Christian values, Chamberlain exerted considerable influence on Germany's educated elites not only through his publications but also through an extensive correspondence with Kaiser Wilhelm II and other high-ranking officials. His religio-racist views justified pan-German imperialism and helped to form the ideology of the National Socialist Party after the First World War. When the Nazis came to power in 1933, Chamberlain was officially celebrated as one of the heralds of the Third Reich.

His most celebrated and widely distributed work was the anti-Semitic tome *The Foundations of the Nineteenth Century,* published in German in two volumes in 1899. Chamberlain interpreted history since the death of Christ as a continuing conflict between the Aryan-Christian worldview of the Germanic race and Jewish secularism and materialism, to which he attributed the degeneration of the modern world. With revivalist zeal, he exhorted his readers to awaken the religio-idealistic powers slumbering within and use them to strengthen the nation. According to Chamberlain, Germanic Christianity was a religion of pure and immediate experience superior to historical, earth-centered, and allegedly materialistic Judaism. Chamberlain helped to popularize the claim of racial anti-Semites that Jesus was Aryan, not Jewish.

For Chamberlain, religion, like racialism, served primarily the purpose of unifying and strengthening the recently united German Reich and justifying authoritarian power politics, thereby counteracting the reformist and revolutionary doctrines of the Left. According to Chamberlain, the Achilles heel of modern German culture was the lack of a religion commensurate with the Germans' unique gifts of freedom and loyalty. A racially conscious Germanic Christianity would promote reverence for the hierarchical monarchical state and purge un-German elements (democracy, liberalism, socialism) from the body politic Although Chamberlain admired Roman Catholicism as a bulwark against liberalism, he accused the church of dogmatism and opposed it as an international institution that competed with the nation for the allegiance of German Catholics. Despite his suspicions of progressive and egalitarian tendencies in the German Lutheran churches, Chamberlain looked to Lutheranism for the doctrinal basis of a German national church. Unlike most *völkisch* publicists of a German-Christian creed, such as Paul de Lagarde (1827–1891) or Adolf Bartels (1862–1945), who blamed St. Paul for introducing Jewish principles into the church, Chamberlain admired St. Paul (to whom he ascribed Hellenic blood) for his rejection of Judaism. His fulsome acclaim of Martin Luther's heroic reassertion of freedom of conscience through the doctrine of justification by faith led George Bernard Shaw to call *The Foundations* "the greatest Protestant Manifesto ever written."

A strong believer in Germany's divinely sanctioned mission to regenerate and lead the world, Chamberlain provided the ideological underpinnings of the "positive Christianity" espoused by the Nazis in their 1920 party program. A Houston Stewart Chamberlain Association for Germanic Christianity was founded in 1940, with several members of the Wagner family as honorary members. By emphasizing the redirection of the will toward action and downplaying the notion of personal sin, Chamberlain hoped to make Christianity useful to German supremacism. His baleful role in twentieth-century German history continues to serve as a cautionary example of the destructive potential in the historic link between racism, nationalism, and religion in right-wing politics.

Bibliography. Field, Geoffrey G. *Evangelist of Race: The Germanic Vision of Houston Stewart Chamberlain.* New York: Columbia University Press, 1981. Stackelberg, Roderick. *Idealism Debased: From Völkisch Ideology to National Socialism.* Kent, OH: Kent State University Press, 1981.

Roderick Stackelberg

CHANNING, WILLIAM ELLERY (1780–1842). Although he was the son of Rhode Island's attorney general and the grandson of a signer of the Declaration of Independence, Channing chose the ministry over politics during his senior year at Harvard because of his concern for the growing influence of French infidelity on American society. Nevertheless, his theology dictated that he be involved in numerous political and social concerns, including public education and antiwar, labor, and antislavery movements.

When he was just twenty-three years old, Channing was ordained minister of the Federal Street Congregational Church in Boston, a position in which he served for the remainder of his life. In his sermons, Channing developed and defended a Unitarian theology that challenged the traditional Calvinist doctrines that dominated New England churches at that time. The point of Channing's message was that Christianity's primary purpose is to cultivate the human soul's innate moral attributes. By developing these attributes, humans become more and more like God, which is precisely what the Father wants. Knowledge of God is not enough. Identity with God is what the Deity desires for His people.

By 1838, Channing's focus had progressed to a concept of "self-culture," or education of the individual. To Channing, self-culture meant a dedication to developing the human faculties (the conscience, the religious principle or sense, and the intellect) together in harmony. Channing believed that proper education subordinated a person's intellectual development to conscience and an innate religious principle, because "reading and study are not enough to perfect the power of thought" (Channing, 16). Thus, Channing's doctrine of self-culture provided a theological justification for his social agenda. While Unitarians and evangelicals shared a goal of reawakening society's religious affections, Channing dismissed the latter's revivalism as emotionalistic and anti-intellectual. Instead, he favored literary and cultural pursuits as the preferred means to cultivate religious and moral sentiments, and by them, to effect change beneficial to society. Writing, preaching, and encouraging the organization of charitable societies were his principle contributions to the various causes he supported.

Early in his ministry, Channing took an interest in the education of children and worked with reformers such as Horace Mann in their efforts to establish public, nonsectarian education for all children. When the War of 1812 broke out, Channing was vocal in his opposition to the conflict, partly because of its harm to the New England economy and partly because he did not consider it a war of self-defense. It came as no surprise when, in 1815, at a meeting in Channing's study, opponents of the war founded the country's first significant peace society.

Channing's greatest social challenge came from the issue of slavery. Raised by his parents' slaves in Newport, he did not fully appreciate the evils of the practice until he spent two years in Virginia following his graduation from Harvard in 1798. Channing began to speak publicly against slavery as early as 1825, but he shunned the **abolitionist** movement because their inflammatory language had precipitated violence at some antislavery meetings.

When one of Channing's disciples challenged him to construct a reasoned criticism of slavery, he responded in 1835 by publishing the book *Slavery*. There he argued that all humans, slave and free alike, share the same spiritual nature and are made in the image of God, with an innate capacity for self-improvement. Slavery is an affront to God, therefore, because it treats humans like property and denies them the spiritual progress God intended. Moreover, Channing insisted, all humans possess inherent God-given, sacred rights, which no society ought to violate. Anyone who had to assess spiritual or political worthiness through the lens of skin color lacked the discernment afforded by true Christianity.

The book outraged some of his parishioners, who deemed it too radical, and disappointed abolitionists, who thought it too moderate. Despite criticism on both sides, Channing continued to press the issue to the end of his life. In *The Duty of the Free States* (1842), Channing argued that the moral law against slavery supersedes the nation's slave laws. Even in his final sermon, preached just two months before his death, Channing called upon the United States to use all peaceful means to bring an end to slavery.

Bibliography. Bressler, Ann Lee. *The Universalist Movement in America, 1770–1880.* New York: Oxford University Press, 2001. Channing, William E. *The Works of William E. Channing.* Boston: American Unitarian Association, 1899. Howe, Daniel Walker. *Making the American Self: Jonathan Edwards to Abraham Lincoln.* Cambridge, MA: Harvard University Press, 1997. Patterson, Robert L. *The Philosophy of William Ellery Channing.* New York: Bookman, 1952. Robinson, David. *The Unitarians and the Universalists.* Westport, CT: Greenwood Press, 1985. Turner, James. *Without God, Without Creed: The Origins of Unbelief in America.* Baltimore: Johns Hopkins University Press, 1985.

Richard A. Koffarnus

CHATEAUBRIAND, FRANÇOIS-RENÉ DE (1768–1848). While Chateaubriand owes his enduring fame to his contributions to French literature, where he ranks as one of the greatest of the romantics, Chateaubriand also played an important role in modern Christian politics, both through his writings defending Christianity and monarchy and as a French statesman in the first three decades of the nineteenth century.

Chateaubriand's life was as romantic as any of the romantic heroes of his novels. Born in St. Malo, the youngest son of a provincial nobleman of ancient lineage who had made a fortune as a privateer and slave trader, Chateaubriand grew up in the medieval castle of Combourg, newly purchased by his father, in the Breton countryside. Educated in various schools in the region, he was successively destined for the clergy, the navy, and finally the army, where he was commissioned in 1786. Presented at court the next year, he was in Paris for the fall of the Bastille in 1789. When his regiment began to disintegrate in 1790, he resigned and departed for the United States.

Landing in Baltimore in July 1791, he traveled as far as Niagara Falls on an ill-conceived project in search of the Northwest Passage but after six months returned to France on news of the king's flight to Varennes. Following a hasty marriage for money (which never materialized), he emigrated, joined a royalist army in Germany, was wounded in battle, nearly died of his injury and dysentery, and finally made his way to England, where he lived in poverty from 1793 to 1800.

It was in England that he turned away from the skepticism of his youth and began the work that became *Le génie du Christianisme* (1802), an aesthetic defense of Christianity. On his return to France, he published first a novel, *Atala* (1801), and then, at the time of Napoleon's Concordat with Rome restoring the church in France, his *Génie.* Utilizing his literary genius and liaisons with politically influential women (a combination that would recur a number of times in his career), Chateaubriand was able to have his name removed from the list of proscribed émigrés and obtain a post as secretary to the French ambassador in Rome. He quit Napoleon's service in protest in 1804 following the execution of the Bourbon prince, the duc d'Enghein, and traveled in Greece and the Near East (1806–1807). At the time of the Restoration, a political pamphlet, *De Buonaparte et des Bourbons,* won him a post as minister to Louis XVIII and a peerage, but he then lost favor because of another pamphlet,

De la monarchie selon la charte (1816), which argued for a British-style constitutional monarchy.

The high point of his political career came during the period of political reaction following the assassination of the heir to the throne, the duc de Berry, when Chateaubriand served as ambassador to Berlin (1821), ambassador to London (1822), French representative to the Congress of Verona (1822), and minister of foreign affairs (1822–1824), presiding over a successful French military intervention in Spain that restored the Bourbon monarchy there. Despite real political talents, he fell from Cabinet largely because vanity made him a difficult colleague. In 1828–1829, he served as French ambassador to Rome, where, after the death of Pope Leo XII, he tried to influence the election of his successor. Following the Revolution of 1830, he refused the oath to the new Orleanist monarch, Louis-Philippe; renounced his pension as a peer; and was twice tried for intrigues in favor of the legitimist line. He spent his last years polishing his most famous literary work, the posthumously published *Mémoires d'outre-tombe,* twelve volumes of beautifully written and fascinating vignettes of the personalities and events of his time.

In politics, Chateaubriand believed in two fundamental principles. First, he embraced legitimacy, because recognition of a specified line of descent would avert political uncertainties over succession to the throne. Secondly, he championed constitutionalism, with a preference for something like the British political system with ministerial responsibility to an elected chamber. Though as a pamphleteer and journalist he could be surprisingly flexible with respect to particular issues, he never varied in his consistent support for these two ideas.

Despite a lifelong indulgence in publicly known love affairs, Chateaubriand appears to have been a sincere believer who advocated Catholicism both for its importance for artistic and cultural inspiration and for its contribution to political stability. Though his political activity and his political and religious views were important during his lifetime, it is his still-popular literary works that have had a continuing influence on French artistic expression, imagination, and sensitivity. **Bibliography.** Clément, Jean-Paul. *Chateaubriand: Biographie morale et intellectuelle.* Paris: Flammarion, 1998. Maurois, André, *Chateaubriand.* Trans. Vera Fraser. London: Bodley Head, 1958. Switzer, Richard. *Chateaubriand.* New York: Twayne, 1971.

Richard A. Lebrun

CHÂTEAUBRIANT, ALPHONSE DE (1877–1951). A Breton by origin, Châteaubriant was born and raised in the conventional Catholic provincial gentry in a young and rapidly evolving French Third Republic. His early writings, which include the prize-winning novels *Monsieur des Lourdines* (1911) and *La brière* (1923), are littered with antimodern, anti-Revolutionary, anticapitalist, anti-individual, and pro-organicist themes that indicate that his roots lay in an intransigent Catholicism. Disappointed with what he saw as the sterility and weakness of popular institutional Catholicism, however, Châteaubriant looked outside the church for a fresh approach to Christianity (a *nouvelle chrétienté,* or a New Christendom, a common quest among Catholics in the 1920s) and advocated complete spiritual renewal and regeneration through the rediscovery and reactivation of medieval values.

The feudal precapitalist Germany he saw in the first decades of the twentieth century matched his Christian requirements. When he finally experienced National Socialism in 1936 (an event he records in his infamous 1937 essay *La gerbe des forces*), he viewed the encounter as a long-awaited meeting of minds. He believed that Hitler was a spiritually guided leader and that the National Socialists were an elite group of reborn heroic warriors who would re-evangelize a newly unified Europe and get rid of its agents of de-Christianization (the Bolshevists and the Jews). The French, associated with the Germans on the grounds of race, would play a significant role.

Châteaubriant's commitment to the National Socialist cause arose from an idiosyncratic reading of Christian doctrine that justified racism and elitism in the name of spiritual regeneration. His spiritualization of politics resulted in his unconventional reception of National Socialism as the concrete incarnation of his desired brand of *nouvelle chrétienté* and culminated in his collaboration with Germany during the Second World War. His collaboration was rooted in his long-standing interpretation of Christianity and fascism played little, if any, role in his commitment.

Far from being the mystical, otherworldly figure generally portrayed, Châteaubriant was in reality a militant and resolute collaborator. He was active and well known in major collaborationist circles, as witnessed by his directorship of the ignominious and widely read newspaper *La gerbe* and his frequent contributions to its columns, as well as by his presidency of the influential Groupe Collaboration, formed in September 1940. Châteaubriant associated with such wartime personalities as Robert Brasillach, Pierre Drieu la Rochelle, Louis-Ferdinand Céline, and Lucien Rebatet. He knew many leading members of the Vichy government, including the head of state, **Philippe Pétain**; Premier Pierre Laval; and **Philippe Henriot,** the "voice" of Radio Vichy and minister of information and propaganda from January 1944. He also knew and socialized with prominent Germans in Paris, such as Otto Abetz, the Reich's ambassador to France. In June 1944, Châteaubriant fled France, finally settling in Austria in April 1945.

Condemned to death as a traitor in his absence, he indulged in an attempt at self-revision and fulminated against his judges until his dying day.

Châteaubriant was not an opportunistic collaborator, but rather one of vocation. He cooperated willingly with the Germans and freely condoned and became increasingly actively engaged in those organizations in which he saw his preferred form of politics. His spiritualization of politics may have been eccentric, but it was neither naive nor harmless. His life illustrates the very dangerous pathway down which idealism can lead.

Bibliography. Chadwick, Kay. *Alphonse de Châteaubriant: Catholic Collaborator.* Oxford: Peter Lang, 2002.

Kay Chadwick

CHÁVEZ, CÉSAR (1927–1993). Farm worker and labor leader, Chávez was born near Yuma, Arizona, in 1927. His grandfather had immigrated to the United States from Mexico in the 1880s and established a freight business in addition to obtaining land to homestead. The Chávez land was possessed by the state in 1937, an event that led César Chávez to become a migrant farm laborer in California with his family members. After being discharged from the U.S. Navy in 1946, Chávez began to work as a labor organizer with the Community Service Organization in Los Angeles. In 1962, he founded the Farm Workers' Association (FWA) and was named its president. The FWA became the National Farm Workers Union (NFWU) and led the Delano Grape Strike and Boycott, which culminated in 1966 in a 250-mile pilgrimage from Delano to the state capital in Sacramento. In the 1970s, the successor to the NFWU, the United Farmer Workers (UFW), aggressively opposed Teamster efforts to organize California farm laborers, and Chávez once again assumed national prominence in leading a strike against the Gallo wine company. In the 1980s and 1990s, the membership of the UFW declined, although Chávez continued to be a prominent advocate for immigration reform and for the rights of migrant farm workers.

César Chávez's activism drew upon the deep religious imagery of Catholicism as expressed within Chicano culture. A banner of Our Lady of Guadalupe was often displayed with the UFW's famous black eagle. Chávez himself would often fast during the strikes and boycotts he organized and would break his fast by partaking of the Eucharist. While César Chávez is often considered to be the pivotal figure in the rise of Chicano consciousness and activism, his significance as a labor leader extends well beyond the confines of the farm workers' movement in California. César Chávez died in April 1993.

Bibliography. Del Castillo, Richard Griswold, and Richard A. Garcia. *César Chávez: A Triumph of Spirit.* Norman: University of Oklahoma Press, 1995. Ferriss, Susan, Ricardo Sandoval, and Diana Hembree, eds. *The Fight in the Fields: Cesar Chavez and the Farmworkers Movement.* New York: Harcourt Brace Jovanovich, 1997.

Mathew N. Schmalz

CHESTERTON, CECIL (1879–1918). Born in Kensington, London, Chesterton was educated at St. Paul's School and the Slade School of Art before becoming a journalist. Early in his career, he joined the Christian Social Union and the Fabian Executive Committee. He was always an eccentric among the Fabians, however, because of his efforts to combine socialism with Tory radicalism and Christianity.

A regular contributor to Alfred R. Orage's *New Age* from 1907 to 1911, most of his articles defended socialism against the criticisms of **Hilaire Belloc** and his more famous brother, **Gilbert Keith Chesterton.** During this period he also anonymously published *G. K. Chesterton: A Criticism* (1908), a widely reviewed book that furthered his brother's literary reputation.

After coauthoring *The Party System* (1911) and launching *The Eye-Witness* with Belloc, Cecil converted to the Roman Catholic faith; took over the journal, which became the *New Witness* (1912–1918); and launched an exposé of government corruption (in language tinged with anti-Semitism), which led to his conviction for libel in the Marconi scandal.

During World War I, he wrote numerous works of anti-German propaganda. His most ambitious wartime book, *A History of the United States,* aimed to demonstrate the British-American cultural and political affinity that he believed formed the underpinning of their military alliance against Germany. Gilbert Chesterton had the book published posthumously in 1919 after Cecil volunteered for service in France, was wounded, and died of pneumonia in a military hospital in Paris. Gilbert also considered himself heir to Cecil's political struggles and managed to keep the *New Witness* going, changing its name to *G.K.'s Weekly* (1925–1938). The journal promoted the cause of Distributism, an economic system based on the social teaching of the Catholic Church, expounded in Pope **Leo XIII**'s *Rerum novarum* (1893).

After his death, Cecil's wife and editorial assistant, Ada Jones, founded hostels to serve the poor and the elderly, named Cecil Houses in honor of her husband.

Bibliography. Chesterton, Cecil. *A History of the United States.* London: Chatto & Windus, 1919. Corrin, Jay P. *G. K. Chesterton and Hilaire Belloc: The Battle against Modernity.* Athens: Ohio University Press, 1981.

Susan E. Hanssen

CHESTERTON, GILBERT KEITH (1874–1936).

Chesterton was a British Catholic journalist, novelist, and poet who reached national prominence in the early twentieth century as a vigorous and colorful polemicist for a range of political causes. His politics were rooted in a particular rendition of Catholicism and yielded an eclectic mix of liberal and conservative, egalitarian and antidemocratic, public doctrine.

Born of Anglican parents in 1874, Chesterton was educated at St. Paul's and at the Slade School for artists. He never worked as an artist but rather dedicated himself to writing. By the age of twenty-six, Chesterton was nationally known for his lively and quirky novels, and he gradually gained popular acclaim, especially as a writer of detective stories. Many of his fictional works showed a propensity to rehearsals of religious themes, and when Chesterton became an essayist for the *Eye-Witness* (later the *New Witness*) and for his own *G.K.'s Weekly,* it was a sustained religio-political commentary that distinguished most of his journalism. He became a Roman Catholic in 1922 and published several important theological works, most notably *Orthodoxy* (1908), *The Everlasting Man* (1925), and *Avowals and Denials* (1934), in which he argued forcefully for a God-centered view of all life and insisted that God was to be encountered in even the most mundane experiences.

But it was Chesterton's political writings that established his reputation as a Christian polemicist. Teaming up with **Hilaire Belloc** to form the so-called Chesterbelloc circle, Chesterton exerted himself in sketching and popularizing the Distributist system of economics. Inspired by neo-Thomist Catholic philosophy, Distributism envisioned the replacement of the modern, nation-state-based capitalist system with locally autonomous communities of peasant proprietors, craftsmen, and shopkeepers. It hoped to avoid what it regarded as the equally disastrous policies of capitalism and collectivism, to undermine materialist thinking and preoccupations, and to reconnect Western peoples to what it regarded as the Christian mores of medieval communitarianism. The movement was institutionalized in 1926 in the Distributist League, of which Chesterton was the president, but in the

1930s its closeness to Catholicism and its increasingly abstruse theories meant that it had only a limited impact on broader Christian social thought.

Chesterton was also a pronounced opponent of imperialism and military establishments and of great concentrations of wealth, and an opponent of constitutional parliamentary democracy. Though no systematician of anti-Semitic theory, Chesterton was profoundly anti-Semitic, and he came to believe that modern nation-states were governed by a hidden and occult, largely Jewish directorate that undermined Christian civilization and chained Christian states to its nefarious purposes. More than anything else, it was this conviction that arraigned Chesterton against parliamentary democracy and all other secular political institutions. His brother **Cecil** and his second cousin, A. K. Chesterton, were even more insistent on this point and became major leaders in the early British fascist movement.

Above all as a prominent polemicist on topical issues, and secondarily as one of the two formulators of Distributism, Chesterton's impact on the Catholic and Anglican political thought of the early twentieth century was significant. It was also very diffuse and never implemented in policy, since he was never trusted by either of the major political parties. Priding himself on his independence, he did not set out to influence party politics in the traditional way. He lived a crowded, colorful life in the center of religious and political polemic but left a profoundly mixed legacy of intellectual brilliance and cogent religious advocacy interspersed with anti-Semitic and antidemocratic opinion.

Bibliography. Corrin, Jay P. *G.K. Chesterton and Hilaire Belloc: The Battle against Modernity.* Athens: Ohio University Press, 1981. Hollis, Christopher. *The Mind of Chesterton.* London: Hollis & Carter, 1970. Ward, Maisie. *Gilbert Keith Chesterton.* London: Sheed & Ward, 1944.

Markku Ruotsila

CHILEMBWE, JOHN (1870?–1915). Chilembwe, a Baptist minister, led a rebellion against British colonial rule and the exploitation of Africans in the territory of Nyasaland (Malawi). Although the revolt failed to bring about social and economic reform for Africans in southern Nyasaland, Chilembwe is remembered as Malawi's first anti-colonial revolutionary.

John Chilembwe was born about 1870 in Sanganu, northeast of Mbombwe near Chiradzulu in what would become British Nyasaland, of a Yao father and a Chewa mother. He received his primary education from a Church of Scotland mission school in Blantyre. About the year 1890, Chilembwe met Joseph Booth, a British evangelical minister whose teachings on human equality regardless of race had a significant influence on Chilembwe's spiritual and intellectual formation. By 1893, Chilembwe had received baptism from Booth and subsequently helped the latter to establish several mission stations and schools, working as a preacher and teacher.

Chilembwe taught at the school in Mitsidi until 1897, when he accompanied Booth to the United States and enrolled as a student at the Virginia Theological Seminary in Lynchburg, which was affiliated with the African American National Baptist Convention. In 1899, he was ordained a Baptist minister. The following year, he returned to Nyasaland and established the Providence Industrial Mission at Mbombwe in Chiradzulu district. It was more than likely in Lynchburg that Chilembwe learned of **John Brown**'s raid on Harpers Ferry, as well as African American interpretations of other aspects of American history and Booker T. Washington's ideology of industrial self-help.

For the next fourteen years, Chilembwe worked quietly as a Baptist missionary, establishing seven independent African schools; earning the respect of the colonial administration; European settlers and missionaries; and gaining followers as far away as Portuguese East Africa (Mozambique). Despite the proliferation of millenarian forms of Christianity associated with Elliot Kenan Kamwana, another disciple of Booth's, Chilembwe preached orthodox Baptist doctrine.

During the years of his mission work, Chilembwe was deeply concerned with the racism of the Nyasaland colonial administration toward Africans, and especially with the oppressive exploitation of African workers by European settlers during the early years of the colonial period. He was particularly appalled by the deaths of fellow Nyasaland Africans in British wars of conquest in Somaliland and the Gold Coast colony, and the ill-treatment of their widows by the colonial administration (e.g., holding them liable for taxes and imprisoning them for failure to pay).

Upon hearing of the outbreak of World War I in 1914, Chilembwe consulted with local African leaders, who asked him to write a letter to the *Nyasaland Times* asking the British government not to recruit local African men to serve in the British army, as they had nothing to do with Anglo-German affairs. Although the editors of the newspaper were prepared to publish the letter in November 1914, it was withdrawn by the censors. Shortly thereafter Chilembwe began plotting his rebellion.

Significantly, Chilembwe did not intend to overthrow the British colonial administration in Nyasaland or to massacre the white settlers therein. Rather, he wanted to strike at those he thought most responsible for the ill-treatment of Africans in order to bring the Africans' poor living and working conditions to the attention of the colonial administration, knowing and accepting that he and his followers would more than likely die as a consequence. Accordingly, he instructed his army not to harm European women or children, or to despoil their property. On January 23, 1915, Chilembwe's army attacked the plantation of A. Livingstone Bruce, which

neighbored the Providence Industrial Mission. They killed three planters and robbed arsenals in Blantyre and Chiradzulu to gain more weapons. These latter raids failed. Further, a group in Ncheu was captured before they could attack, and other detachments failed to attack targets in Nsoni, Mlanje, and Zomba. In their flight toward Mozambique, the rebels also attacked a Catholic mission station, severely wounding one person. Chilembwe was shot to death on February 4, 1915 by African police at Kelinde, north of Mlanje.

Bibliography. Mwase, George Simeon. *Strike a Blow and Die: A Narrative of Race Relations in Colonial Africa.* Ed. Robert Rotberg. Cambridge, MA: Harvard University Press, 1967. Shepperson, George A., and Thomas Price. *Independent African: John Chilembwe and the Origins, Setting and Significance of the Nyasaland Native Uprising of 1915.* Edinburgh: Edinburgh University Press, 1958.

Nicholas M. Creary

CHOMBART DE LAUWE, PAUL-HENRY (1913–1998).

Drawing on his experience in Catholic associations and his reading of Catholic intellectuals, Chombart de Lauwe transformed urban sociology into a vehicle of democratization, changing the way French officials planned cities.

Chombart de Lauwe studied under Marcel Mauss, an ethnologist and Socialist who introduced him to the working class and the issue of democratization. Chombart de Lauwe built on these ideals in the Social Teams (ES), a Catholic association that sent bourgeois students to lead classes of young workers. The ES hoped to introduce workers to bourgeois society, but Chombart de Lauwe changed his own attitude as he began to understand workers.

During World War II, Chombart de Lauwe continued his odyssey as an instructor with the Leadership School at Uriage. Though associated with the conservative Vichy regime of **Philippe Petain,** the school connected Chombart de Lauwe with union leaders and the philosophy of Pierre Teilhard de Chardin, a Jesuit intellectual who promoted popular participation as an instrument of human unity. Uriage reinforced Chombart de Lauwe's devotion to working-class democracy and prodded him to integrate that ideal with sociology.

After the war, Chombart de Lauwe undertook a study of Parisian urban development. To facilitate participatory planning, he conducted interviews with workers. He then recommended reforms, including construction of the social infrastructure missing from recent housing estates. Chombart de Lauwe urged state planners to adopt his proposals, arguing that ordinary individuals could participate in urban design through sociological research.

Chombart de Lauwe gained the support of Robert Auzelle, an old friend who worked for the Ministry of Reconstruction, and began conducting contract studies for state agencies. He helped revise the plans of several cities, and he visited residents of new housing estates to uncover design flaws. Most architects, however, rejected his recommendations, arguing that they understood the cities' true needs better than did the ordinary people whom Chombart de Lauwe consulted.

By the early 1960s, though, social problems in housing estates had grown so bad that even resistant officials began conducting sociological inquiries. By that time, however, Chombart de Lauwe had started calling for the reorganization of local government, not just sociological studies, as the best means to democratize planning. Chombart de Lauwe thus remained a critic of government policies. Despite his frustration, though, he had sparked a significant change as state officials adopted participatory sociology, paving the way for further democratization in the 1970s and 1980s.

Bibliography. Chombart de Lauwe, Paul-Henry. *Un anthropologue dans le siècle: Entretiens avec Thierry Paquot.* Paris: Descartes, 1996.

W. Brian Newsome

CHRISTEN DEMOCRATISCH APPÈL. *See Christian Democratic Appeal*

CHRISTIAN COALITION (UNITED STATES). When **Pat Robertson** ran for president in 1988, he tapped into a preexisting political discontent among evangelical Christians, many of whom viewed the United States as being in a state of moral decline. On the heels of Robertson's run, the Christian Coalition came into existence a year later in 1989.

Robertson founded the coalition with the help of a $64,000 grant from the National Republican Senatorial Committee. During its first eight years in existence, the coalition flourished under the leadership of **Ralph Reed.** Reed, a history PhD from Emory University, knew how to tap into that evangelical discontent and organize around core issues such as abortion and prayer in public schools. The coalition also supported lower taxes and other issues affecting middle-class America. Reed succeeded in creating a sophisticated network of local supporters that stood firmly as one of the most influential lobbying groups in the United States.

At its height in the mid-1990s, the coalition counted 1.7 million members housed in two thousand local chapters. Reed promoted the coalition's causes through a variety of media including telemarketing, cable television, talk radio, the Internet, and, most noticeably, the distribution of millions of coalition voter guides, which discussed candidates' views on issues such as abortion and gay rights. In 1994 alone, the group sent out thirty million postcards opposing President Bill Clinton's health-care plan and made more than twenty thousand phone calls to support a federal balanced-budget amendment.

In its early years, the group's success was measured by its ability to corral supporters to pressure Congress to support or oppose legislation. The coalition's commitment to direct support of political candidates (usually Republicans) helped produce Republican landslides in the South in the early 1990s. The group claimed credit for helping to produce Republican majorities in Congress in 1994, despite the fact that its central issues—prayer in schools and opposition to abortion and gay rights—were not trumpeted by Republicans. All this changed when Reed quit in 1997 to become a political consultant.

With the loss of Reed, the coalition lost its most proficient fundraiser, organizer, and public face and fell on hard times. Budget cuts had already forced the cancellation of outreach programs to African Americans and Catholics in 1997, and this in turn led to layoffs at headquarters. Under the leadership of former Reagan secretary of the interior Donald Hodel, revenues continued to drop and the Christian Coalition magazine ceased publication.

After years of contentious battles, the coalition gave up fighting for its tax-exempt status and replaced Hodel, who had proved to be an inefficient fundraiser and organizer. *Fortune* magazine noted that in its measure of effective lobbying groups, the coalition fell from a seventh-place ranking in 1998 to thirty-eighth place in 1999.

In 1999 Robertson stepped in and hired Roberta Combs, the former head of the South Carolina chapter, to run the organization. In order to retain some solvency and focus, the coalition split into two entities: the Christian Coalition International, which was the taxable political arm, and the Christian Coalition in America, which focused on voter education. Revenues continued to fall from twenty-six million in 1996 to three million in 2000. The coalition had to defend itself against a racial discrimination lawsuit brought by black employees who charged that the coalition denied them health benefits and overtime pay and forced them to enter the workplace through a back door and eat in a separate section. The lawsuit was settled out of court.

Seeking to move back to some of Reed's pragmatic ideas, Combs successfully worked with liberal U.S. senator Charles Schumer (D-NY) to pass a bill that limited both Internet spam and pornography. Most recently, the coalition has committed resources to generating opposition to stem cell research and support for a constitutional amendment that would prohibit gay marriage. While the organization has never recovered the clout it enjoyed under Reed's ascendance, it continues to stand as one of the most visible symbols of modern evangelical political activism.

Bibliography. Martin, William. *With God on Our Side: The Rise of the Religious Right in America.* New York: Bantam Del, 1996. Powell, Leon. "Ups and Downs of the Religious Right." *Christian Century,* 19 April 2000, 462–66. Reed, Ralph. *After the Revolution: How the Christian Coalition Is Impacting America.* New York: W Publishing Group, 1995.

Arlene Sanchez Walsh

CHRISTIAN DEMOCRACY [DEMOCRAZIA CRISTIANA] (ITALY). The Christian Democracy (DC) was a Catholic-inspired party that dominated Italian politics for the half-century following the end of World War II. The party formed clandestinely during the waning years of Benito Mussolini's Fascist regime. As the disaster of Italy's alliance with Nazi Germany and military defeat pointed to national ruin, politically motivated Catholics formed a network of contacts to prepare a postwar role for a party of Christian inspiration.

Among the leadership of this group were veterans of Don **Luigi Sturzo**'s **Italian Popular Party** (PPI), which had been disbanded by the Fascists in the 1920s. **Alcide De Gasperi,** for instance, had served as Sturzo's chief assistant and as the PPI's leader in its last months, and he surfaced as the DC's first chief from the 1940s until his resignation in 1953. Others in that group included **Mario Scelba** and **Giovanni Gronchi.** A younger cadre of leaders was drawn from academia, including professors such as **Amintore Fanfani** and **Giorgio La Pira,** and those who had been active in the Catholic University Federation (FUCI) such as **Aldo Moro** and **Giulio Andreotti.**

By 1942, Christian Democracy was taking shape as one of the political forces that would replace the Fascist regime. On September 9, 1943, the DC joined other anti-Fascist parties, the Communists (PCI), Socialists (PSI), and others in a coalition, the Committee of National Liberation (*Comitato di liberazione nazionale,* CLN). When the Allied armies entered Rome in June 1944, the CLN coalition assumed control of the liberated Italian government. In December 1945, De Gasperi was given the reins of the CLN government and began his long tenure as prime minister. By 1947, he had ejected the PCI and the PSI from the alliance. From then on, the DC enjoyed a status as by far the largest government party, and it would control Rome until the early 1990s, a position that the crucial April 1948 elections confirmed.

With a great deal of support from the United States, Pope **Pius XII,** and **Italian Catholic Action,** and thanks to a peasant and middle-class electoral base (67% of which was comprised of women), the DC acquired an absolute majority in the Chamber of Deputies, a security it maintained until 1953, when it lost its absolute control but perennially formed cabinets either by itself (so-called single-color or *monocolore* ministries) or in coalitions with smaller and weaker partners.

The period 1948 until 1962 might be considered the DC's golden age in power.

De Gasperi called his party one of the center leaning to the left, an attitude dismissed by some as paternalistic but which nonetheless persisted among his successors during this era—Fanfani until 1959 and Moro until 1963. While maintaining a strict anticommunism and a commitment to the American alliance and to European union, the DC governments adopted policies that aided Italy's impoverished zones, particularly in the south; engaged family assistance and low-income housing; and advocated economic planning. Such policies disturbed some American cold war observers. On the other hand, particularly under Fanfani, who announced that the DC must pay more attention to culture, the party was determined to maintain aspects of Italy's traditions through preservation of the sanctity of the family in opposition to divorce, in limited censorship of the arts, and in enforcement of morality laws.

Italy and the DC experienced the same upheavals of the 1960s that affected other nations—the rise of protest movements and a strengthening of the Left—along with industrialization and the rise of a consumer society that eroded the party's peasant base. The Christian Democracy looked to bring the Socialist Party back into the governing coalition. The more relaxed attitudes encountered in the John Kennedy administration in the United States and in the pontificate of **John XXIII** permitted the party to make its overtures, and by 1963 the Socialists entered the coalition in the DC's so-called opening to the Left. Both Socialists and Christian Democrats considered this, from their own perspectives, pacts with the devil that ensured that neither party would ever be the same again. For its part, the DC continued its soul-searching in significant congresses that focused on culture at San Pellegrino in 1961 and at Lucca in 1967.

In the next two decades the Christian Democracy lost its close identification with the papacy, a situation confirmed by Pope **Paul VI** in his 1971 apostolic letter, *Octogesima adveniens,* while it faced stiffer competition from the Communists, who virtually tied it by the mid-1970s. Headaches were compounded when it suffered significant setbacks in debates and referenda over cultural issues that ended with the legalization of divorce in 1974 and of abortion in 1981. The DC, while holding onto its electoral coalition in the 1980s, agreed for the first time that the prime minister's chair would be occupied by figures from other parties, first the Republican Giovanni Spadolini and then the Socialist Bettino Craxi. Prime Minister Craxi signed a new Concordat with the Catholic Church (1984), negotiations for which the Christian Democrats had started in the 1960s. The document terminated the church's official status as the state church, although it acknowledged its special place in Italian society. Despite the new sobering circumstances, glimmers of hope appeared. The Communist threat turned moribund as the party itself collapsed at the end of the 1980s along with the fall of the Berlin Wall, and the DC rallied to a clear leadership over the Italian political spectrum.

Scandal loomed, however, and would trigger the end of DC power and the demise of the party itself. In 1991 an avalanche of exposed corruption, which began with Craxi's misdeeds, soon overwhelmed the Italian political system. It quickly swamped the Christian Democracy. The Northern Leagues of Umberto Bossi were the first to benefit from the catastrophe, taking large numbers of votes in traditional Catholic strongholds (for example, 20% of Lombard ballots) in the 1992 elections. By 1994 the DC leadership acknowledged that its long rule had come to an end and disbanded the party. Its electorate scattered across the spectrum, although some small Catholic splinter parties have continued to form and re-form in the hopes of reconstituting the Christian Democracy.

Bibliography. Furlong, Paul. *The Italian Christian Democrats: From Catholic Movement to Conservative Party.* Hull Papers in Politics 25. Hull, UK: University of Hull, Department of Politics, 1982. Giovagnoli, Agostino. *Il Partito italiano: La Democrazia Cristiana dal 1942 al 1994.* Rome-Bari, Italy: Laterza, 1996. Leonardi, Robert, and Douglas A. Wertman. *Italian Christian Democracy: The Politics of Dominance.* New York: St. Martin's Press, 1989. Malgeri, Francesco. *Storia della Democrazia Cristiana.* 5 vols. Rome: Cinque Lune, 1987–1989. Scoppola, Pietro. *La Nuova Cristianità perduta.* Rome: Edizioni Studium, 1986.

Roy P. Domenico

CHRISTIAN DEMOCRATIC APPEAL [CHRISTEN DEMOCRATISCH APPÈL] (THE NETHERLANDS). In 1980, the three major Dutch Christian political parties— Katholieke Volkspartij (KVP), the Antirevolutionaire Partij (ARP), and the Christelijk Historische Unie (CHU)— united to form an independent party called the Christian Democratic Appeal (CDA). The history of the modern Netherlands' Christian democracy closely mirrors the country's confessional and social fragmentation.

Already in the middle of the 1960s the three parties agreed to work closer together, but the ARP and the KVP could not reach an understanding about a common program. Only in 1976 did the three build an alliance that for the first time took part in the elections to the Dutch Second Chamber in 1977. The oldest of the three parts is the **Anti-Revolutionary Party** (ARP), which dates from 1878. The ARP turned against progressive and republican influences and aimed at Christian conservative solutions to society's problems. The ARP was mostly supported by the pietistic working class and the Protestant middle class. The Christian Historical Union (CHU) split off from the ARP in 1908. Its program scarcely differed from the ARP, but it instead appealed to the upper classes. Founded in 1926 as the Roman Catholic States Party (RKSP), the Catholic People's Party (KVP) was anchored in Catholic social doctrine and gained great status among the Dutch Catholics.

The postwar success of the German **Christian Democratic Union** and the events of the Second Vatican Council in the 1960s spurred interest in a Dutch interdenominational party. After the end of World War II, more or less permanent coalitions among the three Christian parties had already formed, so foundations for union had already been laid. But serious negotiations were started only after the 1967 elections. The conversations took place within the so-called Group of the Eighteen, and the most important point of discussion focused on the contents of Christian politics. The three joined forces with a common program in the 1971 elections; and two of the parties, the ARP and the KVP, participated in the Den Uyl cabinet (1973). In 1977 the CDA for the first time participated in a combined list in the elections for the Second Chamber behind its leading candidate, Dries van Agt. In 1980 more negotiations resolved differences between the ARP and the KVP, and the aim of a Christian-dominated Dutch party was reached.

The architect of the new union was Piet Steenkamp (KVP), who was appointed honorary chairman. Its first chairman was **Ruud Lubbers,** who had directed the alliance since 1978. Lubbers served as prime minister from 1982 until 1994. Between 1994 and 2002 the CDA was the chief opposition during the social democrat Wim Koks's term of office. After the elections of May 15, 2002, the CDA again became the largest parliamentary group in the Commons, and the party leader, Jan Peter Balkenende, became the head of the government, with Maxime Verhagen as the head of the parliamentary group in the lower chamber. The electoral victory of

2002 was reconfirmed in 2003. Although having nearly doubled its number of votes during the 1990s, the party could not reach the results of the 1950s and 1960s, when the three mother parties regularly collected more than 40 percent of all votes.

The CDA and its predecessors were known for particular interest in educational and school reforms. In keeping with Christian Social doctrine, the party promoted confessional schools and the rights of religion and the individual toward the state. The so-called Polders model of state-capital-labor cooperation and the German idea of subsidarisation form cornerstones of its politics, while its state and social politics are conservative. The interdenominational CDA recognizes atheist, Muslim, and Hindu colleagues, and despite rampant Dutch secularization, it has preserved itself as a Christian people's party. European integration and the Atlantic alliance serve as fundamental ideas of the CDA's foreign politics.

Bibliography. Gladdish, Ken. *Governing from the Center: Politics and Policy-Making in the Netherlands.* Dekalb: Northern Illinois University Press, 1991.

Helmut Rönz

CHRISTIAN DEMOCRATIC PARTY [PARTIDO DEMÓCRATA CRISTIANO] (CHILE). Chile's Christian Democratic Party (the PDC) originated in the Conservative Party's youth wing of the 1930s. Many of the founding members of the Conservative Youth, including **Eduardo Frei Montalva,** Bernardo Leighton, Manuel Garretón, and Radomiro Tomic, were also active in the National Association of Catholic Students (ANEC) and in Catholic Action. They were influenced by progressive priests such as Oscar Larson, Fernando Vives, and Jorge Fernández Pradel, who emphasized social Catholic doctrine and reform. The future founders of the Christian Democratic Party rejected socialism but also criticized unrestrained capitalism for its overemphasis on the individual and consequent neglect of the common good. Soon known as the National Falange, they composed a declaration of twenty-four fundamental points that defined the group as one interested in the common good of the nation, beyond the traditional political divisions of left and right, and inspired by Christian thought. It also prioritized the defense of the family, just wages and the right of workers to organize, and a corporativist economy.

The National Falange originally remained part of the Conservative Party but broke with it after a dispute during the presidential elections of 1938. The new party established the magazine *Política y Espíritu* and the publishing house Editorial del Pacífico in the mid-1940s and gained further influence as its leaders were elected to Congress. In July 1957, the National Falange joined with the Social Christian Conservative Party to create the Christian Democratic Party (PDC).

The PDC's Declaration of Principles (1958) emphasized the realization of Christian values as its goal. It prioritized democracy and social justice, stating that a democratic system should not only guarantee individual rights but also ensure equal access to them. The declaration also expressed the party's aspirations for an economy that respected both private and collective property and advocated the rights of workers to organize peacefully. For the Christian Democrats, the ultimate goal of the economy is to achieve the common good and prevent the dominance or oppression of any single group.

The new party grew tremendously between 1957 and 1964. By 1963, it was the largest political party in the country. Spokesmen emphasized that it was not a confessional party, but it did receive support from Catholic laity and some members of the hierarchy, especially as the church's emphasis on reform and *aggiornamiento* during and after the Second Vatican Council grew. Christian Democratic leader Eduardo Frei Montalva won the 1964 presidential elections with an absolute majority, a rarity in twentieth-century Chilean politics. In the 1965 legislative elections, the PDC won a majority in the lower house of Congress and gained seats in the Senate. This facilitated Frei's so-called Revolution in Liberty, which accomplished educational improvements, agrarian reform, and the partial nationalization (Chileanization) of the mining industry. As the party gained power, though, it also suffered some internal conflicts. The Movimiento de Acción Popular Unitario (MAPU) split off from the PDC in 1969, and the Christian Left followed in 1971. Despite this, however, the Christian Democratic Party remained the largest political party in Chile until 2001.

The PDC opposed the Popular Unity (UP) government of Socialist Salvador Allende (1970–1973). When Allende was overthrown, some Christian Democrats initially supported the military government as the only means of restoring order. When they realized that General Augusto Pinochet (1973–1989) did not intend to return the nation to democracy, however, their views changed. The PDC served in a critical role in the opposition at the center of the Democratic Alliance, a coalition of parties and political groups formed in 1983 after a wave of protests against the regime. Before the 1988 plebiscite to determine whether or not Pinochet would stay in power, the alliance became the Concertación for the No and campaigned effectively to force the military dictator to step down. The transition back to democracy was overseen by longtime Christian Democratic leader Patricio Aylwin (1990–1994), and he was succeeded by another PDC leader, Eduardo Frei Ruiz-Tagle (1994–2000), son of the former president. The PDC lost electoral strength during the 1990s, however, perhaps because it has not made adequate internal adjustments to the demands of the new democratic society. Socialist Ricardo Lagos won the presidential elections of 2000, but the PDC continues to have several prominent representatives in government and public life, including Soledad Alvear, Gabriel Valdés, and Alejandro Foxley.

Bibliography. Fleet, Michael. *The Rise and Fall of Chilean Christian Democracy.* Princeton, NJ: Princeton University Press, 1985. Grayson, George. *El Partido Demócrata Cristiano Chileno.* Buenos Aires: Editorial Francisco de Aguirre, 1968. Walker, Ignacio. "The Future of Chilean Christian Democracy." In *Christian Democracy in Latin America: Electoral Competition and Regime Conflicts,* eds. Scott Mainwaring and Timothy R. Scully. Stanford, CA: Stanford University Press, 2003.

Lisa Edwards

CHRISTIAN DEMOCRATIC UNION [CHRISTLICH-DEMOKRATISCHE UNION—CDU] (GERMANY). The German CDU is one of the most successful Christian Democratic parties in Western Europe and, with the exception of the 1972 election, was the strongest German party up to 1998. Founded in 1945, although it stood in the tradition of the prewar Catholic **Center Party** (*Zentrumspartei*), the postwar CDU worked to integrate Protestants into its ranks. The Nazi legacy, the Allied occupation, and the fear of communism helped to unite these different wings during the first postwar years.

CDU programs, its politics, and its proportional system stressed the new union between Protestants and Catholics. In contrast to Christian Democratic parties in other countries, Germany's was less clerical and less connected to trade unions. The CDU's loose organization, furthermore, fostered compromise between the different supporters. It is a characteristic of this structure that Bavaria is represented by a semi-independent party, the *Christlich-Soziale Union* (**Christian Social Union,**

CSU). The loose organization and bid for Protestant votes bore fruit. Although the majority of its voters were still Catholics, the CDU could claim to be a people's party (Volkspartei).

From 1949 until 1963, the CDU governments of **Konrad Adenauer** (party chairman from 1949 to 1963) left their mark on German society by inaugurating a free-market system with social protections (particularly for the retired), refugees, and families. The CDU's foreign policy advocated close economic and military ties with the West and reconciliation with France. As a strict anticommunist party it denied contacts with the Eastern bloc and East Germany. The cultural politics of the CDU supported Christian schools and conservative morals while it improved the rights of women only with hesitance.

During the CDU governments of **Ludwig Erhard** (1963–1966) and Kurt-Georg Kiesinger (1966–1969), the party faced its first serious crises. Conflicts between the different wings increased. Many Catholic workers and members of the Protestant middle classes switched their allegiance to the Social Democrats. Economic stagnation, the decrease of anticommunism, and the reorganization of the churches, moreover, contributed to this situation.

The loss of power in 1969 and the heavy defeat of the new party leader Rainer Barzel in 1972 led to significant party reforms. The party machine was strengthened and the membership increased. The executive party committees obtained more power, and the level of democratic debates improved. Since 1968, the CDU started to discuss its programs and finally passed its first basic program in 1978. During these years the CDU modernized its positions. It stressed social questions and turned away from separate schools for Protestants and Catholics. Finally, the CDU allowed negotiations with the East.

These changes were initiated and supported by **Helmut Kohl,** who was elected as chairman in 1973 and who gave key positions to intellectual reformers. Although Kohl failed to recapture the government for the CDU in 1976, the party reached almost the majority of the voters. Unlike his rival **Franz Josef Strauss**—the chairman of the Bavarian CSU, who failed at the elections of 1980—Kohl looked for compromises. His willingness to deal with the Liberal (Free Democratic) Party produced a coalition in 1982 and the CDU's return to power.

Repudiating many of the programs of the seventies, Kohl's government (1982–1998) initiated strict social cuts and corporate tax reductions. Despite rising unemployment, therefore, the economic upswing and reduced inflation that grew from these actions buoyed the CDU. In foreign policy, Kohl's government showed more continuity. He accepted existing treaties with the Eastern bloc and cultivated dialogue with communist East Germany. At the same time, a close cooperation with the West and a promotion of a European market were central elements of his foreign policy. Environmental policy, frequently stressed in policy speeches, surfaced as another core issue. After 1983, however, the CDU lost members continuously and the party's already loose structure suffered. Programs and party committees became more and more unimportant as Kohl often decided matters on his own or after discussion with his advisers in the Chancellery—not within the party committees. This attitude and setbacks in regional elections led to a party rebellion against Kohl. At the party meeting in Bremen (1989), Kohl managed to save his power and dismiss several mutinous leaders. Kohl's reputation and that of the CDU, nevertheless, remained so bad that most observers expected victory of the rival Social Democrats at the forthcoming election.

The unexpected reunification of 1990 presented Kohl and the CDU with a new chance. Kohl's risky and generous decisions to achieve unification quickly increased his popularity, especially among Eastern voters, although the majority had no Christian background. The new challenges in the East, furthermore, helped to cover the problems in the West. The structure of the CDU was changed after its unification with the formerly communist CDU of the East. The party was reorganized, and its new structure further enhanced Kohl's position.

Since the mid-1990s, the CDU has faced several new problems. After the end of the cold war, its anticommunist appeals lost their integrating power. The high unemployment rate increased, especially in the East, and the CDU's social cuts led to strong and widespread protests. Trade unions and churches, moreover, demanded greater social responsibility from the government. The quite liberal abortion law of the CDU intensified the conflicts with the churches. At the same time, women supported the CDU less often because its family politics seemed too conservative for them.

The loss of power in 1998 triggered several ups and downs for the party. A donation scandal led to a complete turnover of the party elite in 2000. The CDU, furthermore, discussed several programs without finding a significant common direction. Nevertheless, the new party leader Angela Merkel—a divorced Protestant women who grew up in the communist East—became a symbol for a new, more liberal direction. At the same time the party rank and file preferred the more conservative Catholic Bavarian prime minister Edmund Stoiber as its candidate in the 2002 elections. Although the CDU led the polls for month, Stoiber lost, probably on account of defections among northern Protestants, women, and the voters in large cities. Relative to other countries, however, the German Christian Democratic Party remains in a strong position.

Bibliography. Kleinmann, Hans-Otto, and Gunter Buchstab. *Geschichte der CDU.* Stuttgart, Germany: Deutsche Verlags-Anstalt, 1993. Becker, Winfried, et. al., eds. *Lexikon der Christlichen Demokratie in Deutschland.* Paderborn, Germany: F. Schöningh, 2002. Bösch, Frank. *Die Adenauer-CDU: Gründung, Aufstieg und Krise einer Erfolgspartei (1945–1969).* Stuttgart, Germany: Deutsche Verlags-Anstalt, 2001. Bösch, Frank. *Macht und Machtverlust: Die Geschichte der CDU.* Stuttgart, Germany: Deutsche Verlags-Anstalt, 2002.

Frank Bösch

CHRISTIAN DEMOCRATS (DENMARK). Denmark's Christian Peoples Party, as it was initially called, was founded in April 1970 at a meeting held in Aarhus in the presence of the chairman and vice chairman of its Norwegian counterpart and namesake. The immediate occasion was provided by the liberalization of controls on abortion and pornography, which had made Denmark a byword for permissiveness. The nonsocialist coalition (Agrarian Liberals, Conservatives, and Radical Liberals), which had come into office in 1968, had accelerated, instead of braking, the liberalizing trend to the dismay of conservative religious groups such as those found in the Lutheran "inner-mission" lay movement and among members of the free churches. The party presented itself as a vehicle for protest against the permissive trend and called for a return to a traditional morality rooted in Christian values.

Following the lead of the other Christian parties of the Nordic area (Norway, Finland, and Sweden), the party also called for Christianity to be the inspiration of policy in other areas too, making mention particularly of education; the care of the sick, elderly, and poor; and aid for the third world. At its first election in 1971, the party just failed to surmount the 2-percent threshold of the electoral system, and shortly thereafter, internal tensions relating to the appropriate balance between religious and social policy concerns led to the resignation of the first chairman. Despite these uncertain beginnings, in the so-called earthquake election of 1973, the party doubled its support and took seven seats in the Folketing (parliament) and only once since then (1994–1998) has it failed to gain representation by taking over 2 percent of the vote. It has remained a minor party, however, peaking at 5.3 percent in 1975, and most of the time achieving only about half that. In the general election of 2001 it took only 2.3 percent. Despite its small size, the party has enjoyed a share in government office, occupying as it does the center of the left-right political spectrum, where its contribution can be crucial for coalition governments achieving majority status. Between 1982 and 1988, the party was in a Conservative-led "four-leaf clover" coalition, and between January 1993 and September 1994 in a Social Democrat coalition, on both occasions occupying inter alia the housing ministry. In October 2003, the party followed the example of its Swedish and Finnish sister parties and voted to change its name to the Christian Democrats, thereby emphasizing its connection with the wider Christian Democratic movement while also avoiding any confusion with the right-wing populist (and anti-immigrant) Danish People's Party.

Bibliography. Freston, P. *Protestant Political Parties: A Global Survey.* Aldershot, UK: Ashgate, 2004. Madeley, J.T.S. "Reading the Runes: The Religious Factor in Scandinavian Electoral Politics." In *Religion and Mass Electoral Behaviour in Europe,* ed. D. Broughton and Hans-Martein Ten Napel. London: Routledge, 2000.

John T. S. Madeley

CHRISTIAN DEMOCRATS (FINLAND). The party was founded under the name Finland's Christian League in 1958 at a time when a number of religious activists associated with "new pietist" and Pentecostalist movements feared that the country's Christian heritage was in danger. In the elections of that year, the Communist-dominated Finnish People's Democratic League (Suomen Kansan Demokraattinen Liitto, SKDL) advanced to become the largest parliamentary grouping, and there was an acceleration in the rate of people withdrawing from membership of the Lutheran state church.

The party founders looked to the example of the Norwegian Christian Peoples Party, adopting as their program a more or less verbatim translation of the corresponding Norwegian document. At its first three elections, however, the party made little impact, taking less than 1 percent of the votes. During the 1960s the party developed its role as a sort of "moral vigilante" highly critical of various scandals in public life while also pursuing issues such as the defense of religious instruction in schools. It first achieved parliamentary representation in 1970, following a four-year period of leftist government, which had become synonymous with liberalization. The party only achieved a modest 1.1 percent, but the Finnish electoral system had no threshold and allowed for the formation of local electoral alliances between parties. The party leader, Raino Westerholm, was elected on the strength of a local alliance with the (Agrarian) Center Party.

The party has remained represented in Finland's parliament, the Eduskunta, ever since, maximizing the impact of its modest electoral share by means of alliances with other parties. In 1978, Westerholm achieved 8.8 percent in the presidential election of that year when he stood against long-term incumbent President Kekkonen. The following year, the party was able to increase its general election support to 4.8 percent. When the issue of European Union (EU) membership first arose in 1990, the party adopted a firmly Eurosceptic stance in defense of the country's distinctive moral-religious heritage. In 1991, it joined a four-party nonsocialist coalition under the Center Party leader Esko Aho, but its solitary minister, party leader Toimi

Kankaanniemi, minister of overseas development, resigned in 1994 in opposition to the pro-EU line of the rest of the cabinet. With Finland's accession to the EU from January 1995, it has tended vigorously to oppose further installments of integration, such as adoption of the euro currency, while conceding that EU membership itself has to be accepted. Under the new leadership from 1996 of Bjarne Kallis, it has become both less Eurosceptic and less narrowly focused on issues bearing on morality and religion. In December 2001 the party changed its name to the Christian Democrats and moved to a moderately pro-EU stance.

Bibliography. Freston, P. *Protestant Political Parties: A Global Survey.* Aldershot, UK: Ashgate, 2004. Madeley, J.T.S. "Reading the Runes: The Religious Factor in Scandinavian Electoral Politics." In *Religion and Mass Electoral Behaviour in Europe,* ed. D. Broughton and Hans-Martein Ten Napel. London: Routledge, 2000.

John T. S. Madeley

CHRISTIAN DEMOCRATS (SWEDEN). The Christian Democratic Coalition Party, as it was called for the first two decades after its founding in 1964, brought together Christians of different confessional backgrounds in a common political endeavor to protest against the secularization of Swedish society.

In early 1964, a doctors' petition had expressed concern about increasing sexual promiscuity, blaming the Social Democrats' liberal policies. The action of the National Board of Social Affairs advising municipalities to warn young people against attending the "ecstatic" meetings of a Pentecostal sect was also regarded as ominous, while proposals to reduce the time devoted to religious instruction in secondary schools was met with the expression of widespread concern as 2.1 million signatures (in a country with only five million adult citizens) were collected in protest. Finally, a controversy over film censorship also erupted in 1964. The time seemed auspicious for the launching of a party that would lead a fight for the return of conventional Christian values.

At its first election the party achieved only 1.8 percent of the vote, however, and failed to gain representation. Its prospects worsened four years later when a constitutional reform introduced a 4-percent threshold for representation. Only in 1985 did it finally win its first seat on the basis of a local electoral alliance with the (formerly Agrarian) Center Party. The 1990s was by contrast an electoral roller-coaster. Unrepresented since 1989, when it had taken a mere 2.9 percent of the national vote, the party enjoyed a surge of support to 7.1 percent in 1991, dipped to 4.0 percent in 1994 (only just over the threshold for representation), and advanced again to 11.8 percent in 1998 before falling back to 9.1 percent in 2002.

The remarkable expansion of its electoral base in the 1990s reflected a new ability to attract support in the most populous areas, not least around Stockholm, in addition to advances in its traditional areas of support such as the southern county of Jönköping, where revivalist religious movements have historically been strong. In 1996 the party changed its name to the Christian Democrats as part of an attempt to change its profile from that of an issue-based protest movement to one concerned with wider ethical issues across the whole range of public policy.

Symptomatically, the party also embraced representatives of non-Christian religious traditions, in particular Judaism and Islam. In 1991 the party joined the nonsocialist coalition led by the Conservative Carl Bildt, occupying the ministries of communications, the interior, and development aid. Since then they have remained in opposition despite the general popularity of their leader from 1973 to 2004, the Pentecostalist Alf Svensson.

Bibliography. Freston, P. *Protestant Political Parties: A Global Survey.* Aldershot, UK: Ashgate, 2004. Madeley, J.T.S. "Reading the Runes: The Religious Factor in Scandinavian Electoral Politics." In *Religion and Mass Electoral Behaviour in Europe,* ed. D. Broughton and Hans-Martein Ten Napel. London: Routledge, 2000.

John T. S. Madeley

CHRISTIAN LEFT PARTY [IZQUIERDA CRISTIANA] (CHILE). The Christian Left Party (Izquierda Cristiana, IC) arose out of the Chilean Christian Democrats (PDC) after the election of Salvador Allende as president of Chile in 1970. Its formation followed a period of discontent by a group of six Christian Democrat parliamentarians who called themselves the Christian Left within the PDC before the presidential elections.

The Christian Democrats had been in power from 1964 to 1970 and President **Eduardo Frei Montalva** had implemented a program of agrarian reform and a so-called Revolution in Liberty. However, radical factions of the Christian Democrats were uneasy about the slow reforms implemented by Frei and fostered conversations and alliances with the Socialist and Communist parties. Most of them were practicing Catholics who had been influenced by the post-Vatican II reforms within the Catholic Church and had studied the social doctrine of the church concerning freedom, justice, private property, political involvement, and the modern world in general.

In August 1969 the most radical members of the PDC formed the Movement of United Popular Action (MAPU), a group that became part of the Popular Unity (UP) coalition and supported a Marxist creation of society while including many Christians who believed in a socialist framework. Two years later, a member of the lower chamber had to be elected in Valparaiso, and the Christian Democrats formed a coalition with the right-wing parties. Their candidate was elected and as a result nine Christian Democrats, all members of the lower chamber, left the PDC and formed the IC. They had prepared the presidential campaign of Radomiro Tomic and were in absolute disagreement with the alliance between the PDC and the PN. They eventually became part of the UP and included senior figures such as Luis Maira, Jacques Chonchol, Rafael Gumucio, and Sergio Bitar.

While the MAPU supported a Marxist reading of history and politics, the IC fostered their members' commitment to a Christian life and therefore to an active Christian involvement in politics oriented toward socialism rather than capitalism. While the IC was a small party, it brought to the national sphere a radical Christian contribution close to the social values of the Gospel and related to the social doctrine of the Catholic Church. The IC worked closely with the **Christians for Socialism** and became the target of the security services after the military coup of 1973. Most of its leaders lived in exile till the restoration of democracy in Chile.

Bibliography. Aguilar, Mario I. *A Social History of the Catholic Church in Chile.* Vol. 2, *Cardinal Silva Henriquez and the Military.* Lewiston, NY: Edwin Mellon Press, 2005. Alexander, Robert J. *The Tragedy of Chile.* Westport, CT: Greenwood Press, 1978.

Mario I. Aguilar

CHRISTIAN PEOPLE'S PARTY (NORWAY). Norway's Christian People's Party was founded as a regional party in the Western part of the country in 1933 after a number of previous local initiatives had come to nothing. There was intense dissatisfaction with the established parties, which had failed both to uphold the commitment to liquor prohibition and defend the country's religious heritage from vigorous leftist attack.

At its first election, the party succeeded in getting elected its leading candidate in the Hordaland constituency, Nils Lavik, a man who was already prominent in revivalist Christian circles. It was, however, only after four years of Nazi occupation that the party was able to launch itself as a national party and so pioneer what has become—with Finnish, Swedish, and Danish emulators of the Norwegian example—the distinctive brand of Scandinavian Christian Democracy.

The year 1945 was an auspicious time in Norway, as it was across much of Western Europe, during which revulsion against the political extremes of both left and right were very much to the fore, and a reassertion of religious traditions, especially in the guise of Christian Democracy, was looked to for inspiration in postwar reconstruction. Despite not standing for election across the whole country, the party took almost 8 percent of the national vote and went on in the following year to consolidate its base. Its support came principally from lay members of the revivalist organizations, which had arisen in the late nineteenth century among members of the state church, particularly in the south and west of the country. Significant support from the country's small religious dissenting minorities, however, was also directed toward the party. Its electoral fortunes have varied between approximately 8 percent in 1945 and 13.7 percent in 1997; in 2002, it took 12.4 percent.

The party has always occupied a centrist position in left-right terms and has held government office seven times since the early 1960s, in each case in coalition with other nonsocialist parties in the center and on the right. Three times, in 1972–1973, 1997–2000, and since 2002, it has provided the prime minister, on the last two occasions in the person of Kjell Magne Bondevik. The policy stands, which have particularly distinguished it from the other parties, have been on moral-religious issues such as abortion, pornography, drugs, alcohol-related issues, and the place of religion in education. It has also been a strong supporter of foreign aid to third-world countries and has opposed Norway's entry into the European Union in both the1972 and 1994 referendums.

Bibliography. Freston, P. *Protestant Political Parties: A Global Survey.* Aldershot, UK: Ashgate, 2004. Madeley, J.T.S. "The Antinomies of Lutheran Politics: the Case of Norway's Christian People's Party." In *Christian Democracy in Europe: A Comparative Perspective,* ed. D. Hanley. London: Pinter, 1994. Madeley, J.T.S. "Reading the Runes: The Religious Factor in Scandinavian Electoral Politics." In *Religion and Mass Electoral Behaviour in Europe,* ed. D. Broughton and Hans-Martein Ten Napel. London: Routledge, 2000.

John T. S. Madeley

CHRISTIANS FOR SOCIALISM [CRISTIANOS POR EL SOCIALISMO] (CHILE). After the election of the Socialist senator Salvador Allende as president of Chile in 1970, a group of twenty Catholic priests who at that time lived in working-class parishes offered their support to the new socialist government and later formed the group Cristianos por el Socialismo (Christians for Socialism). They were initially known as "the group of the eighty," and later they became "the group of the two hundred," representing the number of priests who had endorsed Allende's road to socialism as the closest political system to Gospel values and to Christianity in general.

Christians for Socialism was a movement that arose out of the post-Vatican II reflections on religion and politics that followed pronouncements on the presence of the Catholic Church in society, mainly *Gaudium et Spes* (1965) and the documents of the second meeting of Latin American Bishops in Medellin, Colombia (1968). Within those documents the church reaffirmed the involvement of Christians in politics and in the shaping of human society.

Most of its members were clergy who had lived in and witnessed the world of the poor and the marginalized and therefore perceived the social world of the poor as the context for Christian commitment and the political world as the context for the creation of a more just and Christian society. Therefore their theology followed the first steps of a theology of liberation from oppression and social injustice that began with the publication of *Teologia de la liberación* (1971) by the Peruvian theologian **Gustavo Gutiérrez.**

It was in April 1971 that a group of priests and lay people met in Santiago in a ten-day meeting that explored the cooperation by Christians on the building up of socialism. Gutiérrez attended the meeting and gave a paper on the Christian-Marxist dialogue. Several of the organizers had studied in France and Belgium and had been influenced by the European dialogue between Christians and Marxists and by the French experience of the worker-priests.

After the military coup of 1973, the military arrested most of the members, and some of them, such as Gonzalo Arroyo, left for exile in Europe. Others, such as Fr. **Michael Woodward,** were arrested and killed. With the end of the Socialist government, the movement ended, and members continued working for human rights and the subsequent restoration of democracy in Chile.

Bibliography. Eagleson, John, ed. *Christians and Socialism: Documentation for Socialism Movement in Latin America.* Maryknoll, NY: Orbis, 1975. *Primer encuentro latinoamericano de Cristianos por el socialismo.* Havana, Cuba: Ediciones Camilo Torres, 1973.

Mario I. Aguilar

CHRISTIAN SOCIALISM (HUNGARY). Hungarian Christian Socialism was born as a reaction to political liberalism and atheistic evolutionary socialism (Marxism) in the middle of the nineteenth century. Its adherents wished to solve major social problems through the application of Christian ideals to society. But while campaigning against the exploitation of the working classes, they also wanted to preserve the principle of private ownership as manifested in Pope **Leo XIII**'s *Rerum novarum* (1891).

The Hungarian public first became informed about Christian Socialism through the writings of Bishop **Ottokár Prohászka,** who was supported by the writings and organizing activities of Canon **Sándor Giesswein.** Many political parties and workers' associations were born under the name of this ideology. The first of these was the somewhat aristocratic Catholic People's Party (1895), followed by the Christian Socialist Workers' Union (1903) and the Federation of Christian Socialist Associations (1904), out of which evolved the social welfare-oriented National Christian Socialist Party (1907). While Giesswein was the moving spirit of Hungarian Christian Socialism, its most powerful prophet was Bishop Prohászka, who elaborated his political philosophy in such influential works as his *Diadalmas világnézet* (Triumphant World Ideology, 1903) and *Modern katholicizmus* (Modern Catholicism, 1904). Prohászka and Giesswein were powerful critics both of exploitive capitalism and atheistic Marxism, but also of reactionary Catholicism.

Following the collapse of Austria-Hungary and the end of the Habsburg dynasty (1918), Christian Socialism was represented in the transitional Hungarian National Council (November 1918–March 1919), which soon veered into the brief but destructive Hungarian Bolshevik Regime under Béla Kun (March–July 1919). The fall of Bolshevism was followed by the establishment of a conservative political system under the regency (1920–1944) of Admiral Nicholas Horthy (1868–1957).

During the interwar years the Christian Socialists split into two camps, one behind Horthy and the other with the Legitimists, who supported the return of the Habsburgs. Although usually calling themselves Christian, they were generally tied to the political activities of the Catholic Church and followed the ideology of political Catholicism. While Catholic in orientation, these Christian Socialist parties as a rule cooperated with the ruling regime until the mid-1930s, when Hungary's move toward right radicalism pushed them to opposition.

During the 1930s the movement was given a boost by **Pope Pius XI**'s encyclical *Quadragesimo anno* (1931), which gave birth to many Christian Socialist organizations, including the National Federation of the Catholic Youth Associations (KALOT), the Federation of Catholic Girls' Associations (KALÁSZ), the Parish Workers' Guilds (EMOSZ), the National Association of Catholic Artisans and Workers (KIOE), and the Evangelical Workers' Federation (EMSZ). Notwithstanding this boost and boom, the Christian Socialist parties could not become significant players on the national scene.

During World War II, growing disenchantment with right radicalism brought many of Hungary's liberal intellectuals into the same camp with the spokesmen of Hungarian political Catholicism, who jointly established the Christian People's Party (1943) with the approval of the primate of Hungary, Justinian Cardinal Serédi (1884–1945). Toward the end of 1944, under German occupation, the Christian People's Party transformed itself into the more inclusive Christian Democratic People's Party (1944), and then, with the country's Soviet occupation, into the Democratic People's Party (1945). This party functioned during the coalition period (1945–1948) under the leadership of István Barankovics (1906–1974), but only as a minor party. Not even the Catholic Church supported it fully, because **Jósef Cardinal Mindszenty** (1892–1975) threw his weight behind the Smallholders' Party as the only viable alternative to the Communist Party and to a total communist takeover.

The establishment of communist totalitarianism (1947–1948) resulted in the elimination or forced merger of all political parties, with the exception of the Hungarian Communist Party, which functioned as the Hungarian Workers' Party (1948–1956), the Hungarian Socialist Workers' Party (1956–1989), and then, after the collapse of communism, as the reorganized Hungarian Socialist Party (1989–).

The Democratic People's Party was liquidated in early 1949 and did not reemerge until 1989, when it joined the Hungarian Democratic Forum (HDF) in the first postcommunist ruling coalition (1990–1994). Following the return of the Socialist Party to power (1994–1998), and then the triumph of the Alliance of Young Democrats (Fidesz, 1998–2002), the Christian Democratic Party barely survived. Segments of the ideology of Christian Socialism, however, have been incorporated into the platforms of both the HDF and of the Fidesz.

Bibliography. Gergely, Jeno. *A keresztényszocializmus Magyarországon, 1903–1923* [Christian Socialism in Hungary, 1903–1923]. Budapest: Akadémia Akadémiai Kiadó, 1977. Gergely, Jenö. *A keresztényszocializmus Magyarországon, 1924–1944* [Christian Socialism in Hungary, 1924–1944]. Budapest: Typovent Kiadó, 1993. Romsics, Ignác. *Hungary in the Twentieth Century.* Budapest: Corvina Press, 2000, chapters 1–3, 7. Várdy, Steven Béla. *Historical Dictionary of Hungary.* Lanham, MD: Scarecrow Press, 1997.

Steven Béla Várdy

CHRISTIAN SOCIALIST PARTIES (HUNGARY). The first political party in Hungary of a Christian Socialist orientation was founded at the urging of Bishop **Ottokár Prohászka,** by Count Nándor Zichy (1829–1911) and Count Miklós Móric Esterházy (1855–1925). Established in 1895 as the Catholic People's Party (CPP), its goals included the defense of the Catholic Church against antireligious trends and the advancement of social welfare reforms. The CPP had been inspired by Germany's **Center Party,** and especially by Pope **Leo XIII**'s encyclical *Rerum novarum* (1891). From the very start, the Hungarian Christian Socialist movement had two rival orientations: a conservative Catholic trend represented by its aristocratic leaders, who tried to preserve the special constitutional position of the Catholic Church, and a social welfare trend embodied in various Christian workers' associations and championed by Canon **Sándor Giesswein** and Bishop Prohászka. Additional points of conflict included the national minority question, Hungary's constitutional position within Austria-Hungary, Christian Socialism's relationship to the Catholic hierarchy, and the nature of the desired social welfare reforms. Especially touchy was the question of land reform, which had an impact upon the Catholic Church. Disagreements on these issues resulted in repeated splits, mergers, and renewed divisions within the movement.

Initially, the CPP functioned successfully, but as the aristocratic faction repressed the movement's social welfare tendencies, the champions of the latter trend established in 1907 the rival National Christian Socialist Party (NCSP). This new party was supported by the National Federation of Christian Socialist Associations (established in 1903) and the National Catholic Federation under the leadership of Count János Zichy (1868–1944). The NCSP's platform included universal and secret suffrage, freedom of association, right to strike, limiting child and female labor, right to private property, and a need for Christian moral renewal. It also demanded that workers share in the profits and the administration of their work. By 1910 the

NCSP had its own newspaper, *A Nép* (the People), wherein Canon Giesswein advocated his own radical views on social reform, his pacifism, and his sympathies for the Social Democratic Party.

Neither of these parties was very successful in attracting sufficient number of voters. Thus in 1918 they merged into the Christian Socialist People's Party (CSPP). Following the collapse of Austria-Hungary, the CSPP threw its support behind the leftist republican government (November 1918–March 1919) headed by Count Michael Károlyi (1875–1955). The growing radicalization of the political situation, however, soon turned them against Károlyi. The situation became worse after the establishment of the Hungarian Soviet Republic (March–July 1919), which dissolved all Christian organizations and political parties and arrested and imprisoned their leaders.

After the collapse of the Bolshevik regime (July 31, 1919), Christian Socialism reemerged in the form of several competing parties, only to merge again into the Christian National Unity Party (CNUP). Although primarily a Catholic party, the CNUP also accepted Protestants. In 1920 the CNUP joined the ruling political coalition and had a lion's share in the country's internal consolidation after historic Hungary's dismemberment. Following the establishment of the government-sponsored United Party (1922), the influence of the CNUP declined. This was followed by the temporary fragmentation of Christian Socialism, and the reemergence of the conflict between the movement's conservative and progressive wings. This conflict was further exacerbated by their diverging views on the possible restoration of Emperor-King Charles to the Hungarian throne.

In 1923, Christian Socialists established two rival parties: the progressive National Christian Socialist Party and the conservative Christian National Economy Party. In 1925 these two parties merged into the National Christian Economy and Socialist Party, which became Parliament's second-largest party in 1926. Although heavily outweighed by the ruling United Party, during the 1920s and early 1930s Christian Socialist were able to push through some social welfare reforms. Losing popularity in the late 1930s and early 1940s, they restructured themselves into the United Christian Party (1937), the Christian People's Party (1943), the Christian Democratic People's Party (1944), and finally the Democratic People's Party (1945). Having fallen victim to communism in 1949, Christian Socialism reemerged four decades later in 1988 as the Christian Democratic People's Party (CDPP). During the first postcommunist government (1990–1994), the CDPP was a member of the ruling coalition, while during the socialist-liberal rule (1994–1998) it was one of the opposition parties. Internal personality conflicts, however, prevented it from gaining any seat in the next parliament (1998–2002), which then led to its virtual demise.

Bibliography. Gergely, Jenö. *A keresztényszocializmus Magyarországon, 1903–1923* [Christian Socialism in Hungary, 1903–1923]. Budapest: Akadémia Akadémiai Kiadó, 1977. Gergely, Jeno. *A keresztényszocializmus Magyarországon, 1924–1944* [Christian Socialism in Hungary, 1924–1944]. Budapest: Typovent Kiadó, 1993. Romsics, Ignác. *Hungary in the Twentieth Century.* Budapest: Corvina Press, 2000, chapters 1–3, 7. Várdy, Steven Béla. *Historical Dictionary of Hungary.* Lanham, MD: Scarecrow Press, 1997.

Steven Béla Várdy

CHRISTIAN SOCIALIST WORKERS AND PEASANTS PARTY (RUSSIA). Authorities of Russia's Provisional Government first registered as the Christian Social Labor Party on June 8, 1917, in Moscow. Founded by Fedor I. Zhilkin, a weaver, the party was based on the principles of Christian faith and love of God, family, and fatherland. It aspired to unite people of all classes in a harmonious, enlightened working family.

In February 1919 the Bolshevik government reorganized the party's program and rules and renamed it the Christian Socialist Workers and Peasants Party, although Zhilkin's position and those of the cofounders remained the same. The new program included chapters on Christian Socialism and Christian Communism, Orthodox Church property, and the social position of workers and peasants. The party called for the improvement of the material position of the communes (*obtshiny*), support for Soviet authorities, and for the "arrange[ment of] a life in accordance with the teaching of the Gospels." The Christian Socialists worked to create popular communist canteens, shops, cooperative societies, workshops, factories, libraries, agricultural storehouses, orphanages, and poorhouses. It also hoped to conduct religious meetings and hold concerts and lectures. In 1919 the party received permission to hold a divine service in Moscow's Kremlin for the Easter days. Later it opened two party branches in Moscow; organized debates, lectures, and tea parties; and published appeals. The party had around twenty activists in 1917, fifty in 1918, and perhaps one hundred permanent members by the summer of 1919; there is no data on the social origin of its members. Despite the small numbers, events organized by the party were attended by thousands of Muskovites. The party existed on money from members' fees, publications, lectures, and other organized events. In summer 1919 the party founded the Peasants' Working Cooperative Society with 863 members with the aim of achieving the organization of the food supply. In June 1919 the party announced a lecture and discussion on the topic "The Worship of Saints and Relics in Connection with Their Examination." An expert of the People's Commissariat of

Justice who had been announced as an official opponent went to court to accuse Zhilkin of "speculation" and "of fostering among the workers a wrong image of Soviet power." On September 30, 1919, the Moscow People's Court heard the case and sentenced "Worker F. Zhilkin" to imprisonment in a concentration camp until the end of the civil war. The party was labeled "anti-Soviet", "injurious," and "hostile" and was ordered to cease its activities. Its funds were confiscated for the benefits of workers' children.

Bibliography. Novichenko, Irina. "A Christian Labor Movement in Eastern Europe?" In *Between Cross and Class: Comparative Histories of Christian Labour in Europe, 1840–2000,* ed. Lex Heerma van Voss, Patrick Pasture, and Jan de Maeyer. Bern, Germany: Peter Lang, 2005.

Irina Novichenko

CHRISTIAN SOCIAL PARTY [CHRISTLICHSOZIALEN PARTEI] (AUSTRIA). Austria's Christian Social Party was born between 1890 and 1893 in Vienna out of earlier organizations (Vereinigte Christen, Christlichsozialer Verein, and Christlich-sozialer Arbeiterverein) that had been close to the Catholic political and social ideas of Baron Karl von Vogelsang and Prince Aloys Liechtenstein. Inspired by Pope **Leo XIII**'s encyclical *Rerum novarum,* these organizations wanted to improve the social situation of the working classes by ethical and religiously based social reforms. **Karl Lueger** succeeded in uniting the disparate organizations of the Christian Social movement into one party. This development was carried by Viennese merchants, public employees, and the lower-middle classes. With their support and anti-Semitic agitation, Lueger managed to destroy the liberal majority in the Viennese district council, and in 1897 he became mayor of Vienna.

The Christian Social Party respected property rights but was at the same time anticapitalist and opposed liberalism as an economic doctrine. This line continued through World War I and was still traceable in the party programs of the Austrian People's Party after 1945. Its merger with the Roman Catholic conservative party in 1907, however, curtailed much of the party's social reformism. It transformed into more of a conservative party representing the Austro-Hungarian German-speaking and property-owning bourgeoisie and the farmers. The party's "great-Austrian" and federalist policy, furthermore, made it attractive among the nobility and at court. This brought the party the electoral victory in the house of representatives in the Reichsrath campaign of 1907, yet it lost its majority of votes in Vienna to the Social Democrats in 1911 after Lueger's death. After this defeat, the Christian Social Party was preferred by the Catholic rural population and the middle class.

During the First World War the Christian Social Party stood loyally by the imperial family. But after the collapse of the Habsburg Empire in 1918, the Christian Socials approved the introduction of a republican governmental system. During the following years, the party temporarily supported union with the Weimar Republic because many in the party and in the total population doubted the viability of a postwar truncated Austria.

From 1918 to 1920, the Christian Social Party formed a coalition government on federal level with the Social Democratic Party (Sozialdemokratische Arbeiterpartei, SDAP) under Chancellor Karl Renner (SDAP). In 1920, under the leadership of Prelate **Ignaz Seipel,** the Christian Social Party became the strongest group in the federal parliament, the Nationalrat, and took charge in a coalition with the Pan-German People's Party (Grossdeutsche Volkspartei) until 1932. Between 1927 and 1934 the Country Party (Landbund) was another coalition partner. From 1920, the Christian Socials provided the federal chancellor, except for the years 1921–1922 and 1929–

1930, when the former Viennese chief of police Johannes Schober led the federal government. For ten years, 1928–1938, the federal president (Wilhelm Miklas) also came from Christian Social benches.

In 1929 Carl Vaugoin took over the party leadership from Ignaz Seipel. Vaugoin approved a closer cooperation with the nationalist paramilitary force Heimwehr. After recognizing that this cooperation with the Heimwehr did not prove useful, the party revived the coalition with the German Nationalists, Deutschnationale (until 1932) and the Landbund. In September 1934 the Christian Social Party was dissolved and incorporated into the Fatherland Front (Vaterländische Front) as a consequence of the end of parliamentary democracy in 1934, and the proclamation of the May Constitution. But the two leaders of the Ständestaat from 1934 until the Nazi takeover in 1938 were Christian Social politicians: **Engelbert Dollfuss** and **Kurt Schuschnigg.**

After the end of the Nazi power in Austria in 1945, mostly former Christian Socialist politicians founded the Austrian Peoples Party (Österreichische Volkspartei), which took over the Christian Social tradition. The new Christian party was committed to democracy and the rule of law.

Bibliography. Berchthold, Klaus. *Österreichische Parteiprogramme, 1868–1966.* Munich: Oldenbourg, 1967. Boyer, John W. *Culture and Political Crisis in Vienna. Christian Socialism in Power, 1897–1918.* Chicago: University of Chicago Press, 1995. Boyer, John W. *Political Radicalism in Late Imperial Vienna: The Origins of the Christian Social Movement, 1848–1897.* Chicago: University of Chicago Press, 1981. Goldinger, Walter, ed. *Protokolle des Klubvorstandes der Christlichsozialen Partei 1932–1934.* Vienna: Verlag für Geschichte und Politik, 1980. Staudinger, Anton, Wolfgang C. Müller, and Barbara Steininger. "Die Christlichsoziale Partei." In *Handbuch des Politischen Systems Österreichs: Erste Republik 1918–1933,* ed. Emmerich Herbert Dachs Tálos and Ernst Hanisch. Vienna: Manz, 1995.

Jürgen Nautz

CHRISTIAN SOCIAL PARTY [PARTI SOCIAL CHRÉTIEN] (BELGIUM). The Parti Social Chrétien (PSC) is Belgium's French-language Christian democratic party, one of a family of parties that have been governing the nation either alone or in coalition almost without interruption since 1884.

Originally called the Catholic Bloc, grouping together Catholics of a variety of persuasions, the party was transformed following the liberation of Belgium at the end of the Second World War, as those of the Christian democratic persuasion became the dominant force, into the PSC, or the *Christelijke Volkspartij* (CVP, Christian People's Party) in Dutch. More than just a change of name, the transformation into the PSC symbolized a shift away from the Catholic hierarchy, and toward the doctrine of Christian democracy, which had long been developed by a minority within the Bloc.

The party was divided in two in 1968 along linguistic and community lines, within a Belgium moving further and further toward federalism. The PSC became the party of French-speaking Wallonia, and the CVP that of Dutch-speaking Flanders, with the two occasionally running candidates against one another in the bilingual region of Brussels. Historically, the party had always enjoyed greater support in Flanders. Since the split, the PSC has been the smaller partner in coalitions. The policies of the two Christian democratic parties have gradually diverged since their official split, especially in light of the closer links of the PSC with trade unions, and the promotion of cultural specificity and the defense of Flemish regional interests on the part of the CVP.

Like the Catholic Bloc before it, throughout the twentieth century the PSC has been composed of quite different groups with a variety of political positions and held together by a basic Christian outlook and the pragmatics of politics. It maintained strong links with the Christian trade unions and sought to broaden its appeal within Belgian society. Within Wallonia, the PSC's electorate is pluralistic in terms of social origin and more female than the average electorate of Belgium as a whole. Ideologically, the PSC developed around the doctrine of personalism, seeking the reconciliation of class interests and the support of the less privileged members of society without major structural changes. The party favors European integration, and one of its leaders, Paul-Henri Spaak, was one of the principle architects of the European Economic Community.

Bibliography. Fitzmaurice, John. *The Politics of Belgium: A Unique Federalism.* London: Hurst, 1996.

Timothy Baycroft

CHRISTIAN SOCIAL UNION [CHRISTLICH-SOZIALE UNION IN BAYERN—CSU] (GERMANY). The Christian Social Union (CSU) emerged in 1945 from various ideological and geographically dispersed groups throughout Bavaria. On the one hand, the party followed the tradition of the Catholic and deeply conservative Bavarian People's Party (*Bayerische Volkspartei,* BVP), the Bavarian equivalent to the **Center Party** (*Zentrum*), which was dissolved in 1933 after the National Socialists had seized power in Germany. On the other hand the CSU attempted from the beginning to be a party representing general Christian values and attractive not only for Roman Catholics but also for Protestants and eventually for the whole nonsocialist population. The party always was and still is an advocate of rural interests, stands against the influence of trade unions, and, most essentially, strictly clings to federalist ideas.

Therefore it did not become part of the **Christian Democratic Union** (CDU), the party established after the Second World War by groups of similar alignment for all parts of Germany except Bavaria.

There is an agreement of the two parties that the CSU does not stand for elections outside Bavaria and that the CDU is not eligible in Bavaria. In the federal diet the CSU forms a united Parliamentary Party with the CDU, and in times of federal administrations led by CDU chancellors, the CSU was always part of the government, participating with three to five federal ministers. In 1980 and in 2002 the two parties even agreed to nominate CSU politicians to run for the chancellorship but lost both times to the Social Democrats, in 1980 to **Franz Josef Strauss,** rather clearly, and in 2002 very narrowly to Edmund Stoiber. The CSU is more than a special regional branch of the CDU. The Bavarian party generally takes a tougher and more conservative ideological position than its nationwide sister party. This was particularly perceptible, for example, in its distinctively uncompromising attitude toward the Soviet Union and its satellites during the cold war decades or in absolute opposition to the legalization of abortion. Regarding industry, the CSU strongly supports innovation such as the technology of nuclear power plants, a highly contested issue in Germany for decades.

The CSU acquired the rather unique position as the quasi-natural Bavarian party. In every federal or Bavarian election since 1962 the CSU has always won the majority, and sometimes even two-thirds, of seats to be gained in Bavaria. At the federal level this arithmetically meant a proportion of about 10 percent of the German electorate until 1990. German unification led to a decrease in the party's strength, for in the former East German parts of the country the conservative political spectrum was covered by the CDU, and the Bavarian portion of the electorate declined against expanded population of united Germany.

In 2003 the party maintained a staff of more than three hundred full-time employees and a membership of approximately 180,000. Despite attempts to attract the whole Bavarian population, the CSU remains a party of old Catholic men: two-thirds of its members are of fifty years old or older, about 80 percent are Roman Catholics, and less than 20 percent are women. Membership and electorate still mainly consists of people with an agricultural background, civil servants, employees, and entrepreneurs. About half of the party's finances are funded by contributions, mainly from large German industrial companies.

The CSU oversees regional subdivisions; organizations for different groups of political interests and ages (e.g., a youth organization); and a closely connected foundation, the Hanns-Seidel-Stiftung, which is financed by public grants and provides scientific analysis, international cooperation, and scholarships.

Bibliography. Burkhard, Haneke, and Hanns-Seidel-Stiftung, ed. *Geschichte einer Volkspartei: 50 Jahre CSU 1945–1995.* Grünwald: Atwerb-Verlag, 1995. Christian Social Union. www.csu.de. Mintzel, Alf. *Die CSU-Hegemonie in Bayern. Strategie und Erfolg. Gewinner und Verlierer.* 2nd ed. Passau, Germany: Rothe, 1998.

Bernd Leupold

CHRISTLICH DEMOKRATISCHE UNION (GERMANY). *See* Christian Democratic Union

CHRISTLICHSOZIALEN PARTEI (AUSTRIA). *See* Christian Social Party

CHRISTLICH-SOZIAL UNION IN BAYERN (GERMANY). *See* Christian Social Union

CHURCH WOMEN UNITED. This worldwide ecumenical organization represents twenty-five million Protestant, Roman Catholic, Orthodox, and other Christian women and is best known as the sponsor of World Day of Prayer.

As war spread around the globe in 1941, three women's organizations met to advance peace through ecumenism. These women's groups, some of which had begun as missionary societies before developing diverse ways to better their communities, shared civic and religious goals and felt the need for a national umbrella organization to provide expertise and coordination. The Council of Women for Home Missions joined with the Federation of Women's Boards of Foreign Missions and the National Council of Federated Church Women to become the United Council of Church Women (later changed to CWU). The groups forming CWU sought to work on a broad range of goals, specifically war relief, then later reconstruction and reconciliation, especially as they affected women and children; efforts for peace; and the cultivation of just racial relations.

Through these founding organizations, CWU acquired its best-known programs: World Day of Prayer, May Friendship Day, and World Community Day. World Day of Prayer is an international prayer movement that began in 1887 as a day of prayer for confession of individual and national sins. May Friendship Day, first observed in 1933, emphasizes creative and healing relationships in local communities. World Community Day, celebrated initially at the start of World War II in 1939, is an occasion for Christian women to pray and work for lasting peace.

While the prayers drew no controversy, CWU made waves by supporting a variety of liberal political causes. CWU strongly supported a goal of racial inclusiveness by declaring that it intended to make the organization open to all women. In 1945, it recognized only those state councils that were open to all races, thereby supporting integration before many other predominantly white organizations did so. In 1961, it began a program called Assignment Race to challenge the vestiges of racism within the CWU movement, the church, and the larger society through consciousness raising and activism. The largest undertaking ever attempted by CWU, it forced both black and white women to define justice and to contemplate power relations within their communities. As women, the members believed that they could act in areas where men feared to tread because it was more difficult to punish women for activism through physical or economic sanctions.

As an organization affiliated with the United Nations, the **National Council of Churches,** and the **World Council of Churches,** CWU has been the target of strong attacks from the Right. Women who left the organization often cited the liberalism of the group as constituting a menace to society. Recently, CWU has drawn the ire of conservatives for opposing the 1991 Persian Gulf war, promoting universal health care, encouraging peace activism, and opposing punitive welfare reform measures. Acting out of deep religious convictions, the members of CWU have attempted to reform society into a more Christian one that affords equal opportunity for all. They bear much responsibility for the integration of the religious community.

Bibliography. Calkins, Gladys Gilkey. *Follow Those Women: Church Women in the Ecumenical Movement, a History of the Development of United Work Among Women of the Protestant Churches in the United States.* New York: United Church Women, 1961. Shannon, Margaret. *Just Because: The Story of the National Movement of Church Women United in the USA, 1941 through 1975.* Corte Madera, CA: Omega Books, 1977.

Caryn E. Neumann

CLAPHAM SECT (UNITED KINGDOM)

The Clapham Sect refers to an extraordinary group of political activists that flourished alongside the evangelical movement in the Church of England. Beginning in the 1780s, they sought to shape government policy and social mores through the regenerative influence of a Christianity that was both serious and practical.

The nucleus of the Sect was formed when **William Wilberforce,** a young graduate of Cambridge University, experienced a conversion to godly religion in 1785. He subsequently paid an extended visit to his cousin **Henry Thornton,** whose family lived in Clapham, south London, and around this pair of friends, a network of like-minded individuals formed. Using their extensive connections among the elite of English society, the so-called Clapham saints exerted steady pressure for the "reformation of manners" and helped to create a constituency for social reform. By the early nineteenth century, the group comprised a half-dozen members of Parliament, reformers, and essayists. In the second generation, it also produced figures like the historian **Thomas Babington Macaulay.**

Much of the Sect's early history parallels the campaign to end the slave trade. Wilberforce entered the House of Commons in 1780 and decided to pursue abolition after his friend Prime Minister William Pitt recommended the antislavery campaign as suitable to his "character and talents" (Howse, 12). Granville Sharp and Thomas Clarkson, though not evangelicals themselves, had pioneered the cause in England and collaborated closely with Wilberforce. By the early 1790s, the campaign had also attracted Zachary Macaulay and James Stephen, both formerly residents of the West Indies, where they had acquired a hatred of slavery. From 1787 onward, Wilberforce regularly introduced bills in Parliament to abolish the trade; all were soundly defeated. Between 1799 and 1804, the group did not bring the bill forward—the war against Napoleon proved a divisive issue—but after Pitt's death, under a new ministry, abolition passed easily in 1807. Wilberforce lived to witness the abolition of slavery itself twenty-six years later.

This opposition to slavery was only part of a larger program to bring about reform at home and abroad. Evangelical religion within the Anglican tradition supplied the impetus behind the Clapham Sect, and their principal motive was to spread the Gospel among all classes. One of their favorite vehicles was education. During the 1780s, Mrs. **Hannah More,** an acquaintance of Thornton and Wilberforce and a close associate in many of the Sect's projects, opened schools for hundreds of students, particularly in rural Somerset. Early members of the Clapham Sect shared similar experiences in the broadening reaches of the empire, and they undertook to send British Protestant missionaries to India. They were thwarted at first by the East India Company, which wanted no part of proselytism, but in 1793, one of their own number, John Shore, became governor general of India. Henry Thornton, also a proprietor of the company, helped to found an expressly Anglican body for evangelism, which later became the Church Missionary Society. He also turned his attention to reviving the African colony of Sierra Leone, first established for freedmen and women by Granville Sharp in 1787. The British and Foreign Bible Society, organized in 1804 with several Clapham men among the founders, had sold over four million copies of the scriptures by 1825.

Claphamites sought their main chance in influencing the elite directly, yet their relationship with the establishment of the day was ambivalent. On one hand, the Clapham leaders were undoubtedly social conservatives. With respect to this world, theirs was no revolutionary creed. Wilberforce told his readers that religion "renders the inequalities of the social state less galling to the lower orders, whom she also instructs, in their turn, to be diligent, humble, patient" (Ford, 120). Doubting the capacity of the lower orders to exercise the vote responsibly, the Clapham leaders did not consistently support the parliamentary reform movement. They were assailed by the radicals for condemning only the pleasures of the poor; indeed, one of their most notorious organizations was the Society for the Suppression of Vice, which undertook to end popular entertainments like cockfighting and bear-baiting, especially on the Sabbath.

On the other hand, the Sect occasionally faced indifference or hostility from the High Church as well. Neither Anglican archbishop joined the Bible Society, and Wilberforce never succeeded in converting the prime minister. The title of Wilberforce's own book, *A Practical View of the Religious System of Professed Christianity Contrasted with Real Christianity* (1797), epitomized their outlook. The world was a moral arena in which the true follower of Christ must demonstrate a daily awareness of God's demand for purity in thought and deed. Evangelicals avoided both the emotional "enthusiasm" of Methodism and the millennialism of some sectarian groups, but they nonetheless believed that the promotion in society at large of acceptance of God's will as revealed in scripture required tireless work. The dry rationalism and conventional piety of contemporary Anglicanism failed to inspire this sense of personal zeal.

Evangelicalism had first taken root in Clapham through the ministry of Henry Venn, whose *Complete Duty of Man* (1763) laid out the basic evangelical theology. John Thornton, a successful Clapham merchant, became Venn's close friend and later presented Venn's son to the same living. Ties of family and friendship also helped to bind members to the group. The elder James Stephen was Wilberforce's brother-in-law, and Zachary Macaulay, father of the historian, was recommended to Henry Thornton by his friend Thomas Babington. Finally, there was a significant Scottish connection: Macaulay, Shore, Grant, and Stephen had all received a godly upbringing north of the border before their various experiences led them to join the Sect. Wilberforce himself moved from Clapham to the City in 1808, soon to be followed by the Thorntons, but the place of the Clapham Sect at the center of nineteenth-century social reform is secure. In 1844, the literary critic Sir James Stephen published a retrospective appreciation that gave the group its enduring name.

Bibliography. Brown, Ford K. *Fathers of the Victorians: The Age of Wilberforce.* Cambridge: Cambridge University Press, 1961. Hilton, Boyd. *The Age of Atonement: The Influence of Evangelicalism on Social and Economic Thought, 1795–1865.* Oxford: Clarendon Press, 1988. Howse, Ernest M. *Saints in Politics: The "Clapham Sect" and the Growth of Freedom.* Toronto: University of Toronto Press, 1952.

John D. Ramsbottom

CLAUDEL, PAUL (1868–1955). A dramatist, poet, and diplomat, Claudel was a leading luminary of the Catholic revival in early twentieth-century France. He was born to a bourgeois family in Villeneuve-sur-Fère, between Paris and Champagne, before moving with his family to Paris in 1881. The brother of sculptress Camille Claudel, whom he eventually committed to an asylum, he was influenced in his youth by the symbolist poetry of Arthur Rimbaud and repelled by the positivism of Ernest Renan and Hippolyte Taine, to which he was exposed in the prestigious Lycée Louis-le-Grand. A plaque in Notre Dame marks the site of the mystical experience on Christmas 1886 that led to his conversion to Catholicism in 1890.

Dissuaded from a monastic vocation, Claudel followed a successful diplomatic career that ultimately lasted over forty years. Consular assignments took him to various posts around the world, including the United States (1893–1894), China (1895–1909), Austria-Hungary (1909–1911),

Germany (1911–1914), Italy (1915–1916), Brazil (1917–1919), and Denmark (1920–1921). He eventually served as ambassador to Japan (1921–1927), the United States (1927–1933), and Belgium (1933–1935). Before assuming his first diplomatic assignment, Claudel had already begun to write plays, including *Tête d'or* (1890) and *La jeune fille violaine* (1892; rewritten and published in 1901). After a shipboard affair with a married woman in 1900, Claudel's plays, beginning with *Partage de midi* (1906), blurred the distinction between loves sacred and profane, returning continually to doomed lovers and Christian transcendence toward the flame of the divine. *Cinq grandes odes* (1910) helped make his reputation as a poet.

Claudel's dramatic and poetic works are infused with a passionate vision of a suffering humanity's inner longing for the love of God, with frequent medieval motifs and allegories, as well as an underlying political conservatism (he was an ardent supporter of **Francisco Franco,** for example). Plays such as *L'Annonce faite à Marie* (1912) and *Le soulier de satin* (1930) found enthusiastic audiences in occupied Paris and Vichy during World War II. Claudel had seen the 1940 destruction of the French Third Republic at the hands of the German Wehrmacht as a providential event, confiding to his diary: "France has been delivered after sixty years from the yoke of the radical and anti-Catholic party (teachers, lawyers, Jews, Freemasons). The new government is invoking God and restoring liberty to the religious orders."

But his effusive—and ultimately embarrassing—poem "Ode au Maréchal" (1940) marked the limit of his political engagement with Marshal **Philippe Pétain**'s collaborationist regime (he proceeded to write an ode to **Charles de Gaulle** as well in 1944), and unlike some other French cultural figures of the period, his reputation emerged largely intact in 1945. He

was elected to the Académie Française in 1946. In his last years, Claudel stopped producing works of drama and poetry and concentrated on writing devotional works, including the book *J'aime la Bible,* published in 1955, the year of his death.

Bibliography. Chaigne, Louis. *Paul Claudel: The Man and the Mystic.* Westport, CT: Greenwood Press, 1978. Knapp, Bettina Liebowitz. *Paul Claudel.* New York: Ungar, 1982.

Richard Francis Crane

COADY, MOSES MICHAEL (1882–1959). A Roman Catholic priest, educator, and social reformer, Coady was born at Northeast Margaree, Cape Breton, Nova Scotia, Canada. He was educated at Margaree Forks High School and then attended the provincial normal college for teachers in Truro. He returned to his native village as principal of the local high school. In 1903 he entered St. Francis Xavier's College in Antigonish, Nova Scotia, from which he obtained the bachelor of arts degree two years later. In October of 1905 he left for the Urban College, Rome, to study for the priesthood. He studied there for five years and obtained the degrees of PhD and doctorate of divinity. He was ordained priest by Cardinal Respighi in the Cathedral of St. John Lateran on May 21, 1910. Coady returned to St. Francis Xavier as a professor of education from 1910 to 1915, and for one year he attended the Catholic University of America for postgraduate studies. He was then appointed principal of the St. Francis Xavier High School from 1916 to 1925 and continued to teach education at the college.

Coady was appointed the first director of the St. Francis Xavier Extension Department in 1928 and held this position until his retirement in 1952. The Extension Department was established primarily to help people establish remedies to the many social and economic problems that the region was experiencing at that time. From 1929 to 1930 he deferred his responsibilities as director to organize the fishermen of the Maritime Provinces. He quickly gained an outstanding reputation as a forceful and dynamic speaker, eminent philosopher, and writer. He received an honorary doctorate from Boston College in 1939. In the same year he published his only book, *Masters of Their Own Destiny*, which was made possible through a grant from the Carnegie Foundation. He was invested as a domestic prelate in 1946 and was invited to speak to the United Nations in 1949.

Coady had many friends and colleagues in both provincial and federal government. He welcomed and embraced relationships with bureaucrats who worked in the areas of agriculture, the fishery, industry, labor, finance, education, and health. They regularly sought his guidance. In 1952, after many years of poor health, he submitted his resignation but continued to provide direction to the Extension Department and others. In 1959, the St. Francis Xavier Coady International Institute was established in his memory.

Bibliography. Johnston, A. A. *Antigonish Diocese Priests and Bishops, 1786–1925.* Ed. Kathleen M. MacKenzie. Antigonish, NS: Casket, 1994. MacLellan, Malcolm A. *Coady Remembered.* Antigonish, NS: St. Francis Xavier Press, 1985. Moses M. Coady Papers, Personal/Professional. Antigonish, Nova Scotia, Extension Department Collection, St. Francis Xavier University Archives. Welton, Michael R. *Little Mosie from the Margaree, A Biography of Moses Michael Coady.* Toronto: Thompson Educational, 2001.

Kathleen M. MacKenzie

COLIJN, HENDRIKUS (1869–1944). Colijn was the greatest leader of the Calvinist political party known as the **Anti-Revolutionary Party** (ARP) in the Netherlands between the First and Second World Wars. Organized by **Abraham Kuyper** in 1879, the ARP joined the **Christian Democratic Appeal** party in 1980.

Colijn was an evangelical believer who served as an military officer and administrator in the Dutch East Indies (1893–1909)

and at home served in Parliament for the ARP and then as minister of war and finances (1909–1913). During and after the war he held directorships in oil companies in his homeland and England. During the war Colijn was an intermediary between the British and the Germans in a failed attempt at peace talks. In 1920 he was elected ARP chairman. Between 1920 and 1940, Colijn was the most important Dutch statesman, serving twice as premier (1925–1926 and 1933–1939) and chairing economic conferences at the League of Nations. He was the first ARP premier to have secular politicians in his governments. His areas of expertise were finances, colonial affairs, and international affairs.

After Kuyper's death Colijn institutionalized the ARP perspective by raising a million guilders to fund the new Abraham Kuyper Foundation think tank, personally buying Kuyper's former home to serve as party headquarters and setting up a theoretical journal to apply party principles. *AR Staatkunde* (AR Politics) was published from 1924 to 1980, except for during the war years. The ARP leader appointed Dr. Herman Dooyeweerd (1894–1977) to the foundation, where he wrote his first articles on Reformational philosophy.

Colijn moved from Kuyper's "Christian nationalism" to a responsible economic and political internationalism. During the Depression he kept faith in the value of the free market and free trade. Although he felt that **Woodrow Wilson** had a naive idea of the League of Nations' effectiveness, he supported it loyally. The ARP leader also recognized in 1918 that the Dutch East Indies would have to be granted independence in the distant future (after the enormous colonial oil resources were used by the motherland). In elections the ARP leader was a great vote-getter for his party, with over 402,000 votes won in 1922 (13% of total vote) and 665,000 in 1937 (16%).

Colijn warned of the disturbing trends in Germany concerning free love, gay marriage, racial breeding theories, anti-Semitism, massive unemployment, and poverty. At one point he met Benito Mussolini and returned home to warn the Dutch people of the antidemocratic nature of fascism.

When the Germans took the Netherlands in May 1940, Colijn made some tactical mistakes. He criticized Queen Wilhelmina in print for fleeing to London. Then his poorly timed pamphlet declaring that the future of Europe was tied to the future of Germany came out. With the help of **Jan Schouten,** Colijn soon realized his mistake and resigned the editorship of the compromised ARP daily *De Standaard* and took the party underground. He held large protest rallies and had his "twelve apostles" carry the resistance message to smaller groups.

In 1941 all democratic parties were banned, and Colijn was interned in Germany, where he died in 1944. In the Colijn obituary, the resistance paper *Trouw* declared, "We did not always agree with all that Colijn wrote in May 1940. But overall he was a patriot and a Calvinist. His principles will make a contribution to national renewal once liberation comes to The Netherlands."

Bibliography. Langley, M. R. "Balance Sheet: Kuyperian Worldview between the Wars, 1920–1932," *Christian Renewal* 23 (April 2005): 28–31. Puchinger, G. *Colijn.* Kampen, Netherlands: J. H. Kok, 1960.

McKendree R. Langley

COMÍN, ALFONSO (1933–1980). Sociologist, journalist, and politician, Comín was born in Zaragoza, Spain, into a traditionally Catholic integralist family; his father Jesús was elected a Carlist deputy in 1933 and 1936. Comín studied with the Jesuits, first in Zaragoza and then in Barcelona, where he moved in 1942 and where he stayed until his death, with the exception of four years that he spent at Malaga (1961–1965). He was influenced by the works of the Catholic philosopher José Luis López-Arangueren Jiménez, and in

1954 he entered the *Servicio Universitario de Trabajo* (University Labor Service), where he met Jesuit father José María Llanos. He was also influenced by the writings of Charles de Foucauld, Jean-Marie Domenach, and **Emmanuel Mounier.** In 1955, Comín joined the staff of *El Ciervo,* which served as his observation post for national affairs (such as the critiques on Spanish Catholicism) and international developments (the war in Algeria, the militancy of French Catholics in the Union de la Gauche Socialiste, worker-priests, the Twentieth Communist Party [Moscow] Convention, and critiques of Stalinism, the Cuban Revolution, etc.). Through contact with Mounier's review, *Esprit,* he met **José Bergamín.** After 1956 he became active in the *Frente de Liberación Popular* (National Liberation Front), an anti-Francoist organization in which many leftist Catholics took part, and was arrested for the first time after participating in a strike. The next year, he contacted the groups of Fr. Foucauld and joined the *Pax Christi.* In 1958 he took part in the initiatives of Fr. Pierre (Henri Gouès), the founder of the Emmaus association. In 1959 he received his degree in engineering. In an article he published in *El Ciervo* in 1958, Comín declared himself against Catholic confessionalist parties and in favor of leftist militancy. In 1961 he briefly stayed at Partinico in Sicily, where he followed the activities of the Italian social activist Danilo Dolci, and then he moved to Malaga with his wife, Maria Luisa Olivares y Sanvicens. While there he participated in the founding of the *Joventud Obrera Católica* (JOC, Young Catholic Workers). During the summer of 1965, he returned to Barcelona, where he worked on the collection *Tiempo de Concilio* for Nova Terra Editions. For a January 1967 article that he wrote for the French Catholic review *Témoignage Chrétien,* Comín was charged with spreading illegal propaganda and sentenced to sixteen months in prison. He began his time on October 7, 1969, but he was released on a pardon on January 24, 1970. Comín, furthermore, had already been arrested in January 1969 along with twenty-two of his friends who met at his house to speak with Mounier's wife. In 1970, he took part in the communist Bandera Roja organization, and in 1972 he founded Laia Editions and became its literary director. In 1973, Comín, along with others, provoked a split in the Bandera Roja and joined the Catalan Unified Socialist Party (PSUC). In 1975, he became a member of the central committee and of the executive branch of the PSUC and the Spanish Communist Party (PCE). In 1976, Comín founded and directed the Taula de Canvi. On March 20, 1980, he was made deputy of the PSUC in the Catalan parliament. In the summer of that year, he died of bone cancer, a disease that had tortured him since 1973.

Bibliography. Carmona Fernández, F. J. *Faith, Political Engagement, and Social Change in Spain: A Partial Social Biography of Alfonso Carlos Comín.* Ann Arbor: University of Michigan Press, 1996 Comín, Alfonso. *Obras.* 7 vols. Barcelona: Fundación Alfonso Comín, 1986–1994. Marzà, A. *Alfonso Comín, esperança en la historia: La persona de Comín y el debat cristianisme-marxisme en la perspectiva d'un christianisme d'alliberament.* Barcelona: Edicions 62, 1995.

Alfonso Botti

COMITÉ DE EMERGENCIA PARA AYUDA A LOS DESAROLLO (CEPAD). *See* Nicaraguan Council of Evangelical Churches

COMMUNION AND LIBERATION [COMUNIONE E LIBERAZIONE] (ITALY). The ecclesial movement popularly known as Communion and Liberation was created in Milan, Italy, at the Liceo Classico Berchet in 1954 as a result of the teachings of the Lombard Monsignor Luigi Giussani. After its creation, the new movement spread through the diocese under the name of *Gioventù Studentesca* (GS). The current name of Communion and Liberation was

adopted in 1969 to symbolize how Christ's sacrifice as shown through communion is at the root of the true liberation of humankind. A characteristic of the movement is the belief that Christianity, as a real and living event, can give meaning to one's life; therefore, faith must be behind every human action.

The pamphlet "Students of Milan" first appeared in 1957 and would continue for the next ten years as the principal voice of the new movement. Soon after began a series of initiatives called *Caritaviva* to help poor and needy people, especially those living in Milan's southern neighborhoods. Thousands of students actively participated in these initiatives.

The first editions of *Traces of the Christian Experience*, the new magazine of the movement, appeared in 1960. In that same year, there were various public meetings where the so-called GSers (or *giessini*), by now numerous in the schools throughout the city and province, spoke of various issues concerning the lives of young students. In 1962, the first mission financed by Communion and Liberation, which sent four *giessini* to Brazil, took place. Also in 1962, the Charles Peguy Cultural Center was founded to propose and expand upon issues that were of the utmost importance to the group. In 1968, the student protests that began at the Catholic University of Milan and spread throughout Italy affected all ecclesial associations, organizations, and movements. Many *giessini* became involved in these protests and left Communion and Liberation to join extreme leftist political organizations. After the turbulence, however, Monsignor Giussani's movement came back to life, especially in the universities, as well as among industrial workers and in residential neighborhoods.

Throughout the 1970s, Communion and Liberation was exceptional in sustaining Christian visibility in an increasingly secular society. Pope **Paul VI** recognized this aspect of the work of Giussani and the *ciellini* (CLers) and, in the holy year of 1975, gave a papal audience to 170,000 movement participants, explicitly recognizing Communion and Liberation in 1977. The movement's relationship with Pope **John Paul II** was even more intense: the *ciellini* knew Cardinal Wojtyla very well, and he appreciated their initiatives. In 1982, John Paul personally attended the Friendship Meeting that Communion and Liberation sponsored every summer.

Besides the Friendship Meeting, other Communion and Liberation initiatives included free schools, centers for the disabled, radio stations, and book publishers such as *Jaka Book.* In the 1980s, the Popular Movement (MP) and **Christian Democracy** were active enough to show a greater influence in the political sphere. The Brotherhood of Communion and Liberation, founded by adult members of the movement, obtained official Vatican recognition in 1983. Today, Communion and Liberation has more than 60,000 participants of all ages in European countries such as Germany, Switzerland, Poland, Ireland, England, and Spain. The movement also has participants in non-European countries such as the United States, Chile, Argentina, Brazil, Paraguay, Uganda, and Kenya. However, Communion and Liberation continues to maintain its movement characteristics—not those of an association—due to the fact that there are no membership fees. The spiritual growth at the core of this movement occurs by members' participation in the community by obeying ecclesiastic authority, diligently receiving the sacraments, and reading scripture; in this way, Christians can develop culture, charity, and missionary spirit.

Bibliography. Bianchi, S., and A. Turchini, eds. *Gli estrimisti di centro. Il neointegralismo cattolico degli anni 70. Comunione e liberazione.* Rimini-Florence, Italy: Guaraldi, 1977. Giussani, Luigi. *Tracce d'esperienza cristiana.* Milan: Jaka Book, 1977. Riva, G. *Don Giussani.* Milan: Rusconi, 1986. Ronza, R. *Comunionee Liberazione: Interviste a Luigi Giussani.* Milan: Jaka Book, 1976.

Eliana Versace

COMUNIONE E LIBERAZIONE. *See* Communion and Liberation

CONE, JAMES (b. 1938). Cone helped to inspire the movement known as black theology of liberation. Through such provocative books as *Black Theology and Black Power, A Black Theology of Liberation,* and *God of the Oppressed,* Cone insists that God is not neutral with respect to social injustice; rather, God stands on the side of the oppressed. Given the legacy and persistence of racism in the United States, God, in this context, is black. In Cone's own words, "Any theology that is indifferent to the theme of liberation is not Christian theology. In a society where men are oppressed because they are *black,* Christian theology must become *Black Theology*" (*Black Theology of Liberation,* 11).

James Cone has, at times, been a lightning rod for controversy. His writings often evoke a significant shock value. Cone's writings build upon two postmodern claims: that all politics is identity politics and that all theology is contextual. Although white Christians have drawn upon their own unique experiences to develop their own theologies, Cone insists, they mistakenly assume that their experiences are objective, neutral, and value-free, even when they clearly defend the interests of the dominant class. Cone has no illusions about the neutrality of his own works. He explicitly draws upon black experience as a source for black theology. Nevertheless, he understands the danger that any theology can become a form of self-justification, so he has engaged in dialogue with others, notably theologians outside the United States, women, and non-Christians, to refine his own theological views. In the process, he has had a profound impact upon third-world, feminist, womanist, and mujerista theologies. His writings have also become required readings for students at most mainline Protestant and Catholic seminaries.

James Cone has sought to reinvigorate the civil rights movement in the United States, in part by contextualizing the lives of the two most influential civil rights leaders. In *Martin and Malcolm and America: A Dream or a Nightmare,* Cone argues persuasively that the ideas of **Martin Luther King, Jr.,** and Malcolm X were converging. In this book he also reveals his conviction that the black community in the United States today could use a little more Malcolm and a little less Martin. Not surprisingly, Cone's own black theology of liberation, with its emphasis upon black power, black experience, and black liberation, resonates more powerfully with the views commonly associated with Malcolm X than with the views commonly associated with Martin Luther King, Jr. From Cone's perspective, racism today may be subtler than it was in the 1960s, "but the black masses remain trapped in a world of poverty and death" (*Malcolm and Martin,* 316). He goes on to conclude, "America is a nightmare for the poor of every race" (*Malcolm and Martin,* 316).

James Cone is an ordained minister in the African Methodist Episcopal Church. He has spent much of his career as the Charles A. Briggs Distinguished Professor of Systematic Theology at the Union Theological Seminary in New York. In 1992, *Ebony* magazine granted him the American Black Achievement Award in the category of religion.

Bibliography. Cone, James H. *A Black Theology of Liberation.* New York: J. B. Lippincott, 1970. Cone, James H. *Martin and Malcolm and America: A Dream or a Nightmare.* Maryknoll, NY: Orbis Books, 1991.

Andrew D. Walsh

CONFEDERACIÓN ESPAÑOLA DE DERECHAS AUTÓNOMAS. *See* Spanish Confederation Of Autonomous Right-Wing Groups—CEDA

CONFEDERACIÓN NACIONAL-CATÓLICA AGRARIA—CNCA. *See* National Catholic Agrarian Federation.

CONFEDERACIÓN NACIONAL CATÓLICA DEL TRABAJO—CNCT. *See* National Catholic Labor Confederation

CONFÉDÉRATION FRANÇAISE DES TRAVAILLEURS CHRÉTIENS—CFTC. *See* French Confederation of Christian Workers

CONNOLLY, THOMAS LOUIS (1814– 1876). The archbishop of Halifax (1859–1876), Connolly enjoyed great influence but modest success in promoting Catholic schools in Canada, the Canadian Confederation, and Canadian Irish loyalty. Born and educated in Ireland as a Capuchin priest, he came to Halifax in 1842 as secretary to Bishop William Walsh. Three years later he was vicar-general of the diocese, then bishop of Saint John, New Brunswick, in 1852 before assuming the archbishopric in 1859.

The Conservative government of Nova Scotia came to power in 1863 and set two major goals. It was committed to joining the Canadian Confederation and to establishing common schools throughout the province. The government assured Archbishop Connolly and Bishop Colin MacKinnon of Antigonish (1852–1877) that Catholic rights would be protected.

Responding to this overture, Archbishop Connolly in 1864 embraced the Tory strategy for confederation of the Canadian provinces. The next year, Connolly wrote to Bishop John Sweeney of Saint John (who opposed confederation) that "confederation is thoroughly sound in almost every point of view" (Flemming, 72–73). Bishops Colin MacKinnon and James Rogers of Chatham joined Connolly in support of a pro-confederation policy.

Connolly also took issue with Catholic editor Timothy Anglin of the Saint John *Freeman,* who opposed Confederation.

In 1866 the charming and intelligent Connolly, with the support of his suffragans, sailed for London to lobby for a legislative provision that would recognize Catholic schools in the Maritime Provinces. The resulting Section 93 of the British North America Act turned out to be a most contentious part of Canadian constitutional history. At the London Conference in 1866, Connolly explained that the denominational schools of New Brunswick and Nova Scotia, as well as those in Quebec and Ontario, should be included in the new Canadian constitution. His proposal called for two educational systems in the Maritime Provinces, one for Catholics and another for Protestants, paid for by the school taxes of their respective denominations. Connolly's proposal was subsequently scaled down by **Thomas D'Arcy McGee,** and the consequent legislation supported schools in Ontario and Quebec but not in New Brunswick and Nova Scotia.

Maritime Catholics thus had to be satisfied with something less than constitutional guarantees and accept a gentleman's agreement as a negotiated settlement. Catholic institutions under these haphazard arrangements had to shift for themselves and provide schools where financially feasible. Committed religious sisters were essential to providing quality education at modest cost. Despite this disappointment, Archbishop Connolly and Irish, Scottish, Canadian, and Aboriginal Catholics remained committed to confederation, believing it was the strongest guardian of religious minorities and would eventually bring economic advantage.

At the First Vatican Council in Rome in 1869, Connolly studied the definition of papal infallibility and sided with the insights of the minority. Owing to the political sensitivities of the time, he believed the definition was inopportune. With many of the minority, Connolly revealed his unhappiness with the majority's decision and returned to his diocese before the vote was taken. He later subscribed to the majority's decision and approved *Pastor aeternus.*

Bibliography. Flemming, David B. "Archbishop Thomas L. Connolly, Godfather of Confederation." *CCHA Study Sessions* 37 (1970): 67–84.

Terence J. Fay, SJ

CONSALVI, ERCOLE (1757–1824). Cardinal Consalvi made it his life's work to preserve and promote the interests of the Roman Catholic Church and the authority of the papacy in an age of political and social upheaval. Consalvi earned the respect of his contemporaries and a place for himself alongside the likes of **Metternich** and Talleyrand in the pantheon of nineteenth-century European diplomats. Stendhal (Marie-Henri Beyle) observed that Consalvi was "the greatest statesman in Europe, because the only honest one" (Robinson, xi).

Born in Rome to a noble family, Consalvi devoted his career to the temporal or political power of the papacy, not the spiritual authority of the successor to St. Peter. For this reason, he has been described as "a secular cardinal" (Robinson, 1). As prosecretary of state to **Pius VII,** a position he occupied from 1800 to 1806 and 1814 to 1823, Consalvi undertook a serious internal reform of papal government and did more than any other individual to restore the international prestige of the papacy. Consalvi implemented financial and administrative reforms to stimulate the economic life of the Papal States. This included the introduction of free trade, the abolition of inequitable taxation and ecclesial privileges, and the inclusion of laypersons in the day-to-day operations of the papal government.

Consalvi was instrumental in defending and enhancing the power and prestige of the papacy in the face of growing secularization, nationalism, and anticlericalism. One of Consalvi's greatest political achievements as a statesman was the negotiation of a concordat with Napoleon's France in 1801. Consalvi refused to consent to Napoleon's demand that the church and the exercise of religion be subject to the state, and to police regulation. Through persistence, flexibility, and creativity, Consalvi negotiated an agreement that satisfied both parties and defended the principle of the church's autonomy from the state.

The Concordat of 1801 served as a model for church-state relations after the French Revolution. Consalvi worked to extend the concordat system to protect the interests of the church and the rights of Catholics throughout Europe. In doing so, he laid the foundations for the centralization of papal authority and church governance in the nineteenth and twentieth centuries. At the Congress of Vienna (1814–1815), Consalvi solidified his reputation as a brilliant statesman. In face-to-face meetings with some of Europe's most experienced diplomats, the cardinal successfully negotiated the restoration of mostly all the Papal States lost during the French Revolution and the Napoleonic Wars.

When his career ended in 1823, Consalvi could count many lasting accomplishments. Perhaps no single individual did more than he did to preserve and promote the temporal power of the papacy against great odds. Not only did he strengthen papal government from within, but he also helped to restore the international prestige of the papacy. Consalvi's career was a watershed in the history of the papacy, the fruits of which are evident today more than ever.

Bibliography. Ellis, John Tracy. *Cardinal Consalvi and Anglo-Papal Relations, 1814–1824.* Washington, DC: Catholic University of America Press, 1942. Robinson, John Martin. *Cardinal Consalvi, 1757–1824.* New York: St. Martin's Press, 1987.

Robert A. Ventresca

CONSELHEIRO, ANTÔNIO (1830–1897).
Antônio Vicente Mendes Maciel, commonly known as Antônio Conselheiro (wise counselor), remains intimately linked to the settlement in the Bahian backlands known as Canudos and its ultimate destruction by regiments of the Brazilian national armed forces in 1894. The event's most famous chronicler, Euclides da Cunha, referred to it as "our Vendée," a reference to the 1793–1796 wars in which armies of the new French Republic defeated a popular uprising in that region.

Like the rebellious folk of the Vendée, Conselheiro and his followers refused to accept the disestablishment of the Catholic Church that occurred when the First Brazilian Republic (known also as the Old Republic) replaced the monarchy in 1789.

Typically described as a mystic, Antônio Conselheiro followed a penitential and millennial tradition that had begun with the activities of Padre Ibiapina (José Antônio Pereira, 1806–1883), a lawyer turned religious missionary who traveled and preached throughout the backland areas of Brazil's northeast. In the early 1870s, Conselheiro took up a life of itinerant lay preaching, living from alms, and repairing churches and cemeteries. Over the course of the ensuing years, he became known throughout the region and gained a number of followers. In 1893, he established the Canudos settlement, which grew in size as poor people from the backlands sought refuge in what they regarded as a holy city. That growth angered area landowners, who regarded it as an affront to their authority and a threat to their ability to extract labor from the masses.

For reasons related to complex state and national political currents, Canudos also came to be seen as a center of rebellion against the new Brazilian Republic, and in 1896 the first of several military expeditions marched on the settlement. Although the residents proved successful in resisting several campaigns, in October 1897 a fourth military expedition destroyed Canudos, killing most of its residents. By that time, Conselheiro already was dead, most probably because of dysentery.

Generations of Brazilian historians, powerfully influenced by Brazilian writer Euclides Da Cunha's portrayal of the destruction of Canudos as representing a struggle between civilization and barbarism, typically portrayed both Conshelheiro and his followers as fanatics. In recent years, however, a reappraisal of popular or "folk" Catholicism and issues of social class and power have sparked reinterpretations that present both Conselheiro and Canudos in a more positive fashion.

Bibliography. Levine, Robert M. *Vale of Tears: Revisiting the Canudos Massacre in Northeastern Brazil, 1893–1897.* Berkeley and Los Angeles: University of California Press, 1992.

Gerald Michael Greenfield

CONWELL, RUSSELL HERMAN (1843–1925). Conwell was born into modest circumstances in Worthington, Massachusetts. After graduating from Wilbraham Academy in 1859, he taught school for a short time before briefly studying law at Yale. During the Civil War, he served as an officer in the Union Army. In the late 1860s, he practiced law, worked as a journalist, and engaged in civic activities in Minneapolis. After traveling abroad as an immigration agent and reporter, he lived for several years in Boston, making a living as an attorney, newspaper editor, author, and lecturer. Ordained as a Baptist minister in 1879, Conwell became pastor of Grace Baptist Church in Philadelphia in 1882. Under his leadership, the church inaugurated innovative programs, including the establishment of a hospital and the launching of a program of education for Philadelphia's working class, which by the late 1880s had evolved into Temple College, now Temple University.

Conwell was best known by his contemporaries as a public speaker, and his name appears today in history texts because of his most famous lecture, "Acres of Diamonds," a paean to the American myth of success. He was, however, more than an apostle of Gilded Age materialism. He was also a proponent of the so-called gospel of wealth, insisting that those who enjoyed worldly success had an obligation to use their wealth in socially responsible ways. At the same time, he cautiously espoused ideas sometimes associated with the **Social Gospel** and progressivism. Although he appreciated the economies of scale inherent in big business and recognized the need for some regulation, he mistrusted the concentration of too much power in business or government. He believed that workers deserved a fair share of the wealth they helped to produce but was wary of the potential tyranny of unions, believing arbitration to be a reliable means of achieving justice for labor. He prized the Baptist principle of rigid separation of church and state but urged Christians to utilize the vote to address such evils as political corruption and the saloon and to support such reforms as more liberal divorce laws, the inheritance tax, and the direct election of senators. Though not free of prejudice, he advocated better education for, and fairer treatment of, African Americans. He supported restrictions on the entry of undesirable aliens into the United States but opposed the wholesale exclusion of immigrants willing to embrace the American way of life. Conwell had misgivings about colonialism and war but believed that his nation had an international obligation to promote civilization and defend victims of oppression and aggression.

Bibliography. Nelson, Clyde K. "The Social Ideas of Russell H. Conwell." PhD diss., University of Pennsylvania, 1968.

Robert F. Martin

COUGHLIN, CHARLES (1891–1979).
Coughlin, the so-called radio priest of the
1920s and 1930s, was the only child of
Irish Americans from Hamilton, Ontario.
Groomed by his devoutly Catholic mother
to become a priest, Coughlin entered seminary as a child and was ordained in 1916.
After some parish work in Canada, Coughlin
transferred to Royal Oak, Michigan, a suburb of Detroit, in 1926 to supply a struggling parish. Coughlin turned to radio
broadcasts as a fundraising measure as well
as a modern effort to combat Royal Oak's
stridently anti-Catholic climate.

Coughlin's radio popularity soon sky-
rocketed. By 1931, the stations broadcast-
ing his *Golden Hour of the Shrine of the
Little Flower*—named after the recently
canonized Therese of Lisieux—ranged
from Maine to Missouri. Other religious
figures preached over the radio, but no
one equaled Coughlin's popularity. He
received over 250,000 letters a week, more
than any other American. Donations
helped build the massive stone Shrine of
the Little Flower in Royal Oak. Besides his

Charles Coughlin. Courtesy of the Library of Congress

velvety baritone voice and on-air demeanor,
Coughlin demonstrated deep pastoral
concern. Coughlin spoke confidently
about the emphasis of the Catholic
Church's social theology upon the divine
right of both private property and just
employment practices. During the
Depression, this empathy for working-
class struggles fueled his exploding popularity. He attacked socialism and
communism as false and irreligious solutions to the economic crisis.

At first Coughlin supported Roosevelt's
New Deal, claiming the nation faced
a choice between "Roosevelt or Ruin."
However, he soon grew increasingly critical of the president's policies. Federal
authorities responded by revealing
Coughlin's speculations in the silver market while he duplicitously argued for
changing the money standard to silver. In
1934, Coughlin formed the National
Union for Social Justice (NUSJ), which
featured a sixteen-point platform of populism and Catholic Social theology. In 1936,
feeling betrayed by Roosevelt, Coughlin
joined **Gerald L.K.
Smith** and Francis J.
Townsend for a hasty
and ill-conceived
third-party presiden-
tial campaign. As a
priest Coughlin could
not run for office, so
a North Dakota con-
gressman, William
Lemke, did so. Wary
of each other,
Townsend and Smith
both wanted to use
Coughlin's popular
NUSJ for their own
political ends. All
of them quickly lost
confidence in Lemke,
who gained only
3 percent of the
popular vote.

Coughlin returned to the radio in early 1937 ready to harangue the Roosevelt administration. His demagoguery helped defeat the New Deal's 1938 Reorganization Bill. However, Coughlin's attacks quickly devolved into anti-Semitic diatribes concerning Jewish conspiracies. He repeatedly blamed Jews for his, and the nation's, reversals. As the Nazis took over Germany, Coughlin praised Hitler's willingness to combat Jewish interests. The Christian Front, populated by Coughlin's listeners, further linked Coughlin to Nazism. FBI agents arrested eighteen Front members in 1940 for suspected subversive activities.

Coughlin appeared unwilling to control his followers, and he seemed to have direct communication with Nazi leaders. Later in 1940 his bishop, Edward Mooney, cancelled Coughlin's radio show. In 1942, Mooney prohibited him from publishing his anti-Semitic magazine *Social Justice.* Coughlin retreated to the quiet routines of Catholic parish life in suburban Detroit. He died in 1979, largely forgotten except by Catholic traditionalists who revered him as a prophet and martyr. Nonetheless, while occasionally credited as the "father of hate radio," Coughlin pioneered the Catholic clergy's use of new media and introduced Catholic Social thought to new American audiences.

Bibliography. Brinkley, Alan. *Voices of Protest: Huey Long, Father Coughlin, and the Great Depression.* New York: Alfred A. Knopf, 1982. Fisher, James Terence. *The Catholic Counterculture in America, 1933–1962.* Chapel Hill: University of North Carolina, 1989. Warren, Donald. *Radio Priest: Charles Coughlin, the Father of Hate Radio.* New York: Free Press, 1996.

Jeffrey Marlett

CRISTEROS MOVEMENT (MEXICO). The Cristeros movement of the 1920s was part of a long struggle for power between Catholic leadership and secular political regimes in Mexico. The Cristeros fought to maintain Catholic rights and political influence in the face of determined resistance from Mexican revolutionary governments.

Spain's monarchs controlled the Catholic Church during Mexico's colonial period (1521–1821). Separate papal bulls acknowledged the Crown's right to serve as apostolic vicar, nominate archbishops and bishops, and collect tithes on behalf of the church. The state directed evangelization efforts, built churches and monasteries, and demarcated dioceses. The church became extraordinarily wealthy and influential; religious orders, most notably Dominican, Franciscan, Augustinian, and Jesuit, acquired vast urban and rural properties, and secular clergy benefited from frequent donations and bequests. Clerics enjoyed special privileges, such as the right to be tried by ecclesiastical and inquisitorial officials rather than by civil and criminal magistrates. During the eighteenth century, however, enlightened Bourbon despots more fully subordinated the regular orders to bishops, expelled the Jesuits in 1767, and diminished church economic influence.

Liberals and freemasons in independent Mexico after 1821 demonstrated increased hostility toward the church, which they said stifled progress and modernization. Constant political upheaval between liberals and conservatives dominated Mexican politics for decades. Liberals achieved their agenda through various reform laws and the constitution of 1857, which granted freedom of religion, abolished ecclesiastical immunities, prohibited religious institutions from owning private property, limited parish fees and services, ended religious instruction in schools, deemed marriage a civil contract, eased restrictions on divorce, secularized cemeteries, and forbade clerics from holding public office. President Porfirio Díaz (1876–1911) sought a policy of conciliation with the church and never enforced most of these anticlerical measures.

The Mexican Revolution (1910–1917) ended Díaz's dictatorship and fostered significant socioeconomic change. Like its predecessor, the constitution of 1917 contained anticlerical measures that secularized education, restricted religious orders, eliminated church properties, forbade clergy participation in politics, and permitted state legislatures to limit the number of priests. Presidents Venustiano Carranza (1917–1920) and Álvaro Obregón (1920–1924) proved unwilling to confront the church. President Plutarco Elías Calles (1924–1928) relished the opportunity, especially given the vocal opposition of Archbishop José Mora y del Río, who frequently criticized the constitution.

On July 2, 1926, Calles proclaimed the government's right to convert churches into government buildings and encouraged governors to limit priestly activity. He also endorsed the formation of a Mexican Catholic Church free of papal influence. Perhaps Calles hoped to end fanaticism and resented the upper clergy's endorsement of conservative politicians. More likely, he attempted to create "new cultural identities and practices through which local patron saints and communal ties would be replaced by secular heroes and a national identity" (Purnell, 179).

Catholics responded vehemently to Calles's enforcement of the anticlerical articles of the constitution. The episcopacy suspended public worship on July 31, 1926, making it difficult for parishioners to receive sacraments for the next three years. Urban Catholic groups such as the Catholic Association of Mexican Youth and the **National Catholic Party** joined forces under an umbrella organization, the National League for the Defense of Religious Liberty. Rural rebellions erupted throughout the country and were especially intense in Colima, Guanajuato, Jalisco, Michoacán, and Nayarit. Fighting to the slogan *Viva Cristo Rey* (Long Live Christ the King), these *Cristeros* repre-sented a significant threat to the revolutionary regime.

The episcopacy never officially sanctioned warfare and began dialogue with government officials. Some National League members favored the overthrow of the government and participated in revolts during the first months of the movement, but most defected after significant government military victories in 1927. Enrique Gorostieta and Jesús Degollado y Guízar provided military leadership. Peasants did most of the fighting and successfully engaged federal troops and agrarian militias. The latter were compelled to defend the regime in order to maintain their land. The 1928 assassination of President-Elect Obregón by a Catholic stalwart may have prompted state and ecclesiastical officials to end the military conflict. Approximately 60,000 government soldiers and 40,000 Cristeros died in battles until the episcopacy signed an agreement with President Portes Gil in June 1929. Church officials demanded that Cristeros put down their arms. The anticlerical articles of the constitution remained, but they would not be enforced vigorously.

Mexican president Lázaro Cárdenas (1934–1940) sought rapprochement with the church. His successor, Ávila Camacho (1940–1946), went as far as to describe himself as a "believer" during his presidential campaign. Recent years have witnessed increased goodwill, as suggested by four papal visits by **John Paul II,** the establishment of diplomatic relations between the Vatican and Mexico, and changes to the constitution that gave priests the right to vote and permitted religious instruction in private schools. These developments have provided a respite for Mexico's 90-percent Catholic populace.

Bibliography. Meyer, Jean A. *The Cristero Rebellion: The Mexican People between Church and State, 1926–1929.* Trans. Richard Southern. Cambridge: Cambridge University Press, 1976. Purnell, Jennie. *Popular Movements and*

State Formation in Revolutionary Mexico: The Agraristas and Cristeros of Michoacán. Durham, NC: Duke University Press, 1999.

Lee M. Penyak

CRISTIANOS POR EL SOCIALISMO. *See* Christians for Socialism

CZECHOSLOVAK PEOPLE'S PARTY (ČESKOSLOVENSKÁ STRANA LIDOVÁ). The Czechoslovak People's Party, sometimes referred to as the Czechoslovak Catholic Party, participated in the multiparty system of the Czechoslovak Republic (1918–1938). The roots of the party originated in the rise of the Christian socialist and clerical movements of the late nineteenth-century Habsburg Empire and the unique national situation in Bohemia and Moravia that occurred with the collapse of the Old Czech Party and the rise of the more secular Young Czech Party.

Not only was Catholicism challenged by the rise of secular politics, but the Czech national revival's focus on the Protestant Hussite tradition, particularly in Bohemia, concerned Czech Catholics. Before World War I, a conservative clerical party was established in Moravia, which had notable success, electing a number of delegates to the provincial and imperial diets. In Bohemia the Catholic political movement followed Christian socialist ideals, but there was extensive factionalism. Such factionalism, combined with Bohemia's secular and Protestant traditions, resulted in a weaker Catholic political movement than existed in Moravia.

With the creation of an independent Czechoslovak state, the Czechoslovak People's Party was established and played a role in the coalition governments that marked interwar Czechoslovakia. Although the party never won more than about 10 percent of the vote in national elections, Monsignor Jan Šramek, the party leader, participated in the coalition governments and held a number of leadership positions in the government and ruling Committee of Five (Petka). He did not always follow Vatican policy, particularly in 1925, when the Vatican reacted strongly to the government commemoration of the five hundredth anniversary of the death of Jan Hus. Šramek's moderation was rewarded when the government preserved certain privileges for the Roman Catholic Church. The party operated independently of the larger Catholic Slovak Democratic Party.

The party did not support the Munich Pact and during World War II was represented in the Czechoslovak exile government in London. Following the defeat of Nazi Germany, the party participated in the democratic coalitions that marked the postwar Czechoslovak government until 1948. Šramek was increasingly in ill health, and others like Monsignor František Hala, Pavel Tirgid, and Adolf Procházka assumed more responsibility. Following the February 1948 communist takeover, the party was banned.

Bibliography. Marek, Pavel. "Emancipation of Czech Political Catholicism, 1890–1914." *East European Quarterly* 37 (1): 1–17. Trapl, Miloš. *Political Catholicism and the Czechoslovak People's Party in Czechoslovakia, 1918–1938.* New York: Columbia University Press, 1995.

Paul Kubricht

D

DAENS, ADOLPHE (1839–1907) Born in the Flemish industrial town of Aalst in a family of six, the abbé Daens dedicated his priesthood to the defense of the working classes as well as the Flemish people. Refusing at times to obey his superiors in the Catholic Church, and also to ally himself with Charles Woeste (also from Aalst, the leader of the mainstream Catholic Party, which had been governing Belgium with a majority since 1884), he founded the Christene Volkspartij/le Parti Populaire Chrétien (the Christian Popular Party) in 1893. In the first Belgian elections with qualified universal male suffrage (1894), he was elected to the parliament as a representative from Aalst.

Inspired by the doctrine of Christian democracy and supportive of the Flemish movement, Daens's party outraged other Catholics by its lack of discipline and its class polemics, felt by the church authorities and the elite of the Catholic party to be too close to socialism. After some gentle encouragement from several of his colleagues, in 1896 he brought his movement into the Ligue démocratique belge, an umbrella organization for several hundred small groups within the Catholic Party. This move signaled his willingness to try to work within the unified Catholic Party structure; however, given the Daensists'

preoccupation with personal rivalries and their confrontational attitude toward the class question, they were expelled from the organization within a year of joining. Fewer than two thousand of the Ligue's ninety thousand members left with Daens, and his party never achieved more than two seats and 3 percent of the vote, never expanding beyond its original base in the southern parts of the Belgian provinces of East and West Flanders.

Although it was condemned by the church before it had achieved any political importance, Daens's movement demonstrates the agitation in favor of Christian democracy that existed behind the facade of the unified Catholic party in Belgium. Its fate also exemplified the impossibility at the end of the nineteenth century of founding any organization dedicated to Christian democracy without the express support of the Catholic hierarchy.

Bibliography. Verdoodt, Frans-Jos. *De zaak-Daens: Een priester tussen Kerk en christendemocratie.* Leuven, Belgium: Davidsfonds, 1993.

Timothy Baycroft

DALLA TORRE, GIUSEPPE (1885–1967). Count Dalla Torre directed the official newspaper of the Vatican, the *Osservatore Romano,* for forty years from 1920 until

1960, and over the pontificates of popes **Benedict XV, Pius XI, Pius XII,** and **John XXIII.**

Born in Padua, he became the director of the city's Catholic daily, *La Libertà,* in 1909. Three years later, Pius X appointed him president of the Popular Union (*Unione Popolare*) of **Italian Catholic Action.** Dalla Torre headed the Popular Union from 1912 and, from 1915, also chaired the directorate of Catholic Action until September 1920, when he became the editor of *Osservatore Romano.* He strongly believed in peace, dialogue, and the respect of human dignity, and consequently he was a strong antiwar advocate, but when the First World War started he volunteered and served in an artillery unit and then at the supreme command.

Dalla Torre played a supporting role to Don Luigi Sturzo in the establishment of the **Italian Popular Party** (*Partito Popolare Italiano,* PPI) in 1919. Hence his editorial in the November 11, 1919, edition of the *Osservatore Romano,* which advocated a number of principles dealing with religious liberty, family law, education system, and labor unions that were in accordance with the PPI's platform. The rise of Italian Fascism triggered a split in the party between those who advocated some measure of sympathy for Fascism, many of whom were active in Catholic Action, and Don Sturzo's more intransigent followers. Dalla Torre favored the former and suggested through his *Osservatore Romano* editorials that his readers remain loyal to Catholic Action and not to any political party.

An avowed anticommunist, Dalla Torre disapproved of the PPI's role in the so-called Aventine crisis (wherein Mussolini's opponents boycotted the Chamber of Deputies), and he considered any type of antifascist coalition with the Left a disgrace. His position strengthened the Vatican and papal position but at the same time meant a great loss for the party, which was soon suppressed by Mussolini's regime. Nevertheless, Dalla Torre continued to support Catholic Action against Fascist measures to curtail it.

After Italy's 1943 collapse in World War II, Dalla Torre was instrumental in securing Allied support for **Alcide De Gasperi** and **Christian Democracy,** although his *Osservatore Romano* positions through the 1950s tended to side with conservatives.

Bibliography. Dalla Torre, G. *Azione Cattolica e Fascismo.* Rome: A.V.E., 1964. Dalla Torre, G. *I cattolici e la vita pubblica italiana.* 2 vols. Rome: Cinque Lune, 1962. Ferrari, F. L. *L'Azione cattolica e il "regime."* Florence: Parenti, 1957. Howard, E. P. *Il Partito Popolare Italiano.* Florence: La Nuova Italia, 1957. Molony, J. N. *The Emergence of Political Catholicism in Italy: Partito Popolare 1919–1926.* London: Croom Helm, 1957.

Efharis Mascha

DAMASKINOS. *See* Papandreou, Demetrios

DAWSON, CHRISTOPHER (1889–1970). Dawson, one of the generation of English Roman Catholic converts influenced by **John Henry Newman,** was an influential historian during the period of the Second World War and the beginnings of the cold war. His work reveals the path taken by many Catholic thinkers, from a criticism of liberal democracy's secularizing and centralizing tendencies to an alliance with liberal democratic thinkers in opposition to the rise of totalitarianism.

He vividly expressed his concerns in *Religion and the Modern State* (1936), where he wrote, "Communism in Russia, National Socialism in Germany, and Capitalism and Liberal Democracy in Western countries are really three forms of the same thing, and they are all moving by different but parallel paths to the same goal, which is the mechanization of human life and the complete subordination of the individual to the state." Dawson, drawing on the social encyclicals of **Leo XIII** and later popes, attempted to outline a corporatist, organic view of society that would respect economic liberty while preserving the agrarian heritage he considered so central to the English tradition of liberty and the spiritual ends of human life.

Beneath his various responses to particular modern regimes, however, the core of Dawson's political thinking was a historical vision of Western civilization as the outgrowth of Christianity. Dawson's conversion and historical vocation can be traced to a visit to Rome during his college years, when he sat on the celebrated steps of the *Ara Coeli* and conceived the idea of writing a counternarrative to Edward Gibbon's famous condemnation of Christianity as the destroyer of civilization.

Dawson was born into a High Anglican family; attended Winchester and Trinity College, Oxford; and converted without fanfare to Roman Catholicism in 1914. John Henry Newman's writings helped convince him that "the Church that made Europe may yet save Europe." Newman also inspired his deep antipathy for the dehumanizing combination of skepticism and conformism he encountered at school, and his close study of scripture that led him to an understanding of the sacramental economy in the life of the church.

In 1929 his book *Progress and Religion,* a study of the secularization of the idea of progress, gave him an audience far larger than did his earlier scholarly and generally non-polemical work. In 1932 he published the second book in a planned multivolume history of the world, *The Making of Europe,* in which he argues contra Gibbon and contra nineteenth-century Teutonic theories that the Christian church preserved the thread of Latin culture through the dark ages. During World War II, as editor of the *Dublin Review* and vice president of an interdenominational group, the Sword of the Spirit, he worked to shape the public's understanding of the war

effort. His 1942 publication, *The Judgment of the Nations,* shows the complexity of his position—his desire to be true to his critique of the totalitarian strain within the secular liberal tradition of the West while supporting the liberal democracies in their struggle with racist, nationalist fascism and international communism.

After the war his reputation for integrity and vision was recognized when he was first invited to give the prestigious Gifford Lectures (published as *Religion and Culture,* 1948, and *Religion and the Rise of Western Culture,* 1950) and later to become the first Chauncey Stillman Chair of Roman Catholic studies at Harvard University (1957–1962). During his years at Harvard, he published *The Crisis of Western Education* (1961), a criticism of American progressive educational reforms and a counterproposal for a curriculum in which the Christian tradition would shape every discipline. From his encounter with American society, he seemed to draw hope in the future of the Christian West while grappling with the difficulties of preserving the political liberalism of limited government and fostering an organic society oriented to spiritual ends.

Bibliography. Allit, Patrick. "The Convert Historians." In *Catholic Converts: British and American Intellectuals Turn to Rome.* Ithaca, New York: Cornell University Press, 1997. Scott, Christina. *A Historian and His World: A Life of Christopher Dawson.* London: Sheed & Ward, 1984.

Susan E. Hanssen

DAY, DOROTHY (1897–1980). Day cofounded the **Catholic Worker movement** in 1933 with the itinerant French philosopher Peter Maurin. The Catholic Worker movement (and monthly newspaper of the same name) promoted the social teachings of the Roman Catholic Church while also performing the gospel works of mercy in urban settings across the United States. Dorothy Day described herself as a

Catholic anarchist and urged followers to eschew participation in electoral politics, but her movement was deeply influential among Catholics across a wide spectrum of political persuasions. The Catholic Workers offered a model of public witness against war and social injustice and encouraged others to practice the social teachings of the church in everyday life.

Dorothy Day was the third of five children of John Day, an itinerant sportswriter, and Grace Satterlee, both from nominally Protestant backgrounds. Day enjoyed an intensely religious orientation from early childhood, but as an adolescent she developed an equally ardent attraction to the urban proletariat; she grew certain that these commitments were irreconcilable. When she converted to Catholicism on Staten Island in December 1927—twenty-one months after offering her infant daughter for baptism and just weeks after ending a common-law relationship with the child's father—she remained unaware that the Catholic Church featured a social doctrine. In 1932, Day met Peter Maurin, who quickly convinced her to turn her lower Manhattan apartment into a "house of hospitality" serving their impoverished and unemployed neighbors. Maurin tutored Day in the message of the church's major social encyclicals, Pope **Leo XIII**'s *Rerum novarum* (1891) and **Pius XI**'s *Quadragesimo anno* (1931). While Maurin felt the encyclicals' critique of capitalism and calls for a more communitarian social order were overly timid, Day blended the message of the encyclicals with the leftist ideology of her pre-conversion years and created an unprecedented movement of Catholic radicals that was at the same time radically Catholic.

In her newspaper and in public forums during the 1930s, Day vociferously defended the rights of workers to organize (especially in places like Jersey City, where a deeply entrenched Catholic political leadership violently resisted organizing campaigns of the Congress of Industrial Organizations). While Peter Maurin described himself as a reactionary seeking a revival of premodern peasant Catholicism, Day was a thoroughly urbanized American with a deeply pragmatic temperament. The Catholic Worker movement grew from the creative tension between Day and her mentor. It was not a labor movement in any sense but rather a communitarian experiment in gospel witness. Day condemned the New Deal for substituting public welfare programs for a Christian model of shared responsibility for the poor and dispossessed. She espoused absolute pacifism during the Second World War, a decision that divided her movement but solidified her reputation as an individual of unwavering integrity.

The political implications of Day's mission emerged most clearly in the 1950s and 1960s. In the 1950s Michael Harrington and Robert Ludlow led a cohort of younger figures intent on applying Catholic Worker radicalism to political issues. Harrington became a socialist and left the movement, but his 1962 book, *The Other America*, was rooted in his Catholic Worker experience and helped spur the 1960s war on poverty. In 1965 Catholic Workers were among the first young Americans to burn draft cards in protest of the Vietnam War. The Second Vatican Council (1962–1965) and the emergence of a theology of liberation in the late 1960s validated the preferential option for the poor that had always been central to the Catholic Worker movement. Dorothy Day remained however a deeply orthodox Catholic and was dismayed by the sexual revolution and the youthful counterculture that some mistakenly believed she had encouraged. Her cause for canonization was introduced by New York's **John Cardinal O'Connor** in 1997.

Bibliography. Fisher, James Terence. *The Catholic Counterculture in America, 1933–1962.* Chapel Hill: University of North Carolina

Press, 1989. Miller, William. *Dorothy Day: A Biography.* New York: HarperCollins, 1984.

James T. Fisher

DE BECKER, RAYMOND (1912–1969). De Becker launched the Catholic personalist movement in Belgium in the early 1930s, although he later ambiguously infused it with a national socialist orientation. In its "communitarian personalism," the influential French review *Esprit,* took a cue from him and promoted a Christian answer to both individualist liberal democracy and collectivistic totalitarianism.

This maverick Catholic Youth leader put forward, as a revolutionary alternative to communism and fascism, an anti-bourgeois, postcapitalist "totalitarian Catholicism" encompassing all aspects of life, while accommodating nonbelievers in a spiritualistic—but not specifically Catholic—New Order. Drawing from the new Christian personalist language developed by thinkers like Nicholas Berdiaev and **Jacques Maritain**, over against the right-wing rhetoric associated with **Charles Maurras** that was preferred by other young Belgian Catholic radicals like **Léon Degrelle**, De Becker led or inspired many movements and publications of French-speaking Belgian Catholic youth. Noteworthy is *L'Esprit nouveau,* a review that he quit as editor in 1933 to undertake a pilgrimage through France, where he encountered several Catholic intellectuals.

Emmanuel Mounier found in him a model for Christian political action. De Becker's project of a personalist lay order—baptized *Communauté* in 1934—was established just as Mounier was defining communitarian personalism as *Esprit's* political philosophy. Mounier lived in Brussels from 1935 to 1938, and his review popularized De Becker's work to an international readership; De Becker's quest for a common front, for example, between young Catholic militants and morally serious young Socialists, outside their own parties, on the basis of Mounier's communitarian personalism, Hendrik De Man's ethical socialism, and state "planism." Other personalists like Maritain became increasingly wary of De Becker's involvement with pro-German leftists, like Hendrick, who called for the unity of all classes and all parties in a "national socialism."

De Becker renounced Christianity in 1938 to support first National Socialism, and then the wartime European New Order—defending Belgium's place in it as collaborationist editor of the main Brussels daily *Le soir* until, disillusioned and outmaneuvered by his old rival Degrelle, he resigned in 1943. Facing a death sentence upon his return from German captivity, he was pardoned in 1950 and wrote many books exploring his pagan Gnostic spirituality and newfound homosexual lifestyle. He committed suicide when his longtime partner left him.

Bibliography. Conway, Martin. "Building the Christian City: Catholics and Politics in Interwar Francophone Belgium." *Past and Present* 128 (August 1990): 117–51.

Christian Roy

DE GASPERI, ALCIDE (1881–1954). De Gasperi was one of the founders of Italian **Christian Democracy** (DC) at the end of World War II and represents one of twentieth-century Europe's most able practitioners of Catholic politics. He was born of middle-class parentage in Pieve Tesino (Trentino) in what was then Austria-Hungary and graduated in 1905 with a degree in philology from the University of Vienna. Six years later he was elected to the Austrian parliament by the Trentine Catholic regionalist party.

After Italy annexed Trentino at the end of the First World War, De Gasperi joined the newly formed **Italian Popular Party**

(PPI) and won election to the Chamber of Deputies in 1921. A collaborator close to the party's founder, **Luigi Sturzo,** De Gasperi served as the PPI's last leader prior to its disbanding in 1926, a victim of the consolidation of Benito Mussolini's Fascist dictatorship. Accused of clandestine activities and then imprisoned for nine months by the regime, De Gasperi was released with Vatican assistance. He spent the next decade working as a librarian at the Vatican and studiously laying the organizational and intellectual foundations for the Christian Democratic party. Much of the DC's postwar program may be traced back to De Gasperi's *Reconstructive Ideas of Christian Democracy,* which circulated in Rome in July 1943, just after Mussolini's fall from power.

Between December 1945 and July 1953, De Gasperi headed eight successive governments, serving as the Italian Republic's first, and to this day most durable, prime minister. His approach to postwar economic reconstruction depended heavily on the austere anti-inflationary liberalism of budget and finance minister Luigi Einaudi, mitigated in part by reform initiatives like the *Cassa per il Mezzogiorno* (Fund for the South). Relying initially on a broad antifascist coalition, including the Socialist and Communist parties, De Gasperi excluded these parties from the government in 1947. Though he mistrusted the Marxists' "Jacobinism," De Gasperi did not want to break with them until the lion's share of the new Italian republican constitution had been drafted—including Article 7, which made the 1929 Lateran Accords and Concordat (preserving the political integrity of the Vatican) an integral part of the new document. The watershed 1948 elections garnered the Christian Democrats an absolute majority of seats in the Italian Chamber of Deputies. Nevertheless, De Gasperi bucked Vatican pressures and retained a multiparty governing coalition with the Social Democrats and several other small centrist lay parties. As the cold war deepened, he endeavored to contain the Marxist Left within a position of ongoing parliamentary opposition. In 1949 he resisted right-wing pressures to outlaw the Communist Party or, in the early 1950s, to accept parliamentary support from the neo-Fascists.

A staunch supporter of the Western alliance and NATO, De Gasperi also espoused European federalism. In the eyes of his countrymen and women, however, he was most appreciated for his leadership in reconciling Italy's Catholic and its liberal, secular national traditions. De Gasperi understood parliamentary politics as a vocation possessing its own professional standards and ethos. During the quiet decade he spent working at the Vatican library, De Gasperi researched the experience of pioneer Belgian, French, and Austrian Christian Democrats, as well as the German **Center Party.** He drew on the legacies of these European forerunners, and on the writings of such contemporaries as French neoscholastic **Jacques Maritain** in refining his own distinctive political philosophy. De Gasperi's celebrated 1948 Brussels address—"The Moral Bases of Democracy"—echoed both Maritain's *Christianity and Democracy* (1943) and the wartime Christmas radio messages of Pope **Pius XII.**

For all his personal piety, however, De Gasperi was no integralist: in biographer Elisa Carillo's words, he disliked those who "say their prayers on street corners." This sensibility contributed in no small measure to the trust he inspired among a broad spectrum of postwar lay political leaders. Even Italian Communist Party chieftain Palmiro Togliatti, writing four years after De Gasperi's death, acknowledged the unusual "disinterestedness" and personal probity of his erstwhile political nemesis.

Bibliography. Carrillo, Elisa. *Alcide De Gasperi: The Long Apprenticeship.* Notre Dame,

IN: Notre Dame University Press, 1965. De Gasperi, Alcide. *De Gasperi scrive: Corrispondenza con capi di stato, cardinali, uomini politici, giornalisti, diplomatici.* Ed. Maria Romana Catti De Gasperi. Brescia, Italy: Morcelliana, 1974. Scoppola, Pietro. *La Proposta politica di De Gasperi.* Bologna, Italy: Il Mulino, 1977. White, Steven. "Christian Democracy versus Pacellian Populism: Rival Forms of Post-war Italian Political Catholicism." In *Christian Democracy: Historical Legacies and Comparative Perspectives,* ed. Thomas Kselman. Notre Dame, IN: Notre Dame University Press, 2002.

Steven F. White

DE GAULLE, CHARLES (1890–1970). Leader of the French Resistance in World War II and founder of the Fifth French Republic, de Gaulle was born in Lille of a royalist and religious family. His father, Henri, a pupil of the Jesuits, became headmaster of the Jesuit College of the Immaculate Conception in Paris and there de Gaulle did his studies from 1901 until 1907, when the Third Republic expelled the Jesuits from France. Transferring to the Jesuit college at Antoing across the border in Belgium, he soon passed the entrance exam for the French military academy at St. Cyr in 1910. Graduating as a second lieutenant in 1912, he served with the French army at Arras under **Philippe Pétain**. During World War I, he fought with distinction but was a prisoner in Germany for its final two years. From 1919 to 1921 Captain de Gaulle spent two years in a French advisory unit helping newly independent Poland fight the Russian Bolsheviks.

During the interwar period, he served on the staff of the Supreme War Council and as lieutenant colonel on the National Defense Council. He wrote a series of books during this period emphasizing mobile and mechanized tank warfare as the wave of the future, as opposed to the static bunker strategy associated with defense minister André Maginot.

Following the outbreak of World War II in 1939, he commanded a tank brigade that fought successfully against the Nazi invasion. Promoted to brigadier general, he was named by Premier Paul Reynaud undersecretary of state for defense, answering to Reynaud himself, who took over the ministry. When Pétain replaced Reynaud as the last premier of the Third Republic and negotiated an armistice with Hitler, de Gaulle refused to accept defeat and flew to London on June 17, 1940. As Churchill was later to write, "He carried with him in this small airplane the honour of France."

Notwithstanding Churchill's initial enthusiasm, de Gaulle soon became alienated from him because of the British sinking of the French fleet at Mers-el-Kebir. De Gaulle's relations with America's President Franklin Roosevelt were even more strained. Nonetheless as leader of the Resistance, de Gaulle succeeded in winning for the once-defeated and occupied France a place at the table of victors, a zone of occupation in Germany, and one of the five permanent seats on the Security Council of the new United Nations.

From September 1944 he headed the provisional government of France but resigned in January 1946 because the political parties planning the Fourth Republic refused to heed his advice for a stronger executive and revised election system in the new constitution so as to preclude the paralysis that had brought the Third Republic to its knees. He retired to his country home at Colombey-les-Deux-Églises in Champagne.

The Algerian crisis of May 1958 and consequent threat of civil war and an army coup brought him out of retirement as the last premier of the Fourth Republic. He and Michael Debré drafted the constitution for a Fifth Republic, which dramatically strengthened the powers of the French president and provided for a run-off election system for the National

Charles de Gaulle during an official visit, 1967. © Bruno Barbey / Magnum Photos

Assembly that was more likely to produce a majority party and diminish deadlock. Over the opposition of the leftist parties, the French people in a referendum approved the new constitution in September 1958. De Gaulle became first president of this Fifth Republic in January 1959 with Debré as his premier. He further strengthened the presidency through a 1962 referendum by which the people would directly elect the president through universal suffrage rather than through the 80,000-member electoral college of local officials that had selected him in 1958.

One of the effects of the growing success of the Gaullist party in the Assembly was to undermine the **Popular Republican Movement** (Mouvement Republicain Populaire, MRP), the center-left Catholic party, which regularly received between 15 and 25 percent of the vote in Fourth Republic elections and along with the socialists and communists was one of the three major governing parties. Now Catholics felt comfortable voting for de Gaulle as a practicing Catholic. Many other French men and women also felt comfortable voting for the party of this nationalist hero who represented the values of both the Center and the Right and would increasingly also articulate economic and social policies that could well be described as center-left. The result was a center-right majority in both presidential and parliamentary elections for the next twenty years.

Among de Gaulle's achievements were the resolution of the Algerian problem by persuading the French people in a referendum to grant independence; the resolution of all of France's colonial problems in West and Equatorial Africa by a referendum that allowed each colony to decide for itself whether it wanted immediate independence or rather to remain in a French Union with certain economic benefits; and the development of a French nuclear weapon that would guarantee French independence for the foreseeable future. His failure to persuade the French electorate in a 1969 referendum to broaden the electoral college, which chose members of the French Senate, caused him to resign. The highly conservative Senate had been blocking many of his progressive economic and social reforms. De Gaulle retired to Colombey and produced one volume of his presidential memoirs before his death in 1970.

Bibliography. Gaulle, Charles de. *Memoirs of Hope, 1958–62.* London: Weidenfeld & Nicolson, 1971. Gaulle, Charles de. *Memoirs of War, 1940–46.* 3 Vols. New York: Simon & Schuster, 1964. Lecoutre, Jean. *De Gaulle.* 2 vols. New York: HarperCollins, 1992.

William J. Parente

DEGRELLE, LÉON (1906–1994). Degrelle's career illustrates how the interwar quest for Christian alternatives to parliamentary democracy and communism could veer into authoritarian politics for its own sake in the hands of a charismatic leader.

In 1930, this student journalist was asked by the Catholic Association of Belgian Youth to revive the small publishing house Christus Rex. Its ensuing politicization, with public meetings where Degrelle honed his oratorical skills, worried Catholic authorities, who distanced themselves from the **Rexist movement** in 1933. Degrelle began openly attacking the Catholic Party establishment. Rex became first the focus of a dissident movement among young Francophone members, and then a populist party in its own right for the 1936 elections, successfully channeling a broader protest vote against a corrupt and dysfunctional party system.

All other parties rallied behind Catholic premier Van Zeeland when he ran against Degrelle to stop him from winning a 1937 by-election, and the Belgian primate condemned Rex when he claimed church support. Degrelle's contacts with Axis powers further marginalized Rex, but this only increased the messianism of remaining Rexists, vindicated by Germany's

seemingly triumphant imposition of a post-liberal, anticommunist New Order in Europe. They became unconditional supporters of this international authoritarian "revolution," and while most saw themselves as good Catholics, they attacked the clergy for not joining it. Degrelle was excommunicated for coming to Mass wearing the SS uniform as general of the Légion Wallonie, formed in 1941 to fight on the eastern front, which he used to stage his comeback from the political wilderness. The Germans finally appointed Degrelle führer of the Walloons in 1944, when they withdrew from Belgium.

Degrelle followed the Germans, escaped through Norway, and lived to a ripe old age in Spanish exile, writing books about his exploits and international fascism—as a defense of Christian civilization.

Bibliography. Bruyne, Eddy de, and Marc Rikmenspoel. *For Rex and for Belgium: Léon Degrelle and Walloon Political and Military Collaboration 1940–45.* Solihull, UK: Helion, 2004. Conway, Martin. *Collaboration in Belgium: Léon Degrelle and the Rexist Movement, 1940–1944.* New Haven, CT: Yale University Press, 1993.

Christian Roy

DELBRÊL, MADELEINE (1904–1964). An atheist who converted to Catholicism, Delbrêl lived for more than thirty years in the Parisian "red belt" suburbs, an area with a strong Communist presence. Originally from Mussidan, a farming village in the southwest of France, Delbrêl moved with her family to Paris in 1916. The Bolshevik Revolution of 1917 strongly influenced the French workers' movement, and for Delbrêl, it was the opportunity to become familiar with the Marxist artists Paul Éluard, Louis Aragon, and Tristan Tzara.

After years of irregular study, she eventually graduated from the Sorbonne with a degree in philosophy. Delbrêl's dealings with Catholic students helped her become aware of the world of scouting and consti-tuted the decisive element in her conver-sion. The direct impact of the stock market crash of 1929 on the poor people of the Parisian metropolitan area inspired her to reflect upon social injustices and to form, with other young people, a focus group on sacred scripture. Three years later this focus group grew into a project for com-munal living. The community expanded thanks in part to the donation of a small house to the group by the parish of Ivry-sur-Seine, a locality known as a center for the formation of Communist party lead-ers. With it, the group created an aid cen-ter for workers and the poor.

In 1935, this community grew even larger and took the name of Équipe (Team) to highlight the idea of the division of work and of bodily spirit. Delbrêl then became a social worker, but contact with working families, the majority of whom were Communists, was not easy. The town council of Ivry gave her the direction of social and family services. This began her collaboration with the town's Communist administration, and because of a new French Communist Party (PCF) initiative in 1936, the Mutual Aid Committee for the Unemployed was founded, giving the chance for Catholics and nonbelievers to work together. The work of Équipe contin-ued in the climate of the Popular Front under Léon Blum. Delbrêl prepared peti-tions to get the government to open dis-pensaries and public libraries as well as to create educational programs for workers.

During World War II she worked for Parisian Social Services to help control the influx of refugees into the city. She also took an active part in the Resistance effort. She was asked to join the PCF and, though tempted, formally refused the invitation. Despite her beliefs in Marxist action, after reading a book on Lenin and religion, Delbrêl discovered a profound difference between Communism and Catholicism, the latter teaching universal love for all human beings, not just a single social class. Delbrêl's actions, therefore, all favored justice for all mankind.

In 1952, Delbrêl asked the French Bishops not to participate in the Eucharistic Conference of Barcelona in the name of Spanish refugees. In the new effervescent climate of the 1960s, Delbrêl continued to fight for Christians and the modern world. Rearmament and nuclear experiments convinced her to participate in the *Mouvement de la Paix* (Peace Movement), which was linked to Communists and, therefore, deplored by Catholics. Delbrêl participated in well-received conferences throughout all of France, where she dis-cussed her experiences as a Christian. In her writings, just as in her life, she opened dialogues with those who had different political or religious beliefs than her own, contesting dominant ideas and fighting for social justice against discrimination.

Bibliography. Delbrêl, Madeleine, and David Louis Schindler. *We, the Ordinary People of the Streets.* Trans. Charles F. Mann. Grand Rapids, MI: William B. Eerdmans, 2000. Mann, Charles F. *Madeleine Delbrêl: A Life Beyond Boundar-ies.* San Francisco: New World Press, 1996.

Ilaria Biagioli

DEMOCRATIC POPULAR PARTY [PARTI DEMOCRATE POPULAIRE] (FRANCE).

The Parti Democrate Populaire (PDP) was the first Christian Democratic party in France and a direct precursor of the **Mouvement Républicain Populaire** (MRP) launched after the Second World War. The PDP was born in the aftermath of the First World War, when Catholic-Republican tensions had largely dissi-pated thanks to the loyal service of Catholics in the French armed forces. This new attitude was underlined by the election of a number of Catholics to the Chamber in 1919 and by plans, subse-quently discarded, for a Catholic parlia-mentary group. In the end, it was not until 1924 that a distinct Catholic political body was created in the establishment of the PDP.

The PDP has traditionally been viewed as among the more conservative elements of French Christian democracy. This image stems from the fact that, while its cousin the *Jeune République* focused on building bridges to the Left, the PDP sought to win over more right-wing Catholics, who had previously been very hostile to the republic. The PDP's refusal to formally support the Popular Front in 1936 is often cited as evidence of the party's conservative leaning. Still, the PDP was not without reformist credentials. It advanced the principle of democracy, favored cooperation between the classes, rejected unbridled capitalism, and supported both the League of Nations and Aristide Briand's attempts to foster better relations with Germany.

The PDP never succeeded in becoming a truly national party. Nevertheless, some of its members—most notably its president, Auguste Champetier de Ribes (1882–1947)—achieved a degree of notoriety. Champetier de Ribes assumed a number of ministerial portfolios in the Third Republic and was among the eighty deputies who voted against the granting of full powers to Marshal **Philippe Pétain** in 1940. This and his subsequent resistance work with Combat led **Charles de Gaulle** to select him as the inaugural president of the Council of the Fourth Republic in 1946.

As with much of French Christian democracy in the interwar period, the significance of the PDP does not lie in its own achievements but in what it foreshadowed. Its philosophy reflected a new synthesis of traditional social Catholicism and Christian democracy that came into full blossom with the emergence of the MRP after 1945.

Bibliography. Irvin, R.E.M. *Christian Democracy in France.* London: George Allen & Unwin, 1973.

Peter Farrugia

DEMOCRAZIA CRISTIANA (ITALY). *See* Christian Democracy (Italy)

DE MUN, ALBERT (1841–1914). Count De Mun was a pioneer French Social Catholic and member of Parliament. Born into an aristocratic family of age-old loyalty to king and church, he began a military career with service in Algeria. He served heroically in the war of 1870 but, with the defeat of the army in 1871, was interned at Metz. There he formed a close friendship with a fellow Catholic officer, **Rene La Tour du Pin.** They read Emile Keller's commentary on **Pius IX**'s *Syllabus of Errors* and were completely persuaded by its thesis that France's dire social conflict was rooted in the false philosophy of liberalism and its corollary economic individualism. De Mun saw this insight confirmed as an officer in the army that put down the workers with great savagery in the rebellion of the Commune in 1871.

As he meditated on the enormous chasm that separated the workers from the middle class, he hit on the idea of bringing workers and employers together. This was the basis of the project he initiated at this point, which he called the *Oeuvre des Cercles.* The Cercles, or Clubs, were designed to provide centers where the workers could relax, find entertainment, get counseling and material help, and have an occasion for friendly dialogue with the employers.

The early success of the Cercles saw the number of clubs climb to 150, with a membership of some 18,000. In fact, as the membership continued to grow, the Cercles remained for twenty years the center of French Social Catholicism. But the political aspects of the movement violated the neutrality of the army, and De Mun was forced to abandon his military career. He decided to run for a seat in the National Assembly and as a victorious candidate was dubbed the "Knight of the Syllabus," a name that summed up the thrust of the

Albert de Mun. © Harlingue / Roger Viollet / Getty Images

first phase of his work in the Assembly, as he regularly engaged in verbal combat with the radical republicans with their quasi-religious faith in the French Revolution. "We are the Counterrevolution!" he would commonly exclaim.

At the same time De Mun's awareness of the misery of the workers and the poor moved him to work indefatigably for social reform. Inspired by Leon Harmel, the Catholic manufacturer and social activist, he supported separate unions for the workers, which he came to see as the more realistic approach. A strange interlude occurred at this point, which involved him in an ignominious episode involving a failed attempt to restore the monarchy with the help of a second-rate ex-general— George Boulanger. The whole affair was a great embarrassment for De Mun, but it prepared him for the next shift in his thought.

This was a follow-up to Pope **Leo XIII**'s call to French Catholics to cease identifying their cause with that of the monarchy and work with the moderate republicans. It was a big leap for De Mun to make, but one that his loyalty to the pope required. He then set about organizing a conservative Catholic party, Action Liberale Populaire, which in a coalition with progressive republicans he hoped might wrest power from the radicals and socialists. It combined the goals of Social Catholicism— living wage, improved working conditions, old-age pensions, and liberal Catholicism— with freedom of education and freedom of worship. Pope Leo blessed it as an expression of the kind of Social Catholicism adumbrated in his encyclical, *Rerum novarum* (1891).

In the elections of 1896 De Mun's coalition seemed ready to defeat the radicals, who had closed down the Catholic schools, confiscated church property, and separated the church from the state, but it was outmaneuvered by Clemenceau. Then as the reactionary policies of the new pope, **Pius X** (1903–1914), set in, the fortunes of the party further declined, as did De Mun's hopes to spearhead social reform. Moreover, the looming war with Germany diverted everyone's attention. De Mun, however, was able to forge an alliance with the moderate republicans and heal the division between clericals and anticlericals on the basis of their mutual commitment to nationalism and rearmament.

Social Catholicism disappeared from the agenda of the ALP, though De Mun continued his personal fight for labor reform. When the war broke out, he devoted himself without stint to the war effort until he suffered a fatal heart attack. De Mun stands out as a pioneer French social Catholic and statesman whose efforts for social reform as well as his efforts to integrate Catholics into French political life bore fruit after his death. In 1920, France reestablished diplomatic relations with the Vatican and incorporated many of de Mun's Social Catholic ideas into reform legislation.

Bibliography. Bokenkotter, Thomas. *Church and Revolution.* New York: Doubleday, 1998. Martin, Benjamin. *Count Albert de Mun.* Chapel Hill: University of North Carolina Press, 1978.

Thomas Bokenkotter

DESJARDINS, PAUL (1859–1940). Trained as a classical philologist, Desjardins abandoned his career as a literary critic in order to organize conferences and societies through which intellectuals, philosophers, and academics might build an independent and scholarly community capable of sustaining a nondenominational Christian humanist outlook.

Following the Dreyfus Affair, Desjardins founded, in 1892, the Union for Moral Order, which became, in 1905, the Servants of Truth. Their meetings and publications defended nondogmatic Christian ethics and discussed how to infuse a spiritual element into contemporary French politics in order to achieve social and moral justice. Starting in 1910, Paul Desjardins hosted annual conferences in the old Cistercian Abbey of Pontigny in Yonne, France. The Pontigny school reflected the efforts of progressive and politically engaged intellectuals to participate in a national discourse concerning French spiritual identity outside existing forums and in conditions that would become increasingly difficult with the political polarizations associated with interwar France. Representatives from several intellectual generations and a handful of European nations convened to discuss topics ranging from the nature of divine grace to the consequences of immigration policies. Attendees enjoyed a sophisticated balance of morning lectures, afternoon teas, and evening soirees.

Following the disruption occasioned by the First World War, summer conferences at Pontigny recommenced in 1922 and lasted until 1939. Three ten-day gatherings—hence the term *décade*—ran through the month of August. While the so-called School of Pontigny had been particularly well attended by writers associated with the *Nouvelle revue française* in the 1910s, its postwar reincarnation was favored by authors associated with the prestigious Gallimard publishing house who sought to (re)produce "a healthy cultural dialogue" (Aron, 401). Leading intellectual figures who attended included Raymond Aron, André Malraux, Charles du Bos, André Gide, Lytton Strachey, François Mauriac, Thomas and Heinrich Mann, Jean Schlumberger, Denis de Rougemont, Jean Tardieu, Raymond Aron, Léon Brunschvicg, Angelo R. Tasca, René Poirier, Gaston Bachelard, Jean Prévost, Antoine de Saint-Exupéry, André Maurois, Jean-Paul Sartre, Alfred Fabre-Luce, Jean Tardieu, and Roger Martin du Gard. The level of intellectual discussion in the 1922 *décade,* for instance, was such that Roger Martin du Gard told André Gide that his participation had left him feeling humbled (Heurgon-Desjardins, 386). Celebrated *décades* included André Malraux and Jean-Paul Sartre in 1926 on communism and the Chinese Revolution; **Gaston Roupnel** in 1929 on pre-Christian pantheism and agrarian civilizations; E. d'Ors on Christianity and baroque art; R. Aron in 1932 on the rise of German nationalist socialism; Angelo Tasca in 1935 on the nature of Italian fascism; and G. Bachelard in 1939 on "anti-Babel."

Desjardins' intellectual and spiritual legacy survives today through annual conferences still hosted by the Pontigny-Cérisy Foundation.

Bibliography. Aron, Jean-Paul. "Les Décades de Pontigny et Cerisy. . . ." In *Histoire sociale, sensibilities collectives et mentalités,* ed. Robert Mandrou. Paris: Presses Universitaires de France, 1985. Chaubet, François. *Paul Desjardins et les Décades de Pontigny.* Villeneuve d'Ascq: Presses Universitaires du Septentrion, 1999. Heurgon-Desjardins, Ann. *Paul Desjardins et les Décades de Pontigny.* Paris: Presses Universitaires Françaises, 1964.

Philip Whalen

DEUTSCHE CHRISTEN (GERMAN CHRISTIANS). Several movements of German Protestants in favor of National Socialism (ca. 1927–1945) have been collectively described as Deutsche Christen (DC). Two main currents of the Deutsche Christen have been identified, the *Kirchenbewegung* and the *Glaubensbewegung.*

The *Kirchenbewegung* was a movement regarding the organization of the German Protestant churches, founded in Thuringia in 1927 by two parsons. This group stood for the union of German Protestants in a single nationwide people's church. Other groups with similar ideas, especially from Wurttemberg and Bremen, joined this branch of the Deutsche Christen. For a time some even advocated the integration of German Catholics into this national German church. The *Glaubensbewegung* was a movement regarding the faith. Under the direct influence of the National Socialist Party this movement developed in Prussia in 1932 and attempted to bring about a synthesis between the National Socialist ideology and Christianity. It identified Germany, for example, as the Holy Land, and Adolf Hitler as the person to finally complete the reformation started by Martin Luther. The importance of the allegedly Jewish Old Testament was depreciated. Both movements were complementary to each other despite different geographical and theological origins, not to mention rivaling leaders.

The Deutsche Christen won a large majority in the Protestant Church election of July 1933 after Hitler in a broadcast had personally called on the German Protestants to vote in favor of the movement. A German national church was established with an empire's bishop, the *Reichsbischof* Hermann Müller. But besides the different *Landeskirchen,* the regional Protestant churches subsisted. Müller tried to impose racist German legislation on the church, excluding from office, for example, people with Jewish ancestors, Jewish spouses, or spouses with Jewish ancestors. He overplayed his hand, however, and stirred up significant and widespread resistance when he attempted to incorporate all the Protestant youth organizations into the Nazi Party's Hitler Youth. The National Socialist leadership, furthermore, was at variance regarding Müller himself, the general role of the church within the führer's state, and the adaptation of party ideology to Christian beliefs. Thus, after 1934 the Deutsche Christen lost direct National Socialist and government support. The minority of the German Protestant clergy who opposed the Nazi regime, at best one-third of the total, and their *Bekennende Kirche*

(Confessing Church) were suppressed by the state.

Officially more than half of the German Protestant churches remained in the hands of the Deutsche Christen until the end of the war. After the collapse of the Third Reich, the Allied powers dissolved the Deutsche Christen. Leading representatives were replaced by personnel recruited from the Bekennende Kirche. In Lower Saxony and in Wurttemberg, however, small communities of the Deutsche Christen survived well into the 1960s.

The movement clearly demonstrates the disruption of the dozens of German Protestant churches, which no longer seemed to be convenient to the country's political condition in the early 1930s. The Deutsche Christen replied to the search for orientation and the demand for unity with the idea of a common ideological and organizational subservience to the state. Yet the Deutsche Christen never served as a pliant tool to the Third Reich. This was certainly due to internal quarrels within the movement and the small but strong opposition within German Protestantism, but hardly less important was the skepticism among the National Socialists themselves.

Bibliography. Meier, Kurt. *Die Deutschen Christen: Das Bild einer Bewegung im Kirchenkampf des Dritten Reiches.* 3rd ed. Göttingen, Germany: Vandenhoeck & Ruprecht, 1967.

Bernd Leupold

DE VALERA, EAMON (1882–1975). De Valera is the most significant Irish nationalist leader in twentieth-century Ireland. Born in New York City of an Irish mother and Cuban father, de Valera was raised in Ireland. Trained as a mathematician, he became involved in Irish nationalist organizations including the Gaelic League and the Irish Volunteers. He participated in the 1916 Easter Rising and was the only major leader to escape execution, primarily because of his American birth. In 1917 he was elected leader of the major nationalist movements, **Sinn Fein** and the Irish Republican Army. In 1919 he was elected by the underground Dail Eireann as president of the Irish Republic. He rejected the Anglo-Irish Treaty in 1921, which ended the Irish struggle for independence. In spite of his opposition to the new Irish Free State, he entered Dail Eireann in 1927, and in 1932 he became president of the executive council. In 1936 under a new constitution this became *Taoiseach,* a position he held from 1936 to 1948 and from 1952 to 1959. After he left this office he was elected for two terms to the largely ceremonial position of president of Ireland. He died in 1975, two years after leaving office.

De Valera invoked strong positive as well as negative feelings among his followers and opponents throughout his long career. In his personal life he was a modest man of strong Catholic faith. As was true of most Irish nationalists, he made little distinction between his faith and his nationalism. In many ways, for these individuals to be Irish meant also to be a Catholic. He was a man of strong convictions, and once he had made up his mind on an issue was not given to reassessments.

De Valera served as primary draftsman of the new constitution, a document that focused primarily on severing links to Great Britain. It also contained sections that reflected his views on the ideal Catholic Irish society. The new constitution, known as *Bunreacht na hÉireann,* was ratified by the people in July 1937 and essentially created a standard British-style parliamentary democracy. It was distinctive because of its section on entrenched rights, which were a mixture of traditional British rights, such as freedom of press, assembly, and speech, with those rights usually associated with Catholic concepts of natural rights. It affirmed the sanctity of marriage, banned divorce, declared the primacy of family in education, and protected the significance of personal property for the use of the individual. Rights in the constitution were rooted in natural law as being "antecedent to positive law" (Article 43). Moreover, the preamble to the constitution clearly lays out the Christian and Catholic basis of the document with its reference to the "most Holy Trinity" and "to Our Divine Lord, Jesus Christ Who sustained our fathers through centuries of trial."

While de Valera was the principal author of the constitution, he did consult others, including members of the civil service, such as John Heron, as well as the Jesuit Edward Cahill and the Holy Ghost priest John Charles McQuaid, who later became cardinal archbishop of Dublin. There was some conflict over the provisions in Article 45, which, while recognizing the significance of the Catholic Church, also guaranteed religious freedom and named several other Christian faiths as well as Judaism in its list of faiths adhered to by Irish citizens.

On other matters, particularly those related to Irish society and moral values, de Valera was quite willing to accept the guidelines of Catholic social and philosophical thought. This is often associated with his broadcast on St. Patrick's Day in 1943, when he talked about what he saw as the ideal life that God desired human beings to live. He described Ireland as "a land whose countryside would be bright with cozy homesteads, whose fields and villages would be joyous with the sounds of industry, with the romping of sturdy children, the contests of athletic youths, the laughter of comely maidens, whose firesides would be forums for the wisdom of serene old age. It would, in a word, be the home of a people living the life that God desires man should live."

De Valera's Ireland was an ideal that was based on a strong alliance between the Irish government, the Catholic Church, and the rural and urban middle class. It

Eamon de Valera. Courtesy of the Library of Congress

came with a certain price. Those who for whatever reason did not fit into the model of patriarchy and small family-owned farms were often isolated, and poverty was widespread. Conflict and unrest were controlled by immigration. At the same time, de Valera as a Catholic leader was more of a Christian democrat and displayed little sympathy for the views of his contemporaries in Spain and Portugal.

Bibliography. Coogan, T. P. *De Valera: Long Fellow, Long Shadow.* London: Hutchinson, 1990. Keogh, Dermot. "Church, State and Society." In *De Valera's Constitution and Ours,* ed. Brian Farrell. Dublin: Gill & Macmillan, 1988.

Gretchen M. MacMillan

DIBELIUS, OTTO (1880–1967). A theologian and one of the principle figures of the German Evangelical Church (Evangelische Kirche Deutschland, EKD) who faced the challenges of war and dictatorship, Dibelius was born in Berlin, the son of a privy government councilor. His theological studies in Berlin (1899 to 1904) and in Giessen led him to the ideas of Adolf von Harnack and **Adolf Stoecker**. He continued his education in Scotland and was ordained in 1906.

After serving as a pastor in Crossen, Danzig, Lauenburg, and Berlin, he was appointed general superintendent of Kurmark in 1925. From 1945 to 1966 he was bishop of the Evangelical Church in Berlin-Brandenburg. He was president of the **World Council of Churches** from 1954 to 1960 and held the highest office (chairman, or *Ratsvorsitzender*) of the Evangelical Church from 1949 to 1961. The relationship between state and church was the central theme of Dibelius's works and the motivating force for his political and organizational activities. In his widely noted book *Das Jahrhundert der Kirche* (1926), he criticized the 1918 November Revolution for its destruction of imperial Germany. At the same time, he argued that this destruction offered the church independence from the state and contained the possibility of a renewed importance of the church as a moral force in a secular state; the church should facilitate a national renewal and unification after the ravages and rifts of war and revolution. Antidemocratic and nationalist sentiments among German Protestants made them susceptible to National Socialist propaganda. Dibelius, for example, refused to support an international campaign championed by **Dietrich Bonhoeffer** in support of nine black Americans who had been sentenced to death. Dibelius initially sympathized with National Socialism, only to be quickly disenchanted by Hitler's attempts to create a unified Reich Church. He was driven from office in 1933.

After a short stay in Italy he returned to Germany, where, as a prominent member of the Confessing Church, he fought Nazi intrusions on church independence. In 1937–1938 he was prosecuted because of a conflict with church affairs minister Hans Kerrl, although the court case ended with an acquittal. As a recipient of the Gerstein reports (named after a member of the Confessing Church who also was a SS officer), Dibelius became aware of the gassing of Jews in Belzec in 1942. After the war, when he was a member of the provisional Council of the Evangelical Church, he participated in the writing of the October 1945 Stuttgart Declaration of Guilt (*Stuttgargter Schuldbekenntnis*).

Dibelius joined the **Christian Democratic Union** and contributed to national reconciliation and to the reconstitution of the Evangelical Church. In his *Grenzen des Staates* (Limits of the State, 1949) he claimed that the Confessing Church's resistance to Nazism constituted a "world historical service" that demonstrated the church's importance as "strong bulwark against the tyranny of state violence." He warned that only the church could limit the claims to power made by modern states in the East and the West. He ignited controversy when he argued that citizens of totalitarian regimes such as that of the German Democratic Republic had the right to resist the state. As president of the World Council of Churches, he was a recognized leader of the ecumenical movement.

Bibliography. Hartmut. Fritz. *Otto Dibelius: Ein Kirchenmann in der Zeit zwischen Monarchie und Diktatur. Mit einer Bibliographie der Verèoffentlichungen von Otto Dibelius, Arbeiten zur kirchlichen Zeitgeschichte.* Göttingen, Germany: Vandenhoeck & Ruprecht, 1998. Stupperich, Robert. *Otto Dibelius: Ein evangelisher Bishof im Umbruch der Zeiten.* Göttingen, Germany: Vandenhoeck & Ruprecht, 1989.

Thomas M. Bredohl

DIEM, NGO DINH (1901–1963). Diem, first president of the Republic of Vietnam, was born near the imperial city of Hue, in central Vietnam. He was a member of a prominent mandarin family that had converted to Catholicism in the mid-nineteenth century. Diem was both a deeply zealous Catholic (he took a vow of celibacy as a young man) and a committed Vietnamese nationalist.

In 1933 Diem resigned his position as minister of the interior in the regime of Emperor Bao Dai after French colonial administrators reneged on promised reforms. Diem was later declared a subversive by French officials and he was also condemned in 1945 by Ho Chi Minh, leader of the communist-nationalist Viet Minh. In 1950, Diem entered an exile that included a notorious stay at Roman Catholic Maryknoll seminaries in Lakewood; New Jersey; and Ossining, New York.

Shortly after the French garrison at Dienbienphu fell to the Viet Minh in April 1954, Bao Dai—from his exile in Paris—appointed Diem prime minister of the portion of Vietnam ceded to pro-Western forces, which became the Republic of Vietnam (better known to Americans as South Vietnam). Diem's fledgling regime was most ardently promoted by U.S. Air Force Colonel Edward G. Lansdale, the CIA's station chief in Saigon. Lansdale was charged to manufacture a pro-American regime under Diem's leadership, a goal made viable by Lansdale's central role in the transplantation of nearly one million Vietnamese from the communist North to the South during the fall and winter of 1954–1955. Lansdale won crucial support for Diem from skeptical figures in the State Department in Washington and also constructed a potent pro-Diem lobby, consisting of liberal anticommunists and prominent Catholics, in the United States. The former were always more influential than the latter despite enduring claims that Diem's ascent was orchestrated by New York's **Francis Cardinal Spellman** and other Catholic anticommunists.

Diem's American public relations were always much more effective than his relations with Vietnamese constituents. The most powerful member of his administration was his brother Ngo Dinh Nhu, a mystic who sought to adapt the French Catholic philosophy of personalism to Vietnamese conditions. Personalism was an unsystematic mélange of "third force" ideas associated with **Emmanuel Mounier** and other French Catholics who rejected both capitalism and Marxism. In the hands of Nhu and Diem, personalism supplied the intellectual foundation for an authoritarian regime that alienated Catholics nearly as badly as South Vietnam's Buddhist majority. At the same time, Diem's American handlers made little effort to understand Vietnamese history or culture, a point Diem made with increasing vehemence until even his lobbyists lost confidence in his leadership. John F. Kennedy was an enthusiastic supporter of Diem in the mid-1950s but was surprised to discover how unpopular his regime had grown by 1960. U.S. policy veered sharply away from unconditional support of Diem after President Kennedy sent Henry Cabot Lodge to Saigon as ambassador in August 1963.

Diem was finally overthrown in a coup and assassinated, along with Ngo Dinh Nhu, on November 2, 1963. Though Kennedy tacitly endorsed the coup, he denied that his fellow Catholic leader and his brother were despots. "No," he said. "They were in a difficult position. They did the best they could for their country."

Bibliography. Hammer, Ellen J. *A Death in November: America in Vietnam, 1963.* New York: E. P. Dutton, 1987. Jacobs, Seth. *America's Miracle Man in Vietnam: Ngo Dinh Diem, Religion, Race, and U.S. Intervention in Southeast Asia 1950–1957.* Durham, NC: Duke University Press, 2005.

James T. Fisher

DOBSON, JAMES C., JR. (b. 1936). A clinically trained psychologist, Dobson is a popular author and radio personality, and the founder of Focus on the Family, a conservative Christian organization. Dobson was the son, grandson, and great-grandson of Church of the Nazarene pastors. The Church of the Nazarene was associated with the Holiness branch of American evangelicalism, and it typically combined a stern moralism with highly effusive displays of emotional faith—qualities personified by Dobson.

Born in Louisiana, he was raised as an only child in several towns across Oklahoma and Texas. Despite the numerous absences of his father, owing to his ministerial duties, the younger Dobson was indelibly influenced by the man's pastoral concern for people, yet abhorrence toward sin. Resisting the expectation that he would follow the career path of his father, Dobson attended Pasadena College (1954–58), a Nazarene institution in California, to study education and psychology. At Pasadena, Dobson met, and eventually married, Shirley Deere in 1960. Upon graduation from college and a short stint in the military, Dobson moved his family to Los Angeles, where he enrolled at the University of Southern California in order to pursue graduate degrees in psychology. After earning his doctoral degree in child development from USC in 1967, Dobson joined the faculty of the USC medical school. By the early 1970s, Dobson had built an impressive academic career. He directed a multimillion dollar project studying children with mental retardation, wrote several articles in prestigious medical journals, and had his research widely recommended by his peers.

In the course of working with numerous parents, Dobson was increasingly dismayed by the highly permissive style of child rearing that was popularized in the 1960s by psychologists like Benjamin Spock. Dobson believed that parents needed to establish boundaries—a clear understanding of what behavior is allowable and what is not—for their children to develop personal security, self-esteem, and self-confidence. As a direct result of his observations and counseling, Dobson wrote his first and ultimately most famous book, *Dare to Discipline,* in 1970. Intended as a conservative Christian alternative to the permissive approach, *Dare to Discipline* combined Dobson's experience as a psychologist with biblical principles to emphasize consistent use of discipline, including a judicious amount of corporal punishment, in parenting. Dobson's book led to a series of workshops on parenting, a video series, and, in 1977, a radio program entitled *Focus on the Family.*

Dobson's effect on his listeners was immediate and intense. He spoke on any and all concerns of the family with an authority that came "from an ability to connect with people right at the level of their problems." The impact of his message was enhanced "by the slight drawl of a country doctor, a radio voice . . . at once effortless and authoritative" (Gerson, 22). Dobson's greatest impact was upon young evangelical Christian parents, particularly mothers, who blamed a host of societal evils at the end of the 1960s on parental permissiveness. Yet his message seemed strangely modern in his emphasis on relationships in addition to rules, and his insistence that the latter without the former would lead to youthful rebellion. Parents, he argued, must be emotionally accessible to their children, and fathers in particular needed to be thoroughly involved in the lives of their families.

Directly as a result of *Dare to Discipline* and its aftermath, Dobson gave up his academic career as a psychologist and founded the organization Focus on the Family in Pomona, California. By the late 1970s, his prominence as a radio commentator led to an appointment to a national task force on children and the family by President **Jimmy Carter.** Additional books like *The Strong-Willed Child* (1978) and *Straight Talk to Men and Their Wives* (1980) built upon and expanded themes explored in Dobson's first book. *Dare to Discipline* eventually sold more than three million copies and was republished in 1994 as *The New Dare to Discipline.*

The prescriptions found in *Dare to Discipline* and Dobson's other books were not well received by everyone, even by some in the evangelical subculture. "Friendly" critics pointed to careless referencing of studies mentioned in his book, a failure to address the needs of families other than those of the traditional or nuclear variety, a disregard for positions different from his own, the lack of a comprehensive philosophy of parenting, and the absence of a strong biblical foundation for his assertions (Addleman, 121–26). More severe critics accused Dobson of offering his readers authoritarian and simplistic answers to difficult behavioral problems.

By the mid-1990s, Dobson supplanted **Jerry Falwell** and **Pat Robertson** as the most formidable political voice in American evangelicalism. Focus on the Family, now headquartered in Colorado Springs, Colorado, was a flagship organization with a $116 million yearly budget. Focus on the Family employed about 1,300 people and promoted a fiercely conservative, or traditionalist, sociopolitical agenda through a myriad of publications for every age group. Dobson's daily radio program reached five million listeners on 2,900 North American radio stations. Despite his continued emphasis on parenting, child rearing, and various family concerns, Dobson was more explicitly political, speaking out stridently against abortion, pornography, and homosexuality. The establishment of a national Family Research Council (1982) and thirty-five state Family Councils, which were officially independent from Focus on the Family, enabled Dobson to promote a conservative "pro-family" political agenda that was highly attractive to the one-third of all Republicans who identified themselves as evangelical Christians. In the

1996 presidential campaign, Dobson's threats to lead his constituency out of the GOP over a perceived softening concerning the Republican Party's antiabortion stand directly influenced the party's presidential nominating convention and platform. Moderate Republicans, who represented a greater diversity of social views than did evangelicals, complained openly about the perceived hijacking of the party by Dobson and his associates.

Bruising political battles in the 1990s with organizations like Americans United for the Separation of Church and State, People for the American Way, and Planned Parenthood, plus the presidential election of 1996 and the impeachment of President Bill Clinton in 1999, took their toll on Dobson. Yet a heart attack in 1990 and a stroke in 1998 seemed barely to slow the pace of this psychologist, counselor, author, entrepreneur, and political strategist. By the turn of the century, however, Dobson seemed to have adopted a less strident and visible political stance. This change was perhaps prompted by the highly controversial presidential election of 2000, which placed the very conservative **George W. Bush,** a political figure who shared many of Dobson's sympathies, in the White House. The change may also be credited to the aftermath of the September 11, 2001, terrorist attacks on America, which shifted the country's collective focus away from domestic sociopolitical issues and toward national security concerns. Along with many evangelical Christian commentators, Dobson was hopeful that the tragedies of terrorism and war in Afghanistan and Iraq would lead to a profound religious revival in the United States.

Ultimately, however, Dobson's subtle shift in emphasis may have been due to a return to his original and greatest concern: the sanctity of the traditional family unit and all the crucial human relationships that found their foci within it.

Bibliography. Addleman, John. "James C. Dobson: Focus of Controversy. A Review Essay." *Brethren In Christ History and Life* 25 (April 2002): 116–30. Gerson, Michael J. "A Righteous Indignation." *U.S. News and World Report,* 4 May 1998, 20–29. Schick, Elizabeth A., ed. "Dobson, James C." *Current Biography Yearbook: 1998.* New York: H.W. Wilson, 1998. Zettersten, Rolf. *Dr. Dobson: Turning Hearts Toward Home.* Dallas, TX: Word Publishing, 1989. Zoba, Wendy Murray. "Daring to Discipline America." *Christianity Today,* 1 March 1999, 31–38.

Robert H. Krapohl

DOLGANOV, GEORGII EFREMOVICH [GERMOGEN] (1858–1918). Dolganov's political activity from 1905 to 1912 represented the most overt alliance of a Russian Orthodox prelate with the radical Right and the boldest attempt to convert Orthodoxy to a political force by superimposing clericalist goals and leadership on rightist groups.

The son of a priest, Dolganov received an education that was unusually broad and secular for the Russian episcopate. After studies in law, mathematics, history, and literature at the universities of Novorossiisk and St. Petersburg, he took monasticism in 1890 and graduated from the St. Petersburg Theological Academy in 1893. Fluent in Georgian, he served in teaching, administrative, and editorial posts in the Georgian dioceses of the Russian Orthodox Church. In 1901, he received his first episcopal appointment in Samara, and in 1903 he was transferred to Saratov, becoming also a member of the Holy Synod in St. Petersburg.

An enemy of church liberals, Dolganov, now Bishop Germogen, attacked lay intellectuals, too, on many occasions. In 1906, with Germogen's blessing, the Monarchist Party, which later became a chapter of the extremist Union of the Russian People (URP), or **Black Hundreds,** was founded in Saratov in 1906. Germogen organized URP brotherhoods at the parish level, headed by priests. This collaboration kept leftist influence away from Saratov clergy, who dominated "patriotic" organizations, not vice versa.

In June 1907 Germogen tried to take control of the URP chapter by substituting his priests for the chapter's council and proposed that the URP be renamed All-Russian Orthodox Fraternal Union of the Russian People: "It is necessary to ensure that Orthodox Christians are given a pre-eminent position," he insisted. "Our members will be not only those who have registered, but all Russian Orthodox people . . . The name change is especially important because now all Orthodox priests will participate [in the Union]" (Stremooukhov, 22). Germogen had national aspirations for this brotherhood in which diocesan bishops would also chair local URP chapters. However, the rightist press protested clerical attempts to dominate politics and civil life, and Germogen ended his association with the URP, though he maintained his connection to right-wing politics.

Not a traditional monarchist, Germogen exemplified a longing for the predominant role the episcopate had enjoyed in all national matters in pre-Petrine Russia. Together with his protégé, populist-rightist monk **Iliodor,** Germogen ushered into Russian church life the modern politics of popular mobilization and mass appeal through editorials, letters, and interviews in the press, exchanging supplication of the czar for influence on the monarchy through control of public opinion. Unsurprisingly, his activity displeased the government. The Saratov governor confiscated several issues of Germogen's inflammatory gazette. His castigation of the monarchy's policy of forcing canonizations that the church considered inappropriate made Germogen notorious across Russia and popular with rightist clergy. It also infuriated the court.

In December 1911 Germogen sent Czar Nicholas II a telegram opposing the introduction of the institution of deaconesses and the mention of the death of non-Orthodox dignitaries in Orthodox churches, measures the czar favored. Germogen's association with Rasputin and his failure to curb Iliodor's anti-hierarchical populism alienated him from the Synod, too, which ousted him in January 1912. A few days later, at Nicholas's behest, Germogen was dismissed from diocesan service and confined in a monastery in Moscow province.

After the February 1917 revolution, Germogen refused to bless the regime change but called on the faithful to pray for the Provisional Government in the interest of avoiding anarchy. Elected bishop of Tobolsk in March 1917, Germogen participated in the All-Russian Church Council of 1917–1918, where he resisted the separation of church and state and advocated participation of prelates in the Constituent Assembly, announcing his desire to run for deputy himself. Having reconciled with the captive imperial family, Germogen boldly protested Bolshevik desecration of churches and persecution of clergymen. He was arrested for counterrevolutionary activity and was later thrown, together with other captives, in the river Turu, near Tobolsk, where his remains were buried on August 23, 1918.

Bibliography. Curtiss, J. S. *Church and State in Russia: The Last Years of the Empire, 1900–1917.* New York: Octagon Books, 1965. Freeze, G. L. "Tserkov', religiia i politicheskaia kul'tura na zakate staroi Rossii." *Istoriia SSSR* 2 (1991): 107–19.

Argyrios K. Pisiotis

DOLLFUSS, ENGELBERT (1892–1934). The Christian Social chancellor of Austria, Dollfuss was born in Texing, a small village in the province of Lower Austria. He was raised Catholic and was determined to become a priest, but he gave up theology

to study law at the University of Vienna and economics at the University of Berlin.

Dollfuss enlisted as a soldier during World War I and was accepted despite his short stature. After the war, he became politically active and joined the **Christian Social Party.** Having served as the secretary of the Peasants' Association of Lower Austria, Dollfuss was elected director of the Lower Austrian Chamber of Agriculture in 1927. He was appointed to serve as minister of agriculture in Karl Buresch's conservative administration in 1931. Since his party felt increasingly threatened by the rising National Socialist Party, Dollfuss took on Buresch's position as chancellor of Austria and formed a new coalition in 1932. While Dollfuss's height triggered insults from the opposition, through remarks and nicknames such as "Milimetternich," he emerged as one of Austria's most authoritarian politicians.

In 1933, he dissolved Parliament, instituted rule by decree, and formed the Vaterländische Front (Fatherland Front), a heavily Catholic, "non-partisan" political organization. He banned the Communist and National Socialist parties and the Schutzbund (Defense League), the paramilitary branch of the Social Democratic Party. At first, the Social Democrats did not voice their protests against Dollfuss's decision. It became clear, however, that the chancellor and his Vaterländische Front opposed democracy. On September 11, 1933, he announced Austria's mission to become a pure Christian Social state. Again, the leaders of the Social Democrats remained calm, despite Dollfuss's intention to introduce a dictatorship. In February of 1934, however, as Dollfuss' paramilitary troops fought against the Schutzbund in Linz, Vienna, and Graz, the Social Democratic Party was banned as well. The brief civil war killed two hundred and injured three hundred Social Democrats. Dollfuss, whose politics received support from the Austrian

Catholic Church, declared the nation a corporative state similar to Mussolini's fascist Italy in April 1934. As a result, Italy became Austria's most important ally, but it did not strengthen Austria's independence from Hitler's Germany.

Although Dollfuss had banned the National Socialist Party, Austrian Nazis recruited more and more followers, and he felt mounting pressure from Adolf Hitler's Germany. On July 25, 1934, eight Austrian Nazis attempted a coup when they entered the Chancellery building. They captured some of the politicians present and assassinated Dollfuss when he tried to flee. He was succeeded by his Christian Social associate **Kurt von Schuschnigg,** although Austria succumbed to Hitler's ambition in 1937. Chancellor Dollfuss was declared a martyr, and some conservative politicians in today's Austria still admire his pluck and zeal despite his fascist dictatorship.

Bibliography. Bischof, Günther, Anton Pelinka, and Alexander Lassner, eds. *The Dollfuss/Schuschnigg Era in Austria: A Reassessment.* New Brunswick, NJ: Transaction: 2003. Steininger, Rolf. "12. November 1918 bis 13. März 1938: Stationen auf dem Weg zum 'Anschluss.'" In *Österreich im 20. Jahrhundert: Von der Monarchie bis zum Zweiten Weltkrieg,* ed. Rolf Steininger and Michael Gehler. Vol. 1. Vienna: Böhlau, 1997.

Gregor Thuswaldner

DONATI, GIUSEPPE (1880–1931). Donati was a leading antifascist Catholic journalist and director of the *Popolo di Roma* who died shortly after a severe beating by Benito Mussolini's henchmen. As a student in Florence, he attended the seminar of Gaetano Salvemini (the biographer of Giuseppe Mazzini), whose influence was evident in Donati's later work regarding the Christian Democrats and the historical role of the church in Jacobinism. In letters to Salvemini, Donati expressed his dissatisfaction with Giovanni Giolitti's liberal governments and later with Fascism.

Donati evolved into one of the key agents for a new political consciousness in Catholic ranks that advocated an Italian Catholic party that could operate independently from the church. He assisted **Romolo Murri** in the Christian Democratic movement and the organization of the Lega Democratica. In 1911, he succeeded Murri in the direction of the League. In 1919 the **Italian Popular Party** (Partito Popolare Italiano) was formed by Don **Luigi Sturzo.** Donati did not join the party immediately, because he considered it a political platform of the moderates. He founded a Christian democratic party (Partito Democratico Christiano), but the failure of his party in the elections opened the way for the support of the Popular Party.

Following the assassination of Socialist leader Giacomo Matteotti in 1924, Donati accused the Fascist leader Emilio De Bono before the High Court of the Senate of connivance in political crime, and the body ordered an enquiry. Although he clearly had support for investigating Matteotti's death, he nevertheless challenged the so-called Aventine secession, during which many antifascist deputies boycotted parliamentary sessions in protest of the Matteotti affair, and called for their return to the chamber. In 1925 the Fascist regime suppressed Donati's *Popolo di Roma* and sent him into exile. He traveled to Paris, London, and Malta. In Paris he edited two antifascist publications, the *Corriere degli Italiani* (1926) and *Il Pungolo* (1928–1930).

Bibliography. Bedeschi, L. *Giuseppe Donati.* Rome: Cinque Lune, 1959. Cannistraro, P. V., ed. *Historical Dictionary of Fascist Italy.* Westport, CT: Greenwood Press, 1982. Rossini, G. G. *Donati: Scritti Politici.* Rome: Cinque Lune, 1956.

Efharis Mascha

DONOHOE, HUGH ALOYSIUS (1905– 1987). Born in San Francisco, Donohoe was a diocesan priest, labor union specialist, professor, editor, chancellor, and bishop. He was a product of the city's Irish Catholic working-class Mission district. He attended St. Paul's elementary school along with John F. Shelley, a lifelong friend who later became president of the state labor federation, state senator, congressman, and mayor of San Francisco. Donohoe was ordained in 1930, earned masters and doctoral degrees at Catholic University under the supervision of Monsignor **John A. Ryan**, and wrote a dissertation on "Collective Bargaining under the NIRA."

From the mid-1930s to the end of the 1940s, Donohoe taught industrial ethics, organized and administered a Social Action School for Priests, drafted Labor Day sermons, delivered public lectures on the labor encyclicals, and represented Archbishop John J. Mitty at local and national labor union functions. In January 1939, Donohoe and John F. Shelley organized a San Francisco chapter of the Association of Catholic Trade Unionists, and Donohoe served as its chaplain during and after World War II. During his tenure as editor of the archdiocesan newspaper the *Monitor* (1942–1948), Donohoe backed organized labor's attempts to maintain its New Deal and wartime gains in the face of organized employer resistance, and the paper opposed such measures as the Taft-Hartley Act of 1947.

Donohoe served as chancellor of the archdiocese from 1948 to 1956 and was pastor of St. Mary's Cathedral from 1948 to 1962, when he became bishop of Stockton, California. In 1969 he was appointed bishop of Fresno, California, a position he held until his retirement in 1980. From the early 1960s through the 1970s, Donohoe supported the efforts of Filipino and Mexican American farm workers to organize labor unions and gain collective bargaining rights under federal and state law. He died on October 27, 1987.

Bibliography. Issel, William. "'A Stern Struggle': Catholic Activism and San Francisco Labor, 1934–1958." In *American Labor and the Cold War: Grassroots Politics and Postwar Political Culture*, ed. Robert W. Cherny, William Issel, and Kieran Walsh Taylor. New Brunswick, NJ: Rutgers University Press, 2004.

William Issel

DONOSO CORTÉS, JUAN (1809–1853). Among Spain's and Europe's most influential thinkers of Catholic politics, Donoso was born at Valle de Serena (Badajoz) to a family of landowners descending from Hernán Cortés, the conqueror of Mexico. Donoso was a tutor in Madrid before studying at Salamanca (1820), Cáceres, and finally at the University of Seville, where he received his degree in law at the age of nineteen. He enjoyed a brief marriage to Teresa Carrasco, who died prematurely in 1835.

Donoso moved to Madrid and became famous following the publication of his *Memoria sobre la situaciòn actual de la monarquía* (1832), which was addressed to Ferdinand VII, the father of young Isabella II, to whom he remained attached after the king's death, and to the regent Maria Cristina. He supported them and the notion of a liberal monarchy against the insurrection of Isabella's uncle, the pretender Don Carlos. Donoso served as secretary to Prime Minister Mendizábal during a wave of *desmortización,* when the government confiscated church property, a process that Donoso supported.

When he was elected deputy in 1837, however, he campaigned against the progressive constitution of that year through the columns of *El Porvenir,* which he founded to assist his campaign. Through various writings that anticipated the evolution of his beliefs, he manifested his own conviction that society needed to be hierarchically ordered and organized with the royal family rather than the Cortes at the top of the pyramid. In 1840, Donoso followed Maria Cristina to her exile in France and became her personal secretary. He returned to Spain in 1843 and became the personal tutor of Isabella II and later made an important contribution to the moderate liberal constitution of 1845. Also significant was his *Discurso sobre la Biblia,* which secured his admission into the Royal Historical Academy in 1846.

The death of Donoso's older brother Pedro in 1847 and his reflections on the revolutions of 1848 caused him finally to break from his previously held liberal ideas. This political and ideological change eventually became a true "conversion," which was made public with the *Discurso sobra la dictadura* that he made in Parliament on January 4, 1849. In that speech, he affirmed his beliefs in the supremacy of the Catholic Church—even in politics—and justified the dictatorship in special circumstances. On January 30 of the next year, after having served as ambassador to Berlin, Donoso made his other important *Discurso sobre la situación de Europa,* in which he predicted the crisis of the British Empire and the Russian Revolution. His most important work is the *Ensayo sobre el catolicismo, el liberalismo y el socialismo* (1851), which was immediately translated into French.

Influenced by the ideas of **Joseph de Maistre** and **Joseph de Bonald,** Donoso believed that the secularization of society and liberalism were the works of human beings who placed themselves ahead of God. For Donoso, punishment for this sin was a revolution that could be avoided by submission to Christianity and to the church. His work was divided into three books, the first of which speaks of the miracle of the church, while the second presents the church's solutions to the problems of good versus evil and of necessity and freedom in opposition to liberalism and socialism. The third book of the *Ensayo* discusses the church's conviction regarding great social questions, family unity, national solidarity, and the experience of hardship.

Donoso's work immediately caused controversy in France and Spain. Bishop **Félix Antoine Dupanloup** and other scholars critiqued his work while **Luigi Taparelli d'Azeglio** in *La Civiltà Cattolica* and **Louis Veuillot** in *L'Univers* both defended him. Cardinal Fornari consulted him in 1852 regarding liberalism, and his response was reflected in Pope **Pius IX**'s *Syllabus of Errors.* Donoso's work exerted notable influence on reactionary and counterrevolutionary thought in Spain as well as in Europe. After World War I, **Carl Schmitt** reiterated Donoso's thoughts in an antidemocratic fashion. Donoso believed in the necessity of uniting the two Bourbons through the marriage of Isabella II to Don Carlos's heir, Carlos VI, the Count of Montemolín, in a proposition that appears to have been approved by Pius IX but opposed by Napoleon II. Donoso corresponded with **Charles Montalembert,** Dupanloup, Monsignor Louis-Gaston Andrien de Ségur, **Giacomo Cardinal Antonelli,** Louis Veuillot, and other representatives of European culture. From 1851 to 1853, Donoso served as ambassador to Paris, where he died.

Donoso was a brilliant writer and speaker, literary critic and philosopher, and a man of thought and action in politics and diplomacy. He is considered the most important representative of Christian romanticism in Spain. As a theologian and political thinker, Donoso considered the church the key to social order and as the principal deterrent to revolution. Because of these beliefs, he occupies a central position in counterrevolutionary Catholic thought and, it can be argued, is the most influential and noteworthy Spanish thinker of the nineteenth century.

Bibliography. Donoso Cortés, Juan. *Obras completas.* Ed. C. Valverde. 2 vols. Madrid: La Editorial Católica, 1970. Hernández Arias, J. R. *Donoso Cortés und Carl Schmitt.* Paderborn, Germany: Schöningh, 1998. Suárez, F. *Introducción a Donoso Cortés.* Madrid: Rialp, 1963.

Alfonso Botti

DOSSETTI, GIUSEPPE (1913–1996)

An atypical politician driven by Christian idealism rather than by the pursuit of power, Dossetti was a founding father of the Italian Republic and a leader of the left wing of the **Christian Democracy** who decided to retire to monastic life when he realized that his plans for Catholic reformism had failed.

A bright intellectual with a law degree from Milan's Catholic University, Dossetti was active in the antifascist Resistance as a representative of the Christian Democracy within the Committee of National Liberation for the province of Reggio Emilia. In the early postwar years, he became a member of both the Constitutional Assembly and Parliament. He also rose to become vice secretary of the Christian Democrat Party in 1945.

In this latter capacity, Dossetti endeavored to make the Christian Democrats into a reformist and anticapitalist force that sided with the destitute and the workers as if it had been a sort of labor party deprived of Marxist ideology. He shared this project with a group of other young university professors that included **Amintore Fanfani, Giorgio La Pira,** and Giuseppe Lazzati. Through their own association, *Civitas Humana,* and journal, *Cronache Sociali,* they spearheaded sweeping reforms in welfare and agriculture that would enable the Italian state to protect the weak, the poor, and the family in compliance with evangelical precepts.

The Italian premier and Christian Democrat leader, **Alcide De Gasperi,** exploited Dossetti's appeal to the working class to win the 1948 parliamentary elections. But, under pressure from the conservatives and the moderates, he eventually did little to accommodate Dossetti's claims besides passing an emasculated agrarian reform in 1950. Dossetti also took issue with De Gasperi in late 1948 by opposing Italy's entry into the North Atlantic Treaty Organization (NATO) on the grounds that the country faced no external threat and the strengthening of her nonmilitary relations with her Western European partners would better suit Italy's interests.

After suffering a defeat on the NATO vote in the Christian Democrat parliamentary caucus, and realizing that De Gasperi intended to practice low-profile politics based on compromise, Dossetti chose not to play the role of minority in Italy's majority party. While his more pragmatic allies, most notably Fanfani, were ready to negotiate with De Gasperi, he dissolved his own faction, resigned from Parliament in 1952, and retired from active politics. As a more effective way of serving the poor, he became a priest in 1959, established a monastic community in Jericho, and worked with the Second Vatican Council.

Dossetti made two brief political comebacks. In 1956, the Christian Democrats slated him for Bologna's city council in the fruitless effort to prevent the incumbent Communist mayor, Giuseppe Dozza, from again securing a large majority there. In 1994, Dossetti resurfaced once more, this time to warn against a strengthened Italian presidency and to endorse the Committees to Defend the Constitution, a movement aimed at safeguarding the institutional framework as it had resulted from the 1948 constitution.

Bibliography. Galli, Giorgio, and Paolo Facchi. *La sinistra democristiana.* Milan: Feltrinelli, 1962. Pombeni, Paolo. *Il gruppo dossettiano e la fondazione della democrazia italiana, 1938–1948.* Bologna, Italy: Il Mulino, 1979.

Stefano Luconi

DOUGLASS, FREDERICK (1818–1895).

An abolitionist, journalist, and civil rights activist, Douglass was born Frederick Augustus Washington Bailey on the eastern shore of Maryland in 1818. His mother, Harriet Bailey, was a slave, and his father an unknown white man. For the first six years of his life he lived with his grandmother,

Betsy Bailey, in comparative comfort. In 1824 he was sent to the plantation of Edward Lloyd to live with his master, Aaron Anthony, where he witnessed some of the horrors of slavery.

In 1826 he moved to Baltimore to live with Hugh and Sophia Auld and serve as companion to their son Tommy. During his seven years there, he learned to read, underwent a religious conversion, joined the Bethel African Methodist Episcopal Church, and found hope in the word "abolition."

Thomas Auld, his new master, had Frederick sent back to the Lloyd estate on Maryland's eastern shore in 1833. Auld considered him insolent and in 1834 hired him out to Edward Covey, known in the area as a "slave breaker." After numerous beatings, Frederick stood up to Covey, fought him, and was no longer whipped. "I was a changed being after that fight," he wrote. "I was *nothing* before. I was a man now." Following an unsuccessful escape plot in 1836, he was sent back to Baltimore to live with Hugh and Sophia Auld. He learned the caulking trade, hired himself out as an apprentice caulker, joined a debating club, and met his future wife, Anna Murray, a free black woman who worked as a domestic.

On September 3, 1838, Frederick escaped north by train and boat, masquerading as a sailor and carrying the free papers of a black seaman he had met in Baltimore. Later that month he married Anna Murray. They settled in New Bedford, Massachusetts, where Frederick found work and changed his last name to Douglass (from Sir Walter Scott's hero in "The Lady of the Lake"), to hide his fugitive status. Within a decade, he and Anna had five children.

In New Bedford, Douglass was drawn into the abolitionist movement. He read **William Lloyd Garrison**'s newspaper, the *Liberator,* and attended meetings. His oratorical skills brought him growing recognition, and in 1845 he published the enormously successful *Narrative of the Life of Frederick Douglass, an American Slave, Written by Himself.* In his powerful appendix to that volume, Douglass made clear his revulsion for the institutional church in America. He had briefly served as a licensed preacher in the African Methodist Episcopal Zion Church before concluding that even that institution's compromises on slavery left it as culpable as other denominations. Douglass acknowledged that "between the Christianity of this land and the Christianity of Christ, I recognize the wisest possible difference." He contrasted his love for "the pure, peaceable, and impartial Christianity of Christ" with his disdain for the "corrupt, slaveholding, women-whipping, cradle-lundering, partial and hypocritical Christianity of this land."

Fearing that his *Narrative*'s disclosure of his identity endangered his freedom, however, he left for an eighteen-month speaking tour in England, Ireland, and Scotland. British admirers raised money for him to purchase his freedom and start his own newspaper. The *North Star* was his four-page weekly, which promoted immediate abolition, temperance, and women's rights, among other reforms.

Douglass's move to Rochester, New York, partly reflected his growing disenchantment with Garrison, the racial inequalities within the American Anti-Slavery Society, and the society's doctrine of nonresistance. By 1849 he endorsed violence to combat the growing belligerence of the Slave Power. He formally broke with Garrison and the society in 1851 (Garrison was its president from 1843 to 1865), joined the National Liberty Party, and changed the name of his newspaper to *Frederick Douglass' Paper* to reflect his commitment to political action.

In 1852 he published *The Heroic Slave,* his only work of fiction and the first African American novella. It explored the virtues of violence and featured an interracial friendship between the "heroic slave" and an abolitionist modeled on **Gerrit Smith,** the white friend to whom he dedicated *My Bondage and My Freedom* (1855). *My Bondage,* the first African American autobiography, highlighted Douglass's revolutionary ethos.

Throughout the 1850s, Douglass was a close friend of **John Brown,** and he helped plan Brown's raid on the federal arsenal at Harpers Ferry. When the raid failed, Douglass fled to Canada and then England for a speaking tour. He considered Brown a hero, referring to him as the "man of this nineteenth century."

During the Civil War, he was invited to the White House three times by President **Abraham Lincoln.** He pressed the administration to make emancipation a war aim and to arm black troops, which he felt would hasten an end to slavery and racism. By the end of the war, he was a committed

Frederick Douglass. Courtesy of the Library of Congress

Republican and remained so for the rest of his life.

During Reconstruction, Douglass advocated black male suffrage and sought to prevent Confederate elites from returning to power. He met with President Andrew Johnson in 1866, urging him without success to endorse these measures. In 1870, he purchased a Washington, D.C., weekly and changed its name to the *New National Era.* Two years later, growing losses forced him to stop publishing it, and he became president of the insolvent Freedmen's Bank.

These failures cost him money and respect among other black leaders, who felt that he had become too moderate on questions of race. He failed, for example, to criticize the Republican Party's abandonment of Reconstruction in 1876 when it removed federal troops from the South. That same year he was appointed marshal of the District of Columbia by President-Elect Rutherford B. Hayes. His appointment masked the concessions Republicans had made to white supremacists to get Hayes elected.

Even after the failure of Reconstruction, Douglass continued to view the Republican Party as the best means for black improvement. In 1881 President James A. Garfield appointed him the recorder of deeds for the District of Columbia. With his Republican appointments, he gave fewer lectures, no longer needing to rely on speaking fees for financial security. His wife died in 1882, and in 1884 he married his white secretary, Helen Pitts, a white woman who was twenty years his junior. The marriage prompted attacks from whites and blacks alike, including members of his own family. His final Republican appointment came in 1889, where he served as U.S. minister to Haiti for two years.

In 1881, Douglass published *Life and Times of Frederick Douglass,* a book that revealed Douglass's vision to now be linear, secular, and progressive. Gone was his hope for a new age and a sharp break with the past. His earlier millennial hopes for a divinely inspired new day of peace and social justice now seemed a sentimental delusion. His faith that God could enter into and affect the affairs of the world, a faith that had guided his actions since his conversion to Christianity, was gone.

Despite his growing moderation and skepticism, Douglass continued to vigorously denounce disfranchisement, Jim Crow laws, and the upsurge of lynchings until his death. He was the most influential African American of the nineteenth century.

Bibliography. Blight, David W. *Frederick Douglass' Civil War: Keeping Faith in Jubilee.* Baton Rouge: Louisiana State University Press, 1989. Douglass, Frederick. *My Bondage and My Freedom.* 1855. New York: Dover, 1969. Douglass, Frederick. *Narrative of the Life of Frederick Douglass, an American Slave.* 1845. Ed. Houston A Baker, Jr. New York: Penguin, 1982. Martin, Waldo E. *The Mind of Frederick Douglass.* Chapel Hill: University of North Carolina Press, 1984. McFeely, William S. *Frederick Douglass.* New York: W. W. Norton, 1991.

John Stauffer

DRUMONT, EDOUARD (1844–1917). To include Drumont in a reference book on Christian politics raises the uncomfortable connection of Christian political movements with anti-Semitism. Drumont was the most prolific, most published, and most read political propagandist of late nineteenth-century France, the era of the Dreyfus Affair, and his public identification with the Catholic Church and great popularity among French Catholics made him, next to **Karl Lueger** in imperial Austria, the most famous Catholic anti-Semite in modern history. But his inclusion is an opportunity to assess the not-inconsiderable contribution of Christian and Catholic anti-Judaism to the development of the racial anti-Semitism that marked the first

half of the twentieth century so profoundly and so tragically.

In the spring of 1886 Drumont's massive volume *La France juive* appeared and became a rapid best seller, with many editions and several translations into other languages. Drumont used prejudice, history, anecdotes, financial disasters, and religion to compose a vast exposé of the alleged Jewish assault on the body of France. For all those concerned about the present state of France among the nations and its perilous future confronted by powerful rivals and enemies, Drumont found the secret key to all anxieties and troubles: the dangerous activities of the Jews, whose emancipation by the French Revolution had not led to their assimilation into French life but had made the French their victims—economically, politically, and culturally.

The modern anti-Semitism he propagated brought traditional beliefs and fears up to date with contemporary concerns. Drumont found a willing audience among workers, clerics, and patriots. Workers learned that it was not capitalism but Jewish finance that oppressed them. Ecclesiastics, particularly the much harried lower clergy, had their millennial suspicions of the perfidious Jews enhanced by revelations about their new methods of anti-Christian action and thought. And for patriots, the hated rivals in London and Berlin could be portrayed in league with Jews who had planted themselves in every capital and within every government.

It was Drumont's anti-Semitic daily newspaper, *La libre parole,* that on October 29, 1894, first revealed that a Jewish officer, Alfred Dreyfus, had been arrested for espionage on behalf of imperial Germany. Virtually no one doubted Dreyfus's guilt except his own family, for he was wealthy, Jewish, and Alsatian and had relatives in Germany—the perfect villain for workers, priests, and patriots alike. The affair seemed providential for the vindication of anti-Semitism, and Drumont became the leading propagandist of anti-Jewish agitation, propelling him into prominence, election to the Chamber of Deputies from anti-Semitic Algiers, and wealth. While an effective and brilliant journalist and propagandist, Drumont lacked the skills for a successful political career, and the last twenty years of his life were marked by loss of readership, financial distress, and political oblivion. He lacked the skills but preached the same message as the extremely successful Karl Lueger in Vienna: the unification of the nation around an internal enemy, the Jews, in place of class struggles and religious rivalries.

Drumont was a populist. He loved and sympathized with the common people and was suspicious of all elites, particularly the bourgeoisie and the upper clergy, who could always be relied on to betray the trust placed in them. Even when it came to the Jews and their activities, he found the uneducated worker and peasant more instinctively attuned to what was happening than was the fearful bourgeois or the opportunistic bishops or archbishops. He sincerely believed that France's economic distress, its poverty, its oppression, its financial scandals, and its foreign adventures gone bad were the result of Jewish harmfulness, which neither emancipation nor even baptism could really eradicate. In this he was a racist anti-Semite.

Many historians, not only Catholic ones, have rejected the connection between traditional anti-Judaism taught by the church and modern racial anti-Semitism that emphasized the alien nature of the non-Aryan in the midst of Europeans. Catholic theology to be sure taught that in Christ's church "there is neither Jew nor Greek," but in practice this distinction between unbelieving Jews and believing Jews did not often hold water. Few Jews were converted to Catholicism in nineteenth-century France, since they could enjoy all

the benefits of liberty, equality, and fraternity while remaining Jews. The baptismal option seemed theoretical, while real Jews continued to trouble Christian French souls. On the contrary, in late medieval Castile and Aragon, too many Jews had sought baptism, and the result was that anti-Jewish Old Christians had to invent a threat of crypto-Judaism in order to maintain the old hostility to the alien Jews. Whether baptized or not, Jews still troubled Christians with suspicions of their anti-Christian purposes; therefore, the enemy for Drumont and his followers had to be the Jews because of their race, not their particular religious allegiance, real or feigned. Drumont even went out of his way to deny his hostility to the Jewish religion, focusing instead on the evil and dangerous racial-ethnic characteristics that made Jews alien, inassimilable, and threatening. He thus modernized anti-Judaism into modern anti-Semitism.

Christian Democrats on the left and Social Christians on the right might differ on exactly how the church should confront the challenges of industrialization and Socialism, but they agreed that the Jews were the models of unchristian economic and financial exploitation and the oppressors of the Catholic masses of France. In looking for a third way between capitalism and Socialism, they discovered anti-Semitism. They agreed that the struggle the church was losing against anticlericalism, radicalism, and Socialism were the work of the Jews in league with Protestants and anticlerical politicians. There was very little expression by Catholics of anything other than anti-Jewish belief and feeling, and all of them were ready for an understanding of the Jewish Question stripped of outdated, anachronistic, traditional dress.

Drumont more than any other provided a potent brew that any kind of anti-Semite could drink with satisfaction. Some twenty years after his death, Drumont's *La France juive* would find new appreciative readers in the France of Marshal **Philippe Pétain** and Pierre Laval, who put into effect many of the measures that Drumont and his circle recommended but could not get past a ruling class not yet convinced of the Jewish menace. It took Catholics a long time, perhaps even longer than others in France, to abandon an anti-Semitism that had nourished them for centuries in its traditional and then its modern version.

Bibliography. Byrnes, Robert Francis. *Antisemitism in Modern France.* New Brunswick, NJ: Rutgers University Press, 1950. Pierrard, Pierre. *Juifs et catholiques français: De Drumont à Jules Isaac (1886–1945).* Paris: Fayard, 1970. Sternhell, Zeev. *La droite revolutionnaire: 1885–1914, 1885–1914. Les origines françaises du fascisme.* Paris: Éditions du Seuil, 1978. Wilson, Stephen. *Ideology and Experience: Antisemitism in France at the Time of the Dreyfus Affair.* Rutherford, NJ: Fairleigh Dickinson University Press, 1982.

Norman Ravitch

DUMONT, FERNAND (1927–1997). Dumont significantly contributed to the development of French Canadian self-consciousness during the crucial years of Quebec's Quiet Revolution (1960–1970). His most important political action certainly remains his contribution to the writing of the White Paper under the invitation of the Parti Québécois. The White Paper was to be the cornerstone for the elaboration and legitimization of the French language Charter (Bill 101, 1977). It stated that Quebec should be a French unilingual province in the realms of work, education, and communication.

More than for his political actions, Fernand Dumont should be remembered for his political stands. One of the most prestigious French Canadian social scientists, and the author of deep and abstract works, he did not believe science should be an excuse to avoid taking position in public debates. His Christian convictions were no strangers to his commitments, for he very early convinced himself that science should be a way to foster love, and that the role of a Christian is always to place himself in what **Charles Péguy** called the *axe de détresse*.

In the 1950s, Quebec was a priest-ridden province (one out of eighty-nine believers was a religious figure). Addressing the issue of the Roman Catholic Church thus contained an important political charge. Dumont, who headed the Commission d'Étude sur les Laïcs et l'Église (1968–1972), criticized the clergy's monopoly on various social activities. In *Maintenant,* a magazine devoted to popularizing the themes of the Second Vatican Council, he wrote several articles (1967–1975), all inspired by his conviction that faith is an "adventure," a special calling and not something that can be imposed.

Dumont enjoyed repeating how his Catholic faith got him interested in the fate of the working class. In his eyes, the longing for the kingdom of heaven should not distract Christians from the fulfillment of a better life on earth. He proposed a planned economy that would help create a real solidarity, not only by achieving a better wealth distribution, but also by making sure the entire population would have a say in the making of governmental policies.

Finally, the dream of an independent Quebec animated Dumont's commitments. It seemed for him a necessity in order to protect the French population of Quebec from being engulfed by the surrounding Anglophone tide. Moreover, given a history of grievances and continuous misunderstandings, he was disillusioned by the possibility to build a true political community with the English Canadian population.

Fundamentally, Dumont's work is structured by two concepts borrowed from Catholic philosophy. On one hand, against the materialism of mass culture and the ideology of neoliberalism, Dumont made sure people remembered what he called a "transcendence without a name." Man, repeated Dumont, cannot live on bread alone. On the other hand, he also insisted on the need for traditions. Against the heralds of the "end of history," Dumont wrote that authentic traditions handed down from the past were the only way to define a common culture that was not artificial. Traditions to keep one's feet on solid ground, a transcendence to raise one's eyes to the sky, thus can briefly describe the political philosophy of this sociology professor, who left us an inexhaustible work to dwell on.

Bibliography. Dumont, Fernand, *Raisons communes*. Montreal: Boréal, 1995. Warren, Jean-Philippe, and Simon Langlois. "Mémoire de Fernand Dumont." Special issue, *Recherches sociographiques* 42 (May–August 2001).

Jean-Philippe Warren

DUPANLOUP, FÉLIX ANTOINE PHILIBERT (1802–1878). A leader of liberal Catholics in nineteenth century France, Dupanloup began life as the illegitimate child of a young peasant girl and a father who was probably a member of the higher nobility. His teachers recognized his exceptional intelligence and guided him to the priesthood. After ordination, he demonstrated his talents as a popular preacher and educator.

As rector of the seminary of Saint Nicholas du Chardonnet from 1837 until 1845, he secured his reputation as a brilliant educator. He gained particular limelight in 1838 when he reconciled the aged Charles de Talleyrand (the wizard of French diplomacy) with the church. At the same time, association with **Charles Montalembert** won Dupanloup over to the cause of liberal Catholicism.

Dupanloup displayed his considerable polemical abilities in the controversy over freedom of education and authored the Falloux Law, which granted Catholics freedom in secondary education. His manifest literary talent and liberal credentials won him a seat on the French Academy. He became canon at Notre Dame Cathedral in 1845, and then bishop of Orléans from 1849 until 1878. There he proved to be a zealous administrator, pioneering in more effective pastoral methods while also elevating the intellectual and spiritual quality of his priests.

A major issue at the time was the fate of the Papal States in the face of Italian unification. Dupanloup proved to be a resolute defender of the pope's right to keep his territory intact. But he also spoke in powerful terms to defend modern freedoms. In *Pacification religieuse,* he hailed the church as a bastion of freedom. Hence when Pope **Pius IX**'s reactionary *Syllabus of Errors* (1864) appeared, with its apparent condemnation of modern freedoms, and unleashed an enormous storm of controversy, Dupanloup rushed to print with *La convention du 15 septembre* (1865), which put an ironic spin on the text by means of ingenious distinctions between papal hypotheses and actual realities. The ultramontanes at the time, however, were determined to reinforce a less benign interpretation of the *Syllabus* through a conciliar definition of papal infallibility. Dupanloup felt this would disastrously pit the papacy and church against the best thought of the modern world, but he intervened maladroitly with a publication that argued against a definition. At the First Vatican Council (1869–1870), matters came to a head. Dupanloup could only alert the French government and urge the minority in Rome to abstain from voting on a definition of papal infallibility. Later as a member of the French National Assembly, his interventions proved counterproductive for the church.

Dupanloup was widely revered as a distinguished orator, a passionate churchman, a brilliant educator, a liberal statesman and, above all, a sensitive director of souls.

Bibliography. Faguet, E. *Mgr. Dupanloup: Un grand évêque.* Paris: Librairie Hachette, 1914.

Thomas Bokenkotter

DWIGHT, TIMOTHY (1752–1817). American clergyman and theologian, Federalist leader, and the eighth president of Yale College, Dwight was born into a prosperous family in Northampton, Massachusetts. His mother was the daughter of Jonathan Edwards. An intellectual prodigy, Dwight was already adept at classical languages when he entered Yale in 1765 at the age of thirteen. After finishing his bachelor's degree in 1769, Dwight remained at Yale as a tutor while continuing his studies. He received his master's degree from Yale in 1772 and was later awarded the doctor of divinity degree by Princeton. He left Yale in 1774, exhausted and suffering from a visual problem that plagued him for the remainder of his life. After being ordained as a Congregationalist minister in 1777, Dwight served briefly as a chaplain to the Continental army until his father's death in 1778 forced him to return to Northampton. In 1783, he accepted a call to the pastorate of Greenfield Hill, a congregational church in Fairfield, Connecticut. During his ministry at Greenfield Hill, he founded Greenfield Academy and became widely known as an educator as well as a preacher. Dwight was appointed president of Yale College in 1795 and remained at that post until his death. Under his leadership, Yale became one of the top schools in the country and a bulwark of religious and social conservatism.

Despite his intellectual heritage, Dwight was a moderate Calvinist whose thought differed significantly from the consistent Calvinism of his maternal grandfather. While Calvinism emphasized human depravity and divine sovereignty, Dwight believed that God's grace worked indirectly through human institutions and that religious nurture could facilitate conversion. Consequently, Dwight developed a keen interest in the spiritual benefits of education and social institutions. As a clergyman and educator, he sought to reconcile the discoveries of modern science with his religious beliefs. Perceiving no conflict between reason and revelation, he defended Christianity on rational grounds and held that common sense supported Christian faith. Dwight argued that reason could generate virtuous behavior as well as foster Christian belief. His departure from consistent Calvinism had a distinctly practical element: he placed greater value on winning converts and unifying evangelical churches than he did on promoting doctrinal consistency. The greater dangers for Dwight were the pluralist and libertarian tendencies inherent in democracy and, from his perspective, the morally corrupting influences of skepticism, deism, and liberal Christianity.

Dwight completely supported American independence but opposed popular democratic governance. Like his Puritan forebears, he understood democracy to be contrary to the will of God. Dwight envisioned the ideal society as a harmonious social order in which individual liberty would always remain subservient to Christian morals and the common good. This society would combine the scientific advances of the Enlightenment with a respect for tradition and virtue. Its members would accept the paternalistic guidance of clergymen and appointed leaders, and the society as a whole would be governed by the word of God. Dwight's allegiance to the established authorities and traditions of Puritan New England made him a Federalist. Federalism, social conservatism, religious orthodoxy, and a distain for speculative philosophy tended to coalesce in his sermons, lectures, and published writings. Primarily during the 1770s, he composed pro-Federalist poetry that expressed his hopes as well as his fears for the new nation. By the end of eighteenth century, however, he had become profoundly critical of the American political system. In his view, Americans were overstepping the bounds of liberty, and the country was on the brink of utter moral decay.

Upon the death of Ezra Stiles, a religious and political liberal, Dwight was named president of Yale College. As president and professor of divinity for twenty-two years, he exerted a profound influence over an entire generation of Yale students. Dwight was one of the catalysts of the Second Great Awakening, which began early in his tenure at Yale. His four-year sermon cycle provided each graduating class with a full course in biblical theology, and students were sometimes converted by a single sermon or lecture. Dwight's political opponents accused him of teaching Federalism and referred to him as "Pope Dwight."

Shortly after his death, the traditional institutions and models of authority that Dwight had been determined to defend and maintain faded from American politics. However, his influence on American society endured. His followers, including Yale graduates Nathaniel Taylor and **Lyman Beecher,** continued to emphasize revivalism and evangelical unity, and, through the benevolent movement, established the type of institutions that Dwight viewed as essential for fostering Christianity and promoting virtue.

Bibliography. Berk, Stephen E. *Calvinism versus Democracy: Timothy Dwight and the Origins of American Evangelical Orthodoxy.* Hamden, CT: Archon Books, 1974. Cuningham, Charles E. *Timothy Dwight.* New York: Macmillan, 1942. Fitzmier, John R. *New England's Moral Legislator: Timothy Dwight, 1752–1817.* Religion in North America. Bloomington: Indiana University Press, 1998.

Susan J. Hubert

E

EHLERS, HERMANN (1904–1954). Evangelical leader of the German **Christian Democratic Union (CDU)** and president of the German Bundestag, Ehlers was born in Schöneberg, the son of a postal clerk. As a pupil at the Berlin-Steglitz secondary school, he joined the Student's Bible Circle, which exerted great influence on his development, and by 1925, he assumed its leadership. Having finished his studies in law at Berlin and Bonn, Ehlers at first worked as an administrative officer and later as judge in Berlin. After the Nazis came to power, he joined the Confessing Church for freedom of conscience and religion and as a result was arrested, accused, and removed from his position.

Ehlers was drafted in 1940. In 1945, be became a member of the Oldenburg Lutheran Church Council and later of the all-German Protestant synod, and chairman of a church disciplinary court. He joined the CDU, working closely and successfully with Bishop Hermann Kunst and **Konrad Adenauer.** in cultivating a Protestant wing of the party. In 1952, his organization of a CDU/CSU Protestant committee earned the mistrust of Adenauer, although the relationship between the two eventually matured into a partnership. Ehlers became a member of the Bundestag in 1949 and a year later became the president of that body. It was widely assumed that Ehlers would succeed Adenauer as party chief, but he died suddenly and prematurely in Oldenburg.

Bibliography. Meier, Andreas. *Hermann Ehlers: Leben in Kirche und Politik.* Bonn, Germany: Bouvier, 1991. *Spotts, Frederic. The Churches and Politics in Germany.* Middletown, CT: Wesleyan University Press, 1973.

Andrea Rönz

ELLUL, JACQUES (1912–1994). As a lay theologian, sociologist, and professor at the University of Bordeaux and its Institute for Political Studies (where he taught Roman law, Marxism, propaganda, technology, and history and sociology of institutions), Ellul made political analysis a regular theme in his voluminous published works. He paid particular attention to the high status accorded politics in the modern world, and to the sort of political involvement appropriate for Christian believers.

Ellul held that politics should remain relative, as a means to certain ends, rather than playing a dominant role and being formally allied to the state. Rather than embracing political "solutions" in critical situations, Ellul called for placing political activity in the context of realism, not ideology.

Illustrations of this principle abound in Ellul's writings, especially in his theological and ethical works. Since Christians' fundamental allegiance lies elsewhere, they can participate in politics without giving it ultimate significance. This stance enables them to understand their real motivations when they form an opinion or join a party. They can view differences of opinion with good humor and associate freely with believers of widely different political persuasions, since they know that what unites them matters infinitely more than their politically adversarial relationship. Such contact can reduce tensions as it engenders respect, communication, discernment, and reconciliation. When the church functions as a haven for unfettered dialogue among believers who participate in different or opposing political camps, it can serve as a witness to people who believe that political conviction must preclude such free association. Ellul named prayer the most significant political action of all.

A supporter of the separation of church and state, Ellul recommended that believers join existing groups instead of forming Christian political parties. He doubted, however, that they could function as "model" party members, since their commitment would never become absolute. He argued that Christians opposing oppression by aligning themselves with a revolutionary struggle should logically switch their loyalties to the opposite side if a revolution triumphed, since winning would transform the formerly oppressed group into the new oppressors.

Ellul vehemently opposed modern developments in Marxism, but he often attributed much of his understanding of society, technique, and the importance of the poor to his youthful encounters with Marx's writings. A proponent of many socialist ideas, such as the importance of mutual care and economic justice, Ellul surprised many by advocating a modified anarchist stance. Although he abhorred violence and did not desire the disappearance of the state, he claimed that the adoption of certain anarchist positions, especially by small groups, could reduce the modern state's power, which he believed had grown dangerously.

In his personal involvement in politics, Ellul practiced the principle "think globally, act locally." His brief stint as adjunct mayor of Bordeaux, immediately following his participation in the Resistance in World War II, taught him the severe constraints under which politicians operate, so that thereafter he steadfastly refused to run for office and exerted his influence from the outside. In addition to his frequent political commentaries in newspapers and journals, he established a center for delinquent youth in his hometown and worked as leader of autonomous groups toward specific goals, often ecological in nature, such as the preservation of the Atlantic coastal area near Bordeaux, which the national government had decided to develop for tourism and recreation.

In a typical effort, as a lay preacher who had held local and national office in the denomination, Ellul proposed that the Reformed Church of France reinvent itself through a grassroots consultation, thus subordinating its bureaucracy and power to the expressed desires of the individuals it served. Despite widespread enthusiasm and anticipation regarding the so-called Estates General of Protestantism, the project failed to prosper, and the church remained much as before, with decisions routinely made by an aloof hierarchy.

Bibliography. Ellul, Jacques. *Anarchy and Christianity.* Trans. Geoffrey W. Bromiley. Grand Rapids, MI: William B. Eerdmans, 1991. Ellul, Jacques. *The Politics of God and the Politics of Man.* Trans. Geoffrey W. Bromiley. Grand Rapids, MI: William B. Eerdmans, 1972.

Joyce M. Hanks

EMERSON, RALPH WALDO (1803–1882). In the mid-nineteenth century, Emerson, America's foremost poet, essayist, and philosopher, became a prominent spokesperson for what we know today as liberal democracy.

In 1844, when he began his personal campaign against slavery, Emerson declared that "government exists to defend the weak and the poor and the injured party; the rich and the strong can better take care of themselves." In speech after speech thereafter, he consistently attacked an American government that was dominated by conservative slaveholding interests. He demanded not only the liberation of the slaves, but also that they be provided with educational and economic support and the benefits of full citizenship, including the vote.

As a means toward this end, in the spring of 1851 Emerson mounted a stump campaign in an effort to get his friend John Gorham Palfrey elected to Congress on the Free-Soil ticket. The speech that Emerson used in his campaign was a bitter attack on the recently passed Fugitive Slave Law and one of its chief supporters, Massachusetts

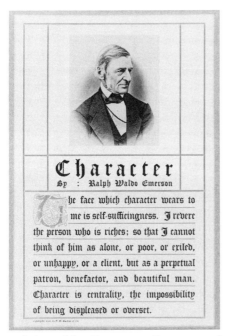

Ralph Waldo Emerson. Courtesy of the Library of Congress

senator Daniel Webster. Emerson demanded that his listeners defy the law at every opportunity, asserting that "If our resistance to this law is not right, there is no right." Such civil disobedience, Emerson held, was sanctioned by a "Higher Law" than the Constitution, one that resided in the hearts of all moral persons.

Emerson's opposition to slavery and his promotion of freedom and equality for all Americans, regardless of race or gender, evolved directly from his early religious training and his later transcendental philosophy. Emerson graduated from Harvard Divinity School and was ordained a Unitarian minister in 1829. Following the death of his first wife, he became increasingly disillusioned with the Unitarian Church and its increasing emphasis on doctrine rather than the spirit. He left the church in 1832 and soon became the recognized leader of a new movement that sought to promote the spirit of religion without its formality. This movement came to be known as transcendentalism. Emerson's liberal notion of democracy was a direct outgrowth of his transcendental philosophy.

The core of transcendentalism is a belief in the divinity, unity, and equality of humankind. This unity derives from the fact that all human beings participate in a universal, spiritual dynamic that Emerson often called the "Over-Soul." In a classic essay by that name, he defines this entity as "that great nature in which we rest, as the earth lies in the soft arms of the atmosphere; that Unity, that Over-Soul, within which every man's particular being is contained and made one with all other." Emerson believed that *all* people share in this divinity. It is this fundamental belief that informs his concept of democratic equality, as well as his opposition to slavery. As he noted in an early journal entry, "Democracy/Freedom has its root in the Sacred truth that every man hath in him the divine Reason." This is "the equality &

the only equality of all men, [and] because every man hath in him somewhat really divine therefore is slavery the unpardonable outrage it is."

Emerson fought a long battle against slavery throughout the tumultuous 1850s. At the beginning of the Civil War, he established a de facto alliance with the Radical Republicans in Congress, who were led by his friend and fellow **abolitionist** Massachusetts senator Charles Sumner. When he visited Washington in January of 1862 to speak at the Smithsonian, Emerson urged immediate emancipation both as a moral imperative and as a war measure. He insisted that "the end of all political struggle is to establish morality as the basis of all legislation," and morality demands freedom, equality, and justice for all. This was the original promise of the founding fathers, and it is because of this ideal that "our whole history appears like a last effort of the Divine Providence in behalf of the human race." This promise of equality is all-inclusive and, as Emerson observed in a later war lecture, "American genius finds its true type—if I dare tell you—in the poor Negro soldier lying in the trenches by the Potomac, with his spelling book in one hand and his musket in the other." In another lecture, he insisted that in a reconstructed America, every "sane and innocent man, have an equal vote in the state, and a fair chance in society."

For Emerson, because of the war, America was finally "passing out of old remainders of barbarism . . . into freedom of thought, of religion, of speech, of the press, of trade, of suffrage, or political right." Indeed, with a Union victory, "a new era of equal rights [will] dawn on the universe," one that will eventually include women as well as men.

As a result of the war, the passage of the thirteenth, fourteenth, and fifteenth amendments to the Constitution ended slavery forever, granted equal protection to all citizens, and guaranteed suffrage to all adult males "without regard to race, color, or previous conditions of servitude." Reflecting on all this in 1871, Emerson took comfort that a truly great victory had been won, and American democracy had been reinvented in the process. Slavery was defeated, and "the Constitution not only amended, but construed in a new spirit." That universal spirit was at once both liberal and moral, promising "every race and skin, white men, red men, yellow men, black men; hospitality of fair field and equal laws to all."

Bibliography. Garvey, T. Gregory, ed. *The Emerson Dilemma: Essays on Emerson and Social Reform.* Athens: University of Georgia Press. 2001. Gougeon, Len. *Emerson and Eros: The Making of a Cultural Hero.* Albany: State University of New York Press, forthcoming, 2007. Gougeon, Len. Introduction to *Emerson's Antislavery Writings,* ed. Len Gougeon and Joel Myerson. New Haven, CT: Yale University Press. 1995. Gougeon, Len. *Virtue's Hero: Emerson, Antislavery, and Reform.* Athens: University of Georgia Press. 1990. Richardson, Robert. *Emerson: The Mind on Fire.* Berkeley and Los Angeles: University of California Press. 1995.

Len Gougeon

ENGLAND, JOHN (1786–1842). Bishop England was born in Cork, Ireland, to Thomas and Honora (Lordan). In 1802, he began studies for the priesthood at St. Patrick's College, Carlow, and was ordained in 1808. As a young priest, England was assigned to the cathedral in Cork, where he earned respect as a preacher, minister to the imprisoned, and president of a new seminary. While engaged in these various pursuits, England also found time to edit a religious magazine and manage a secular newspaper. While working in the prison, England learned of the plight of many of the convicts who would eventually be sent to Australia and was able to convince the House of Commons to allow Catholic priests to go to the penal colony. England again gained national prominence for his

vocal support for rights for the Irish people as well as his strong stand against
British government influence in the selection of Irish bishops. At first Rome and the
Irish bishops supported the Crown's
involvement in this process, and England's
opposition led to his exile to a small country parish. Eventually the church authorities reversed themselves and came to agree
with his position.

While a young priest, England twice
sought permission to go to America as a
missionary but was refused both times.
After a time, however, his prayers were
answered. In 1820, Pope **Pius VII** sent
England to the United States not as a
priest, but rather as the first bishop of
Charleston, South Carolina. Upon his
arrival in his new diocese, which then
comprised both Carolinas as well as the
entire state of Georgia, the new bishop
found he had a total of three priests to
minister to a flock of about five thousand
Catholics. He immediately began making
pastoral visits to the different parts of his
diocese. He encouraged his flock to continue their practice of the Catholic faith,
despite their paucity of numbers and the
fact that they might go months without
seeing a priest. In response to the impossibility of regular attendance at Mass for
many of his faithful, he organized groups
of laypeople to meet on Sundays for
prayer. Also toward this end, he started
the first regularly published Catholic newspaper in the country, the *United States
Catholic Miscellany,* which he hoped
would forge greater unity among his far-
flung flock.

In addition to throwing himself into sacramental and catechetical work, England
assumed that his responsibilities as a church
leader included understanding the democratic spirit of his new nation and how
American Catholics should relate to it.
Despite what most in Rome thought,
England believed the separation of church
and state to be beneficial for both

John England. Courtesy of the University
of Notre Dame Archives

institutions. He spoke in favor of freedom
of religion, a position the church would not
officially adopt until the Second Vatican
Council (1962–1965). Respected by others
for his progressive views, in 1826 he
addressed the U.S. Congress, defending the
inherent compatibility between the Catholic
Church and the American system of government. England also made public his views
on the burning political issues of the day.
Although he believed slavery to be evil, he
considered immediate abolition unfeasible
and declared the state legislature to be
responsible for regulating the peculiar institution. As far as what he could do for African
Americans, in addition to urging both Rome
and the other bishops about the need to
evangelize this oppressed population, he
opened a school for free blacks in
Charleston. Fierce opposition from many
whites, however, forced its closing.

In dealing with unruly lay trustees who
demanded an excessive amount of control
over church affairs, England borrowed a
page from the nation's founders and wrote

a constitution for his diocese that articulated a legitimate power-sharing role for laypeople in the church. In keeping with this, more than two dozen annual diocesan conventions were held during his tenure as bishop, which brought together both clergy and laity to deliberate over the affairs of their local church. Such innovations earned England the displeasure of his fellow bishops, who believed in breaking the will of "upstart" laypeople rather than finding a role for them in church governance.

Active also in international affairs, England was chosen by Pope **Gregory XVI** as apostolic delegate to the new state of Haiti, but the pope ultimately rejected the concordat he proposed. Although forever a son of Ireland who continually spoke out for the people of his homeland, England chose to remain in his missionary diocese even though Rome offered a see back home. He died in his adopted country.

Bibliography Carey, Patrick. *Immigrant Bishop: John England's Adaptation of Irish Catholicism to American Republicanism.* Yonkers, NY: U.S. Catholic Historical Society, 1982. Guilday, Peter. *Life and Times of John England, 1786–1842.* 2 vols. New York: America Press, 1927.

Anthony D. Andreassi

ERHARD, LUDWIG (1897–1977). Erhard served as German chancellor and commerce secretary of the **Christian Democratic Union** (CDU). Besides Chancellor **Konrad Adenauer,** Erhard was the most important and popular German politician during the 1950s and 1960s. He was called the father of the German economic miracle, of the social market economy, and the strong German Mark.

Erhard, son of a Catholic shopkeeper and a Protestant mother, was not a particularly devout member of the Protestant Church. After his dissertation on national economy (1925) he worked at an economic institute, a position he maintained under National Socialism, although he was not a member in Nazi organizations. In 1942 Erhard was employed by an industrial consortium to develop plans for a postwar economy, a task that later would prove key to his quick success. In 1945–1946 he was Bavarian commerce secretary. He lost this position, although the Americans nominated him to prepare a new currency (1947).

In the next year he was elected as the director of administration and economy in the British and American Zone. His major initiative was the sudden lifting of price controls and economic restrictions during the invention of the new currency. Although prices and unemployment rose immediately, Erhard kept to his decision to develop a free-market economy. In 1951, the results of his politics started to bear fruit, and the strong German Mark and economic prosperity were connected with his name.

The German minister of economics Ludwig Erhard during a press conference in Vienna. © National Library of Vienna

Between 1949 and 1963, Erhard was commerce secretary in Konrad Adenauer's governments. He was not a member of a party until 1963 but was then highly responsible for the electoral success of the CDU. Erhard continued his liberal politics and fought many conflicts with the CDU's social wing. He called his politics "social market economy," but many major social decisions (like pension reform in 1957) were taken against him. At the same time, Erhard fought against the Federation of German Industry to prevent cartels. He also opposed European economic integration in favor of worldwide free trade. In these questions, Chancellor Adenauer forced Erhard to compromise.

The popular Erhard became chancellor in 1963, over the opposition of Adenauer. Erhard however, proved to be a weak chancellor, particularly in foreign policy, which favored a stronger relation with the United States and Britain instead of France and led to protests from his own party. His most important programmatic effort (*Die formierte Gesellschaft,* or the formed society, 1965) demanded harmonious social balance and led Erhard unsuccessfully to style himself as the "chancellor of the people." Opposition from his Free Democratic Party allies in 1966 led to the downfall of his ministry.

Bibliography. Hentschel, Volker. *Ludwig Erhard: Ein Politikerleben.* Munich: Olzog, 1996. Laitenberger, Volkhard. *Ludwig Erhard: Der Nationalökonom als Politiker.* Göttingen, Germany: Munster-Schmidt, 1986.

Frank Bösch

ERZBERGER, MATTHIAS (1875–1921). In 1903, at age twenty-eight, Erzberger of the **Center Party** (Zentrum) became the youngest member of the German parliament, where he immediately made a name for himself as a fierce polemicist and a man with a great capacity for work. He went on to achieve fame as a key public figure at the end of the German Empire and the birth of the Weimar Republic.

Born to Catholic parents in the small south German village of Buttenhausen in Württemberg, Erzberger enjoyed a modest upbringing. From an early age he displayed great ambition, intellectual capability, and industriousness, which made up for his lack of formal education. In the mid-1890s, after brief careers as a teacher and journalist, he discovered politics as his calling. Due to his strong Catholic faith, the Center Party was his only political option. He dedicated his first few years in Parliament to colonial politics, becoming the leading critic of Germany's management of its colonial empire. After having established himself on the national political stage, Erzberger embarked on developing a comprehensive social and economic policy on which the heterogeneous Center Party could unite. His Catholicism influenced many of these policies, as he remained a strong protectionist who championed social insurance, an independent trade union, and an end to the anti-Catholic discrimination in the bureaucracy. In the last few years before the First World War, he became increasingly interested in foreign policy and diplomacy. His belief that a militarily strong Germany was one of the prerequisites for a stable Europe paralleled the views of the majority of Germans.

Although Erzberger was primarily responsible for propaganda toward neutral countries, he also engaged in a variety of diplomatic activities during the war. His attitude toward Germany's war aims underwent a dramatic change during the conflict. An extreme annexationist at the outbreak of war, by 1915 his pragmatism had forced him to revise his ideas. By 1917 Erzberger became one of the best-known public figures in Germany, as he was deeply involved in the controversy over submarine warfare. He opposed the use of submarines, arguing that it would ultimately lead to German defeat because it would force the United States into the war. He was also involved in the crisis that brought down the government of Chancellor Theobald Bethmann-Hollweg. In a famous speech to Parliament in mid-1917, Erzberger maintained that Germany was in such bad military shape that it must renounce all annexationist claims and sue for a negotiated peace. Amidst the controversies that followed, Emperor William II forced Bethmann-Hollweg to resign and introduced a more democratic franchise. Erzberger's actions had the dual result of gaining him great support among the war-weary lower classes while making him the most despised man in Germany among the powerful elements of the upper classes who still sought an annexationist peace.

In 1918–1919, Erzberger was placed in charge of the armistice negotiations for the nascent Weimar Republic. Although he realized that it would compromise his political future, his patriotism convinced him to accept the position as armistice commissioner. Despite applying all his diplomatic skills during the negotiations, he proved unable to limit the harsh conditions the Allied powers imposed upon Germany. Ironically, his greatest achievement was probably to convince German politicians to ratify the treaty, yet this deed essentially doomed his political future and made him a marked man for conservatives and nationalists.

In 1919, Erzberger became finance minister of the Weimar Republic, which forced him to confront the disastrous German economic situation. In an increasingly hostile climate in which his political opponents initiated a campaign to portray him as the main traitor who had stabbed Germany in the back by signing the Versailles Treaty, he still managed to implement a uniform tax code that applied to all Germans, irrespective of their residence.

This modern and efficient tax system constituted one of his most important accomplishments.

In 1920, Erzberger's involvement in a libel suit against the former finance minister for all practical purposes ended his political career. Although Erzberger was never proven guilty of any crimes, his personal honor was beyond repair, and in 1920 he took what he assumed would be a temporary leave of absence from national politics. However, he was assassinated in 1921.

Bibliography. Epstein, Klaus. *Matthias Erzberger and the Dilemma of German Democracy.* Princeton, NJ: Princeton University Press, 1959. Eschenburg, Theodor. *Matthias Erzberger: Der Grosse Mann des Parlamentarismus und der Finanzreform.* Munich: R. Piper, 1973.

Pontus Hiort

ESCRIVÁ DE BALAGUER Y ALBÁ, JOSEMARÍA (1902–1975). Escrivá was a priest, founder of the Roman Catholic religious order Opus Dei, and a canonized Roman Catholic saint. Born in the province of Aragon, Spain, he studied at the Pontifical University of San Valero and San Braulio before being ordained a priest in 1925.

While in Madrid in 1928, Escrivá founded Opus Dei (the Work of God, or simply the Work) as an organization dedicated to the sanctification of work and ordinary life. According to official Opus Dei publications, while at a retreat house Escrivá "saw" the future structure of Opus Dei, even though it would be over a decade later that Opus Dei began to achieve legal recognition by the Roman Catholic Church. With the outbreak of the Spanish Civil War in 1936, Escrivá went underground and eventually escaped over the Pyrenees after hiding in the Honduran consulate in Madrid.

In 1943, Opus Dei received approbation from the Vatican, and in 1944 its first priests were ordained. Under Escrivá, Opus Dei developed a structure with a variety of categories of membership: "numeraries," priests and laypeople who live lives of celibacy in Opus Dei centers; associates, who live celibate lives either alone or with their families; "supernumeraries," who are married; and cooperators, sympathizers who need not be Catholic or even Christian. In addition to the sanctification of work, divine filiation ("intimate spiritual connection") with Christ and filiation with Escrivá as the founder are central components of Opus Dei spirituality. Josemaría Escrivá de Balaguer y Albá died in Rome on June 26, 1975, and in 1982 Opus Dei was named a personal prelature by Pope **John Paul II.** Escrivá was beatified in 1992 and was canonized in 2002.

Escrivá is a particularly controversial figure because of allegations of his support of the dictatorship of Generalissimo **Francisco Franco.** In his voluminous writings, Escrivá often relates nationalist fervor to zeal for Christ, a zeal that will return Spain to its original grandeur. Of course, one of the key ideological elements of the Franco regime was National Catholicism, in which being Catholic was seen as an integral part of Spanish identity. Certainly, Escrivá's valorization of *Hispanidad* (Spanishness) was quite in keeping with the rhetoric of the Franco regime. Furthermore, key figures in Franco's cabinet were members of Opus Dei.

Yet the question of the extent of Escrivá's specific support for Franco is less clear. For example, Peter Berglar defends Escrivá from charges of "Franco-philia" by emphasizing how Escrivá himself understood Opus Dei as "supernatural" and incompatible with anything "not spiritual or apostolic in character." The political activities of members of Opus Dei, including those in Franco's cabinet, are thus presented as an inevitable consequence of the absolute freedom given to members of Opus Dei in secular matters. The weight of the hagiographical literature surrounding Escrivá is counterbalanced by an equally large collection of works and Web resources that liken Opus Dei to a cult and accuse it and its founder of supporting right-wing political forces and of recruiting politicians in order to gain influence. Given the extreme positions held by Opus Dei and its critics, it is clear that a balanced study of Escrivá's political commitments has yet to be written.

Bibliography. Berglar, Peter. *Opus Dei: Life and Work of its Founder Josemaria Escrivá.* Princeton, NJ: Scepter Books. 1989. Walsh, Michael. *Opus Dei: An Investigation into the Secret Society Struggling for Power within the Roman Catholic Church.* New York: Harper-Collins, 1989.

Mathew N. Schmalz

ESPADA Y FERNANDEZ DE LANDA, JUAN JOSÉ DIAZ DE (1756–1832). Bishop Espada was prelate of Havana, Cuba, for thirty years. He was instrumental in promoting public education, vaccination of the general population, and for establishing the first general cemetery in Cuba.

Born in Arróyabe, Alava, Calahorra, Spain, Espada studied at the University of Salamanca, in Spain, where he earned a doctorate in theology. He was ordained in 1782 by the bishop of Segovia. Afterwards he held various offices and titles including rector of the Colegio Mayor de San Bartolome, vice secretary of the archbishopric of Plasencia, and chaplain of the Armada.

After the death of the first bishop of Havana in 1799, King Carlos IV submitted Espada's name as a candidate to Pope Pius VII. He was named bishop on August 11, 1800. His arrival in Havana did not occur until February 25, 1802. In 1803 he set out to visit all the parishes in his diocese. This was quite a feat since it extended from the westernmost province of Pinar del Rio to the next to last in the east, Camagüey. He instituted various reforms including the order to ring the church bells the same amount of times for the poor as for the rich.

To promote healthier conditions within churches, he prohibited burials within their buildings or in their immediate surroundings. Instead, Bishop Espada founded the first general cemetery in Cuba in February 1806. It became known as the Espada Cemetery and was in use for more than sixty years. Additionally, he promoted the vaccination against small pox for the general population. He founded the first hospital for the mentally ill in Cuba.

Bishop Espada was laid to rest in the cemetery he founded. In 1881, after the closure of the Espada Cemetery, his remains were transferred to the new cemetery of Cristóbal Colón. Bishop Espada's legacy of working for the welfare of the poor, in life and death, attests to his humanitarianism.

Bibliography. Garcia Pons, César. *El obispo Espada y su influencia en la cultura cubana.* Havana, Cuba: Ministerio de Educación, 1951.

Peter E. Carr

EUGÉNIE, EMPRESS OF FRANCE [EUGENIA-MARIA PALAFOX DE MONTIJO] (1826–1920).

On January 30, 1853, the twenty-seven-year-old Countess Eugenia-Maria Palafox de Montijo of Spain married Emperor Louis Napoleon (Napoleon III) of France and ascended to the imperial throne. Although sometimes considered to be more influential than she actually was, the empress was both a symbol and an occasional practitioner of Catholic power during the French Second Empire.

Since Napoleon I, the relations between the Bonapartes and the Catholic Church had been strained (examples of this tense relationship include the arrest of Pope **Pius VII** and the excommunication of Napoleon I). The reign of Napoleon III (1852–1870) was dogged by Italian affairs, particularly the question of Rome's status as a papal state or as part of a unified Italian kingdom, a matter not only of French foreign policy, but an issue of

internal dispute in a mostly Catholic France. Although Napoleon III did not allow the Italians to enter Rome and to make it part of Italy (which only happened after the defeat of the Second Empire in 1870), neither could he in practical politics nor by the beliefs expressed in his theoretical writings be seen as overly favorable to the papal position. Eugénie, rather, was identified by many critics of the regime to be the Catholic behind the emperor and thus responsible for the protection of Rome as well as for the failed Mexican adventure of the 1860s, which was presented as her wish to deliver an American Catholic empire to the pope.

With little factual basis for such allegations, however, they were based largely on her Spanish descent and her Catholic devotion. She did, nevertheless, ensure that a pro-papal policy was maintained in the foreign ministry by her support for the Catholic Edouard Drouyn de Lhuys in the

Eugénie.   Courtesy   of   the   Perry-Casteñeda Library

1860s over Edouard de Thouvenel. Her image as the ardent Catholic empress, moreover, was not to be underestimated as propaganda for Napoleon's rule in France.

After the collapse of the empire, Eugénie devoted much of her remaining (very long) life to fostering relations between Catholicism and Bonapartism, which she saw not as much as a political issue but as the conservation of the memory of the Second Empire. In her British exile she inspired a Benedictine monastery at Farnborough and built St. Michael's Abbey, which became the final resting place for the late emperor, the prince imperial (her son, who died as a youth), and for herself. Eugénie did not engage directly in French politics after 1870 but continued to be a symbol for the Catholic element in the Bonapartist movement.

Bibliography. Les Amis de Napoléon III, ed. *Napoléon III, l'Église et Rome.* Paris: Nouveaux Cahiers du Second Empire, 2000. Monks of St. Michael's Abbey. *St. Michael's Abbey, Farnborough.* Andover, UK: Pitkin Unichrome, 1998. Smith, William. *The Empress Eugénie and Farnborough.* Winchester, UK: Hampshire County Council, 2001. Smith, William. *Eugénie.* Paris: Bartillat, 1998.

Oliver Benjamin Hemmerle

EUROPEAN PEOPLE'S PARTY. The European People's Party (EPP) represents the endeavors of European Christian Democratic parties to engage in dialogue, coordinate common goals, and organize their representation in the European Parliament, an impetus that mirrored activity by, among others, communist, socialist, liberal, and far-right groups toward the same end.

Some early attempts at coordination, the work of the exiled Italian Don **Luigi Sturzo** and of the French **Democratic Popular Party,** occurred in the 1920s. An International Congress of People's Parties was first held in Paris in December 1925.

Arguments over Catholic authoritarian regimes, however, particularly in Austria, crippled these early efforts, and a headquarters established in Paris ceased to function in 1939. Postwar roots of the EPP can be found in part in the Geneva Discussions, a Franco-German initiative that brought together many of the continent's Christian Democratic leaders and their representatives. These informal meetings lasted from 1947 until 1956 and provided a forum that contributed to the creation of both the European Coal and Steel Community and the Common Market.

On the more public level, the *Nouvelles Équipes Internationales* (NEI) formed in Montreux, Switzerland, in 1946. It was closely connected to the Geneva Discussions and held its first congress in Chaudfontaine, Belgium, in May 1947. The NEI identified with the recent antifascist resistance and thus took on an antiauthoritarian mentality, although postwar Christian Democracy was still frequently criticized for its lukewarm endorsement of democratic institutions. The NEI, on the other hand, maintained a close relationship with the Christian Democratic Union of Central Europe, formed in New York in 1950 and comprised mainly of exiled parties from Eastern Europe. At its seventeenth congress at Taormina, Italy, in 1965, the NEI dissolved and was re-formed as the European Union of Christian Democrats, which proclaimed in its charter the goal of a "common political program." Christian Democratic electoral reversals in many nations, particularly West Germany and France, in the 1960s, and the 1973 enlargement of the European Union led to an acceleration of an all-European Christian Democratic Party. In 1976 the European People's Party was created to meet these new needs. It merged with the European Union of Christian Democrats in 1983. In 1999 the EPP formed an alliance in the European Parliament with the conservative European Democrats (ED). In 2005, the EPP/ED group formed the largest voting bloc in the parliament.

Bibliography. Dechert, Charles. "The Christian Democratic 'International.'" *Orbis* 11 (1) Spring, 1967. European People's Party. www.epp-eu.org. Gehler, Michael. "The Geneva Circle of West European Christian Democrats." In *Christian Democracy in Europe Since 1945,* ed. Michael Gehler and Wolfram Kaiser. Vol. 2. London: Routledge, 2004. Kaiser, Wolfram. "Transnational Christian Democracy: From the Nouvelles Équipes Internationales to the European People's Party." In *Christian Democracy in Europe Since 1945,* ed. Michael Gehler and Wolfram Kaiser. Vol. 2. London: Routledge, 2004. Papini, Roberto. *The Christian Democrat International.* Trans. Robert Royal. Lanham, MD: Rowman & Littlefield, 1997.

Roy P. Domenico

EVARTS, JEREMIAH (1781–1831). The Congregationalist writer, social reformer, and opponent of Cherokee removal was born and raised on a Vermont farm but found his calling in urban philanthropy. In September 1798, he entered Yale. President **Timothy Dwight** tightly controlled the students and had an enormous influence. Evarts's graduate's address in 1802 stressed the need to purify the nation of sinful behavior to avoid God's judgment, and his subsequent writings held to these goals. He initially returned to Vermont to become a schoolmaster but instead returned to New Haven to obtain his master's degree from Yale and to train for the law with Charles Chauncey.

Evarts was admitted to the bar in June 1806 but found himself far more interested in writing articles urging religious conversion, social order, and moral legislation to create a Christian republic. These principles guided the rest of his life. In January 1810, he accepted an offer from Jedidiah Morse to edit the *Panoplist,* since 1805 a Calvinist counterweight to Unitarianism. Evarts thus became an influential voice in the Awakening that was emerging as a national movement. His primary interests were the education of children, promotion of Calvinist religion, the recruitment of properly trained ministers, Sabbatarianism, temperance, and foreign missionary efforts.

Evarts's efforts beyond his writing exemplified the tendency in the Second Great Awakening to forge voluntary organizations transcending denominational boundaries to better reform the world. Shortly after arriving in Boston, Evarts helped to establish the ABCFM (American Board of Commissions for Foreign Missions), becoming its treasurer one year later and a board member the following year. He also served as treasurer of the Boston-area Foreign Mission Society. Between 1812 and 1816, he helped to create the Massachusetts Society for the Suppression of Intemperance; the Charlestown Association for the Reformation of Morals, which battled idleness, intemperance, gambling, Sabbath breaking, profanity, and disobedience to one's parents; the New England Religious Tract Society, forerunner of the American Tract Society; and the American Education Society, designed to encourage more young men to become ministers. In 1815, he also organized (with **Lyman Beecher**) a nationwide petition campaign to halt Sunday mail delivery and one year later became manager of the American Bible Society. But his work with benevolent societies did not prevent his occasional condemnation of Unitarianism, which he viewed as unchristian and a threat to a nation dependent on New England's moral compass.

Evarts put most of his effort into the ABCFM after the end of the War of 1812 and was at the forefront of the organization when it became involved with southeastern Indian tribes. In 1816, the Board began establishing missions among the Cherokees and opened a school for Indian students in Cornwall, Connecticut. Their goal was to "civilize" Indians by persuading them to embrace the universe of reformist causes as well as Anglo-American gender roles. The board also sent missionaries to India, Ceylon, Palestine, and the Sandwich Islands (Hawaii)—the latter effort particularly capturing the attention of the American public. But Evarts's focus, and that of the ABCFM (despite its name), was clearly on Native Americans. In 1821, he was elected corresponding secretary of the ABCFM and remained in that leadership position until his death. Despite growing health problems, Evarts frequently visited Board facilities and missionaries in the southeast. By 1826, the ABCFM had missions scattered among the Choctaws in Mississippi, and the Cherokees in Tennessee, Alabama, and Georgia.

The Board's efforts became part of a brewing political battle over U.S. Indian policy as western and Southern politicians pushed for tribes to be "removed" west of the Mississippi River, and resistance increased among the acculturated Cherokee leaders (who were the missionaries' allies) to further land sales. Evarts and the ABCFM tried to straddle the issue by supporting voluntary removal until 1827, but Cherokee resistance, Georgia's militancy, and Andrew Jackson's election drove Evarts to Washington in January 1828 to lobby for the tribe and against removal. One year later, he returned to Washington, initially to lobby against proposed Sunday mail delivery, but soon again focused on helping the Cherokees. Evarts became the leader of opposition to removal. In 1829, he published many writings, including "Essays on the Present Crisis in the Condition of the American Indians," under the pseudonym William Penn, in which he reviewed U.S. Indian policies and attacked Removal as illegal and immoral. He also helped organize public meeting and petition drives and advised missionaries and tribal leaders on tactics to use in lobbying Congress. Despite such intense opposition, the Indian Removal Bill became law on May 26. Evarts continued organizing support for the Cherokees' efforts before the Supreme Court and advised ABCFM missionaries to resist through civil disobedience. His tuberculosis grew worse, however, and he died on May 10.

Bibliography. Andrews John A., III. *From Revivals to Removal: Jeremiah Evarts, the Cherokee Nation, and the Search for the Soul of America.* Athens: University of Georgia Press, 1992. McLoughlin, William G. *Cherokees and Missionaries, 1789–1839.* New Haven, CT: Yale University Press, 1984.

Daniel R. Mandell

EVLOGII. *See* Georgievskii, Vasilii Semyonovich

F

FALWELL, JERRY (b. 1933). Baptist pastor and founder of the **Moral Majority,** Falwell built a career that in many respects typifies the journey of American evangelicalism in the twentieth century. After graduating from Bible Baptist College in Springfield, Missouri, he committed himself to evangelism and "winning souls to Christ" and founded the Thomas Road Baptist Church in 1956. With the onset of the civil rights movement at the same time, political activism by pastors and priests of the theological Left increased. Falwell famously remarked from the pulpit in 1965 that "preachers are not called upon to be politicians but to be soul winners. Nowhere are we commissioned to reform the externals."

Falwell articulated the fundamentalist aversion to political involvement extant at that time. Like many in his subculture, however, Falwell was alarmed at the cultural and political trends of the 1960s and 1970s, especially the legalization of abortion, the gay rights movement, and the banning of organized prayer and Bible reading in public schools. In 1967, Falwell founded a Christian day school and in 1971 founded Liberty Baptist College—now Liberty University—as an alternative for evangelical young people to an educational system seen as increasingly riddled with secularism. Denouncing self-proclaimed

born-again presidential candidate **Jimmy Carter** in 1976 for giving an interview to *Playboy* magazine, Falwell learned that he could command a national stage when the Carter campaign contacted him to protest. With what he and other evangelicals perceived as the leftward drift of the Carter administration, and with a growing national grassroots tax revolt and calls for greater national defense, Falwell in 1979 teamed with other evangelical leaders and national conservatives such as Paul Weyrich to form the **Moral Majority.** The Moral Majority emerged as a key player in the 1980 elections, strongly supporting the Reagan candidacy and working to defeat liberal Democratic senators such as George McGovern. Falwell held "I Love America" rallies around the nation and encouraged pastors to register their congregants to vote. Significantly, Falwell reached across previously uncrossed theological lines to enlist antiabortion Roman Catholics and conservative Mormons and Jews to the Moral Majority. The organization's strong antiabortion stance, pro-family agenda, and strong commitment to Israel appealed to these groups. Many observers credited the Moral Majority with helping to create **Ronald Reagan**'s electoral landslide in November 1980.

Falwell emerged as the public face of the Religious Right in the 1980s. Strongly supporting the Reagan administration, Falwell continued to speak out on issues such as school prayer, abortion, gay rights, and the tide of what evangelicals called "secular humanism." By 1986, however, Falwell's controversial stance had caused his ministries in Lynchburg to suffer financial decline. Sidetracked in 1987 by his involvement in wresting control away from the discredited Jim and Tammy Bakker's Heritage Ministries, Falwell formally ended the Moral Majority in 1989.

Politics was never far away, however. Falwell became embroiled in controversy again in 1994 when his Liberty Alliance— the remains of the Moral Majority—funded a video series entitled *The Clinton Chronicles,* which accused President Bill Clinton and wife Hillary of participating in numerous nefarious activities.

The September 2001 Al Qaeda attacks upon the World Trade Center and the Pentagon also thrust Falwell back into the center of controversy. Appearing on **Pat Robertson**'s *700 Club* television program just two days after the attacks, Falwell said, "And, I know that I'll hear from them for this. Throwing God out successfully with the help of the federal court system, throwing God out of the public square, out of the schools. The abortionists have got to bear some burden for this because God will not be mocked. And when we destroy forty million little innocent babies, we make God mad. I really believe that the pagans, the abortionists, and the feminists, the ACLU, People for the American Way, all of them who tried to secularize America— I point the finger in their face and say 'you helped this happen.'" Falwell backtracked when a public outcry ensued, but a year later he referred to the Prophet Mohammed as a "terrorist."

Falwell continues as pastor of Thomas Road Baptist Church and chancellor of Liberty University. His life and career provide a snapshot of the journey many American evangelicals took away from the enclave mentality of the 1920s and 1930s toward a reengagement with political activism and reform—legacies of their nineteenth-century Protestant heritage.

Bibliography. Falwell, Jerry. *Strength for the Journey: An Autobiography.* New York: Simon & Schuster, 1987. Harding, Susan. *The Book of Jerry Falwell: Fundamentalist Language and Politics.* Princeton, NJ: Princeton University Press, 2002.

Mark Taylor Dalhouse

FANFANI, AMINTORE (1908–1999). A Catholic thinker, politician, and one of the most important leaders of Italian **Christian Democracy** (Democrazia Cristiana, or DC), Fanfani was born in Pieve Santo Stefano in Tuscany's Arezzo province into a large family. His father was a lawyer and notary and actively participated in the **Italian Popular Party** after World War I.

In 1926, Fanfani moved to Milan to study economics at the Catholic University of the Sacred Heart, one of the few Italian cultural institutions that resisted Benito Mussolini's Fascist regime. He graduated in 1930 with a thesis on the origins of capitalism. In exploring these issues he developed a neo-voluntarist vision in which people should modify natural laws when such laws become perilous to humankind. He then published *Cattolicesimo e Protestantesimo nella formazione del Capitalismo* (Catholicism and Protestantism in the Formation of Capitalism), which was translated into English and Spanish, where he explained that economic supremacy needed to be replaced by religious ethics. Several years later, he was given a position as a professor of economic history of economy at Genoa and then at the Catholic University of Milan.

While at the Catholic University of Milan, Fanfani met other university professors, like **Giuseppe Dossetti,** Giuseppe Lazzati, and **Giorgio La Pira,** with whom he engaged in social arguments, and in 1945, following the end of World War II, they joined the Christian Democracy. Party secretary **Alcide De Gasperi** called Fanfani and Dossetti to Rome to the Office of Press and Propaganda (SPES), where Fanfani demonstrated his organizational skill. In 1946 he became a member of the DC's National Council and its National Direction. Representing the Siena-Arezzo-Grossetto electoral district, a position he would retain until 1968, Fanfani attended the Constituent Assembly, where he contributed to the drafting of the new Italian constitution and formulated the expression in the document's first article that defined Italy as a republic founded on labor.

In De Gasperi's fourth government, formed in May 1947 without communists and socialists, Fanfani received his first job as minister of labor. Reconfirmed to this position after the 1948 elections, Fanfani approved a seven-year plan that favored jobs for workers and housing construction for them. This measure was known as the Fanfani Plan and even obtained support from communists and socialists. During the 1949 DC party congress the so-called *Cronache Sociali* leftist faction, founded by Fanfani and Dossetti, was very successful, and Dossetti was elected the party's vice secretary. While Dossetti grew disillusioned in his political aspirations, temporarily abandoning politics in 1951, Fanfani grew closer to De Gasperi's moderate line while remaining convinced that political power needed to maintain control over the economy. After Dossetti left politics and the *Cronache Sociali* was dissolved, Fanfani, along with **Aldo Moro,** Mariano Rumor, and Paolo Emilio Taviani, formed the *Iniziativa Democratica,* which was supported by De Gasperi. In 1953, Fanfani became minister of the interior, and in January of the next year he was asked to form a government, but it did not receive the approval of the Houses. Fanfani then dedicated himself to the DC and at the 1954 Naples congress established himself

as leader of the party's second generation. Despite leftist opposition by **Giovanni Gronchi** and some representatives of the party's Right, Fanfani successfully succeeded De Gasperi as party secretary.

Above all, Fanfani worked for a solid party structure by making the party independent from industrial groups through a campaign of self-financing by party members. The new party leaders were more sensible to Christian social thought and against both communism and conservatism. For Fanfani the social programs of the Democrazia Cristiana, which were based on the social doctrines of the Catholic Church, were enough to reform Italy by conquering the popular masses without alliances with communists and ideological concessions toward Marxism. As secretary of the Democrazia Cristiana, Fanfani energetically faced the campaign for the 1958 elections and used as his slogan the search for a "progress without adventures," which greatly benefited him with an unequaled success and damaged the leftist parties. After the elections he became prime minister and foreign minister, but his activism earned him hostile reactions from many quarters, and in 1959 he vacated the prime minister's chair as well as the position of DC party secretary following the dissolution of the Iniziativa Democratica by the *dorotei* faction (named for the Roman convent of Santa Dorotea sul Gianicolo, where this group first met). Moro became party secretary, while Fanfani returned to politics during the DC Florence congress by presenting himself as a reference for the leftists in the party. In opposition to Moro, Fanfani founded a new current in the spirit of the *Cronache Sociali,* called the *Nuove Cronache.* After Fernando Tambroni's tormented ministry (summer of 1960) when the DC turned, for the first and only time, to the neo-Fascist party for support, Moro asked Fanfani to head a government of "parallel convergences" with the support of centrist parties and the abstention of monarchists and socialists. With this new government, Fanfani led Italy from De Gasperi's centrist policy in place after World War II to a new center-left one due, in part, to the favorable climate and good relationships with President Kennedy (who knew Fanfani as a politician and studied him as an economist) and Pope **John XXIII,** which opened a period of openness and dialogue. In 1963 there was a hard political fight on the nationalization of electric energy, which met opposition from the Liberals, some DC deputies, and much of the press and led to Christian Democratic losses in the 1963 elections. Fanfani was forced to cede his prime minister's chair to Moro, who formed the first government with socialists since 1947.

Fanfani then became foreign minister and in 1965 was elected president of the General Assembly of the United Nations, where he received Pope **Paul VI,** who visited the UN for the first time. Also in 1965, Giorgio La Pira pushed Fanfani to try mediation regarding the Vietnam War, but this was unsuccessful and garnered him many criticisms, forcing him to resign his position as foreign minister. In 1968, Fanfani became senator and was elected president of the Senate. He was the DC candidate for the president of the republic but was not successful. In 1973, he became secretary of the Democrazia Cristiana once again and involved his party in the campaign for the repeal of the new law on divorce even though other parties were against him.

After this defeat and after his party lost the regional elections in 1975, Fanfani definitively left the leadership of the Democrazia Cristiana. When the Red Brigade terrorist group kidnapped Moro in 1978, Fanfani was one of the most determined people who planned for his rescue, but his hopes were shattered when Moro's dead body was found in the trunk of a car parked near the DC headquarters. In 1982 and again in 1987, he formed his last (fifth

and sixth) governments, and in 1987, while part of the Goria government, he once again became minister of the interior. Following these experiences, becoming senator for life, Fanfani began to express himself more freely on issues he felt were important, such as the increased participation of citizens in political and social choices. He died at age ninety-one in November of 1999.

Bibliography. Fanfani, A. *Da Napoli a Firenze (1954–1959): Proposte per una politica di sviluppo democratico.* Milan: Garzanti, 1959. Filizzola, R. *Amintore Fanfani: Quaresime e resurrezioni.* Rome: Editalia, 1988. Galli, G. *Fanfani.* Milan: Feltrinelli, 1975. Ottone, P. *Fanfani.* Milan: Longanesi, 1966.

Eliana Versace

FAULHABER, MICHAEL (1869–1952). One of the most powerful Catholic preachers in Germany during the era of the World Wars, Faulhaber was also an able public defender of the church's position amid wartime political upheaval.

After an education in grammar schools in Schweinfurt and Würzburg and one year of military service (1889), Faulhaber entered the seminary in Würzburg. Ordained in 1892, he became the prefect at the Kilianeum in Würzburg in 1893 after a year as chaplain. Following a study visit in Rome and receipt of his postdoctoral lecture qualification in Würzburg, Faulhaber taught Old Testament exegesis starting in 1899. From 1903, he was an ordinary in Strassburg, where his reputation as a magnificent preacher was cemented.

On November 11, 1911, he became bishop of Speyer (with the campaign slogan *Vox temporis—vox Dei*), and after the outbreak of World War I in 1914 he headed the Office of the Bavarian Field Provost. His transformation into the archbishop of Munich-Freising took place on July 24, 1917. He formed a lasting mutual trust with the nuncio in Munich (1917–1929),

Eugenio Pacelli, later Pope **Pius XII.** Shaken by the disappearance of the monarchy in 1918, Faulhaber tried to contribute to a reorganization of the state-church relationship in the Weimar Republic (1919–1933). The chairman of the Freising (Bavarian) Bishops' Conference in 1921, he received the cardinal's hat. In 1923 and 1926 he visited the United States.

After the appointment of Hitler as Reich chancellor, Faulhaber retracted his earlier warnings against National Socialism and welcomed the conclusion of the Reich Concordat in 1933. However, his criticism of Nazi ideology resurfaced in his Advent sermons of that year. In 1937, he composed the draft of **Pius XI**'s encyclical against the Nazi regime entitled *Mit brennender Sorge*. Still, the cardinal refrained from discussions within the German episcopacy about the church's proper behavior toward the Nazis. He supported individual opponents of the regime but condemned the assassination attempt on Hitler in 1944.

Following World War II, Faulhaber pushed for the rebuilding of the church in the German desert of rubble and was responsible for the alleviation of much hardship. He criticized anti-church measures of the U.S. occupation force and called for the reestablishment of the status quo in terms of the Bavarian Concordat of 1924. Faulhaber ranks among the most important princes of the church in the twentieth century.

Bibliography. Forstner, Thomas, Susan Kornacker, and Peter Pfister. *Faulhaber, Michael Kardinal von: Eine Ausstellung des Erzbistums München und Freising, des Bayerischen Hauptstaatsarchivs und des Stadtarchivs München zum 50.* Munich: Generaldirektion der Staatlichen Archive Bayerns, 2002. Forstner, Thomas, Susan Kornacker, and Peter Pfister. *Michael Kardinal von Faulhaber (1869–1952): Beiträge zum 50: Todestag und zur Öffnung des Kardinal-Faulhaber-Archivs.* Munich: Generaldirektion der Staatlichen Archive Bayerns, 2002.

Rudolf Morsey

FEIJÓ, DIOGO ANTONIO (1784–1843). Born in the southern Brazilian state of São Paulo, Feijó was famous in Brazilian history as an antislavery advocate and regent in the independence period of the early nineteenth century. Ordained as a Catholic priest in 1807, Feijó had been a staunch advocate of Brazilian separatism under Portuguese rule, and as such he was persecuted but escaped prison by seeking refuge in England. After Brazil attained its independence in 1822 under Dom Pedro I, son of the Portuguese king, Feijó became active in politics as a Radical Party member and deputy from São Paulo.

He advocated the abolition of clerical celibacy, a popular idea among liberals in nineteenth-century Latin America. A prolific author of philosophical and theological books, his most famous work was *Demonstracão da Necessidade da Abolicão do Celibato Clerical,* a vigorous polemic against clerical celibacy that was later denounced by the pope. Feijó's liberal attitude on this subject may have stemmed from the fact that he was the son of a priest and was himself the father of several children.

Feijó later became Brazil's minister of justice, maintaining public order during disturbances in Rio de Janeiro and suppressing separatist movements that threatened the authority of the central government during the reign of Dom Pedro I (1822–1831). From 1835 until 1837, he served as regent during the minority of Dom Pedro II, but, according to the historian Roderick Barman, he lacked the educational sophistication, vision, and flexibility to lead Brazil, so he was replaced by more liberal statesmen until the young emperor could assume the throne in 1840.

Although he was chosen bishop of Mariana in Minas Gerais in 1835, he did not accept the position, preferring the world of politics to ecclesiastical office. He did on occasion, however, involve himself in church politics, promoting his choice for bishop of Rio in the 1820s and 1830s.

In 1842 Feijó was imprisoned, accused of conspiracy against the young Emperor Dom Pedro II, and exiled to the state of Espirito Santo for six months. Later he defended himself before the Brazilian Senate and was exonerated of the charge. Ill health forced him out of politics at the end of his life.

Bibliography. Barman, Roderick J. *Citizen Emperor: Pedro II and the Making of Brazil, 1825–91* Stanford, CA: Stanford University Press, 1999. Burns, Bradford E. *A History of Brazil.* New York: Columbia University Press, 1970. *Dicionario de Historia do Brasil.* 4th ed. pšo Paulo, Brazil: Edicoes Melhoramentos, 1976.

Patricia A. Mulvey

FERNANDEZ DE LA MORA, GONZALO (1924–2002). One of Spain's preeminent conservative theorists of the late twentieth century, and a founder of Spain's **Popular Party** (Partido Popular), Gonzalo Fernandez de la Mora was born in Barcelona, came to Madrid with his parents when he was two years old, and then spent his decisive childhood years in Galicia, the land of his mother. His father was a Castilian monarchist whose ideas exerted a great influence on the youth. He received a formal Jesuit high school education and went on to the University of Madrid, where, in 1945, he received diplomas in law and philosophy. The following year he entered the Spanish foreign ministry and eventually served as its general director of foreign affairs and head of its diplomatic school. His linguistic and literary gifts, recognized by many, led to his collaboration and direction of the newspaper *ABC* .

As a young man, he joined the Catholic *Acción Española* and acquired the reputation of a moderate monarchist. Later, as minister of public works (1970), he played an outstanding role in Spain's economic expansion and helped to prepare the way for Juan Carlos's accession to the throne after Franco's death in 1975.

The legacy of Fernando de la Mora, however, emerges most impressively in his role as a political thinker and philosopher, solidly rooted in Christianity. This intellectual foundation informed his newspaper columns, his articles, analytical commentaries, and book reviews, all of which fill seven volumes. Based on his familiarity with Aquinas, Fernandez criticized leftist egalitarianism as a manifestation of political and social envy. Among his best-known works are *Ortega y el 98* (1961) and *El Crepúsculo de las idealogías* (1965) as well as his presentations at the Academy of Moral and Political Sciences. His *Envidia igualitaria,* however, on the role of envy, prompted great discussion among those interested in political philosophy at the end of the century.

Bibliography. Fernandez de la Mora, Gonzalo. *La Envidia Igualitaria.* Barcelona: Planeta, 1984. Translated as *Egalitarian Envy: the Political Foundations of Social Justice.* New York: Paragon House, 1987.

Fernando Murillo Rubiera

FIANNA FAIL (IRELAND). This is usually translated into English as "Soldiers of Destiny" or "Soldiers of Ireland." Founded as a political party in 1927 by **Eamon de Valera**, it has been the largest and most successful political party in the Irish Republic. The party was established following a breakdown in the coalition that opposed the 1921 treaty with Great Britain that had established an autonomous Irish Free State in the predominantly Catholic areas of Ireland in 1922. They first formed a government following the 1932 general election and by 2004 had governed Ireland for over fifty of the past seventy years. It is not surprising that they have often been referred to as the natural governing party of Ireland.

The source of their electoral strength has been in their ability to build a strong populist platform, which was built on the traditional strengths of Irish society. These include traditionally popular positions on the national question of sovereignty, unification, and neutrality. More importantly, the party's platform was built around the values of a traditional Irish Catholic society with rural roots.

A major component of Irish Catholic society has been the tradition of granting the Catholic hierarchy, clergy, and institutions the major role in policy making in areas of learning and private morality. The result was that for most of the first decades following independence, the state was willing to recognize the church's dominance over educational facilities and Catholic values on marriage and divorce, contraception, and birth control.

This model of state acquiescence in church control of education and morality had widespread support among the rural base of the Fianna Fail electorate. The nationalist agenda was of much less importance than the Catholic moral agenda, but this began to shift in the 1960s. The position of the church on issues of poverty, if not morality, began to change following the Second Vatican Council. The nationalist position underwent change as well. Part of this was the result of the beginnings of the Troubles in Northern Ireland. This led to a reevaluation of the party's own traditionally republican and violent roots. Further change came with the admission of Ireland into the European Community in 1972.

Fianna Fail adjusted to the new order. Their position on the nationalist issue was deftly handled in the 1990s by Albert Reynolds and Bertie Aherne. Morality issues have created more difficulties for the party, which supported the constitutional ban on abortion in 1993. While opposed to removing the constitutional ban on divorce, it ultimately supported the removal of the ban in the 1995 referendum.

On the whole, the success of Fianna Fail has been linked to their ability to mirror the image of an Ireland that has had the support of the rural and urban Catholic middle class. Traditionally this group did not support expenditure on the poor, or deviant behavior. As long as church, state, and middle class agreed upon what was important, this arrangement worked. This alliance has broken down, however, since the 1980s. The cultural power of the church in the community has weakened with the development of an urban educated society less interested in the strict morality of rural Ireland. Although Fianna Fail maintains its links with the church, the growth of the Celtic Tiger and the development of a secular-oriented middle class has shifted its attention away from reinforcing the church's view of Irish society.

Bibliography. Coogan, T. P. *Ireland in the Twentieth Century.* London: Hutchinson, 2004.

Gretchen M. MacMillan

FINE GAEL (IRELAND). Fine Gael, or Tribe of the Gaels, is the second major political party in the Republic of Ireland. Originally known as Cumann na nGaedhael, it represented the faction within the independence movement that supported the treaty with the British in 1921. The party governed the Irish Free State from 1922 to 1932, when it lost power to **Fianna Fail**. In the conflict that followed with Fianna Fail over the nature of the relationship with Britain under the treaty, several different factions developed. In 1935, they joined together to form a new party known as Fine Gael. The party has never managed to form a government on its own. It has been the principal party in several coalitions, most of these including parties on the left of the political spectrum, particularly the Irish Labour Party.

The party, like Fianna Fail, represents sections of the Catholic community in

Ireland. It is the differences in these groups that have made them less representative of the community, not because of their Catholicism but because of their less mainstream views on the national question. Moreover, their tendency to ally themselves with the Left on questions of morality and education has often alienated them from their own more conservative supporters as well as from the centrists who supported Fianna Fail.

While the party is also the political heir of Michael Collins, it has always taken a pragmatic view of their relationship with Great Britain and on the issue of Northern Ireland. In 1948 the *Taoiseach* John Costello, as head of a coalition government, unilaterally announced that Ireland would leave the British Commonwealth and become the Republic of Ireland. In the 1980s the coalition under Garret FitzGerald signed the Anglo-Irish Accord, which provided the basis for the future negotiations over the status of Northern Ireland within the United Kingdom.

On moral issues, the party's position on Catholic traditional morality is similar to those expressed by Fianna Fail. The strength of Fine Gael, however, is to be found in the upper echelons of the rural and urban middle classes of Catholic background. It also became the de facto home of the small Protestant groups in Ireland and the traditional supporters of the old Irish Parliamentary Party of the pre-1918 period.

The problem for the Fine Gael party in coalition with more radical parties in government is that despite the Catholic conservatism of its leaders, it became embroiled in conflicts with the church on family and sexual issues. One of these was the failed Mother and Child Health Scheme in 1951, which would have provided free care to pregnant women and newborn children but was seen as state interference with family life. In the 1980s and 1990s the party was less supportive of the amendment regarding the ban on abortion and put forward the ultimately successful referendum removing the constitutional ban on divorce.

Bibliography. Coogan, T. P. *Ireland in the Twentieth Century.* London: Hutchinson, 2003.

Gretchen M. MacMillan

FINNEY, CHARLES GRANDISON (1792–1875). Finney, the most successful revivalist of the Second Great Awakening in America, was also instrumental in creating a politically viable antislavery movement. Born in Warren, Connecticut, to parents of modest means, Finney's intelligence and ambition enabled him to pursue a career in law through apprenticeship rather than the Yale University education he had originally planned. A dramatic religious conversion in 1821 convinced him to cut short his legal career and pursue the ministry under the Presbyterian banner.

The orthodox Calvinism and the Westminster Confession of his denominational home proved a very uncomfortable fit for Finney. With a coercive pulpit style marked by rigorous logic and an unswerving focus on immediate spiritual conversion, Finney served up a Gospel message of individual accountability that melded easily with the Jacksonian democratic spirit of the times. His techniques included advance publicity announcing revivals, an "anxious bench" at the front of the church to accommodate penitent seekers, women praying publicly, and an open message of salvation to all who seemed to defy Calvinist doctrine. These new measures became signatures of his revivals in upstate New York. They earned sharp rebuke from establishment luminaries such as Asahel Nettleton and **Lyman Beecher,** but they also made Finney a regional celebrity with enormous popular influence.

Finney's mission turned westward in 1835 when he accepted a professorship at

Oberlin Collegiate Institute in Ohio. This most liberal of American colleges welcomed African Americans, awarded the nation's first bachelor's degrees to women in 1841, and had become a seedbed of antislavery sentiment by the time Finney arrived. Finney, first as professor of theology and later as president of the institution (1852), embraced the cause, but he also jealously maintained a clear distinction between Christian evangelism and political reform.

Finney's most important contributions to antebellum American political culture were twofold: First, he smoothed the raw edges of radical abolitionism and made the antislavery message palatable to a wider Northern audience; Secondly, he provided early leadership in claiming "higher law doctrine" as a sound basis for attacking a political system that supported slavery. Finney employed simple but forceful logic. All laws that violated godly moral principles were necessarily "null and void," since they violated "the prerogative of God." (Hardman, 170). While he pulled no punches in condemning Southern slaveholders, Finney traced the root of the problem to sin and human selfishness. Consequently, expunging this blight from the American landscape required individual spiritual conversion as the first and essential step toward change.

Radicals such as **William Lloyd Garrison,** Finney believed, elevated abolitionism to a "sacred cause" and polluted the primary Christian message of salvation. Provided there was no distortion of priorities, however, the pulpit could be effectively employed to champion Christianity as the foundation of all moral reform. In his 1852 sermon "Guilt Modified by Ignorance," Finney rebuked both Whig and Democratic politicians for passing the compromise of 1850, a series of measures mandating Northern cooperation in the return of fugitive slaves. Praising the pulpit luminaries of the Revolutionary era, Finney reminded his contemporaries that the "tallest statesmen of the land heard the gospel of liberty proclaimed from the sacred desk. Who needs be told that ministers then met their responsibilities to the state and to the public weal, fearlessly and boldly?" True repentance, Finney believed, shed corresponding light on the social sins of the age and demanded a response from believers. "Where repentance is genuine, there will be and must be external reformation," he concluded.

Echoing the evangelical hope that marked the times, Finney looked forward to a millennial age of peace and prosperity as believers accepted the Great Commission and spread the message of salvation to the ends of the earth. Christian failure to employ the Gospel in the antislavery cause paralyzed that effort and invited national calamity. Wherever humankind recognized truth, experienced guilt, and failed to reform, Finney warned, "God's chariot will grind them into powder!"

Finney's reform interests extended beyond the slavery issue. He also supported the early temperance movement, promoted public education for women and men, and, in his last years, spoke forcefully against Freemasonry as a false religion that threatened Christian civilization. During the Civil War, he withheld support for **Abraham Lincoln,** claiming the president would neither punish the South adequately nor sustain the political agenda of Radical Reconstructionists, who wanted blacks fully incorporated into the nation's social and political life. Finney nevertheless stepped cautiously with regard to black social and political equality. The man who encouraged Oberlin to accept African Americans also insisted that racial segregation was a social and political concern that did not constitute a moral transgression comparable to slavery.

Throughout his career, Finney's zeal remained fixed upon evangelism, not politics or social reform. Political zealotry, however worthy the cause, served only to exalt human effort and deny the divine will and personal spiritual conversion as the only basis for earthly reform. Finney's ability to combine determination in principle and moderation in method gave the antislavery message credibility in mainstream Northern society that the shrill attacks of the radicals could never achieve.

Bibliography. Finney, Charles G. *Memoirs of Rev. Charles G. Finney, Written by Himself.* New York: Barnes, 1876. Hardman, Keith J. *Charles Grandison Finney.* New York: Syracuse University Press, 1987. Weddle, David L. *The Law as Gospel: Revival and Reform in the Theology of Charles G. Finney.* Metuchen, NJ: Scarecrow Press, 1985.

Mark Y. Hanley

FRANCO, FRANCISCO (1892–1975). General and dictator of Spain (1936–1975), Franco rose rapidly through merits in the colonial wars in Morocco, becoming at thirty-two the youngest general in Europe in 1926. In Africa he was known for both his ruthlessness and personal probity. At least until his marriage in 1923, his religious devotion was mild at best.

Like other officers formed in the African campaigns, Franco developed a strong caste identity that included disdain for liberal values, and he resented the arrival of Spain's democratic Second Republic in 1931. Nevertheless, he formally accepted the new regime, becoming head of the general staff. In October 1934, troops under his direct command distinguished themselves for the cruelty with which they repressed a left-wing revolution in Asturias.

When the Popular Front won the general elections of February 1936, the most conservative members of the army and leading politicians started to plot the overthrowing of the republic. Franco only committed himself to the conspiracy a few days before action started on July 17, 1936. The planned coup succeeded only partially and gave way to the Spanish civil war. A set of chance opportunities made it possible for him first to take charge of the rebels' most formidable force, the colonial army posted in Morocco, and then to get crucial help from Adolf Hitler and Benito Mussolini. This situation and the prolongation of war inclined his fellow generals to elect him the leader of the rebels in October 1936. From then on, his political power increased, and at the end of the war in April 1939, he became the undisputed dictator of the country.

From the start, most of the church backed the July rebellion, the main exception being some sectors of the Basque clergy. This position became more determined when news started to spread of the widespread killing of religious personnel on the Republican side, which resulted in the murder of some seven thousand members of the clergy. Those killings were part of both sides' ferocious repression behind the lines that took the lives of perhaps 150,000 people, two-thirds of them at the hands of the Francoists. The church started to use the word "crusade" to define the Francoist cause, and in June 1937, a formal letter of support for the rebels was signed by all the Spanish bishops except for two. Franco's victory in 1939 was publicly celebrated by **Pius XII.** For most Catholics in Spain, it was a moment to celebrate rather that to reflect on the reasons behind the recent tragedy.

The quasi-Fascist tendencies of the regime caused some reservations in the Vatican, which would have preferred a more traditional system in Spain rather than the single-party dictatorship imposed in 1939. This is why, instead of a Concordat, the Vatican opted for reaching an agreement with the regime in 1941. With the Allied victory in 1945, Franco's regime adopted a survival strategy that sought to dispose of its more strident Fascist features and emphasize its Christian values. The

Spanish church assisted this project by allowing Alberto Martin Artajo, one of the most influential leaders of the Catholic Action, to become minister of foreign affairs. The United Nations saw to it that the late forties was a time of isolation for the dictatorship, but for the Spanish church they were, at least in material terms, very good years. The church was generously financed by the regime and given a prominent role in both society and education. Temples were rebuilt, new seminaries opened, and vocations were plenty. Critics called this arrangement National Catholicism. The only discordant voices toward this close relationship between church and state came from the Workers Brotherhood of the Catholic Action (HOAC), which by the end of the decade experienced its first serious problems with the authorities.

The Francoist strategy of survival finally paid off during the cold war. As a result, the regime underwent a semi-rehabilitation that was formalized with the signing of an agreement between the United States and Spain in 1953. In the same year, the Vatican fully endorsed the now-solid regime with a Concordat that extended the privileges obtained in 1941. This close identification between the dictatorship and the church remained remarkably stable throughout the 1960s, during the papacies of **John XXIII** and **Paul VI.**

It was not until after the Second Vatican Council that Spanish Catholicism started to reexamine itself and to distance itself from the dictatorship. This was so much the case that in the late sixties and early seventies, the regime grew alarmed at the increasing number of priests involved in left-wing democratic, and Basque and Catalonian nationalist activities. At this time there were also many prominent Catholic leaders who openly called for democratization and for the immediate end of National Catholicism. As a result, when Franco died in 1975, the relationship between church and State was in deep crisis.

Bibliography. Callahan, William. *The Catholic Church in Spain, 1875–1998.* Washington, DC: Catholic University of America Press, 2000. Preston, Paul. *Franco: A Biography.* London: HarperCollins, 1993. Tusell, Javier. *Franco y los católicos: La política exterior española entre 1945 y 1957.* Madrid: Alianza, 1984.

Antonio Cazorla Sanchez

FREI MONTALVA, EDUARDO (1911– 1982). Frei is a well-known and well-respected figure in Chile and in Latin America because of his leading role in the development of Chile's **Christian Democratic Party** (PDC) and the far-reaching Christian-inspired reform program he developed as president of the nation from 1964 to 1970.

Frei initially became involved in social activism and politics as a law student at the Catholic University of Chile, where he joined the National Association of Catholic Students (*Asociación Nacional de Estudiantes Católicos,* ANEC). Frei's social and political thought was influenced by progressive priests such as Father Oscar Larson, ANEC's adviser, as well as by **Jacques Maritain,** whom Frei met in Europe. Frei and his fellow students, including Bernardo Leighton, Radomiro Tomic, and Manuel Garretón, formed the youth branch of Chile's Conservative Party in 1934. Four years later this semi-autonomous group evolved into an independent political party, the National Falange.

During this time, Frei was completing his law degree and writing for newspapers such as *Lircay* (the organ of the Conservative Youth) and *El Diario Ilustrado.* From 1935 until 1937, he directed the newspaper *El Tarapacá* in the northern city of Iquique. He was able to continue his political work throughout the country by traveling frequently for meetings and speeches. His book-length essay *Chile desconocido* (1937) examined Chile's economy, society, and politics with suggestions for change. This was only the first of Frei's many books and collections of essays and lectures, which included *La política y el espíritu* (1940), *América Latina tiene su destino* (1967), and *América Latina: Opción y esperanza* (1977).

When Frei returned to Santiago at the end of 1937, his leadership role in the National Falange and in national-level politics became even more prominent. He was elected president of his party in 1941. When President Juan Antonio Rios invited him to serve as minister of public works in May 1945, Frei accepted the position, though he resigned in January 1946 after the police used violence to end a political demonstration that Frei considered legal.

His ability to influence the future of Chilean social and political life increased when he entered the Senate in 1949 as a representative for Atacama and Coquimbo and, in 1957, when he was elected senator for Santiago. The latter seat, especially, provided him with more national recognition, important for his election to the presidency in 1964. By that time, the National Falange had merged with another party to become the **Christian Democratic Party** of Chile.

Frei's goal as president from 1964 until 1970 was a so-called Revolution in Liberty emphasizing modernization and reform. His program was made easier when the 1965 parliamentary elections gave the Christian Democrats a majority in the lower house of Congress and an increase in the Senate. In office, President Frei was particularly interested in creating community groups and enacting social reform. This part of his program was called *promoción popular* and included maternal-child programs, sports associations, and youth groups. Educational and health-care systems were expanded significantly and a ministry of housing was established.

Since the 1930s, Frei and his colleagues had been interested in the improving opportunities for those in rural areas. Along these lines, the Revolution in Liberty fostered agricultural unionization and agrarian reform, initially using previous legislation and then passing additional laws in 1967. Frei also enacted the partial nationalization, or Chileanization, of the mining industry, in which the government acquired 51-percent interest in mining companies. Despite the many successes of Frei's government, opposition from both the Left and the Right remained, and inflation rose during the latter half of his term.

After he left office and after his March 1973 reelection to the Senate from Santiago, Frei worked in the opposition to Allende's Popular Unity (UP) government. When Allende was overthrown in September 1973, Frei attended the Te Deum for the military government on September 18. When it became clear that the military was not moving the nation back to democracy, however, Frei openly turned against the regime. He died in January 1982 due to complications after surgery, unfortunately several years before Chile's return to democracy in 1990. His son, Eduardo Frei Ruiz-Tagle, continues his legacy as a leader in the Christian Democratic Party and served as Chile's president from 1994 until 2000.

Bibliography. Gazmuri, Cristián, Patricia Arancibia, and Álvaro Góngora. *Eduardo Frei Montalva (1911–1982)*. Mexico City: Fondo de Cultura Económica, 1996. Moulián, Luis, and Gloria Guerra. *Eduardo Frei M. (1911–1982): Biografía de un estadista utópico*. Santiago, Chile: Editorial Sudamericana Chilena, 2000.

Lisa Edwards

FRELINGHUYSEN, THEODORE (1787–1862).

Manifold public service and deep personal piety earned Frelinghuysen the epithet of "the Christian Statesman." His life personified Protestant evangelical political involvement in antebellum America.

Frelinghuysen's finest hour came in April 1830. In a speech on the floor of the U.S. Senate, he attacked the efforts of President Andrew Jackson and his Southern allies to forcibly remove the southeastern Indian tribes to the trans-Mississippi west. Frelinghuysen denounced these moves as a naked land grab that violated earlier treaties and the Indians' sovereignty. Such injustice, especially against tribes that had advanced so far toward civilization and Christianity, threatened divine wrath, he warned.

The great-grandson of a renowned revivalist, and son of a Revolutionary War officer and U.S. senator, Theodore Frelinghuysen was born into a distinguished family. He graduated from the College of New Jersey (now Princeton) in 1804 and began a career as a lawyer in Newark. He served as New Jersey's attorney general from 1817 to 1829 before his election to the U.S. Senate for one term. There he affiliated with those critics of Jackson who would soon coalesce in the Whig Party. He opposed Jackson's banking policies, supported a proposal to halt the U.S. mails on Sundays, and endorsed Henry Clay's call for a national fast day in the face of a looming cholera epidemic in 1832. None of these efforts or his opposition to Indian removal succeeded, but all of them grew out of his Christian faith. A devout layman of either the Dutch Reformed or Presbyterian church, Frelinghuysen made a habit of daily Bible study and prayer. He long taught Sunday school and founded a Congressional prayer meeting. His piety and prominence both brought him to leadership positions in a variety of evangelist and reform organizations, including the presidency or vice presidency of the American Bible Society, American Board of Commissioners for Foreign Missions, American Colonization Society, American Sunday School Union, American Temperance Union, and American Tract Society. This nongovernmental activity would help to safeguard republican institutions by instilling morality.

Frelinghuysen's prominence further led to his nomination as the Whigs' vice presidential candidate in 1844. He appealed to the party's evangelical wing and offered sectional balance to his running mate, Kentuckian Henry Clay. His integrity additionally balanced Clay's somewhat checkered past of gambling and dueling. However, he also sparked fears of religious intolerance among Roman Catholics and criticism from **abolitionists** over his support of colonization. The resultant loss of Irish and Liberty Party voters contributed to the Whig ticket's narrow defeat in New York State, tipping the election to James K. Polk and the Democrats. Frelinghuysen ended his career as chancellor of New York University from 1839 to 1850 and as president of Rutgers College from 1850 to his death.

Bibliography. Carwardine, Richard J. *Evangelicals and Politics in Antebellum America.* New Haven, CT: Yale University Press, 1993.

Theodore Frelinghuysen. Courtesy of the Library of Congress

Chambers, Talbot W. *Memoir of the Life and Character of the Late Hon. Theo. Frelinghuysen, LL.D.* New York: Board of Publication of the Reformed Protestant Dutch Church, 1863.

Jonathan D. Sassi

FRENCH CONFEDERATION OF CHRISTIAN WORKERS (CONFÉDÉRATION FRANÇAISE DES TRAVAILLEURS CHRÉTIENS—CFTC). This trade union confederation was founded in France in November 1919 to coordinate the activities of the Catholic trade unions that had been established since the 1880s. Begun at a moment of intense anticommunism among French Catholics, the CFTC based its workplace action on Christian morality and the principles of Catholic social doctrine, especially as articulated in Pope **Leo XIII**'s 1891 papal encyclical *Rerum novarum.* The confederation thus opposed class struggle, promoted negotiation over strikes, and sought a third way between socialism and capitalism.

The CFTC struggled to establish itself during its first decade. It was attacked by the other trade union confederations, the *Confédération Générale du Travail* (CGT) and the newly formed communist-controlled *Confédération Générale du Travail Unitaire* (CGTU), and by Catholic employers in northern France, some of whom lodged an official complaint with the papacy in 1924. Only in 1929 did Catholic officials in Rome declare their official support for the CFTC.

During the 1920s and 1930s, the CFTC recruited most strongly among white-collar workers (*employés*) and in Paris, northern and southeastern France, and Alsace-Lorraine. Women, who were active within all-female trade unions, constituted between one-quarter and one-third of CFTC members. During the massive strike movement of May–June 1936, the CFTC leadership, which expressed initial reservations about the factory occupations, was excluded from negotiations among employers, government officials, and trade union leaders that led to the Matignon Accords. Nonetheless, young militants from the Jeunesse Ouvrière Chrétienne (JOC, **Young Christian Workers**) defended the CFTC and its program in a range of strike situations, and the CFTC saw its membership increase by 180,000 between mid-June 1936 and the end of April 1937.

The events of the Second World War and the liberation helped the CFTC gain a more respected place within French trade unionism and gave rise to tensions over the CFTC's status as an explicitly Christian trade union confederation. During the early phases of the war, CFTC leaders joined CGT leaders to defend the principle of free independent trade unions against initiatives taken by the Vichy government, while CFTC leaders and members participated in Resistance networks. By the liberation, the CFTC was issuing joint strike calls with the CGT, while CFTC leaders and members were represented in such bodies as the *Conseil National de la Résistance* (CNR) and the Consultative Assembly. However, tensions soon emerged over the CFTC's fundamental orientation, with a younger generation of activists forged during the strikes of 1936 and the war in the forefront of those arguing for a reconceptualization of the confederation's relationship to religion and the working class.

Those who argued for deconfessionalization of the CFTC gathered support in the late 1940s and 1950s, and the CFTC split at an extraordinary congress of November 1964, when the majority voted to create the *Confédération Française Démocratique du Travail* (CFDT). Three hundred delegates agreed to maintain a CFTC that would remain true to its explicitly Catholic roots and inspiration.

Bibliography. Adam, Gérard. *La C.F.T.C., 1940–1958: Histoire politique et idéologique.*

Paris: Librairie Armand Colin, 1964. Launay, Michel. *La C.F.T.C.: Origines et développement, 1919–1940.* Paris: Publications de la Sorbonne, 1984.

Susan B. Whitney

FRIEDRICH WILHELM III (1770–1840). Friedrich Wilhelm III was the king of Prussia. He was born in Potsdam, the son of crown prince, later king, Friedrich Wilhelm II and his second wife, Friederike Luise of Hessen-Darmstadt. The prince's youth was dominated by a shy and disapproving distance toward the eighteenth century's courtly life, its intrigues, mistresses, and decadences. In March 1793 he met his future wife, Luise, duchess of Mecklenburg-Strelitz (1776–1810), and married her on Christmas Eve of the same year.

There were ten children of this love match, among them the later king **Friedrich Wilhelm IV** and the first German Emperor Wilhelm I. In 1797 Friedrich Wilhelm III was crowned and bought the Paretz estate that the architect David Gilly converted to a model village and where he often spent the holidays and participated in the rustic life together with his family. His accession to the throne, however, occurred at a time when courtly Europe was challenged by revolutionary France. Already since 1794, French forces had occupied Brandenburg-Prussia's western provinces. Domestically, Friedrich Wilhelm III adopted an austerity program. While abroad, he pursued a fickle and hesitating strategy that resulted in the loss of large parts of his country after the defeat near Jena and Auerstädt on October 14, 1806. On July 7, 1807, he concluded the Peace of Tilsit. Luise's effort to persuade Napoleon to be lenient earned her the people's reverence, and a so-called *Luisenkult* developed around her.

After Napoleon's defeat in the Battle of the Nations near Leipzig in 1813 and the

Vienna Congress in 1815, Prussia received some of its lost territories and some others in the Rhineland. The liberation struggle against Napoleon, furthermore, brought Friedrich Wilhelm III close to Czar **Alexander I,** and he joined the postwar Holy Alliance. The king adopted a reactionary policy against liberal and nationalist movements such as the Freikorps, which had been important in the victory over the French. As a result of the Carlsbad Decrees of 1819, many scientists, politicians, and writers, such as the historian Ernst Moritz Arndt and the theologian **Friedrich Schleiermacher,** were arrested and fell victim to the persecution.

One of Friedrich Wilhelm's main achievements was the union of the Prussian Protestants so that on May 27, 1816, he issued a cabinet's ordinance that mandated a new church constitution for a united Protestant church. Most Prussian parishes joined this church. Against the kingdom's expanded Catholic population, on the other hand, Friedrich Wilhelm pursued a rigid politic, often dominated by lack of understanding and distrust. To some degree he succumbed to an aggressive missionary zeal against the strange new Rhinelanders and Westphalians that was manifested in numerous church political initiatives. Most notorious were the provisions on marriage between Protestants and Catholics in which Friedrich Wilhelm opted for a model that in the western provinces favored the Protestants and that Rome could not possibly accept. As a result of this quarrel, Cologne's Archbishop Klemens August von Droste zu Vischering was arrested, and many bishop's sees (Treves, Cologne) were left vacant. The conflict was settled only during the reign of **Friedrich Wilhelm IV.**

Friedrich Wilhelm III died in the forty-third year of his reign (second in length only to Friedrich the Great) on June 7, 1840, in Berlin and was buried in the mausoleum in the park of Charlottenburg Castle.

Bibliography. Stamm-Kuhlmann, Thomas. *König in grosser Zeit: Friedrich Wilhelm III, der Melancholiker auf dem Thron.* Berlin: Seidler, 1992.

Helmut Rönz

FRIEDRICH WILHELM IV (1795–1861). Friedrich Wilhelm IV, the king of Prussia, was born in Berlin, the oldest son of **Friedrich Wilhelm III** and Luise von Mecklenburg-Strelitz. At first his parents intended Friedrich Delbrück to be their son's educator, and later Jean Pierre Frédéric Ancillon, to whom Friedrich Wilhelm was attached his whole life. When he was twenty-eight he married the Catholic princess Elisabeth von Bayern, who as a result had to convert to Protestantism. The marriage resulted in no children.

Friedrich Wilhelm IV was a child of his time, and the events of the French Revolution and the wars against Napoleon deeply affected him. His family's flight from the French forces into East Prussia left the youth with a deep aversion to the revolution and change. Already at the end of the wars, as crown prince he declared himself against Prime Minister Karl von Hardenberg's progressive reforms. He was, however, an enthusiast for the graphic arts, architecture, and romantic literature, which led to wish for a return to what he considered medieval social and religious models.

As a young man Friedrich Wilhelm discovered architecture as a particular interest. His Charlottenhof estate and its surroundings turned with the help of Karl Friedrich Schinkel and Peter Joseph Lenné into an Italianate vision. Also important as the king's architects were Friedrich August Stüler, Ludwig Persius, Christian Daniel Rauch, and Hermann von Pückler-Muskau. Friedrich Wilhelm's most important building project was the completion of the Cologne Cathedral, which would also serve as a national symbol for union and was supported by many with contributions and subscriptions for its construction. The structure illustrated Friedrich Wilhelm's enthusiasm for religion as well as his romantic and medieval notions that kingdom and church are united within the sovereign's anointed person. For him the divine right of kings was axiomatic of the Prussian monarchy.

Nevertheless, many liberal hopes for a united Reich rose with Friedrich Wilhelm's accession to the throne on June 7, 1840. He issued a general amnesty for political prisoners, lifted censorship with the exception of the press, and resolved the so-called Cologne disorders that had clouded relations between the Catholic Church and the Prussian state since 1836. Before the United Prussian parliament in 1847 his repeated rejection of a constitution made the revolution of 1848 unavoidable. Bloody barricade fighting made the king withdraw his forces from Berlin. His ride through the city wearing a black, red, and golden sash, and his solicitous appeal to the citizens of Berlin, however, were well conceived. Berlin that summer was controlled by a civic guard while an assembly worked on a constitution.

The following autumn, however, Friedrich Wilhelm returned with his troops. On April 3, 1849, the Frankfurt National Assembly offered the crown of the German emperor to Friedrich Wilhelm, but he refused on the grounds that God alone had made him king and that he could not accept a "crown from the gutter." After the constitutional campaign and the revolution of May 1849 were suppressed, the German revolution definitely failed. On December 6, 1849, a new Prussian constitution guaranteed a free press, the right of assembly, an independent judiciary, and an elected parliament but left the power mainly in the hands of the sovereign. This constitution stayed in force until the end of World War I.

After 1857, several strokes impaired the health of the harshly criticized king, so that his brother, Wilhelm, took the governmental power. Friedrich Wilhelm IV died in Sanssouci and was buried in the Potsdam Peace Church. His heart rests at his parent's resting place in the mausoleum of Charlottenburg Castle.

Bibliography. Barclay, David E. *Frederick William IV and the Prussian Monarchy, 1840– 1861.* Oxford: Clarendon Press, 1995.

Andrea Rönz

FRINGS, JOSEF (1887–1978). Among the leading ecclesiastics of twentieth-century Germany, Cardinal Frings participated extensively in his nation's church and political life.

Upon completion of studies at Neuss and theology studies in Innsbruck, Freiburg/Breisgau, and Bonn as well as being in the seminary in Cologne, Frings was ordained in 1910. After further studies in Rome and receiving a doctorate in Freiburg/Breisgau in 1916 (doctor of theology), as well as pastoral activity in Neuss, Frings took over the parish of St. Joseph in Cologne-Braunsfeld in 1924. From 1927 on he was in charge of the seminary and was elected archbishop of Cologne in 1942 by the cathedral chapter and ordained the same year.

Frings leveled criticism at the National Socialist regime, particularly in December of 1942 when he insisted from the pulpit that those "who are not of our blood" be treated with basic human dignity. Shortly after the war, however, Frings denied collective responsibility for Nazi crimes, criticized denazification, and spoke to an audience of the barbarity of the Soviet soldiers who had killed his brother in eastern Germany. In 1945, after a brief period at Bad Honnef following the destruction of his apartment in the war, Frings returned to the destroyed cathedral-city and soon took the leadership of the Fulda bishops' conference as well.

In 1946, faced with the problem of populations in flux, Pope **Pius XII** named Frings cardinal and protector for refugee questions, and he became a spokesman for the Germans vis-à-vis the occupation forces during the governmental interregnum of 1945–1949. He promoted the reconstruction of the church (163 destroyed churches and 33 chapels) but also for the rebuilding of church life, advocating, for instance, social balance. He frequently intervened in German politics on behalf of social, family, education and labor reform and at one point joined the **Christian Democratic Union,** although Rome advised him to suspend his membership.

Frings sought connections to the world church, furthermore, and took many trips to foreign countries. In 1954, a partnership arose between his archdiocese of Cologne and that of Tokyo. Frings founded the international relief organizations Misereor (1959) and Adveniat (1961) and supported the founding of the neighboring diocese of Essen (1958). Along with his advisor, Josef Ratzinger, Frings was an active participant in the deliberations of the Second Vatican Council, particularly in the reform of the church commissions. He delivered a particularly controversial speech, said to have been written by Ratzinger, highly critical of the Holy Office. The cardinal, however, was not in any way associated with the "progressives" and, for example, had difficulties at first with the acceptance of ecumenicalism and freedom of religion. He could only comprehend with difficulty, moreover, the changes within the church, which had accelerated in the mean time due to the encroachment of new committees.

Bibliography. Spotts, Frederic. *The Churches and Politics in Germany.* Middletown, CT: Wesleyan University Press, 1973. Trippen, Norbert.

Josef Kardinal Frings (1887–1978). Paderborn, Germany: Schöningh, 2002–2005.

Rudolf Morsey

FRUTOS DE MEYER, MARÍA CELIA (b. 1946). Born in Asunción, Paraguay, Frutos de Meyer began to be politically engaged through the Catholic Youth at a time when the Catholic Church was a major protagonist in the resistance to the dictatorship of General Alfredo Stroessner (1954–1989). In the years of authoritarian government, Frutos de Meyer assumed important functions in the Latin American Council of Catholic Bishops' Department of the Laity. Through her engagement in church politics, she has continuously invigorated the process of redemocratization in her native Paraguay.

Frutos de Meyer graduated in pharmaceutics and chemistry at the National University in Asuncion, and completed her graduate degree in ethics and theology at the Catholic University. Her work with the Catholic University Youth Movement gained new importance when the church became a central force in the struggle for democratization, opposing the human rights violations under the Stroessner dictatorship.

In 1987, Frutos de Meyer joined the Christian Democratic Party and also worked with the National Confederation of Workers (CNT), a group inspired by Christian humanist principles, and one of the most important labor organizations in the country. Her political engagement continued in the role of organizer and educator. Frutos de Meyer was one of the founders of the national teachers union and became director of the Paraguayan Center for Social Studies, an educational institute within the CNT. She has continued to lead workshops and training groups, promoting grassroots organizing and the mobilization of the poor.

Since 1995, Frutos de Meyer has been a member of the Partido Encuentro Nacional (PEN), a driving force in the ongoing democratizing efforts, which brings together Social Christians, Social Democrats, and Independents, thereby presenting an alternative to the traditional political parties in Paraguay. She accepted the position of general secretary of the Federation of Associations for Life and the Family and teaches social ethics at Catholic University in Asunción.

Jadwiga E. Pieper Mooney

FUMET, STANISLAS (1896–1983). The son of an anarchist composer who converted to Catholicism, from a young age Fumet took part in the Parisian cultural world, showing a great talent for art and literature. After World War I, he became involved in the apostolate for the unity of the church and for the conversion of Israel through prayer and writing. Fumet then found his way to politics through the journalistic profession.

He collaborated with the magazine *Les lettres,* which was directed by Gaëtan Bernouville, and was a journalist for *L'Intransigeant.* With **Jacques Maritain,** Henri Massis, and Fédéric Lefèvre, he produced the collection *Le reseau d'or* (The Golden Network) for Plon Éditions in 1925. Among the published authors of *Le reseau d'or* were **Paul Claudel, Georges Bernanos,** Jean Cocteau, Nicolas Berdiaeff, **G. K. Chesterton,** and T. S. Eliot, and its point was to show the universality of Catholicism.

In his home on rue Linné, Fumet welcomed various artists and Catholic intellectuals, as Maritain did at Meudon. After *Le reseau d'or,* Fumet became the literary director for Desclée-de-Brouver and collaborated with *Sept* until its final edition. After his experience there, Fumet founded and directed the political weekly *Temps Present.* Throughout the 1930s, he joined other Catholic intellectuals in antifascist denunciations, such as 1937's "For the

Basque People" after the bombing of Guernica.

Fumet also consecrated himself to propaganda by traveling throughout France and preaching ideas of a new Christianity against liberalism, Nazism, and communism. In December of 1940, he founded *Temps nouveau* in Lyon, which was suppressed by the next year. He also cofounded the *Cahiers du téimoignage chrétien* and participated in the founding of the **Popular Republican Movement (MRP),** which was inspired by the principles of Christian Democracy and of Sillon.

In 1943, the Gestapo arrested Fumet in Paris and imprisoned him for a few months. At the end of World War II, he, Pierre-Henri Simon, and André Frossard founded a movement of public opinion to continue to promote the ideas of the Resistance and to help the nation's rebirth. His Gaullist ideas emerged when he became literary director of *Temps present,* which ceased publication in 1947. With Claude Mauriac, who was the secretary to General **Charles De Gaulle** from 1944–1947, he was a writer for the magazine *Liberté d'esprit,* a publication intended to persuade young members of the leftist intelligentsia to join the Gaullist cause. By collaborating with *Notre république,* Fumet showed himself truly to be on the side of the Gaullists.

His work as an art and literary critic continued with the publication of books as well as the production of various radio broadcasts. Although he was a member of the board of directors of the Catholic Center of French Intellectuals, he no longer considered himself a part of the post-Vatican II Catholic Church and so left the faith. Fumet's abundant writings, such as his autobiography, *The History of God in My Life,* and his vast personal archive, housed in France's National Library, serve as testimonies of his vocation as intellectual mediator in the changing atmosphere of literary, spiritual, artistic, and political ideas of his era.

Bibliography. Germain, Marie-Odile. *Stanislao Fumet ou La présence au temps.* Paris: Cerf–Bibliothèque Nationale de France, 1999.

Ilaria Biagioli

FURDEK, ŠTEFAN (1855–1915). No one has exerted a greater impact on the life of Slovaks in America than the Reverend Furdek. As the founder of the largest Slovak fraternity in the United States, Furdek clearly was the leading spiritual and political leader of the first generation of Slovak immigrants. He spearheaded the founding of the Slovak League of America, which unified Slovaks in America to support their countrymen in their struggle against oppression and Magyarization in Hungary.

Born in Trstená, Orava County, Furdek received his secondary education in Slovakia and continued his theological studies in Budapest (1877–1879). Upon completing his seminary work in classical philology in Prague (1879–1882), he answered a call from Bishop Gilmour of the Cleveland Diocese to minister to immigrants in the rapidly growing city. He assumed the pastorship of a Czech Catholic church, Our Lady of Lourdes. As the Slovak and Magyar migration to Cleveland escalated, Furdek organized in 1888 the first Slovak-Magyar parish, St. Ladislaus.

Within a short time, Furdek acquired a reputation as a great national spokesman and writer. In addition to founding the First Catholic Slovak Union in 1891, he promoted the establishment of a women's auxiliary, which eventually formed an independent fraternal benefit society. First writing for a Czech Catholic newspaper, after 1891 Furdek edited the publication *Jednota* (Union). In 1896 he established and wrote voluminously for the Slovak annual *Kalendár Jednota,* the humorist weekly *Šip* (Arrow, 1901), and the religious magazine *Viera* (Faith,

1901–1902). Authoring numerous articles and songs, Furdek also wrote the first Slovak grammar and textbooks in America. One of his poems, "America, the Distant Land," provided the lyrics for what became the first anthem of American Slovaks.

Furdek was the leading personality in the Slovak American community in the United States, and Slovak Americans looked to him as their guiding shepherd. The bishop also tapped his talents as an advisor, particularly in ethnic affairs. His suggestions to the hierarchy proved instrumental in defusing potentially explosive ethnic tensions and establishing Slovak parishes with Slovak priests and nuns he recruited from Europe.

Known not only for wit but also wisdom, Furdek served as an intermediary between the ethnic community and the municipal government. When the Magyars attempted to raise a statue to Louis Kossuth in Cleveland Public Square in 1902, he adroitly organized a petition drive that unified many nationalities by stating that "only American heroes" should occupy such an esteemed place.

Always a Catholic and a priest first, he represented Slovak interests in America and assumed a pioneering role in organizing a unified response to Magyar attempts to assimilate Slovaks in Hungary. At the national level, Furdek organized the Matica slovenská (Slovak Cultural Society) in America in 1893, which the Hungarian government had disbanded. As Magyarization accelerated in Hungary, in 1907 he pioneered the creation of the Slovak League of America, which united Slovaks across the country in a nondenominational political association. Serving as its first chairman, he organized nationwide protests and established a Slovak fund to provide financial aid to Slovak politicians and the national movement in Hungary. Simply put, nobody in America did more to promote the national cause, and his work inspired generations afterward.

Bibliography. Matovčík, Augustín, et al. *Slovak Biographical Dictionary.* Martin, Slovakia: Matica slovenská, 2002. Strhan, Milan, and David P. Daniel, eds. *Slovakia and the Slovaks: A Concise Encyclopedia.* Bratislava, Slovakia: Goldpress, 1994. Van Tassel, David D., and John J. Grabowski, eds. *Encyclopedia of Cleveland History.* Bloomington: Indiana University Press, 1987.

Michael J. Kopanic, Jr.

FU TIESHAN, MICHAEL (b. 1941). Fu Tieshan served as Catholic patriotic bishop of Beijing and vice president of the National People's Congress. After the success of the revolution in 1949, the Chinese Communist Party began a process of purging Catholicism of foreign influence. Central to this effort was the creation of an indigenous Chinese Catholic Church called the Chinese Catholic Patriotic Association (CPA). The CPA was founded as a Catholic entity fully independent of ties to the Vatican that would uphold the four principles of socialism, the People's Democratic Dictatorship, the Communist Party, and the thought of Mao Zedong.

Ordained in the CPA, Fu Tieshan quickly rose to become bishop of Beijing and president of the Chinese Catholic Patriotic Association. He was part of Premier Jiang Zemin's Shanghai Circle and exercised considerable influence in the Permanent Committee of the Politburo. In spite of Rome's recent efforts to find a rapprochement with the CPA, Bishop Fu has publicly criticized the Vatican, not only for meddling in Chinese affairs, but also for canonizing Chinese "martyrs," which he argued was an affront to Chinese national sensibilities. Bishop Fu has spoken internationally to defend the actions of the Chinese government in Tiananmen Square and has supported governmental suppression of the Falun Gong movement and Tibetan Buddhism. On March 13, 2003, Fu Tieshan became the first religious leader to be elected vice president of the National People's Congress.

Bibliography. Leung, Beatrice. *Sino-Vatican Relations: Problems in Conflicting Authority 1976–1986.* Cambridge: Cambridge University, 1992.

Mathew N. Schmalz

G

GALEN, CLEMENS AUGUST VON (1878–1946). Clemens August count von Galen, bishop of Münster and cardinal of the Catholic Church, was born at Castle Dinklage, the eleventh of thirteen children of a German Reichstag member, Ferdinand Heribert von Galen, who was a member of the **Center Party**'s parliamentary group and was respected as a distinguished political leader. Clemens August attended the Jesuit secondary school in Feldkirch from 1890 until 1894 and then, with his younger brother Franz, the Catholic secondary school in Vechta, where in August 1896 he finished. In 1897 he studied at the University of Freiburg (Switzerland), although he decided that year to enter the priesthood and thereafter entered the Benedictine abbey Maria Laach, a decision confirmed by a journey to Rome and a private audience with Pope **Leo XIII** in February 1898. That year Galen began to study theology at the Jesuit university in Innsbruck and in 1904 was ordained and soon joined his uncle, the Münster suffragan Bishop Maximilian Gereon Graf von Galen, as chaplain. In 1919 he became priest at St. Matthias Church in Berlin. In 1929 Galen returned home and took an important ecclesiastical post at St. Lambert's in Münster. On September 5, 1933, he was appointed bishop by pope **Pius XI** and consecrated on October 28 by archbishop Karl Joseph Cardinal Schulte of Cologne. On February 18, 1946, one month before his death, Galen was appointed cardinal by **Pius XII.**

As a convinced and courageous opponent of the National Socialist church, and racial and euthanasia policies, Count Galen earned his soubriquet the "Lion of Münster." True to his motto *Nec laudibus, nec timore,* as early as 1933 he publicly and bluntly criticized the German dictatorship. In a pastoral letter of 1934 he castigated the National Socialists' ambiguous "confession" of a "positive Christianity" and, with other members of church, he fought against the National Socialist's chief ideologist Alfred Rosenberg and his *Myth of the Twentieth Century,* based on the ideas of **Houston Stewart Chamberlain.** In the spring of 1937 Galen instructed that the papal encyclical *Mit brennender Sorge* be read from all the bishopric's pulpits. In his three famous homilies of July and August 1941 against the requisition of church possessions and the use of euthanasia in Westphalia's sanatoriums he took the offensive and charged the government with murder. The homilies were distributed throughout Germany and were later used by the Allies as propaganda leaflets. The Nazis did not arrest the popular and distinguished bishop in order not to disturb or weaken Catholic loyalty during the

Second World War, so the believer's support preserved him for what he had called "possibly my fate, but possibly my most beautiful reward—that I got the torture crown." But the prophecy of Dr. Josef Goebbels, that after the final victory Galen would hang from Münster's highest pole, did not prove true. After the war Galen appealed to the Allied forces to treat with decency Germany's population and prisoners of war, a plea that earned him the resentment of the British military administration. The British Foreign Office described him as "the most outstanding personality among the clergy in the British zone. . . . Statuesque in appearance and uncompromising in discussion, this oak-bottomed old aristocrat . . . is a German nationalist through and through." Galen died only a few days after he returned from Rome on March 22, 1946. He was buried in the Ludger chapel of Münster's cathedral. In November 2004 he was beatified.

Bibliography. Kuropka, Joachim. *Clemens August Graf von Galen: Menschenrechte, Wilderstand, Euthanasie, Neubeginn.* Münster, Germany: Regensberg, 1998.

Helmut Rönz

GAPON, GEORGII APOLLONOVICH (1870–1906). Gapon was a priest in the Russian Orthodox Church best known for leading a demonstration to the Winter Palace on January 22, 1905, to present a petition to Czar Nicholas II. The imperial guards dispersed the crowd by force, and several hundred people were killed or injured. This so-called Bloody Sunday massacre touched off the 1905 Revolution.

Gapon was born into a modestly prosperous peasant family in Poltava province. He was educated in the church school system, graduating from the Poltava seminary in 1893. Initially, he worked as a rural statistician, but in 1897 he took clerical vows and was appointed to serve in the town of Poltava. In 1899, he moved to St. Petersburg, where he entered the elite Ecclesiastical

Academy, from which he graduated in 1903.

Gapon was ambivalent about becoming a priest. His fundamental desire was to serve the people, but he saw the church as isolated from the world and criticized the clergy as ignorant, hypocritical, and careerist. Yet he believed passionately in what he considered the central value of Christianity: self-sacrificing service to others. In this, he saw Jesus Christ and the saints as models for his own life.

He lived out his ideal in words and deeds. In Poltava, he became well known for his stirring sermons on compassion and service; in St. Petersburg, he regularly attracted hundreds to his humble church in the docks district. He also displayed an impulse to organize. In 1898, he proposed a mutual aid society for the poor in Poltava, followed in 1899 by a mutual aid society for St. Petersburg workers, a Christian holiday society in 1900, and a network of Christian workhouses in 1901. None of these projects won official approval.

In the fall of 1902, the secret police chief approached Gapon with a plan to establish a workers' society under clerical leadership. Gapon eventually rejected the plan because it was not in the workers' best interests. Local church leaders participated, but the project attracted little other support and was soon abandoned. Shortly afterwards, Gapon organized his own society for workers' education and self-help, the Assembly of Russian Factory Workers. Approved in February 1904, it held its first public meeting in April. The initially slow expansion led Gapon to meet secretly with radical workers to formulate the Program of the Five, which called for political and social reform along socialist lines. By June, the Assembly had seven hundred members.

The next fall, the Assembly's growth increased dramatically in response to widespread agitation in the capital for political reform. In August, it had one thousand members; by October, seven thousand. Gapon wanted to take advantage of the moment to publicize the secret program in the form of a petition to the czar. The opportunity arose when four Assembly members were wrongfully dismissed from the Putilov factory in late December. The Assembly called a strike, which began January 16 and quickly spread. Negotiations stalled while Gapon worked on a petition that called on the czar to fulfill his duty as a Christian ruler to establish a just political and economic order for his people. The day before the march, the petition was presented and discussed at dozens of Assembly meetings throughout the city. On January 22, tens of thousands of people holding icons and religious banners rallied behind Father Gapon to march to the Winter Palace and demand Christian justice and mercy.

Gapon escaped harm in the massacre that followed and fled Russia. For months, he traveled around Europe seeking to organize a new revolutionary party. After the October Manifesto, which established a limited constitutional regime, he returned to Russia, hoping to revive the Assembly, but neither the government nor the revolutionary parties trusted him. In March of 1906, he was assassinated. Despite his sad end, his example inspired some other young Orthodox priests to devote themselves to continue his work for social justice in the name of Christianity.

Bibliography. Gapon, Georgii. *The Story of My Life.* New York: E. P. Dutton, 1906. Hedda, Jennifer. "Good Shepherds: The St. Petersburg Pastorate and the Emergence of Social Activism in the Russian Orthodox Church, 1855–1917." PhD diss., Harvard University, 1998. Sablinsky, Walter. *The Road to Bloody Sunday.* Princeton, NJ: Princeton University Press, 1976. Surh, Gerald D. *1905 in St. Petersburg.* Stanford, CA: Stanford University Press, 1989.

Jennifer Hedda

GARCÍA MORENO, GABRIEL (1821–1875). President of Ecuador (1861–1865, 1869–1875), García Moreno was born into a socially prominent Guayaquil family of modest financial means. After being tutored at home, he went to Quito, where he earned a law degree from the Central University, and in 1846 he married Rosa Ascásubi Matheu, a member of Ecuador's aristocratic class.

García Moreno's early career was in journalism, and from 1844 to1855 he published a number of anti-government newspapers. García Moreno was in France during the Revolution of 1848 and was appalled by the chaos that emerged. This experience led to his adoption of an ultramontane philosophy of government and his later determination to use Catholicism as the moral basis of his governments. In 1856, García Moreno became rector of the Central University, was elected to the Ecuadorian Senate, and became head of the Conservative Party. He assumed the presidency in 1861 after several years of civil unrest. García Moreno's administrations were noted for their clericalism, modernization schemes, and repression. He allowed the Jesuit order to return to Ecuador and, in 1862, negotiated a new concordant with the Holy See that greatly expanded the power of the Catholic Church to include authority over clerical appointments, collection of tithes, censorship of educational materials, and the administration of public schools. García Moreno also led a campaign to reform and rejuvenate Ecuador's notably corrupt ordered clergy, thus establishing the church as a key component of state power. Additionally, he declared Ecuador to be a republic dedicated to the Sacred Heart of Jesus.

García Moreno also spearheaded efforts to modernize Ecuador, initiating construction of a wagon road to link Quito with Guayaquil, starting Ecuador's first railroad, building a state of the art astrological observatory, establishing a military academy and polytechnic school, implementing prison reform, and further modernizing the Central University. Although his governments were relatively free of corruption, García Moreno increasingly used repression and a secret police force to remain in power. Although he left office in 1866, he ruled from behind the scenes and seized the presidency again in 1871. His authoritarianism resulted in a fervent opposition, symbolized by Ecuador's famous expatriate writer, Juan Montalvo, whose pamphlet *La dictadura perpetua* (The Perpetual Dictatorship) inspired a group of young radicals to assassinate García Moreno.

Bibliography. Pattee, Richard. *Gabriel García Moreno y el Ecuador de su tiempo.* Quito, Ecuador: Editorial Ecuatoriana, 1941.

George M. Lauderbaugh

GARRISON, WILLIAM LLOYD (1805–1879). Garrison was the best-known, the most influential, and the most controversial name in the **abolitionist** movement. He was born in Newburyport, Massachusetts. Because his father deserted the family before William was three, poverty dictated that he receive meager schooling. He was placed under the care of Deacon Ezekiel Bartlett, who saw to it that the lad was instructed in orthodox theology and ethics.

At age thirteen, Garrison began seven years of apprenticeship at the *Newburyport Herald.* He became an accomplished compositor and writer, authoring some anonymous articles for the paper under the pseudonym "An Old Bachelor." In 1826, he became the editor of another local paper, *Free Press,* which published some of John Greenleaf Whittier's earliest poetry. The paper soon folded due to poor management and some controversial views on various reform issues. He became coeditor of the *National Philanthropist* in 1828, a reformist paper devoted to such issues as intemperance, lotteries, Sabbath breaking, and opposition to war.

It was in 1828 that Garrison met Benjamin Lundy, a Quaker who during the 1820s was the most outspoken antislavery voice in America. It was Lundy who persuaded Garrison to become involved in the antislavery movement. The two men joined in publishing the Baltimore *Genius of Universal Emancipation.* Garrison's writings were harsh and uncompromising, some even vitriolic. He was convicted of libel, and because he was unable to pay his fine, he spent seven weeks in a Baltimore jail. **Arthur Tappan,** a wealthy New York businessman and ardent abolitionist, paid Garrison's fine, and the fiery publisher was released. On July 4, 1829, at Boston's Park Street Church, Garrison delivered his first public antislavery address. Hundreds more would follow. Garrison and Lundy severed their relationship over differences in opinion as to the best way to combat slavery. One of those differences concerned the American Colonization Society, an organization committed to raising money and developing the material resources to resettle American blacks in Africa. Lundy supported the plan, while Garrison opposed it. Throughout his career, Garrison often withdrew his support and friendship from other abolitionists with whom he differed over the means to accomplish their common goal.

On January 1, 1831, in Boston, Garrison published the first issue of *Liberator.* Some are persuaded that this date marks the formal beginning of the abolitionist movement. That first issue carried Garrison's famous statement: "I am in earnest—I will not equivocate—I will not excuse—I will not retreat a single inch—and I will be heard." The paper would continue for thirty-five years, until the completion of the Civil War. Constantly in financial trouble (the circulation was never over three thousand), the paper was underwritten by generous and sympathetic contributors.

Garrison's methodology was "moral suasion." He believed the South could be shamed into ending the "peculiar institution," and he wanted the North to unite in the shaming process. He was opposed to force and believed that abolitionists should not be involved in politics, which he viewed as extremely corrupt. Garrison made many enemies. The state of Georgia offered $5,000 for his arrest and conviction. His writings were banned throughout most of the South. Many in the North opposed him, fearing he would irreparably divide the nation. In 1835, at an antislavery rally in Boston, Garrison was seized by a mob and dragged through the city streets. Boston's mayor stopped the mob action and placed Garrison in the city jail in order to protect him.

Though at one time "ultra orthodox" in his religious views, Garrison the abolitionist spoke vehemently against the established churches for their failure to be more active in the antislavery movement. Among other accusations, Garrison called the churches "implacable foes of God and man." Many clergymen responded to Garrison with equal vehemence. For the rest of his life, Garrison drifted further and further away from his previous orthodoxy. Nevertheless, members of established churches played a major role in the abolitionist movement. Over time, Garrison began to gain more support in the North, including the churches. Events such as the Fugitive Slave Law (1850), the Kansas-Nebraska Act (1854), the caning of Charles Sumner (1856), and the Dred Scott decision (1857), forced many Northerners to think seriously about the merits of abolitionism.

In 1832 Garrison was instrumental in the formation of the New England Anti-Slavery Society and became its paid secretary. The following year the American Anti-Slavery Society was founded, and Garrison played a dominant role in this national organization. About 1839, a rupture developed in the abolitionist movement over the question of political involvement. Garrison strongly opposed any involvement. Other abolitionists, such as **Frederick Douglass,** believed that political involvement was imperative to the eradication of slavery. The bitter division was not healed until Lincoln announced the Emancipation Proclamation in September of 1862.

In 1841, Garrison became a disunionist. Realizing the South was not going to change its views on slavery, he recommended that the North secede from the South. The "unholy alliance," he declared, must be dissolved. Because the U.S. Constitution recognized the legitimacy of slavery, Garrison labeled it "an agreement with hell." On July 4, 1854, he publicly burned a copy of the Constitution in Framingham, Massachusetts, declaring, "So perish all compromises with tyranny."

When the American flag was raised over Fort Sumter on April 14, 1865, after a four-year absence, Garrison was invited to briefly address the audience. In the speech he noted, "I hate slavery as I hate nothing else in the world. It is not only a crime, but the sum of all criminality." In the years following the war, Garrison twice more traveled to England, where he had always been greeted as a hero by most of the population. He became involved in other reform issues: prohibition, woman's suffrage, justice for Native Americans, and the elimination of prostitution.

On September 4, 1834, Garrison married Helen Benson. The couple settled in a house called Freedom's Cottage in Roxbury, Massachusetts. Seven children were born to them, two of whom died in infancy. Helen died in January of 1876, spending her last several years as a nearly helpless invalid. Garrison died on May

24, 1879, at the home of his daughter in New York. He is buried at the Forest Hills Cemetery in Boston.

Garrison was radical, uncompromising, and stubborn, often offending even his friends. On the other hand, he was courageous and insightful, a man who pricked the American conscience as to the evils of slavery.

Bibliography. Mayer, Henry. *All On Fire: William Lloyd Garrison and the Abolition of Slavery.* New York: St. Martin's Press, 1998. Merrill, Walter M. *Against Wind and Tide.* Cambridge, MA: Harvard University Press, 1963. Stewart, James Brewer. *William Lloyd Garrison and the Challenge of Emancipation.* Arlington Heights, IL: Harlan Davidson, 1992.

David B. Chesebrough

GARVEY, MARCUS MOSIAH (1887–1940). Garvey's reputation among his followers as the "Black Moses" suggests that religious ideology was an important element in his political nationalism. Garvey successfully integrated religious ideology into his unique form of black nationalism and produced a practical theology that empowered urban working-class African Americans and enabled him to create the Universal Negro Improvement Association (UNIA), the largest African American support organization in U.S. history dedicated to black economic self-determination and racial pride.

During his years in the United States (1918–1927), Garvey constructed an organization that, although aimed at social uplift and political nationalism, resembled a religious movement in various ways. UNIA meetings were highly liturgical in nature. They opened with a hymn followed by a prayer, were most often held in community churches, and always included an address by the local minister. The UNIA also boasted a Universal Negro Catechism outlining the organization's principles of religious and historical knowledge. Moreover, the UNIA's deification in 1924 of Jesus Christ as the Black Man of Sorrows and the Universal Negro Catechism's construction of God as a black man revealed the role of religious symbolism in inspiring racial pride and empowerment among Garvey's followers.

More important than these symbolic manifestations was Garvey's integration of religious ideology into the movement. Garvey's ideas, preached widely and powerfully by Garvey and other leaders of the UNIA, revealed a theology of empowerment that drew on African American's deep religiosity, on black Christianity's tradition of protest, and on the widespread dissatisfaction with otherworldly religion. Garvey envisioned God as impartial to the actions of men, whose duty is to tame the material world. He preached a doctrine of free will and self-reliance as well as a doctrine of this-worldly salvation. Garvey also provided a religious justification for the acquisition and legitimate use of secular power as a means for achieving his nationalist goals. For example, his essay "God as a Warlord" effectively reoriented the Christian creation myth to justify the righteousness of violence in the cause of the black race, especially for the purpose of constructing a black African nation.

Moreover, Garvey's religious ideology functioned as an important element in the African American culture of protest during the 1920s. Following World War I, African Americans hoped to take advantage of their participation in and support of the war in order to realize their political aspirations. Race riots and lynching, however, dashed those hopes and inspired a more militant response to racial discrimination. By voicing the concerns of African Americans in language and symbols they readily understood, Garvey's ideas inspired self-respect, self-reliance, racial solidarity, and activism against discriminatory practices and nourished black militancy during the 1920s and after.

After Garvey's departure in 1927, his doctrine of the more militant "New Negro" remained influential in African American communities throughout the country. Garvey's contribution to black racial pride formed one basis for the development of the civil rights activities during the 1950s and 1960s. Garvey's ideas also heavily influenced the Nation of Islam as well as the Jamaican Rastafarian movement, both of which grew out of the UNIA.

Bibliography. Burkett, Randall K. *Garveyism as a Religious Movement: The Institutionalization of a Black Civil Religion.* Metuchen, NJ: Scarecrow Press, 1978. Stein, Judith. *The World of Marcus Garvey: Race and Class in Modern Society.* Baton Rouge: Louisiana State University Press, 1986.

William L. Glankler

GASPARRI, PIETRO (1852–1934). Through various roles as a member of the Vatican's secretariat of state, Cardinal Gasparri helped to lay the foundations for papal diplomacy and Catholic Church governance in the twentieth century. From his leading role in the formulation of the 1917 Code of Canon Law, to his attempts to broker an end to the First World War on behalf of Pope **Benedict XV,** to his role in the establishment of Vatican City in 1929, Cardinal Gasparri played a seminal role in defining the nature of church governance and church-state relations in the first half of the century.

Born in Capovallazza di Ussita (diocese of Norcia, Italy) in 1852, Pietro Gasparri was the youngest of nine children born to Bernardino Gasparri and Giovanna Sili. He was educated at the Pontifical Roman Seminary and the Pontifical Roman Athenaeum S. Apollinare, where he completed doctorate degrees in theology and philosophy as well as canon and civil law. Ordained a priest in 1877, Gasparri went on to teach canon law at the Catholic Institute in Paris (1879–1898) before being named apostolic delegate in Peru, Ecuador, and Bolivia. Returning to Rome, Gasparri was named secretary of extraordinary affairs in 1901, serving as deputy to the cardinal secretary of state charged with the supervision of relations with foreign governments. In 1904 Pope **Pius X** asked Gasparri to undertake the task of organizing about fifteen hundred years of canon law into a single code. Gasparri took thirteen years to complete the project, but the result was worth the effort. The 1917 Code of Canon Law governed the Roman Catholic Church for sixty-give years, until it was revised and replaced by the 1983 code authorized by Pope **John Paul II.**

Gasparri went on to serve as cardinal secretary of state for Benedict XV and **Pius XI,** a position he held from 1914 until his retirement in 1930. As secretary of state, Gasparri played a central role in Benedict XV's efforts to broker a peaceful end to the Great War. Under Pius XI, Gasparri helped to define church-state relations in the era of the fascist dictators, playing a key role in the negotiations that culminated in the 1929 Lateran Agreements between the Holy See and Mussolini's Italy. These agreements were a watershed in the history of church-state relations. They established Vatican City as an independent state and also established formal relations between the Holy See and the Italian government, thereby ending the dispute caused by Italian unification and the dissolution of the Papal States in the nineteenth century.

As a leading figure of papal diplomacy in the first half of the twentieth century, Pietro Cardinal Gasparri was cut from the same cloth as an entire generation of papal diplomats who took a cautious, even legalistic approach to their mission. Like other papal diplomats of his generation, Gasparri was suspicious of overt church involvement in the moral and political issues of the time. In this view, Gasparri reflected that element of papal governance that placed a premium on establishing formal ties between the Holy See and the modern states of the world but was also reticent to take sides or to be perceived to be taking sides in political or ideological struggles of the day. To those who suggested that the pope render moral judgments on political matters, Gasparri warned of the dangers inherent in such an approach. "It would mean," he observed, "we would no longer be at peace with anyone . . . since to get to the bottom of the problem, we would have to condemn one by one and with great clamor, all peoples, all social classes and all types of sinners." The ongoing controversy over papal reaction to the totalitarian dictators of the twentieth century has called into question the moral and political wisdom of Gasparri's cautious, diplomatic approach. Yet, as Gasparri himself remarked, "this century seems to want to ask of the papacy the very thing which the previous century criticized the papacy." Whatever the judgment of history, it is a testament to Gasparri's enduring legacy that the debate still continues. Pietro Cardinal Gasparri died in Rome in November 1934.

Bibliography. Alvarez, David. *Spies in the Vatican: Espionage and Intrigue from Napoleon to the Holocaust.* Lawrence: University Press of Kansas, 2002. Bokenkotter, Thomas. *A Concise History of the Catholic Church.* New York: Doubleday, 1990 Riccardi, Andrea. *Il Potere del Papa da Pio XII a Giovanni Paolo II.* Bari-Rome, Italy: Laterza, 1993.

Robert A. Ventresca

GAY, FRANCISQUE (1885–1963). Editor, journalist, and militant, Gay actively participated in the renewal of the Catholic mentality and the reconciliation of the church with democracy by working to help people better understand Christ's message and by fighting to make the French social and economic system more humane.

After the completion of his secondary studies with the Lazarin priests at Lyon in 1903, Gay's parents sent him to Paris, where he embraced the Christian democratic ideals of **Marc Sangnier,** whom he had recently met and who eventually influenced his ideas and actions. After a year in the seminary, he took a position in the Bloud bookstore in 1909 which became the Bloud and Gay booksellers and publishers in 1911. He also edited the work of many Catholic writers. In the years leading up to World War I, Bloud and Gay edited works for the "Catholic Committee of French Propaganda Overseas," which was created by **Paul Claudel** in 1915 at the request of the office of the political affairs of the French foreign minister and was directed by Monsignor **Baudrillart.** Gay worked with the Spanish aspect of the Committee and traveled there to convert neutrals to the French cause. While in Barcelona he opened a branch of Bloud and Gay and founded the *Revista quincenal* (Fifteenth Review).

After the war, under the new political climate in which diplomatic relations were reestablished between France and the Holy See, he continued his editorial activities and in 1924 founded *La vie catholique* (The Catholic Life). Even though the review was religious in character, it treated political themes and joined the campaign against the **Action Française** (1926–1929), as well as the moderate Catholic arguments over peace and education (1930–1931). It also discussed Catholic situations in Spain, Germany, Italy, and the Soviet Union until it was absorbed by *Present Time* in 1938.

In 1932, Gay and **Georges Bidault** cofounded *L'Aube* as a new journal with a political character. Although it suspended publication when the Germans occupied France, *L'Aube* was designed to appeal to readers who did not recognize themselves in Catholic journals and attempted to unite disparate Christian Democrats. Activities such as this continued with the foundation, along with Bidault, of

Nouvelles Équipes Françaises, in 1938. In 1936, Gay presented himself as a candidate for the legislative elections but suffered a heavy defeat. His editorial activities continued with the publication of *Dans les flammes et dans le sang* (In Fire and In Blood), which spoke out against the Spanish civil war. After the aerial bombing of Guernica, the leadership of *La vie catholique* and *L'Aube* signed petitions for peace. During World War II, Gay participated in the French Resistance, secretly published *La France continue* (France Continues), and contributed to the first steps of the French Christian Democratic Party, the **Mouvement Republicain Populaire** (MRP). In 1944, Gay revived *L'Aube* and became press director for the provisional government's ministry of information. He also served as a deputy to two assemblies, vice president of Felix Gouin's cabinet, and minister in the Bidault cabinet (June 1946). In 1948, Gay was named French ambassador to Canada before leaving politics permanently in 1949. He retired in 1954 after the purchase of Bloud and Gay by Desclée Éditions.

Bibliography. Terrenoire, Eléonore. *Un combat d'avant-garde: Francisque Gay et "La vie catholique."* Paris: Bloud and Gay, 1976.

Ilaria Biagioli

GAYED, NAZEER. *See* Shenouda III

GEDDA, LUIGI (1902–2000)

Gedda was one of the most important lay figures of Italian Catholicism, and in his tenure at the helm of **Italian Catholic Action** (Azione Cattolica Italiana), he aided in ensuring Italy's place in the cold war's Western alliance. Gedda was born in Venice and spent his childhood moving with his family because of his father's work as a customs inspector. The family eventually settled in Turin, where Gedda's mother, Marianna Calderini, passed away in 1916. While in Turin, Gedda began to attend meetings of the Catholic Action's

youth branch, the Gioventù Cattolica, to which he was introduced through a family friend who served as the association's regional president and who nominated him secretary.

In 1918, Gedda and his family moved to Milan, where he attended meetings of the city's chapter of the Gioventù Cattolica, giving him the opportunity to meet Father **Agostino Gemelli,** who founded Italy's Catholic University there. Gedda then studied medicine, first at the University of Pavia and then at Turin, from which he graduated in 1927. In 1933, Gedda obtained his university teaching certificate in special medical pathology. During this time, Gedda also wrote *Gioventù Pura,* a book that expressed his ideas on the diocesan Gioventù Cattolica. Toward the end of World War II, he and some medical colleagues founded the Association of Catholic Doctors (Associazione dei Medici Cattolici) in Rome, which worked in the fields of genetic engineering and biotechnology.

In 1948, Pope **Pius XII,** worried over the outcome of the political elections that seemed to favor the Communists and Socialists rather than the Christian Democratic bloc, asked Gedda to assist the Italian **Christian Democracy** with its propaganda. In response to the pope, Gedda founded the Civic Committees (Comitati Civici), which helped the Christian Democrats win 48 percent of the vote and an absolute majority in the Chamber of Deputies. The next year, Gedda left his position as president of the Catholic Action Men's organization to become first vice president and then president of the Catholic Action until 1959, when he was replaced by Agostino Maltarello.

While president of the Azione Cattolica, Gedda enjoyed a different career in science. His interest in genetics led him to launch the *Acta Geneticae Medicae et Gemellologiae* and create the Twins Study Center (Centro di Studio Gemellare).

Gedda was also instrumental in the creation of the first Italian chair of medical ethics. In the 1960s, he began to write his multivolume *Treatise on Genetic Medicine* (*Trattato di Genetica Medica*), which involved the best geneticists throughout the world.

After having been a member of Father Gemelli's Regalità di Cristo for several years, in 1942 Gedda founded his own lay group called the Società Operaia, which recalled the spirituality of Gethsemane, the fundamental prayer of various religious communities, which was repeated by Jesus in the olive garden: "Father, let not mine but your will be done." By law, both religious and lay people, regardless of gender, could join the Società Operaia. Gedda also founded *Tabor*, a journal that nourished the spirituality of Gethsemane, which was directed by Sister Maria, also called Mary, who is in the process of being beatified.

Gedda devoted the last part of his life to his studies, publishing over six hundred works on genetics and the studies of twins. Collaborating with the Mendel Institute, he founded the International Society of Twin Studies, which sponsored numerous international conventions. Gedda died in Rome with his wife, whom he married later in life, at his side.

Bibliography. Falconi, Carlo. *Gedda e l'Azione Cattolica.* Florence: Parenti, 1958. Gedda, Luigi. *18 aprile 1948: Memorie inedite dell'artefice della sconfitta del Fronte Popolare.* Milan: Mondadori, 1998. Gedda, Luigi. *Problemi di frontiera della medicina.* Turin, Italy: Borla, 1963.

Eliana Versace

GEMAYEL, BACHIR (1947–1982). One of six children born in Bikfaiya, Lebanon, to **Pierre Gemayel,** Gemayel served as his father's paramilitary commander and later as president of Lebanon. At age fifteen, he joined the youth wing of the Kataeb (Phalange), a party founded in 1936 by his father to promote Christian interests. He was exposed to the debates between Nasserist students and Lebanese nationalists during his university education in the 1960s.

Gemayel was trained as a lawyer, earning degrees in political science and law from Saint Joseph University in Lebanon. He was admitted to the bar in 1971 after a three-year stint as a civil administration teacher. He was kidnapped in 1970 by the Palestine Liberation Organization and held for eight hours at the Tal el-Zaater refugee camp. The experience, as his own supporters acknowledge, colored his perception of the Palestinians.

He practiced law until 1974, when the clouds of civil war appeared on the horizon. He thereupon formed a paramilitary unit called BG in the Achrifiyeh section of Beirut. In 1976, he became the deputy commander of the Kataeb military wing and, after the death of William Hawi, rose to the rank of commander. He forced other Christian paramilitaries to join the Lebanese Forces militia, which combined the Phalange with other Christian parties. He essentially ran the Christian enclave of Mount Lebanon until the Israeli invasion removed the Palestine Liberation Organization from the country.

In 1982, he was elected Lebanese president but was soon assassinated, killed in an explosion at Kataeb Party headquarters by forces believed to have been loyal to Syria. His brother, Amir, succeeded him as president. Gemayel's untimely death transformed him to a hero and martyr for many, but not all, Lebanese Christians. It is still common to find his pictures at souvenir stands in the Christian stronghold of Mount Lebanon. His death led many to forget that his primary military targets were more often than not other Christian factions and communities. His death also perpetuated Syrian influence in Lebanon and shattered the possibility of an independent Lebanese policy concerning Israel.

Bibliography. Lebanese Forces. "About Bashir Gemayel." www.lebaneseforces.com/bachir.asp. Sélim, Abou. *Béchir Gemayel, ou l'esprit d'un people.* Paris: Anthropos, 1984.

Jack V. Kalpakian

GEMAYEL, PIERRE (1905–1984). Gemayel was born in the village of Bikfaya, in the heights above Beirut in Ottoman Lebanon. He was the son of a Lebanese Maronite notable and in the tradition of his family bore the title of sheik. During the Ottoman Empire's last phase, the Lebanese Maronites were targeted for decimation, and the Gemayel family fled to Egypt for the duration of World War I. The experience of being persecuted for professing Christianity may have politicized the young Gemayel. After the war, the Gemayels returned to Lebanon. After attending universities in France and Lebanon, Gemayel became a pharmacist, and in 1936 he established the Al-Kataeb (Phalange) Party. Opinions differ about the nature of the Phalange. For some, it represents a Fascist tendency, and for others it stands for secular Lebanese Social Democracy. It is certain, nevertheless, that Al-Kataeb stood for an independent Lebanon and for a special relationship between the state and the Maronites.

Pierre Gemayel's party grew rapidly and began to challenge French rule. After Lebanon's independence, however, the party did not play a central role. Pierre Gemayel's direct involvement with the state materialized during the civil war of 1958. Pierre Gemayel sided with the government of President Chamoun against the pan-Arabists and the Nasserists. Later that year, he was appointed a cabinet minister. His importance to the stability of the state was underlined by his election to Parliament in 1960 and his participation in every subsequent Lebanese cabinet until his death in 1984.

When the second Lebanese civil war erupted in April 1975, Pierre Gemayel's Phalange became the nucleus of a Lebanese Front, which contained Christian factions and their allies, and of a Lebanese Forces militia that promoted the Christian community's interests in the country. The militia maintained a clandestine alliance with Israel, which provided it with both training and arms. The 1982 Israeli invasion appeared to herald the end of the civil war on terms favorable to the Lebanese Christian community. Accusations leveled at the Phalange concerning the Sabra and Chatila massacres need to be evaluated in the context of the Lebanese civil war, during which such events were sadly all too common. That same year, **Bachir Gemayel,** Pierre's son, was elected president of Lebanon. Bachir, however, was assassinated by forces fearing Lebanese peace with Israel. Amin replaced his brother as president but could not stabilize the country without Syrian cooperation, despite the departure of the Palestine Liberation Organization, which had been seen as a threat to Lebanese independence by the Phalange.

Bibliography. Fisk, Robert. *Pity the Nation.* 4th ed. New York: Thunder Mouth Press, 2002. Kataeb and Lebanese Forces Ottawa. *Kataeb.* September 2001. http://azzirob.freeyellow.com/kataeb.htm (accessed January 2004).

Jack V. Kalpakian

GEMELLI, AGOSTINO (1878–1959). Among the most prominent and controversial Catholic intellectuals of twentieth-century Italy, Gemelli was born Eduardo Gemelli in Milan, where, as a youth, he embraced the positivist and socialist values prevalent in turn-of-the-century Lombardy. In 1902 Gemelli graduated with a degree in medicine from the University of Pavia. The following year, however, he experienced an intense spiritual conversion and entered the Franciscan novitiate at Rezatto (near Brescia), taking the name Agostino. Franciscan spiritualism and neo-scholasticism were to inspire him throughout the remainder of his professional and public life.

In characteristic Thomist fashion, Gemelli argued that the ends and larger meaning of human existence were governed by Christ's message and by the church—but that the physical and psychological mechanisms of human behavior were best understood through empirical and reasoned scientific investigation. As an experimental psychologist, Gemelli made significant contributions in the areas of developmental psychology, attitudinal and vocational testing, and perception.

His research accomplishments were overshadowed by his militancy within wider intellectual, cultural, and political circles. In 1914, he and two associates founded the journal *Vita e Pensiero*. The journal's inaugural manifesto, entitled "Medievalism," urged Italians to return to the theocentric values of the Christian Middle Ages. In 1921, he founded Milan's Catholic University of the Sacred Heart. As its rector, he enthusiastically supported the policies of the Fascist regime, but not the neo-fascist Republic of Salò. Accused of clerico-fascism, he was briefly suspended as rector by Allied authorities in 1945 but was reinstated after Vatican intervention. In personality and outlook, Gemelli combined a forceful, outspoken temperament reminiscent of that of **Pius XI** with **Pius XII**'s organizational zeal and intellectual ambition.

Under his aegis, the Catholic University of Milan became the intellectual matrix for many key figures of post-1945 Italian political Catholicism. Two such individuals embodying Gemelli's protean, but ambiguous, ideological legacy were **Luigi Gedda,** the physician turned Catholic Action organizer and leader, and **Amintore Fanfani,** the economist turned Christian Democratic party chieftain. **Communion and Liberation,** the conservative, integralist lay organization close to Pope **John Paul II,** also echoes many of Gemelli's

values and commitments within the contemporary Italian context.

Bibliography. Cosmacini, Giorgio. *Gemelli: Il Machiavelli di Dio.* Milan: Rizzoli, 1985.

Steven F. White

GEORGIEVSKII, VASILII SEMYONOVICH [EVLOGII] (1868–1946). Vasilii Georgievskii, Bishop Evlogii, was one of the most prominent rightist political activists among Russian prelates. Born to a Russian Orthodox priest's family in Tula Province, Vasilii Georgievskii graduated in 1892 from the Moscow Ecclesiastical Academy with the master's degree. After taking the monastic name Evlogii in 1895, he worked as a seminary teacher and administrator in the Orthodox dioceses of Warsaw and Kholm, becoming that city's bishop in 1905.

While associating himself early with conservative circles of the elitist, high-class brand, such as the Russian Assembly, he understood well the potential benefits from the clergy's participation in the post-1905 political reforms, at a time when the very existence of a Duma was anathema to many leaders of the Right. Elected to the second and third State Duma (1907–1912) by the Orthodox population of the Lublin and Siedlce provinces, Evlogii served on the committees on the land question, legislation, proposals, religious affairs, and Old Believer affairs.

Though a member of the monarchist-nationalist faction, Evlogii was not a mouthpiece for the autocracy's policies but devoted his energy to what the conservative clergy considered the interests of the Orthodox Church. Chief among them was the reversal of Orthodoxy's threatened monopoly over missionary activity after the 1905 decree on "freedom of conscience [religion]." Evlogii wrote in his memoirs that, although he "was not in principle an opponent of the freedom of conscience," he "advocated gradualism in the process," accepting the freedom to confess any religion but fearing that this could give other religions the right to proselytize freely from the Orthodox flock. Evlogii's successful promotion of an individual project that initially seemed improbable exemplifies the confidence with which even conservative clergy leaders in the late empire were beginning to make church support for government policies contingent upon state help in purely church matters. Evlogii championed the separation of Kholm Province (Polish Chelm) from Poland, so that his Orthodox constituents would not be a minority in a Catholic administrative unit. Resisting the liberal criticism of wanting to "fence in his flock with the help of the policeman," Evlogii emphasized the need to safeguard the Kholm Orthodox from conversion to Catholicism. Deputies representing the landed nobility also attacked Evlogii as an enemy "of the established order" as the bishop flirted with pro-peasant populism and its quest for land against the mostly Polish landowners of Kholm Province. Evlogii's plan nonetheless prevailed, but he did not participate in the fourth Duma after he resisted the officialdom's plans to organize a national clericalist party that would back the government in Duma debates.

Although he did not welcome the fall of the Romanovs, by the end of 1917 Evlogii, like other Orthodox churchmen, was sympathetic to the liberal Kadets over the Bolsheviks. During the civil war he served in the Whites' High Ecclesiastical Command in southern Russia, and in 1920 he emigrated to Serbia. When emigration divided the Russian Church in different jurisdictions throughout the interwar, Evlogii, who had been primate of the Russian parishes of Western Europe since 1921, switched his allegiance several times between the Soviet-dominated Moscow Patriarchate, the monarchist Russian Orthodox Church Abroad, and the

Ecumenical Patriarch of Constantinople. The first of émigré prelates to be reconciled with the Soviet state after the end of World War II, Evlogii died in Paris, the seat of his jurisdiction area, having rejoined the Moscow Patriarchate.

Bibliography. Curtiss, J. S. *Church and State in Russia: The Last Years of the Empire, 1900–1917.* New York: Octagon Books, 1965. Evlogii [Georgievskii, Vasilii]. *Put' moei zhizni.* Paris: YMCA Press, 1947.

Argyrios K. Pisiotis

GERLACH, LEOPOLD (1790–1861) AND ERNST LUDWIG (1795–1877) VON. Known as the "brothers Gerlach," they were descended from a German Prussian family of civil servants appointed from nobility. Leopold von Gerlach was born in Berlin, attended military academy in 1803, and was a sergeant in the Prussian Army. Between 1808 and 1811, his studies at Göttingen and Heidelberg gave him an appreciation of political romanticism. Later, he took part as an officer in the wars of liberation against Napoleon. This experience enforced his Prussian-monarchic and clearly anti-revolutionary stance. After the war, he joined Crown Prince Friedrich Wilhelm's circle, one steeped in Romantic poetry and deep religiousness. In 1826, he became the adjutant of the younger Prince Wilhelm, later Emperor Wilhelm I, with whom he held a position of trust. But his friendship with the older brother and successor to the throne was even closer and was not even interrupted by Gerlach's posting as chief of the general staff of the Second Army Corps in Frankfurt an der Oder in 1838. After **Friedrich Wilhem IV** accessed to power in 1840, he employed his intimate friend in small diplomatic missions, until Gerlach became an aide-de-camp in spring 1848. When watching over the king, who died in mental derangement at the beginning of 1861, the pressure of Gerlach's helmet caused an erysipelas (rose) on his head, which he disregarded.

In chilling cold, he took part at Friedrich Wilhelm's burial and died himself in consequence of the exertions on January 10, 1861—nine days after his king.

Leopold von Gerlach was the most important personality in the "circle of fellows at the court" who, especially from 1850 on, had the strongest influence on the decisions taken by the monarch. This shadow regiment wanted to preserve the "principle of legitimacy" in the sense of an authoritarian state of ranks wanted by God. With this aim, Leopold supported the career of his young friend Otto von Bismarck, who admittedly did not stick to the norms of the "Gerlach party" and who turned out to be a conservative revolutionary. This development, however, did not interfere with their friendship.

Among other things, this made a difference to Leopold's brother Ernst Ludwig von Gerlach, his senior by five years, who made a complete enemy of Bismarck after the latter's ascent, and then liberal change. Ernst Ludwig, who was born in Berlin, was more radical than Leopold, being a fanatic Old Conservative (*Altkonservativer)* and romantic zealot with strong Catholic tendencies. He studied jurisprudence at the newly founded University of Berlin in 1810, continued in Göttigen and Heidelberg, and volunteered in the liberation wars from 1813 to 1815. He then entered the Prussian judiciary service and joined a circle of romantic-conservative friends. By marriage, he gained a relationship with Adolf Ferdinand von Thadden-Trieglaff, whose religiously enthusiastic and revivalist conferences he especially enjoyed. He converted to the neo-Pietist revivalist movement and spent his spare time in local groups of Pietist circles. A district court director since 1829, in 1830 he sharply attacked local liberal-theological rationalism, which almost put an end to his career. Under the impression of the July Revolution in France, both brothers were among the founders of the

interdenominational and conservative *Berliner politisches Wochenblatt* (Berlin Political Weekly). Here, he joined other Catholic traditionalists in support of traditional social ranking, against the spirit of revolution. In 1835, Ernst Ludwig was made vice president of the Higher Regional Court in Frankfurt an der Oder, and in 1840 he was called to the ministry of justice, where he dealt with legislative tasks. In 1844, he was promoted to the position of president of the Higher Regional Court in Magdeburg, where he stayed he for thirty years. During the March Troubles of 1848, this Old Conservative was supposed to be put out of harm's way, but he refused to leave and, in June 1848, founded the *Neue Preussische Zeitung* (New Prussian Paper, called *Kreuzzeitung,* the Cross Paper)—the organ for the protection of kingdom and church. With political "sermons calling to repentence" against the liberal spirit of the times, he soon gained a European reputation, distinguishing himself as friend of British evolutionist theory, and exerting decisive influence as the king's legal counselor. He became a force in the Conservative Party, even after he lost his seat in 1858, although he still exerted his influence on the party from behind the scenes. Gerlach finally broke with Bismarck over the Prussian-Austrian War of 1866, the founding of the North German Confederation, and the introduction of universal suffrage, and he gave up his work for the *Kreuzzeitung.* The Franco-Prussian War and victory over Napoleon III brought the two together again when Gerlach conceded that Bismarck had smashed the "incarnation of revolution." But the Kulturkampf (cultural struggle between the Catholic Church and the new state), which started in 1872, lead the Old Conservative into the ranks of the Catholic **Center Party.** From there, he attacked those responsible for the Kulturkampf's secularizing legislation (such as the introduction of civil marriage) with endless polemic and resigned in 1874. Three years later he died of the consequences of a traffic accident.

Bibliography. Clark, Christopher M. "The Politics of Revival. Pietists, Aristocrats, and the State Church in Early Nineteenth-Century Prussia." In *Between Reform, Reaction, and Resistance: Studies in the History of German Conservatism from 1789 to 1945,* ed. Larry Eugene Jones and James N. Retallack. Providence, RI: Berg, 1993, 31–60. Kraus, Hans-Christof Kraus. "Ein altkonservativer Frondeur als parlamentarischer Publizist—Ernst Ludwig von Gerlach (1795–1877)." In *Idem, Konservative Politiker in Deutschland: Eine Auswahl biographischer Porträts aus zwei Jahrhunderten.* Berlin: Dunker & Humbolt, 1994.

Gerhard Besier

GERMOGEN. *See* Dolganov, Georgii Efremovich

GESAMTVERBAND DER CHRISTLICHEN GEWERKSCHAFTEN DEUTSCHLANDS. *See* League of Christian Trade Unions of Germany

GIESSWEIN, SÁNDOR (1856–1923). Sándor Giesswein was a linguist, social philosopher, church historian, and one of the founders of Hungarian **Christian Socialism.** Consecrated a Catholic priest (1878) with a doctorate in theology (1880), he joined the faculty of Györ Teachers' College (1881) while also serving as the bishop of Györ's liaison to the Holy See. In 1897 Giesswein became a canon, then a titular abbot (1902), papal prelate (1909), president of the National Catholic Education Council (1912), corresponding member of the Hungarian Academy (1914), president of St. Stephen Academy (1916), and member of the board of directors of the Gratz-centered Catholic International (1922).

Giesswein's interest in Christian Socialism was aroused by Pope **Leo XIII**'s *Rerum novarum* (1891), which prompted him to establish Hungary's first Christian

Workers' Association in 1897. By 1904, it had evolved into the Federation of Christian Socialist Associations. In 1905, Giesswein was elected to the Hungarian parliament, but becoming disenchanted with the Catholic People's Party's conservatism, he shifted his allegiance in 1910 to the National Christian Socialist Party. He championed universal suffrage, right of free assembly, right to form labor unions, and the right of the rural proletariat to strike. He also organized land-renting associations to aid landless peasants.

Working in close cooperation with Bishop **Ottokár Prohászka** (1858–1927), Giesswein advocated his socially progressive views orally and in writing. The latter included such revolutionary works as his *Munkásvédelem* (Protection of Workers, 1901), *Társadalmi problémák és a keresztény világnézet* (Social Problems and Christian Worldview, 1907), *Keresztény-szocialista törekvések a társadalmi és gazdasági életben* (Christian Socialist Aspirations in Social and Economic Life, 1913), and *A szociális kérdés és a kereszténysocializmus* (Social Problems and Christian Socialism, 1914).

While serving as the champion of the downtrodden, Giesswein became an advocate of pacifism, which he expressed in several of his works, including *Kereszténység és békemozgalom* (Christianity and the Peace Movement, 1913) and *A háború és a társadalomtudat* (War and Social Consciousness, 1915).

Following Austria-Hungary's collapse, Giesswein joined the left-leaning National Council (November 1918–March 1919), for which the Catholic hierarchy ostracized him. Subsequently he served in the Hungarian parliament as a representative of the Christian National Unity Party (1920–1923). Giesswein died in 1923 fully aware that his version of Christian Socialism was still unwelcome in Hungary.

Bibliography. Gergely, Jenö. *A kereszté-nyszocializmus Magyarországon, 1903–1923* [Christian Socialism in Hungary, 1903–1923]. Budapest: Akadémiai Kiadó, 1977. Romsics, Ignác. *Hungary in the Twentieth Century.* Budapest: Corvina Press., 2000, chapters 1–2. Várdy, Steven Béla. *Historical Dictionary of Hungary.* Lanham, MD: Scarecrow Press, 1997.

Steven Béla Várdy

GIL ROBLES Y QUIÑONES, JOSÉ MARÍA (1898–1980).

Gil Robles was brought up in an academic family in Salamanca, Spain. He followed his father into the law and even changed his name to adopt both his father's surnames. Gil Robles did not share his family's Carlism, but he shared his father's "robust faith … consolidated by reason as well as by study and experience," so different from his mother's "simple" beliefs (*La fe,* 51). He attended Salamanca's Salesian college, an education he believed had taught him "the lesson of true Christian democracy" (*No fué,* 21), but he was also profoundly influenced by the socially exclusive Jesuit order, joining the Marian Congregations as a schoolboy and remaining an active member as a young lawyer in Madrid. Here he became close to **Ángel Herrera,** joining in 1920 the ACNP (**National Catholic Association of Propagandists**).

In 1922, Gil Robles collaborated with an initiative to establish a Spanish equivalent to **Luigi Sturzo**'s **Italian Popular Party** (Partito Popolare Italiano). The People's Social Party (Partido Social Popular, PSP) reflected contemporary understandings of Christian democracy, but its adoption of the liberal language of political parties was too much for many, including Herrera. Even Gil Robles preferred to regard the new grouping as a "'meeting of 'men of goodwill'" (*La fe,* 82). General **Miguel Primo de Rivera**'s coup d'état in 1923 provided the ACNP with a more congenial political opportunity. The dictator's single

party, the Patriotic Union (Unión Patriótica, UP), had no truck with liberalism but looked to mobilize citizens behind the regime. Gil Robles was among several Propagandists who were instrumental in launching the UP, making skillful use of the Catholic agrarian syndicates established by the **CNCA** (National Catholic Agrarian Foundation). By 1930, when Gil Robles became the CNCA's first general secretary, a new style of politics had been inaugurated.

After Primo's fall in 1930, Gil Robles campaigned for the monarchy in the municipal elections of April 1931. The sudden, and entirely unforeseen, installation of the Second Republic after those elections took Gil Robles and his coreligionists by surprise. However, it also provided an extraordinary political opportunity. As the monarchical Catholic right regrouped in the first months of the republic, Gil Robles emerged as its leader. A talented orator and able political tactician, Gil Robles had the full backing of the ACNP and Herrera's newspaper, *El Debate.* At only thirty-three years old, Gil Robles became leader of Popular Action (Acción Popular, AP), later the CEDA (**Confederación Española de Derechas Autónomas**), and one of the most prominent politicians in Spain. A new man for a new age, Gil Robles modernized the Spanish Right with pioneering forms of electoral campaigning. Effective use of the media, particularly the radio, and modern communications, notably air transport, made him a truly national figure.

The political program espoused by AP/CEDA also had a popular appeal. A robust defense of landed property enabled Gil Robles to mobilize the CNCA networks, just as in the 1920s. Defense of religion, and of public order, was the other main plank of the party platform, and here the CEDA was aided by the overt anticlericalism of the republic. In areas of traditional Catholic practice, constitutional clauses banning public manifestations of religious cult (including processions and bell ringing) appeared to be an onslaught against God. However, Gil Robles's opposition to those clauses that separated church and state and introduced freedom of worship to Spain was just as vociferous. Though a man of deep faith and genuine social conscience, Gil Robles was not a democrat in the 1930s, at least not in the sense of accepting the cultural and religious pluralism on which democracy is based. He was genuinely impressed by the authoritarian corporative solutions being introduced in Benito Mussolini's Italy and **António Salazar**'s Portugal and was flattered by the cult that developed around him, particularly among the party's youth movement (JAP). In government after the Left's electoral defeat in November 1933, Gil Robles proved willing to countenance authoritarian solutions. As minister of war he ordered General **Francisco Franco**'s colonial African troops to crush resistance in Asturias after the ill-fated rising of October 1934.

New elections called for February 1936 were fought by Gil Robles on a manifesto promising to revise the constitution on confessional, corporatist lines. As the JAP claimed absolute power for their *jefe*, Gil Robles, so he guaranteed voters an absolute majority and a revised republic. But when he lost the elections, his demagogic career was over. His party fell apart, and, in June 1936, Gil Robles finally transferred CEDA funds to the army conspirators plotting against the republic. When the generals rose on July 18, Gil Robles was already in Portugal, where he remained in exile until 1953. His relations with Franco could best be categorized as those of mutual mistrust and, despite declaring his loyalty to the *generalísimo,* he found no official role in the new state. Returning to his monarchical roots, Gil Robles developed an anti-Francoist political option around the Bourbon heir to the throne, Don Juan.

His proposed corporative constitutional monarchy was still inspired by Salazar, but Gil Robles gradually moved closer to Christian democracy, becoming increasingly prominent in moderate opposition circles within Spain. He had little time for those who collaborated with the regime, even his former mentor, Angel Herrera, and this affected his relationship with the main center party, the UCD, during the transition to democracy. In 1977, Gil Robles stood for election alongside the Christian Democrat **Joaquín Ruíz-Giménez** but failed to revive his parliamentary career.

Bibliography. Gil Robles y Quiñones, José María. *La fe a través de mi vida.* Bilbao, Spain: Desclée de Brouwer, 1975. Gil Robles y Quiñones, José María. *La monarquía por la que yo luché.* Madrid: Taurus, 1976. Gil Robles y Quiñones, José María. *No fué posible la paz.* Barcelona: Ariel, 1968. Montero, José Ramón. *La CEDA: El catolicismo social y político en la Segunda República.* Madrid: Revista de Trabajo, 1977. Tusell, Javier. *La oposición democrática al franquismo.* Barcelona: Planeta, 1977.

Mary Vincent

GIOBERTI, VINCENZO (1801–1852). Gioberti was one of the leading Catholic voices during the Italian struggle for unity and independence. Born in Turin (Piedmont) and educated by priests, he received a degree in theology (1823), was ordained into the priesthood (1825), and continued his theological studies at the University of Turin. In 1831 he was appointed to teach theology at that university and as court chaplain to King Charles Albert (1831–1849).

What looked like a promising career for one born to a family of modest means was cut short by his political connections. The suspicion that he had ties to secret societies deemed subversive in the conservative atmosphere of the early years of Charles Albert's reign and that he was a contributor to **Giuseppe Mazzini**'s proscribed journal, *La Giovine Italia,* led to Gioberti's arrest in June 1833. Released for lack of conclusive evidence but irremediably compromised in the eyes of the government, he left the country in September of that year, settled in Brussels until 1846, taught in a private school, and wrote the important work that established him as a primary figure on the Italian political scene.

Del primato morale e civile degli italiani (On the Moral and Civil Primacy of the Italian People, 1843) argued that Catholicism was the key to the Italian national character, that the papacy was therefore the natural leader of the movement for Italian political independence, and that under papal leadership the Italian people could achieve independence peacefully. Gioberti maintained that the pope could be compensated for the loss of temporal power over the Papal States by assuming the presidency of an Italian federation.

Gioberti's championing of the papacy as national leader appealed to politically moderate Italians who wanted independence but feared revolution and war. Gioberti's opponents, who by this time included Giuseppe Mazzini, applauded the concept of an Italian civil and moral primacy but rejected papal leadership as an unrealistic and visionary notion, pointing out that the ultraconservative pope **Gregory XVI** (1831–1846) was hardly likely to take up the cause of Italian independence. But the election in 1846 of a seemingly liberal pope in the person of **Pius IX** (1846–1878) gave greater credibility to Gioberti's argument and to the so-called Neo-Guelf movement inspired by Gioberti's ideas that looked to the papacy for national leadership. Gioberti moved from Brussels to Paris in 1846 to be in closer contact with Italian political exiles present in the French capital and returned to Italy after revolution took hold in Lombardy and Tuscany in March 1848.

Welcomed as a reformer wherever he went, it was in his native Piedmont that his political career burgeoned with surprising rapidity. The Piedmontese constitution (*Statuto*) granted by Charles Albert in March 1848 provided for an elected parliament. Although the king retained the power to appoint and dismiss prime ministers, Parliament exercised considerable power, and it was in Parliament that Gioberti found his supporters. He held a ministerial post in the short-lived government headed by Gabrio Casati in July 1848. As minister without portfolio, Gioberti was instrumental in convincing the government to send the theologian Antonio Rosmini-Serbati (1787–1855) to Rome to negotiate the formation of an Italian league that would enable the Italian states to cooperate in prosecuting the war against Austria and lay the foundations of an independent Italian state.

The mission failed, but Gioberti found support among the democrats in the Piedmontese parliament, who called for a national war against Austria. With their support, Gioberti assumed the post of prime minister in December 1848. His prime ministry was controversial, for Gioberti enjoyed neither the confidence of King Charles Albert, who did not trust him, nor of most democrats, who found him too moderate. He stepped down as prime minister in February 1849, his political career cut short by political rivalries, the pope's rejection of the liberal cause, and the hardening of ideological lines in the course of the revolutions of 1848.

The new government sent Gioberti to Paris on a diplomatic mission that served mostly to get him out of the way. In Paris, where he spent the rest of his life, he lived at the margins of poverty and continued to write, often in a polemical tone. He intensified his attacks against the Jesuits, begun in 1847 with the publication of *Il gesuita moderno* (The Modern Jesuit) and reiterated in 1849 in the ironically entitled

Apologia del gesuita moderno (Apologia of the Modern Jesuit), which accused the Jesuits of corrupting church and papacy. His new vision of Italy's future, articulated in his *Rinnovamento civile d'Italia* (Civil Renewal of Italy, 1851), no longer rejected war and looked to Piedmont, rather than the papacy, as the natural leader of the national movement. Catholicism he still regarded as the fundamental component of Italian identity, but he harbored no illusions about the role of the papacy and called on Catholics to bring about a reform of the papacy in a liberal direction. His writings were now on the Index.

In the last years of his life, Gioberti also addressed the need for social reform, influenced perhaps by French socialist writers critical of capitalism. But Gioberti's most important contributions occurred in the context of the Italian Risorgimento. There, he sought to tie the movement for national independence to papal leadership. When that failed, he looked to the Kingdom of Piedmont-Sardinia, which eventually did fulfill the role that he envisaged. Despite his undeniable political shortcomings, Gioberti saw clearly that avoiding the conflict of church and state was of critical importance to the future of a united Italy. The founders of the Italian nation did not take that lesson to heart.

Bibliography. Gianturco, Elio. "Gioberti and the Contra-Revolutionary Doctrine." *Romantic Review* 24 (October–December 1933): 329–35. Rumi, Giorgio. *Gioberti.* Bologna, Italy: Il Mulino, 1999.

Roland Sarti

GLADDEN, SOLOMON WASHINGTON (1836–1918). Gladden was born in Pottsgrove, Pennsylvania, and spent most of his youth there and on a farm near Oswego, New York. After graduating from Williams College, he taught briefly at an academy in Oswego and then, with minimal theological instruction, began a career as a Congregational minister.

Gladden pastored two churches in the greater New York City area in the early and mid-1860s, during which time he took a few courses at Union Theological Seminary and studied independently in an effort to strengthen the theological underpinnings of his ministry. While serving a church in Springfield, Massachusetts, during the late 1870s, his theological liberalism and growing awareness of the problems of urbanizing-industrializing America began to develop into the religious and social message that would reach its full flowering during his years as minister of the First Congregational Church in Columbus, Ohio, between 1882 and 1918.

Through his roughly forty books and hundreds of articles and in his service to his denomination, Gladden espoused the message that there was an economic and social dimension to Christianity. He recognized the complexity of the problems confronting his nation and labored to address them in a thoughtful and humane way. Although he had some misgivings about the large numbers of immigrants pouring in upon the nation's shores and approved of legislation to bar undesirable aliens, he never succumbed to the nativism rampant in some quarters. On matters of race, he shrank from attacking segregation directly but assumed a more liberal posture than did his contemporaries on questions of African American education, economic opportunity, and political participation. He condemned the injustices inherent in unfettered capitalism and objected to philanthropy based on the fruits of that injustice. He supported municipal reforms (such as home rule), nonpartisan local elections, and the commission form of government. He advocated either public ownership or strict regulation of utilities and urban transit systems. He also called for changes in state and national politics including women's suffrage, judicial reform, the initiative and referendum, the short ballot, and the direct primary.

Internationally, Gladden accepted a humane colonialism, by means of which the superior would uplift the inferior. He was initially optimistic about the potential for international peace, but events such as the Balkan Wars and deteriorating U.S. relations with politically unstable Mexico in the 1910s caused him to grow more pessimistic. Gladden was shocked by the outbreak of war in Europe in 1914 and opposed American involvement prior to 1917. Once the United States entered the war, however, he seems to have accepted the Wilsonian view that something constructive might come out of the catastrophe. His hope for a better world in the aftermath of the Great War was merely another manifestation of the optimism that had characterized his understanding of the **Social Gospel** for almost four decades.

Bibliography. Dorn, Jacob H. *Washington Gladden: Prophet of the Social Gospel.* Columbus: Ohio State University, 1968. Knudten, Richard D. *The Systematic Thought of Washington Gladden.* New York: Humanities Press, 1968.

Robert F. Martin

GLADSTONE, WILLIAM EWART (1809–1898). Gladstone was the outstanding Christian statesman of nineteenth-century Britain. Prime minister on four separate occasions, he also transformed the role of chancellor of the exchequer into one of the great offices of state. Gladstone's earnest religiosity was unusual even by the standards of Victorian Britain. Despite being at the forefront of politics for most of his adulthood, Gladstone always considered his spiritual life to be more important than his public life. Even when busy with matters of state, he found time not only to ponder the scriptures but also to write sermons and works of theology.

Gladstone was born into a Liverpool shipping family. In his early life, he tended toward the evangelical wing of the Church of England. He initially hoped to become an Anglican minister but abandoned this because he concluded he did not have a vocation. His turn to politics was not, however, a great shift, as he endeavored throughout his life to moralize the state and spread Christian values. Politics was his pulpit. He shifted away from Evangelicalism (adopting a moderate High Church position) and distanced himself from his youthful belief that the English state should be essentially Anglican. Instead, he came to stand for religious liberty for all, which made him a hero to nonconformists.

Gladstone entered Parliament as a Conservative in 1832. His talent allowed him quickly to climb the ministerial ladder. He became a supporter of the Conservative prime minister Sir Robert Peel in the 1840s and an advocate of free-trade and laissez-faire economics. After the Conservative party split in 1846, he was chancellor of the exchequer from 1852 to 1855 and from 1859 to 1866 in the Whig-Liberal governments, where he slashed duties on goods and cemented free trade as the basis of Britain's economic strategy. He helped found the modern Liberal party in 1859 and was elected prime minister in 1868.

His first government was characterized by bold reforms, including modernizing the army and the civil service, introducing the secret ballot for elections, and instituting the first mass elementary education system. He dealt with unrest in Ireland by disestablishing the Church of England in Ireland to mollify the Catholic majority of the Irish population. He retired from politics on losing the 1874 election, but his campaign against the Bulgarian atrocities in 1876 brought him back to public life. The most significant achievement of his second Liberal government, formed in 1880, was to extend the vote to rural workers in 1884. Losing power briefly in 1885, Gladstone came to the view that the only solution to the ongoing Irish problem was home rule. Returning to government in 1886, he introduced a Home Rule Bill, which not only failed to get through Parliament but split his party, with a significant number leaving to establish a separate party, the Liberal Unionists. Gladstone's dedication to home rule was undimmed. Forming a fourth ministry in 1892, he introduced a second Home Rule Bill that again failed to get through Parliament in 1893. He resigned a year later and died in 1898. Gladstone dominated the political landscape of Victorian Britain.

Bibliography. Jenkins, Roy. *Gladstone.* London: Macmillan, 1995. Matthew, H.C.G. *Gladstone, 1809–1898.* Oxford: Clarendon Press, 1997.

Rohan McWilliam

GOJDIČ, PAVOL PETRO (1888–1960). Gojdič was the chief voice of Carpatho-Rusyn nationality and the Greek Catholic Church in Czechoslovakia during the first half of the twentieth century. Clinging to his national and religious ideals, he rejected Communist pressures to merge with the Orthodox Church, and on January 10, 1951, a Czech court tried and convicted Gojdič and two other bishops of state crimes. Despite his ill health, the Communists abused him and denied him proper medical attention.

Born in Ruské Pekl'any in eastern Slovakia, Gojdič finished his theological training in Prešov (1907) and Budapest (1911). From 1902 on, he actively participated in the administration of the Greek Catholic Church in Hungary and became a monk of the Order of St. Basil. After Czechoslovak independence he served as an archivist and a director of the bishop's office in Mukachevo, Ruthenia. In 1926 the Holy See named him auxiliary bishop and apostolic administrator for the diocese of Prešov, where he became bishop in 1940.

A deeply spiritual man devoted to the Blessed Virgin Mary, Gojdič expanded the influence of the Greek Catholic Church with new parishes in Prague, Brno, and Bratislava, as well as many new convents and monasteries. He encouraged the use of the Rusyn language in the religious press and schools and helped found a Rusyn High School, a home for girls, and an orphanage in Prešov.

His religious activities irritated governments because of their political overtones. Even in interwar Czechoslovakia, Gojdič outspokenly supported the movement for an autonomous Ruthenia. Moscow's annexation of the region after the Second World War made him persona non grata. Despite repeated threats and attempted bribes, Gojdič refused to sanction the Communist regime's forced merger of the Greek Catholic and Orthodox churches. As a result, the Czechoslovak government incarcerated him for life. Considered a holy man and a martyr for the faith, Gojdič is under consideration for canonization.

Bibliography. Mat'ovčík, Augustín, et al. *Slovak Biographical Dictionary.* Martin, Slovakia: Matica slovenská, 2002. Strhan, Milan, and David P. Daniel, eds. *Slovakia and the Slovaks: A Concise Encyclopedia.* Bratislava, Slovakia: Goldpress, 1994.

Michael J. Kopanic, Jr.

GOMÁ Y TOMÁS, ISIDRO (1869–1940). Pope Pius XI caused surprise in Spanish ecclesiastical circles when he promoted Gomá, elderly bishop of the obscure diocese of Tarazona, to the archbishopric of Toledo in 1933. But it was not an accidental choice. Following the passage of the Law on Religious Congregations and Confessions by the republic in 1933, with its severe restrictions on the religious orders, the Vatican signaled a significant change in direction in its relations with the republican government.

Gomá, as archbishop of Toledo, primate of Spain, and president ex-officio of the

Committee of Metropolitans, displaced Francisco Cardinal Vidal y Barraquer, archbishop of Tarragona, as leader of the hierarchy. Since the republic's proclamation in 1931, Vidal y Barraquer had sought to reach an accommodation with the new regime with the support of the Vatican. By 1933, this strategy had produced few results. The appointment of Gomá, who had long entertained reservations about this approach, to the Toledo archdiocese and his elevation to the rank of cardinal in 1935 showed that the Vatican wanted a tougher figure at the head of the Spanish hierarchy.

Gomá was fortuitously absent from Toledo on July 18, 1936, when the generals rose against the republic. He would have almost certainly been arrested had he been in Toledo as a wave of reprisals against the clergy swept through areas under republican control. Gomá escaped this fate to play a key role in relations between the new Spanish military government, led by General **Francisco Franco,** and the church, especially after being appointed the pope's personal representative to Franco in December 1936. Gomá's role during the civil war (1936–1939) has generated controversy. Critics at the time and since have accused him of being an unabashed apologist for the rebellion, particularly through the collective letter (1937) of the Spanish hierarchy to Catholic bishops throughout the world, a document he wrote. But this view is simplistic. It is now known through publication of documents from the cardinal's archive that he was uneasy about the regime's intentions with respect to the church from the moment the insurrection began. Although he did not publicly acknowledge this apprehension until 1939, he feared the creation of a totalitarian state on the Italian or German model through the regime's quasi-fascist party, the Falange. Moreover, civil-ecclesiastical relations were far from smooth over a number of issues, including the execution in September 1936 of Basque priests accused of separatism and the regime's failure to abrogate the republic's anticlerical legislation as rapidly as the bishops wished. Indeed, Gomá urged the Vatican not to extend full diplomatic recognition to the Franco government until such issues were resolved.

Gomá's concerns with the nature of the regime deepened in 1939. The regime's suppression of Catholic student associations, its rigid censorship of ecclesiastical publications, and the increasingly totalitarian tone of official rhetoric led him to publish a pastoral letter criticizing the regime, albeit discreetly. The response was immediate. Government censors ravaged the text until the authorities prohibited its publication altogether, while Franco gave the cardinal a severe dressing down. Gomá paid the price of underestimating the regime's determination to keep the church on a tight leash.

Bibliography. Andrés-Gallego, José. *Fascismo o Estado católico?* Madrid: Ediciones Encuentro, 1997. Rodríguez Aisa, María Luisa. *El Cardenal Gomá y La Guerra de España: Aspectos de la gestión pública del Primado, 1936–1939.* Madrid: Instituto Enrique Flórez, 1981.

William J. Callahan

GONZÁLEZ SUÁREZ, FEDERICO (1844–1917). Archbishop of Quito (1906–1917) and celebrated Ecuadorian historian, González Suárez at the end of the nineteenth century was Ecuador's leading religious figure as well as a staunch opponent of attempts by the liberal President Eloy Alfaro (1895–1901, 1906–1911) to secularize Ecuadorian society.

The liberal agenda sought to separate church and state; promote religious toleration; provide for civil registration of births, marriages, and deaths; establish public education and permit divorce. González Suárez opposed these measures and the admission of Protestant missionaries into

Ecuador because he realized the liberals intended to diminish the influence of the church in Ecuador forever. At times he proved to be conciliatory. He was a peacemaker during politically turbulent periods and served as a figure of national continuity. In large measure, he was the last of the politically powerful church officials in Ecuador's history.

His eight-volume *Historia general de la República del Ecuador* (General History of Ecuador) is a masterpiece of meticulous research, objective analysis, and literary style. Of particular note was his methodology of gathering facts before arriving at conclusions. González Suárez was openly critical of the Catholic Church's record exposing abuses and sins of priests and monks during the colonial period. His writings initially earned him condemnation by superiors, but his honesty was vindicated by the Vatican, which ultimately approved his findings. His exhaustive scholarship, political acumen, and indomitable commitment to the Catholic faith distinguish González Suárez as one of the most prominent men in Ecuador's intellectual, political, and ecclesiastical history.
Bibliography. Brubaker, George A. "Federico González Suárez, Historian of Ecuador." *Journal of Inter-American Studies* 5 (1963): 235–48.

George M. Lauderbaugh

GORE, CHARLES (1853–1932). An Anglican theologian and bishop in the Anglo-Catholic tradition, Gore was a leading early twentieth-century protagonist for systematic social renovation in church and state. His witness to radical Christian social ethics began in the 1870s and lasted to his death in 1932, making him one of the most persistent and politically the most influential British clerics of his lifetime.

Gore was born in 1853 and began his public career as a clergyman and a fellow in the Oxford of the 1870s, becoming the first principal of the Anglo-Catholics'

academic center, the Pusey House, in 1884. In the same year he founded the monastic Community of Resurrection for socially interested clergy. However, he fell under the sway of modernist biblical criticism, and as the editor of the controversial *Lux Mundi* (1889) he endorsed an evolutionary, rationalist, and scientific approach to the Christian faith. Forced to leave the conservative Pusey House, Gore emerged as a key clerical publicist for an Anglo-Catholic sacramental socialist movement that blended ritualist ecclesiological doctrines, modernist views on biblical inspiration, and a new Christian social witness.

While serving as bishop of Worcester (1902–195), Birmingham (1904–1911), and Oxford (1911–1919), Gore also led the Christian Social Union. The organization tried to devise strategies for replacing capitalist laissez-faire with alternative social ethics that would be based on cooperation, self-abnegation, and purposeful socioeconomic reform. Gore's primary interest was with what he called "moral regeneration," not with party politics, but he also publicized the plight and inherent rights of the working classes and called for an alliance of clerical social reformers with socialist activists. He always maintained that a peaceful yet very real socioeconomic revolution was requisite if his concept of Christianity was to be truly implemented, but he believed that this could come about only through the inspiration of socially aware churches.

While bishop, Gore campaigned also for women's suffrage, for the disestablishment of the Anglican Church in Wales, against birth control, and for disarmament and the League of Nations. In *The League of Nations: The Opportunity of the Church* (1918), he portrayed the world organization as the institutional manifestation of universal fellowship and advocated a broad agenda of international social and industrial reform. He left the episcopacy in 1919 but continued his activities as a preacher; a lecturer at King's College, London; and an activist of the Industrial Christian Fellowship. Some of his most significant work yet took place under the auspices of the 1924 interdenominational Conference on Politics and Economic Cooperation (COPEC), which drafted proposals for increased state and church involvement in social and industrial reform.

Gore is often seen as an early champion for a modern welfare state, and he was instrumental in converting the Anglican Church to a radical social reform program and consciousness. His eloquence and persistence ensured that long after his death Gore continued to inspire generations of socially oriented Anglicans and other English-speaking Christians.

Bibliography. Crosse, Gordon. *Charles Gore.* London: A. W. Mowbray, 1932. Prestige, George L. *The Life of Charles Gore.* London: William Heinemann, 1935.

Markku Ruotsila

GÖRRES, JOHANN JOSEPH (1776–1848). Görres, a German Catholic publicist and historian, was born in Coblenz to the lumber merchant Moritz and his wife, Helena Theresia. From 1786 to 1793 he attended the Jesuit secondary school that today is named after him, a place that brought him into touch with Enlightenment ideas. After he left the school, he educated himself in medicine, natural science, and history. Görres sympathized with France's revolutionary republican currents and approved the annexation of his homeland to the adjacent republic. He embraced revolutionary ideals, devoted himself to political journalism, and, for a time, abandoned his Catholic faith.

A stay in Paris in 1798–1799 by order of Coblenz's Jacobin Patriotic Club, however, left him disappointed by the despotism and arbitrariness that he witnessed there. He gave up journalism and, in 1800, began work as a physics teacher at Coblenz's secondary school. In 1801 he married his publisher's daughter, Katharina von Lassaulx, who came from a well-known family of architects and clergy. Between 1806 and 1808 he worked at the University of Heidelberg as a private lecturer in philosophy, aesthetics, and Old German literature, lectures on which illustrated his turn to romanticism. He returned to Coblenz and worked for a free and united Germany and toward that end created one of his best-known works, the daily paper *Rhenish Mercury* (still in operation today).

At the end of French rule, Görres's efforts for union and freedom led to the ban on the *Rhenish Mercury* by Prussia, and, after the 1819 publication of his "Germany and the Revolution," he had to flee the country to Aarau (Switzerland) and then to Strasbourg. Collaborating on the strictly Roman Catholic periodical the *Catholic,* Görres made his peace with the church in 1824. Together with the entrepreneur and municipal councilor Hermann Joseph Dietz and the poet Clemens Brentano he founded the Charitable Women's Club and other welfare associations. In 1827 Görres was appointed professor at the new-founded university of Munich. In Strasbourg and Munich he published many papers that dealt with his interest in Christian and Far Eastern mysticism. In Munich he was the center of a Christian conservative circle to which Ignaz von Döllinger, **Wilhelm Emanuel von Ketteler,** Franz von Baader and **Adolph Kolping** also belonged. The circle's voices were the periodical *Eos* and since 1838 the *Historic Political Journal for Catholic Germany,* the most important Catholic organ of the pan-Germanic liberation movement.

Görres's most effective publication was the polemic *Athanasius,* which was edited in 1838 after the arrest of Cologne's Archbishop Clemens August Droste zu Vischering in 1837. This paper gave the so-called Cologne disorders their historical sense and made them a turning point in the relationships of church and state and of laymen and church. In 1839, he was ennobled by the Bavarian king. Until his death Görres remained concerned with Catholic politics. In his posthumously published work, *The Pilgrimage to Treves* (1854), he turned against rationalism and a German national Catholicism and toward the religion's goal of living together peacefully. On January 29, 1848, Görres died in Munich, where he was buried. The city of Coblenz maintains a large Görres archive.

Bibliography. Vanden Huevel, Jon. *A German Life in the Age of Revolution. Joseph Görres, 1776–1848.* Washington DC: Catholic University of America Press, 2001.

Andrea Rönz

GRAHAM, WILLIAM FRANKLIN "BILLY" JR. (b. 1918). Born and reared on a farm outside Charlotte, North Carolina, Graham became the most famous and successful evangelist of the twentieth century. He preached the gospel of Christ in person to more than eighty million people and reached countless more millions via radio, television, films, books, magazines, and newspaper columns. Successful revivals (called crusades and, in later years, missions) and international conferences sponsored by his ministry fostered widespread ecumenical cooperation, particularly among evangelical Christians. His worldwide fame and popularity, his association with a series of presidents and other political leaders, and his unofficial but widely recognized status as chaplain to the nation provided him with considerable political influence.

During the late 1940s and early 1950s, Graham laced his sermons with political themes, with emphasis on the threat from nuclear-powered communism and the superiority of the free-enterprise system. He also eagerly sought ties with political leaders. President Harry Truman rebuffed him as a crass publicity seeker, but other politicians saw him as a valuable ally and warmly supported his 1952 crusade in Washington, D.C. Such attention convinced Graham that he wielded substantial clout. Though he professed neutrality in the 1952 presidential campaign, he clearly favored Dwight Eisenhower and even traveled to Paris early in the year to convince the general to run for office. His support of Eisenhower's campaign and administration led to frequent visits to the White House, unofficial diplomatic errands during his foreign travels, and a close friendship with Vice President Richard Nixon, whom he hoped would succeed Eisenhower as president.

John F. Kennedy's defeat of Nixon in the 1960 presidential election attenuated Graham's ties to the White House, although he and Kennedy maintained a polite association. When Lyndon Johnson became president after Kennedy's assassination in 1963, Graham began a decade-long association with power that cemented his enduring identity as pastor to the president. The famed evangelist provided valuable support and legitimation for major Johnson causes, including the war on poverty, the Civil Rights Act, and the war in Vietnam.

When Johnson announced his decision not to seek reelection in 1968, Graham urged Richard Nixon to make another run at the presidency. After his old friend was elected, Graham proved to be one of his staunchest and most public allies. He invited Nixon to speak at a nationally televised crusade in Knoxville, Tennessee. He helped organize and spoke at Honor America Day, a patriotic extravaganza held in front of the Lincoln Memorial on July 4, 1970. And he gave his blessing to an extended series of White House church services, which many critics regarded as a conscious, calculating use of "civil religion" as a political instrument.

Before the 1972 election, Graham informed Nixon's staff that he perceived a significant move to the right among religious people in America and indicated he felt he could mobilize his audience on the president's behalf, but not if the administration began making too many concessions to liberal critics. In the months prior to the election, H. R. Haldeman, Nixon's chief of staff, called Graham frequently to discuss the political situation, giving him inside information and asking for his feedback on a wide range of matters.

Graham's unyielding admiration and defense of Nixon in the face of mounting criticism, particularly of the administration's handling of the war in Vietnam and its harsh treatment of critics, drew sharp disapproval from those who felt he had compromised his ability to speak with a prophetic voice. As the war dragged on, Graham's support for the war began to wane, but his confidence in Nixon remained strong—until Watergate. His first response to the infamous break-in and cover-up was to assert confidently that the president could not have been seriously involved. When he finally read the transcripts of the White House tapes in the late spring of 1974, what he found devastated him, though he seemed to have been more troubled by Nixon's profanity than by political espionage, suborning perjury, bribery, and other strikes at constitutional government.

Deeply stung by his own disillusionment with Nixon and the criticism he had received for his defense of the president, Graham drew back from overt political involvement, rarely visiting the White House during the Gerald Ford and **Jimmy Carter** administrations. When the movement known as the Religious Right surfaced in the late 1970s, he declined to participate in it, warning his brethren to "be wary of exercising political influence," lest they lose their spiritual impact. He returned to Washington more frequently and more publicly during the presidencies of **Ronald Reagan** and George Bush, both

of whom had been friends since the 1950s, but his contribution appears to have involved symbolic legitimation rather than strategic counsel. In 1988, he attended the Republican National Convention, led prayer after Reagan spoke, then sat in the box with Barbara Bush as her husband gave his acceptance speech. Subsequently, Graham prayed at Bush's inauguration and, on the evening the president announced the launching of Desert Storm, the 1991 war in Iraq, Graham was on hand at the White House and, the next morning, led a prayer service heavily loaded with civilian and military leaders. At Bush's 1992 State of the Union address, the evangelist was once again shown seated next to the president's wife, conveying a powerful symbolic blessing.

Graham's connections and unique stature enabled him to break down many formidable barriers. Beginning in 1978, virtually every Soviet-controlled country progressively gave him privileges that no other churchman, including the most prominent and politically docile native religious leaders, had ever received. These efforts culminated in state-broadcast services in packed stadiums in Budapest (1989) and Moscow (1992). In 1992 and 1994, he made more-limited but still unprecedented visits to Pyongyang, North Korea. Graham used these visits to preach, to encourage Christian believers, and to explain to communist leaders that their restriction of religious freedom was counterproductive, hampering diplomatic relations with America. He also spoke repeatedly in favor of nuclear disarmament, a surprise to many who remembered the aggressive anticommunism of his early years.

When the nation proved unwilling in 1992 to choose Bush to fill a second term in the White House, Graham found much to admire in Bill Clinton and was pleased to lead prayers at both of his inaugurations. He also joined Clinton in a moving prayer service in the aftermath of the bombing of the Oklahoma City federal building in April 1995.

Parkinson's Disease and other health problems took their toll on Graham in the late 1990s, keeping him from leading prayer at the 2001 inauguration of **George W. Bush,** though his familiar role was filled by his son and successor, the Rev. Franklin Graham. Later that year, however, three days after the terrorist attacks on the World Trade Center and the Pentagon on September 11, Billy Graham once again served as the People's Pastor at the National Day of Prayer and Remembrance in Washington, speaking healing words to a wounded nation.

Despite increased wariness of excessive involvement in the political realm, Billy Graham encouraged evangelical Christians to assume greater responsibility for social and economic justice, as well as other temporal problems, including, most notably, nuclear disarmament. In recognition of his achievements and influences, Graham received, among many accolades and prizes, both the Presidential Medal of Freedom (1983) and the Congressional Gold Medal (1996), the highest honors these two branches of government can bestow upon a civilian.

Bibliography. Graham, Billy. *Just as I Am: The Autobiography of Billy Graham.* San Francisco: HarperCollins, 1997. Martin, William. "Fifty Years with Billy." *Christianity Today,* 13 November 1995, 20–29. Martin, William. *A Prophet with Honor: The Billy Graham Story.* New York: William Morrow, 1991.

William Martin

GRANT, GEORGE (1918–1988). Viewing himself as a "political philosopher within Christianity" (less its Anglican wing than a "Hindu wing" or "Greek Christianity" defined with Weil in Platonic terms), Grant was arguably English Canada's best-known public intellectual before Charles Taylor—another Christian communitarian

philosopher. Grant however was a "Red Tory"—a term first coined about the typically Canadian political sensibility he expressed, where conservatism and socialism overlap in distrust of liberalism. His *Lament for a Nation* (1965), subtitled *The Defeat of Canadian Nationalism,* became its enduring manifesto. Claiming the impossibility of conservatism in our era is the impossibility of Canada, Grant aspired to maintain particular historic identities within an orderly whole for the common good, even in the shadow of the dynamic center of technological society: the American empire at the vanguard of modernity, with no history prior to the age of progress. As Puritanism's secular heir, liberalism fosters rugged individualism, scientific management, and reckless expansionism, leading to the tyranny of the "universal homogeneous state." Grant sees technology as the "triumph of the Will," defining modernity's aimless activism over against contemplation and faith as "intelligence illuminated by love" for the other—be it nature, the neighbor, or God—as absolute limits to human manipulations. If Grant was briefly popular with Canada's New Left for supporting anti-American protests, they parted ways over his antiabortion stance. He favored an egalitarian welfare state to mend the fabric of industrialized society and saw the equality of humans before God as the theological foundation of democracy. Without this base, liberalism enables a definition of freedom that endorses each person's ability to shape reality according to his or her own values. Rejecting talk of values as legitimizing the modern primacy of subjective evaluation, Grant turns to the ancient language about objective good by which humankind is measured, and which we first encounter through love of one's own being. Hence he defends the nation's cultural heritage (and consequently, Quebec nationalism) against rootless cosmopolitanism, and wariness of personal/technical "creativity" as an acceptable replacement for the wonder of divine Creation. Grant wanted to show God shining by his very absence in the wake of Western Christianity's slide into voluntaristic nihilism due to the fatal confusion of ultimate good with personal necessity, as well as the sacralization of temporal success. A prophet calling on both Athens and Jerusalem, "Grant ends up with a metapolitical position which sees philosophy as more important than politics, and classical political thought as more true to reality than any of the modern political options" (A. James Reimer, in Schmidt, 57). Yet Grant continues to inspire English (and recently French) Canadians seeking to restore meaning to political citizenship, beyond technocratic business administration.

Bibliography. Angus, Ian, ed. *Athens and Jerusalem: The Philosophy and Theology of George Grant.* Toronto: University of Toronto Press, 2004. Schmidt, Larry, ed. *George Grant in Process: Essays and Conversations.* Toronto: Anansi, 1978.

Christian Roy

GREGORY XVI [BARTOLOMEO CAPPELLARI] (1765–1846). Born Bartolomeo Cappellari at Belluno in Venetia, the future pontiff became a Camaldolese monk in 1783. During the revolutionary era he won a reputation as a defender of the papacy by his works, especially his *Trionfo della Santa Sede* (1797). Persecution by Napoleon only increased his prestige in Catholic circles and, after the Restoration of 1814, he rose steadily in rank at Rome, receiving the red hat in 1825.

At the conclave of 1831 he was elected pope as Gregory XVI. Soon afterwards, revolt broke out in the Papal State, and all but Rome was lost. Only Austrian intervention restored papal authority. A conference of the Great Powers urged reforms on the pontiff to prevent further revolts, but the

essentially conservative pope rejected fundamental changes. In consequence, discontent grew steadily. Uprisings in 1843 and 1845 were suppressed, but discontent continued to grow. In reaction, Gregory became increasingly hostile to change, indeed, to modern civilization in general. Politically, he aligned the church with the conservative powers, most notoriously by an encyclical, *Cum primum* of 1832, which directed the Polish clergy to preach submission to the Orthodox Czar, Nicholas I, who after crushing the Polish revolt of 1831 was now persecuting the Polish Catholic Church. Gregory was equally hostile to currents within the church that sought to reconcile it with modern civilization, as shown by his condemnation of **Félicité Lamennais,** the founder of liberal Catholicism, generally in the 1832 encyclical *Mirari vos* and specifically in *Singulari nos* of 1834. The effect of his pontificate was to make the papacy seem the enemy of modern civilization, and to stimulate in the Papal State the popular hostility that was undermining the temporal power. He died in Rome on June 1, 1846.

Bibliography. Bartoli, ed. *Gregorio XVI: Miscellanea commemorativa.* 2 vols. Rome: Pontificia Universita Gregoriana, 1948. Federici, Domenico. *Gregorio XVI fra favola e realta.* Rovigo, Italy: Istituto padano di arti grafiche, 1948.

Alan J. Reinerman

GRILLPARZER, FRANZ (1791–1872). An Austrian Catholic dramatist, Grillparzer was born, raised, and educated in Vienna. He studied German philology (1807–1809) and law (1807–1811) at the University of Vienna before he began his lifelong career working for the Austrian government. Grillparzer was a civil servant in Vienna's court library before he became director of the Hofkammerarchiv (the Emperor's Archives), an office he held until his retirement in 1856.

His tragedy *Die Ahnfrau* (The Ancestress) of 1813 was Grillparzer's breakthrough as a dramatist. This typical *Schicksalstragödie* (fate tragedy) was a very popular genre at that time, resembling in many ways the features of the Catholic *barockes Trauerspiel* (baroque tragedy). Among his other plays are *König Ottokar's Glück und Ende* (1825, King Ottocar, His Rise and Fall), *Der Traum ein Leben* (1834, A Dream Is Life), and the posthumously published *Die Jüdin von Toledo* (The Jewess of Toledo).

As an author, Grillparzer was constantly pressured by the rigid censorship Prince **Metternich** had introduced. During his lifetime, Grillparzer witnessed the Enlightenment movement, the Napoleonic Wars, and the Restoration period after the Congress of Vienna (1815). Privately he opposed the restoration monarchy of Francis I and criticized it at length in his diaries. As an author and public servant, however, Grillparzer's criticism was much more subtle. In his Austrian patriotic dramas, he alluded to a utopian past and idealized the Habsburg monarchy before the restoration.

Although there is little proof that Grillparzer was a devout Catholic, his oeuvre is clearly shaped by Austria's Catholic culture. Thus, his literary expression emphasizes images and not abstract concepts, which were associated with Protestantism. Grillparzer, who identified with the Catholic Enlightenment, viewed both the Habsburg monarchy and the Catholic Church as the most important pillars of Austria's society.

Bibliography. Haider-Pregler, Hilde, and Evelyn Deutsch-Schreiner, eds. *Stichwort Grillparzer.* Vienna: Böhlau, 1994.

Gregor Thuswaldner

GRIMKÉ, SARAH MOORE (1792–1873) AND ANGELINA EMILY [WELD] (1805–1879). Born in Charleston, South Carolina, Sarah and Angelina Grimké were the sixth and last children, respectively, of Mary Smith Grimké and John Faucheraud Grimké. Their father was a Revolutionary War veteran, slaveholding planter, and South Carolina Supreme Court justice. The sisters departed the South, physically and ideologically, and became outspoken advocates of abolition and women's political rights. They distinguished themselves as the first female **abolitionists,** and the only prominent white female Southern abolitionists. Their carefully crafted Bible-based arguments in favor of women's full political participation, particularly Sarah's *Letters on the Equality of the Sexes* (1837), anticipated by at least a decade those by mid-nineteenth-century feminists (Bartlett in Grimké, 5). Even among their abolitionist colleagues, the Grimké sisters broke new ground in protesting racism in the North and South. Their public work spanned a relatively brief period, but they inspired Lucretia Mott, **Elizabeth Cady Stanton,** and other well-known reformers of the nineteenth century.

Sarah began her education alongside elder brother Thomas Smith Grimké, enjoying richer curricular fare than that usually offered to girls. Thomas's departure for Yale when Sarah was twelve deprived her of a friend and partner in intellectual inquiry. Sarah soon found new purpose as baby sister Angelina's godmother.

Unable to square the family's Episcopal professions with its slaveholding, Sarah experienced an evangelical conversion and in 1817 joined the Presbyterians. Angelina refused Episcopal confirmation in 1818 and joined the Presbyterians in 1826.

In 1819, a gravely ill Judge Grimké requested that Sarah accompany him to Philadelphia to obtain treatment. Sarah made her first contacts there with the Society of Friends. After her father's death, she boarded for two more months in Philadelphia with a Quaker family. Quaker

Angelina Grimké. Courtesy of the Library of Congress

Israel Morris (who would later twice unsuccessfully propose marriage to Sarah) gave her John Woolman's memoirs, which featured his antislavery ideas. After her return from Philadelphia, Sarah converted to Quakerism in 1820. Unable to tolerate life in Charleston among family members who disapproved of her abolitionism and her new religious affiliation, Sarah departed in 1821 for Philadelphia with her widowed sister, Anna Frost.

Meanwhile, Angelina's active participation in her Charleston Presbyterian congregation included lively debate about abolition with her minister and unreceptive elders. With Sarah's encouragement, Angelina began attending a Friends meeting in Charleston in 1828. Early in 1829, the Presbyterians expelled Angelina for religious neglect. In November, she moved to Philadelphia.

The sisters attended the conservative Fourth and Arch Street Meeting. The meeting frequently discouraged the sisters' antislavery sentiments and career aspirations—Sarah's, to become a Quaker minister; Angelina's, to train as a teacher at Catharine Beecher's Hartford Female Seminary. In 1832, Angelina began reading abolitionist newspapers and recognized her and Sarah's sympathies with the abolitionist movement.

In response to an escalation of Northern antiabolitionist violence in August 1835, Angelina wrote to radical abolitionist **William Lloyd Garrison,** who then published the letter in the *Liberator.* This exposure brought Angelina more squarely into abolitionist networks. In 1836, she composed *An Appeal to the Christian Women of the Southern States,* the only abolitionist tract written by a Southern woman to Southern women. It argued, from skilled exegesis of the Hebrew scriptures, slavery's injustice and the Southern women's duty to fight it.

Angelina also accepted an invitation from the American Anti-Slavery Society to speak to women in New York. Sarah agreed to accompany her. The two spent November 1836 at a workshop for antislavery agents run by Theodore Dwight Weld, the "Lane rebel" leader. They itinerated in January and February 1837, speaking to female audiences. When their Quaker meeting objected to this public work and requested their resignations, the sisters refused, asserting their continued loyalty to Quaker belief and discipline.

They then set off for what would become an organizationally important but exhausting speaking tour of Boston and its environs. The sisters addressed "mixed" audiences of men and women, a practice that threatened to divide abolitionists. Widely publicized criticisms had come from Congregational ministers in Connecticut in 1836, and from those in Massachusetts in 1837, the same year **Catharine Beecher** attacked Angelina for such public work. In her response, *Letters*

Sarah Grimké. Courtesy of the Library of Congress

to Catherine [sic] E. Beecher (1837), Angelina argued from the Bible against racism and for women's political equality. Depending "solely on the Bible" (Grimké, 31), Sarah too responded to the various clerical attacks in her *Letters on the Equality of the Sexes* (1837). Angelina spoke before the Massachusetts legislature in February 1838, becoming the first woman in the country to address such a body (Lerner, *Grimké Sisters,* 218).

In 1838, Theodore Dwight Weld confessed in a letter his love for Angelina. On Monday, May 14, 1838, before an interracial gathering at sister Anna's Philadelphia home, they married. The Quakers expelled her for marrying outside the Society; they expelled Sarah for attending the ceremony. On May 16, Angelina, in her last public address for years, spoke to the American Anti-Slavery Society in the Pennsylvania Hall. The next evening, antiabolitionist rioters burned the hall to the ground.

In 1839, conservative and radical abolitionists in the American Anti-Slavery Society officially divided over strategy (including women's involvement). Theodore Weld, temperamentally with the conservatives but opposed to their stand against women's public participation, could not ally wholeheartedly with either side, so he and the sisters withdrew from both societies' activities.

After their marriage, the Welds, with Sarah, moved to Fort Lee, New Jersey. The Welds had three children, in whose upbringing Sarah played a large part: Charles Stuart Faucheraud, Theodore Grimké, and Sarah Grimké. They moved in 1840 to a farm in Belleville, New Jersey. In 1854, Angelina and Theodore moved to the Raritan Bay Union at Eagleswood, New Jersey, where Weld ran a school until they moved to Massachusetts in 1862. Sarah initially resisted the move to Eagleswood and, as long-simmering family and financial tensions with Angelina climaxed, struck out on her own to write and explore a career in law or medicine. Finding her options few, Sarah made peace with Angelina and joined the Welds at Raritan Bay.

Beginning in the 1850s and continuing through the 1870s, the sisters lent occasional support to the women's rights movement. In the 1860s, the Welds and Sarah supported the Civil War but only as the last resort for ending slavery.

In 1868 the sisters were informed by their nephews that their brother Henry had fathered a child by one of his slaves. They assumed active roles in the lives of Archibald Henry Grimké and Francis James Grimké (another nephew, John, kept his distance). These men, rather than the Welds' children, picked up the sisters' reformist mantle. Archibald graduated from Harvard Law School and became an editor, author, political activist, and leader in the National Association for the Advancement of Colored People (NAACP).

Francis attended Princeton Theological Seminary and served as pastor of the Fifteenth Street Presbyterian Church, Washington, D.C., for almost fifty years. Sarah wrote but never published a novel based on their experiences (Lerner, *Grimké Sisters*, 363–66).

In addition to many articles, Angelina also wrote *An Appeal to the Women of the Nominally Free States* (1837) and *A Declaration of War on Slavery* (1862). Sarah wrote an *Epistle to the Clergy of the Southern States* (1836), an *Address to Free Colored Americans* (1837), and a translation of the life of Joan of Arc (1867). The two sisters also researched and contributed to Weld's *American Slavery as It Is* (1839), one source for **Harriet Beecher Stowe**'s *Uncle Tom's Cabin* (1852).

Bibliography. Barnes, Gilbert H., and Dwight L. Dumond, eds. *Letters of Theodore Dwight Weld, Angelina Grimké Weld, and Sarah Grimké.* 2 vols. New York: D. Appleton-Century, 1934. Ceplair, Larry, ed. *The Public Years of Sarah and Angelina Grimké: Selected Writings, 1835–1839.* New York: Columbia University Press, 1989. Grimké, Sarah. *Letters on the Equality of the Sexes and Other Essays.* Ed. Elizabeth Ann Bartlett. New Haven, CT: Yale University Press, 1988. Lerner, Gerda. *The Feminist Thought of Sarah Grimké.* New York: Oxford University Press, 1998. Lerner, Gerda. *The Grimké Sisters from South Carolina: Pioneers for Woman's Rights and Abolition.* New York: Schocken Books, 1971.

Anne Blue Wills

GROEN VAN PRINSTERER, GUILLAUME (1801–1876). Groen was the founder of the **Anti-Revolutionary Party** (ARP) in the Netherlands. He articulated the Calvinist worldview and principled activism that **Abraham Kuyper** organized into a national party in 1879. The ARP was dissolved in 1980 to join the **Christian Democratic Appeal** party.

Groen rejected upper-class frivolity to call the nation back to its Christian moral foundations. Educated at Leiden University,

he served as secretary to King Willem I and as the national archivist. Edmund Burke and **Félicité de Lamennais** were early influences. With an evangelical conversion, he looked deeply into the causes of secularism and decline. In *Unbelief and Revolution* (1847), he analyzed the Enlightenment's secularization process and concluded that the cause of both radical revolution and moderate secular Liberalism was "unbelief," or the secular humanist worldview's rejection of the entire Christian tradition. His slogan, the "Gospel versus the Revolution," captured his concern to defend the Christian worldview from all attacks and to pit principle against principle. Secular Liberalism was a danger since it also denied an explicit biblical moral foundation. Principled pluralism, not theocracy, was his approach, for he appealed to public opinion to promote a reformist ARP program.

Groen's prediction of the continuing revolutionary cycle from terror to ruthless pragmatism makes his thought relevant for postcommunist Europe and Russia. Likewise his crediting of Liberalism's decline to voting solely on pragmatic grounds still describes Western democracy.

In Parliament the ARP leader was a champion of constitutional and educational reforms. But when the Primary Education Act (1857) opted for a religiously "neutral" public school, Groen resigned for a time and worked for a pluralist educational system incorporating Protestant, Catholic, and secular components with the "free school as the rule and the public school as the supplement." This goal was not realized until after his death.

In 1871 he endorsed three independent ARP candidates (including Kuyper) for Parliament, thus breaking with Burkean-type natural law Conservatives on the platform of biblical principles, freedom for Christian schools, and suffrage reform. They lost but gained five thousand votes, forming the core group for publishing *De Standaard* newspaper in 1872 and the nucleus for the national organization of the ARP under Kuyper.

Bibliography. Van Dyke, Harry, *Groen van Prinsterer's Lectures on Unbelief and Revolution.* Jordan Station, Ontario: Wedge Publishing Foundation, 1989.

McKendree R. Langley

GRONCHI, GIOVANNI (1887–1978). Born in Pontedera (Pisa), Gronchi was a founding member of the **Italian Popular Party** (*Partito Popolare Italiano,* PPI), established in 1919, and a leading figure in the Catholic labor movement of the pre-Fascist era. Gronchi also helped establish Italy's **Christian Democracy** during the Second World War. He was elected president of the Italian Republic in 1955. His vision of Catholic-socialist cooperation to build a new post-Fascist Italy failed to fully materialize during his career, but it offered a viable alternative to the ideological polarization and parliamentary stalemate that characterized Italy's postwar system.

Gronchi cut his political teeth in the early decades of the twentieth century as an active member of **Italian Catholic Action** and the Federazione Universitaria Cattolica Italiana (FUCI, Catholic University Federation of Italy) as well as an early supporter of Don **Luigi Sturzo**'s PPI. Gronchi was attracted to Sturzo's vision of a new movement that could provide the working class with a Catholic alternative to the socialist parties. Like Sturzo, Gronchi saw a need for the church to address the social and economic issues affecting the lives of working people at the turn of the century. Gronchi soon became a leader of Italy's Catholic labor movement on the eve of the Fascist rise to power in 1922.

As a labor leader, Gronchi found himself in conflict with the main body of Catholic Action, which was closely aligned to the Vatican. In opposition to Pope **Pius XI,** Gronchi advocated autonomy for Catholic labor unions from Catholic Action. He also warned of the danger in forging official ties between the Catholic Church and Mussolini's Fascist state. Gronchi saw the dangers that Fascism presented to Italy's democracy and worried that a formal relationship between the pope and the duce would return to haunt the church, as well as ordinary Italians, since Fascist talk of foreign conquest and acts of domestic repression were sure to bring Italy to ruin.

When Gronchi's warnings went unheeded, he left active politics. He reemerged along with other Catholic politicians and intellectuals only after the fall of Mussolini in 1943. Together with former members of the PPI, such as **Alcide De Gasperi, Aldo Moro,** and **Giulio Andreotti,** Gronchi helped establish Democrazia Cristiana, Italy's Christian Democratic party.

Giovanni Gronchi, 1944. © Time Life Pictures / Getty Images

Gronchi's left-of-center leanings kept him at odds with De Gasperi and the main body of Christian Democracy. Where De Gasperi forged an intimate relationship with the United States, Gronchi advocated Italian autonomy in foreign affairs. Where centrist and rightist elements of the Christian Democracy opposed political collaboration with the revolutionary socialist parties, Gronchi urged it, to the dismay of powerful members of the Roman Curia, such as cardinals **Ottaviani** and **Tardini.**

Despite considerable opposition, Gronchi won the support of enough left-leaning Christian Democrats, together with socialists and communists, to be elected president of the Italian Republic in 1955, a post he kept until 1962. The highlight of his presidency was his controversial trip to the Soviet Union in February 1960, which solicited the criticism of anticommunists in Italy, including elements of Catholic Action and the Vatican. Historians acknowledge that Gronchi's presidency was an important step forward for Italy's postwar republic, a move beyond the ideological polarization of the immediate postwar period. Because of his reputation as a moderate Catholic, Gronchi offered a model of political cooperation between sworn enemies that anticipated the "historic compromise" of the mid-1970s. Though it ended in political failure, this compromise was a viable alternative to the ideological polarization that crippled Italian politics and society during the cold war, and a model for Catholic participation in Italian political life. Giovanni Gronchi died in Rome in 1978.

Bibliography. Colarizi, Simona. *Storia dei partiti nell'Italia repubblicana.* Bari-Rome, Italy: Laterza, 1996. Gilbert, Martin F., and Robert Nilsson, K. *Historical Dictionary of Modern Italy.* Lanham, MD: Scarecrow Press, 1999.

Robert A. Ventresca

GROPPI, JAMES E. (1930–1985). Groppi was one of the United States' most prominent Catholic priests involved in the civil rights struggle. He gained notoriety as a radical priest willing to engage in direct confrontations with police and other authorities to protest racial and social injustices.

Groppi was born in Bay View, a working-class Italian neighborhood of Milwaukee, Wisconsin. He attended seminary in Wisconsin and was ordained a Roman Catholic priest in 1959. Four years later, Groppi moved to St. Boniface Church, an African American parish in inner-city Milwaukee. Quickly appreciating the black community's dire need of better housing and economic opportunities, he also recognized an implicit link between the civil rights movement's biblical roots and the social theological tradition of Roman Catholicism. Unlike older generations of Catholic clergy who withdrew from public life, Groppi engaged unreservedly. He embarked on a decade of intense work on behalf of all urban blacks, especially in Milwaukee. His youthful fire fit the new confidence of Vatican II perfectly. To supporters, Groppi's activism proved the Catholic Church could speak directly to urgent contemporary crises.

Groppi attracted local and national attention for his advocacy for civil rights. He participated in the 1963 March on Washington, and the following year with the Council of Federated Organization's work in Mississippi. In 1965, Groppi figured prominently in two significant civil rights events: in March in full clerical garb he walked in the Selma-Montgomery March, and that summer he assisted the voter registration project of the **Southern Christian Leadership Conference.** Groppi received support from **Martin Luther King, Jr.**, and other black civil rights leaders, and in fact presented himself as their white Catholic counterpart. Back in Milwaukee he became the advisor for the city's NAACP Youth Council. In this role he organized the Milwaukee Commandos, an all-black male group charged with protecting protesters and preventing violence. The group kept busy as Groppi organized several protests against the city's segregated public schools and public housing system. They could not prevent Groppi from being arrested several times. From 1965 to 1966, Groppi also served as second vice-president to the Milwaukee United School Integration Committee. In July 1967 a race riot erupted in Milwaukee. In the aftermath, Groppi and the NAACP Youth Council led marches—often through Milwaukee's predominantly white South Side—for two hundred consecutive days to protest the segregated housing, which helped spark the riot. Defending the rioters' needs, Groppi openly identified himself with black power. The city passed an open housing law in 1968. The following year he led over a thousand marchers to the state capitol in Madison to protest welfare cuts. Groppi was jailed after the crowd held an eleven-hour sit-in strike in the state assembly chamber. Groppi said going to jail "was a holy act." He felt the same way about his arrests for organizing protests against the Vietnam War.

Many white Catholics in Milwaukee reviled Groppi for his activities. His multiple arrests and associations with urban unrest seemed to embody everything dangerous about progressivism in the 1960s. Throughout these controversies, Groppi enjoyed the quiet support of Milwaukee's archbishop, William Cousins, who resisted repeated requests to sanction Groppi. Cousins rarely endorsed Groppi's aggressive outspokenness, but he did agree with the priest's larger goal of opening Milwaukee's housing opportunities. Despite his detractors, Groppi also inspired many Milwaukee residents—Catholic or not—to become involved with social justice causes. A 1972 issue of the *New York Times* featured Groppi along with Gay Talese, Frank Sinatra, and Lee Iacocca as prominent Italian Americans who had "made it."

Groppi left St. Boniface in 1970 for another Milwaukee parish. In the 1970s his street activism paid fewer dividends. In 1971 he was arrested after attempting to disrupt Yale University's commencement. A 1972 antiwar rally at the Pentagon was broken up as police resisted the protesters' charges. In the mid-seventies Groppi worked with volunteer services for southeastern Wisconsin. In 1976 Groppi left the priesthood, married, and became a parent. He contemplated pursuing ordination in the Episcopal Church but after a year of seminary study returned to Milwaukee and Roman Catholicism. In 1979, he took a job as a bus driver for the Milwaukee region's transit authority but rekindled his activist past two years later as he led protests against police brutality in Milwaukee. By then the so-called Milwaukee Commandos was one of the city's most respected urban agencies.

Bibliography. Di Salvo, Jackie. "Father James A. Groppi (1930–1985): The Militant Humility of a Civil Rights Activist." In *The Lost World of Italian-American Radicalism,* ed. Philip Cannistraro and Gerald Meyer. Westport, CT: Praeger, 2003. Di Salvo, Jacqueline. "Father James Groppi: Portrait of a 1960s Activist." In *The Lost World of Italian-American Radicalism,* ed. Phillip Canistraro and Gerald Meyer. Westport, CT: Praeger, 2003. Gambino, Richard. "Twenty Million Italian-Americans Can't Be Wrong." *New York Times,* 30 April 1972.

Jeffrey Marlett

GROULX, LIONEL (1878–1967). Groulx was a Quebecois intellectual, a member of the Catholic clergy, a historian, and, at least from the 1920s until his death, an influential nationalist leader. He was a prolific author, writing scientific studies, historical essays, novels, and many public and personal letters. He also wrote under various pseudonyms, and his writings remain controversial to this day. For some commentators, he is a messiah, a giant, or a visionary, while for others he is just a racist and grumpy reactionary thinker promoting a form of anti-Semitic nationalism. The question can hardly be settled since both assertions can be sustained by Groulx's abundant writings.

Above all Groulx was a man of action involved in many areas of social and intellectual activism, from the setting up of Catholic youth movements to the directing of a nationalist journal, from the teaching of Canadian history (at Université de Montréal) to acting as founding president of the Franco-American History Institute. In addition, he was an accomplished polemicist and lecturer, eager to influence public opinion in a very distinct way.

Groulx took to heart the task of regenerating the French Canadian nation, trying to extricate it from what he believed was a nasty mediocrity. From his viewpoint, the British Conquest (1760) brought only subservience to French Canadians, and he aimed at shaking off his compatriots' defeatism, without hesitating to admonish them whenever necessary. According to his Catholic beliefs, a nation ought to enhance its own dignity and reach for emancipation and justice; otherwise, it is not worthy of God's love. A national mysticism must then be devised to provide body and direction for the nationalistic project of recovering a mastery of politics and economics. It is from this perspective that Groulx undertook the long-term enterprise of redirecting French Canadian history.

Bibliography. Boily, Frédéric. *La pensée nationaliste de Lionel Groulx.* Sillery, Quebec: Septentrion, 2003.

Sylvie Lacombe

GRUNDTVIG, NICOLAI FREDERIK SEVERIN (1783–1872). Prominent clergyman, poet, historian, philosopher, educator, hymn writer, and politician, Grundtvig has been called a creative genius and the spiritual founder of modern

Denmark after its crushing defeat and emasculation by the Prussians in 1864.

Born on the island of Sjaelland, he received a formal and conventional education culminating in university studies in Copenhagen. After a brief spell as pastor in a country parish, he became chaplain to the Church of the Savior in Copenhagen in 1822. In a pamphlet he published three years later, he mounted a vigorous attack on the rationalism he saw prevailing in the state church. He disputed the idea that Christianity consisted in holding orthodox beliefs, or in undergoing a conversion experience, or in being attached to a system of ethics, claiming instead that it consisted in the lived experience of "the living word" heard at baptism and in Holy Communion.

The pamphlet raised a storm of controversy, which eventually led to his being deprived of his church office. He soon became a champion of civil and religious liberty, advocating separation of church and state. As a member of the national assembly in 1849, he helped to draw up the country's first liberal constitution. He was by turns a romantic, a nationalist, a liberal, and sometimes all three at once. Grundtvig is most remembered, however, as the pioneer and inspirer of the influential Folk High School movement, an effort that began in the mid-nineteenth century and subsequently spread beyond Demark. The Folk High Schools provided and still provide a unique system of adult education. Especially when the movement first got underway, they helped young farmers develop both practical skills and wider horizons in literature, politics, religion, and culture. Grundtvig called it "education for life." Those supporters who followed him set up the most successful schools and developed his ideas. Eventually he was reinstated in church office and made a titular bishop in 1861, albeit without a see.

His followers are called Grundtvigians and still constitute a significant wing of the

Danish national church. In addition to his public activities, he studied and wrote about ancient Norse traditions, collected and transcribed folk songs, wrote a number of hymns still in wide use in the Danish church, and published several volumes of poems.

Bibliography. Allchin, A.M. *N.F.S. Grundtvig: An Introduction to His Life and Work.* London: Darton Longman Todd, 1997. Knudsen, J. *Danish Rebel.* Philadelphia: Muhlenberg, 1955.

John T. S. Madeley

GRUTKA, ANDREW G. (1908–1993). Bishop Grutka ranks among the most influential clergyman of Slovak descent in America. He acquired a national and international reputation for his dedication to ecumenism, civil rights, and racial equality long before they became fashionable or politically acceptable. Grutka also became the foremost representative of Slovak Americans among the clergy and was the driving force behind the founding and funding of the Slovak Institute of Saints Cyril and Methodius in Rome, a training ground for seminarians from Slovakia, where religion suffered communist persecution. He promoted religious freedom for Communist Czechoslovakia in his articles and speeches, and on Vatican Radio. The Communist government singled him out and labeled him a public menace and a threat to socialism.

Born in Joliet, Illinois, Grutka was the son of Slovak parents from Spišská Stará Ves. After completing studies at St. Procopius Benedictine in Lisle, Illinois, the Diocese of Fort Wayne, Indiana, sponsored him as a seminarian at the North American College in Rome, a training ground for episcopal leaders. He began his career as a very active and popular priest at a non-Slovak parish in Elkhart, Indiana, where he organized a variety of youth groups and community activities. Transferred to Slovak parishes in east

Chicago (1942–1944) and Gary, Indiana (1944–1956), he worked to settle the labor and racial conflicts that were unfolding in a changing urban environment. In doing so, he cooperated with black and white ministers from a variety of denominations to maintain safe, racially integrated neighborhoods. Gary became one of the few American cities to never experience a racial riot, for which Grutka deserves part of the credit.

As bishop (1956–1984) of the new Gary diocese, Grutka promoted youth programs like summer camp and oversaw the building of twenty-two new parish churches, fifteen elementary schools, and two new Catholic high schools. He promoted a dynamic Catholic Charities program, expanded the Catholic hospitals and invited the Albertine sisters from Poland to staff a home for the elderly. He frequently spoke out for human rights and the rights of the unborn and sought compassion for prisoners. As moderator of the American Catholic Correctional Chaplains, he advocated reforms in American criminal law. In 1970, he chaired the Catholic Federation for Communication and Mass Media and was an active participant the American Council of Bishops.

At the Second Vatican Council in 1964, Grutka made a lasting contribution to the Catholic Church's social teaching by raising the race issue and subsequently drafting the Second Vatican Council's statement on race and social justice. He insisted on its application in specific church policy and for "equal opportunities for housing, education, culture and employment" as essential to building a just society. He addressed the council with the famous words, "No one would look for beauty on a garbage dump, and no one can expect virtue in a slum."

During the Vietnam War, Grutka strove to promote a peaceful resolution to the conflict. At the National Council of Catholic Bishops meeting in 1967, Grutka headed the committee, which drafted a Peace Resolution, urging a negotiated end to the conflict and "a just and lasting peace." His involvement in the peace movement led to an ecumenical visit to Hanoi in 1974, and upon his return to the United States, he organized charitable relief for the war-torn country.

As the first bishop in the United States of pure Slovak ethnic background (Bishop Joseph Durrick of Alabama was half Slovak), Grutka provided a rallying point of pride for Slovak Americans. Although he had first shunned involvement with Slovak connections, he did an about-face and became the Slovak American voice in Catholic America. In 1970 he played a key role in founding the Slovak World Congress and served as its first chairman. His continual financial and very personal support for students at the Slovak Institute trained many priests for future work in Slovakia and in missions around the world. The institute also published religious and cultural literature unavailable in Communist Slovakia.

Bishop Grutka was well known for his very personal and compassionate manner as a champion of the rights of the common person and average worker. He strove to touch the lives of individuals of all races, creeds, and nationalities in America and throughout the world. He is often remembered for the motto by which he strove to live: "Where there is Love, there is God."

Bibliography. Kopanic, Michael. "Rev. Andrew G. Grutka, D.D.: Slovak-American Bishop of Gary Indiana." *Národný Kalendár* 109 (2001): 111–18. Matovčík, Augustín, et al. *Slovak Biographical Dictionary.* Martin, Slovakia: Matica slovenská, 2002. Strhan, Milan , and David P. Daniel, eds. *Slovakia and the Slovaks: A Concise Encyclopedia.* Bratislava, Slovakia: Goldpress, 1994.

Michael J. Kopanic, Jr.

GUARESCHI, GIOVANNI (1908–1968).

A celebrated Italian journalist, novelist, and humorist who often wrote from a Catholic perspective, Guareschi was the son of a landowner and his wife, a teacher. The inflation crisis of 1926 bankrupted the Guareschi family and forced the young Giovanni to end his formal studies. After a job as a doorman in a sugar refinery, then as a boarding school teacher, Guareschi found a position with a local newspaper and later on in 1929 he became the editor of the magazine *Corriere Emiliano.*

From 1936 to 1943 he coedited the Milanese satirical weekly magazine *Bertoldo.* Its political satire landed the magazine in trouble, and Guareschi joined the army in order to avoid imprisonment by the Fascist regime. In 1945 he founded another satirical weekly journal, *Candido,* which strongly attacked both the government, the communists, the Italian **Christian Democracy,** and more specifically **Alcide De Gaspari.** He accused the latter of cooperating with the Nazis during the invasion of Rome, accusations that landed Guareschi in a libel trial and earned him a year in prison.

By 1948 he published his most famous best seller, *The Little World of Don Camillo,* the first book of a series that has been translated in many languages and established Guareschi as a famous novelist. The short stories center on Don Camillo, a parish priest, and take place in a small Italian village. Don Camillo's nemesis is Peppone, the Communist mayor, who strongly disagrees with everything the priest says or does. Guareschi tried to make fun of both sides, but his audience was more sympathetic toward Camillo's side, and Guareschi's Catholic motivations are always evident. He can be remembered as an independent gadfly of Italian Catholicism. In 1957 he stepped down as editor of *Candido* but did not retire immediately. He continued to write articles and columns for the magazine. His books include *Il destino si chiama Clotilde* (1942), *Diario Cladestino* (1946), *Lo Zibaldino* (1948), and *Mondo piccolo: Don Camillo* (1948).

Bibliography. Gnocchi, Alessandro. *Giovannino Guareschi: Una storia italiana.* Milan: Rizzoli, 1998. Guareschi, G. *Il decimo clandestino: Piccolo mondo borghese.* Milan: Rizzoli, 1982.

Efharis Mascha

GUTIÉRREZ, GUSTAVO (b. 1928). Born in Peru, Gutiérrez helped to inspire the movement known as liberation theology. Drawing upon the work of **Jurgen Moltmann** and other political theologians after World War II, Gutiérrez rejects the image of a distant God who silently ignores the suffering of God's children.

If post-Holocaust theology insists that God was in the crematoriums, suffering with the people of God, liberation theology insists that God is in the slums of Peru, suffering with the people of God. Whereas Christians have sometimes appealed to wealth or power as a sign of God's grace and misfortune as a sign of God's displeasure, Gutiérrez points to the image of a crucified God, who suffers for and with humanity, to show that God stands in solidarity with the oppressed. Looking at the effects of globalization upon Latin America, Gutiérrez preaches that God stands in solidarity with the poorest of the poor. Poverty, he insists, is a spiritual issue that affects the Christian conscience. Inasmuch as the causes and solutions to poverty are social, political, and economic, then religion and politics become inevitably intertwined. Reminding us that Jesus's preaching about the kingdom of God has obvious political implications, Gutierrez states, "The struggle for a just world in which there is no oppression, servitude, or alienated work will signify the coming of the Kingdom. The Kingdom and social injustice are incompatible" (Gutiérrez, 168).

While the majority of people in the United States and Europe may be unfamiliar with his name, Gutiérrez is better known among Christians throughout the third world and among the leaders of the Catholic and mainline Protestant churches in the United States. Because Gutiérrez's writings have become required reading at most Catholic and mainline Protestant seminaries, his ideas will continue to shape a new generation of church leaders. As a Catholic, Gutiérrez has developed an ambivalent relationship with the Catholic Church. On one hand, he and others have inspired the Catholic Church to embrace a "preferential option for the poor." On the other hand, some Catholic Church leaders have criticized Gutierrez for relying too heavily upon Marxist economic analysis as he exposes the systemic injustices of globalization.

The works of Gutiérrez have inspired numerous theologians to apply the basic principles of liberation theology to a variety of social contexts. Consequently he has had a major influence on black theology of liberation, feminist theology of liberation, *mujerista* theology, and womanist theology, among others. For most of his academic career, Gustavo Gutiérrez served as a professor of theology at the Pontifical University of Peru. After serving as a visiting professor at Union Theological Seminary, he accepted the position as John Cardinal O'Hara Professor of Theology at the University of Notre Dame. In 1993 the French government awarded him the Legion of Honor.

Bibliography. Gutiérrez, Gustavo. *A Theology of Liberation: History, Politics, Salvation.* Ed. and trans. Caridad Inda and John Eagleson. Maryknoll, NY: Orbis Books, 1973. Hartnett, Daniel. "Remembering the Poor." *America* 188 (February 2003): 12–16.

Andrew D. Walsh

H

HAAS, FRANCIS J. (1889–1953). Emerging from the Catholic social justice tradition of **Leo XIII, Pius XI,** and Father **John A. Ryan,** Haas combined priesthood and public service in the New Deal era. An appointee to several government and Catholic social service agencies, he translated Christian Social teachings into practice as a voice for working class Americans.

Born in Racine, Wisconsin, Haas entered St. Francis Seminary in 1904 and was ordained to the priesthood in 1913. His intellectual acuity carried him beyond the duties of a parish priest and into the Catholic University of America, where he absorbed the Catholic Social Gospel according to Father John Ryan. Haas returned to St. Francis Seminary for another nine years, but his lectures and writings, particularly *Man and Society* (1931), bore the stamp of Catholic social consciousness. Appointed director of the National Catholic School of Social Service in Washington in 1931, Haas acquired a reform profile that brought him to the attention of Frances Perkins, secretary of labor in Roosevelt's New Deal administration.

The priest from Wisconsin found himself recruited into the Labor Advisory Board of the experimental National Recovery Administration. Through public hearings and insider meetings, the board represented American workers in the NRA's struggle to establish production codes that would stimulate industrial demand and spark economic recovery. Father Haas supervised twenty codes and participated in formulating several others. Following the approval of the codes, which occupied the board's attention in 1933, he and other appointees represented workers through amendment proceedings and code-related investigations. The work was exhausting: by November of 1933, nearly ten million workers had been included under the umbrella of NRA protection for minimum wages, maximum hours, and union organization. Despite the strain, Haas kept the issues in perspective: "The tragic fact is that twelve millions of people are out of employment and something has to be done to get them back to work, and done now" (Blantz, 576). Following his work with the Labor Advisory Board, Haas joined Senator Robert Wagner's National Labor Board, followed by appointments to the Wisconsin Labor Relations Board, the Works Progress Administration, and the Fair Employment Practice Committee. By 1945, Haas had expended his political capital and became bishop of Grand Rapids, Michigan. Although never a leading figure in the New Deal, he used his government appointments to apply Christian principles to the struggle for industrial democracy.

Bibliography. Blantz, Thomas. "Francis J. Haas: Priest and Government Servant." *Catholic Historical Review* 57 (January 1972): 571–92.

Michael Dennis

HAMER, FANNIE LOU (1917–1977). Hamer, an African American grassroots activist and eloquent spokesperson for the American civil rights movement, was as famous for her political labors as for her personal suffering under the tyrannies of Southern segregation.

The granddaughter of slaves, Hamer was the youngest of twenty children. Her parents were sharecroppers, and she joined them in the field at age six. Hamer's mother encouraged her to take pride in her race and to take comfort in the transforming power of the Gospel message even in the face of endless disparity and insult. Although baptized at the Stranger's Home Baptist Church, Hamer had a vehement distaste for "chicken eatin' Baptist preachers," whom she felt frequently took advantage of their authority at the expense of meaningful spiritual labor. Nevertheless, she remained a deeply spiritual woman, using the scriptures to motivate and endure.

By her mid-forties, Hamer was "sick and tired of being sick and tired." She toiled relentlessly in the fields for insignificant recompense and was unable to bear children since a white doctor had sterilized her without permission. Thus, when the Student Nonviolent Coordinating Committee (SNCC) arrived in her county for a voter registration drive in 1962, she attempted to join their cause. While traveling to the courthouse in order to register, she and several others were jailed and brutally beaten on orders from white police officers in Winona, Mississippi. Although the incident led to her dismissal from the plantation where she had worked for decades, it also led to her entrance into the political arena. She became the SNCC field secretary, managing their summer training camp. To those Northerners under her care, she inculcated them with black Southern religiosity, frequently encouraging rousing renditions of "This Little Light of Mine" and offering fiery speeches sparked by biblical metaphors. "Christ was a revolutionary person," she explained.

Although under constant death threats, Hamer persisted in her work, gaining a national reputation following her testimony before the Credentials Committee at the 1964 Democratic Convention. As cofounder of the Mississippi Freedom Democratic Party (MFDP), Hamer had gone to the convention to challenge the official all-white delegation from Mississippi. She provided eloquent testimony about how blacks were prohibited from voting through illegal tests and taxes. Following her speech, she returned to her home in Ruleville, where she initiated grassroots antipoverty projects. She started several cooperatives, including the Freedom Farm

Fannie Lou Hamer. Courtesy of the Library of Congress

Cooperative, a project through which five thousand African Americans came to grow their own food and collectively own 680 acres of land. Although she would occasionally participate in larger events, such as the formation of the National Women's Political Caucus, Hamer focused her remaining days on the local fight against social discrimination. At her death, she was remembered as a passionate and spiritual advocate for the rural disinherited.

Bibliography. Kai Lee, Chana. *For Freedom's Sake: The Life of Fannie Lou Hamer.* Urbana: University of Illinois Press, 2000. Mills, Kay. *This Little Light of Mine: The Life of Fannie Lou Hamer.* New York: Dutton, 1993.

Kathryn Lofton

HARTLEY, FRANK JOHN (1909–1971). Hartley was a Methodist minister, president of the Democratic Rights Council (1950–1951), superintendent of the Prahan Methodist Mission (1954–1971), and Australian representative to the World Peace Council (1950–1971). Residing the first twenty years of his life in the Victorian coal-mining town of Wonthaggi, Hartley committed to serving the Methodist Church by the age of sixteen. He attended Otira Methodist Mission College before graduating with a divinity degree from Queens College, Melbourne University.

Hartley served as chaplain with the Twenty-seventh Australian Division Cavalry Regiment and as senior chaplain with the Seventh Division in the Ramu Valley Campaign during World War II. One of the few Australian survivors on the Sanananda Road (New Guinea), he was traumatized by his own experience of the Pacific War, which he described in *Sanananda Interlude* (1949). In the immediate postwar period, Hartley helped to establish the Australian Peace Council (APC) and contributed as joint secretary to the development of this pacifist body.

He was elected member of the World Peace Council in November 1950 and represented Australia at the WPC meeting in Vienna in November 1951. Influenced during his adolescence by the miners' struggles, Hartley's engagement with the sociopolitical life of Melbourne was accentuated in 1951 when he became president of the Democratic Rights Council (DRC). He published *In Quest of Peace* in 1951 and was subsequently nominated executive officer of the newly formed Australian and New Zealand Congress for International Cooperation and Disarmament (ANZCID). This position expanded his international pacifist reputation and helped him earn the Joliot Curie Gold Peace Medal and later the Lenin Gold Peace Medal.

In addition to his international peace activities, Hartley served in the 1950s as administrator of the Prahan Mission, dedicated to the welfare of underprivileged citizens. As a Methodist evangelist for more than fourteen years, he preached a peace message from Moscow to Melbourne that combined strong political advocacy with occasional appeals for general disarmament. He died at a Prahan city council meeting.

Bibliography. Hartley, Frank J. *In Quest of Peace.* Melbourne, Australia: Australian Peace Council, 1956. Hartley, Marion. *The Truth Shall Prevail: A Noble Life in Quest of Truth, Reconciliation and Peaceful Co-existence.* Melbourne, Australia: Spectrum Publications, 1982.

Jérôme Dorvidal

HEER, FRIEDRICH (1916–1983). Catholic author, editor, and publicist, Heer was born, raised, and educated in Vienna. While still in high school, he developed a fascination with the Greek church fathers and with Christian mysticism. These interests blossomed in October 1934, when he began his study of history, German literature, and art history at the University of

Vienna. After Adolf Hitler took over Austria in 1938, Heer joined a group of resistance fighters and was arrested six times. In 1940 he was drafted to serve in the German army.

After the war Heer was imprisoned by the British and released in 1946. From 1949 until 1961 he served as editor of *Die Furche,* a Catholic weekly newspaper. In 1961 Heer was elected as dramaturge at Austria's most important theater, the Viennese *Burgtheater,* an office he held until 1971, when he became associate professor at the University of Vienna.

Throughout his adult life Heer was both a dedicated Catholic and an outspoken critic of the institutional Catholic Church. An extremely prolific writer, he published numerous articles and books on such diverse issues as anti-Semitic notions in the Catholic Church, Hitler's belief system, abortion, Austrian identity, and spirituality. He was deeply influenced by Teilhard de Chardin, Hans Urs von Baltasar, and Erastian humanism and always propagated the separation of faith and theology. As a convinced ecumenical Christian he also fought for a united Christendom without any denominations. Shortly before his death, Heer vehemently supported the pro-choice movement in Austria. He was continuously criticized by conservative Catholics and church officials there. Heer also had a lasting influence on European and American intellectuals, including Gabriel Marcel and Pierre Bertaux in France and Arthur A. Cohen in the United States.

Bibliography. Adunka, Evelyn. *Friedrich Heer (1916–1983): Eine intellektuelle Biographie.* Innsbruck, Austria: Tyrolia, 1995.

Gregor Thuswaldner

HENRIOT, PHILIPPE (1889–1944). Born into a military family in the Gironde region of southwest France, Henriot was raised in a classic right-wing Catholic environment.

Rather than pursue the family tradition of a career in the army, Henriot became a teacher in a private Catholic school. He found a natural outlet for his political leanings in the conservative, anti-German, and anticommunist Fédération Nationale Catholique (FNC), set up in 1925 and headed by the First World War veteran Général Edouard de Castelnau.

Then, in 1932, Henriot was elected as deputy for Bordeaux in the seat vacated by the unexpected retirement of abbé Bergey, a powerful orator and a principal figure in the FNC. Henriot sat in parliament with Louis Marin's right-wing Fédération Républicaine, of which he became vice president. By the mid-1930s, Henriot had established himself as a highly visible and eloquent speaker for the Right. His anticommunism and antirepublicanism prompted tirades against the French Popular Front government of 1936–1938. Internationally, he opposed the Spanish Republic, supporting **Francisco Franco**'s Nationalists instead. In 1938, Henriot defended appeasement and supported Munich. Two years later, the defeat of France by Germany confirmed his antirepublican prejudices. He welcomed the armistice, immediately becoming an ardent Pétainist and one of the great rhetoricians for Vichy's program of national revolution.

Henriot was one of a minority of prominent conservative, Catholic, and anti-German nationalists (including the historian Louis Bertrand, and Cardinal **Baudrillart,** the aged rector of the Catholic Institute in Paris) who converted to the National Socialist cause around 1940 as a direct result of their anticommunism. In Henriot's case, the cause was nothing less than a crusade. He sought to unite France and Germany in the struggle against Communism as the enemy of Christianity, reconciling his Catholic beliefs with National Socialism in the process. Henriot was obsessed by the Communist threat.

Germany's invasion of Russia on July 22, 1941, further radicalized his position, and by 1942, he was well known as a zealous advocate of collaboration. He made frequent contributions to such collaborationist newspapers as *Gringoire* and *Je suis partout.*

Henriot took on the mantle of propagandist for Radio Vichy in 1943, the role for which he remains best known on account of his striking voice, eloquent delivery, and rhetorical power. In his weekly broadcasts he played on traditional Catholic fears and prejudices, painting Communism as the monster of the modern age and indulging in virulent anti-Semitism. By all accounts, huge audiences were attracted to what were widely regarded as compelling broadcasts.

On January 6, 1944, in line with German wishes, Henriot was appointed Vichy's minister of information and propaganda. His broadcasts on Radio Vichy now became twice-daily events, increasingly moralizing in content and passionate in tone. He also joined the infamous *Milice française,* whose trademark black shirt he regularly donned in public. Henriot's reputation and influence as a propagandist made him a natural target for the Resistance in the final months of the war, and he was assassinated in his ministerial apartment in Paris on June 28, 1944. In what is widely regarded as Vichy's last act, a state funeral was held in Notre Dame on July 1, presided over by the archbishop of Paris. The "voice" of collaboration had finally been silenced.

Bibliography. Kedward, H. R. "The Vichy of the other Philippe." In *Collaboration in France: Politics and Culture during the Nazi Occupation, 1940–1944,* ed. Gerhard Hirschfeld and Patrick Marsh. Oxford: Berg, 1989.

Kay Chadwick

HERRERA ORIA, ÁNGEL (1886–1968). Herrera was a lawyer, journalist, and Catholic priest (made cardinal by **Paul VI** in 1965). His prominent role in developing and modernizing the Spanish Catholic Action started in 1910 when, jointly with Father Ayala, he founded the elitist **National Catholic Association of Propagandists** (ACNP), an organization aimed at recruiting a select minority with the ultimate objective of assuring the prevalence of Catholic values in both society and the state.

In 1911 he created the Catholic Publishing House (*Editorial Católica*), which soon published *El Debate.* He directed this most prominent Catholic newspaper in the country until1933. In 1926, Herrera also founded a school of journalism attached to *El Debate* that greatly raised the quality and professionalism of Spanish journalism. In 1933, he became president of the board of the Spanish Catholic Action.

After the abdication of King Alfonso XIII, Herrera and *El Debate* adopted a position of critical accommodation toward Spain's secular and democratic Second Republic. He also worked to establish a new, modern conservative party, which could galvanize and reorganize Catholic opinion. This party, National Action (Acción Nacional) of which Herrera was first president, became core of the **Confederación Española de Derechas Autonómas (CEDA)** that was led by ACNP member **Jose Maria Gil Robles.** The CEDA became Spain's largest political party and successfully opposed some of the Republic's key reform projects such as land distribution.

The majority of the CEDA party leaders preferred an authoritarian, corporative political system, similar to the Austrian dictatorship, rather than democracy. The victory of the leftist Popular Front in the February 1936 elections was received by many of the CEDA supporters as a sign that strong action was now the only alternative available to prevent revolution. Accordingly, they backed the military rising of July 1936 that degenerated into a civil war that lasted until 1939. For Herrera, even if he shared most of the rebels' values, it was a personal defeat. In 1936 he left for Freiburg to become a priest. He returned in 1943, distinguishing himself, both as a priest and later as a bishop, for his charitable work with the poor and the illiterate.

Bibliography. Herrera, Ángel. *El pensamiento de Ángel Herrera: Antología política y social.* Madrid: BAC, 1987. *Ángel Herrera Oria, adelantado de nuestro tiempo: Ante los nuevos modos de comunicación y relación social / José María García Escudero.* Madrid: Universidad Pontificia de Salamanca en Madrid: Fundación Pablo VI, 1996.

Antonio Cazorla Sanchez

HIDALGO, MIGUEL (1753–1811). Father Miguel Hidalgo y Costilla, born into a Creole family in the present-day state of Guanajuato, Mexico, is known as the father of his country for initiating Mexico's independence movement against Spain on September 16, 1810. He led Creoles, Indians, and mixed-blood peoples against Spanish rule until his capture and subsequent execution in July 1811.

Creoles, or colonists of Spanish descent born in the Americas, resented the political and ecclesiastical domination of Peninsular Spaniards. Indians and mixed-blood peoples knew that Hidalgo promoted social justice. His unique background, personal experiences, and position as a Catholic priest enabled him to bring together, albeit temporarily, these diverse and even antagonistic groups. His leadership suggests that the independence movement was neither hostile to the Catholic Church nor anticlerical in nature.

Hidalgo's father served as administrator on a rural estate and Miguel understood from an early age the difficulties of agricultural production and the plight of peasants. He even learned to speak Otomí, an indigenous language. Because of his privileged socioeconomic background, he received a first-rate education at the Jesuit College of San Francisco Xavier and the College of San Nicolás Obispo, obtaining a baccalaureate in arts in 1770, and another in theology from Mexico's prestigious Royal and Pontifical University in 1773. He became a priest in 1778 and taught courses and became rector at the College of San Nicolás Obispo. His brilliant academic career was cut short, however, because of his controversial teaching, suspect bookkeeping, frequent gambling, and notorious womanizing; he was reassigned to parishes in Colima and Dolores in 1792 and 1803, respectively. Hidalgo's parish house in Dolores became a meeting ground for Creoles who enjoyed his wit, intellectual curiosity, knowledge of several languages, and interest in Enlightenment principles. Poorer parishioners appreciated Hidalgo's promotion of agriculture, industry, and genuine concern for their well-being. While in Dolores, he was denounced before the Holy Office for making dangerous political and religious statements and for possessing prohibited books, but inquisitors pursued no formal action at this time.

Bourbon monarchs throughout the eighteenth century strengthened the political, economic, and military position of the Crown vis-à-vis the colonies; curtailed the aspirations of Creoles who desired home rule; and more fully subordinated the church to the state by ending ecclesiastical privileges, confiscating and administering church wealth and property, and expelling the Jesuits in 1767. Napoleon's 1808 invasion of Spain and the abdication of Ferdinand VII exacerbated tensions between Spaniards and Creoles.

Royalists in Mexico squelched various plots by autonomists in 1808 and 1809. On September 16, 1810, however, Miguel Hidalgo, who had conspired with other Creole leaders during the previous several months, began military operations, when a traitor divulged their plans to imperial authorities. Hidalgo issued a call to arms from his church in Dolores and encouraged his parishioners, mostly indigenous and mixed-blood peoples, to overthrow the colonial regime. In nearby Atotonilco, Hidalgo took the image of the Virgin of Guadalupe from the local church and adopted this proud symbol of Catholicism and Mexican identity as the movement's flag. Hidalgo was named General of America and recognized as the leader of the movement.

Creoles sought political revolution and the application of liberty and equality to members of their own group. Peasants desired social revolution, access to land, and better working conditions. Hidalgo's control of the movement meant that the insurgency, as originally planned by the Creoles, would change in tenor and focus, since Hidalgo's concern for the rural populace was not "characteristic of the bulk of American *criollos*" (Hamill, 53). Unfortunately, he proved to be a poor military strategist and incapable of resolving the "important contradictions within the insurgency, " as demonstrated on September 26, 1810, when Hidalgo's peasant forces, now estimated at fifty thousand, sacked and captured the important silver-mining city of Guanajuato (Guedea, 119). Peasant insurgents killed Spaniards and Creole royalist sympathizers indiscriminately, which prompted most Creoles to abandon the movement, join the royalists, and help preserve the status quo. They received additional support from Manuel Abad y Queipo, the bishop-elect of Michoacán, who excommunicated Hidalgo and his partisans.

Hidalgo's undisciplined troops proved no match for the royalist army under the command of Brigadier General Félix María Calleja. After establishing a provisional government in Guadalajara, abolishing slavery, and ending tribute payments by Indians, the royalists defeated and captured Hidalgo and other Creole leaders at Acatita de Baján on March 21, 1811. Hidalgo was tried by the Inquisition, handed over to magistrates, and shot on July 30. His severed head was placed on a post in Guanajuato as a reminder of Spanish domination until independence was achieved in 1821. Hidalgo's efforts contributed to Mexico's political independence, but not to socioeconomic reform in favor of the indigenous and mixed-blood peoples for whom he sacrificed his life.

Bibliography. Guedea, Virginia. "The Process of Mexican Independence." *American Historical Review* 105 (February 2000): 116–30. Hamill, Hugh M. Jr. *The Hidalgo Revolt: Prelude to Mexican Independence.* Gainesville: University of Florida Press, 1966.

Lee M. Penyak

HISTORICS (SPAIN). A faction of Spanish politics that held a conservative vision of Catholic power in the face of liberal assaults in the 1870s, the Historics identified with the semi-dictatorial state created between 1866 and 1868 by General Ramón Narváez and dominated by the Moderate party, a government which made substantial concessions to the church, although it did not succeed in eliminating widespread support for Carlism among Spanish Catholics.

The Glorious Revolution (1868) overthrew Queen Isabella II and the regime in favor of a progressive liberal government that introduced religious liberty for the first time in the kingdom's history in 1869. Clerical and lay reaction to these reforms and to the proposed separation of church and state by the First Republic (1873–1874) increased the determination of the hierarchy and a variety of Catholic political groups to force the creation of a rigidly Catholic state obligated to sustain the church's religious monopoly. Bishops and Catholic politicians identified with this approach wished to have nothing to do with the religious liberty established by the 1869 constitution. But there was little unity among the diverse currents of Catholic opinion before the installation, as a result of a military coup in 1874, of Isabella II's son, Alfonso XII, as king and a liberal ministry directed by Antonio Cánovas del Castillo.

Given their dynastic preoccupations, Carlists rejected the liberal monarchy outright, while Catholics willing to accept it entertained reservations about the sincerity of the prime minister's commitment to defend the interests of the church. Cánovas, a middle of the road Moderate who disagreed with the repressive policies pursued by Narváez, wished to create a constitutional system embracing the two liberal parties that had dominated politics since the 1830s, the Moderates and the Progressives. But he also recognized the need to pacify Catholic opinion on the issue of religious liberty. Foremost among his critics in 1875 were members of the Moderate party who had supported Narváez. Known as Historics, they wished to return to the political model of 1866–1868. They rejected the progressive 1869 constitution and wanted to settle accounts with those responsible for it. They preferred Isabella II to her son and deeply mistrusted Cánovas, particularly on the issue of religious liberty. In 1875 and 1876, the Historics began a determined campaign through their press to force the prime minister to abrogate the religious liberty introduced in 1869 and immediately restore the 1851 concordat, which recognized the state's official confessionality. The Historics expected, said their Madrid newspaper, that all laws, dispositions, and government acts should be moved by a Catholic spirit.

The offensive of the Historics in alliance with some members of the hierarchy posed a serious political danger to Cánovas during the first year and a half of his ministry. But the prime minister employed his well-honed political skills to balance the interests of liberals from the Progressive party, whose political support he needed, with those of the church through Article 11 of the 1876 constitution. It established Catholicism as the religion of the state and prohibited the public exercise of any other religion than that of the state. But Article 11 also declared that no one could be prosecuted for personal religious beliefs nor for their private exercise. This clause led to a renewed and vociferous campaign by the Historics and their clerical allies but to no avail. Cánovas won his political gamble. A majority of former Moderates and Progressives accepted Article 11, although some did so with reservations.

The Vatican was unhappy with the concession allowing the private practice of religion by non-Catholics, but in the end it accepted Article 11 grudgingly. Cánovas succeeded in consolidating his version of a liberal constitutional monarchy, thereby leaving by the wayside the ambitions of the Historics for a return to the political system of Narváez.

Bibliography. Campomar Fornieles, Marta M. *La cuestión religiosa en la Restauración.* Santander, Spain: Sociedad Menédez Pelayo, 1984. Robles, Cristóbal. *Insurrección o legalidad: Los católicos y la Restauración.* Madrid: CSIC, 1988.

William J. Callahan

HLINKA, ANDREJ (1864–1938). Hlinka was born in the village of Černová, in northern Hungary (today's Slovakia). Ordained in 1889, he was pastor at the Roman Catholic parish in Ružomberok from 1905 to 1938, as well as a political activist on behalf of the Slovak minority, both in Austria-Hungary (to 1918) and Czechoslovakia (1918–1938).

Hlinka began his political career in the 1890s as a Catholic activist but soon joined the Slovak nationalist movement. In 1906, he was imprisoned for nationalist agitation. When Hungarian gendarmes shot and killed over a dozen pro-Hlinka protestors in Černová, he briefly became known across Europe as a symbol of Hungary's oppression of its minorities. After the war, now in Czechoslovakia, he continued his career as a Slovak Catholic activist, founding his own Slovak People's Party. As the charismatic leader of Slovakia's largest party, Hlinka pursued a dual program of defending the church against anti-Catholic legislation and advocating autonomy for Slovakia and national recognition for Slovaks, a people regarded as Czechoslovakians in the state's constitution.

Though a staunch Catholic and ardent Slovak nationalist, whose religious faith and nationalism were inextricably intertwined, Hlinka often proved to be more nationalist than Catholic. On two occasions, under two different regimes, his bishop reprimanded him on account of his nationalism. He was manifestly unable to develop political alliances with Catholics of non-Slovak nationality, but fairly successful in cooperating with Slovak Lutherans and even those Czech anti-Catholics willing to support Slovak nationalism. Within his own party, he favored the promotion of young lay radicals for whom nationalism was a religion in itself, at the expense of traditionally minded older clerics.

During 1938, as Nazi Germany put Czechoslovakia under increasing pressure, Hlinka's main concern was how to exploit Czech misfortune to get Slovak autonomy, though his Catholic outlook kept him from cooperating with anti-Catholic Nazism. He died in August 1938, just a few weeks before Germany began its dismemberment of Czechoslovakia. Though Hlinka surely saw no conflict between his Catholicism and his nationalism, in fact, when the two came into conflict, he habitually opted for the latter. The Hlinka Guard, a fascist militia that bore his name, was founded after his death and bore no relation to Slovakia's priest politician.

Bibliography. Felak, James Ramon. "Priests in Central European Politics: Ignaz Seipel, Jan Šrámek, and Andrej Hlinka." In *Render Unto Caesar,* ed. Sabrina Petra Ramet and Donald W. Treadgold. Washington, DC: American University Press, 1995.

James Ramon Felak

HLOND, AUGUST (1881–1948). Throughout the interwar years and during the Second World War, Hlond served as the primate of the Roman Catholic Church in Poland. He used his authority to steer the clergy away from explicit or direct engagement with the newly independent Polish state, even as he advanced a policy agenda rooted in modern Catholic social and political thought. He exemplified the two faces of early twentieth-century Polish Catholicism: on one hand, he did much to promote the concerns of workers and peasants who were harmed by the era's rapid industrialization and urbanization and tried to adapt church institutions to this changing environment; on the other hand, he allowed the church to become affiliated with a narrow, often xenophobic and anti-Semitic, understanding of the Polish national cause.

Hlond was raised by pious working-class parents in Upper Silesia (then a part of Germany), and of his twelve siblings, four entered the priesthood. He distinguished himself early and was sent to Italy at age twelve to pursue his education at a school run by the Salesian order. He obtained a doctorate in philosophy from the Gregorian University of Rome in 1900 and taught in a number of Salesian schools after his ordination in 1905. Hlond rose rapidly in the church hierarchy after the establishment of Polish independence in 1918, becoming apostolic administrator for Silesia in 1922, then bishop of Silesia in 1925. He became archbishop of Gniezno/Poznań and primate of Poland a year later, and in 1927, he was named a cardinal.

His selection as primate was politically significant, because only a month beforehand the Polish government had been overthrown in a military coup led by Józef Piłsudski, a hero of the independence movement who had once been a prominent socialist, and who was nominally a Protestant. Many in the church were deeply hostile toward the new regime, and there was a great deal of support among the clergy for a right-wing anti-Semitic party known as the National Democrats. Hlond himself made a number of infamous anti-Semitic pronouncements, and he was certainly not a supporter of Piłsudski, but he nonetheless advocated a nonpartisan stance for the church and worked to achieve a rapprochement with the new government. He tried to keep a tight reign on the more explicitly politicized members of the clergy, and he enforced the Vatican's policy of cooperation with the Polish state.

While striving to keep the church out of partisan politics, he was nonetheless a key figure in moving Polish Catholicism toward a greater engagement with the social and cultural issues of the modern world. He created a Social Advisory Council, which continues to work with the episcopate to this day; he brought the Catholic Action movement to Poland; and he started to move the clergy away from a narrow understanding of their sacramental function to a more socially engaged approach to pastoral work.

Bibliography. Hlond, August. *Na straży sumienia narodu: Wybór pism i przemówień.* Warsaw: Ad Astra, 1999. Kant, Bronisław. *Sztygar Bożej kopalni: Obrazki z życia Ks. Kardynała Augusta Hlonda.* Lodz, Poland: Wydawnictwo Salezjańskie, 1980.

Brian Porter

HODGE, CHARLES (1797–1878). For a Princeton professor whose lifelong work lay chiefly in the field of conservative Calvinist theology, Hodge sustained a remarkable interest in politics. During an adulthood that saw the advent of mass democracy, territorial expansion, stunning economic change, a technological revolution, abrasive sectionalism, and civil war, Hodge the engaged citizen actively sought to shape the events through which he lived and remained true to the Reformed tradition and to Princetonians' fusion of American republicanism, civil liberty, and Protestant Christianity. He felt acutely, as he confided to his brother, that "real politics, . . . when connected with morals and the . . . interests of the country, is a subject second only to religion in importance." Through the *Princeton Review,* in particular, he stepped into the political daylight, notably during the crisis over slavery and the Union, when he adopted positions more radical than he was temperamentally equipped to hold and from which he would retreat only with the coming of peace.

Hodge followed a party political route common to many Northern evangelicals, whose affiliations ranged from Federalist to Whig to Republican. In his youth he absorbed the Federalism of his family's commercial-professional Presbyterian circle in Philadelphia. He welcomed John Quincy Adams's presidency, sharing the National Republicans' disdain for Andrew Jackson and the new class of party professionals who sustained him. Hodge's brand of ethical anti-Jacksonianism explains much about the embryonic Whig party, for it initially drew its power from the Democratic administration's indifference to Reformed protests over the movement of mails on Sundays, and from the president's forced and "un-Christian" removal of Indians from their historic settlements. Fusing conservative social principles with a faith in commercial progress, Hodge regarded the Whig party as the best means of developing the nation's economy and protecting its propertied interests. He cast Whigs, by contrast with rabble-rousing

Democrats, as agents of moral order, benev-olence, respectability, and social harmony. Determined to ensure the hegemony of the Protestant virtues of personal self-disci-pline, industriousness, self-improvement, and responsibility, he sought to stiffen the naturalization laws, especially after foreign and Catholic votes had helped defeat the party's great presidential hope, Henry Clay, in 1844.

For Hodge, the 1850s marked a political watershed. As a conservative antiabolition-ist in the 1830s he had bought slaves for his domestic use and—in a Southern-oriented seminary—articulated a theologi-cal defense of slavery. Now, in the party flux of the mid-1850s, he did not follow the many conservative Whigs (his own brother included) who endorsed the nativ-ist American Party but instead adhered to an infant Republican organization dedi-cated to choking slavery within its existing limits. It was the decision of a man stunned by the Kansas-Nebraska Act and its open-ing up of the western territories to slave-holding settlers. Fearing that the republic had fallen under the malign influence of a slave power—in which, to his dismay, his Southern Old School Presbyterian col-leagues seemed complicit—Hodge voted for John C. Frémont in 1856 and **Abraham Lincoln** four years later. He continued to see himself as a conservative defender of the federal Constitution, in this case against the South's radical leadership, but in reality he had moved to new ground.

The months following Lincoln's elec-tion drew Hodge into what was, politically, the most controversial phase of his life. For over three decades he had pursued intersectional bridge building in both church and state to protect a priceless Union, his natural emollience reinforced by geographical location and professional milieu. Secession he deemed in prospect a criminal absurdity, but faced with its real-ity, he toyed with peaceful separation, only to adopt an unwavering Unionism after

the shots at Fort Sumter. In wartime Hodge the moral expositor sought to galvanize support for Lincoln's administration in its "Herculean task." He defended the Emancipation Proclamation and the ero-sion of civil liberties as legitimate means of saving the nation; his essays played a part in Lincoln's reelection and eventual Union victory. After Robert E. Lee's formal surren-der to Union forces at Appomattox Court House in 1865, Hodge's conservatism reasserted itself. He endorsed Lincoln's reconciliationist approach to national reconstruction and, after the president's assassination, sympathized with Andrew Johnson in his struggle against Republican radicals. At the same time, he recovered his essential optimism. The cause of Christ was on the advance, encouraged by resil-ient republicanism, striking economic progress, and a more profound nation-hood. "I really believe," he wrote in his final years, "that the world, on the whole, is getting better" (Hodge, 566).

Bibliography. Hodge, Archibald Alexander. *Life of Charles Hodge.* New York: Charles Scribner's Sons, 1880. Stewart, John W., and James H. Moorhead, eds. *Charles Hodge Revis-ited: A Critical Appraisal of His Life and Work.* Grand Rapids, MI: William B. Eerdmans, 2002.

Richard J. Carwardine

HOLLAND, HENRY SCOTT (1847–1918). Holland was an Anglican cleric, theolo-gian, and social commentator active in the latter part of the nineteenth and the early twentieth centuries. He is generally recalled as a leading pioneer of modern Christian Socialism.

Originally a university lecturer in phi-losophy, Henry Scott Holland began his Christian social witness in the early 1870s when he joined the settlement movement in London. In 1884, he was appointed to the canonry of St. Paul's, where he made a reputation as a cogent social critic as well as the leader of the group of young

Anglican theologians who wrote the controversial manifesto of modernist biblical theory, *Lux Mundi* (1889). This book developed the so-called Incarnationalist or sacramental socialist case for social reform. Supporters, claiming that God's incarnation in the human Christ had made the church a partaker of Christ's ethical perfection, nevertheless emphasized that the church could remain true to its redeemed nature only if it corporately ushered in a world of human cooperation, fellowship, and equity. With Holland as one of the founders and early leaders, the Christian Social Union became the main organization of such sacramental socialist advocacy. Holland edited its periodical *Commonwealth* from 1896 to his death in 1918.

In 1910 Holland was transferred to the canonry of Christ Church, Oxford, and elected as the Regius Professor of Divinity at the University of Oxford. There, together with his close friend and collaborator **Charles Gore,** he did probably more than anyone else to convert the younger academic generation of Anglicans to Christian Socialist views. He published few systematic theological or political writings but did take a key part in many of the political and ecclesiastical controversies of the 1910s, making a name for himself as a critic of laissez-faire capitalism, a supporter of the organized labor movement, and a pioneering publicist for a statutory minimum wage and for unemployment compensation.

Although Holland called himself a socialist, he was a disbeliever in the state ownership of the means of production and a consistent critic of all materialist theories of life and society. Originally a student and disciple of the Idealist philosopher T. H. Green, his social thought was characterized by the desire to infuse capital and organized labor alike with a moral vision of cooperation and to wean both away from the pursuit of only material gains.

Like Green, Holland wanted to employ a very strong state to foster this kind of ethical social cooperation.

Holland never aspired to public political leadership, but his impact was felt behind the scenes of the Church of England. There he helped to reshape the church's social teaching and make it into that major promoter of radical social reform that it continued to be for decades after his death.

Bibliography. Heidt, John H. "The Social Theology of Henry Scott Holland." DPhil thesis, University of Oxford, 1975. Paget, Stephen. *Henry Scott Holland, Memoir and Letters.* New York: E. P. Dutton, 1921.

Markku Ruotsila

HONG, XIUQUAN (1814–1864). Hong was leader of the Taiping Uprising (1851–1864), a movement that sought to overthrow the Qing dynasty and establish a "Heavenly Kingdom of Great Peace" *(Taiping Tianguo)* in China.

Hong's early life made him a marginal figure in Chinese society. Born into a farming family in Hua County, Guangdong Province, he was from the Hakka minority ("guest peoples" who were said to have emigrated southward from north China). Frustrated by his failures in the government examination, Hong had visions of ascending to heaven and being anointed by God to exterminate "demons" on earth. Influenced by a Christian tract entitled "Good Words for Exhorting the Age," written by the evangelist Liang Fa (1789–1855), Hong believed himself to be the son of God, the younger brother of Jesus.

Hong went to Canton in 1847 and studied the Bible with Isaacher Roberts, an American Southern Baptist missionary. Later that year, Hong left Canton and joined one of his followers, who had founded the Society of God Worshipers in Guangxi Province. The society was a militarized league of religious congregations. Proselytizing among Hakkas and mountain tribes, Hong required his followers to attend Christian ceremonies, convinced them to cut their queues and let their hair grow, and segregated women into a separate camp run by female officers. These actions aroused state suspicion, and in 1850, the Qing government decided to suppress the movement. On January 11, 1851, Hong gathered his God Worshipers and declared himself the heavenly king of the Taiping Tianguo. Forced out of their base by larger government forces, the Taipings fought northwards to central China. They captured Nanjing in March 1853 and renamed it "Heavenly Capital."

Drawing on Hong's revelation and his interpretation of the Bible, the Taipings propagated the universal brotherhood and sisterhood under one true and only God. They banned opium smoking, foot binding, prostitution, dancing, and alcohol consumption. Women were to be treated as equals of men and were permitted to hold office, fight in the army, and take the government examinations. Civil service examinations were based on Christian rather than Confucian principles. More remarkable was the Taiping land reform, which divided all land among families of the Taipings and their supporters according to family size, with men and women receiving equal shares. Factional struggles among the leaders and lack of support from the West, however, undermined the Taiping domination of central China. In 1864, the Qing troops stormed into Nanjing and crashed the uprising. Hong Xiuquan died in the siege, and most of his followers were killed.

Bibliography. Spence, Jonathan D. *God's Chinese Son: The Taiping Heavenly Kingdom of Hong Xiuquan.* New York: W. W. Norton, 1996.

Joseph Tse-Hei Lee

HOSSU, IULIU (1885–1970). Hossu was the leading churchman and spokesman of the Romanian Uniate Church until its suppression by the communists in 1948. Owing their spiritual allegiance to Rome, while adhering to the Eastern Christian rite, the Uniates had been at the forefront of efforts to unify the Romanian-speaking lands since the national awakening in the eighteenth century. Because they supported Western values, however, Moscow considered their suppression an imperative task when it imposed its control on Romania after 1945.

Hossu received a doctorate in theology in 1910 after six years of study at the Vatican. He was appointed a bishop in 1917 and, in December 1918, he read the declaration of unity at the mass gathering in Blaj, the spiritual capital of the Romanian Uniates. This signified the transfer of the province of Transylvania from Hungarian to Romanian rule.

Hossu became the bishop of Cluj-Gherla in 1930, and he served in Parliament before a dictatorship was imposed in Romania in 1938. Two years later, Hungary reoccupied northwest Transylvania, and Hossu regularly interceded with the occupiers in order to shield Romanians from persecution.

The 1.5 million Uniates (1930 census) were nearly all located in Transylvania where they made up at least 40 percent of the Romanian population. Once again under Romanian (and Soviet) rule from 1944, their church was suppressed in 1948, and Hossu was placed in confinement for the rest of his life. He rejected inducements from the state to restart a puppet church beholden to the communists after Romania broke free from Soviet control in the early 1960s. The imprisoned Hossu was made a cardinal by the Vatican in 1969. His deathbed words reportedly were "My struggle has ended. Yours continues."

Bibliography. Prundus, Silvestru, ed. *Cardinalul Iuliu Hossu.* Cluj, Romania: Editura Unitas, 1995.

Tom Gallagher

HROMÁDKA, JOSEF LUKL (1889–1969).
Hromádka was a Czech theologian recognized for his ecumenical efforts and his attempts to encourage Christian-Marxist dialogue following the 1948 communist takeover in Czechoslovakia until his death in 1969. His activities created controversy during the cold war, especially in the West, where some theologians and politicians felt he was a tool of the Czechoslovak communist regime. Hromádka also had critics within Czechoslovakia, who questioned whether he had made too many compromises with the communist government.

Hromádka was born in Hodslavice, Moravia. He studied theology at universities in Vienna, Basel, Heidelberg, and Aberdeen and received his doctoral degree in philosophy from Charles University in Prague in 1920. Although reared in the Lutheran Church, he spent his adult life serving the Czech Brethren Church. Theologians such as **Karl Barth,** the **Niebuhr** brothers, and **Ernst Troeltsch** influenced his thinking, but he also was shaped by the writings of Vladimir Soloviev, Nicholas Berdyayev, and Thomas G. Masaryk. Before World War II he taught at the Comenius Protestant Seminary in Prague. During the Nazi occupation of Czechoslovakia, he was guest professor at Princeton Theological Seminary. Hromádka returned to Czechoslovakia in 1947, only to face the 1948 communist takeover of the country.

Following the communist takeover, he became dean of the Comenius Protestant Seminary and was a leader in the **World Council of Churches.** Later he was a key organizer and leader of the Christian Peace Conference, founded in 1958 and headquartered in Prague. He played a leading role in promoting Christian-Marxist dialogue during the cold war. The Soviet Union awarded him the Lenin Prize for his efforts to promote world peace. However, after the Soviet invasion of Czechoslovakia in 1968, he wrote a letter to the Soviet ambassador in Prague questioning Moscow's decision to invade Czechoslovakia.

Bibliography. Hromádka, Josef. L. *Looking History in the Face.* Trans. Margaret Pater. Madras, India: Christian Literature Society, 1982.

Paul Kubricht

HUGHES, HUGH PRICE (1847–1902).
Hughes was a preacher and social reformer who led the Methodist Forward movement in late nineteenth-century Britain, which sought to infuse Methodism with **Social Gospel** principles and reshape British Nonconformity into a national force for social reform. He was born in Wales but spent his adult life in England. He founded the West London Mission of the Wesleyan Methodist Church in 1887 and served as its superintendent until his death in 1902. He was elected president of the National Council of the Evangelical Free Churches for the year 1896–1897 and also served a year's term as president of the Wesleyan Methodist Conference in 1898–1899.

Hughes's preeminence was based upon charismatic oratory, forceful journalism, and innovative ideas. By the 1880s, he was Methodism's most famous preacher and orator, drawing large audiences to his Sunday afternoon "conferences" to hear him speak on the political, social, and theological issues of the day. His ideas and opinions reached a national audience through his weekly journal, the *Methodist Times,* which he founded in 1885 and edited until his death.

The central idea of his career was "social Christianity," which was the title of his first collection of published sermons (1889). In its theological dimension, social Christianity involved a gospel of social salvation rooted in the notion that Jesus Christ was the "greatest of all social reformers" (the title of one of his sermons). Christians were called upon to defeat the forces of "pauperism, ignorance, drunkenness, lust, gambling, slavery, mammonism, war and disease."

In its practical dimension, Hughes's social Christianity took the shape of new institutions, ecclesiastical reforms, and political activism. Hughes began as a moral reformer. In the 1870s he emerged as the leading Methodist exponent of both the temperance movement and the campaign to repeal the Contagious Diseases Acts, which mandated regular examinations of prostitutes in garrison towns and their forcible detention if diseased. As editor of the weekly journal *Protest* (1876–1883), which was established to attack the acts, Hughes denounced the government for enabling immorality among the troops and for assaulting the dignity of women.

By 1884, however, Hughes had become aware that agitation on moral questions was not enough. In that year he declared himself a Christian Socialist, and he began to plan for what became the West London Mission in 1887. The mission was intended to model new methods of preaching and social service among the poor and featured a group of full-time female volunteers called the Sisters of the People under the direction of his wife, Katherine. Hughes sought a number of ecclesiastical reforms. He worked to increase the participation of the laity, especially women, at all levels of Wesleyan Methodism. He was also a great enthusiast for ecumenism. He was instrumental in founding the National Council of Evangelical Free Churches and served as its first president. He hoped that this body would become a sort of Nonconformist parliament that would give direction to greater ecclesiastical cooperation and political dynamism. Indeed, this emerging Nonconformist unity shaped a potent, if somewhat inchoate liberal constituency that supported the Liberal party and nourished the careers of many politicians, most notably David Lloyd George, who was a great admirer of his fellow Welshman Hughes.

Politics were central to Hughes's vision of social Christianity. In addition to his efforts to regulate drink, gambling, and vice, he pressed for greater investments in public services and public education, as well as support for international arbitration, labor unions and home rule for Ireland. A signal moment in Hughes's advocacy of Christian politics occurred in 1890, when he and other Nonconformist clergy successfully demanded that the Liberal party disassociate itself from Charles Stuart Parnell, the leader of the Irish Nationalist Party, after Parnell was accused of adultery. On that occasion Hughes memorably declared that "what is morally wrong can never be politically right." The term "Nonconformist conscience" was coined to describe this principle and has been a commonplace of the British political lexicon ever since.

Bibliography. Bebbington, David. *The Nonconformist Conscience.* London: George Allen & Unwin, 1982. Oldstone-Moore, Christopher. *Hugh Price Hughes: Founder of a New Methodism, Conscience of a New Nonconformity.* Cardiff: University of Wales Press, 1999.

Christopher Oldstone-Moore

HUGHES, JOHN JOSEPH (1797–1864). Hughes emigrated to the United States in 1817 and was ordained a priest of the Catholic archdiocese of Philadelphia in 1826. His rise to the episcopacy was rapid. In 1838, he was consecrated coadjutor to Bishop John Dubois of New York, succeeded Dubois as bishop in 1842, and became the first archbishop of New York in 1850. Between 1840 and 1844, Hughes's involvement in two local political events propelled him to national prominence.

Hughes triggered the first event when he challenged the control of the public educational system in New York City by the Public School Society, a sectarian Protestant organization. The twenty-one-month conflict climaxed in 1841 when the state legislature delayed passage of a bill to replace the Public School Society with elected school boards. Angered by the failure of the Democrats to support the proposed legislation, Hughes helped to organize a Catholic political party in New York City, the Carroll Hall ticket. The Catholic party got only 2,200 votes in the state election, but the Democrats lost New York City by a mere 290 votes.

The following spring the redrafted school legislation, now known as the McClay Bill, failed to secure a majority in the state senate. The Catholics reacted by organizing another ad hoc political party for the municipal elections scheduled for April 12, 1842. On April 9 the state senate passed the McClay Bill, whereupon the Catholics withdrew their slate from the municipal elections.

The legislative leaders consulted Hughes on the formulation of the McClay Bill, which was widely regarded as a Catholic victory despite the fact that it forbade public funding of religious schools. Hughes's encouragement of a Catholic political party, even as a temporary tactical device, was perhaps the most blatant example of the direct intervention of an American Catholic bishop in partisan politics.

The second event that propelled Hughes to national prominence stemmed from his opposition to nativist bigotry. In 1844, nativist riots in Philadelphia resulted in the death of fourteen people and the destruction of two Catholic churches. When the nativist leaders threatened to repeat their performance in New York City, Hughes placed armed guards around his churches and threatened to turn New York City into "a second Moscow" (i.e., to burn the city to the ground) if the municipal authorities failed to protect his churches. As a result, the peace was preserved and New York City was spared the anti-immigrant violence that occurred in other American cities.

For the next twenty years Hughes was the best-known Catholic prelate in the United States. His belligerent defense of Catholic interests led many Catholics to admire him but also led many non-Catholics to fear him and potential Catholic political power.

Bibliography. Hassard, John. *Life of the Most Reverend John Hughes, First Archbishop of New York.* New York: D. Appleton, 1866.

Thomas J. Shelley

HURLEY, DENIS EUGENE (1915–2004).

Catholic archbishop of Durban, South Africa, from 1947 to 1992, Hurley was, together with Anglican archbishop of Cape Town **Desmond Mpilo Tutu,** one of the most outspoken internationally recognized Christian opponents of apartheid.

Born in South Africa to Irish immigrants, he attended primary school on Robben Island, later to become the notorious prison in which Nelson Mandela was incarcerated for twenty-seven years. He attended St. Charles College in Pietermaritzburg,

Denis Hurley. Courtesy of the University of Notre Dame Archives

Natal, and at age seventeen entered the novitiate of the Oblates of Mary Immaculate in Ireland. He studied philosophy at the Angelicum and earned a licentiate in sacred theology from the Gregorian University in Rome, where he was ordained in 1939. Five years later he was elected to head the Oblates' scholasticate in Pietermaritzburg, and in 1947, Pope **Pius XII** appointed him bishop of Durban. At age thirty-one, he was the youngest bishop in the world. He became archbishop in 1951 when the South African hierarchy was established.

As president of the South African Catholic Bishops Conference (SACBC) from 1952 to 1961, Archbishop Hurley decried the South African National Party's policy of apartheid, or separation of the races, as "intrinsically evil," speaking out against the Group Areas Act and its associated forced removals of nonwhites, and working to block draft legislation that would have banned interracial worship. He also established the SACBC's Justice and Peace Department, serving as chair until 1997.

Hurley was frequently critical of the apartheid regime's military actions. He testified on behalf of conscientious objectors to mandatory military service in 1974, and later—following the government reprisals in the wake of the Soweto uprising and massive arrests of antiapartheid leaders in the 1980s—supported the movement to abolish military conscription. He testified in court on behalf of conscientious objector Charles Yeats, declaring South Africa's war against the Southwest African Peoples Organization (SWAPO) in Namibia unjust. In 1983, the government prosecuted the archbishop for allegedly defaming the notoriously brutal South African paramilitary *koevet* units by claiming that they had committed atrocities in Namibia. The prosecution dropped the case shortly after the trial began.

He served as SACBC president a second time from 1981 to 1987, the period when apartheid was in its death throes, most especially following the imposition of states of emergency in 1985 and 1986. He continued to serve as archbishop until 1992, when apartheid was in the process of being dismantled and the transition to democracy in South Africa was well underway.

Bibliography. Abraham, Garth. *The Catholic Church and Apartheid: The Response of the Catholic Church in South Africa to the First Decade of Nationalist Party Rule 1948–1957.* Johannesburg: Ravan Press, 1990. Page, John. "A 'Giant' of the Church and South Africa." *National Catholic Reporter* 40 (February 2004). *Trefoil: The South African Catholic Quarterly.* Special edition, June 2004.

Nicholas M. Creary

I

ILIODOR. *See* Trufanoff, Sergei Mikhailovich

IRELAND, JOHN (1838–1918). Ireland emigrated to the United States with his parents in 1848. Ordained a priest of the Diocese of St. Paul on December 22, 1861, he was consecrated coadjutor bishop of St. Paul in 1875 and succeeded to the see in 1884, becoming the first archbishop of St. Paul on May 4, 1888.

As one of the leading figures in the Americanist, or liberal, wing of the American hierarchy, Ireland supported such progressive causes as the labor movement, civil rights for African Americans, public education, the temperance movement, and the establishment of the Catholic University of America. Unfortunately, as a result of his desire to make Catholicism appear thoroughly American, he displayed marked insensitivity to the language concerns and religious culture of German and Slavic Catholic immigrants, especially the Eastern-Rite Ukrainian and Ruthenian Catholics.

Ireland's service as a chaplain with the Fifth Minnesota Infantry Regiment for nine months during the Civil War cemented a lifelong association with the party of **Abraham Lincoln** and the Grand Army of the Republic. In the 1880s and 1890s he minimized the influence of the anti-Catholic American Protective Association within the Republican Party. His intervention in New York State politics in 1894 on behalf of the Republican Party earned him a public rebuke from Bishop Bernard McQuaid of Rochester. Ireland defended himself in Rome by saying: "I am a citizen of the nation."

Unlike most U.S. Catholic bishops, who committed themselves to creating a comprehensive parochial school system at the Third Plenary Council of Baltimore in 1884, Ireland preferred to explore some kind of cooperation between parochial and public schools. Two such experimental arrangements in his own diocese won guarded Roman approval in 1892 but proved to be ephemeral for reasons beyond his control.

In 1898, the Holy See asked Ireland to use his political connections with the White House to avert war between the United States and Spain. His last-minute intervention with President William McKinley failed to prevent the war and may have cost him the cardinal's red hat that he so much coveted. Nevertheless, after the war President Theodore Roosevelt appointed Ireland to the commission that adjudicated the dispute between the United States and the Holy See over the status of the former friars' property in the Philippines.

John Ireland. Courtesy of the University of Notre Dame Archives

The condemnation of "Americanism" by Pope **Leo XIII** in the apostolic letter *Testem Benevolentiae* of 1899 was a heavy blow to Ireland because of his identification with many of the condemned propositions, such as his positive view of the American system of separation of church and state. An ardent Francophile from his student days in France, Ireland urged French Catholics to imitate the example of American Catholics and embrace political democracy. One of his proudest moments occurred in 1900 when he served as the official American emissary to present the French people with a statue of the Marquis de Lafayette.

Bibliography. O'Connell, Marvin R. *John Ireland and the American Catholic Church*. St. Paul: Minnesota Historical Society, 1988.

Thomas J. Shelley

IRON GUARD (ROMANIA). The League of the Archangel Michael, better known by the title of its political section, the Iron Guard, headed a backlash in Romania against Western values and political arrangements in the 1930s. It purveyed conspiracies, prejudices, and Orthodox sentiments, many of which had originated in Russia.

Despite being suppressed in 1940, it greatly influenced the communist regime when it entered a long nationalist phase under Nicolae Ceausescu from 1965 until his overthrow in 1989. The greatly enlarged Romania that emerged from the First World War provided the background for the emergence of a movement that wished to remove the country from the liberal and Western-leaning path it had been on for nearly a century. The Iron Guard capitalized on the anti-Semitism then widespread among lower-middle-class Romanians, who were finding it difficult to obtain a secure footing in the labor market. Jews were depicted as the mortal enemies of Romania because of their perceived identification with anti-Christian communism as well as liberal democracy. Founded on June 24, 1927, the Iron Guard mobilized alarming support from the early 1930s onwards without assistance from the fascist powers. Its leader, Corneliu Zelea Codreanu (1899–1938), a law graduate from the University of Iasi, built up a following among young graduates attracted by his call to cleanse the country of allegedly alien and urban influences. He benefited from the strong appeal of thinkers like Nichfor Crainic and Nae Ionescu, who claimed to promote an essentially Romanian spirituality shaped by the values of the Orthodox Church. The Iron Guard acquired a mass following in the 1930s when Romania was devastated by the great depression. Perhaps as many as one-fifth of Romania's ten thousand Orthodox clergy belonged to it. The Iron Guard provided social mobilization and dynamic leadership lacking in Orthodox Christianity.

Green-shirted young fascists, Romania's Iron Guard, standing side by side with tradition-ally dressed men in the Place de Minai Viteazu in Bucharest, 1940. © Getty Images

When the Iron Guard made striking gains in the January 1938 election (the last free one seen in Romania until the 1990s), King Carol II imposed a royal dictatorship, suppressed the Iron Guard, and had Codreanu murdered. Following Carol II's abdication in September 1940, the Iron Guard briefly shared power with General Ion Antonescu until it was forced underground following a failed coup in January 1941. Many Guardists rose in the professions during the latter stages of communist rule in Romania and contributed to the defiant nationalism that remained a disturbing feature of public life in the country after the end of the cold war.

Bibliography. Gallagher, Tom. *Romania After Communism: Distrusting Democracy.* London: Hurst, 2003. Veiga, Francisco. *Istoria Garzii de Fier 1919–1941: Mistica ultranacio-nalismului.* Bucharest: Humanitas, 1993.

Tom Gallagher

ITALIAN CATHOLIC ACTION (AZIONE CATTOLICA ITALIANA). Italian Catholic Action (ACI) is the chief lay organization of Catholic children, women, and men. Early forms of lay mobilization appeared in **Cesare Taparelli d'Azeglio**'s *Amicizie Cattoliche,* based in Piedmont between 1820 and its dissolution in 1827 (recalling an earlier Piedmontese version established in 1775).

Italy's nineteenth-century national unification (the *Risorgimento*) presented many challenges to the Catholic Church, particularly the Holy See and the lands that it directly controlled. While some Catholic thinkers, such as **Cesare Balbo** and **Vincenzo Gioberti,** urged a significant papal role for the new nation; the creation of the Italian Kingdom between 1859 and 1870 instead resulted in the extinction of the Papal States. Many Catholics consequently rallied to defend their church and its traditional privileges.

The first important undertaking was the creation of the Society of Italian Catholic Youth, founded in Bologna on June 29, 1867, by Count Mario Fani and Giovanni Acquaderni, a lawyer. The organization spread quickly and received the blessing of Pope **Pius IX** in his 1868 letter, *Dum filii Belial.* In parallel developments, a broad-based lay movement, the *Opere dei Congressi,* formed under Acquaderni in 1875, and the Catholic intellectual **Giuseppe Toniolo** established the Catholic Union for Social Studies (Unione Cattolica per gli Studi Sociali) in 1889. Pope **Pius X** reorganized the lay Catholic movement in 1904, ending the Opere, which had been too independent for his liking. Nevertheless, with his 1905 encyclical, *Fermo proposito,* he aimed to "reintroduce Jesus Christ in the family, in school and in society." As a result, in March 1906, along with Catholic Youth (*Gioventù cattolica*), three unions formed for the adult laity—a popular one under Toniolo, an electoral one under Filippo Tolli, and an economic-social one under Stanislao Medolago Albani. In 1909 Pius X approved the addition of a Women's Union, headed by Maria Cristina Giustiniani-Bandini, and **Pius XI** then established a Catholic Men's Federation in 1922.

Pius XI was closely identified with Catholic Action, particularly as a force of lay Catholics during the Fascist regime of Benito Mussolini. Pius entrusted his secretary of state, **Pietro Gasparri,** to restructure the organizations and created a Central Junta of Italian Catholic Action, chaired by Luigi Colombo, an old Milanese friend of the pope, which sat for the first time in December 1922. The following October the reorganized society was divided into six groups: for adult men and women, boys and girls, and male and female university students. Many other units, for small children, university graduates, and workers, were added later.

When the Lateran Accords (1929) between the church and the Italian government established the Vatican City State and sanctioned Catholicism as the state religion, the ACI was allowed to function as an apolitical and purely religious entity, although confrontations, often over education, soon marred the relationship between church and state. Open fighting broke out in 1931, and the Fascists briefly suspended Catholic Youth activity, prompting Pius to issue his encyclical *Non abbiamo bisogno* (1931), which criticized the regime. An alternative Catholic idea to Mussolini's dictatorship, moreover, informally developed during the 1930s within the ACI's male university federation, the FUCI.

When Mussolini's government collapsed in 1943, Catholic Action developed a more openly political role. Under the energetic leadership of **Luigi Gedda,** the organization existed in a strange relationship with Italy's new **Christian Democracy** (DC). The two collaborated successfully for the crucial cold war 1948 elections that witnessed the defeat of the left-wing alliance. Gedda organized and led the *Comitati civici* (Civic Committees), which were crucial to the Christian Democratic victory over the Communists and Socialists. By the early 1950s, however, Gedda's ACI and *Comitati civici* were positioning to replace the DC and assume the political leadership of Italian Catholics. Pope **Pius XII,** Gedda and factions of the Jesuit review *Civiltà cattolica* were concerned that, under **Alcide De Gasperi**'s direction, the Christian Democracy had drifted too far to the political left. Using the aged Catholic leader,

Luigi Sturzo as a cover, Gedda and his allies prepared to form a right-wing alternative to the DC. While it finished in failure in 1952, this so-called Operation Sturzo ended the golden age of Catholic Action political activity.

After Pius's death, Gedda relinquished the Catholic Action leadership in 1959 to the more moderate Agostino Maltarello, who in turn was replaced in 1964 by Vittorio Bachelet. The two post-Gedda decades were ones of ACI retrenchment; its membership dwindled from over three million at the beginning of the 1960s to about 800,000 in the mid-seventies. In 1969 more modest statutes were adopted that reflected Maltarello and Bachelet's less political and more spiritual orientations. Secularization and the consumer culture have taken their toll on Italian Catholic Action, which, in 2005, has declined to between 300,000 and 400,000 members.

Bibliography. Casella, Mario. *L'Azione cattolica nell'Italia contemporanea (1919–1969).* Rome: A.V.E., 1992. De Antonellis, Giacomo. *Storia dell'azione cattolica, dal 1867 a oggi.* Milan: Rizzoli, 1987.

Roy P. Domenico

ITALIAN POPULAR PARTY (PARTITO POPOLARE ITALIANO). The Partito Popolare Italiano (PPI, 1919–1926) is an Italian political party of Catholic inspiration. After the unification of Italy, the Holy See forbade Catholics from participating in Italian national politics by the *Non expedit* decree, because of the so-called Roman Question. But Catholics organized charitable, social, intellectual and youth groups and newspapers. Under the influence of **Leo XIII**'s social encyclical *Rerum novarum,* trade union and peasant cooperative organizations sprang up as well. By 1900, a reforming Christian Democratic group led by two priests, **Romolo Murri** and **Luigi Sturzo,** had emerged as a strong influence inside the entire Italian Catholic movement.

At a local electoral level, Catholics cooperated with liberal conservatives in "clerico-moderate" electoral alliances against radicals and socialists, who threatened their common interests. The rise of an anarchist/Marxist movement dominated working-class agitation in the 1880s and 1890s. In particular, the Italian Socialist Party, which entered the parliamentary arena, persuaded Pius X to relax the *Non expedit* in 1905. Then in1913, the Giolitti-Gentiloni Pact ensured the election of twenty-nine Catholic deputies to the Italian parliament and buttressed the liberal-conservative majority against a high tide of Socialist votes in the first elections to be held under virtual adult male universal suffrage.

The emergence of the PPI was partly a result of this development but also an effect of the First World War. **Woodrow Wilson**'s Fourteen Points led to demands for democratic reform in Italy, and with the consequent introduction of proportional representation in 1919, Fr. Sturzo believed that only a mass party of Catholic inspiration could compete with the Socialists. The Vatican helped by abolishing the *Non expedit* altogether. The PPI attracted support from all the prewar Catholic deputies, a dozen Catholic senators, the entire Catholic press, and a vast network of Catholic organizations, and in the November elections of 1919 it won 20 percent of the votes and one hundred out of the five hundred seats in the lower house of Parliament, the Chamber of Deputies. Its support was concentrated in the "white" provinces of northeastern Italy and Le Marche, and the PPI electorate was characterized by the strong support of the peasantry and lower-middle class, with a smattering of support from the intelligentsia and upper class.

The party suffered from three serious weaknesses. First, it was regarded with diffidence in the Vatican on account of its declaration of "aconfessionality," and for the lack of attention it gave to the Roman Question. Secondly, it was a very heterogeneous movement representing at one extreme landless laborers of the Po Valley and large landowners and bankers at the other. On the left, peasant leader Guido Miglioli had wanted to call the PPI the Party of Catholic Workers. On the center-right was a group of clerico-moderate notables, and further to the right there was an intransigent faction centred around Fr **Agostino Gemelli,** a friend of **Pius XI.** Finally, the fact that Luigi Sturzo, who dominated the Christian Democratic center, was prevented by the ecclesiastical authorities from sitting in Parliament because he was a priest, posed a serious problem for the party.

Given its size, parliamentary government in Italy could not function without PPI participation, but it had an unhappy experience of coalition government: the demands of a modern mass party with a fixed program did not square with the traditional transformist tactics of a succession of liberal-conservative prime ministers—Francesco Saverio Nitti, Giovanni Giolitti, and Ivanoe Bonomi. On the other hand, in the context of the "red two years," spontaneous working-class militancy manifested itself in the form of strikes, bread riots, acts of violence by individuals and groups and ultimately the occupation of the factories in the summer of 1920. As a result, the party was increasingly censured by the Vatican and local hierarchy for refusing to enter blindly into cleric-moderate alliances with liberal-conservative forces in order to prevent the Socialist Party from triumphing at the polls.

The violent Fascist reaction against working-class militancy, especially in the countryside, had an impact upon government at a national level, and it became harder and harder to construct durable and effective coalitions to tackle Italy's problems. The king called upon the PPI to assume the leadership of the government on three occasions, but each time, the parliamentary leader of the party, **Filippo Meda,** declined the responsibilities of the premiership. Sturzo would not have hesitated.

The PPI felt obliged to enter Benito Mussolini's coalition government of November 1922, only to insist upon merely "conditional" support the following year, whereupon Mussolini evicted the PPI ministers. In the summer of 1923, the party split over the Acerbo electoral law, and in June 1924, during the Matteotti Crisis, it was publicly forbidden by Pius XI from entering into a coalition with the Reformist Socialists, which was the last remaining hope of overthrowing Mussolini and Fascism. In 1926, the PPI was dissolved along with the other antifascist parties, and its leaders went into exile.

Bibliography. Molony J. N. *The Emergence of Political Catholicism in Italy.* London: C. Helm, 1977. Pollard, J. F. "Italy." In *Political Catholicism in Europe, 1918–1965,* ed. T. Buchanan and M. Conway. Oxford: Clarendon Press, 1996.

John F. Pollard

IZQUIERDA CRISTIANA. *See* Christian Left Party

J

JACKSON, JESSE LOUIS (b. 1941). Jackson strongly influenced the African American community as well as national politics and race relations as a minister, as founder of Operation PUSH-Excel and the National Rainbow Coalition, and as a two-time candidate for president of the United States. Jackson's political engagement derived from his religious ideology, a "gospel populism" that mandated grassroots political involvement guided by Christian morality as the means for improving African Americans' situation and redeeming America and the world.

After graduating from North Carolina Agricultural and Technical State College in 1964, Jackson attended the Chicago Theological Seminary. Although he left the seminary six months prior to receiving a degree, Jackson was ordained in the Fellowship Missionary Baptist Church in Chicago in 1968. While at seminary, Jackson distanced himself from civil rights activities, but his interest revived when he participated in the historic civil rights march in Selma, Alabama, in 1965 and met **Martin Luther King, Jr.**, president of the **Southern Christian Leadership Conference** (SCLC). Jackson identified with King's philosophy of nonviolent resistance and his vision of the active moral reconstruction of America. For Jackson, King also represented the model for a minister's social responsibility.

Jackson's passion for civil rights led him to embrace the SCLC as an opportunity to fulfill his leadership ambitions and to utilize the free-form black evangelicalism he had begun developing as a youth in his hometown church in Greenville, South Carolina. He left the seminary in 1966 to head the Chicago branch of Operation Breadbasket, a group committed to improving the economic situation of the local African American community. As head of this organization Jackson successfully pressured several large Chicago corporations into hiring more African Americans, an achievement that garnered him much local fame. Despite friction between himself and SCLC leadership after King's assassination, Jackson remained with the SCLC and continued to run Operation Breadbasket under what he called "the Kingdom Theory," a plan of black economic self-sufficiency similar to the economic black nationalism espoused by the Nation of Islam. By 1971 Jackson left the SCLC to pursue a national leadership position and formed Operation PUSH (People United to Serve Humanity), claiming King's mantle of moral leadership as his own.

Operation PUSH linked economic empowerment and electoral activity by mobilizing black voters to support black candidates, most notably in the reelection of Carl Stokes as mayor of Cleveland. PUSH weekly prayer meetings attracted large, enthusiastic crowds, and Jackson's influence and celebrity grew rapidly. Although PUSH's motto, "I am Somebody," resonated somewhat with the more militant spirit of black power and black nationalism, Jackson advocated political action over militant activism and effectively crafted an appeal to both radicals and conservatives. In 1977, with a federal grant from the Department of Health, Education and Welfare, Jackson expanded the aims of PUSH to include education programs and voter registration drives and renamed the program PUSH for Excellence (PUSH-Excel). Jackson, building on the success of PUSH, became increasingly involved in politics serving as a recognized voice for minorities and the poor and appeared often in the national media, supporting various political candidates.

Jackson's venture into electoral politics began in 1984 when he competed for the presidential nomination of the Democratic Party. In this campaign, Jackson attempted to become a credible political figure as well as an authentic social apostle. Moreover, Jackson saw his campaign as an effort to make Martin Luther King's dream a political reality. He declared, "This ain't no ordinary campaign; it's about finding the light!" During the campaign Jackson emphasized his interest in the situation of America's poor and forged around his black base of support a "rainbow coalition" committed to biracial political cooperation, resulting in a populist social protest movement that assumed electoral form. Lacking both an experienced national organization and the funds to operate it, Jackson's campaign failed, although he won more delegates (384) than anyone expected. In 1986, Jackson institutionalized his rhetoric by founding the National Rainbow Coalition, a popular front political organization, and sought the Democratic nomination again in 1988. Although he lost this bid as well, he fared

Jesse Jackson. Courtesy of the Library of Congress

much better than in 1984, winning primaries in Alaska and Delaware and finishing second in twenty-three other states. Despite Jackson's failure to secure the Democratic nomination, his attempts were politically significant. Through his campaigns and because of their unique religious character, Jackson mobilized unprecedented black political participation, inspired other blacks to seek political office, opened the way for future presidential challenges, and nationalized many social and racial issues.

Following his presidential bids Jackson returned to the more comfortable role of social evangelist but did not altogether abandon politics. In 1989 he served as a "statehood senator," lobbying for the statehood of the District of Columbia. Jackson also resumed his role as an unaligned diplomat as a means of extending his moral vision to a global congregation. In 1991, he secured the release of hundreds of hostages held by Iraqi president Saddam Hussein and three American members of United Nations peacekeeping forces in Yugoslavia in 1999. Jackson traveled to Israel in 1994, at the request of both the Israelis and the Palestinians, to apply the principles of nonviolent moral witness to the region's disputes.

Jesse Jackson's gospel populism, primarily because of its grounding in black Christianity, resonated with both Southern blacks and those in Northern urban ghettoes. His effortless integration of biblical allusion and analogy into his political rhetoric further endeared him to his ever-growing constituency, black and white. Moreover, Jackson's adoption of Martin Luther King's moral vision enabled him to become a dominant African American political and religious figure, a position he maintains at the beginning of the twenty-first century.

Bibliography. Frady, Marshall. *Jesse: The Life and Pilgrimage of Jesse Jackson.* New York: Random House, 1996. House, Ernest R. *Jesse Jackson and the Politics of Charisma: The Rise and Fall of the PUSH/Excel Program.* Boulder, CO: Westview Press, 1988. Reed, Adolph, Jr. *The Jesse Jackson Phenomenon: The Crisis of Purpose in Afro-American Politics.* New Haven, CT: Yale University Press, 1986.

William L. Glankler

JEUNESSE OUVRIÈRE CHRETIENNE. *See* Young Christian Workers

JOHN XXIII [ANGELO GIUSEPPE RONCALLI] (1881–1963). A pivotal pope from his coronation in 1958 until his death five years later, John XXIII began life as Angelo Roncalli, born to a peasant family at Sotto il Monte near Bergamo, Italy. He entered the diocesan seminary at the age of twelve and after ordination in Rome was appointed secretary to the bishop of Bergamo, Count Giacomo Radini-Tedeschi, a forward-looking, socially aware prelate who had a profound influence on Roncalli.

As a young priest Roncalli embarked on his chief scholarly work, *Charles Borromeo's Visitations to Bergamo.* He taught in the seminary and served as a chaplain in the Italian army during World War I. He then moved to Rome (1921) as national director of the Society for the Propagation of the Faith. Roncalli was an ardent supporter of Don **Luigi Sturzo**'s Christian Democratic **Italian Popular Party** (PPI) and lamented its demise at the hands of **Pius XI** and Mussolini.

In 1934 Roncalli was made archbishop and posted as apostolic delegate to Bulgaria and its tiny community of Latin and Slav Catholics. There he had his ecumenical apprenticeship in opening up dialogue with the Bulgarian Orthodox Church. Moved to Istanbul as apostolic delegate to Turkey and Greece, he had to contend with the antireligious reforms of Kemal Atatürk's secularized republic while he cultivated better relations with the Greek Orthodox. During the Second World War he had to cope with the thick and heavy intrigue of neutral Istanbul. He ministered to troops of both sides and administered food relief while also saving thousands of Jews in exit to Palestine—an effort recognized and highly commended by Dublin's ex-chief rabbi, Yitzhak HaLevi Herzog.

In 1944 after twenty years in the East, Roncalli was appointed papal nuncio to France at age sixty-three. He adroitly dealt with the problem of those bishops who had collaborated with the Vichy regime. He also dealt sensitively with the "worker priests," those who had taken up factory work to evangelize the dechristianized workers, although the initiative troubled his sense of tradition. However, he formed a close friendship with Cardinal Suhard, the innovative archbishop of Paris, who inspired the priest-worker movement. Suhard urged the need for the church to learn from the modern world in a dialogue with it. His influence on Roncalli was substantial. At the same time he managed to evade the issue caused by a number of French theologians who were under fire from the Vatican. The influence of their historical approach to theology, nevertheless, is quite discernible in Pope John's opening address to the Second Vatican Council.

Made cardinal and patriarch of Venice in 1953, Roncalli made a great hit with his jovial style and pastoral zeal, but he infuriated right-wing Italian Catholics when he welcomed the delegates of the Italian Socialist Party to the city in 1957. He was elected pope in 1958 after a three-day conclave and took the name John XXIII. Many expected him to be an amiable transition pope, and he astonished everyone by calling an ecumenical council. At the solemn opening he delivered one of the most remarkable addresses in the entire history of the church. In subtle but unmistakable language he disassociated himself from the Roman Curia's bureaucratic, narrow, and defensive views and urged the bishops to undertake an updating (*aggiornamento*) of the church, using a pastoral approach with the ultimate goal of unity of all Christians. His death occurred before the second of the four sessions that were held between 1962 and 1965.

John made his own contributions to the social doctrine of the church in two major encyclicals. In *Mater et magistra,* he pointed to the enormous gap between the rich and the poor nations and emphasized the responsibility of the richer nations to aid the poor ones. He also dealt with such concerns as the rights and duties of capital and labor, and problems of agriculture. He also espoused the welfare-state model of society and upheld the rights of labor.

Pacem in terris also received a tremendous hearing for its message focused on the rights and duties of humans, women, and colonial peoples, and the evils of racism and condemnation of the arms race. John continued these themes in prayers for a more effective United Nations, and in the Cuban missile crisis of 1962, when he publicly urged caution on the leaders of the United States and the Soviet Union.

Bibliography. Hebblethwaite, Peter. *Pope John XXIII, Shepherd of the Modern World.* New York: Doubleday, 1987. Pope John XXIII. *Journal of a Soul.* London: Geoffrey Chapman, 1965.

Thomas Bokenkotter

JOHN PAUL II [KAROL WOJTYLA] (1920–2005). John Paul II, born Karol Wojtyla in Wadowice, Poland, served as pope of the Roman Catholic Church from 1978 to 2005. In a long and eventful life, he experienced and engaged the century's two most notorious totalitarian regimes; shaped and developed Catholic teaching on politics, economics, society, and culture; and made his influence felt not only in his native Poland, but across the globe.

From 1939 to 1945, Wojtyla endured the Nazi German occupation of Poland, where he was forced to work in a quarry and chemical plant. He supported the Polish cultural resistance through the underground theater and entered the secret seminary in Krakow in response to a priestly vocation. These experiences, along with his Catholic faith, helped shape his views on human dignity, the evils of totalitarianism, workers' rights, and the primacy and power of culture, themes that would run through his life's work as priest, professor, and pope.

At war's end, Wojtyla saw Poland forcibly incorporated into the Soviet empire. He spent the next three decades serving the Catholic Church under the Communist regime. During this period, he was a key player in efforts by Poles to carve out a space for themselves in accordance with a vision of reality that challenged Communist ideology on religious, moral, cultural, national, and social grounds. Wojtyla lectured on social ethics as professor of philosophy at the Catholic University in Lublin, wrote important works on moral theology, and advanced in his ecclesial career from priest (1946) to bishop (1958) to archbishop (1964) to cardinal (1967). He was a key participant in the Second Vatican Council, where his personalist views on religious freedom and human dignity helped prepare the groundwork for a renewed Catholic engagement with the modern world. In Poland, Wojtyla engaged in dialogue with non-Catholic intellectuals, helping facilitate cooperation among Poles looking for political change and a life of dignity.

On October 16, 1978, Wojtyla was elected Pope John Paul II. This had an enormous impact on Poland and over the course of the 1980s played a pivotal role in undermining Soviet and Communist authority there. John Paul's position, the greatest ever held by a Pole, boosted the patriotism and confidence of his compatriots. His immense personal charisma, athletic vigor, and unique popularity with both intellectuals and the common people enhanced his widespread appeal. Not a distant Italian bureaucrat who understood little of life under Communism, John Paul

was a Pole who knew firsthand the hopes and fears, challenges and temptations of life under a totalitarian regime. His election brought world attention to Poland, where a worsening economy, growing worker unrest, and burgeoning dissident movement were already giving the Communist regime more than it could handle. His pilgrimage to his native land in June 1979, with its message of human rights and encouragement to Poles to "Be not afraid," helped plant the seeds that grew into the Solidarity movement, a massive patriotic Catholic-inspired workers movement founded in 1980. John Paul helped the church play a key role in Poland's dramatic political evolution away from Communism. Following a course dating from the 1950s, the church in Poland defended human rights and advocated reforms while simultaneously denouncing violent resistance and urging societal peace, thereby winning both popularity with the population and grudging recognition by a regime that needed the church's cooperation. In the 1980s, John Paul checked Communist efforts to co-opt the church, keeping Polish Catholicism solidly on the side of forces for constructive change.

Underlying John Paul's approach to Poland, and indeed to the world as a whole, was his vision of Catholic social doctrine. In a series of encyclical letters, most significantly *Centesimus annus* (1991), he laid out a position on social-economic policy, human rights, development, and other pressing questions. He reaffirmed and reapplied the inherited Catholic principles of solidarity (concern for the least among us) and subsidiarity (that this concern is best addressed through means closest to those affected, i.e., local and private, not distant and governmental). He argued that Marxism's chief error was anthropological—an erroneous understanding of humankind (e.g., deterministic denial of his freedom; utopian

Pope John Paul II. Courtesy of the Library of Congress

failure to recognize the effects of original sin; denial of human dignity along with its foundation, God). He denounced attempts to adulterate Christianity with Marxism, such as liberation theology in the developing world, or the pro-government organizations of "progressive clergy" set up by Communist regimes. Perhaps most significantly, John Paul departed from a decades-long Catholic search for a "third way" between communism and capitalism by affirming the superiority of the free-market economy, while warning that it could only function properly within a just legal, moral, and cultural framework.

In still other ways, John Paul influenced the times in which he lived. He confirmed and expanded Catholicism's global nature through the beatification or canonization of hundreds of saints, most from the non-Western world. He cooperated with Islamic states at UN conferences against Western efforts to use financial pressures to impose morally permissive values on the developing world. He traveled extensively, visiting a variety of regimes and "speaking truth to power" as the situation required—denouncing the death penalty in the United States, the Mafia in Sicily, and violations of human rights in Cuba. He issued encyclicals that forcefully defended truth against relativism (*Veritatis splendor*), championed the right to life (*Evangelium vitae*), sought reconciliation among Christians (*Ut unum sint*), and elaborated on the dignity of work (*Laborem exercens*).

John Paul II was one of the dominant intellectual and moral figures of his time. By his own admission, he regarded his pontificate as destined to bring the church and the world across the threshold of the third millennium, an event he welcomed not with apprehensions about the coming of the year 2000, but with the confident hope that the church and world were entering a springtime of Christian evangelization. Though suffering from a crippling disease during his later years, he continued to preach, teach, and travel, bringing to a world anxious about a number of disturbing postmodern trends a message of joy and hope.

Bibliography. Buttiglione, Rocco. *Karol Wojtyla.* Grand Rapids, MI: Willian B. Eerdmans, 1997. John Paul II. *Crossing the Threshold of Hope.* New York: Alfred A. Knopf, 1994. Szulc, Tad. *Pope John Paul II: The Biography.* New York: Simon & Schuster, 1996. Weigel, George. *Witness to Hope.* New York: HarperCollins, 2001.

James Ramon Felak

JONES, ROBERT "BOB" (1883–1968). Jones, evangelist and founder of Bob Jones College, was born to Alex Jones and Georgia Creel Jones in southeast Alabama. Bob Jones grew up at a time when the post-Reconstruction South still visibly reeled from the Civil War and where revivalist Christianity provided both community and meaning. Raised around daily Bible reading, prayer, and regular attendance at church and revival meetings, Jones experienced his call to the ministry at age fifteen. Jones distinguished himself early with his speaking ability and began traveling the evangelistic circuit throughout Alabama. He attended Southern University (now Birmingham-Southern) from 1900 to 1903 but did not earn a degree. In 1908, while preaching a revival in Uniontown, Alabama, Jones met and married Mary Gaston Stollenwerck. Their son, Bob Jones, Jr., was born in October 1911.

Jones's fame as an evangelist spread, and he soon began receiving numerous speaking invitations. Remaining an evangelist for most of his life, Jones's most active years of preaching ranged from 1900 to 1927. Simultaneously, the nation experienced great transition as waves of southern European Roman Catholic immigrants came to urban centers of the North. These industrial urban centers claimed predominance over rural America, as the United States fought a war in Europe, and as a growing sense of intellectual crisis gripped many of the nation's churches and seminaries. The wide acceptance of Darwinism and the rise of critical biblical scholarship exacerbated this sense of crisis.

Jones's preaching reflected these anxieties. Decrying the influence of Darwin, Roman Catholics, "loose" women, and cities, Jones also actively participated in the campaign against Democratic candidate and Roman Catholic **Al Smith** in the 1928 presidential election. Jones traveled throughout the southeast attacking Smith, declaring that "the things that made America great are the very things Al Smith's religion opposes." The Smith candidacy was, in Jones' view, a "challenge to pure, old time, honest-to-God Americanism." Jones also actively opposed the 1960 Kennedy candidacy.

Jones founded Bob Jones College (BJC) in Panama City, Florida, in 1927 to combat these theological, social, and political challenges. In addition to a strident theological separatism and ironclad student life regulations, BJC also advocated a militant political conservatism. The school sponsored annual "Americanism" conferences featuring speakers such as Strom Thurmond, Billy James Hargis, and Dan Smoot. Bob Jones University awarded George Wallace with an honorary doctorate in 1964. Most famously, BJU maintained a segregationist stand. Jones referred to civil rights activists as "satanic propagandists," and the school refused to admit African Americans until 1970 and then banned interracial dating until 2000. This stance resulted in a 1983 Supreme Court decision stripping BJU of its tax exemption.

Jones served as president of the college until 1947, when his son, Bob, Jr., assumed leadership and the school acquired university status. Jones first and foremost remained an evangelist, traveling and speaking, helping found the National Association of Evangelicals in 1941, and always endeavoring, in his words, to "keep the chapel platform hot." Referring to himself as "the Founder," Jones until his death in October 1968 advocated a traditionally Southern separatist revivalism that reflected the persistent currents of the fundamentalist-modernist controversy in American religious life.

Bibliography. Dalhouse, Mark. *An Island in the Lake of Fire: Bob Jones University, Fundamentalism and the Separatist Movement.* Athens: University of Georgia Press, 1996.

Mark Taylor Dalhouse

JOYNSON-HICKS, WILLIAM (1865–1932). An evangelical layman of the Church of England and a Cabinet minister, Joynson-Hicks, first Viscount Brentford, was an early twentieth-century British politician who combined evangelical Christian beliefs and Conservative politics. His major prominence dated to his service as home secretary (1924–1929), during which time he tried to implement his conservative Christian beliefs through vigorous enforcement of moral legislation and the restriction of Jewish immigration.

Joynson-Hicks was elected to the House of Commons in 1908. There he quickly established himself as a member of the Conservatives' die-hard faction, which argued to return the Conservative party to its putative roots in nationalist, imperialist, and Christian conservatism.

Appointed to the Cabinet in 1923 in a junior position, Joynson-Hicks rose to the Home Office a year later and there acquired a reputation as a puritanical guardian of public morals. A teetotaler and against gambling, he moved aggressively to employ the powers of the state to shut down nightclubs and to curb the availability of sexually explicit or unusual literature, plays, and films. Joynson-Hicks acted forcefully to restrict the immigration and naturalization of foreign-born Jews, whom he believed to form a worldwide semi-communist anti-British and anti-Christian conspiracy. In the process he gave frequent expression to economic, racialist, and religious anti-Semitic prejudices, at least some of which were grounded in his evangelical Christian beliefs and prompted by his membership in agencies dedicated to converting Jews to Christianity. He was also a forceful opponent of proposed changes in the Book of Common Prayer and, convinced that such changes would undermine popular inculcation in Protestant paradigms, he led the 1927 parliamentary effort that defeated a proposed revised prayer book.

Known as Jix, and frequently referred to as "Mussolini Minor," Joynson-Hicks was a controversial, alternately feared or admired figure whose anti-Semitic beliefs, insistence on the continued establishment of Protestant faith, and bent for vigorous moral legislation made him a particularly consistent representative of a very conservative form of evangelical Anglicanism. His embrace of the political means of effecting religious change was exceptionally pronounced throughout his public career and his evangelical convictions among the primary prompters of his politics.

Bibliography. Cesarini, David. "Joynson-Hicks and the Radical Right in England after the First World War." In *Traditions of Intolerance: Historical Perspectives on Fascism and Race Discourse in Britain*, ed. Tony Kushner and Kenneth Lunn. Manchester: Manchester University Press, 1989. Taylor, H. A. *Jix: Viscount Brentford.* London: Stanley Paul, 1933.

Markku Ruotsila

K

KAAS, LUDWIG (1881–1952). Kaas studied for the priesthood in Trier and Rome and became professor of canon law at the University of Trier in 1918. He entered Parliament for the **Center Party** (Zentrum) in 1919 and became its chief spokesperson for foreign policy, supporting Gustav Stresemann's efforts to promote reconciliation with France.

Kaas also served as personal advisor to the papal nuncio to Germany, Eugenio Pacelli, and traveled often to the Vatican to discuss how to secure recognition by the secular powers of the new Code of Canon Law adopted in 1917. A tense party congress drafted him as chair of the Center Party in 1928, because he was thought to stand above the conflicts between trade unionists and other interest groups that threatened to tear the party to pieces. Kaas then promoted **Heinrich Brüning** to parliamentary leader of his party, urged him in March 1930 to agree to form a new government, and became the closest political advisor to the German chancellor at a critical juncture. At the same time, Pacelli became the Vatican secretary of state, and Kaas found his advice more sought after than ever in Rome. The nervous strain caused by these conflicting responsibilities contributed to periodic bouts of illness, followed by lengthy periods of convalescence incommunicado in the Italian Alps.

According to the uncorroborated testimony of Brüning's memoirs, Pacelli began in August 1931 to pressure Brüning to terminate all forms of cooperation with Social Democrats and seek an understanding with the Nazi Party; there is corroboration for Brüning's related assertion that Kaas weakened markedly in his support for the chancellor's policies soon thereafter. Brüning later concluded that Kaas and Pacelli had become obsessed with concordats and subordinated all other considerations to the hope that a right-of-center parliamentary majority including the Nazis would accept certain provisions of canon law that had always provoked opposition from liberals and Social Democrats. Kaas continued nevertheless to support Brüning's course and worked closely with him to oppose his reactionary Catholic successor, Franz von Papen.

After Hitler's appointment as chancellor, Kaas soon concluded that the Nazis would inevitably suppress all other political parties. He believed, however, that Hitler would keep his promises to respect the autonomy of religious bodies and retain Catholic civil servants in office, and he offered a rosy assessment of the consequences of the Lateran Treaties between the Vatican and Fascist Italy. Over Brüning's strenuous objections, Kaas persuaded his parliamentary delegation to approve the

Enabling Act of March 23, 1933, which gave Hitler dictatorial powers. Kaas left for Rome the next day and was drawn into the negotiations for a Reich Concordat. Kaas helped to persuade the German episcopate to accept the resulting agreement, but by the time it was ratified in September 1933, Catholic organizations were experiencing a wave of violent harassment that discredited his optimistic view of Hitler's intentions. Center Party colleagues reproached Kaas bitterly for abandoning them, and he lived in Rome for the rest of his life, devoting himself to archeological research. Kaas's shortcomings are one reason why German Catholic politicians after 1945 agreed wholeheartedly with Pacelli (now Pope **Pius XII**) that priests should never again play an active role in party politics.

Bibliography. May, George. *Ludwig Kaas: Der Priester, der Politiker und der Gelehrte aus der Schule von Ulrich Stutz.* 3 vols. Amsterdam: Grüner, 1981. Morsey, Rudolf. *Der Untergang des politischen Katholizismus: Die Zentrumspartei zwischen christlichem Selbstverständnis und "Nationaler Erhebung" 1932/33.* Stuttgart, Germany: Belser, 1977.

William Patch

KAISER, JAKOB (1888–1961). A labor leader, nationalist, and committed Catholic, Kaiser is also one of the most underappreciated German Christian politicians of the twentieth century. In large part, this is due to the fact that he was on the losing side of a long-running argument with **Konrad Adenauer,** postwar Germany's first chancellor, about the nature of Christian democracy and the future of Germany. His views on social policy and his continued insistence on German reunification proved prescient. Kaiser was committed to the **Social Gospel,** to the importance of German national unity, and Germany's bridge function between East and West in Europe.

Beginning in the early years of the twentieth century, Kaiser, by trade a bookbinder, was active in the leadership of the Christian Trade Union movement. After World War I,

he actively supported the development of a comprehensive trade union coalition based not on political ideology, but on the need for an integration of workers into the social fabric of society. Kaiser was influenced by Adam Stegerwald's call for an interdenominational Christian party and developed his own idea of a participatory democracy based on social welfare.

Beginning in 1920, Kaiser was a leading member of the Rhenish **Center Party,** Germany's Catholic Party, for which he was elected to Parliament in 1933. Shortly thereafter, despite agreeing to an integration of the Christian Trade Unions into the German Labor Front, Kaiser joined the active resistance against the regime. In 1938, he was jailed for six months for treason, which did not deter him from becoming actively involved in circles planning to overthrow Hitler. He went into hiding in 1944.

After the war, Kaiser returned to politics, first through a newly integrated labor union movement, the Freie Deutsche Gewerkschaftsbund, and then through the foundation of the Christlich-Demokratische Union (CDU, **Christian Democratic Union**) in Berlin, parallel to similar foundations in the western zones of occupation. Kaiser believed the time had come to realize his vision of a socially integrated Germany by means of an interdenominational party, consisting of both Catholics and Protestants, committed in particular to the social teachings of contemporary Christianity. Kaiser argued that the best guarantee for peace and social justice in Germany was a noncapitalist economy.

Furthermore, he believed that Germany should play a particular role as bridge between East and West and thus should maintain good relations with all the occupying powers. Furthermore, as chairman of the CDU in both Berlin and the Soviet zone of occupation, Kaiser's words carried much weight in the national discussions about the future of Germany. Given Konrad Adenauer's commitment to an antisocialist, westward-oriented democracy and a free-market economy, relations between the two quickly soured. Adenauer campaigned hard to undermine Kaiser's national leadership aspirations.

In 1947, Kaiser's increasing criticism of the heavy-handed repression of political freedom in the Soviet zone led the Soviet Military Administration to depose Kaiser as leader of the CDU in the East. Kaiser now had to work within a political framework increasingly dominated by Adenauer. Although Kaiser still had much influence on the first party program of the CDU, the *Ahlener Programm,* by the time the Federal Republic of Germany was established in 1949, Kaiser's continued insistence on social justice and German unity led him to oppose Adenauer's policies. Largely for intraparty reasons, however, Adenauer appointed Kaiser minister for all-German affairs, a position he held until his ill health forced his resignation in 1957.

Until his death, Kaiser struggled within the CDU for labor rights and against what he considered to be Adenauer's sacrifice of German unity in favor of alliance with the West. While neither politician could foresee that it would take forty years to reunify Germany, Kaiser's influence caused the CDU to adopt labor and welfare policies that fundamentally changed the nature of German politics by laying the groundwork for the social market economy that grew out of the postwar economic miracle.

Bibliography. Conze, Werner, Erich Kosthorst, and Elfriede Nebgen. *Jakob Kaiser.* 4 vols. Stuttgart, Germany: W. Kohlhammer, 1969–1972. Morsey, Rudolf et al., eds. "Jakob Kaiser." In *Zeitgeschichte in Lebensbildern: Aus dem deutschen Katholizismus des 19. und 20. Jahrhunderts.* Vol. 2. Mainz, Germany: Mathias-Grunewald-Verlag, 1974.

Martin Menke

KARAMANLIS, CONSTANTINE (1907–1998). Arguably the most influential and respected politician in Greece in the second half of the twentieth century, Karamanlis belonged during his career of sixty years to successive political parties that represented the country's parliamentary conservative forces. He was prime minister from October 1955 until June 1963, and from July 1974 until April 1980. During the second period he did much to shape the present democratic system. He was then president of Greece from 1980 to 1985 and from 1990 to 1995.

As a conservative, he was naturally faithful to the Orthodox Church of Greece, though in a conventional and undemonstrative way. He accepted without question that its faith was integral to most Greeks' national identity and before 1975 followed precedent in treating the church as a virtual arm of the state. The constitution of 1952—enacted shortly after the defeat of communist-led forces in a civil war—adopted "Helleno-Christian civilization" as the ideological basis of the political system. However, the church's political role was seriously discredited by the unpopular military dictatorship of 1967–1974, which interfered extensively in church government and aggressively used Orthodox Christianity as part of its ideology.

After the dictators' ignominious downfall, Karamanlis and his colleagues recognized the need to strengthen both civil liberties and the church's autonomy through the constitution that they designed in 1975. To these ends, they deliberately weakened the relationship of church and state, although in the parliamentary debates over the constitution they were not allowed by their supporters to go as far as they originally intended. The 1975 constitution was the first in Greek history to guarantee freedom of conscience, although the practical implementation of this guarantee is even now incomplete. Karamanlis's government, led by his newly organized party, **New Democracy,** established a practice by refraining from intervention in the appointment of bishops and guaranteed that the church would be self-governing in the charter of 1977, which is still in force. After 1974, Karamanlis accepted a new spirit of independence among bishops, who have since then expressed their views on diverse issues with increasing vigor and frequency. Among their complaints against Karamanlis's government were its establishment of diplomatic relations with the Holy See and its introduction of divorce by consent.

The relationship between church and state, over which Karamanlis presided after 1974, was a confused compromise, which he recognized as unsatisfactory but seems to have accepted as politically inescapable.

Bibliography. Close, David H. *Greece since 1945.* London: Longman, 2002. Woodhouse, C. M. *Karamanlis: The Restorer of Greek Democracy.* Oxford: Clarendon Press, 1982.

David H. Close

KARAVAGGELIS, STYLIANOS [GERMANOS] (1866–1953). Karavaggelis was a Greek Orthodox metropolitan and exarch and a key figure in the struggle to assert Greek national claims in the Ottoman province of Macedonia at the beginning of the twentieth century.

Karavaggelis was born on the island of Lesbos. After his graduation from the Chalki Theological Seminary of Marmara near Constantinople, the ecumenical patriarchate in 1888 anointed him as Germanos, a deacon of the Orthodox Church. He thereafter pursued and attained a doctorate in philosophy at the University of Leipzig (1889–1891). In 1896, Germanos was elected bishop of Peran, a district of Constantinople.

The apex of his political career came when the patriarch appointed Germanos metropolitan of Kastoria, a town in Western Macedonia, in 1900. At the time, the Ottoman province of Macedonia was a hotbed of ethnic and religious strife, as the bordering states of Greece, Bulgaria, and Serbia, sensing the imminent collapse of Ottoman authority in the region, sought to establish their respective ethnic claims in the hopes of acquiring as much Macedonian territory as possible in the event of an Ottoman withdrawal.

In Kastoria, Germanos cooperated closely with a Greek officer, Pavlos Melas, in the organization of local resistance to the roving bands of Bulgarian *comitadji*, irregulars covertly armed and supplied by the Bulgarian government whose ultimate purpose was to raise the local population's Bulgarian consciousness, often using violence. Frustrated by the Greek state's initial moribund approach to the Macedonian issue, Germanos attempted to promote the Greek nationalist cause single-handedly, at one point even espousing and nurturing the growth of armed Greek bands to counter the Bulgarian challenge. Germanos's efforts to involve the Greek government in Macedonia met eventually with success, and this was, undoubtedly, his greatest political contribution to the Greek state.

At the behest of the Turkish authorities, the Holy Synod removed Germanos from Kastoria in 1907 and named him metropolitan of Amaseia, a district in the Pontus region of Asia Minor, in 1908. There, he defended the rights of the local Greek and Armenian populations, but the rising tide of Turkish nationalism eventually thwarted his efforts. Under penalty of death, Germanos fled Turkey in 1923. The patriarch thereafter appointed him Orthodox exarch to Central Europe in 1924, a title he retained until his death in 1953.

Bibliography. Karavaggelis, Germanos. *O Makedonikos Agon: Aponemoneymata.* Thessaloníki: Etairia Makedonikon Spoudon, 1959.

Kyriakos Nalmpantis

KHRAPOVITSKII, ALEKSEI [ANTONII] (1863–1936). One of the most influential Russian Orthodox prelates of the twentieth century, Khrapovitskii (Aleksei Pavlovich Khrapovitskii) was born in Novgorod province. He owed his meteoric rise to ecclesiastical leadership to noble origin (a rarity in the Russian episcopate), his elite education and outstanding performance in secular and church schools, and his connections to the capital's high society and officialdom.

After tonsure in 1885, Khrapovitskii took teaching and administrative appointments at the seminaries of Kholm (Poland), St. Petersburg, Moscow, and Kazan and at the St. Petersburg Theological Academy. He was promoted to full bishop (of Ufa) in 1900, and two years later church leaders transferred him to Volynia, hoping that Khrapovitskii's energy, erudition, and connections could counter Uniate influence in that Ukrainian province. In 1906, considered one of Russia's most politically astute churchmen and erudite theologians, he became Archbishop Antonii at the age of forty-three. His post in a borderland, however, brought him in direct contact with nationalist tensions.

During the revolutionary unrest of the last Romanov decades Khrapovitskii's monarchist views did not set him apart from the majority of the episcopate, but his distinctive forcefulness attracted the interest of rightist parties such as the Union of the Russian People, (URP) or **Black Hundreds.**

In 1905, in a letter to Boris Nikol'skii, one of the URP leaders, Khrapovitskii revealed his penchant for repression, advocating martial law across the land, the closing of three quarters of all publications, and, if necessary, an autocratic appeal to the whole population to armed self-defense and the lynching of revolutionaries (Levin, 167–68). Khrapovitskii encouraged support for the autocracy everywhere and addressed many URP meetings, referring to his sermons in private correspondence as "ultra-reactionary." In his diocese of Volynia, the Pochaev

monastery was converted to a "Black Hundred" center, publishing the inflammatory *Pochaev* leaflet and *Pochaev News*, which opposed constitutional reforms for allegedly opening the door to a Polish or Jewish yoke over Russians. In July 1908, a congress of missionaries chaired by Khrapovitskii in Kiev encouraged Orthodox missionaries to turn to monarchist-patriotic societies for help in their proselytizing work. He expected patriotic unions to support a new concept of Russian national identity that he and other conservative church leaders were elaborating. He called on rightists to subject nationalist feeling to the church's universalist teaching and to base Russian nationalism on religion rather than ethnicity and language: "Russians define themselves before all else as a religious community, as a confessional community, which includes even Georgians and Greeks who are unable even to speak the Russian language" (Antonii, 447).

Antonii's interference in social and political life was occasionally so provocative that local governors warned him to refrain from inciting a pogrom atmosphere and to censure clergy for moderate liberal views. He nevertheless exhorted state authorities to prosecute the notorious Beilis affair, a blood libel case in Ukraine. Still, his anti-Semitism was selective and tactical, as he also castigated pogroms from a Christian viewpoint. In church politics Antonii led the opposition to the more liberal metropolitan of St. Petersburg, Antonii Vadkovskii, and terrorized his subordinate priests for demanding introduction of the elective principle in church government. Besides political conviction, Khrapovitskii feared that Vadkovskii was in line to assume the patriarchal throne as soon as it was restored. In 1912 he was transferred to Kharkov and was appointed to the Russian Church's governing body, the Holy Synod in St. Petersburg.

The All-Russian Church Council of 1917–1918 promoted Archbishop Antonii to metropolitan. In the summer of 1918, the Ukrainian Church Council elected him metropolitan of Kiev and Galicia, while the episcopate in the All-Russian Church Council voted him first among three candidates to the patriarchal throne. After losing the throne to Tikhon (Bellavin), Khrapovitskii headed the Whites' High Ecclesiastical Command during the civil war. In 1920 he emigrated to Serbia and founded the Episcopal Synod of the Russian Orthodox Church Abroad (the ROCA or the so-called Karlovac Synod), progressively severing allegiance to Tikhon and his successor Sergii (Stragorodskii) for their declarations of loyalty to the Soviet regime. Still a hero to all ROCA faithful, Antonii Khrapovitskii is buried in Sremski Karlovci, near Belgrade.

Bibliography. Agursky, Mikhail. "The Jewish Problem in the Russian Religious Radical Right: The Case of Metropolitan Antonii (Khrapovitskii)." *Ostkirchliche Studien* 36 (1987): 39–44. Arkhiepiskop, Antonii. "O svobode veroispovedanii." In *Polnoe sobranie sochinenii.* 2nd. ed. Vol. 3. St. Petersburg: Universiteta, 1911. Regel'son, Lev. *Tragediia russkoi tserkvi 1917–1945 gg.* Paris: YMCA Press, 1977. Levin, S. "Materialy dlia kharakteristiki kontr-revoliutsii 1905 g. Iz perepiski Borisa Nikol'skogo s Antoniem Volynskim." *Byloe* 21 (1923): 167–68.

Argyrios K. Pisiotis

KHRIMIAN, MKRTICH (1820–1907). Khrimian was born in Ottoman Armenia. His life spanned eighty-seven years, and he was fortunate enough to avoid the Armenian Genocide of 1915, but many events during his long ministry foreshadowed that event.

During the 1850s, he worked as a teacher in the Ottoman Armenian province of Vaspurakan, where he published a journal called *Vaspurakani Atrziv* (Vaspurakan Eagle). As a priest, he worked out of a local monastery there and actively participated in one of the most dramatic changes in Armenian society.

The mid-nineteenth century saw the opening of dozens of schools in Ottoman Armenia, the decline of illiteracy, and the rise of political consciousness among Armenians in the Ottoman Empire who soon demanded basic equality and human rights. Particularly troublesome were nomadic tribesmen, who regularly raided Armenian settlements but could not be sued for torts under the Ottoman Empire's confessional court system due to their Muslim faith. Such injustice helped to trigger a dramatic shift in Armenian attitudes from quietism and acceptance of second-class status to resentment, anger, and demands for equality. These demands were fueled by an educational revolution in Armenian life, and Khrimian became a central figure in that revolution.

Khrimian was elected the Armenian patriarch of Constantinople in 1869 and tried to use his office to persuade the Ottoman government to protect its Armenian people from the nomad depredations, but Sultan Abdul Hamid II, himself born of an Armenian mother, refused to listen and in 1873 deposed Khrimian. The priest spent the next nineteen years opening schools in both Russian and Ottoman Armenia as well as fundraising and writing poetry.

His chief and everlasting contribution to the evolution of the Armenian worldview was his "iron ladle" sermon. In 1878, he was asked by the new patriarch to represent the Armenian people of the Ottoman Empire at the Congress of Berlin. He found it very hard to be taken seriously there, because he had a "ladle of paper," which represented his commission. He noted how the Montenegrin and Bulgarian delegates helped themselves to the "porridge," with their blood-dripping swords serving as "iron ladles."

His perspective on the relationship between power and the ability to secure justice continues to inform Armenian foreign policy today. Khrimian was elected catholicos and supreme patriarch of all Armenians in 1892. He had to fight Czar Nicholas II to retain the Armenian Church's property in the Russian Empire. The czar was keen on homogenizing Christianity in his domains, and the Armenian Church was an obstacle. His Holiness Mkrtich I advised the Armenian clergy of the Russian Empire to disregard the czar's decrees and engage in passive resistance. The Japanese victory over Russia led the czar to reconsider his policy of confiscating Armenian property. In recognition of his courage in defying both the czar and the sultan, the catholicos came to be known as "hayrig," or little father; he is second only to the mythical Haik as the nation's father figure.

Bibliography. Danielian, Emil. "Iron Ladle: The Historic Roots of Armenia's Tough Line on Karapakh." *Prism* 4 (27 November 1998). http://161.58.193.170/pubs/view/pri_004_023_005.htm. Grigoryan, Vardan. *The Archive of Mashtotz Matendaran: Archive of Catholicos Mkrtich Khrimian.* 1999. www.matenadaran.am/en/departments/archive/#9. Hovannisian, Richard. *Armenian Van/Vaspurakan.* Costs Mesa, CA: Mazda, 1999. Khrimian, Mkrtich. "The Paper Ladle." Trans. Father Vazken Movsessian. *Window Quarterly* 1 (2). www.sain.org/WINDOW/Documt2.txt. Papazian, Dennis. "The Armenians." 8 September 1987. www.umd.umich.edu/dept/armenian/papazian/armenia.html.

Jack V. Kalpakian

KIM SOU-HWAN, STEPHEN (b. 1922). As cardinal archbishop of Seoul, Kim Sou-hwan was a leading promoter of human rights during authoritarian rule in South Korea during the 1970s and 1980s. The now-retired archbishop of Seoul, South Korea, was born in Tae Gu in 1922. He studied philosophy at the Jesuit Sophia University in Tokyo and was ordained a priest in 1951. After serving as bishop of

Masan, Kim Sou-hwan was promoted to archbishop of Seoul in 1968 and was made a cardinal by Pope **Paul VI** in 1969.

Sou-hwan is often credited for trying to prevent the violent suppression of the pro-democracy movement in the city of Gwangju. He also maintained close relationships with labor unions and was instrumental in negotiating the end of a number of nationwide strikes. The cardinal also wrote extensively on the reforms of the Second Vatican Council and was recognized as their foremost advocate among the Asian Catholic hierarchy. After his retirement as archbishop, he continued as an outspoken advocate of human rights, the abolition of capital punishment, and the eventual unification of North and South Korea.

In 2004, he spoke publicly of the dangers of facing South Korean society not only from the increasingly polarized rhetoric surrounding North Korea's nuclear weapons program but also from an uncritically sympathetic attitude toward North Korea

Stephen Kim Sou-Hwan. Courtesy of the University of Notre Dame Archives

among South Korean youth. As a result, according to a report in the *Korean Herald,* Kim was strongly criticized by the left-wing Uri Party as an "obstacle to the people's tomorrow." In a response, the leader of the opposition Millennium Democratic Party pointed to Cardinal Kim's iconic significance in Korean society by observing, "Our society's last symbol of authority is being abused."

Bibliography. Hanson, Eric O. *Catholic Politics in China and Korea.* Maryknoll, NY: Orbis Books, 1980. So-young, Kim. "Debate Rages over Criticism of Cardinal Kim." *Korean Herald.* 3 February 2004.

Mathew N. Schmalz

KING, MARTIN LUTHER, JR. (1929–1968). King believed that Christian faith compelled sociopolitical involvement in the quest for justice. His early models and mentors shaped his ideas about how Christian love could function as a force for sociopolitical change. King became a master at using nonviolent protest, including civil disobedience, to make America's power structures reflect upon the injustices inherent within them, and, at times, make constructive change. As his focus moved from dismantling Jim Crow laws in the South to ending poverty and monopolies on power nationally, he became more radical and despairing. Nevertheless, his faith always drove his political goals, methods, choices, and actions. It also fueled his perseverance and hope.

King's maternal grandfather and father each pastored the prestigious Ebenezer Baptist Church in Atlanta, Georgia. Both were leaders within the NAACP and organized protests to win local battles against discrimination. King grew up in middle-class comfort with these examples and with constant affirmation from his church community that he was somebody special. He enrolled at Morehouse College at age fifteen. There he studied under modernist theologians who demonstrated how to blend faith and reason, make ministry relevant, and use the pulpit to propagate ideas and change. He explored how capitalism anchored an exploitive system that supported racism. He also critiqued black pastors who taught accommodation to injustice while awaiting rewards in heaven. He absorbed Henry David Thoreau's advocacy of civil disobedience. This strategy called for filling jails with just men to protest an unjust society and igniting moral revolution through individual acts of conscience. After graduation, he moved North to pursue a bachelor's degree in divinity at Crozer Seminary and a PhD at Boston University. While there, he embraced **Walter Rauschenbusch**'s idea of the **Social Gospel.** He rejected Karl Marx for condoning materialism, supporting violent methods of social change, denying human conscience, and crippling freedom. Gandhi captured King's imagination through his use of nonviolent resistance and "soul force" to impel change while redeeming one's enemy. This paralleled Jesus's sermon on the mount; Jesus also illustrated that suffering was redemptive, both for sufferer and persecutor. Friedrich Hegel's writings taught him that conflict propelled change, that social answers could be found in the synthesis of opposites, and that social prophets could serve as change agents by tapping into the zeitgeist of their times. The fact that God governed history gave King faith that righteousness would prevail.

King began his ministerial career in Montgomery, Alabama, in 1954, the year the Supreme Court declared segregated schools unconstitutional. In 1955, Rosa Parks refused to surrender her bus seat to a white person and was arrested. The NAACP launched a court case to fight the segregation statute, while several local black leaders, including King, formed the Montgomery Improvement Association to organize a bus boycott. Elected its president, King shaped the nonviolent strategy they used and articulated the spiritual basis of their motivation and methods. During the boycott, King suffered a crisis of confidence. Then one day in his kitchen, he experienced a divine presence that told him to stand up for righteousness and truth, and that God would be by his side. That experience remained a source of strength for him until his death. The boycott's success affirmed the practicality of his nonviolent strategy and was imitated around the nation.

King's articulate visible leadership transformed him into a spokesperson for the movement. In 1957, he helped create the **Southern Christian Leadership Conference** (SCLC) to organize similar protests throughout the South. He also aided others' civil rights efforts such as student sit-ins, voter registration drives, and Freedom Rides. His SCLC joined forces with local

Martin Luther King speaking at a Civil Rights March on Washington, D.C. Courtesy of the National Archives and Records Administration

organizations in a civil rights campaign in Albany, Georgia. Lessons learned from that failed endeavor were employed into one of King's greatest successes in Birmingham, Alabama, in spring 1963. King used nonviolent confrontational protest to expose the virulent racism in that town. When city official Bull Connor used police dogs and fire hoses on the demonstrators, many of them children, the media transmitted those images nationally and globally. This occurred during the peak of the cold war. America's claims of being a bastion of freedom were undercut by the hypocrisy exposed in her sanctioned racist practices. Moral outrage and public outcry, combined with cold war pressures to make claims of freedom credible, compelled President Kennedy to submit a strong civil rights bill to Congress a month later. King's "Letter from a Birmingham Jail," written during the campaign, addressed white clergymen who opposed his confrontational tactics. His response presented the Christian argument for his goals and tactics so convincingly that it drew many religious white people actively into the movement. In August, King participated in the March on Washington for Jobs and Freedom. His keynote "I have a dream" speech tied his vision of racial harmony so closely to American ideals that few white Americans could disagree with its premise, even though many resisted its practice. It aimed to build support for the Civil Rights Bill, which became law in 1964. King used similar nonviolent confrontational tactics in Selma, Alabama, to create conditions that made it politically expedient for President Johnson to press a Voting Rights Bill into law in 1965.

Race riots began in ghettos outside the South, areas left largely unchanged by previous civil rights legislation. From 1965 until his assassination, King addressed the economic and housing issues plaguing blacks in inner cities. King's Christian critique of capitalism sharpened as he called for a revolution in values, and a Bill of Rights for the poor, which would include a guaranteed income, jobs for all, and funding for ghetto schools. He tried similar tactics in Chicago that had been effective down South. Unfortunately, success was limited, and King grew frustrated. As black violence rose along with white backlash, King admitted that he had underestimated black anger and overestimated the racial goodwill of whites. He began to believe that only nonviolent civil disobedience on a massive scale—a strategy capable of stalling the system—would force government action. Therefore he planned to bring thousands of poor people to camp in Washington, D.C., in the summer of 1968 until government addressed their needs. A year earlier, King had angered the Johnson administration, as well as many civil rights leaders, for criticizing the violence, immorality, racism, and wastefulness inherent in America's war in Vietnam. When warned that this could hurt him politically, King admitted being politically stupid but morally smart by opposing the war. In the end, he said that only God's judgment mattered and that being a servant for justice on a world scale was more important than being popular, profitable, or nationalist. King was assassinated April 4, 1968, while in Memphis to aid a sanitation strike. Many consider King one of America's greatest prophets of nonviolence and social justice.

Bibliography. Ansbro, John. *Martin Luther King, Jr.: Nonviolent Strategies and Tactics for Social Change.* New York: Madison Books, 2000. Garrow, David. *Bearing the Cross: Martin Luther King Jr., and the Southern Christian Leadership Conference.* New York: Vintage Books, 1986. Oates, Stephen B. *Let the Trumpet Sound: The Life of Martin Luther King Jr.* New York: HarperPerennial, 1994.

Jill K. Gill

KINGSLEY, CHARLES (1819–1875). Kingsley was an Anglican clergyman, novelist, and founding member of the Christian Socialist movement. He studied at private schools and at King's College, London before entering Magdalene College, Cambridge, in 1838. In 1842, he was ordained to the curacy of Eversley in Hampshire, and two years later to the rectory, where he stayed for the remaining thirty-three years of his life. In 1844, he married Fanny Grenfell and they had four children.

Kingsley was one of the first churchmen to support Darwin's theories and call for reconciliation between modern science and Christian doctrine. In 1848 he was among the founders of the Christian Socialist movement, which sought to correct the evils of industrialism through measures based on Christian ethics. He participated, together with **John F. D. Maurice** and J. M. Ludlow, in publishing the newspaper *Politics for the People* (1848–49) and was among the founders of the Society for Promoting Working Men's Associations (1850–1854). As an extension of this work he contributed to the *Christian Socialist* (1850–1851), *Tracts by Christian Socialists* (1850), and *Tracts on Christian Socialism* (1850) under the pseudonym "Pastor Lot." In his novels *Yeast* (1848) and *Alton Locke* (1850), he showed sympathy with the Chartists and attempted to awaken members of his class to their responsibilities to the workers. He advocated adult education, improved sanitation, and the growth of the cooperative movement, rather than political change, for the amelioration of social problems.

Maurice and Ludlow had more powerful intellects, but in some ways Kingsley had wider influence, especially through his popular social novels, pamphlets, and polemical articles. As a preacher, his vivid language was plainspoken and uncompromising.

After 1852, he left the movement and sought influence through the writing of social and historical novels such as *Hypathia* (1853), *Westward Ho!* (1855), and *Hereward the Wake* (1866), in addition to the children's books *The Heroes* (1856) and *Water Babies* (1863). He became chaplain to Queen Victoria in 1859 and served as professor of modern history at Cambridge during the 1860s.

In later years he became involved in controversy with Cardinal **Newman,** who in reply to Kingsley's critic of Catholicism wrote his *Apologia pro vita Sua* (1864). He was a broad churchman, bitterly opposed to what he considered the medievalism and narrowness of the Oxford Tractarian movement, and canon of Chester (1870) and Westminster (1873). The valuable inspiration he contributed to the development of social welfare was undermined by his intellectual limitations, by the inconsistencies of his class and race prejudices, and by his aggressive patriotism. *Charles Kingsley: His Letters and Memories of his Life* (London, 2 vols.) was written by his widow in 1877.

Bibliography. Chitty, Susan. *The Beast and the Monk: A Life of Charles Kingsley.* London: Hodder & Stoughton, 1974.

Irina Novichenko

KIRK, RUSSELL AMOS (1918–1994). One of the foremost intellectual figures of the conservative revival in the United States after the Second World War. Born in the Detroit suburb of Plymouth, he lived most of his life in his ancestral home of Piety Hill in the north central Michigan village of Mecosta, a deliberate decision on his part to maintain a sense of continuity with his own familial roots and local community.

Kirk was educated at what was then known as the Michigan State College of Agriculture and Applied Science, Duke University, and St. Andrew's University in Scotland, where he received a doctor of letters. He began an academic career at his undergraduate alma mater, Michigan State, where he taught the history of civilization

from 1946 until his resignation in 1953. The latter year saw the publication of his seminal book, *The Conservative Mind,* which brought him fame and a secure position within the movement he helped to define and defend.

In 1964, at age forty-six, he married Annette Courtemanche, with whom he had four daughters. His marriage provided an occasion for his reception into the Roman Catholic Church, toward which he had already been moving for some years. Kirk's conversion thus paralleled those of other conservative intellectuals of the twentieth century, most notably **G. K. Chesterton** and Malcolm Muggeridge. Among his many accomplishments, Kirk edited the quarterly journal the *University Bookman* and was founding editor of *Modern Age.*

Many observers have noted the tension among American conservatives between traditionalists and libertarians, the former defending inherited institutions, customs and mores, and the latter embracing as wide as possible a range of individual liberties. As an unequivocal traditionalist, Kirk plays down the vaunted novelty of the American founding, emphasizing instead the continuities tying America to its British and European origins. Similarly, in the debate between old-line conservatives and neoconservatives, Kirk takes the part of the former, believing that the latter, in Marxist fashion, improperly apply the capitalist label to the whole of society in all its complexity, as well as esteeming too highly democracy as more than a mere form of government flowing out of what he calls the politics of prudence.

His economic ideas borrow heavily from the Swiss economist Wilhelm Röpke, whose humane economic vision accords with his own professed localism. Rejecting both the bureaucratic statist economy and the impersonal corporate economy, Kirk shares much with the southern agrarian movement of the early twentieth century, as well as with the English Distributism of Chesterton and **Hilaire Belloc**. Although he naturally sympathizes with the antistatist impetus of such libertarians as Friedrich von Hayek and Ludwig von Mises, Kirk is highly critical of the libertarian doctrine of "universal selfishness" (*Politics of Prudence*, 171), as well as of the tendency to reduce so much of life, in all its rich diversity, to mere market values.

Above all, Kirk is opposed to ideology. Although he himself wrote *A Program for Conservatives* (1954), he resists the tendency to reduce conservatism to one more effort to implement a form of utopian politics. For Kirk ideology is an "inverted religion" denying the cardinal Christian doctrines and offering a false hope of worldly salvation to its followers. Moreover, it erects its own absolute truth rooted in secular revelation, from which deviance is not tolerated. Ideology facilely dismisses the imperfect compromises necessary to a modest conception of politics as the art of the possible, or, once more, the politics of prudence, as Kirk prefers.

With respect to foreign policy, Kirk's politics of prudence counsels against any effort to make of the United States the world's police force. He is particularly critical of American presidents committing troops abroad for the sake of abstractions, such as the spread of democratic values or the construction of a new world order.

Finally, Kirk must be understood as the quintessential renaissance man, attached to what he calls the "permanent things," but as mediated through the particular traditions of the West, a civilization built on the synthetic heritage of Greek philosophical reflection, Roman political institutions, and Judeo-Christian religion.

Bibliography. Kirk, Russell. *America's British Culture.* New Brunswick, New Jersey: Transaction Publishers, 1993. Kirk, Russell. *The Conservative Mind from Burke to Eliot.* 7th rev. ed. Chicago: Regnery, 1986. Kirk, Russell. *The Politics of Prudence.* Bryn Mawr, PN: Intercollegiate Studies Institute, 1993. Kirk, Russell. *A Program for Conservatives.* Chicago: Regnery, 1954. Kirk, Russell. *The Roots of American Order.* 3rd ed. Washington, DC: Regnery Gateway, 1992. Kirk, Russell. *The Sword of Imagination.* Grand Rapids, MI: William B. Eerdmans, 1995, 2002. Person, James E., ed. *The Unbought Grace of Life: Essays in Honor of Russell Kirk.* Peru, IL: Sherwood Sugden, 1994. *Russell Kirk: Man of Letters.* A tribute issue. *Intercollegiate Review: A Journal of Scholarship and Opinion* 30, 1 (Fall 1994).

David T. Koyzis

KOHL, HELMUT (b. 1930). West German politician and Christian Democrat, Kohl was born the Roman Catholic son of a civil servant of a local revenue office. He grew up in Ludwigshafen/Rhine in what was then the Bavarian Palatinate. The young Kohl studied history, political science, and law at the universities of Frankfurt and Heidelberg and received a doctorate from the University of Heidelberg in 1958.

From 1959 until 1969 he held a position in a Federation of Chemical Industries in Ludwigshafen. His father, a former member of the **Center Party** (Zentrum), was one of the founders of the **Christian Democratic Union** (CDU) in Ludwigshafen, and Helmut Kohl himself joined the CDU in 1947. Immediately he took a leading role in the establishment of the party's local youth organization (Junge Union). He was elected to the Rhineland-Palatinate state parliament in 1959 and one year later became a member of the Ludwigshafen city council. From 1969 until 1976, Kohl served as premier of Rhineland-Palatinate, and from 1976 until 1982 he led the opposition in the German federal parliament.

After a close failure at the polls in 1976, in October 1982, he became German federal chancellor (head of the German government), by a change of the coalition. The

Liberals, who had cooperated with the Social Democrats before, quit this alliance and helped to form a new administration under the leadership of Helmut Kohl. This coalition was reelected in 1983, 1987, 1990, and narrowly in 1994. In September 1998, Kohl's coalition clearly lost the general election to an alliance of Social Democrats and Greens. After the defeat, he stepped back from the national chairmanship of the CDU, a post he had held since 1973. In 2002, he did not stand for reelection in the Diet. In the United States he received the Presidential Medal of Freedom in 1999 and honorary doctorates from more than twenty universities, including the University of Maryland, Harvard, and Brandeis.

During the Second World War Kohl's older brother, who as a pupil had helped to save injured persons and recover corpses after air strikes against Ludwigshafen, fell in action in autumn 1944. From the beginning, Kohl's strong political convictions came from his Catholic family background and his deeply held detestation of National Socialism and any other form of dictatorship. Soon after the war he advocated close friendship with the democratic neighbors and later partners of Germany, especially France and the United States. This vision was demonstrated by his ardent activism in physically bringing down toll and frontier barriers at the German-French border in 1950. In the 1970s and more prominently in the 1980s, Kohl proved to be a staunch pillar in the Western diplomatic and military alliance, including his support for the modernization of NATO's missile systems on German territory.

When the East German political system crumbled and the Berlin Wall came down on November 9, 1989, Chancellor Kohl quickly reacted with an elaborate program for German reunification and presented it to the public on November 29. It was to his merit that the great powers acquiesced to a fast incorporation of East Germany into the Federal Republic within the Western frame of institutions, primarily the European Union and NATO. The foundation of this success was to be seen in his deep and trusting personal ties with politicians such as the U.S. president George H. W. Bush, French president François Mitterrand, and Russian president Mikhail Gorbachev.

During the second half of his administration German territorial unification was followed by attempts to promote economic, social, and emotional unity. This was accompanied by powerful momentum in favor of further European unification, irreversible with the treaties of Maastricht and the treaties for the common European currency, the Euro. Kohl's government, furthermore, pressed for determined negotiations with former socialist middle and eastern European countries as applicants for membership in the European Union.

Kohl became embroiled in a financial scandal in 1999 as secret campaign contributions to him and other financial irregularities became public. He strictly refused and as of 2003 still refused to disclose the sources of these funds; instead he preferred to pay a fine to keep his silence.

He was married in 1960 to Hannelore Renner, a Protestant Berlin-born war refugee with a Saxonian family background, who died in 2001. The couple had two sons, neither of whom took a prominent role in politics or the German public.

In the collective memory, Helmut Kohl is the chancellor of German reunification. Likewise he was one of the decisive architects and most effective active promoters of the European integration for at least one decade. With Konrad Adenauer, he shares the renown as one of the most important German Christian Democrats after the Second World War.

Bibliography. Bahners, Patrick. *Im Mantel der Geschichte. Helmut Kohl oder Die Unersetzlichkeit.* Berlin: Siedler, 1998. Bering, Henrik.

Helmut Kohl. Washington, DC: Regnery, 1999. Kohl, Helmut. *Die Deutsche Einheit: Reden und Gespräche.* Bergisch Gladbach, Germany: Lübbe, 1992. Kohl, Helmut. *Mein Tagebuch.* Munich: Droemer, 1998–2000.

Bernd Leupold

KOLPING, ADOLPH (1813–1865). Kolping, known as the "Journeymen's Father" and one of the founders of nineteenth-century Germany's key Catholic clubs, was born in Kerpen, the youngest son of Peter, a shepherd and small farmer, and his wife, Anna Maria. Their large religious family was the root and model for Kolping's later organization.

As the youngest child in fragile health, he was permitted to visit the local single-grade elementary school. He then apprenticed for a shoemaker, and in 1829 he became a journeyman, experiencing the hardship of the workman's life. But since this profession did not fulfill him, he decided to continue his education and become a priest. In 1837, the twenty-four year old Kolping passed the entrance examination of Cologne's Marzellen Secondary School, and after he graduated in 1842 he continued studies in Munich, Cologne, and Bonn. Kolping's ordination on April 13, 1845, was overshadowed by his father's death the day before.

At first, Kolping became curate at St. Laurentius in Elberfeld, an industrial city dominated by growing textile concerns and a place that confronted Kolping daily with the worker's hardships. A journeymen's club, founded by the teacher Johann Gregor Breuer in 1846, attempted, through prayer and discussion, to counteract "proletarianization" and elevate the workers in spirituality and in good citizenship. In 1847, Kolping became the club's second chairman and used it as a model to spawn more such associations. Having been appointed Cathedral curate in Cologne in 1849, he struggled and eventually succeeded in realizing this plan. Kolping circulated his ideas

in his paper, the *Journeymen's Club* (1848/49). So-called Kolping Clubs soon spread across Germany and into other European countries. In 1859, the first one in the United States opened. In 1862 Kolping was appointed chamberlain of Cologne's Franciscan (minors) church.

Before his death, Kolping left a well-organized association that changed its name to Kolping Family in 1933 and today unites more than 300,000 members in Germany, Austria, Hungary, Switzerland, and the United States in the international Kolping Work. Women now join the Kolping Work, which represents the model of a Christian layperson's club under ecclesiastical leadership and attends to employee interests. Especially in the third world, the Kolping Work has been exemplary in development aid. On October 27, 1991 Adolph Kolping was beatified by Pope **John Paul II.**

Bibliography. Kracht, Hans-Joachim. *Adolph Kolping: Priester, Pädagoge, Publizist im Dienst christlicher Sozialreform. Leben und Werk aus den Quellen dargestellt.* Freiburg, Germany: Herder, 1993.

Andrea Rönz

KOREC, JÁN CHRYZOSTOM (b. 1924) Cardinal Korec stands out as a prominent Catholic leader of the underground church in Slovakia after the communist takeover in Czechoslovakia. Secretly ordained in 1950 and shortly thereafter consecrated by the Vatican as a secret bishop, he catered to the spiritual needs of Slovak Catholics despite the high risks involved during the last days of Stalinist terror. Arrested by the dreaded secret state police in 1960, Korec was sentences by the courts to a dozen years in prison.

Rehabilitated during the 1968 reform movement, he again assumed his ecclesiastical duties of ministering, teaching, and writing while dodging the ever-present spies of the state police. His samizdat publications garnered world attention by the

1980s, and, in the United States, the University of Notre Dame awarded him, in absentia, an honorary doctorate of law. Pressures on the bishop mounted until the Communist regime crumbled in the 1989 Velvet Revolution. Shortly thereafter, Pope **John Paul II** appointed him bishop of Nitra and bestowed on him the title of cardinal. A living symbol of how one man can make a difference in nurturing the spiritual life of his people, Cardinal Korec continues to write and work to rebuild the church in a free Slovakia.

Born the son of a tannery worker in Bošany, a village thirty miles north of Nitra, Korec grew up in a deeply religious community. Deciding to become a priest, he attended a Jesuit institution in Ružomberok and in 1944 finished high school in Klážtor pod Znievom. He continued his studies in theology and philosophy in both Trnava and Brno. As a young seminarian, he assisted in the publication of religious magazines and was one of the founders of a new journal, which responded to the intellectual challenges posed by atheistic communism. Upon seizing power in 1948, the new communist regime quickly banned one of his earliest works, *The Philosophical Principles of Dialectical Materialism.*

Luckily spared prison during the 1950 raids on religious houses because he was not yet ordained and suffered from a heart condition, Korec secretly received the sacrament of Holy Orders while he worked as manual laborer. After the infamous 1951 trials against Bishops Buzalka, **Gojdič**, and Vojtaššák, the church recognized his talents as it conferred upon him the office of bishop. Though continuing to work at labor jobs, Korec illegally trained young seminarians for the priesthood until the suspecting secret police nabbed him after a decade of dangerous service for the church. Finally freed from confinement, Korec attracted international attention when Pope **Paul VI** recognized his pastoral achievements and took the unprecedented step of presenting

Korec with a ring, a pectoral cross, the pope's own crosier, and two mitres.

Under constant surveillance, even after his rehabilitation, Korec had to return to working at hard labor jobs. Yet he continued to train young men, using a tube to talk to his students to avoid detection from bugging devices. Defying authorities, during the 1980s he went public with his efforts to reinvigorate the church. Even though his car was blown up in an attempted murder by authorities, Korec remained undeterred in his efforts to spread the Gospel and protect the rights of the church to an independent existence.

Korec's numerous studies stand as a testament of his unfailing devotion to the faith and his courage in the face of repeated threats to his personal safety. His most famous writings include the many samizdat manuscripts published under the title "Library of Faith": *Jesus from Afar and Near* (1981), *The Resurrected Christ and His Church* (1983), *The Life of the Consecrated* (1990*), The Struggle of the Church over the Centuries* (1990), *From Nero to the Enlightenment* (1990), *Marriage and the Family* (1990), *The Path to Eternity* (1991), *The Night of the Barbarians* (1990–1993), *Reflections on Man and Who He Is* (1992), *The Philosopher of Common Sense, G.K. Chesterton* (1993), and other works.

Today Korec remains an inspiration for the faithful of Slovakia and continues his work as the moving force of the Catholic Church's postcommunist rebuilding.

Bibliography. Korec, Jan Chryzostom Cardinal. *The Night of the Barbarians: Memoirs of the Communist Persecution of the Slovak Cardinal.* Trans. Peter-Paul Siska, Richard Guaghran, and Jeff Schmilz. Chicago: Bolchazy-Carducci, 2002. Strhan, Milan, and David P. Daniel, eds. *Slovakia and the Slovaks: A Concise Encyclopedia.* Bratislava, Slovakia: Goldpress, 1994.

Michael J. Kopanic, Jr.

KORFANTY, WOJCIECH (1873–1939). As leader of the Christian Democratic movement in Poland between World War I and World War II, Korfanty was one of the most important Catholic politicians of his day. Despite his modest background as the son of a Silesian coal miner, he managed to obtain degrees from the Charlottenburg Polytechnic and the University of Breslau (Wrocław). While still a student, Korfanty became involved with a right-wing, anti-Semitic movement known as National Democracy, but during the years leading up to World War I he drifted away from that formation and toward the Christian Democratic Party.

He entered Prussian and German politics in the early years of the twentieth century as an advocate for Polish national rights and rose to prominence following World War I as the leader of the Polish uprising in Silesia—a revolt responsible for obtaining a large part of that territory for the newly re-created Polish state. From 1922 to 1930 he was a parliamentary delegate, and he served briefly as vice premier in 1923. He was opposed to the military coup of Marshal Józef Piłsudski in 1926, as well as the authoritarian regime that followed. This eventually led to his arrest in 1930 and his exile from Poland in 1935.

In his writings and speeches, Korfanty stressed what he considered to be the two main dangers facing Europe in the early twentieth century: from one side, the dehumanization and pauperization caused by liberal capitalism, and from the other, the anti-Christian totalitarianism of both fascism and communism (which he invariably linked as manifestations of the same fundamental evil). Korfanty advocated a corporatist organization of the state and propagated to a Polish audience the social and political teachings of the contemporary Catholic Church (citing often such key papal texts as **Leo XII**'s *Rerum novarum* of 1891 and **Pius XI**'s *Quadragesimo anno* of 1931).

Korfanty echoed the anti-Semitism that was so common among Catholic circles in interwar Poland, but he strongly opposed the racism and brutality of the Nazis and warned against the temptation of turning to the radical Right as a means of resisting the radical Left. His efforts to defend a political stance that was equally opposed to liberalism, fascism, and socialism proved to be extraordinarily difficult in the context of interwar Poland, and Korfanty remained far from the corridors of power. Nonetheless, he enjoyed a substantial core following during his lifetime, and since his death on August 17, 1939 (less than two weeks before the invasion of Poland by Nazi Germany), his stature has grown to the point where he is routinely included within the pantheon of Polish national heroes.

Bibliography. Balawajder, Edward. *Wojciech Korfanty: Myśl katolicko-społeczna i działalność.* Katowice, Poland: Księgarnia św. Jacka, 2001. Orzechowski, Marian. *Wojciech Korfanty: Biografia polityczna.* Wrocław, Poland: Ossolineum, 1975.

Brian Porter

KU KLUX KLAN. On Christmas Eve 1865 in the small town of Pulaski, Tennessee, the Ku Klux Klan was born. Its founders, the majority of them former Confederates, fashioned their name on the Greek term *kuklos,* meaning a band or circle. This reconstitution of classical culture was typical of the perspective espoused by Klansmen, who saw themselves as essential nobility and protectors of the highest attainments of Western civilization. As self-appointed police, they saw themselves as enforcers of the law and social order rather than vigilantes.

Initially conceived as area associations (later known as dens), they shared little or no overarching organization, discipline, or purpose. But as Radicals ascended Congress in 1867, displacing state governments throughout the South, the Klan's message quickly spread as its mission crystallized against freed blacks, Northern carpetbaggers, Loyal Leagues, and organizations espousing Union Rule. By April of that same year, representatives from throughout Tennessee met and elected former confederate general Nathan Bedford Forrest as their first grand wizard.

In these initial years, the implementation of Reconstruction and its purported outcome of "black lawlessness" drew considerable response from the Southern Klansmen. Verbal threats, militia violence, torture, and death were all tactics employed by the Klan to nullify and reverse the programs of Radical Reconstruction. These activities were carried out by members from varying backgrounds whose allegiances to such rhetorical and intellectual constructs such as "proper limits," "prudent authority," "innocence," "the weak," and "the oppressed" galvanized them into a formidable movement. These converts to the cause included disgruntled Southern Protestants. While successful in its mission, the Klan's autonomous and localized organizational structure proved to be unwieldy. By January 1869, Grand Wizard Forrest disbanded the Klan, later explaining it had become perverted in its mission, as violence perpetrated by members was getting out of control. Forrest's decree apparently liquidated the Klan's activities throughout much of the South with the exception of the Carolinas, where the Federal Force Act, mass arrests, and martial law eventually brought an end to activities in 1872.

Southern Protestant sensibilities helped to revitalize the organization by the second decade of the twentieth century. With the release of D. W. Griffith's 1915 motion picture *The Birth of a Nation,* based on a work written by the popular Baptist minister and orator Thomas Dixon Jr., the emotive power of modern filmmaking techniques was unleashed. Griffith's film and Dixon's story portrayed white Southern vigilantes as the last saviors of American civilization, who valiantly fought to save the nation from the scourge of African Americans and Reconstruction. By the time the movie had left theaters, it had grossed nearly $18 million nationwide and encouraged countless numbers to join the cause.

With the resurgence of the Klan came a broadening of its range of hostility. In addition to African Americans, other enemies of the Klan's Anglo-Saxon Protestant dream now included Jews, Roman Catholics, and other immigrant groups. As these groups increasingly became the target of Klan hatred, long-standing and deep-seated religious bigotries surfaced attracting greater numbers of churchmen to the Klan. Large numbers of Baptist, Church of Christ, Disciples of Christ, and Methodist families joined the ranks of the Klan. Significantly fewer converts came from the Episcopal, Lutheran, and Presbyterian denominations. The pull of members from these broader constituencies reflected a fundamental trait of the Klan during its second manifestation: an ability to align itself and play upon the fears of many mainstream white Americans.

Members of the resurgent Klan were largely Anglo-Saxon Protestants who were especially motivated by the fear that federal efforts would eventually secure the rights of American citizenship for the freedman. It was believed that these efforts were not only in violation of the Constitution but also the divine design for the nation. But the relationship between religion and the Klan went far beyond an intellectual framework that gave such racist sentiments a divine charge. Protestantism provided significant numbers of members to the cause and also the symbolic world upon which devoted Klansmen carried out their charge. Regional business was conducted in so-called tabernacles, an oblique reference to the Hebrew prophet Amos (9:11), who proclaimed the chosen people of God had been charged with restoring the house of David. These carefully constructed symbolic arenas featured elaborate rites devised to strengthen the bonds of members while securing the zeal of would-be candidates.

Sustaining these quasi-religious ties was part of the Klan's institutional makeup. Each chapter of the Klan had its own "kludd," or chaplain, many of them officially ordained ministers. Clerical representation in the Klan played a significant role in other ways. Of the thirty-nine national lecturers touring the country to proclaim the message of the KKK, nearly two-thirds of these leaders were also ordained Protestant ministers. By 1924, clergy Klansmen were claimed to have numbered around thirty thousand airing a sectional brand of Christian fundamentalism that lauded the superiority of the white race, Protestantism, and the Democratic Party. This belief had a particularly Southern expression as well that called for "pure Americanism" to be constituted by patriotism and a revival of that "old time religion."

In the years following World War II, ties between the KKK and American Protestantism continued dramatically to shape the character of the organization. Klan membership in the twentieth century expanded geographically as the self-proclaimed adherents were charged with maintaining the country's "Christian civilization" in the face of newly perceived threats of communism and socialism. Such perceived threats continued to induce and create religious leaders in the South, such as the fundamentalist J. Robertson Jones, or **Bob Jones,** who took up the Klan's mantle.

Yet on other fronts the relationship between Protestantism and the Klan was strained. With increasing media exposure to the cause of civil rights, the demands of African Americans in the segregated South exposed Klan tactics and their racist senti-

ments to national audiences. During these decades the Klan encountered active even virulent resistance from several quarters of the wider society, including from within Protestant circles. No longer capable of enjoying the social dominance it once held, the organization splintered into numerous factions with varying objectives, thus curbing its power as a social force.

Bibliography. Chalmers, David M. *Hooded Americanism: The History of the Ku Klux Klan.* 3rd ed. Durham, NC: Duke University, 1987. Maclean, Nancy. *Behind the Mask of Chivalry: The Making of the Second Ku Klux Klan.* New York: Oxford University Press, 1994. Sims, Patsy. *The Klan.* New York: Stein & Day, 1978.

Kent A. McConnell

KUNG (GONG), IGNATIUS PIN-MEI (1901–2000).
A Roman Catholic cardinal and Chinese dissident, Kung was born in Shanghai. He was ordained in 1930 and appointed bishop of Shoochow in 1949, and then bishop of Shanghai in 1950. Shanghai became central to Catholic efforts to resist the aim of the People's Republic to create an indigenous Chinese Catholic Church free of foreign influence.

The Chinese Communist Party first began to confiscate Catholic educational and social institutions and then, in Shanghai, used the Religious Affairs Bureau to attempt to penetrate and control Catholic institutional activities. Upon his appointment as bishop of Shanghai, Kung reestablished the Legion of Mary and encouraged public displays of Catholic devotion as a mode of resistance to communist authority. Kung also denied communion to those associated with the Catholic Patriotic movement. These acts led to a sentence of life imprisonment for him in 1955.

During his imprisonment, Kung refused to renounce papal authority and support the Chinese Patriotic Catholic Church.

Kung's case became an international cause, with organizations such as an Amnesty International campaigning for his release. He emigrated to the United States after his release in 1985. In 1991, it was revealed that Pope **John Paul II** had named Kung a cardinal *in pectore* in 1979. The activist cardinal died in Stamford, Connecticut.

Bibliography. Haberman, Clyde. "Pope Names 22 Cardinals; Chinese Prelate Identified." *New York Times,* 30 May 1991. Hanson, Eric O. *Catholic Politics in China and Korea.* Maryknoll, NY: Orbis Books, 1980.

Mathew N. Schmalz

KUYPER, ABRAHAM (1837–1920). Kuyper, a Dutch Calvinist theologian, philosopher, church reformer, journalist, and statesman, served as prime minister of the Netherlands from 1901 to 1905. He addressed and proposed responses to the rapidly shifting relationship between faith and culture in the Western industrializing nations.

Born in the pastorate of Maassluis, he finished his high school education at the Middelburg Gymnasium (1855) and graduated from Leiden University, completing a divinity degree at the Leiden Divinity School in 1861, and a doctorate in 1863 on a comparative study of the ecclesiology of John Calvin and Johan a Lasco. A succession of pastorates followed at Breesd, Utrecht, and finally in Amsterdam in 1870. His pastoral experience exposed him to the simple piety of parishioners from the lower classes and led to his conversion from modernist liberal theology to orthodox Calvinism. During this period he met the Dutch politician **Groen van Prinsterer,** joined his **Anti-Revolutionary Party,** and become the editor of *De Heraut* and *De Standaard.*

Elected in 1874 to represent Gouda in the Dutch parliament, he resigned from the Amsterdam Church and eventually led the party, in coalition with the Roman Catholics, to election victories in 1888 and again in 1901, on which occasion he became prime minister. He was instrumental in the *Dolenatie* schism from the Dutch Reformed (*Hervormde*) Church in 1886 and in 1892 led this church into union with the earlier schism formed by the 1834 *Afscheiding,* to form the Gereformeerde Kerk.

His political platform, molded by his Calvinism, primarily involved the rejection of the dominant nineteenth-century views, colored by secularism, which either prioritized the individual (individualist liberalism) or the collective (state sovereignty of Hegel or forms of socialism). Both of these extremes he argued, ultimately denied the sovereignty of God over all spheres of life and, in addition, the individual worth and social nature of the human person. His interests and belief in the efficacy of Christian education led to the founding of the Free University of Amsterdam in 1881, upon which occasion he delivered the famous inaugural lecture on "sphere sovereignty." In this Calvinist version of the Catholic subsidiarity principle, all domains ("spheres") of civilization are understood as autonomous, inspired by God, and guided toward the common good of a society. His reinterpretation of Calvinism became well known in the English-speaking world through his Stone Lectures of 1898 at Princeton Theological Seminary, published in English as *Lectures in Calvinism* (1920).

Through his prodigious editing and publishing efforts, his thought in many fields was widely dispersed, the effects of his theology in the church and political spheres resonating in the twentieth century in the Netherlands, as well as in South Africa and the United States. The last decade of the twentieth century witnessed increased interest in his theological and political views by both Protestants and Roman Catholics interested in his alternative to the rather similar positions that have come to dominate contemporary Western life.

Bibliography. Bratt, James D., ed. *Abraham Kuyper: A Centennial Reader.* Grand Rapids, MI: William B. Eerdmans, 1998. Heslam, Peter S. *Creating a Christian Worldview: Abraham Kuyper's Lectures on Calvinism.* Grand Rapids, MI: William B. Eerdmans, 1998. Lugo, Luis E. *Religion, Pluralism, and Public Life: Abraham Kuyper's Legacy for the Twenty-first Century.* Grand Rapids, MI: William B. Eerdmans, 2000. Rullmann, J. C. *Kuyper-Bibliografie.* 3 vols. 's-Gravenhage: J. Bootsma, 1940.

Iain S. Maclean